1981

Strategies of Community Organization
Third Edition

A Book of Readings·Third Edition

Strategies of Community Organization

Fred M. Cox
Michigan State University

John L. Erlich
California State University, Sacramento

Jack Rothman
John E. Tropman
University of Michigan

 **F. E. PEACOCK PUBLISHERS, INC.**
ITASCA, ILLINOIS 60143

Contents

v

Preface to the Third Edition

This collection of writings deals with the theory and practice of community organization and social change. For this third edition, the collection has been revised and updated substantially to take into account new developments and trends. A completely new section has been added on the common elements of community intervention. While the book is an anthology, it is not a disjointed aggregation of articles. Rather, it is a coherent collection bound together by a perspective on community organization practice forged over a number of years by colleagues at the University of Michigan and, more recently, at California State University, Sacramento, and Michigan State University as well.

Three intersecting perspectives shape the conceptualization that informs this presentation. These include an orientation towards different approaches to community organization, a view of the nature of interorganizational linkages among key community-based social units, and a focus on the practitioner and his or her intellectual equipment.

We have singled out three modes of community practice for attention, referring to them as locality development, social planning, and social action. These are further defined and elaborated in the first chapter of Part One. This approach enables us to embrace and at the same time distinguish a wide variety of activities that have fallen haphazardly under such rubrics as community action, social planning, social action, community development, and the like. Such a structure is badly needed in a field that suffers from considerable conceptual looseness and confusion.

Chapter II, the new section, looks at key elements of community work—particularly as they can provide leverage on the day-to-day pressures, constraints, and possibilities with which the practitioner must live. Neglected areas such as the use of interpersonal skills (an arena in which community practitioners are often regarded as seriously deficient), organizational maneuvering, and conducting program evaluations are given special attention. The relationship of the field to its knowledge base is also addressed. More generally, what we have tried to do in this section is deal with basic professional concepts and issues that confront any change agent who attempts to affect community life.

Part Two attends to two significant kinds of social units comprising American communities—formal organizations and primary groups. We will be concerned with the linkages among these groups as well as the community context in which these linkages are played out.

The community serves as both a context and a target in this scheme. While the urban community receives the greatest emphasis, attention is also paid to the suburban situation. The community is experienced as a complex and fluid social configuration, but we find it useful, for analysis and practice, to select certain variables that are functionally important, accessible, and manipulable. We view a community in terms of the types and numbers of primary groups and formal organizations and their patterns of interrelationship. Practice consists of interventions that enhance, sustain, or sever existing linkage patterns between these social units and establish new linkages or units. Potential interrelationships between the units identified include: primary groups with one another, primary groups with formal organizations, and formal organizations with other such organizations. Each of these possibilities involves different strategic and programmatic actions.

The heart of the book, Part Three, deals with various strategies of action in the community as they relate to the three models of practice. Most of the articles in each chapter are new. They are intended to delineate emerging action approaches, with particular reference to potential roles, practice, and policy alternatives.

It is our aim to distinguish this volume from other works on the subject by an emphasis on tactical considerations in planned community change. We conceive of a practitioner based in an organizational structure (social agency, indigenous action group, and so forth) that sets policy and provides intervention opportunities and resources, while at the same time imposing constraints. The major resource the practitioner brings to his or her task is the ability to engage the self analytically, with skill and commitment, in what is often an extremely fluid and tension-ridden community setting. We offer the individual (or group) performing this role conceptual tools and guides to strategic planning. At the same time, we have tried to take account of societal shifts in the direction of slower and more controlled growth, reduced resource consumption, and environmental protection. The post-Watergate skepticism about not only national and statewide "movers and shakers," but also bureaucrats and politicians at the local community level, is reflected in a number of the articles presented. In addition, we note some resurgence of interest in neighborhoods, from the highest levels of government to the grass roots.

A great debt is owed to a number of people who have contributed to the preparation of this book. Our colleague, Louis Ferman, first pointed to the need for such a collection from his perspective as a consultant to several agencies of the federal government, and he urged us to ready for publication a manuscript that we had been using for teaching purposes. Fedele Fauri and Robert Vinter, former deans of the University of Michigan's School of Social Work; Phillip

Fellin, the current dean; Jesse McClure, former dean of the School of Social Work at California State University, Sacramento, and Wanda Collins, the current dean, provided invaluable assistance, making time and other resources available to us that considerably eased the task of completing each edition. Mitchel Lazarus, who worked with us on the first edition of the book until he returned to professional practice, made his wise counsel available throughout the initial stages of the undertaking. Ted Peacock and Tom LaMarre, our publisher and editor, were most encouraging in the early stages of the project. Their continued support throughout the development of the third edition, with the assistance of Joyce Usher, the managing editor, has done much to sustain us through this publication effort. A very large number of people have helped with typing portions of the manuscript, obtaining permissions from authors and publishers, and a welter of clerical detail. To all of them we are most grateful. Our wives—Gay Cox, Sue Erlich, Judy Rothman, and Penny Tropman—have, with supportive cheerfulness, suffered the disruptions of family life that made this third edition possible. Gay Cox deserves special thanks for her work in coordinating permissions and proofreading substantial portions of the revised manuscript.

Most of what is good about this book we owe to the authors of the readings published here. However, we must bear full responsibility for their selection and organization and the preparation of introductory materials, together with whatever faults may be found.

FRED M. COX
JOHN L. ERLICH
JACK ROTHMAN
JOHN E. TROPMAN

PART ONE:
OVERVIEW

Introduction

Concepts of Community Organization and Trends in Practice

Our interest here is community organization. It has also variously been termed community planning, community relations, planned change, and community work. Others have preferred terms such as neighborhood work, social action, intergroup work, and community practice. Under whatever label, we will be dealing with intervention at the community level oriented toward improving or changing community institutions and solving community problems. This activity is performed by professionals from many disciplines—social work, public health, adult education, public administration, city planning, and community mental health—as well as by citizen volunteers in civic associations and social action groups.

These activities aim at a wide range of purposes. Among them are included establishing new community services and programs; managing existing community organizations or programs and facilitating relationships among them; or building the capacity of grass roots citizens' groups to solve community problems. Other purposes entail seeking justice for oppressed minorities, bringing about social reform, or conducting programs of community relations or public education.[1]

Because of the many and varied approaches to community organization practice, both students and practitioners have often experienced considerable uncertainty and confusion. This uncertainty has been played out historically.

---

[1]Arnold Gurin presents a useful review of emerging efforts to define the field in "Social Planning and Community Organization," *Encyclopedia of Social Work* (New York: National Association of Social Workers, 1971), pp. 1324–37.

Multiple Models and Common Dimensions of Community Intervention

The historical roots of various orientations to community organization practice and the conditions under which they arose are sketched by Charles Garvin and Fred Cox (Reading 2). One dilemma in community organization, particularly in social work, is whether community intervention should stress the delivery of services to individuals in need or the modification of social conditions that predispose some people to inequity or dysfunction.

Social work, from its earliest inception, has had two aspects: the care and rehabilitation of troubled individuals and the elimination of social conditions that bring on hardship—that is to say, *treatment and reform.* These approaches are complementary and ultimately may be viewed as seeking a single purpose—the well-being of the individual.

In our view, change-oriented practice and treatment-oriented practice take place in different kinds of organizations or subunits. The approaches, however, may be viewed as complementary rather than in basic conflict. Further, they may be encompassed in their various dimensions within professions dedicated to social betterment. Optimal community well-being requires the coexistence of multiple community intervention approaches to deal with different problems and to draw in different segments of the population. The following statement by a respected social work leader vividly articulates this perspective:

> I view these two aspects of social work—practice and policy, psychological individ-ualization and social reform, improvement of the individualized services and improve-ment of social conditions, direct rendering of services and broader programs of prevention, personal therapy and social leadership—as a coordinated approach to the solution of these problems, individual and community, with which social work is concerned.[2]

While the casework aspect has tended to dominate, in the recent past opportu-nities have arisen for social work to strengthen its reform dimension. The social sciences, which had a great spurt following World War II, provide a knowledge base for the planning and social change areas comparable to the base provided the field of treatment earlier by psychoanalysis.

Furthermore, society's disenfranchised groups are exerting heavy pressures on the professions to address themselves to discrimination, social injustice, and social dysfunction. Contemporary problems such as poverty, blight, racism, delin-quency, automation, and educational disability simply do not lend themselves to solution through individualized services. The revolt of people of color, as well as the welfare rights, peace, and student movements, created a supportive climate for community change efforts. While in the past the professions, including social work, have not fully embraced controversial areas such as civil rights, more recently they have begun to respond to such challenges. Despite the conservative

---

[2]Charles I. Schottland, "Our Changing Society Challenges Social Work," keynote address, Univer-sity of Pittsburgh School of Social Work Faculty-Alumni Conference, Pittsburgh, Pa., March 30, 1962 (mimeographed).

reversals of the Nixon years, we believe that these responses have modified the perspective of community organization practice for the foreseeable future.

A Three-Model Approach

In this volume we attempt to achieve increased conceptual clarity by treating all of community organization not as a single undifferentiated phenomenon, given new and disparate tendencies, but rather as three somewhat distinct modes of community intervention. This approach implements a suggestion by Alfred J. Kahn: "Perhaps it is more realistic to think in terms of several kinds of community organization agencies or structures with different values and objectives."[3] Further, we are concerned with a professional function, that is the direction or stimulation of community intervention by an individual with responsibility to guide such processes. The practitioner and the alternative roles and strategies that he may choose become a focal point in our conceptual scheme. The three models of community organization practice that form the framework for this book are termed *locality development, social planning,* and *social action.* These are described in the first article in Part One and may be summarized as follows:

Locality Development

Locality development presupposes that community change can be pursued most effectively by involving a wide spectrum of local people in goal determination and action. We find its prototype in the literature of a segment of the field commonly termed "community development." As stated in a major United Nations publication, "Community development can be tentatively defined as a process designed to create conditions of economic and social progress for the whole community with its active participation and the fullest possible reliance on the community's initiative."[4] Themes emphasized in locality development include democratic procedures, voluntary cooperation, self-help, development of indigenous leadership, and education. Self-help traditions of the American frontier have contributed to the emergence of this approach.

Social Planning

Social planning emphasizes a technical process of solving social problems such as delinquency, housing, or health. Rational deliberation and controlled change have a central place in this model. Community participation may vary from much to little, depending on how problems present themselves and what organizational variables are present. This approach assumes that planned change in a complex industrial environment requires experts who guide change processes through the

[3]Alfred J. Kahn, "Social Science and the Conceptual Framework for Community Organization Research," in Leonard S. Kogan (ed.), *Social Science Theory and Social Work Research* (New York: National Association of Social Workers, 1960), p. 79.

[4]United Nations Secretary General, *Social Progress Through Community Development* (New York: United Nations Bureau of Social Affairs, 1955), p. 6.

exercise of technical skills, including the ability to manipulate large bureaucratic organizations. Planners, especially in social work, are concerned with the provision of goods and services to people who need them. Enhancing the community's capacity for constructive problem solving or promoting fundamental social change do not play a central part.

Social Action

Social action presupposes a disadvantaged segment of the population that needs to be organized, perhaps in alliance with others, to make adequate demands on the larger community for increased resources or treatment more in accordance with social justice or democracy. Its practitioners aim at basic changes in major institutions or community practices and policies. They seek redistribution of power, resources, or decision making in the community or changes in basic policies of formal organizations. Examples of groups using the social action approach include racial and ethnic minorities (black, Native American, Latino, and Asian power groups), the student movement, certain elements of the women's movement, radical political parties, neighborhood action groups, labor unions, the National Welfare Rights Organization, Nader's Raiders, Grey Panthers, environmental protection groups, and so forth.

Identification of these separate strategies does not imply their existence in "pure" form always, nor does it suggest that practitioners and change agents should necessarily design intervention programs in tightly distinctive ways. As will be brought out, the skillful blending and interdigitation of various action initiatives is as important as is the recognition of their differing characteristics.

Common Dimensions of Practice

It should be recognized that there are basic dimensions of practice that are common and cut across particular approaches or models. For example, all community practitioners operate out of some kind of organizational base or sponsoring structure. The ability to function skillfully within such an organizational framework, constrained but not imprisoned by it, is characteristic of all community organizers. Similarly, all practitioners, consciously or unconsciously, pursue particular ideologically tinged goals or are informed in their work by given systems of values. Nevertheless, such precepts as concern for human worth, confidentiality, and fairness apply generically. Also, a practitioner may emphasize the role orientation of enabling, advocating, or fact finding. It is the ability to analyze a practice situation in order to design a role and to implement the components of the role that is a vital skill for all professionals in community intervention. In other words, there are both variations and uniformities in the performance of community organization practice. To overemphasize either the common or the distinct features distorts the character of practice. In the sections that follow this introduction both the variations expressed in separate models and common dimensions will be presented. The general structure of the book places greater emphasis on specialized approaches and strategies. The substantial section on common dimensions, however, is intended to provide balance and perspective in understanding community organization practice, as is the concluding section on mixing and phasing.

Some Recent Trends in Practice

Conceptions of practice are in reality an analytical reflection of the existential flow of community organization activity. As an aspect of definition, and as an introduction to major programs and approaches, we will summarize some past trends in community organization.

Greater External Influence on Local Community Organization

Numerous federal government programs, as well as the activities of national voluntary agencies and state governments, are increasingly influencing local community organization. At one time, the local community was viewed as a somewhat independent and autonomous entity that could plan for and maintain itself. A strong trend in American political philosophy has emphasized local initiative and control. This image has been rapidly vanishing. In *The Community in America,* Roland L. Warren highlights the impact of "extra-community forces" on the local community:

> It is a thesis of this book that the "great change" in community living includes the increasing orientation of local community units toward extra-community systems of which they are a part, with a corresponding decline in community cohesion and autonomy. As the relation of community units to state and national systems becomes strengthened, the locus of decision making with regard to them often shifts to places outside the community.[5]

Thus, in the social services, some local communities were profoundly influenced by voluntary organizations such as the Ford Foundation through its Gray Areas community development projects and programs in aging. City planning was similarly modified by federal urban renewal legislation, and public welfare is currently influenced by Title XX of the Social Security Act.

More and more, local community organization is influenced by outside pressures, initiatives, and opportunities to which the local community responds. External monetary inputs have had a large impact, partially because of an inadequate and outmoded system of public finance at the municipal level. Because organizing and planning efforts often require interest group mobilization across community lines, Gilbert and Specht state, "The original notion of community as a small geographic area is no longer useful to distinguish the practice settings of social planning-community organization."[6] An example is the interdependence

---

[5]Roland L. Warren, *The Community in America,* 2d ed. (Chicago: Rand McNally & Co., 1972), p. 53.

[6]Neil Gilbert and Harry Specht, "Social Planning and Community Organization: Approaches," *Encyclopedia of Social Work* (Washington, D.C.: National Association of Social Workers, 1977), p. 1413.

of central cities and suburbs for certain services, notably solid waste disposal, transportation networks, and crime control.

The Economic Opportunity Act (or War on Poverty) was a landmark external stimulus to local community organizing. Through the Office of Economic Opportunity (OEO), a variety of programmatic efforts were stimulated, including Job Corps, residential training centers for disconnected youth, Neighborhood Youth Corps, rural assistance, and the like. Of special note was the Community Action Program (CAP) which emphasized a community organization approach to the problem of poverty. The approach highlighted "maximum feasible participation" of residents and clients in policy formulation and program implementation. Arthur Dunham has described the CAP program as follows:

> According to the law, the purpose of CAP was to provide stimulation and incentive for urban and rural communities to mobilize their resources to combat poverty through community action programs. CAP was conceived of as a local agency receiving technical and financial assistance from the federal government. The approach was flexible; the community was to mobilize its own governmental and voluntary resources and try to coordinate existing local, state, and federal programs in a concentrated drive against poverty. . . . The local anti-poverty agencies [were] . . . the most important local governmental agencies with primarily community organization functions that have ever appeared.[7]

It is clear by this time that the achievements of this new endeavor could not match its objectives or the political rhetoric that adorned it. It became bogged down in political controversy and clashes among various interest groups. Dunham appraises its effects as follows:

> The available evidence regarding the poverty program suggests that (1) The program has helped large numbers of people in one way or another, though the permanency of such results is still uncertain in many cases. (2) The appropriations of about $1.5 billion a year have been totally inadequate in comparison with the extent of the problem. (3) The program has made no revolutionary impact on poverty or on the conditions of the poor. Ben Seligman estimates that it has not reached more than 6 percent of the poor. . . . (4) The results of the poverty program for the country as a whole are probably quite spotty. (5) The program has incurred bitter political attacks on both the national and local levels. . . . The program has established the policy of maximum feasible participation by the poor, and it has, to a substantial degree, applied that policy in practice. This may have revolutionary implications for the future, in terms of consumer participation in social welfare programs.[8]

From a community organization point of view, the program encouraged a tremendous amount of experimentation and innovation at the local level, trained leaders of minority groups in community action, and raised the level of expectations of disadvantaged populations. It has also helped to institutionalize the notion of citizen and client input in federal programs of many kinds. The impact of these effects will likely grow. We have here an example of external influences

---

[7]Arthur Dunham, *The New Community Organization* (New York: Thomas Y. Crowell, 1970), p. 74.

[8]Dunham, *New Community Organization*, p. 74.

on the local community fostering greater vitality at the local level. Revenue sharing has generated some similar reactions, but on a more modest scale.

Multiple Centers of Planning and Action

Primarily as a result of new external influences, a variety of social planning centers are springing up in American communities. Among them we find crime and delinquency concerns in one locus of planning; mental health, poverty planning, and health care programs as examples of other loci; and we can add the mayor's office, revenue sharing, community development programs, city and regional planning commissions, programs for the aged, substance abuse, etc. Meanwhile, community welfare councils, on the scene for many years, remain loci of planning that often relate to these newer ventures in a multiplicity of ways. Individual agencies and civic organizations have likewise become more attuned to and engaged in planning activities.

At one time the community welfare council aspired to be the exclusive agent for comprehensive local health and welfare planning. This aim is now functionally dubious and philosophically in contention. Two statements made in the same month in the early 1960s dramatize the controversy. Gordon Manser restated the traditional point of view when he declared the council should—

> address itself to comprehensive community planning. By this I mean addressing itself to a major community problem, whether it be public welfare, chronic illness, juvenile delinquency, urban renewal, or services to the aged. . . . Whatever steps taken, it is important that the council should be looking to the future, that the council be in the forefront and that the council be the effective central point around which all affected interests of the community can be mobilized and put to work in problem solving.[9]

In that same month in Cleveland, Robert Morris and Martin Rein asserted a contrary opinion in an address:

> It is also possible to envision a continuation of the present competitive situation between various centers for planning with each focused on a special interest. Political scientists frequently seem to agree that the essence of democracy is the freest competition between special interests. In this view, special interests are neither evil nor undesirable but are the best assurance that the great variety of human needs will be ultimately served by the expression of differences free to compete with each other.[10]

A more contemporary assessment is as follows:

> Although community welfare councils remain among the array of local planning organizations, they are increasingly feeling the pressure of competition for resources and domain. . . . At this point it is difficult to predict how local coordination and planning functions will finally be structured.[11]

---

[9]Gordon Manser, "New Opportunities Through Comprehensive Community Planning," address to Rhode Island Council of Community Services, Providence, R.I., May, 1963 (mimeographed).

[10]Robert Morris and Martin Rein, "Emerging Patterns in Community Planning," *The Social Welfare Forum 1963* (New York: Columbia University Press, 1963), p. 174.

[11]John E. Tropman and Elmer J. Tropman, "Community Welfare Councils," *Encyclopedia of Social Work,* 1977, p. 188.

Among all observers there seems to be agreement that in point of fact there is a proliferation of different social planning centers, but there is disagreement about the extent to which this can be modified and the desirability of modifying it.

New Forms and Structures

Not only are there additional loci of community organization, but the structures of community planning bodies have been considerably changed. Professional planning to a greater degree has been built around a single problem, such as housing or poverty or mental health. A structure has been devised to bridge the gap between public and private social service. The political enterprise is more likely to be involved in an important way. Representation on these new structures is broader than was traditional, including people from education, employment, city planning, and civil rights in an ad hoc coalition of interests. These new instrumentalities often provide direct services, in addition to engaging in coordination and planning. The more established welfare councils are usually involved in some way, varying from a central role with much authority to a peripheral position. Resources are often quite substantial, and much of the recent funding has been from outside the community, giving the new structures considerable influence and some degree of independence from local pressures. Warren characterized the new structures as follows:

> A closely related characteristic of the present scene is the development of *ad hoc* coalitions of agencies and organizations in relation to some of these specific problem areas. Often, these are not in the form of committees of divisions within the community welfare council, but are coalitions formed outside it, in a variety of relationships to the council. Each is in some ways a little council of its own, circumscribed by its specific problem area, limited, presumably, in time, and performing some but not all of the usual council functions. Each constitutes a potential threat to the council's ability to achieve a modicum of coordination in the health and welfare field.[12]

Other new structures have emerged from the youth and radical counterculture development. These are represented by such alternative quasi institutions as free health clinics and drug help organizations. These structures are informal, flexible, and decentralized. One can also include women's centers, Nader's spin-offs, and prisoners' unions as new forms. Emerging forms of state and regional planning should also be noted.

Some of the newer forms of social planning and service delivery are imaginative and improve upon structural arrangements previously devised by welfare councils. A question arises concerning the staying power of these new structures. Do they see themselves as permanent or as ad hoc arrangements, and which of the two is more appropriate for their purposes? What will happen as the economy

---

[12]Roland L. Warren, "The Impact of New Designs of Community Organization," *Child Welfare* 44 (November 1965): 494–500.

fluctuates or political regimes change? Considerable erosion of new programs took place under the Nixon administration. Can these new forms be institutionalized in the community? Can or should some be incorporated into welfare councils and other local institutions?

These developments can be characterized as part of a larger social phenomenon —increased specialization of function with separate administrative structures for different social tasks. Certain efficiencies may arise from this type of specialized attention and/or expertise, but problems of coordination thereby created need also to be attended to.

Greater Governmental Activity in Local Community Organization

For many years community organization and local social planning and policy making were the domain of voluntary agencies and private civic groups. Starting with the 1935 New Deal programs, the federal government has entered public welfare and the human services on a large scale. Government programs, however, were often rigidly administered, precluding citizen involvement and manifesting little concern for interagency planning and coordination. Each bureau attended to its own affairs, without relating to other governmental bureaus or voluntary agencies. In a remarkably short period of time, this has changed. More than a decade ago Charles Schottland outlined the growing social planning enterprise of the federal government and its powerful impact on local communities:

> Federal agencies are spending millions of dollars in social planning either directly or through grants to local and state agencies; they are employing social workers called community organization specialists or by some similar title; their programs are directly affecting planning of public and voluntary organizations, at the local, state, federal and national levels; the literature issued by the federal agencies on social planning and community organization is finding its way into the curriculum of schools of social work and other educational programs; and these activities of the federal government in the social planning area seem likely to expand, and increasingly to influence the scope, direction and content of health and welfare planning throughout our social welfare structure.[13]

A more current appraisal reaffirms this trend:

> Recent developments, particularly the enactment of special planning legislation, are a strong indication that all levels of government will intensify their social planning efforts. Public administrators, legislators, program participants, beneficiaries, and the general public can be expected to intensify their demands for a more comprehensive and effective system of human services. There will be increased demands for program accountability and more coordination of services. Social planning will be an essential element in all these efforts.[14]

---

[13]Charles I. Schottland, "Federal Planning for Health and Welfare," *The Social Welfare Forum 1963* (New York: Columbia University Press, 1963), p. 97.

[14]John E. Hanson, "Social Planning, Governmental: Federal and State," *Encyclopedia of Social Work,* 1977, p. 1448.

Several of the governmental programs were deliberately designed to alter the normal service modes of agencies and to influence local social planning patterns. The projects of the President's Committee on Juvenile Delinquency and Youth Crime were in this category, as were the community action programs of the Office of Economic Opportunity. Sargent Shriver, then serving as director of OEO, made this explicit. The main function of the act that established his agency, he asserted, was "a shakeup of the entire system of services that has served the poor. . . . We must change traditional piecemeal approaches and gain a coordinated program."[15] It is clear that this newer approach was no more successful than were the established ones.

The Model Cities program, under the Department of Housing and Urban Development, represented a major concerted effort by government to develop "planning coalitions" to alleviate slum conditions and renew blighted areas. According to its stated objectives the program aimed to "remove or arrest blight or decay and make a substantial impact on the physical and social problems in entire sections or neighborhoods."[16] It was specifically geared toward social conditions such as educational disadvantage, public health, and underemployment. Like the poverty program, Model Cities placed a premium on participation by local residents. New programs replace the old, but the momentum of governmental responsibility and involvement—of states as well as the federal government—continues.

Social Policy Perspectives

Social policy has moved closer to the center of stage of social work, as a practice mode, an intellectual preoccupation, and an area of curriculum development. A spate of books on social policy have been produced by people such as Schorr, Gil, Rein, Tropman et al., and Gilbert and Specht.[17]

Baumheier and Schorr indicate that social policy has "become a matter of world-wide interest" and that "since the mid-1960's, the social work profession has come under considerable pressure to become more credible and effective in social policy, both locally and nationally. It has responded to these pressures ideologically, in its programs of professional activities, and in the direction of interest of its younger members."[18]

While in Great Britain social policy has been highly developed as an academic discipline (social administration) and as an applied area, it has lagged behind in

---

[15]Sargent Shriver, Director of Office of Economic Opportunity, quoted in the *Detroit News*, March 14, 1965, p. 17B.

[16]U.S. Department of Housing and Urban Development, *Programs of HUD* (Washington, D.C.: U.S. Government Printing Office, 1967), p. 6.

[17]Alvin Schorr, *Explorations in Social Policy* (Washington, D.C.: Brookings Institution, 1968); David G. Gil, *Unraveling Social Policy* (Cambridge, Mass.: Schenkman, 1973); Martin Rein, *Social Policy: Issues of Choice and Change* (New York: Random House, 1970); John E. Tropman, et al., *Strategic Perspectives on Social Policy* (New York: Pergamon, 1976); Neil Gilbert and Harry Specht, *Dimensions of Social Welfare Policy* (Englewood Cliffs, N.J.: Prentice-Hall, 1974).

[18]Edward C. Baumheier and Alvin L. Schorr, "Social Policy," *Encyclopedia of Social Work*, 1977, pp. 1453–62.

the United States. Definitions and conceptualization of social policy are varied and somewhat inchoate. Programs of training are emergent and ill defined. Coherent national programs reflecting rational social goals are viewed by politicians and professionals as a necessary approach to problem solving (e.g., in the provision of adequate health services to all). It is recognized that national policy planning and local initiative must be articulated, sometimes collaboratively, sometimes on an adversary basis, for the achievement of maximum social benefits.

While social policy is not yet a clearly defined occupational role in social work, and while training procedures are still in a developmental stage, social policy is an area whose time has clearly arrived. Graduate programs and policy institutes have mushroomed in recent years in specialized areas such as public health, education, aging, and environmental studies. As social policy is so intertwined with politics and government, its evolution will depend on the character of administration empowered by the electorate, the political ideologies that crystallize in coming years within the body politic, and the effects of social movements in influencing these developments.

Increased policy consciousness should not necessarily be read as the road to more rational or humane social welfare programs. Because of the tangled interrelationship of government and industry, policy choices have often tended to be dominated more by the calculations of corporations than the concerns of the clients. Charles Lindblom discusses this relationship in a penetrating theoretical analysis.[19] He finds that market systems such as our own have dual structures of authority. Conventional government is one. The other is the system of business, which both rivals and complements governmental authority. Neither can operate without the cooperation of the other. The values of the business community shape the world view of the government. Lindblom concludes that "a market-oriented system may require for its success so great a disproportion of business influence ... that even modest challenges to it are disruptive to economic stability and growth." This association, he says, may be crippling to both systems.

Michael Harrington has spoken to the same issue as follows:

> America has a planning system that is dedicated to unbalanced—and sometimes socially catastrophic—growth. It follows a hidden agenda in which Government policy reinforces corporate priorities that ... maximize profits.[20]

Two examples can be given. The Urban Renewal Housing policy insisted on a program grounded in economic gains for private investors and builders. The result has been the wholesale destruction of districts in which poor people resided, the construction of civic centers, and a net reduction in the number of dwelling units for low-income and minority populations. Another example is the uncontrolled predilection of corporations to abandon old regions having weak economies and strong unions, and to relocate plants in regions that feature low wages.

---

[19]Charles Lindblom, *Politics and Markets: The World Political-Economic Systems* (New York: Basic Books, 1978).

[20]*New York Times,* January 29, 1978, p. E17.

Government policy is reactive to this, attempting through social welfare to cope with the misery left behind, or through economic incentives to revitalize the economic wasteland. As Harrington continues in his statement, "the long run solution is a complete democratization of basic investment decisions, which are too important to be left in the board room."

The main point is that democratic social planning without democratic economic planning results often in a hodgepodge of distorted and self-defeating policies, no matter how energetic the effort and sophisticated the planning activities. The character of planning, not just its volume and the number of professional jobs that are generated, should be of concern to community organization practitioners and educators.

Efficiency, Accountability, Evaluation

A distinguishing mark of human services work in the 1970s has been the marked preoccupation with accountability and concern for efficient management of programs. Accompanying this is a concentration on evaluation of program outcomes, with cost effectiveness as a central consideration. The emergence of this trend may be seen to emanate from two sources, quite different in character.

The trend toward efficient management stems in part from the era of the Nixon administration. As a means of reducing the scope and costliness of social programs, Nixon and his lieutenants made a deliberate effort to remove as heads of social programs professionals with human service orientations, and to replace them with business-minded executives who had a predilection for the niceties of accountancy. The Nixon administration's ideological preference for the "hard-nosed" ways of the business world in part accounted for this stance, but also involved was a wish to cut back or dismantle many of the programs that had come into being during the Great Society period of the 1960s.

Nixon's gambit was given impetus by the overinflated claims of those programs, their inadequate funding, the hastily conceived, poorly managed quality of many of them, and the political and organizational conflict that surrounded them. The increasingly bad name of public assistance also tended to discredit social programs and the way they were directed. Accordingly, when a liberal Carter administration replaced a conservative Ford administration, it was on the basis of a platform promising to bring better order and managerial acumen to the federal programs than could the Republicans.

The accountability push came in part from these sources, but it was also joined by radical, minority, and locality-based groups who expressed great distrust of professionals and bureaucracies. Professionals and bureaucrats, it was contended, were overwhelmingly focused on their own occupational interests and unresponsive to the needs and wishes of the clients whom they purported to serve. Accountability, in this case, had a service rather than a fiscal basis: it did not mean cheap services, but meaningful ones. Liberal and moderate groups were concerned about the high cost of programs, their seeming inability to make drastic changes, and the need to be more discerning in a time of shrinking resources.

Also, already in the Johnson era, Program Planning and Budgeting System (PPBS) and other management tools were being introduced, but not with a reductionist purpose. The convergence of sentiment from the left, center, and right on making services more effective and responsive has been a strong stimulus to the contemporary "efficient management" school of thought in the human services.

Improvements in the technology of evaluation research have contributed to this movement. This has been a circular development. Calls for more effective management placed demands on evaluation researchers to provide better tools. Availability of these tools has led to demands for their use by managers. Both formal requirements and informal pressures have stimulated program evaluation efforts. Some federal statutes, such as those related to community mental health centers, mandate evaluation as a requisite for receiving funds. In other instances, applicants for federal funding have the implicit understanding that without firm evaluation provisions their proposals are less likely to receive serious consideration, even though this is not a legal requirement.

One sign of this trend has been the proliferation of administration specializations within schools of social work. Two leading schools, Columbia and Chicago, have instituted programs that are run jointly with schools of business administration. The University of Michigan established a new separate concentration in evaluation research. Within agencies a range of structured administrative procedures is being applied commonly—including management by objectives, the Delphi technique, nominal group process for problem formulation, program budgeting (PPBS), and the like. These techniques have infused all the human service fields.

Some discordance may be observed: on the one hand many governmental and voluntary programs call for increased client and community participation, a position that encourages flexibility, pluralism, and the playing out of political and interest group forces. On the other hand there are pressures for orderliness, predictability, and administrative control in the running of programs. These thrusts have some mutual contradictions or at least create major tensions in their simultaneous execution. Nonetheless, they have both emerged as strong intellectual and operational currents in the 1970s.

Fluctuating Neighborhood and Grass Roots Community Organization

Community development and social action at the local neighborhood level reached an apex in the late 1960s, although certain precursors existed in the preceding decade and other developments have followed into the middle and late 1970s. Both social agency programming and independent social forces have contributed to this phenomenon of grass roots citizen involvement. For example, Point 7 of the Urban Renewal Act of 1954 required citizen participation in redevelopment as a condition of federal support. The Housing and Urban Development Act of 1968 reinforced this principle. Urban renewal authorities involved citizens at the grass roots in renewal planning in various degrees and with varying consequences.[21] Programs of the Office of Economic Opportunity gave considerable momentum to the idea of including the poor in policy making and administration. There is evidence that Revenue Sharing is continuing this trend to some degree. Settlement houses increased organizational efforts in the neighborhoods and diminished their preoccupation with small-group activities within their buildings.

Meanwhile, other forces accelerated the grass roots trend, particularly in the area of social action. The civil rights movement gave great impetus to social action in the black community. Some civil rights groups moved from tactics of protest to neighborhood community organization and political action.[22] Growing black nationalism stimulated the beginnings of separatist institutions and programs, with a strong impetus for local control. Black social action touched off similar activity among other oppressed racial minorities as well as among white ethnics. Student activism on hundreds of campuses underlined the participation concept. The women's movement became a powerful force for mobilizing local participation, as did organizing among gays. Grass roots approaches also developed in fertility control, community mental health, housing, public health, environmental protection, political practices reform, consumerism, and other institutional areas. Also of great significance was the peace movement, aimed at ending the war in Vietnam, with its political ramifications in the McCarthy and McGovern presidential campaigns and related ventures.

Grass roots civic action is often likened to a falling star, reaching its heights in the 1960s and plummeting to earth, burned out and dissipated with the transition into the 1970s. A closer look reveals that the legacy of the earlier period has been carried forward, not in as dramatic or comprehensive a way, but nevertheless with vitality and prevalence.

One element of this is the inclusion of provision for citizen involvement in governmental programs of all sorts. A kind of participation revolution has been carried out, often somewhat imperceptibly, but usually at least at the level of formal specification or requirements. The participatory aspects of recent governmental programming have been described as follows:

> Federal and state governments now encourage or require citizen participation structures and processes in most of their funded social programs, including health, mental health, housing, manpower development, education, welfare, aging, economic development, and environmental and consumer protection. Recent evidence of federal support for community development and the necessity for local participation in governmental decision making and program development is found in the State and Local Fiscal Assistance Act (federal revenue sharing) of 1972 and the Housing and Community Development Act of 1974. Legislation and ordinances have been passed in many states that encourage or require the development of not only state and

---

[21]James Q. Wilson, "Planning and Politics: Citizen Participation in Urban Renewal," *Journal of the American Institute of Planners,* 3 (November, 1963): 242–49. For a review of renewal planning, see Herbert Gans, "The Failure of Urban Renewal: A Critique and Some Proposals," *Commentary* 39 (April, 1965): 29–37.

[22]Bayard Rustin, "From Protest to Politics: The Future of the Civil Rights Movement," *Commentary* 39 (February, 1965): 25–31.

municipal, but regional and neighborhood or submunicipal structures to deal with such concerns as education, delinquency, and mental health.[23]

An even broader assessment, which takes into account both governmental factors and general community aspects, describes recent grass roots activity as follows:

> Despite a weakening of citizen input in many programs, new legislation in the mid-1970's strengthened the citizens' role in some instances; therefore, the situation remained mixed. Changes in Title XX of the Social Security Act mandated a period of public review before state plans for a variety of social service programs could be adopted. A majority of the members of health planning agencies must now be consumers. Almost nine hundred community action agencies still exist, providing employment, community organization, and social services. Some citizens continue to be active in decentralized city halls and neighborhood service centers. Others participate in consumer cooperatives or community development corporations in an attempt to make their neighborhoods more self-sufficient economically. Many citizens have turned to mass consumer education or political activities such as lobbying and legal action.[24]

Neighborhood-oriented thinking and activity is a social current that cannot be ignored.[25] Liberals from the 1960s, disillusioned with the antipoverty and urban renewal outcomes, increasingly have turned to the neighborhood approach to urban revitalization and urban reform. They have been joined by masses of ordinary Americans who long have wanted little more than a fit and pleasant place to live, and in recent years have become determined to get it.

Neighborhood organizations in great variety have proliferated around the nation, and many of them have taken a new course. They have moved to a position of formal recognition by city councils, mayors, and/or charters. In effect some of them have become embryo neighborhood governments. The phenomenon of neighborhood government is described, with many case examples, by Howard Hallman in his recent book.[26]

Two new national organizations have come into being to promote the interests of neighborhoods. One is the National Conference of Neighborhood Councils, whose members are largely professionals in local government who work in the area of citizen participation and/or neighborhood development. The other organization is the National Association of Neighborhoods with its political action arm, the Alliance for Neighborhood Government. This association involves volunteer neighborhood organizations and individuals actively working with them.

There is a steady stream of serious books on neighborhoods. The Warrens' *Neighborhood Organizer's Handbook*[27] is a good example, as are Morris and

---

[23]Irving Spergel, "Social Planning and Community Organization: Community Development," *Encyclopedia of Social Work,* 1977, pp. 1428–29.

[24]Peggy Wireman, "Citizen Participation," *Encyclopedia of Social Work,* 1977, pp. 178–79.

[25]This discussion on neighborhoods is informed by a personal communication from James Cunningham, which is either quoted directly or paraphrased.

[26]Howard Hallman, *The Organization and Operation of Neighborhood Councils* (Washington, D.C.: Center for Governmental Studies, Box 34481, 20034, 1977).

[27]Rachelle Warren and Donald Warren, *The Neighborhood Organizer's Handbook* (Notre Dame, Ind.: University of Notre Dame Press, 1977).

Hess's *Neighborhood Power, The New Localism*[28] and David O'Brien's *Neighborhood Organization and Interest-group Processes.*[29] James Cunningham is coauthor of two books on neighborhoods, one with Roger Ahlbrandt, Jr., on neighborhood preservation, and one with Milton Kotler on neighborhood organizing.

The Carter administration has given high priority to neighborhoods in its appointments. People like Jan Peterson on the White House staff and Gene Baroni and Joe McNeilly in HUD are strong advocates. ACTION also is beginning to reflect this orientation.

Direct funding of neighborhoods by the federal government is a future possibility. Sen. William Proxmire has introduced the idea into a community development bill, and it will be with us for a while. This issue will terrify the mayors.

In all this local ferment there will be a large variety of roles for social workers who have a neighborhood orientation or a wish to engage in aspects of grass roots community organizing.

Some concrete results have come about through these efforts. Wireman lists the following achievements of participation:

1. Bureaucrats are becoming sensitive to the need to take citizen and client opinions into account in planning and delivering services.
2. Improvements have been made in services in accordance with client needs and wishes.
3. Groups are learning how to influence and bypass traditional political and administrative channels.
4. A generation of leaders, especially from minority groups, holds positions of political or administrative authority in federal, state and local government.[30]

Having said this, it is also obvious that locality-based actions have not brought about either powerful social reform or a new unified national political ideology. Much agency posturing regarding participation smacks of tokenism. It has become increasingly clear that local efforts must be linked with broader social policy change efforts.

Social Action–Social Change Perspectives

Some of the newer approaches gave increased attention to changing aspects of the social system and deemphasized the provision of individualized services or the coordination of treatment programs. Mobilization for Youth (MFY) was probably the foremost illustration in the last twenty years of the change approach in social work. The project did not primarily attempt to bring treatment services to delinquent youth. It approached delinquency from the perspective of sociological, rather than psychological theory. Delinquency was seen as arising primarily from

---

[28]David Morris and Karl Hess, *Neighborhood Power, the New Localism,* Institute for Policy Studies Series (Boston: Beacon Press, 1975).

[29]David J. O'Brien, *Neighborhood Organization and Interest-group Processes* (Princeton, N.J.: Princeton University Press, 1975).

[30]Wireman, "Citizen Participation."

social arrangements that block access to opportunities, rather than from personal characteristics of the delinquent. Thus MFY made efforts to change aspects of the social system in order to provide better opportunities for low-income youth to rise in the system. One program attempted to influence employers to open additional jobs for these young people, and another sought institutional change in the school system so that children would be better prepared to take those opportunities that became available to them. Youth and adults were trained in methods of protest and social action in order to develop the skills and power to call forth greater resources from the broader society. MFY was a kind of proving ground for such an approach, and the lessons of its roller-coaster history have been taken into account by other organizations. The potentials of social action programs under governmental sponsorship or financial support have been called into question as a result of experiences like this one.

On the heels of MFY came the large radical movements involving minorities, students, and peace advocates. While the highly visible and confrontive radicalism of the 1960s has gone into sharp decline, efforts in that direction still exist. Radicalism has taken a more political grass roots form, as exemplified by the effort to obtain "life line" utility rates for small (noncorporate) energy users and by the community-based political organizing carried out by Tom Hayden in his bid to become governor of California. Cesar Chavez's United Farm Workers Union continues to build an organization and serve as the official bargaining representative for an increasing number of workers. Blacks, Chicanos, Native Americans, and other minorities maintain their thrust for equality and justice, carrying out their programs in more complex, varied, and sophisticated forms. Movements composed of women, gays, consumers, seniors, tax reformers, and other interest groups are in motion. Even within the political mainstream one finds an organized socialist caucus in the Democratic party, with former dissident radicals such as Zolton Ferency in Michigan working in proximity to the party machinery. Social action, while diminished in scope and visibility, appears transmuted rather than eliminated as a contemporary force. The absence of grandstand histrionics in the press is in part a reflection of the establishment of viable underground and alternative media as means of communication within and among movements. The achievements of these multiple thrusts have sometimes been impressive, even though they never match the hopes of enthusiasts. In addition, they are only one component of a blurred and fluctuating political picture composed of simultaneous currents from the left, center, and right, together with mixed expressions that can hardly be identified, for example, the Carter administration.

An extremely informative report on the status of local social action in the mid-1970s has been presented by Janice Perlman,[31] who studied sixty action groups across the country. (See Reading 26.) After examining numerous aspects of their organizing styles and techniques, Professor Perlman states:

---

[31]Janice E. Perlman, "Grassrooting the System," *Social Policy,* (September/October 1976), pp. 4–20.

The seventies are spawning a plethora of grassroots associations involving local people mobilized on their own behalf around concrete issues of importance in their communities. . . . Evidence thus far shows that not only have the groups been growing rapidly but also that participant turnover in the groups has been relatively low.[32]

Among groups described and their major activities are the following:

ACORN, Association of Community Organizations for Reform
NOW (Arkansas)—utilities reform, generic drugs
Massachusetts Fair Share—utilities reform
Mississippi Action for Community Education—municipal services
Save Our Cumberland Mountains—tax reform
The Rhode Island Workers in Action—medical care
Southern Cooperative Development Fund—cooperative housing

Perlman classifies currently operating groups into five types: (1) direct action —multi-issue: (2) direct action—single issue; (3) electoral efforts: (4) alternative institutions—cooperatives; (5) alternative institutions—community development corporations.

The author indicates that the 1960s set the stage for these groups and that some of the old leaders are in evidence. However, the style of operation is different: issues are rooted in the daily lives of participants, there is a longer time perspective, people's consciousness is raised through participation on a concrete issue at the community level, a mass base rather than a minority base is sought, rhetoric is toned down and ideology kept in low key. The groups function independently of government sponsorship (as in Model Cities) and are free as well from a national voluntary superordinate structure (as with a local chapter of NAACP). New methods of indigenous fund raising are being devised.

The researcher especially connects up this activism with economic constrictions. She describes the recent period as characterized by—

unemployment, inflation, and the first decline in real wages in 25 years . . . The fiscal crisis of the state and cities has meant a decline in the quality and quantity of public services coupled with an increase in taxes. People watch their neighborhoods deteriorate from lack of funds for services. . . . Given the widespread disillusionment with existing institutions . . . A tremendous surge of neighborhood vitality in the United States had expressed itself through grass roots associations.[33]

Within social work, professional writings have appeared, taking an avowedly socialist slant.[34] A new journal of Marxist social work thought has emerged (*CATALYST: A Socialist Journal of the Social Services*), sponsored by a number

---

[32]Perlman, "Grassrooting the System," pp. 4, 19.
[33]Perlman, "Grassrooting the System," pp. 7–8.
[34]Roy Bailey and Mike Brake, eds., *Radical Social Work* (New York: Pantheon Books, 1975); Jeffry H. Galper, *The Politics of Social Services* (Englewood Cliffs, N.J.: Prentice-Hall, 1975); Frances Piven and Richard Cloward, *Poor People's Movements: Why They Succeed and How They Fail* (New York: Pantheon Books, 1978).

of well-known social work educators and practitioners. While the pitch of radical community organization and activity has been reduced, there is probably more substance and sophistication in what currently exists.

Having said this, it is also obvious that locality-based action has not brought about either powerful social reform or a new national left-leaning political alignment. It has become increasingly clear to analysts that local efforts must be linked with broader social change efforts. Nevertheless, there has been a significant politicization of the citizenry in the sense of greater awareness of social issues and of the social and economic dimensions of social problems. Veterans of the student, peace, civil rights, poverty, and other movements are an informed segment of the citizen body. The new public awareness includes greater appreciation and use of group action and advocacy methods as a means of dealing with social dissatisfactions. Tom Hayden has said, "The radicalism of the '60's has become the common sense of the '70's." There is good reason to believe it will continue on as part of the politics of the 1980s.

Keeping Up with the Changing Scene

In summary, we have been through a shifting period of community organization activity. The human service professions have been giving greater attention to social problems, social change, planning, citizen and client input, and other community-relevant considerations. As Warren puts it, we have left behind a period when individual agencies were fishing in a placid brook. "Now the brook has become agitated, various agencies get the hook, others find difficulty casting in their lines—in short, an exciting turmoil!"[35] This turmoil creates daily on-the-job difficulties for professional planners and community activists attempting to get their bearings and make hard programmatic decisions. It also disturbs the complacency of the academician who strains to achieve clear and stable definitions.

We have set down some guidelines to aid in the conceptualization of this amorphous and changing area of social practice, recognizing that the ground is shifting under our feet as we write. We believe that the approach we are taking, represented in the first article in Chapter I, which views the field not in monolithic terms but as encompassing several differing and somewhat distinct modes of practice, offers a useful point of departure for understanding the tangle of American community organization practice.

In the light of fluctuating economic conditions, ideological turns and programmatic fads, there are those who see a decline in the prominence of community organization. If the field is viewed in the broad, variegated way suggested here, one can only conclude that community organization is alive and vigorous. From a locality development point of view, much ferment exists. Governmental guidelines of all kinds are insisting on the inclusion of clients and citizens in the

---

[35]Roland L. Warren, "The Impact of New Designs of Community Organization," *Child Welfare* 44 (November, 1965): 495.

planning and provision of services. Neighborhood groups are making claims for a voice in matters affecting their lives. Minority and ethnic concerns have been salient in many of these developments. Consumer and environmental considerations have also been prominent. In social planning there has been a maturation in social policy perspectives. As old federal programs die out, new ones replace them, many geared to state and regional levels. The trend toward efficiency, accountability, and evaluation brings a new level of rigor and potentially much benefit to the delivery of services to client groups. Social action, while diminished in scope and visibility, appears transformed rather than eliminated as a social force. Nevertheless, progress overall is halting and unpredictable. The achievements of these multiple thrusts have sometimes been impressive but never match the hopes of enthusiasts. New challenges and roles ever appear.

Definitions and conceptualizations will need to be reformulated in response to the flow of these events in the shifting stream of community action. In a worldly profession such as community organization, this is as it should be.

JACK ROTHMAN

CHAPTER I

Variations, Conceptual and Historical

We have organized this volume around a particular approach to community organization practice. We suggest that there are three different models of practice. These models, discussed by Jack Rothman in the first selection, are termed locality development, social planning, and social action.

Rothman provides another useful perspective on practice, specifying a set of practice variables which are highly relevant for analyzing community intervention. These practice variables, which are elaborated upon in the article, include the following:

Goal categories of community action.
Assumptions concerning community structure and problem conditions.
Basic change strategy.
Characteristic change tactics and techniques.
Salient practitioner roles.
Medium of change.
Orientation toward power structure(s).
Boundary definition of the community client system or constituency.
Assumptions regarding interests of community subparts.
Conception of the public interest.
Conception of the client population or constituency.
Conception of client role.

These practice variables operate differently, with some regularity, in each model of community organization practice. Further, each is associated with different sorts of sponsoring agencies, practitioner positions, and professional analogues. Rothman also discusses and illustrates mixing and phasing of the three modes of practice.

Rothman views practice from the perspective of the community practitioner and the analytical and functional tasks in which he engages. Said another way, practice is viewed from the eyes of an individual with professional responsibilities to discharge under varying circumstances. Of course, one might approach the task from other points of departure. For example, Mayer N. Zald, in Chapter IV, constructs his practice concepts from an organizational analysis, viewing organizational goals and structural constraints as critical. David L. Sill's study of a voluntary association in the welfare field is another example of this approach.[1] Alternatively, one might start from the vantage point of community problems or the needs and characteristics of different constituencies or target populations. In any case, if the concern is professional intervention, one must specify appropriate operations and tactics to be utilized under varying conditions and not stop at the level of sociological analysis that gives no behavioral guidelines to the practitioner.

Fred M. Cox and Charles Garvin provide an overview of the broad cultural and social factors that have shaped community organization, particularly as it has developed in social work. They give particular attention to some of the institutions that emerged in the latter part of the nineteenth century in England and in North America which were the crucible out of which community organization grew. These institutions—charity organization societies, social settlements, councils of social agencies, community chests—gave birth to much of social work and most of what came to be called community organization in social work. The unique role of racial and ethnic groups in the development of community organization is portrayed. Finally, Cox and Garvin discuss the growth of professional community organization practice, and a few of the main ideas that inform that practice.

A number of groups have had a significant impact on the development of community organization practice. These include adult educators and those who, over many years, have worked through agricultural extension and land-grant college–sponsored community development programs serving rural areas of the United States. Labor leaders with their methods of organizing for social action have added a significant dimension. In addition to organizing increasing numbers of white-collar workers, including nurses, teachers, and social workers, some unions have aided the organization of marginal workers. The organization of farm workers in California is a notable recent example. The United Nations, foreign governments, and a variety of private groups such as the Asia Foundation and the American Friends Service Committee have conducted significant community development programs overseas. Other contributions are discussed in the Introduction to Part One.

Social workers are one of many groups that have helped to develop community organization practice. They have been among the self-conscious practitioners of the art, not content merely to act, but recording their activities, ordering their practice, and searching for general principles to guide intervention. Community practice is not confined to social work, but social workers have made a unique contribution which is the focus of the historical selection in this chapter.

---

[1]David L. Sills, *The Volunteers: Means and Ends in a National Organization* (Glencoe, Ill.: The Free Press, 1957).

1.

Jack Rothman

THREE MODELS OF COMMUNITY ORGANIZATION PRACTICE, THEIR MIXING AND PHASING

A welter of differing, contrasting, and sometimes clashing formulations of community organization practice exists, and this condition has been a source of immense perplexity and discomfort to the struggling practitioner and to the teacher of community organization. Harper and Dunham[1] in their anthology listed 13 different definitions of community organization and indicated that at least 50 to 100 definitions had been projected in social welfare and sociological literature in the previous thirty-five years.

Inadequate conceptual development prevails in professional areas which have community organization and planning aspects. In fields such as social work, education (adult education), and public health (public health education and planning), the community organization dimension is somewhat peripheral and outside the main thrust of the profession. These areas have accordingly suffered from inadequate conceptualization and research efforts. The social planning aspects of city planning have similarly been neglected. Human relations training has stressed social psychological factors. Community psychology and community psychiatry are newly arrived on the scene.

An examination of present practice reveals a considerable degree of variation, transition, and confusion. One observer aptly describes the situation:

> From a method confined largely to Chest and Council social planning and the staffing of national social welfare agencies, it has moved into extensive grass roots organization and participation in political areas. From a method concerned largely with the orderly dispensation of existing welfare services, it has added an emphasis on social change and serving groups in the community by altering institutions and other aspects of their environment. From a method largely utilizing amelioration and consensus, it has consciously moved to include the use of conflict and power. Community organization has added initiating to enabling. It has added working with the impoverished poor to work with the elite; and social agency criticism to social agency support.[2]

One scholar has been led to characterize "macro social work" as "a practice in search of some theory."[3]

With the foregoing as backdrop, we shall endeavor to achieve some greater measure of clarity in conceptualizing community organization practice. One of the difficulties

---

Jack Rothman, "Three Models of Community Organization Practice," from National Conference on Social Welfare, *Social Work Practice 1968* (New York: Columbia University Press, 1968). Copyright © 1968, National Conference on Social Welfare. Revised, 1978.

[1] Ernest B. Harper and Arthur Dunham, *Community Organization in Action: Basic Literature and Critical Comments* (New York: Association Press, 1959).

[2] Charles Grosser, "The Legacy of the Federal Comprehensive Projects for Community Organization," Twenty-fifth Annual Program Meeting, Council on Social Work Education, 1967, p. 2.

[3] Edward E. Schwartz, "Macro Social Work: A Practice in Search of Some Theory," *Social Service Review,* 51, No. 2 (1977), pp. 201–27.

has been that writers on the subject have attempted to set forth a single model or conception of community organization which was presumed to embrace all forms of professional practice. Often these models were actually disparate, touched on different aspects of practice, or made discrepant assumptions about goals, methods, or values. The position advanced here holds that in empirical reality there are different forms of community intervention and that at this stage in the development of practice theory it would be better to capture and describe these rather than to attempt to establish a grand, all-embracing theory or conception. The implication is that we should speak of community organization *methods* rather than *the* community organization method. At the same time the actual and theoretical blending of alternative approaches should be acknowledged. Indeed, a basic intent of this analysis is to encourage purposeful and skilled mixing of different strategies. The analysis will culminate in just such a discussion.

THREE MODELS OF INTERVENTION

There appear to be at least three important orientations to deliberate or purposive community change in contemporary American communities, both urban and rural, and overseas. We may best refer to them as approaches or models *A, B,* and *C,* although they can roughly be given the appellations respectively of *locality development, social planning,* and *social action.* We will use these terms in a particularistic way, as will become clear in the passages which follow. For present purposes, therefore, the reader is cautioned not to interpret these terms in his or her usual way. These three modes of action are not seen as exhaustive of all actual or potential possibili-

ties. Because of their contemporary significance they have been selected for analysis; for reasons of economy in a single presentation, others have been excluded.

It should also be noted that we are referring to community action which is of a somewhat continuing nature and which includes staff (professionally trained or not) who are responsible for planning or sustaining action processes. Thus the category of events which include sporadic, *ad hoc,* voluntary civic action to obtain a new traffic light or displace an arrogant public official is not included.

Model *A,* locality development, presupposes that community change may be pursued optimally through broad participation of a wide spectrum of people at the local community level in goal determination and action. Its most prototypic form will be found in the literature of a segment of the field commonly termed "community development." As stated by a major U.N. publication: "Community Development can be tentatively defined as a process designed to create conditions of economic and social progress for the whole community with its active participation and the fullest possible reliance on the community's initiative."[4] According to Dunham, some themes emphasized in locality development include democratic procedures, voluntary cooperation, self-help, development of indigenous leadership, and educational objectives.[5]

Some examples of locality development as conceived here include neighborhood work programs conducted by settlement houses; Volunteers in Service to America; village-level work in some overseas commu-

---

[4]United Nations, *Social Progress through Community Development* (New York: United Nations, 1955), p. 6.

[5]Arthur Dunham, "Some Principles of Community Development," *International Review of Community Development,* No. 11 (1963), pp. 141–51.

nity development programs, including the Peace Corps; community work in the adult education field; and activities of the applied "group dynamics" professionals. Four representative books that express and elaborate community organization method according to Model *A* are those by the Biddles,[6] Goodenough,[7] Cary[8] and Clinard.[9] We will draw on the Biddle volume in particular for illustrative purposes.

Model *B,* the social planning approach, emphasizes a technical process of problemsolving with regard to substantive social problems, such as delinquency, housing, and mental health. Rational, deliberately planned, and controlled change has a central place in this model. Community participation may vary from much to little, depending on how the problem presents itself and what organizational variables are present. The approach presupposes that change in a complex industrial environment requires expert planners who, through the exercise of technical abilities, including the ability to manipulate large bureaucratic organizations, can skillfully guide complex change processes. The design of social plans and policies is of central importance, as is their implementation in effective and cost efficient ways. By and large, the concern here is with establishing, arranging, and delivering goods and services to people who need them. Building community capacity or fostering radical or

fundamental social change does not play a central part.

Within the field of social work the Brandeis University Florence Heller Graduate School for Advanced Studies in Social Welfare has come to typify this approach, and it also finds expression in university departments of public administration, urban affairs, city planning, and so forth. It is practiced in numerous federal bureaus and departments, in social planning divisions of housing authorities, in some community welfare councils, and in various facets of community mental health planning. Some writings which reflect Model *B* include Morris and Binstock,[10] Wilson,[11] Perloff,[12] and Delbecq.[13]

Model *C,* the social action approach, presupposes a disadvantaged segment of the population that needs to be organized, perhaps in alliance with others, in order to make adequate demands on the larger community for increased resources or treatment more in accordance with social justice or democracy. It aims at making basic changes in major institutions or community practices. Social action as employed here seeks redistribution of power, resources or decision-making in the community and/or changing basic policies of formal organizations. Examples of the social action approach include civil rights and black power

[6]William W. and Loureide J. Biddle, *The Community Development Process: The Rediscovery of Local Initiative* (New York: Holt, Rinehart and Winston, 1965).

[7]Ward H. Goodenough, *Cooperation in Change: an Anthropological Approach to Community Development* (New York: Russell Sage Foundation, 1963).

[8]Lee J. Cary, ed., *Community Development As a Process* (Columbia, Mo.: University of Missouri Press, 1970).

[9]Marshall Clinard, *Slums and Community Development* (New York: Free Press, 1966).

[10]Robert Morris and Robert H. Binstock, *Feasible Planning for Social Change* (New York: Columbia University Press, 1966).

[11]James Q. Wilson, "An Overview of Theories of Planned Change" in Robert Morris, ed., *Centrally Planned Change: Prospects and Concepts* (New York: National Association of Social Workers, 1964), pp. 12–40.

[12]Harvey S. Perloff, ed., *Planning and the Urban Community* (Pittsburgh: Carnegie Institute of Technology, 1961).

[13]Andre Delbecq et al., *Group Techniques for Program Planning: A Guide to Nominal Group and Delphi Processes* (Glenview, Ill.: Scott, Foresman and Co., 1975).

groups, La Raza, Alinsky's Industrial Areas Foundation projects, labor unions, consumer and environmental protection, the welfare rights movement, women's liberation, social movements and political action groups, and student groups associated with the New Left. Alinsky's *Reveille for Radicals* and *Rules for Radicals*[14] and scattered writings among the New Left[15] typify the orientation of the social action model. Some writings by professionals also reflect this orientation.[16]

Several schools of social work have developed specialized programs for training according to these three models. Thus the community development program at the University of Missouri has emphasized Model *A*; the doctoral program in planning at Brandeis University, Model *B*; and the social action program which was based at Syracuse University, Model *C*.

Morris and Binstock suggest a similar threefold division of the field of community planning and action:

> [*A*] . . . to alter human attitudes and behavioral patterns through education, exhortation and a number of other methods for stimulating self-development and fulfillment. [*B*] . . . to alter social conditions by changing the policies of formal organiza-

tions. It is undertaken to modify the amount, the quality, the accessibility, and the range of goods, services, and facilities provided for people. [*C*] . . . to effect reforms in major legal and functional systems of a society. It relies upon political agitation . . . and a host of other instruments for coping with powerful trends and developments.[17]

Having isolated and set off each of these models or ideal-types, it would be well to reiterate that we are speaking of analytical extremes and that in actual practice these orientations are overlapping rather than discrete.

Practice in any of these orientations may require techniques and approaches that are salient in another orientation. For example, neighborhood social actionists may be required to draw up a social plan in order to obtain funding for desired projects from HUD or HEW (Models *C* and *B*). Or social planners may decide that the most effective way of solving the problem of resistant attitudes toward family planning is through wide discussion and participation in developing a community program (Models *B* and *A*). While such mixtures occur in reality, many organizations in their central tendency may be characterized as reflecting one or another model.

On the other hand, community welfare councils, particularly of the older type that emphasize functional divisions rather than project committees, organizationally represented a blending of Models *A* and *B*. Community development as conducted overseas in developing countries also represents a composite of localized community organization along the lines of Model *A*, together with broad social and economic planning at the national level incorporating Model *B*. This blend may actually consti-

---

[14]Saul D. Alinsky, *Reveille for Radicals* (Chicago: University of Chicago Press, 1946), and *Rules for Radicals* (New York: Vintage Books, 1972).

[15]*Thoughts of the Young Radicals* (Washington, D.C., *The New Republic*, 1966).

[16]Warren Haggstrom, "The Power of the Poor," in Frank Riessman, Jerome Cohen, and Arthur Pearl, eds., *The Mental Health of the Poor* (New York: Free Press, 1964), pp. 205–23; Charles F. Grosser, "Community Development Programs Serving the Urban Poor," *Social Work, X*, No. 3 (1965), 15–21; Richard A. Cloward and Richard M. Elman, "Advocacy in the Ghetto," *Trans-Action, IV*, No. 2, (1966), 27–35; Douglas Glasgow, "Black Power through Community Control," *Social Work, XVII*, No. 3 (1972), 59–65; Jeffry H. Galper, *The Politics of Social Services* (Englewood Cliffs, N.J.: Prentice Hall, 1975); Roy Bailey and Mike Brake, *Radical Social Work* (New York: Pantheon Books, 1975).

[17]Morris and Binstock, *op. cit.,* p. 14.

tute a distinct additional model whose characteristics could be explicated independently.

Here, however, we will not attempt to deal with variants or mixed forms which may constitute unique separate models. Instead, for analytical purposes, we will view the three approaches as "pure" forms. The virtue in this is suggested by Morris and Binstock when they refer to their own classification system:

> The categories are somewhat arbitrary, for it is sometimes difficult to say that a particular planning experience fits one category but not another. For these reasons it is particularly important to achieve as narrow a focus as possible in analyzing planning; otherwise a systematic treatment is virtually impossible.[18]

To proceed with the analysis, we will attempt to specify a set of practice variables which will help to describe and compare each of the approaches when they are identified in the ideal-type form. Each of the orientations makes assumptions about the nature of the community situation, the definitions of one's client population or constituency, goal categories of action, conceptions of the general welfare, appropriate strategies of action, and so on. A set of such variables will be treated in the passages that follow. (The reader may find it useful to scan Tables 1.1 and 1.2 at this point.)

1. Goal Categories. Two main goals which have been discussed recurrently in the community organization literature are referred to frequently as "task" and "process." Task goals entail the completion of a concrete task or the solution of a delimited problem pertaining to the functioning of a community social system—delivery of ser-

vices, establishment of new services, passing of specific social legislation. Process goals or maintenance goals are more oriented to system maintenance and capacity, with aims such as establishing cooperative working relationships among groups in the community, creating self-maintaining community problem-solving structures, improving the power base of the community, stimulating wide interest and participation in community affairs, fostering collaborative attitudes and practices, and increasing indigenous leadership. Murray Ross characterizes this set of goals as "community integration" and "community capacity." Process goals are concerned with a generalized or gross capacity of the community system to function over time; task goals, with the solution of delimited functional problems of the system.[19]

In locality development, process goals receive heavy emphasis. The community's capacity to become functionally integrated, to engage in cooperative problem-solving on a self-help basis, and to utilize democratic processes is of central importance. Community practice in adult education makes citizen education the cardinal aim. The applied "group dynamics" professionals likewise assert the priority of "methodological" goals over "substantive" goals, viewed in terms of personal or community growth.[20] The same orientation is found in the theoretical writings in the field of community development proper where improving the

---

[18]Morris and Binstock, *op. cit.,* p. 15.

[19]For a more extended discussion of this subject see Jack Rothman, "An Analysis of Goals and Roles in Community Organization Practice," *Social Work,* IX, No. 2 (1964), 24–31. Also Neil Gilbert and Harry Specht, "Process Versus Task in Social Planning," *Social Work,* XXII, No. 3 (1977), 178–83.

[20]Kenneth D. Benne, "Deliberate Changing as the Facilitation of Growth," in Warren G. Bennis, Kenneth D. Benne, and Robert Chin, eds., *The Planning of Change* (New York: Holt, Rinehart and Winston, 1961).

TABLE 1.1

Three Models of Community Organization Practice
According to Selected Practice Variables

	Model A (Locality Development)	Model B (Social Planning)	Model C (Social Action)
1. Goal categories of community action	Self-help; community capacity and integration (process goals)	Problem-solving with regard to substantive community problems (task goals)	Shifting of power relationships and resources; basic institutional change (task or process goals)
2. Assumptions concerning community structure and problem conditions	Community eclipsed, anomie; lack of relationships and democratic problem-solving capacities; static traditional community	Substantive social problems; mental and physical health, housing, recreation	Disadvantaged populations, social injustice, deprivation, inequity
3. Basic change strategy	Broad cross section of people involved in determining and solving their own problems	Fact-gathering about problems and decisions on the most rational course of action	Crystallization of issues and organization of people to take action against enemy targets
4. Characteristic change tactics and techniques	Consensus: communication among community groups and interests; group discussion	Consensus or conflict	Conflict or contest: confrontation, direct action, negotiation
5. Salient practitioner roles	Enabler-catalyst, coordinator; teacher of problem-solving skills and ethical values	Fact-gatherer and analyst, program implementer, facilitator	Activist-advocate: agitator, broker, negotiator, partisan
6. Medium of change	Manipulation of small task-oriented groups	Manipulation of formal organizations and of data	Manipulation of mass organizations and political processes
7. Orientation toward power structure(s)	Members of power structure as collaborators in a common venture	Power structure as employers and sponsors	Power structure as external target of action: oppressors to be coerced or overturned
8. Boundary definition of the community client system or constituency	Total geographic community	Total community or community segment (including "functional" community)	Community segment
9. Assumptions regarding interests of community subparts	Common interests or reconcilable differences	Interests reconcilable or in conflict	Conflicting interests which are not easily reconcilable: scarce resources
10. Conception of the public interest	Rationalist-unitary	Idealist-unitary	Realist-individualist
11. Conception of the client population or constituency	Citizens	Consumers	Victims
12. Conception of client role	Participants in an interactional problem-solving process	Consumers or recipients	Employers, constituents, members

TABLE 1.2
Some Personnel Aspects of Community Organization Models

	Model A (Locality Development)	Model B (Social Planning)	Model C (Social Action)
Agency type	Settlement houses, overseas community development; Peace Corps, Vista, Friends Service Committee, Model Cities, health associations, consumers' co-ops	Welfare council, city planning board, federal bureaucracy, environmental planning bodies, regional planning groups	Alinsky, black power, welfare rights councils, cause and social movement groups, women's movement, trade union insurgent movements, consumer's movements, radical political groups.
Practice positions	Village worker, neighborhood worker, consultant to community development team, agricultural extension worker	Planning division head, planner	Local organizer
Professional analogues	Adult educator, nonclinical group worker, group dynamics professional, agricultural extension worker	Demographer, social survey specialist, public administrator, hospital planning specialist	Labor organizer, minority group organizer, welfare rights organizer, tenants' association worker

community's "mental health," *qua* community, is sometimes viewed as primary.[21]

In the social planning approach, stress is placed on task goals, oriented toward the solution of substantive social problems. Social planning organizations often are mandated specifically to deal with concrete

---

[21]See, for example, Alan M. Walker, "Some Relations between Community Development and Rogers' Client-centered Therapy," *Community Development Review,* VI, No. 1 (1961), 20–28. ("Community development is essentially a process of community therapy. One of its chief aims as a therapeutic process is the development of more mature individuals through the medium of community betterment. It will, therefore, be helpful to compare theories and methods of community development with those of individual psychiatric therapy, which claims to have much the same end in view.") For a similar position closer to the adult education tradition, see John F. McNaughton, "Seeking Solutions through a Community Workshop in Human Relations," *Adult Leadership,* XI (1963), 227–28, 244. ("This workshop represents the first step in an attempt to improve the psychological health of this community ... resulting from insufficient understanding of each other among the various segments of the community.")

social problems, and their official names signify this—mental health departments, city planning and housing authorities, commissions on physical rehabilitation, or alcoholism, and so on.

The social action approach may lean in the direction of either task goals or process goals. Some social action organizations, such as civil rights groups and cause-oriented organizations (welfare rights, trade unions), emphasize obtaining specific legislative outcomes (higher welfare allotments) or changing specific social practices (preferential hiring). Usually these objectives entail the modification of policies of formal organizations. Other social action groups lean more in the direction of process goals —building a constituency with the ability to acquire and exercise power—as exemplified by Saul Alinsky and the Industrial Areas Foundation or the early black power movement. This objective of building local-based power and decision-making centers transcends the solution of any given problem situation. Goals are often viewed in terms of changing power relationships rather than tinkering with small-scale or short-range problem situations. These small-scale activities are often pursued, however, because they are feasible and they help to build an organization. Creating power may also be associated with building personal self-esteem. Warren Haggstrom states this proposition as follows: "One way in which the poor can remedy the psychological consequences of their powerlessness and of the image of the poor as worthless is for them to undertake social action that redefines them as potentially worthwhile and individually more powerful."[22]

2. Assumptions Regarding Community Structure and Problem Conditions:

In Model *A* (locality development) the local community is frequently seen as overshadowed by the larger society, lacking in fruitful human relationships and problem-solving skills and peopled by isolated individuals suffering from anomie, alienation, disillusionment, and often mental illness. As Ross develops this theme, technological change has pressed society toward greater industrialization and urbanization with little consideration of the effects on social relations:

> The processes of urbanization have almost destroyed "man's feeling of belonging to" a community. . . .
> The problem of developing and maintaining common or shared values (the basic ingredient for cohesion) is made vastly more difficult by industrialization and urbanization. . . .
> The tendency for large subgroups to develop cohesion as separate entities in the

community produces social tension, potentially dangerous in any community. . . .
> Democracy will weaken, if not perish, unless supporting institutions are supported and new institutions (to meet new ways of living) are developed. . . .
> The barriers that prevent active participation in the direction of social change inhibit personal development.[23]

Ross sums up his basic assumptions regarding the contemporary community situation:

> This is the problem of man's loss of his essential human dignity. For surely man is being overwhelmed by forces of which he is only dimly aware, which subjugate him to a role of decreasing importance and present him with problems with which he has no means to cope. Aspects of this central problem are the difficulty of full expression of a democratic philosophy and the threats to the mental health of individual members of societies.[24]

Alternatively, the community may be seen as tradition-bound, ruled by a small group of conventional leaders, and composed of illiterate populations who lack skills in problem-solving and an understanding of the democratic process. Community development in developing nations frequently proceeds from this supposition.[25]

The planner represented in Model *B* comes to his situation with quite a different viewpoint. He is likely to see the community as comprised of a number of substantive social problem conditions, or a particular substantive problem which is of special interest to him, such as housing, em-

---

[22]Warren G. Haggstrom, "The Power of the Poor," in Louis A. Ferman *et al.,* eds., *Poverty in America* (Ann Arbor: University of Michigan Press, 1965), p. 332.

[23]Murray G. Ross, *Community Organization: Theory and Principles* (New York: Harper & Brothers, 1955), pp. 80–83.

[24]*Ibid.,* p. 84.

[25]See Goodenough, *op. cit.*

ployment, recreation. Warren, while taking account of the outlook set down by Ross, expresses also a perspective that is more congruent with that of the social planners:

> It is apparent that certain types of "problems" are broadly characteristic of contemporary American communities. While most noticeable in the metropolitan areas, most of them are apparent in smaller communities as well. They appear in such forms as the increasing indebtedness of central cities, the spread of urban blight and slums, the lack of adequate housing which people can afford, the economic dependence of large numbers of people in the population, poorly financed and staffed schools, high delinquency and crime rates, inadequate provisions for the mentally ill, the problem of the aged, the need for industrial development, the conflict of local and national agencies for the free donor's dollar, the problem of affording rapid transit for commuters at a reasonable price and at a reasonable profit, and the problem of downtown traffic congestion. This list is almost endless, and each of the problems mentioned could be subdivided into numerous problematical aspects.[26]

The social action practitioner in Model *C* has still a different mind-set. He would more likely view the community as comprised of a hierarchy of privilege and power. There exist islands of oppressed, deprived, ignored, or powerless populations suffering social injustice or exploitation at the hands of oppressors such as the "power structure," big government, corporations, the establishment, or the society at large. (Oppression can imply material deprivation or a more psychological state of disaffection.)

Todd Gitlin, a former president of the SDS put it this way:

> In a supposedly fluid America, it is class that apportions a man's share of justice, health, culture, education, ordinary respect —as any visit to a jail, an emergency room, a theatre, a college or a municipal bureau will illustrate.... *Power must be shared among those affected, and resources guaranteed to make this possible.*[27]

Again, we caution that the above describes dominant motifs rather than discrete categories. Many social actionists are greatly concerned about apathy and substantive problems, even as some social planners are concerned about both the quality of social relations and specific problems. We are defining dominant central tendencies rather than mutually exclusive properties.

3. Basic Change Strategy. In locality development the change strategy may be characterized as, "Let's all get together and talk this over"—an effort to get a wide range of community people involved in determining their "felt" needs and solving their own problems.

In planning, the basic change strategy is one of "Let's get the facts and take the logical next steps." In other words, let us gather pertinent facts about the problem, then decide on a rational and feasible course of action. The practitioner plays a central part in gathering and analyzing facts and determining appropriate services, programs, and actions. This may or may not be done with the participation of others, depending upon the planner's sense of the utility of participation in the given situation and the organizational context within which he functions.

In social action the change strategy may be articulated as, "Let's organize to over-

---

[26]Roland L. Warren, *The Community in America* (Chicago: Rand McNally & Company, 1963; rev. 1972), p. 14.

[27]Todd Gitlin, "Power and the Myth of Progress," in *Thoughts of the Young Radicals, op. cit.,* pp. 20, 22.

power our oppressor"—crystallizing issues so that people know who their legitimate enemy is and organizing mass action to bring pressure on selected targets. Such targets may include an organization, such as the welfare department; a person, such as the mayor; or an aggregate of persons, such as slum landlords.

4. Characteristic Change Tactics and Techniques.

In locality development, tactics of consensus are stressed—discussion and communication among a wide range of different individuals, groups, and factions.

Warren underlines the importance of cooperative, inclusive techniques for the practice we are designating as locality development:

> Because it seeks to organize people to express their own needs and to consider action alternatives with respect to them, the term has been applied to the organization of social action groups of the poor. However, such usage is misleading, since the *organization of one segment of the population in a contest relationship to other segments* which have not been brought into the process violates the major tenet of inclusiveness in community [locality] development principles. This passes no judgment on its desirability or feasibility, but simply, indicates that in the commonly accepted sense of the term, it is *not* community [locality] development.[28]

In social planning, fact-finding and analytical skills are important. Tactics of conflict or consensus may be employed depending upon the practitioner's analysis of the situation.

In social action, conflict tactics are emphasized including methods such as confrontation and direct action. Ability to mobilize relatively large numbers of people is necessary to carry out rallies, marches, boycotts, and picketing. In his usual direct and colorful way, Alinsky states the issue as follows:

> A people's organization is a conflict group. This must be openly and fully recognized. Its sole reason for coming into being is to wage war against all evils which cause suffering and unhappiness. A people's organization is the banding together of multitudes of men and women to fight for those rights which insure a decent way of life. . . . A people's organization is dedicated to an eternal war. . . . A war is not an intellectual debate, and in the war against social evils there are no rules of fair play . . . there can be no compromises.[29]

Elsewhere he adds:

> Issues which are non-controversial usually mean that people are not particularly concerned about them; in fact, by not being controversial they cease to be issues. Issues involve differences and controversy. History fails to record a single issue of importance which was not controversial. Controversy has always been the seed of creation.[30]

Warren, in his discussion of types of purposive social change, suggests a variation among conflict tactics: campaign strategies when there are differences among parties but issue consensus can eventually be reached; and contest strategies when the external group refuses to recognize the issue or opposes the change agent's proposal so that issue dissensus is quite pervasive and

---

[28]Roland L. Warren, "Types of Purposive Community Change at the Community Level," Brandeis University, Papers in Social Welfare, No. 11; Florence Heller Graduate School for Studies in Social Welfare, 1965, p. 37. Italics added.

[29]Alinsky, *op. cit.,* pp. 153–55.

[30]Saul D. Alinsky, "Citizen Participation and Community Organization in Planning and Urban Renewal" (Chicago: Industrial Areas Foundation, 1962; mimeographed), p. 7.

inherent.[31] Specht analyzes a variety of disruptive tactics.[32]

5. Practitioner Roles and Medium of Change.

In locality development the practitioner's characteristic role is that of an "enabler" or, as more recently suggested by Biddle, "encourager." According to Ross, the enabler role is one of facilitating a process of problem-solving and includes such actions as helping people express their discontents, encouraging organization, nourishing good interpersonal relationships, and emphasizing common objectives.[33] It has a procedural focus and has little to do with selecting specific task objectives or dealing with concrete substantive problems. The Biddles see the encourager as one who

> . . . has been responsible for initiating a growth of initiative in others. He has been party to a process of participant-guided learning of the habits of responsibility, of applied intelligence, and of ethical sensitivity. The indigenous process he has started, or helped to implement, is one of the growth in democratic competence.[34]

The practitioner gears himself to the creation of manipulation of small task-oriented groups, and he requires skill in guiding processes of collaborative problem-finding and problem-solving. This role resembles that of Selznick's "institutional leader"—"one who is primarily an expert in the promotion and protection of values" and whose "task is to smooth the path of human interaction, ease communication."[35]

In social planning, more technical or "expert" roles are emphasized, such as fact-finding, implementation of programs, relationships with various bureaucracies and with professionals of various disciplines and so on. Referring again to Ross, the expert role is suggested as containing these components: community diagnosis, research skill, information about other communities, advice on methods of organization and procedure, technical information, evaluation. In Model *B* the practitioner gears himself to the manipulation of formal organizations (including interorganizational relationships) and to data collection and analysis.

The social action model is likely to incorporate what Grosser calls the "advocate" and "activist" roles. According to Grosser, the advocate is "a partisan in social conflict, and his expertise is available exclusively to serve client interests."[36] The roles in Model *C* entail the organization of client groups to act on behalf of their interests in a pluralist community arena. The practitioner gears himself to creating and manipulating mass organizations and movements and to influencing political processes. Mass organization is necessary because the constituency has few resources or sources of power outside its sheer numerical strength.

Gamson makes an interesting commentary on the need for mass organization and support in social action projects as he discussed his impressions of a workshop of local social action participants:

> I was reminded of a reaction that I had at the time of the [Cleveland] workshop. We asked the various participants from these groups to describe their successes; I was struck at the time that the descriptions of successes usually did not directly involve

[31]Warren, *op. cit.*

[32]Harry Specht, "Disruptive Tactics," *Social Work*, XIV, No. 2 (1969), 5–15.

[33]Ross, *op. cit.*

[34]Biddle and Biddle, *op. cit.*, p. 82.

[35]Philip Selznick, *Leadership in Administration: a Sociological Interpretation* (Evanston, Ill.: Row, Petersen & Co., 1957), pp. 27–28.

[36]Grosser, *op. cit.*, p. 18.

influence but other things, things that generated a lot of publicity or involved large numbers of people. My first reaction was, "Aren't they missing something? Shouldn't success be defined in terms of some kind of policy influence rather than this other type of thing?" But I thought about it some more and I decided that they really did have certain kinds of goals, even though they were not articulating them, and that there was something egocentric about my applying my conception of success to them. In fact, I think that they had their finger on something that was quite important. One way of formulating it is to see them as working on a shorter range goal that has to do with mobilization of a constituency or the creation of resources. If you ask what resources these groups have, the major one is the ability to command the energy of a large number of people in the community. This energy will, they hope, eventually get converted into influence.[37]

6. Orientation toward Power Structure(s).

In locality development the power structure is included within an all-embracing conception of community. All segments of the community are thought of as part of the client system. Hence, members of the power structure are considered to be collaborators in a common venture. One consequence of this might well be that in Model *A* only goals upon which there can be mutual agreement become legitimate or relevant, the goals which involve incompatible interests are ignored or discarded as inappropriate. Values and constraints narrow the goals to those upon which all factions can agree. Hence, goals involving shifts in casting configurations of power and resource control are likely to be excluded.

In social planning, the power structure is usually present as sponsor or employer of the practitioner. Sponsors may include a voluntary board of directors or an arm of city government. Morris and Binstock state the case this way: "Realistically, it is difficult to distinguish planners from their employing organizations. In some measure, their interests, motivations, and means are those of their employers."[38] Planners are usually highly trained professional specialists whose services require a considerable financial outlay in salary as well as support in the form of supplies, equipment, facilities, and auxiliary technical and clerical personnel. Frequently, planners can only be supported in their work by those in a power position in the society, especially with regard to the possession of wealth, control of the machinery of government, or a monopoly of prestige. As Rein suggests, much planning is by "consensus of elites" who are employers and policy-makers in planning organizations.[39] Usually this consensus is clothed in strong factual data.

In social action the power structure is seen as an external target of action; that is to say, the power structure lies outside the client system or constituency itself, as an oppositional or oppressive force vis-à-vis the client group. Jack Minnis, a former organizer for SNCC, states the position pointedly:

> Community organization for action must be approached with the assumption that someone, or group, in the community has the power to make decisions and to implement them. . . . When this identification has been made it will frequently develop that the groups whose interests will be adversely affected are the same groups who have the power to decide whether or not the objective will be achieved.[40]

---

[37]William Gamson, in John Turner, ed., *Neighborhood Organization for Community Action* (New York: National Association of Social Workers, 1968), p. 131.

[38]Morris and Binstock, *op. cit.,* p. 16.

[39]Martin Rein, "Strategies of Planned Change" (American Orthopsychiatric Association, 1965).

[40]Jack Minnis, "The Care and Feeding of Power Structures" (Economic Research and Action Conference, 1964; mimeographed), p. 6.

The power structure, then, usually represents a force antithetical to the client or constituent group whose well-being the practitioner is committed to uphold. Those holding power, accordingly, must be coerced or overturned in order that the interests of the client population may find satisfaction.

A practitioner's attitude toward power structures and his capacity to utilize one or another strategy with reference to these are conditional upon the organization within which he operates. The organizational base or structure supporting or sponsoring the practitioner thus is an extremely important variable. In order to attack existing bureaucracies that possess considerable resources and legitimacy the practitioner needs an autonomous power base, perhaps growing out of an indigenous population. (Several excellent treatments of organizational variables have been made by Zald,[41] Grosser,[42] Brager,[43] and Hasenfeld and English.[44])

7. Boundary Definition of the Community Client System or Constituency.

In locality development the total community, usually a geographic entity, such as a city, neighborhood, or village, is the client system. According to Dunham, "Community Development is concerned with the participation of *all* groups in the community—with both sexes, all age groups, all racial, nationality, religious, economic, social and cultural groups."[45] It places "emphasis on the unity of community life."[46]

In social planning the client system might be either a total geographic community or some areal or functional subpart thereof. Community welfare councils and city planning commissions usually conceive of their client groups as comprising the widest cross section of community interests. On the other hand, sometimes the client populations of social planners are more segmented aggregates—a given neighborhood, the mentally ill, the aged, youth, juvenile delinquents, the Jewish community.

In social action the client is usually conceived of as some community subpart or segment which suffers at the hands of the broader community and thus needs the special support of the practitioner. Richard Flacks indicates that the objective of action involves "the task of organizing the politically disenfranchised and voiceless so that they can independently and effectively pursue their interests and rights."[47] In social action, practitioners are more likely to think in terms of constituents or fellow partisans[48] rather than in terms of the "client" concept, which may be patronizing or overly detached and clinical.

8. Assumptions regarding Interests of Community Subparts.

In locality development the interests of various groups and factions in the community are seen as basically reconcilable and responsive to the influences of rational persuasion, communication, and mutual good will. The Biddles present a representative set of as-

[41]Mayer N. Zald, "Sociology and Community Organization Practice," in Zald, ed., *Organizing for Community Welfare* (Chicago, Quadrangle Books, 1967), pp. 27–61.

[42]Charles Grosser, "Staff Role in Neighborhood Organization," in Turner, ed., *op. cit.*, pp. 133–45.

[43]George Brager, "Institutional Change: Perimeters of the Possible," *Social Work*, XII, No. 1 (1967), 59–69.

[44]Yeheskel Hasenfeld and Richard English, *Human Service Organizations* (Ann Arbor: University of Michigan Press, 1974).

[45]Dunham, *op. cit.*

[46]Arthur Dunham, "Community Development," in *Social Work Yearbook, 1950* (New York: National Association of Social Workers, 1960), p. 184.

[47]Richard Flacks, "Is the Great Society Just a Barbecue?" in *Thoughts of the Young Radicals, op. cit.*, p. 53.

[48]William Gamson, *Power and Discontent* (Homewood, Ill.: Dorsey Press, 1968).

sumptions concerning differing interests in the community:

> There will always be conflicts between persons and factions. Properly handled, the conflicts can be used creatively.
>
> Agreement can be reached on specific next steps of improvement without destroying philosophic or religious differences.
>
> Although the people may express their differences freely, when they become responsible they often choose to refrain in order to further the interest of the whole group and of their idea of community.
>
> People will respond to an appeal to altruism as well as to an appeal to selfishness.[49]

In social planning there is no pervasive assumption about the degree of intractability of conflicting interests; the approach appears to be pragmatic, oriented toward the particular problem and the actors enmeshed in it. Morris and Binstock set down the social planning orientation as follows:

> A planner cannot be expected to be attuned to the factional situation within each complex organization from which he is seeking a policy change; nor can he always be aware of the overriding interests of dominant factions. Considerable study and analysis of factions and interests dominant in various types of organizations will be needed before planners will have sufficient guidance for making reliable predictions as to resistance likely in a variety of situations.[50]

The social action model assumes that interests among community subparts are at variance and not reconcilable, and that often coercive influences must be applied (legislation, boycotts, political and social upheavals) before meaningful adjustments can be made. Those who hold power or privilege and profit from the disadvantage of others do not easily give up their advantage; the force of self-interest would make

it foolish to expect them to do so. Saul Alinsky states:

> All major controlling interests make a virtue of acceptance—acceptance of the ruling group's policies and decisions. Any movement or organization arising in disagreement, or seeking independent changes and defined by the predominating powers as a threat, is promptly subjected to castigation, public and private smears, and attacks on its very existence.[51]

9. Conception of the Public Interest.

In his brilliant analysis Schubert concludes that the various strands of thinking and writing on the subject can be grouped into three categories in terms of conceptions of the public interest: the rationalist, the idealist, and the realist.[52] The rationalist view postulates a common good that can be arrived at through deliberative processes involving a cross section of interest groups within the population. The common good is determined through expression of various majoritarian interests. The instrumentality of a parliament or congress symbolizes the rationalist outlook. The idealist view holds that the public interest can be best arrived at through the exercise of judgment and conscience on the part of knowledgeable and compassionate advocates of the public interest. This does not necessarily mean communion with the various publics comprising the community. Rather, a small professional or political elite may draw on scientific knowledge, the workings of a higher intellect, and a steadfast moral position to develop decisions or actions on behalf of the public interest.

The realist position views the community

---

[49]Biddle and Biddle, *op. cit.,* p. 61.

[50]Morris and Binstock, *op. cit.,* p. 112.

[51]Alinsky, "Citizen Participation and Community Organization in Planning and Urban Renewal," *op. cit.,* p. 6.

[52]Glendon A. Schubert, *The Public Interest* (Glencoe, Ill.: Free Press, 1960).

as made up of a multitude of conflicting publics or interest groups which endlessly contend with one another in the public arena. Public officials respond to these pressures. Public policy decisions thus register the balance of power at a given point in time. Accordingly, the public interest exists only as a particular transitory compromise resulting from the conflictual resolution of group interaction. Bentley was an early advocate of this position, which is reflected by more recent writers who conceive of American society in pluralist terms.

Meyerson and Banfield[53] add to these notions those of unitary and individualist conceptions of the public interest. The unitary conception implies a choosing process in which the outcome is derived from a single set of ends through a central decision. It implies legislators or administrators who are presumed to know the ends of the body politic as a whole and to strive in some central decision-making locus to assert the unitary interests of the whole over the competing lesser interests. The individualist conception acknowledges a valid place for these "lesser" interacting interests and holds that the public interest can only come into being through the "social choice" interplay of these forces upon one another. No single central locus of authority or decision-making can take the place of the free and open pluralistic interplay in arriving at the common good.

Combining the Schubert and Meyerson-Banfield conceptions, then, and applying them to our models of community organization practice, we conclude as follows:

Locality development has a rationalist-unitary conception of the public interest. It would structure a broad cross section of community groups, focused on the general welfare, utilizing a cooperative decision-making process. The Biddles state it well:

> When the people are free of coercive pressures, and can then examine a wide range of alternatives, they tend to choose the ethically better and intelligently wiser course of action.
>
> There is satisfaction in serving the common welfare, even as in serving self-interest.
>
> A concept of the common good can grow out of group experience that serves the welfare of all in some local area.[54]

The social planning model tends to have an idealist-unitary view of the public interest. Planners, often in collaboration with social scientists, place great stress on the power of knowledge, facts, and theory in arriving at a view of the public interest which is free of the influences of political self-seeking or popular mythology. Thus Morris and Binstock suggest that the planner who seeks to establish goals should base his decisions on an estimate of community need. This is determined through four major avenues: "evidence of demand from the records of service agencies; judgments of experts; population studies; and reanalysis of basic demographic studies."[55] The authors point out that goals cannot be determined by facts alone and that the planner usually arrives at "preference goals" through decisions based on value-tinged judgments as well as on knowledge. And one might add also the sometimes subtle, sometimes strongarm influence of the "consensus of the elites."

The social actionists in Model *C* are usually well acquainted with the grueling interplay of conflicting forces in community change activity. They can be said, in the short run, to take a realist-individualist view of the public interest. As expressed by Tom Hayden, "Realism and sanity would

---

[53]Martin Meyerson and Edward C. Banfield, *Politics, Planning and the Public Interest* (Glencoe, Ill.: Free Press, 1955).

[54]Biddle and Biddle, *op. cit.,* p. 61.
[55]Morris and Binstock, *op. cit.,* p. 42.

be grounded in nothing more than the ability to face whatever comes" in the confrontation with a multiplicity of community forces and interests.[56] Having no control of, and little access to, a central decision-making apparatus in the community, and usually comprising a small minority of the population, Model *C* practitioners can be effective only as a special interest group confronting others, sometimes attempting to make *ad hoc* coalitions and alliances in the community market place. Rein and Morris refer to this as an "individual rationality" and describe it as follows:

> Individual rationality . . . starts with predetermined, specialized, vested interests . . . places greater stress on pluralistic values and the inherent legitimacy of each unique and special objective. Proponents of this strategy focus on a rationality of "realism"; it is rooted in tough-mindedness which tries to respond to the world in terms of how it does function rather than how it *ought* to function.[57]

It is the contention of Morris and Rein that change-oriented organizations are most effective when they utilize this individualistic rationality as opposed to a cooperative one, as reflected in the rationalist position.

In long-range terms some social actionists may view the public interest from an idealist-unitary view, with decisions emanating from a revolutionary elite, the working class, clients, and so on.

10. Conception of the Client Population or Constituency. In locality development, clients are likely to be viewed as average citizens who possess considerable strengths which are not fully developed and who need the services of a practitioner to help them release and focus these inherent capabilities. The Biddles express this viewpoint as follows:

> 1. Each person is valuable, unique, and capable of growth toward greater social sensitivity and responsibility.
>   a. Each person has underdeveloped abilities in initiative, originality, and leadership. These qualities can be cultivated and strengthened.[58]

In social planning, clients are more likely to be thought of as consumers of services, those who will receive and utilize those programs and services which are the fruits of the social planning process—mental health, public housing, recreation, welfare benefits, and so forth. Morris and Binstock specifically refer to "consumers" rather than "clients" in their social planning analytical framework.

In social action, clients or constituents are likely to be considered as victims of "the system," most broadly, or of portions thereof, such as slum landlords, the educational system, city government. Those on behalf of whom action is initiated are often characterized in "underdog" terms.[59]

11. Conception of Client or Constituent Role. In locality development, clients are viewed as active participants in an interactional process with one another and with the practitioner. Considerable stress is placed on groups in the community as the media through which learning and growth take place. Clients engage in an intensive group process of expressing their "felt

---

[56]Tom Hayden, "The Ability to Face Whatever Comes," in *Thoughts of the Young Radicals, op. cit.,* p. 42.

[57]Martin Rein and Robert Morris, "Goals, Structures, and Strategies for Community Change," in *Social Work Practice, 1962* (New York: Columbia University Press, 1962), p. 135.

[58]Biddle and Biddle, *op. cit.,* p. 60.

[59]These categories are similar, respectively, to those of: (1) clients or patients; (2) customers; and (3) victims as described by Martin Rein, "The Social Service Crisis," *Trans-Action,* 1, No. 4 (1964), 3–6.

needs," determining desired goals, and taking appropriate conjoint action.

In planning, clients are recipients of services. They are active in consuming services, not in the determination of policy or goals, a function reserved for the planner or some policy-making instrumentality, such as a board of directors or a commission. According to Morris and Binstock:

> Opportunities for members and consumers to determine policy are severely limited because they are not usually organized for this purpose. If they are organized, and if the central issue which brings them together is sufficiently strong, they are likely to withdraw to form a separate organization. If the issue is weak the opportunity to control policy is short-lived because the coalition will fall apart, lacking sufficient incentive to bind together the otherwise diverse constituent elements.[60]

Policy, then, is made through the planner in collaboration with some community group, usually composed of elites, who are presumed to represent either the community-at-large or the best interests of the client group.

In social action the benefiting group is likely to be composed of employers of the practitioner or constituents. In unions the membership ideally runs the organization. Alinsky's Industrial Areas Foundation will ideally not enter a target area until the people there have gained a controlling and independent voice in the funding of the organization. The concept of the organizer as an employee and servant of the people is stressed. SDS neighborhood functionaries saw themselves as peers and co-partisans working on the basis of complete parity with a constituency of neighborhood residents. This meant living in the neighborhood, on a similar income level, and suffering the same deprivations and hard-

ships. The client group, whether employers or constituents, is in the position of determining broad goals and policies. Those not in continual or central participatory roles may participate more sporadically in mass action and pressure group activities, such as marches or boycotts.

A SOCIAL REFORM MODEL

It would be useful here to point out another model of social action (best referred to as *social reform*) which is close to Model C but varies in one important aspect related to the variable under discussion. A common mode of social action involves activity by a group or coalition of interests which acts vigorously on behalf of some outside client group (community segment) which is at risk or disadvantage. Organizational activity and goal determination take place within the entities who act on the behalf of others, not within the client group itself. Social action to obtain social security legislation, child welfare legislation, better standards of public education, fall into this category. Nader consumer protection activities are largely of this character. The action system is usually comprised of civic improvement associations (League of Women Voters), liberal politically-oriented organizations (Americans for Democratic Action), special interest groups (the Public Education Association), labor organizations, and the like, individually or in coalition. Social action efforts by NASW chapters most frequently take this form.[61] Historically, particularly within social work, many social reform efforts followed this pattern.

Social reform constitutes, in part, a mixture of social action and social planning.

---

[60]Morris and Binstock, *op. cit.*, pp. 109–10.

[61]Daniel Thurz, "Social Action as a Professional Responsibility," *Social Work,* XI, No. 3 (1966), 12–21.

Goal categories are of a task nature, social provision for a disadvantaged group. Assumptions concerning the community situation include both substantive social problems (inadequate housing) and disadvantaged populations (poor people who can not afford decent housing). The basic change strategy involves the organization of a coalition of concerned interests. Change techniques utilize in large measure campaign tactics, the employment of facts and persuasion to apply pressure on appropriate decision-making bodies. Salient practitioner roles encompass the coalition-builder, fact-gatherer, and legislative technician. The medium of change is through the manipulation of voluntary associations, mass media, and legislative bodies. The power structure is viewed neutrally in "gatekeeper" terms as decision-making centers that can be influenced through persuasion and/or pressure. The community client system is defined in community segment terms as a population at disadvantage or risk. Interests of community subparts may be reconcilable or in conflict. The conception of the public interest is, as in social action, realist-individualist. Clients are considered victims, and their role is defined as that of potential consumers or recipients.

THE MODELS VIEWED VERTICALLY

We have examined the three models horizontally; that is, we have looked at them comparatively in a way that has cut across the practice variables. We may also view the models from a vertical standpoint, by describing each separately in terms of all the listed practice variables. Doing this illustratively in two instances yields a product as follows:

In Model *A,* locality development, goals of action include self-help and increased community capacity and integration. The community, especially in urban contexts, is seen as eclipsed, fragmented, suffering from anomie, and with a lack of good human relationships and democratic problem-solving skills. The basic change strategy involves getting a broad cross section of people involved in studying and taking action on their problems. Consensus strategies are employed, involving small-group discussion and fostering communication among community subparts (class, ethnic, and so forth). The practitioner functions as an enabler and catalyst as well as a teacher of problem-solving skills and ethical values. He is especially skilled in manipulating and guiding small-group interaction. Members of power structures are collaborators in a common effort since the definition of the community client system includes the total geographic community. The practitioner conceives of the community as composed of common interests or reconcilable differences, and has a rationalist-unitary view of the public interest. Clients are conceived of as citizens engaged in a common community venture, and their role accordingly is one of participating in an interactional problem-solving process.

In the social action model, goals include the shifting of power, resources, and decision-making loci in the society as well as, on a short-range basis, changing the policies of formal organizations. System change is viewed as critical. The community is conceived of as being composed of a hierarchy of privilege and power, with the existence of clusters of deprived populations suffering from disadvantage or social injustice. The basic change strategy involves crystallizing issues and organizing indigenous populations to take action on their own behalf against enemy targets. Change tactics often include conflict techniques, such as confrontation and direct action—rallies, marches, boycotts (as well as "hard-nosed" bargaining). The practitioner functions in the role of activist, agitator, broker, negotiator, and partisan. He is skilled in the manipulation of mass organizations and political processes. Power structures are viewed as an external target of action—oppressors or exploiters who need to be limited or removed. The client group or constituency is a given community segment at disadvantage (blacks, the poor, women, gays, workers). It is assumed that interests among related parties are at conflict or not easily reconcilable since those who possess power, resources, and prestige are reluctant to relinquish or share them. The conception of the public interest is realist-individualist. Clients are viewed as victims of various forces and interests in the society, and their role is that of employer or constituents with regard to the practitioner, as well as participants in mass action and pressure group activities.

IMPLICATIONS OF A MULTI-MODEL APPROACH

Having come this far, the reader may inquire about the implications of constructing a typology like the foregoing.

In the first place, it is important for a practitioner immersed in the organizational and methodological vortex of one of these models to be aware of his grounding. What are the basic assumptions, orientation toward clients, preferred methods of action, of the situation he is in? In this way, he may perform appropriately, consistent with the expectations of other relevant actors.

Going beyond conformance to what exists, the practitioner may be in a position to create a model of action to deal with specific problems. Some rough rule-of-thumb guidelines can be sketched out in this connection. When populations are homogeneous or when consensus exists among various community subparts and interests it would be useful to employ locality development. When subgroups are hostile and interests are not reconcilable through usual discussional methods, it may be functional

to use social action. When problems are fairly routinized and lend themselves to solution through the application of factual information, social planning would appear to be the preferred mode of action. When the objective is to enhance civic responsibility and competence, Model *A* would be employed; when to make long-range and unpopular institutional and structural change, Model *C;* when to solve specific short-and middle-range substantive problems, Model *B.*

By assessing when one or another mode of action is or is not appropriate, the practitioner takes an analytical, problem-solving stand and does not become the captive of a particular ideological or methodological approach to practice. Practitioners, consequently, should be attuned through training to the differential utility of each approach and should acquire the knowledge and skill which permit them to utilize each of the models as seems appropriate and necessary. Specific strategies and techniques for shifting organizational goals and changing roles are presented elsewhere.[62]

Mixing and Phasing of Models

The community practitioner should also become sensitive to the mixed uses of these techniques within a single practice context; for problems require such blending, and organizational structures may permit adaptations. Thus the practitioner would be able to make adjustments in a social planning approach that is heedless of meaningful participation of people, a community development approach that stresses endless group discussion at the expense of addressing compelling community problems, or a

---

[62]Jack Rothman, John L. Erlich and Joseph G. Teresa, *Promoting Innovation and Change in Organizations and Communities: A Planning Manual* (New York: John Wiley and Sons, 1976).

social action approach that utilizes conflict when avenues are open for fruitful resolution of issues through discussion or negotiation. Within any given model, aspects of other models may play an important part. Thus in social action the practitioner may employ locality development techniques to a considerable degree within and among his own constituency. A community mental health planner, limited largely to consultation regarding services, might appreciate the contribution to his efforts of external social action programs, viewing them in a positive, supportive way rather than with suspicion or hostility.

The point being made has been stated by Gurin as follows:

> Our field studies have produced voluminous evidence that (various) roles are needed, but not always at the same time and place. The challenging problem, on which we have made a bare beginning, is to define more clearly the specific conditions under which one or another or still other types of practice are appropriate. The skill we shall need in the practitioner of the future is the skill of making a situational diagnosis and analysis that will lead him to a proper choice of the methods most appropriate to the task at hand.[63]

Certain types of mixtures may be more feasible than others. For example, a synthesis of locality development and social planning in the same organization may be fairly easy to effect. As the Mobilization for Youth experience has demonstrated, social action approaches do not blend readily with either of the other two modes of action. Here, separation in funding, geographical location, or sponsorship may permit dual use of approaches.

In addition to mixing, there is a phasing relationship among the models. A given change project may begin in one mode and then at a later stage move into another. For example, as a social action organization achieves success and attains resources, it may find that it can function most efficiently out of a social planning model. The labor union movement to a degree demonstrates this type of phasing. The practitioner needs to be attuned to appropriate transition points in applying alternative models.

In the past, professional practices and conceptualizations in community organization were colored by particular value orientations to practice. The value system of the social work profession was seen as restricting practice to a particular formulation. Thus, for many years, the enabler role, and interventions emphasizing cooperative relationships among and across diverse community subparts, was considered the only valid and legitimate avenue of approach in social work. A newer perspective accepts varying value orientations and emphasis within the framework of the profession. The following comment states this proposition well:

> Social work values provide some of the framework for decisions, but they are too broad to provide the specific answers. Social work has general commitments both to the improvement of social institutions and to the enrichment of individual and family life, but no specific formula for determining how these goals can best be achieved at any particular time, not even in an area as central to social work as income maintenance. The profession must therefore be able to encompass a range of ideologies, some of which may be in conflict with one another at certain points.[64]

[63]Arnold Gurin, "Current Issues in Community Organization Practice and Education," Brandeis University Reprint Series, No. 21, Florence Heller Graduate School for Advanced Studies in Social Welfare, 1966, p. 30.

[64]Wyatt C. Jones and Armand Lauffer, "Implications of the Community Organization Curriculum Project for Practice and Education," Professional Symposium of NASW, National Conference on Social Welfare, 1968, p. 9.

This author's examination of empirical findings on professional values leads to the conclusion that "human service professions do not appear to be highly integrated with regard to the existence of a delimited uniformly accepted value system."[65] The three models suggested in this presentation are in the spirit of such a position. The locality development practitioner will likely cherish that aspect of the social work value system that emphasizes harmony and communication in human affairs; the social planner will build on social work values that encourage rationality, objectivity, and professional purposiveness; the social actionist will draw on social work value commitments that stress social justice and equality. Each of these value orientations finds support and

justification in the traditions of the human service professions. It would be difficult to claim a priority preeminence for one or another. Mixing may occur when more than one value is being pursued at a given time.

However, it is clear that all three models, despite divergent value emphases, can be applied in such a way as to foster and support social change. The position taken here accepts the validity of each of these value orientations and encourages the simultaneous and interrelated development of varying community intervention models which stem therefrom. In the absence of research or experience which confirms the overarching superiority of only one, change agent competency can only be enriched and the community benefited by such multiple and concurrent development of practice technologies. Appropriate mixtures and phasing can be attended to within such a development.

---

[65]Jack Rothman, *Planning and Organizing for Social Change: Action Principles from Social Science Research* (New York: Columbia University Press, 1974), p. 100.

2.

Charles D. Garvin and Fred M. Cox*

A HISTORY OF COMMUNITY ORGANIZING SINCE THE CIVIL WAR WITH SPECIAL REFERENCE TO OPPRESSED COMMUNITIES

This paper traces the development of community organization within American communities since 1865. It is concerned not only with community activities in which professionals were engaged but also with indigenous community efforts with similar goals, efforts to which professionals often related their activities. These

goals include enhancing citizen participation in making decisions about community problems, obtaining rights for minorities, and securing changes in relevant social institutions.

We will emphasize the many important community efforts in which ethnic communities have been engaged. Such organizing has occurred in virtually all ethnic communities. For example, there are many organizations devoted to improved conditions within Jewish, Italian, and Polish enclaves. The emphasis here, however, will be upon

---

*The authors are grateful to John Erlich for his careful reading and detailed suggestions for improving this paper, and to Pauline Bush for her editorial assistance.

the history of organizing in ethnic communities which are now economically and socially oppressed. These include black, Chicano, Native American, and Asian American areas.

Other categories of people with a common identity also have organized to secure their rights, such as Puerto Ricans, women, the elderly, gay persons, and the handicapped. Space limitations, however, make it impossible for us to explore each in detail. As an illustration, the women's rights movements have been selected for discussion.

For purposes of this analysis, we identify four stages of American history since the Civil War. First we outline the social forces and ideologies present during each stage which affected community organizing. Then we identify the specific community organization activities during each period, and the institutions within which organizers functioned. We present the types of organizing occurring in oppressed communities, and analyze the effects of these social forces, activities, and institutions upon the education of community organization practitioners.

Community organization practice is a fairly recent specialization within social work, the first professional organization of practitioners having come into existence in 1946. However, there have been many activities which anticipated contemporary issues in community organization. An understanding of these will enhance the reader's comprehension of current issues in the field.

1865 TO 1914

During the period between the end of the Civil War and the beginning of World War I, a number of social issues emerged in the United States which had strong impact upon welfare practices. Ideologies developed in response to these social conditions, and solutions were proposed for those defined as problematic. These social issues were the rapid industrialization of the country, the urbanization of its population, problems growing out of immigration, and changes in oppressed populations after the Civil War. These will be described briefly, highlighting their relevance for the emergence of community organization practice.

Social Conditions

Industrialization. The growth of technology and the centralization of industry brought with them a wide range of social problems. These included problems of working hours and conditions, safety, and child labor.[1]

Urbanization. A direct consequence of industrialization was the movement of large parts of the population from the country to the city.[2] The many unskilled workers who moved into the city from rural areas, particularly from the South and from Europe, were often forced to take up residence within the oldest and most crowded sections of the cities. These districts were inadequate in sanitation, building conditions, and city services for the large numbers of people which they were forced to accommodate. As Jane Addams wrote:

> The streets are inexpressibly dirty, the number of schools inadequate, sanitary legislation unenforced, the street lighting bad, the paving miserable, and altogether lack-

---

[1]For a social worker's perception of these conditions, see Jane Addams, *Twenty Years at Hull House* (New York: The Macmillan Co., 1910), pp. 99, 198ff.

[2]For details, see Allan Nevins and Henry Steele Commager, *The Pocket History of the United States* (New York: Pocket Books, 1942), pp. 326–57.

ing in the alleys and smaller streets, and the stables foul beyond description. Hundreds of houses are unconnected with the street sewer.[3]

Immigration. In the early part of the nineteenth century, many immigrants came from northwestern Europe, spreading out across the country to work the land. By 1890 the frontiers were gone. Larger proportions of southern and eastern European people came to the United States and remained in its cities until the tide of immigration was stemmed by legislation passed shortly after World War I. Asian and Mexican people also came to the West and Southwest, and Puerto Ricans in small numbers to the East.

These people brought with them, not only their own social and religious institutions, but a variety of problems. Coming from peasant origins, many sought a rural environment. However, most of those who came in the later waves were unable to escape the cities where they landed. Impoverished and often sick from the crossing, they were forced to take whatever work they could find. They clung to their former ways. This brought them into conflict with their children, who took on American habits and manners.[4]

Minorities after the Civil War

Blacks. During reconstruction there were many organizations which sought to support and sustain newly won civil rights. After the period of reconstruction there were many efforts on the part of black people to organize themselves "to the point where they could demand those rights which had slipped away since reconstruc-

tion."[5] The Supreme Court decision which declared the Civil Rights Act of 1875 unconstitutional was a major source of difficulty. Thus, the responsibility for protecting the rights of black people rested largely with the states.

During this period, the Populist Movement in the South was a major political force which attempted to secure black support. According to Leslie H. Fishel, Jr., and Benjamin Quarles, the white president of a Populist convention in Texas said that the black "is a citizen as much as we are." However, these authors noted that "the elections of 1892 saw their [Populists'] defeat in the South and the end of any political effort to work with the Negro on an equitable basis."[6]

A major concern of the black community was to solve the problem of educational deficits, particularly in vocational and higher education. In this context, an important event was the founding of Tuskegee Institute in 1881. It must be remembered that in the fifteen years before 1900 over fifteen hundred black people were lynched, and between 1900 and 1910 another nine hundred black people perished in the same way. "The sickening brutality of the act of lynching was matched only by its lawlessness and, in too many cases, the innocence of its victims."[7] Emerging concern and support of other oppressed minorities is well illustrated by black poet Alberry Whitman's *The Rape of Florida,* an exposition of white degradation of the Seminoles, published in 1884.

Toward the end of this period many industries encouraged black people to take positions in the North created by the termi-

---

[3]Addams, *op. cit.,* pp. 97–100.

[4]See Oscar Handlin, *The Uprooted* (New York: Grossett and Dunlap, 1951).

[5]Leslie H. Fishel, Jr., and Benjamin Quarles, *The Negro American: A Documentary History* (Glenview, Ill.: Scott, Foresman and Co., 1967), p. 308.

[6]*Ibid.,* p. 309.

[7]*Ibid.,* p. 358.

nation of the large European immigrations and the expansion of war industry. This ushered in the next phase for blacks, one in which their urban living condition also became a concern.

Chicanos. [8] Although we describe community organizing primarily since the Civil War, we must recognize that the history of protest among Chicanos began with the Treaty of Guadalupe Hidalgo, signed on February 2, 1848, which brought a formal end to the Mexican-American War. Under this treaty, Mexico lost 45 percent of its territory including the wealth of the oil fields of Texas and the gold of California. More than a hundred thousand persons were added to the United States who had previously been citizens of Mexico. From this beginning, the rights of these "conquered" people were heavily infringed upon with little legal redress available. Protest took the form of guerrilla activity by so-called bandits. Although armed rebellions also occurred they were vigorously repressed by the government. According to one authority, "Organized hunts, murders, robberies, and lynchings of Mexicans were everyday happenings, and cattle rustling and assaults on Mexican merchants were carried out with brutality and savagery."[9]

Native Americans. In the period just before the Civil War, the status of Native Americans was largely determined by the Removal Act of 1830. This act gave the president the right to remove any Indians

who continued to survive east of the Mississippi.[10] Some fought, as did the Seminoles of Florida and the Sac and Fox of Illinois, but most moved. A particularly horrible event was the action taken against the Cherokees who, despite an enormous effort to adapt their culture, were forcibly removed in 1838 from Georgia to what was to become Oklahoma with a great loss of lives on the way.

After the Civil War, this pattern continued until the passage of the Dawes Act of 1887 which authorized the president to distribute 160 acres to each Indian adult and 80 acres to each child. This act followed a series of major fights with tribes such as the Sioux in 1876, Nez Perce in 1877, Cheyenne in 1878, and Apache a few years later.

The Dawes Act was a failure in that it did not convert the Indians to agriculture as intended. Much of the land given was poor, and funds for its development were unavailable. As a result, between 1887 and 1932, "approximately 90 million acres out of 138 million initially held by Indians passed to white ownership."[11] In view of the exploitation they suffered the survival of many Indian tribes seems miraculous, indeed.

Asian-Americans. The Chinese, the first immigrants from Asia to come in large numbers, arrived on the west coast in the 1840s. Their labor was sought after as the California economy soared with the gold rush. It was in the mining regions that serious hostility to the Chinese first developed. When the Civil War began there were more than fifty thousand Chinese in California, mostly men. By the 1870s violence was directed at Chinese, intensified by an eco-

---

[8]Although the term *Chicano* has not been used throughout all of the historical periods described in this chapter, we use it whenever we refer to those United States residents and citizens who are descended from Mexicans. For details of the evolution of the Chicano movement, see Gilberto Lopez y Rivas, *The Chicanos: Life and Struggles of the Mexican Minority in the United States* (New York and London: Monthly Review Press, 1973), pp. 57–74.

[9]*Ibid.*, p. 33.

[10]John R. Howard, ed., *Awakening Minorities: American Indians, Mexican Americans, Puerto Ricans* (New Brunswick: Transaction Books, 1970), p. 17.

[11]*Ibid.*, p. 19.

nomic depression. For example, "some twenty Chinese were killed by gunfire and hanging on October 24, 1871."[12]

Agitation continued for the rest of the decade from workers who sought anti-Chinese legislation. In 1882, Congress enacted the Chinese Exclusion Act, which was renewed in 1892 and made permanent in 1902.

About two hundred thousand Japanese arrived in America between 1890 and 1924 in an atmosphere hostile to Orientals. The early immigrants were mostly young males from rural backgrounds. Like the Chinese, they were recruited as a source of cheap labor. However, the migration of Japanese women was soon encouraged.

Perhaps California's Alien Land Bill of 1913 best exemplifies general attitudes toward the Japanese. It provided that Japanese aliens could lease agricultural lands for a maximum of three years, and that lands already owned or leased could not be willed to other persons. As the California attorney general indicated in a public speech, the intention was to limit the number of Japanese who would come to or stay in California.[13]

Ideological Conditions

These, then, are some of the major sources of social problems during this half century. Solutions of these problems were relevant to the emergence of community organization practice and were greatly affected by ideological currents prevalent during this period. These currents included Social Darwinism, radicalism, pragmatism, and liberalism. These ideologies were, at least in part, a response of individuals and groups to problems of industrialization,

poverty, urbanization, race relations, and cultural conflicts brought on by immigration. However, the focus here will not be upon the relationship between social problems and ideology. Rather, the task is to show how these two forces interacted to produce specified approaches to community organization practice. First, however, these ideologies will be briefly described.

Social Darwinism. As Max Lerner pointed out:

> When the gap between *laissez faire* and social welfare became too obvious after the Civil War, conservative thought called into play the new popular interest in Darwinian theories. The jungle character of the economic struggle was frankly admitted, but it was justified and even glorified by Social Darwinism on the ground that nature had decreed it. The new natural law came to be "natural selection" and the triumph of the "fit" who survived.[14]

This philosophy, then, led to the view that social failure was due to some inherent inferiority in the individual and that assistance to such people was an interference with natural law. This approach was also compatible with the the theme of "rugged individualism" which was prevalent in American economic ideology. Another outcome was the principle of minimum government. Under this doctrine the role of government was to protect property and ensure the enforcement of contracts, but not to interfere in any way with their terms.

Radical Ideology. While Social Darwinism may have served the interests of the highly placed and the economically secure, other ideologies provided a rationale for the activities of those who sought to change the

---

[12]Harry H. L. Kitano, *Race Relations* (Englewood Cliffs, N.J.: Prentice-Hall, 1974), p. 196.

[13]Harry H. L. Kitano, *Japanese Americans* (Englewood Cliffs, N.J.: Prentice-Hall, 1969), pp. 7, 17.

[14]Max Lerner, *America As a Civilization: Life and Thought in the United States Today* (New York: Simon and Schuster, 1957), p. 722.

lot of the "unfit." One indigenous American radical, Henry George, according to Lerner, "spoke for a 'reforming Darwinism' which saw the social order as the outgrowth of evolution but wanted to use it deliberately in a humanizing effort for the weakest as well as the strong."[15] Perhaps the most significant radical ideas of this period stemmed from labor organizers. A Socialist Labor Party (SLP) was organized in the United States in 1876.[16] Within this group were Marxist as well as other ideological influences. Among the demands of the party were that "all industrial enterprises be placed under the control of the government as fast as practicable operated by free cooperative trade unions for the good of the whole people."[17] The Socialist party was founded in 1900 and united several groups, including the SLP.

This discussion cannot deal thoroughly with the history of American Labor. However, an important heritage of the kind of community organizing aimed at mobilizing the underdog rests with this movement. Labor organizing, along with the struggles of black people, provided inspiring and effective ideas for more recent grass-roots organizers.

Pragmatism. This indigenous philosophy, first articulated by Charles S. Peirce and William James and developed by such men as John Dewey and George Herbert Mead, anticipated the social sciences which underlie many efforts at social engineering. As Lerner stated:

Through these variations there ran the common thread of the "revolt against formalism" and against fixed principles or rules—that truth did not lie in absolutes or in mechanical formulas but in the whole operative context of individual growth and social action in which the idea was embedded. This movement of thought was, in a sense, the American counterpart to the Marxist and historical schools of thought in Europe which tried to apply the evolutionary process to social thinking. This intellectual base made possible, as it also expressed, the political reform movement from Theodore Roosevelt to Franklin Roosevelt.[18]

Liberalism. The last deeply rooted ideology to be mentioned here is liberalism. Lerner describes it thus: "Its credo has been progress, its mood optimist, its view of human nature rationalist and plastic; it has used human rights rather than property rights as its ends but has concentrated on social action as its means."[19] Despite its problems, Lerner concludes, "However vulnerable, liberalism has nevertheless emerged as a central expression of the American democratic faith."[20] Liberal ideas have been important in building support among the privileged for the right of the under classes to be heard in the councils of government and ultimately to reap some of the benefits bestowed by government.

Community Organization Institutions

Community organization activities during the period between the Civil War and World War I can be divided into two categories. The first are those which were carried on by individuals or institutions directly related to present-day social welfare activities. The charity organization societies, settlement houses, and urban leagues are important examples.

A second category of activities are those that were conducted by institutions with no direct connection to contemporary community organization programs but which have

---

[15]*Ibid.,* p. 726.

[16]Called for one year the Workingman's Party of America.

[17]*The Socialist,* July 29, 1876. See also John R. Commons, *History of Labor in the United States,* Vol. II (New York: The Macmillan Co., 1935), p. 270.

[18]Lerner, *op. cit.,* pp. 722–23.

[19]*Ibid.,* p. 729.

[20]*Ibid.,* p. 730.

become areas of interest for community practitioners. Examples include the organization of political, racial, and other action groups for specific locales or purposes.

The Charity Organization Society. A number of factors noted above contributed to the climate in which charity organization societies developed first in England in 1869 and, by 1873, in the United States.[21] These societies came into existence initially to coordinate the work of the multitude of private agencies which had developed to provide for the needs of the poor. Soon, however, these organizations began to offer direct relief and other services, as well as coordinate the work of other agencies.[22] Murphy summarized their program as follows:

> They established social service indexes or exchanges listing individuals or "cases" known to cooperating agencies. They evolved the "case conference," in which workers from different agencies interested in the same "case" or the same family—workers from the settlement house, the relief-giving agencies, the child-placing agencies, the agencies established to protect children from cruelty, the visiting nurse association, and others—would meet to plan a constructive course of action in behalf of the "case." In some instances, too, the charity organization societies made broad studies of social and economic problems and recommended specific remedial measures.[23]

The social forces described earlier contributed to this development in several ways. The movement of large populations into the cities, as well as the waves of immigration which met the manpower needs of growing industries, led to many social problems associated with poverty, inadequate housing, illness, and exploitation. Both humanitarian impulses and fear of what these people might do in desperation produced agencies directed to ameliorating conditions. In a sense, this was an effort to counter the more radical ideologies.

Separate efforts also were made by groups associated with different neighborhoods and ethnic and religious groups, and those with different problems. Difficulties which arose repeatedly in the course of such developments were: (1) The same people were approached over and over again to provide resources for such agencies, and they began to look for ways to make charitable solicitations more efficient and less demanding on the few. (2) Duplication of aid was apparent, and those who offered it sought ways to avoid this and prevent the pauperization of the recipients which they believed was the inevitable result of indiscriminate relief. (3) Paid functionaries arose who sought to rationalize these activities, drawing their inspiration from the same wellsprings that fed a developing pragmatic philosophy. (4) The resources of some charitable societies were insufficient for the maintenance of required services, prompting an incessant search for new sources of funds.

During this period, leaders of charity organization societies harbored serious reservations about the wisdom of public activity on behalf of the poor. In general, they doubted government's ability to administer aid so that it would be rehabilitative. Darwinian ideology and a hedonistic theory of motivation strongly influenced their views on the matter. The Social Darwinians regarded relief as interference with the operation of natural law, and the hedonists held that the only assurance of hard work among the poorer classes was the fear of hunger and exposure. This was tempered

---

[21]Charles Loch Mowat, *The Charity Organization Society, 1869–1913* (London: Methuen and Co., 1961), pp. 16–21 and 94.

[22]The direct services which had significance for the emergence of social casework will not be pursued in this paper. Only the community organization antecedents will be noted.

[23]Campbell G. Murphy, *Community Organization Practice* (Boston: Houghton Mifflin, Co., 1954), p. 35.

somewhat by humanitarian impulses. The charity organization societies distinguished between the "worthy" and the "unworthy" poor and chose to aid the former who, for reasons beyond their control, were unable to support themselves and who, through the moral example of the societies' "friendly visitors" could be rescued from pauperization. The rest—the vicious poor—were relegated to the not-too-tender mercies of the public poor law authorities, never to be supported at a level equal to the lowest wages in the community so that they would constantly be goaded toward self-support.

Another function of the charity organization societies was cooperative planning among charitable institutions for the amelioration or elimination of various social problems, together with a variety of efforts to create new social agencies and reform old ones. Charity organization leaders were actively engaged in securing reforms in tenement housing codes, developing anti-tuberculosis associations, obtaining legislation in support of juvenile court and probation workers, establishing agencies and programs for the care of dependent children, cooperating with the police in programs for dealing with beggars and vagrants, and supporting legislation requiring absent fathers to support their children.[24]

One of the most significant contributions of the charity organization societies to community organization was the development of community welfare planning organizations and social survey techniques. One of the earliest and most important examples was in Pittsburgh. Writing from his perspective in 1922, Frank Watson discussed the significance of the Pittsburgh survey:

Few of the offspring of the charity organization movement have had more far-reaching consequences or given greater promise of the future than the Pittsburgh Survey, the pioneer social survey in this country. Interpretation of hours, wages, housing, court procedure and all the rest, in terms of standards of living and the recognition that the basis for judging of social conditions is the measure of life they allow to those affected by them, constitute the very essence of the developments that have since taken place in social work.[25]

Out of the Pittsburgh survey came a council of social agencies which took upon itself the responsibility for acting upon the recommendations of the survey and conducting additional studies and reforms.

The Social Settlements.[26] Settlements emerged fifteen years after charity organization societies. Samuel Barnett opened Toynbee Hall, one of the first settlements, in the slums of East London in 1884. Stan-

---

[24]For details on these activities see Frank D. Watson, *The Charity Organization Movement in the United States* (New York: The Macmillan Co., 1922), pp. 288–323.

---

[25]*Ibid.*, pp. 305–6.

[26]This section rests heavily on the analysis of Allen F. Davis in his *Spearheads for Reform: The Social Settlements and the Progressive Movement 1890–1914* (New York: Oxford University Press, 1967). Although Toynbee Hall is commonly referred to as the first social settlement, it was opened, although only half-completed, on Christmas Eve of 1884 by two Oxford University students (see Davis, p. 3). A. F. Young and E. T. Ashton, in their *British Social Work in the Nineteenth Century* (London: Routledge and Kegan Paul, 1956), claimed that Oxford House was opened in October 1884, while Toynbee Hall was not opened until January 1885 (p. 230). Thus Toynbee Hall was *one* of the first settlements to open its doors. Although Oxford House was technically the first, Samuel Barnett, who fathered the settlement house movement in Great Britain, was associated with Toynbee Hall. This may account for the fact that a number of scholars erroneously regard Toynbee Hall as the first settlement house. See: Frank J. Bruno, *Trends in Social Work* (New York: Columbia University Press, 1948), p. 114; Arthur Hillman, "Settlements and Community Centers," in Harry L. Lurie (ed.), *Encyclopedia of Social Work* (New York: National Association of Social Workers, 1965), p. 690. The authors thank David Gilbert for bringing this to our attention.

ton Coit, who visited Toynbee Hall in 1886, established the University Settlement on the Lower East Side of New York later that year. Although charity organization societies and social settlements were prompted by the same social conditions, their analyses of the problems created by industrialization and immigration were quite dissimilar, leading them to different objectives and programs. Barnett, an Anglican clergyman, influenced by the Christian Socialists and John Ruskin, sought to bridge the gap between the social classes and restore human values in a society dominated by materialism. Coit, strongly affected by Felix Adler and the Society of Ethical Culture, believed that nothing short of a moral and intellectual renaissance in city life was required. This could best be approached, he believed, by bringing together people of all descriptions into joint efforts, breaking down the barriers of interest, age, social class, political and religious affiliations, etc.[27] Rather than looking to individual character as the root cause of social problems, settlement house leaders typically found environmental factors responsible for the conditions they deplored.

Thus, while the charity organization societies seemed more ideologically related to the Darwinian ideology, the settlements appeared to draw more heavily upon the liberal, or even the radical, ideologies of the day. The types of individuals who became involved in these two movements also were different. Charity organization leaders were persons closer to the upper classes in society and epitomized noblesse oblige. They favored either reforming the poor or modifying the most adverse of their social circumstances. Although exceptions on both sides can be cited, the settlement house

workers were a different breed. Typically well educated and drawn from the middle classes, they were frequently critics of the social order who identified with and shared the lives of the poor in some measure. Their writings usually lack the condescension so often found in those of the charity organization workers.

Perhaps the most striking quality of the settlement program was its pragmatism. Unlike the charity organization societies, settlements had no predetermined scheme for solving the problems of society. In fact, they had no coherent analysis of the problems they confronted. Instead, with a general concern about the impact of such phenomena as industrialization, urbanization, and immigration upon society, they searched for answers that would be both feasible and effective.

Services were a major theme in their activities. They organized kindergartens and clubs for children, recreational programs, evening schools for adults, public baths, and art exhibitions.[28]

Social reform was, perhaps, the most basic and self-conscious thrust of the settlements. Services were often initiated as experiments which, if successful, could serve as models for other institutions. Indeed, many of the programs demonstrated by the settlements were taken over by other agencies.

The settlements' reform efforts went much beyond the organization of new or improved services. They included legislative and administrative innovations at the local, state, and national levels. In the field of education, they worked for the develop-

---

[27]Stanton A. Coit, *Neighborhood Guilds: An Instrument of Social Reform,* 2d ed. (London: Swan, Sommerschien and Co., 1892), pp. 7–16; 46–51.

[28]Contemporary group work also traces its origins to these settlement activities. On the other hand, the function of group work, particularly as conceptualized at the University of Michigan, is oriented toward personal and interpersonal problems, and community organization, toward social conditions in a wider context.

ment of vocational education and guidance in the public schools, as well as school nurses, hot lunch programs, and education for the retarded and handicapped. They urged the creation of small neighborhood playgrounds, housing code improvements, reduction of congestion through city planning, and the transformation of public schools into neighborhood social centers. Although settlement workers could not agree on the wisdom of immigration restrictions, they organized such groups as the Immigrant Protective League to ease the immigrant's adjustment to the new world. Settlement workers fought for laws to protect employed women and abolish child labor, and they helped organize the National Child Labor Committee and the National Women's Trade Union League. They were often involved in municipal reform activities, both at the ward and the citywide levels, and many contributed to the platform and organizational work of the Progressive party in 1912.[29]

One theme ran through both the service and reform efforts of the settlements—participation and democracy. Many of their service activities were designed to permit dialogue between working people and settlement residents. The residents involved themselves in the life of the community so that they might know what services were needed. They worked to reduce the barriers that separated them from their neighbors, and the neighbors from one another. They invited labor leaders and radicals of their day to use their facilities.

Finally, in everything they undertook, settlements tried to help their neighbors develop their potentialities to the fullest.

There was great emphasis on education of all kinds. One of the major reasons for opposing child labor was its negative effects upon the development of children. Municipal reform was viewed, in part, as a process of helping communities gain the capacity to deal with their problems more effectively.

The settlement idea spread rapidly. In 1891 there were six settlements in the United States; by 1910 the number had jumped to over four hundred. Most of them were located in the large industrial cities of the East and Midwest; there were very few in the South or West.

The Organization of Ethnic Minorities and Women. A variety of forms of organization among black Americans was tested during this period as black people coped with their shifting status in American life. One of the earliest of these forms was developed by a group of prominent black people in 1865 and led by Frederick Douglass and George T. Downing who were "charged with the duty to look after the best interests of the recently emancipated."[30] Almost twenty-five years later, in 1883, a very different kind of step was taken by the Louisville Convention of Colored Men which "concentrated on large issues of political, as distinct from partisan, rights, education, civil rights and economic problems."[31] Five years later, the Colored Farmers Alliance and Cooperative Union came into existence. In 1890, the Afro-American League organized in another direction, emphasizing legal redress rather than politics.[32] In 1890, blacks from twenty-one states and the District of Columbia organized the Afro-American League of the United States. Issues which

---

[29]A recent study indicates that, after his defeat in 1912, Roosevelt terminated his relationship with social workers and returned to a more traditional Republicanism. See W. I. Trattner, "Theodore Roosevelt, Social Workers, and the Election of 1912: A Note," *Mid-America* 50, No. 1 (1968), pp. 64–9.

[30]Fishel and Quarles, *op. cit.,* pp. 259–60.
[31]*Ibid.,* p. 308.
[32]*Ibid.,* p. 312.

this group was concerned about included school funds, and legal and voting rights. In 1896, the National Association of Colored Women was formed.

Crosscurrents similar to those which affect the organizations of black people today were operative between the Civil War and World War I. On the one hand, many efforts were under the influence of Booker T. Washington, who sought an accommodation with white interests in order to maintain their support. In contrast, W. E. B. DuBois epitomized an opposition to this approach in 1905 when he called for "a conference 'to oppose firmly the present methods of strangling honest criticism.' "[33] The Niagara movement grew out of this meeting and by 1909 resulted in the formation of the National Association for the Advancement of Colored People. Such social workers as Jane Addams, Florence Kelly, and Lillian Wald assisted in these organizing efforts.

The Committee on Urban Conditions among Negroes in New York City, later to become the National Urban League, was another organization in which social workers were involved during this period. Its first executive, George Edmund Haynes, "was on the faculty of Fisk University and particularly interested in training black social workers."[34]

As noted earlier, Mexican-Americans were confronted, as were the Native Americans, with successful efforts to take away their lands. One response to this was the development of small groups for protection and support. Some, for survival, became bandits. Organized protest, however, for Mexican-Americans began in agriculture or, as Howard states, "The roots of the Chicano movement lie in the fields."[35]

In 1903, for example, Mexican- and Japanese-American sugar beet workers struck in Ventura, California.[36] In addition, throughout this period but particularly from the 1880s on, many organizations came into existence whose function was, according to Alvarez, to preserve a Mexican-American way of life through "celebrations, social events, provision of facilities, information and communication networks."[37] The function of such organizations was to preserve a bicultural and bilingual existence. Some examples include the Penitente Order in New Mexico in the 1880s and Mano Negra, also in New Mexico, in the 1890s.[38]

The Native Americans during this period continued to have well-developed forms of tribal organization, partly as a heritage of their early struggles for survival against white encroachment. However, the tribes were separated from one another geographically and structurally, thus often rendering them easy prey for governmental manipulation. Nevertheless, the militancy of the period in actual warfare, as well as persistent legal action, represents an impressive, though unsuccessful, effort to secure a greater measure of justice from American society.

The early Chinese immigrants were organized into family or benevolent associations, tongs, or business interests.[39] For the Japanese, the Japanese Association for Issei

---

[33] *Ibid.,* p. 357.
[34] *Ibid.,* p. 361.
[35] Howard, *op. cit.,* p. 95.

[36] *Ibid.*
[37] Salvador Alvarez, "Mexican-American Community Organizations," in *Voices: Readings from El Grito, A Journal of Contemporary Mexican American Thought, 1967–1973,* ed. Octavio Ignacio Romano-V (Berkeley: Quinto Sol Publications, 1971), pp. 205–14.
[38] *Ibid.,* p. 209.
[39] For a discussion of evolving forms of Chinese-American community organizations, see Melford S. Weiss, "Division and Unity: Social Process in a Chinese-American Community," in *Asian Americans: Psychological Perspectives,* ed. Stanley Sue and Nathaniel N. Wagner (Palo Alto: Science and Behavior Books, 1973), pp. 264–273.

(first-generation Japanese in the United States) had some similar functions.

Thus, for these Asian groups, a major function of community organizations during this period was mutual benefit and cultural participation. For example,

> people from the same *ken,* or Japanese state, often cooperated in various ways, and this was noticeable in particular trades. For example, Miyamoto writes that the first Japanese barber in Seattle was from Yamaguchi-ken. After he became established, he helped his friends from the same ken with training and money, so that, eventually, most of the Japanese barbers in Seattle were from Yamaguchi-ken.[40]

During this era, when associations existed or were created in many ethnic groups, organizations for the benefit of women also emerged. In 1868, Susan B. Anthony was a leading organizer of a working women's association to fight economic discrimination against women. In addition, during the next decade unions of women working in a number of industries such as laundries and shoe factories were organized. By 1886, there were 113 women's assemblies in the Knights of Labor.[41] Other organizations also were concerned about the poor working conditions of women. For example, in 1894, the New York Consumer's League presented information on these conditions. By 1896, this organization had branches in twenty states. In 1900, the International Ladies Garment Workers Union was organized and throughout the pre–World War I period it continued to organize despite many obstacles.[42]

While working women were organizing themselves in their workplaces, more affluent women organized to secure the vote. The women's suffrage movement and the movement for the abolition of slavery had originally been one. The split came partially because Northern business interests stood to gain from the black vote but could see no value in women having the same right.[43] This was symbolized when the American Equal Rights Association, working for black and women's rights, split in May, 1869. Later that year moderate women organized the American Woman Suffrage Association while radical women formed the National Women Suffrage Association. These organizations remained separate until 1890 when they merged to form the National American Woman Suffrage Association. Unfortunately, the class bias of these organizations was evident in attacks on blacks as less fit to vote than women and in other statements made to ensure the acceptability of the women suffrage movement in the South.

The women's suffrage movement was able to see to it that the Nineteenth Amendment was proposed every year from 1886 to 1896, although it was defeated each time. The lack of strength to pass the amendment, according to one authority, was due to "their own conservative tactics and racist, elitist positions, which alienated their potential allies."[44] With the emergence of militant supporters, however, such as radical farmers, the Progressive Party, and the socialists and a shift to more militant leadership, many states did come to adopt woman suffrage. By 1916, both major parties supported suffrage. In 1917, the Women's party turned to more militant tactics and picketed the White House. Partly, also, because of women's activities in the war

---

[40]Kitano, *Japanese Americans, op. cit.,* p. 19.

[41]For details of these and other endeavors, see "A Century of Struggle: American Women, 1820–1920," in Barbara Deckard, *The Women's Movement: Political, Socioeconomic, and Psychological Issues* (New York: Harper and Row, Publishers, 1975), pp. 243–284. This section draws heavily on that chapter.

[42]*Ibid.,* p. 270.

[43]*Ibid.,* p. 262.

[44]*Ibid.,* p. 269.

and the public support of President Wilson, the House of Representatives finally passed the Nineteenth Amendment in January, 1918. It took, however, another eighteen months for Senate approval.

Development of The Profession and Professional Education

For this period it is impossible to discuss community organization as a specialization in social work, which had itself not yet emerged as a separate entity. There were individuals concerned with coordinating charity, organizing neighborhood settlements, or mobilizing protest in racial matters, but these people had little common professional identity. Some training activities began to emerge in 1898 when the New York Charity Organization Society started a summer training course. This was expanded to a one-year program a few years later and by the end of World War I, seventeen schools of social work had come into existence in the United States and Canada. The Association of Training Schools for Professional Social Work was formed at that time also. The emphasis, however, was more on what became casework than on methods of community organization.

1915 TO 1929

Social Conditions

Some social conditions in the period just described developed further after World War I and several new conditions emerged —all having a significant impact on community organization practice. Urbanization increased markedly, industrial potential escalated, and racial conflicts intensified.

By 1920 more than half of the population of the United States lived in cities. Industrial innovations were accelerated by the heavy demands on production created by World War I.

The twenties formed a decade of confidence in the economic system. As Lerner stated, "Big business of the 1920's, certain that it had found the secret of perpetual prosperity, claimed the right to the policy-making decisions not only in the economy but in the government."[45]

Ironically, this period also brought some major crises in civil liberties. "After World War I there was a wave of raids and deportations; it arose from the uneasy feeling that the Russian Revolution had caused a shift in the world balance of power and spawned a fanatic faith threatening American survival."[46] The period also witnessed the intensification of activities of groups such as the Ku Klux Klan with antagonism directed against blacks, Jews, and the foreign born.

The Condition of Minorities

Blacks. This was a period during which black Americans made strong attempts to improve their lives and were simultaneously subjected to major efforts at repression. Seventy-six black people were lynched in 1919,[47] and "the white national secretary of the NAACP was badly beaten on the streets of Texas."[48] Chicago experienced a severe "race riot" in 1919 which resulted in the death of 15 white and 23 black persons as well as injury to an additional 537.[49]

However, progress occurred in many spheres of American life. The term *the New Negro* became prevalent in the 1920s, and this bore some relation to the increased self-respect of many black war veterans. During this period, distinguished people such as Langston Hughes, Countee Cullen, and

---

[45]Lerner, *op. cit.*, p. 279.
[46]*Ibid.*, p. 455.
[47]Fishel and Quarles, *op. cit.*, 403.
[48]*Ibid.*
[49]*Ibid.*, p. 405.

Paul Robeson began their careers. Black school attendance jumped between 1910 and 1930 from 45 to 60 percent of the eligible school population.[50] In fact, in many ways the current emphasis on black power and black identity has ideological antecedents in this period.

Chicanos. These years saw a large immigration of persons from Mexico into what had become the United States. Between 1910 and 1919, almost two hundred and twenty-five thousand persons came and in the next decade, the number was almost double.[51] According to one writer, "that striking increase is directly related to the miserable economic conditions in Mexico after ten years of armed struggle."[52] Specifically, the Mexican economy was in a poor state after the Mexican Revolution while the southwestern United States was experiencing considerable growth economically.

There was an expansion and development of nonagricultural worker organizations during this period. As Moore notes:

> In 1920 Mexican workers struck the Los Angeles urban railway. In later years the strikes in the fields and mines of the Border States were both more numerous and more sophisticated. The earlier ones were significant, however, because Mexicans were generally denied normal channels of political expression in any of the Border States except New Mexico.[53]

Native Americans. During this period, the conditions of Native Americans continued to deteriorate as the government persisted in its policy of implementing the Dawes Act of 1887 which distributed land to individuals. The attempt to undermine the widely practiced custom of holding land in common for the good of all was maintained. The act not only created severe economic problems but eroded traditional tribal government.[54] In fact, "the Indian Agent and his staff were 'the government' for most tribes from the cessation of treaty making to the 1930's."[55]

In addition to the effects of the Dawes Act, two other actions also diminished tribal ties. From 1917 to 1921, the trust on land allotments of Indians of less than one-half Indian blood was terminated. Many Indian agents were also eliminated and their wards placed under school superintendents and farmers reporting directly to the Commissioner of Indian Affairs.[56] This focused activities on individuals, not tribes, and presumably moved Indians as individuals into non-Indian education and agriculture.

Asian Americans. The Immigration Act of 1924 epitomized the attitudes of the American government, if not of the society, to the foreign born. No immigration was to be permitted for Asians; low quotas were set for southern Europeans, and high ones for northern Europeans. This made it impossible, particularly for the Chinese who had not come as families, to form or reunite families. In Japanese communities, these years marked the birth and early development of many *Nisei,* or second-generation Japanese-Americans. With great determination, many Nisei moved into middle-class occupations.

Ideological Currents

Several ideologies which were prevalent in the earlier period continued to exert an

---

[50] *Ibid.*

[51] Lopez y Rivas, *op. cit.,* p. 85.

[52] *Ibid.,* p. 39.

[53] Joan Moore, *Mexican-Americans* (Englewood Cliffs, N.J.: Prentice-Hall, 1970), p. 24.

[54] Theodore W. Taylor, *The States and Their Indian Citizens* (Washington, D.C.: United States Department of the Interior, Bureau of Indian Affairs, 1972), p. 17.

[55] *Ibid.*

[56] *Ibid.,* pp. 17–18.

influence. The sense of complacency and optimism stemming from economic growth and affluence did find perceptive social critics. The following are some ideas which prevailed during this period and which helped to mold social work practice.

Psychoanalysis. Some may find it strange to regard psychoanalysis as an ideology; nevertheless, the conditions of the period were conducive to the introduction of psychoanalysis as a major intellectual force in social work. This was a period of affluence, and many believed that the social environment offered so many opportunities and was otherwise so benign that any problems must be the result of individual failure. Psychoanalytic practice was clearly oriented toward changing the individual and not the system. Social workers, as Jesse Taft observed, became preoccupied with the person and all but forgot the situation: "The most daring experimental caseworkers have all but lost connection with social obligation and are quite buried in their scientific interest in the individual as he has evolved through his own unique growth process."[57] The social worker dissociated herself from charity to be reborn a psychotherapist.[58]

Anti-Intellectualism. Despite the increasing popularity of Freud's ideas, this was not a period of intellectual activity in the United States. Vice-President Coolidge attacked the colleges and universities as "hot beds of sedition."[59] Many intellectuals fled to Europe, finding America, along with T. S. Eliot, a "wasteland."[60] American writers such as Sinclair Lewis castigated the American middle class, as F. Scott Fitzgerald did the upper class. It should also be remembered that the Scopes trial took place in 1925. According to one authority "only one event in the 1920's succeeded in arousing intellectuals of every kind of political loyalty: the arrest, trial and execution of two Italian anarchists, Nicola Sacco and Bartolomeo Vanzetti."[61]

Development of Community Organization Institutions

The Community Chest and United Fund. This period saw a continued increase in the number of welfare institutions. This proliferation of agencies generated insistent demands for coordination. The increase in such institutions was prompted primarily by accelerating urbanization. The war increased the pace as "some three hundred American communities organized war chests to cope with the mounting flood of appeals from national and local agencies."[62] The agencies' increasing needs for financing, despite the affluence of the period, prompted demands from both the philanthropists and the professionals for better fund-raising methods. The interests of these two groups were not identical, and this led to the development of two separate yet interrelated institutions—the community chest or united fund, on the one hand, and the community welfare council on the other. The separation of interests between the suppliers of philanthropic dollars and the dispensers of them had effects which can be seen to this day in community welfare institutions.

[57]Roy Lubove, *The Professional Altruist: The Emergence of Social Work As a Cause, 1880–1930* (Cambridge, Mass.: Harvard University Press, 1965), p. 89.
[58]*Ibid.*
[59]Samuel Eliot Morison, *The Oxford History of the American People* (New York: Oxford University Press, 1965), p. 909.
[60]*Ibid.*, p. 910.

[61]For a brief summary of the case and its effects on opinion, see Frederick J. Hoffman, *The Twenties: American Writing in the Post War Decade* (New York: The Viking Press, 1955), pp. 357–64.
[62]Lubove, *op. cit.*, p. 189.

Lubove reflected this situation accurately when he declared:

> Financial federation captured the imagination of businessmen by promising efficient coordination and organization of the community welfare machinery, immunity from multiple solicitation, economical collection and distribution of funds, and the development of a broad base of support which would relieve the pressure on the small circle of large givers. The corporation, increasingly regarded as a source of gifts, appreciated the conveniences of federated finance.[63]

There was also opposition to this development. National organizations resented the competition for local funds. Of particular importance to current issues in community organization was resistance to the erosion of "democracy" implicit in the development of a fund-raising bureaucracy. Lubove cited one chest executive who stated, "We are facing here the age-long and inevitable conflict which exists in any society between the urge for individual independence and initiative on the one hand, and the need for social control on the other."[64]

Philanthropists wanted their funds spent efficiently and desired relief from the constant appeals of charitable solicitors. United appeals for financial support were created to serve these objectives, originating with the United Jewish Appeal in Boston in 1895.[65]

Community chests evolved in several ways. First, welfare agencies joined to solicit funds, hoping to raise more money than each could obtain separately. In 1887, the Charity Organization Society in Denver initiated joint fund-raising among fifteen of its twenty-three cooperating agencies, an effort which proved financially successful in its first year of operation.[66] Community chests have also been organized by councils of social agencies. In 1915, two years after its organization, Cincinnati's Council of Agencies brought twelve agencies together in a united appeal for funds. Before 1927, councils in St. Louis, Minneapolis, Columbus, New Haven, and Detroit had followed suit.[67]

For the most part, however, community chests were initiated by large contributors. Often their first step was a charity endorsement bureau which later reorganized as a community chest. Businessmen and industrialists believed that welfare services, like public utilities, should be held accountable to the public. Because contributors rarely had time to investigate agencies that asked for support, local chambers of commerce organized bureaus to (1) establish standards for welfare agencies; (2) investigate individual agencies and measure their operations against their standards; (3) recommend those agencies that met the test; and (4) encourage members and the public to support organizations that received endorsement.[68]

The endorsement bureau had its critics. Because it represented mainly the large business and industrial contributors, agencies viewed the bureaus as potentially autocratic and a threat to their autonomy. Furthermore, agencies believed that the organization might dampen contributors' interest and enthusiasm.[69] The demands upon a small number of contributors also became very great. The first major effort to

---

[63]*Ibid.*, p. 183.

[64]*Ibid.*, p. 196. Lubove, here, was quoting Raymond Clapp, "Who Shall Decide Personnel Policies?" *Survey* 65 (1930), p. 103.

[65]Lyman S. Ford, "Federated Financing," in Harry L. Lurie (ed.), *Encyclopedia of Social Work* (New York: National Association of Social Workers, 1965), p. 331.

---

[66]William J. Norton, *The Cooperative Movement in Social Work* (New York: The Macmillan Co., 1927), pp. 50–54.

[67]*Ibid.*, pp. 93–99

[68]*Ibid.*, pp. 24–29.

[69]*Ibid.*, pp. 29–30.

remedy these conditions was taken by the Cleveland Chamber of Commerce. After initiating a study of the problem in 1907, the chamber launched the Federation for Charity and Philanthropy in 1913. Cleveland's federation is generally considered to be a major landmark in the history of community chests,[70] a name which was first used in Rochester, New York, in 1919.[71]

Community chests were dominated by three kinds of people: contributors, particularly those who gave large sums; solicitors, the small businessmen, service club members and middle management types who helped to raise the chests' funds; and volunteers representative of the health, welfare, and recreation agencies which were supported by the chests. The membership delegated much of the decision making to a board of directors, which hired an executive. In the beginning, much of the work was done by volunteers, and volunteers continue to play an important part in community chests.

World War I gave a great impetus to the development of chests. Overseas relief and other war-created welfare needs stimulated the development of nearly four hundred "War Chests." During the 1920s the number of communities with community chests increased from 39 to 353.[72]

The Council of Social Agencies and Community Welfare Council. The first decades of the twentieth century saw the development of an increasing professionalism among those who helped the poor. The friendly visitor was replaced by the paid agent. The charity organization societies founded schools of philanthropy which be-

ginning around the turn of the century became graduate schools of social work. The development of the social survey—a disciplined effort to obtain facts necessary for planning—was another manifestation of the growing professionalism. In short, the growing cadre of welfare professionals, with the support of many volunteers who served as board members of charitable societies, was interested in organizing a rational, systematic approach to the welfare needs of communities, providing for the gaps in service, detecting problems, and looking to future needs. The council was one expression of this concern. The first councils were organized in Milwaukee and Pittsburgh in 1909. By 1926 there were councils in Chicago, Boston, St. Louis, Los Angeles, Detroit, Cincinnati, Columbus, and New York.[73]

Because of the potential conflicts noted earlier, one of the problems experienced by councils was their relation to community chests or united funds. Often councils have been regarded as the planning arm of the chest or fund, and this made their relation to publicly supported health and welfare agencies difficult. Yet when councils maintained some degree of independence from chests and funds, they seldom were provided with the incentives necessary to gain compliance with their plans. Those councils that were heavily influenced by chests or funds were often assigned responsibility for distributing the money raised in the united appeal, a function seldom performed by independent councils.

Another problem of welfare councils was their relation with constituents. In the beginning, most councils were confederations of welfare agencies, largely those supported by chests. Within such a federated structure, councils often found it difficult to take forceful action, not wanting to seriously

---

[70] *Ibid.,* pp. 68–71.

[71] Guy Thompson, "Community Chests and United Funds," *Social Work Year Book, 1957,* ed. Russell H. Kurtz (New York: National Association of Social Workers, 1957), p. 176.

[72] Ford, *op. cit.,* pp. 327–28.

---

[73] *Ibid.,* p. 37.

offend their agency constituents, which had a major stake in welfare plans. With the growing professionalization of councils, they often were reorganized as councils of individual citizens with an interest in welfare problems and services. This shift was indicated in the change in name from "council of agencies" to "community welfare council." Efforts were made to recruit those with a reputation for influence, and decisions have increasingly reflected the views of professional planners and their volunteer constituents rather than welfare agencies. In spite of this, welfare councils have not enjoyed a reputation for effective planning.[74]

The Social Unit Plan.

Roy Lubove[75] described a local development which anticipated one trend that later became important in community organization. This plan was launched in 1915 when the National Social Unit Organization was founded. A pilot area was selected in Cincinnati. The sponsors desired to test—

> the theory that a democratic and effective form of community organization which stimulated people to define and meet their own needs has to divide the citizens into small, primary units, organize the occupational specialists, and insure an "organic" and coordinate working relationship between the representatives of groups having special knowledge or skill for service to the community and the representatives of the residents.[76]

The social unit plan led to the development of block councils, block workers, and federations of such groups, referred to as the Citizens Council of the Social Unit. Occupational groups also elected a council.

This program lasted three years and "concentrated on health services."[77] The movement did not expand in this form, perhaps indicative of the fact that the time for this idea had not yet come.

The Organization of Ethnic Minorities and Women.

Particularly in the South, many institutions developed among blacks because of the patterns of discrimination and segregation which existed during this period. Out of school segregation, educational organizations arose. Black newspapers also came into existence because news of the black community was ignored by the white press. The exclusion of blacks from white churches led to a variety of black religious organizations.[78]

Many black soldiers hoped that their return from World War I would see a change in the patterns of racism they had suffered for so long. This was not to occur, as the Klan and other groups intensified their campaigns and "returning Negro soldiers were lynched by hanging and burning, even while still in their military uniforms."[79] One reaction to this was the Universal Negro Improvement Association of Marcus Garvey. This organization rapidly became the largest nonreligious black organization. The purpose of the movement was to send blacks back to Africa, and the attraction of this to many blacks was a clear indication of their disaffection with America.

There was also militancy, and as Franklin stated:

> This was the spirit of what Alain Locke called "The New Negro." He fought the Democratic white primary, made war on the whites who consigned him to the

---

[74] The changes noted here did not occur until the late 1940s and 1950s, but are reported here to complete the discussion of community welfare councils.

[75] Lubove, *op. cit.*, pp. 175–78.

[76] *Ibid.*, p. 176.

[77] *Ibid.*

[78] Much of the material in this section has been drawn from John Hope Franklin, "The Two Worlds of Race: A Historical View," *Daedalus* 94, No. 4 (Fall 1965), pp. 899–920.

[79] *Ibid.*, p. 912.

ghetto, attacked racial discrimination in employment, and pressed for legislation to protect his rights. If he was seldom successful during the postwar decade and the depression, he made it quite clear that he was unalterably opposed to the un-American character of the two worlds of race.[80]

During this same period, a major thrust of Mexican-American organization was toward integration.[81] This represented the desires of the growing middle class to secure their share of the American wealth. An example was the Order of the Sons of America, founded in San Antonio in 1921. An intent of this organization was to show Anglos that its members were different from Mexicans who cause problems.[82] The League of Latin American Citizens had similar objectives.

Meanwhile, Chicano laborers were waging their own struggle. Lopez y Rivas points out that "all over California, Arizona, Texas, New Mexico and other states they went on strike for better wages and living conditions as well as an end to racist employment practices." These efforts, however, met with "violent repression."[83] Nevertheless, an important development was the founding in 1927 of *La Confederación de Uniones Obreras Mexicanos*. This organization held its first general convention in May, 1928. Delegates attended from twenty-one unions as well as mutual aid societies. Farm labor groups also struck the fields throughout California. The Confederación itself engaged in major organizing activities throughout the 1920s and 1930s.[84]

The actions of the federal government which had the effect of undermining Native American institutions continued during this period. One piece of legislation, the Snyder Act of 1921, continued to affirm the objective of the Bureau of Indian Affairs to provide "for the general support and civilization of Indians."[85] However, the Meriam Report of 1928 recommended "an acculturation program based on an understanding of the Indian point of view."[86] Even though these actions may have been inspired by good intentions, their patronizing nature was unsupportive of indigenous institutions.

One author, in an attempt to characterize efforts to organize women after the adoption of the Nineteenth Amendment, titles her chapter "Forty Years in the Desert: American Women, 1920–1960."[87] In the first place, there was no indication of a women's block vote, which some had feared. This was not to deny the fact, however, that in specific elections, the proportions of women voting differently than men made a difference in the outcome. An example was the defeat of antisuffrage senator John Weeks in 1918.[88]

The National Women's Party, however, continued to operate. It maintained a platform committed to full equality and supported the first introduction of the Equal Rights Amendment into Congress in 1923. However, it was quite small and in 1923 had only eight thousand members as compared to fifty thousand three years before.[89]

The League of Women Voters was founded in 1920. This group was much less militant than the National Women's Party and it declared in 1931 that "nearly all discriminations have been removed."[90] The League was less concerned about women's

---

[80]*Ibid.*, p. 913.
[81]Lopez y Rivas, *op. cit.*, p. 62.
[82]*Ibid.*
[83]*Ibid.*
[84]Alvarez, *op. cit.*, pp. 211–212.

[85]Taylor, *op. cit.*, p. 19.
[86]*Ibid.*
[87]Deckard, *op. cit.*, p. 285.
[88]*Ibid.*, p. 286.
[89]*Ibid.*, p. 287.
[90]*Ibid.*

issues than child labor laws, pacifism, and other general reforms.

The general conservatism of the 1920s took its toll in the women's movement. The prohibition against child labor, which women's groups favored, was attacked as a subversive plot.[91] It was even charged that all liberal women's groups were part of a communist plot.[92] Despite this, women continued to found organizations including the National Federation of Business and Professional Women's Clubs (1919) and the American Association of University Women (1921).

Development of the Profession

Most of those who trained for social work in the first two decades of the twentieth century were studying to become caseworkers. However, by 1920 Joseph K. Hart had written a text entitled *Community Organization,* and between then and 1930 at least five books were written on the subject.[93] It is easy to see why the casework emphasis existed in view of the prevalent ideologies and issues of the period emphasizing individual conformity to the "system." In fact, community organization practice during this period was aimed largely at enhancing agencies oriented toward personal adjustment. Except, perhaps, for the workers in settlement houses, the "social unit plan," and the organizations developing in the black community, little thought was given to changing social institutions to meet the needs of individuals. Even in the case of settlements, the workers there often thought of themselves as educators, recreation leaders, or group workers. In the black community, organizers rarely identified with social work.

Nevertheless, some different ideas were beginning to emerge. Mary Follett foresaw the advantages to democracy of the organization of primary groups in the local communities.[94] Eduard Lindeman, who taught for many years at the New York School of Social Work, also spoke of the value of "an attempt on the part of the people who live in a small, compact local group to assume their own responsibilities and to guide their own destinies."[95]

The emphasis of this period, however, was aptly summed up by Lubove when he wrote the following:

> Federation employed the rhetoric of the early community organization movement, but its intensive concern with the machinery and financing of social welfare diverted attention from cooperative democracy and the creative group life of the ordinary citizen to problems of agency administration and service. It substituted the bureaucratic goal of efficiency through expert leadership for what had been a quest for democratic self-determination through joint efforts of citizen and specialist. Community organization had barely emerged as a cause before it had become a function absorbed into the administrative structure of social work.[96]

1929 TO 1954

Social work, as well as other institutions in the United States, was deeply affected by the two major cataclysms of this period: the depression and World War II. To regard these years as a single period in American history may seem odd to some readers, but they cover a coherent period in the develop-

---

[91] *Ibid.,* pp. 288–289.

[92] *Ibid.*

[93] Meyer Schwartz, "Community Organization," *Encyclopedia of Social Work, op. cit.,* p. 177.

[94] See for example, her book *The New State: Group Organization the Solution of Popular Government* (New York: Longmans, Green and Co., 1918), p. 217.

[95] Eduard C. Lindeman, *The Community: An Introduction to the Study of Community Leadership and Organization* (New York: Association Press, 1921), p. 58.

[96] Lubove, *op. cit.,* p. 180.

ment of ideas and issues in community organization practice. A departure from this pattern took place in the fifties, marked by the desegregation decision of the Supreme Court and the end of a period of ideological repression, which received its name as well as much encouragement from the late Sen. Joseph McCarthy of Wisconsin.

Social Conditions

To set the stage for the discussion of the history of community organization during the period, one should call attention to several contemporary social forces.

Depression Issues. The most apparent of the social forces at play was the vast increase in unemployment. The bank and stock market failures also removed whatever reserves people might otherwise have utilized in such a crisis. Mortgage foreclosures deprived many of their homes, farms, and small businesses.

The Growth of Government. The expansion of government programs was a direct result of the depression. Government expenditures, programs, and controls grew in unprecedented ways. The government became an employer, a producer of goods and services, and a vast resource to restore the industrial processes. Also, for the first time the federal government became the most significant planner and promoter of welfare programs, through the enactment in the mid-thirties of such legislation as social security and the minimum wage.

The Growth of Unionism. The depression also stimulated a major upsurge of trade unionism. The founding of the CIO showed that the labor movement was at last free from the limits of a craft basis for organization. The passage of the National Labor Relations Act in 1935 marked the begin-

ning of an era in which government facilitated the development of unions and thereby became less the biased protector of business interests. The development of strong unions in the auto, steel, electrical, meat-packing, and other industries had a major impact upon the industrial scene. The organization of the Brotherhood of Sleeping Car Porters gave the black community an important labor spokesman, A. Phillip Randolph.

The International Scene. During this period, it became evident that the Communist party was firmly entrenched in the USSR. In Spain, Italy, and Germany, fascist governments seized power. American counterparts of these movements were apparent in the developments within the United States.

On the international level, these developments had consequences of the most serious nature for the United States. Just at the time in the thirties that many programs to solve the social problems of the country were being tested, the need to prepare for and then wage World War II increasingly absorbed the attention and resources of the American people. In fact, only with the war did the country clearly come out of the depression.

The Condition of Minorities

Blacks. The creation of many New Deal agencies "added credence to the emergent fact that for the first time the federal government had engaged and was grappling with some of the fundamental barriers to race progress."[97] On the other hand, there were many times when Roosevelt, who was highly regarded by many black leaders, failed to deliver on expectations because of political considerations. Where lo-

---

[97]Fishel and Quarles, *op. cit.,* p. 447.

cal control was strong, the effect of some of those programs was to continue the exclusion of black people from necessary benefits.

It is undeniable, however, that important strides were made during this period. There was a considerable expansion of opportunities for black people in important governmental positions. Civil service brought many black people into white-collar positions in government. World War II increased this momentum. The Committee on Fair Employment Practice, established by Roosevelt in 1941 to improve employment opportunities in defense industries, was a significant development. In 1948, Truman created the civil rights section of the Justice Department and established the President's Committee on Equality of Treatment and Opportunity in the Armed Services. The courts struck down restrictive housing covenants and outlawed segregation on buses in interstate travel.

Chicanos. During this period, Chicanos began to move beyond the Southwest into many parts of the United States. This was due in part to the processes of acculturation but also to the fact that new Mexican immigrants were willing to work for lower wages than second-generation persons, who then tended to move to new areas. Particularly in the North, jobs were more available and wages better. A pattern of migrant farm labor was also established emanating from the Southwest and spreading to other parts of the country, as Chicanos followed the crops.

Much of the immigration during this period was illegal but responsive to employers seeking cheap labor. Employers aided the smuggling in of such persons.[98] The need for labor was heightened as Asian immigration ended.

In summarizing the period prior to 1940, however, one authority stated:

> The lot of the Mexican-Americans, except as they were affected by the immigration, changed little during this period prior to 1940. In a real sense, they were forgotten Americans; there was little assimilation to the majority society. They remained a Spanish speaking, largely rural, and generally poor minority. The decline of the small farmer and sheepherder forced many off the land altogether. But even as wage earners, they received no proper return in comparison to their contribution to the building of the economy of the Southwest.[99]

Native Americans. Early in the period being described here, a new approach was adopted to Native Americans: the Indian Reorganization Act of 1934. The intent of this act was to reverse the land policy of the Allotment Act of 1887 and the intent of trying to "stamp out everything that was Indian."[100] The 1934 act specifically provided authorization for the purchase of new land, the initiation of tribal organization, the creation of loan funds for individuals *and tribes,* and extended the trust of Indian lands "until otherwise directed by Congress."[101]

This new policy of a more humane concern for Indians was a part of FDR's New Deal. The Commissioner of Indian Affairs from 1933 to 1944, John Collier, was an anthropologist with a long career of interest in Indian affairs, and this may also have made a difference. Collier was critical of many American values and was identified with the aspirations of many Indian groups, and he had some utopian ideas about the potential of Indian society.[102]

---

[98]Wayne Moquin with Charles Van Doren, *A Documentary History of the Mexican Americans* (New York: Fraeger Publishers, 1971), p. 252.

[99]*Ibid.,* p. 253.
[100]Taylor, *op. cit.,* p. 20–26.
[101]*Ibid.*
[102]*Ibid.,* p. 22.

Tribal governments established under this act were helped to develop constitutions and carry on many operations required of modern governments, economic as well as political. In contradiction to this, however, was the policy of promoting assimilation by urging states to provide the same services for individual Indians as for other citizens.

Asian-Americans. This period saw the gradual improvement of the economic status of Chinese-Americans although not necessarily of their social status. As Kitano states:

> In the late 1930's and during World War II the Chinese became our friends and allies, although the general tone of the friendship was condescending. . . . Their peace loving nature was emphasized; they had fought valiantly against the "sly, tricky Jap"; they were different from their more aggressive neighbor. . . . In many ways, this praise deflected from the everyday humiliation, harassment, and deprivation faced by many Chinese, even with the relatively favorable attitude toward all Orientals (except the Japanese) at this time.[103]

The most devastating event affecting the Japanese-American community was the wartime evacuation of all persons with as little as one-eighth Japanese blood from the West Coast. By March 1942, one hundred and ten thousand such persons, most citizens of the United States, were in virtual concentration camps in such states as Colorado, Utah, and Arkansas. There was widespread compliance by most Japanese-Americans, even though they had to abandon their homes and possessions. This terrible injustice continued until 1944 when the Supreme Court revoked the policy. Most families who survived the experience had to begin all over again. Little remained of their property or belongings.

Ideological Currents

The most important ideological issues of the period were those stimulated by the conditions of the depression. The emphasis of the twenties upon the individual's responsibility for his or her own destiny could not hold up under the circumstances of the thirties. The literature of this period emphasized the effects of the social order on people and the need to modify that order to solve the spiritual as well as the economic problems which plagued Americans.[104] Many came to regard government, rather than business, as the preferred means for developing a better society. However, except for small minorities, people wanted their government to operate through much the same political processes as it always had, and the economy to remain capitalist, though under strong government controls.

These ideas were not basically shaken by the war. Fascism as an international enemy was further proof that there are forces which transcend the individual and must be controlled by collective action. Although congressional investigations of "un-American activities" received much popular support, the external enemy and wartime prosperity took many people's attention away from problems within the United States. Moreover, Americans' faith in their own political and economic system may have been reinforced by wartime victory. However, the specter of an external enemy acting in concert with internal agents returned with a vengeance with the cold war and the Korean War, dampening criticism of the "American way of life" and making it difficult to gain support for proposals to attack the country's social problems.

---

[103]Kitano, *Race Relations, op. cit.,* p. 200.

[104]It was noted earlier that the ideological antecedents of some Negro militancy were in the twenties. Current white militancy may be traced to the thirties.

Development of Community Organization Institutions

Community organization agencies, like others in social welfare, found themselves unable to cope with the massive needs of the country during the depression. This period marked a shift of emphasis in operations from local and private to regional or national and public. The federal government through its agencies became the main impetus for social planning. At first through the Federal Emergency Relief Administration and later through the Federal Security Agency, standards for welfare activity were set, coordination was promoted, fact finding was conducted, and plans for public education were launched.

World War II advanced the trend toward community planning under national auspices, both public and private. The need for welfare services grew as new and expanding communities of defense workers and soldiers sprang up. The Office of Community War Services in the Federal Security Agency was created to handle some of the planning for recreation and public health needs in affected areas.

Organization of Ethnic Minorities and Women. Organization in the black community remained primarily on a national level, and some authorities have noted a degree of apathy regarding anything beyond that.[105] The NAACP continued to wage campaigns for the rights of blacks in the courts, the Congress, and the press. The Urban League expanded its programs of employment, family welfare, health, and education. The thirties and forties did not foster any prominent new organizational efforts. In addition to the external threats noted earlier, this may have been due to the development of governmental programs, trade union activity, and local activity, which black people believed would provide long-hoped-for access to the "American Dream."

During the 1930s, the organizing activities of the Confederación de Uniones Obreras Mexicanas continued. Efforts to build union organization also included those of the National Farm Workers' Union. Other organizations emerged, and some examples of these are the League of United Latin American Citizens (Texas, 1929), the Associación de Jornaleros (Texas, 1933), the Sociedad Mutualista Mexicana (Ohio, 1936), the Pan American Student Forum of Texas (1943), and the Community Service Organization (California, 1947).[106] The vitality of Chicano life is apparent in the organizations that were created during these years. These developments may well have provided support for the new programs which emerged in the 1960s.

These years also saw such movement within Native American tribes. Through new government policies, many tribal governments were established or strengthened. Tribes assumed authority to—

> employ legal counsel; prevent sale or encumbrance of tribal land or other assets without the consent of the tribe; negotiate with Federal, State, and local governments; determine tribal membership; assign tribal land to individuals; manage economic affairs; appropriate money for salaries or other public purposes; levy taxes, license fees, or community labor in lieu thereof; control conduct of members of the reservation by enactment or ordinances. . . .[107]

As was true of Mexican-Americans, it seems likely that the organizational development of the depression, war, and postwar years was a precursor to militant organizing in the next decade.

---

[105]Fishel and Quarles, *op. cit.,* p. 450.

[106]Alvarez, *op. cit.,* pp. 209–210.
[107]Taylor, *op. cit.,* pp. 23–24.

A somewhat different type of organizational experience characterizes Chinese-American life. Chinese-Americans had been living within their own communities, but a trend toward some dispersion began at this time. The control exerted by the traditional associations weakened in many Chinese-American communities. Some who had gained status in the broader community did not have it in the ethnic community because of age and cultural difference including language. Thus, new institutions began to emerge to meet their needs.[108] In many ways, the situation was similar for Japanese-Americans, although recovery from the "relocation" of the war years was a long and hard process.

The period between the depression and the 1950s was not a good one for the women's movement. During the war years many women were employed, and this may have diminished demands for equal employment opportunities for women. However, such issues as adequate child care were central. The conservative swing after the war discouraged militancy among women. Even the League of Women Voters, hardly a radical organization, showed a decline in membership during this time.

Development of the Profession and Professional Education

This, while not a period of innovation in community organization beyond the shift from a local to a national emphasis, was a time of intensive efforts to conceptualize the nature of community organization practice. Some of the ferment which was occurring among students of community organization is summarized below.

Those who wrote about community organization gave evidence of three overriding concerns. The *first* bore upon the relation between community organization and social work. Some writers contended that community organization was not really a legitimate form of social work practice, and others took pains to establish community organization's affinity to the basic values and concerns of social work. The *second* was an interest in the objectives of community organization. On the one hand, practitioners regarded the Industrial Revolution as destructive of personal, face-to-face relations between people and believed that community organization practice should strengthen community cohesion. At the same time, they were disturbed about a number of social problems and thought that community organization practice should prevent or at least ameliorate them. *Third,* they struggled with the appropriate role for the practitioner. Neighborhoods and communities needed the help of practitioners, it was assumed, if localities were to achieve their objectives. And yet practitioners must not impose their views on those served. One must somehow strike a balance between giving help and fostering self-determination.[109]

1955 TO 1977

Less emphasis will be given this period because it constitutes the subject matter of the rest of this volume. However, the major social and ideological conditions will be indicated, and a few observations on community organization and education for practice will be offered.

Social Conditions

The beginning of this period coincides with the end of the McCarthy era and the

---

[108]For a discussion of this development, see Weiss, *op. cit.,* pp. 264–273.

[109]For further details, see Schwartz, *op. cit.,* pp. 177–90.

Supreme Court decision on school desegregation. Whether or not causally related, these events appear to have anticipated a number of other phenomena.

The Growth of the Civil Rights Movement. Marked by the 1954 Supreme Court decision ending legal school segregation, the rising dissatisfaction of black Americans gave birth or renewed vitality to a number of organizations which have sought to end the inequality of opportunity afforded black people. The Montgomery, Alabama, bus boycott, which began in December of 1955, brought Martin Luther King, Jr., and the Southern Christian Leadership Conference forward as leaders in the civil rights struggle.[110] The Congress of Racial Equality (founded in 1943) sponsored nonviolent resistance in the form of sit-ins, freedom rides, and demonstrations.[111] The Student Non-Violent Coordinating Committee, the Mississippi Freedom Democratic party, the Black Panther party, the Black Muslims, the Republic of New Africa and other black nationalist groups, and the NAACP were among the organizations affected by the rising tide of civil rights activities. The quest for black power grew out of the experiences of the Student Non-Violent Coordinating Committee and other active groups who came to despair of achieving genuine integration. As they began to fight for black pride and capability, they demanded autonomy in black affairs, including neighborhood control of schools and economic institutions.[112]

Subsequently other minority groups asserted themselves, claiming their rights and

developing pride in their special identity. The Chicanos of the Southwest made substantial progress in organizing. Stimulated by Cesar Chavez and his success in organizing California farm workers, Chicanos organized groups such as *La Raza Unida* in many places, including south Texas, New Mexico, and even the places where migrant farm workers traveled in search of employment, such as Michigan, where many Chicano farm workers settled down and sought education and regular jobs. American Indians, whose living conditions are generally worse than those of any other minority in this country, likewise demonstrated solidarity in such ways as occupying Alcatraz Island in San Francisco Bay and obtaining legislative support for expanded fishing rights in Michigan.

As the period continued, one trend was clear: a growing effort to create ethnic minority institutions. Examples include neighborhood control of schools, black-owned business, black professional societies, black-led Model Cities programs, powerful interest groups such as the National Welfare Rights Organization, and black labor unions. Nevertheless, conflicts were evident among the leaders of these groups, often traceable to ideological differences. For example, some black leaders sought parallel black economic organizations, i.e., black capitalism, while others worked for changes in the power bases of all American institutions to include major input from black people and other minorities.

Late in this period, other groups asserted themselves, feeling deprived in comparison with their fellow citizens and encouraged by the achievements of blacks and other minorities. Homosexuals demanded social and economic rights and fought discrimination in jobs and housing. The elderly, sometimes with the support of Grey Panther groups, demanded greater attention to their needs, especially for health care. The handi-

[110]Martin Luther King, Jr., *Stride toward Freedom* (New York: Ballantine Books, 1958).

[111]James Peck, *Freedom Ride* (New York: Simon & Schuster, 1962).

[112]Stokely Carmichael and Charles V. Hamilton, *Black Power: The Politics of Liberation in America* (New York: Vintage Books, 1967).

capped also drew attention to the discrimination they suffer in education, employment, and public facilities. Women, oppressed by the requirements of their traditional roles, demanded liberation and equality. Perhaps their most notable achievement was congressional approval of the Equal Rights Amendment to the federal Constitution and its ratification by many state legislatures. (At this writing the fate of ERA is in doubt, the feminists having inadvertently stimulated formidable opposition from more traditional women who have succeeded in defeating ERA in several state legislatures.) "Middle America" became a potent political force. Disgruntled citizens such as Irene McCabe mobilized large numbers of people who opposed the busing of school children to achieve racial integration. Political candidates (George Wallace, for example) captured the support of large numbers of disenchanted voters who felt strongly about school busing and high taxes and were distrustful of government. An anti-gay movement secured defeat of legislation favoring gay rights in Florida.

The Growth of Student Movements.

Stimulated by student involvement in the civil rights movement, student activism among whites as well as blacks and across the whole political spectrum increased phenomenally until the early 1970s. Many student activists turned to social work and particularly to community organization in search of a career compatible with their personal commitments. Some students entering school in the mid-1960s were affected by the community organization projects carried out by the Students for a Democratic Society. Many had experiences relevant to community organization through the Peace Corps or VISTA.

Increasing numbers of black students sought admission to professional schools, including programs offering training in community organization. Puerto Rican and Chicano students did likewise, and there is an indication of similar developments among Japanese- and Chinese-American students, particularly on the West Coast.

Federal Programs to Improve Social Conditions.

The federal government took increasing responsibility for dealing with a wide range of domestic social problems, primarily through grants-in-aid to state and local governments. This had an important bearing on the growth of community organization practice. For example, early in this period the federal government sharply increased appropriations for mental health, primarily for research, professional training, and mental health clinics. More recently, federal programs encouraged preventive measures and efforts to treat the mentally ill in their local communities, a process requiring community organization skills. Similar developments occurred in programs for the mentally retarded, the physically disabled, and the alcoholic. The construction of hospitals and other health facilities, together with encouragement of health services planning at the state level, also received federal support. Programs of slum clearance, urban renewal, neighborhood development, housing subsidies, and regional planning were created and expanded with federal assistance. Although by no means exhaustive, this list of activities exemplifies the role of the federal government in the fields of health and urban development. Similar changes in related fields such as education and child welfare also occurred, which stimulated additional demand for community organization skills.

The trend toward federal responsibility for welfare problems was escalated by the War on Poverty, a product of the Kennedy and Johnson Administrations. This program captured the interest of many community organizers. Among the specific programs were Head Start; VISTA; Neighborhood Youth Corps, Job Corps and other work-training programs; adult basic education; assistance to the rural poor, including migrant farm workers; and a wide variety of locally conceived "community action programs" offering opportunities for local initiative in legal aid, health, housing, consumer education, and so forth. Perhaps the single most important influence these programs had on community practice was the very large number of jobs they offered for people trained as organizers. One much-debated ingredient of these programs was the provision for "maximum feasible participation" of service recipients in program decisions. The how, where, and why of this was often confusing to both professionals and citizens.

The Nixon administration which followed had its own set of concerns and priorities which did not articulate fully with the programs generated by Kennedy and Johnson. Funds for many programs of the Office of Economic Opportunity and the Department of Health, Education, and Welfare shrank as resources for activities of the Departments of Labor and Justice increased. The more generously supported programs included manpower training and subsidized employment by the federal government and a number of activities aimed at crime control. Among these were the programs of the Law Enforcement Assistance Administration. This agency provided funds to develop innovative approaches including community organization programs for dealing with offenders in localities throughout the country.

Other programs created during this period tried to solve urban problems, which continued to intensify. A major effort was the Model Cities program, which provided funds to groups representative of particular neighborhoods within cities. These groups used such funds either to develop new programs within existing civic institutions or to create new institutions where necessary.

In some Model Cities neighborhoods, a vision grew of a "parallel" government manned by the poor within the neighborhoods. This vision was muted, however, by developments which made the existing city governments powerful partners in any operation, under the rationale that coordination and accountability were necessary. This challenged community organizers to help constituents exert influence under these newly instituted rules. A general revenue sharing plan and later a community development block grant program were adopted as alternatives to the Model Cities program.

All of these moves to solve urban problems raised the same issues: Which strata of society will have power? How are the poor to be represented? How are priorities to be determined? Community organizers were involved in answering all these questions, offering a variety of answers to each of them.

The Vietnam War. It is difficult to judge the impact of this war on social work and community organization. Nevertheless, seldom in American history have so many felt so antagonistic to a major involvement of their country. Aside from concerns about the justice of the war, its implications for the allocation of resources to deal with problems on the home front were of grave concern. Some regarded this war and, more generally, what President Eisenhower had referred to as the expanding influence of the "military-industrial complex" and the consequent retreat from dealing effectively with problems of our cities, as the most serious crisis the nation had faced. Certainly, the war led many to doubt the citizen's ability to influence governmental decisions.

Ideological Currents

This was a time in which virtually all the previous ideas about community organization practice reappeared. On the one hand this was a period in which the American people supported the development of vast new responsibilities for government in solving the problems of welfare. On the other hand, there was a renewed emphasis, at least until the early 1970s, upon participatory democracy. Local organization, black power, community control, and such concepts as "maximum feasible participation" (which Daniel P. Moynihan has paraphrased "maximum possible misunderstanding") had a wide appeal.

As might be anticipated, those ideological developments were reflected in the political groupings of the period. The Eugene McCarthy campaign for president in 1968 brought together many who saw themselves, at least for the moment, as working within existing institutions. Various groups identified with "the New Politics" continued this effort, including those who worked for Shirley Chisholm and George McGovern in their efforts to win the Democratic presidential nomination in 1972. On the other hand, as frustration over the lack of federal commitment to civil rights and ending the Vietnam war grew, violent ideologies and solutions also were perpetuated. An alternative "dropout" culture grew as a spin-off of this process. Some community organizers, for example, developed and lived within a growing network of communes.

Alongside interests in added government responsibility and participation of the people has been a strong tide of disengagement from society on the one hand, largely in the aftermath of Watergate, and of violent opposition to those who control society on the other. These currents were reflected in social work, with some students planning government jobs, others looking forward to participation in anti-establishment grassroots organizations, and still others asking if social work and "revolution" are compatible orientations. At this writing it appears that moderation and social planning form the dominant orientation of community organization students, while social work as a whole has experienced a marked increase of interest in professionalization, psychotherapy, self-realization and "making a good living."

Development of the Profession

Training for community organization practitioners in social work grew markedly at first. Both the number of programs and the number of students rose sharply. By 1969 the number of schools of social work providing training programs for community organizers increased to forty-eight, from thirty-six in 1965.[113] It is difficult to estimate the number of schools offering community organization in 1977 because of changes in training programs and the terms used to describe them in the literature. Community organization is taught in some form in virtually all schools.

There are similar difficulties in estimating the number of students enrolled in community organization training programs, but the numbers have undoubtedly increased during this period.[114]

Parallel with the increase in numbers were efforts to clarify the nature of community organization, identify what community organizers need to know to be effective, and give recognition to the development of community organization as a specialized

---

[113]Arnold Gurin, *Community Organization Curriculum in Graduate Social Work Education: Report and Recommendations* (New York: Council on Social Work Education, 1970), p. 10.

[114]See Council on Social Work Education *Statistics* for each year, especially Table 254.

form of practice within social work. In the late 1950s, the Council on Social Work Education embarked upon a wide-ranging study of the curriculum in schools of social work which included separate attention to community organization.[115] The National Association of Social Workers created a Committee on Community Organization which prepared working papers and bibliographies designed to codify practice knowledge and establish the position of the community organization specialty within social work.[116] In 1962 the Council on Social Work Education gave formal recognition to community organization as a method of social work comparable with casework and group work.[117]

To date, the most ambitious effort to develop curriculum for training community organizers was initiated in 1963. It, too, was sponsored by the Council on Social Work Education and received financial support from HEW's Office of Juvenile Delinquency and Youth Development.[118] This study culminated in the publication of five book-length reports and numerous journal articles and conference reports.[119] Earlier efforts pointed up the similarities of community organization practice and other forms of social practice. Perhaps the most significant theme of this latest curriculum study was the recognition that community organization practitioners require professional training that is, in many ways,

differentiated from training for other social work specializations.

A trend toward conceptualizing all social work in "systems" terms became strong in the 1970s.[120] Presumably, all social workers should see the necessity for systems changes and client participation in these changes. Nevertheless, diminishing student activism, focus upon career advancement, and renewed emphasis upon "therapy" began to diminish commitments to community organizing among social work students. The termination of the War on Poverty reduced job opportunities for community organizers. It also set back creativity in community organization practice.

SUMMARY AND CONCLUSIONS

Community organization practice has been examined in its social and ideological context during four periods of its history, separated by events with particular significance for that practice: the First World War and the end of the Progressive Era (1914); the stock market crash (1929) and the Supreme Court decision ending legal racial segregation in the public schools (1954).

It is impossible to understand community organization as an isolated phenomenon or merely as a technique of social engineering, for it is so closely related to what is most important in the lives of those it touches. Industrialization, urbanization, immigration, and minority emancipation created great opportunities and problems. The perspectives of Social Darwinism, socialism, pragmatism, and liberalism through which social conditions were per-

[115]Harry L. Lurie, ed., *The Community Organization Method in Social Work Education*, Vol. IV, Project Report of the Social Work Curriculum Study (New York: Council on Social Work Education, 1959).

[116]See especially National Association of Social Workers, *Defining Community Practice* (New York: 1962).

[117]Council on Social Work Education, *Curriculum Policy Statement*, (New York: 1962).

[118]Gurin, *op. cit.*, pp. vii–viii.

[119]For a summary and reference to the various publications of this project, see Gurin, *op. cit.*

[120]See Gordon Hern, ed., *The General Systems Approach: Contributions toward an Holistic Conception of Social Work* (New York: Council on Social Work Education, 1969).

ceived set the stage for many institutional developments important for community organization practice. Among these were charity organization societies, designed to coordinate unplanned efforts to rescue the poor, and social settlements intended to help the urban poor get themselves together, unite rich and poor in a common enterprise, and reform the oppressive conditions of life that victimized the poor. Minorities organized, in some cases to accommodate themselves to the system and in others to fight it.

Following World War I, the American people expressed a strong desire to return to "normalcy" and the principles of free enterprise, and they developed a sense of profound optimism toward capitalism. The newly emerging profession of social work withdrew from its prior efforts to change pernicious social conditions. In its place, the profession cultivated a preoccupation with the individual psyche. In this context, efficiency-oriented community chests were organized by businessmen to spread the cost and reduce the annoyance of charitable solicitations. A growing cadre of welfare professionals promoted councils of agencies to rationalize their efforts, fill the gaps in services, and promote disinterested and effective services supported by dependable and expanding resources. The social unit plan, oriented toward grass-roots participation, found little sympathy in the climate of the times.

The depression brought the federal government into welfare planning and strengthened grass-roots activities, particularly through the labor movement. World War II and the government's response to the demands of blacks and others for equality were the beginning of important developments in community organization. Small

programs for training community organization practitioners to work with community chests and welfare councils were organized, and their teachers produced the beginnings of a professional literature.

The recent period is characterized first by the civil rights and movements of oppressed minorities and by student activism and discontent with the war in Vietnam, generating strong professional interest in grass-roots organizing and planning with local citizens, plus a pervasive sense of anger and alienation.

This was followed by major reverses in the government's commitment to community organizing during the Nixon years. Shifts in social attitudes, particularly among young people, were not conducive to organizing. Nevertheless, particularly within ethnic groups and among women, these commitments have been kept alive.

Where does all this lead? We are in the midst of a period of retrenchment in community organization programs. Several major questions dangle precariously overhead like the sword of Damocles: How will impatient underclasses, and particularly the large ethnic minorities, respond to current social conditions? Will the necessary wisdom and determination be forthcoming to put our limited resources to work on the social problems that threaten to divide the nation? What are the most effective ways to accomplish our objectives consistent with our values? The first is a question that only those who are oppressed can answer, and the most persuasive answers are likely to be deeds rather than words. The second is a question for the whole nation, especially the president and Congress, the governors and state legislatures. The last is a particular responsibility of social practitioners, including community organizers.

CHAPTER II

Common Elements of Practice

Among practitioners and teachers of community organization there is little consensus about which practice aspects bear most heavily on the success or failure of any range of interventive efforts. In part, this lack of agreement has been a function of the continuing struggle to define and describe what ought to be included under the practice rubric. Also, the widely varying perspectives of organizers, planners, administrators and policy makers have contributed to the difficulty of sorting out which aspects are central and which should be peripheral.

At the same time, the historical development of community organization has —in a number of ways—made the task of seeking out and identifying common practice elements more difficult. While specification of a set of distinguishing community organization characteristics was occurring, there was also a vigorous attempt to separate "CO" from the "interpersonal" fields of practice. One consequence was a tendency to discard some potentially very useful ideas developed in casework and group work.

This section seeks to remedy some of the oversights of the past twenty-five years (as well as the earlier editions of this book) by emphasizing some of the common elements of practice. While we do not claim to have touched on *all* the aspects of practice that are vital to day-to-day work in the community arena, we do believe that the areas considered in this chapter constitute an important part of what must be taken into account if interventive approaches are to have any reasonable level of success. These areas are: the influence and uses of knowledge from the social sciences in practice; the significance of professional ethics and values; interpersonal and small-group practice components; working within the organizational context; development of program in community practice; some approaches to systematic evaluation of agency and practitioner efforts; and a general guide to problem solving.

Community organization is, ultimately, based upon theories of social organization and disorganization. While community theory is especially important, many other aspects of social science are vital as well. The Spiro and Warren pieces suggest some specific uses of this knowledge. To the harried practitioner, theory is typically an annoyance and a distraction. Often, the practitioner is right, for much knowledge has not been formulated for application or written in a language that seeks to enlighten rather than mystify. On the other hand, it is all too easy to throw out the proverbial baby with the bathwater. If community organization is to be based in science, then we must work toward practical formulations and test out such formulations in practice.

Like the rest of the social work profession, community organization is self-conscious about values and professional ethics. However, the tendency has been for those in positions of power to define which values are most important and what constitutes ethical conduct. The thin line between values, ethics, and ideology has often been breached. Murray Ross, for example, looked askance at community organization practice in which the practitioner took major responsibility for setting goals, preferring to reserve for social-work-based community intervention a facilitative modality.[1] The antipoverty efforts of the last two decades have vividly depicted the many and various ways in which the poor get the short end of any stick, and prompted numerous community agencies to borrow and adapt advocacy ideas from the legal profession. The selections by Gilbert and Specht, and Morris, point to some of the ethical (and operational) problems of advocacy.

In separating itself from interpersonal modes of practice, the community organization field adopted a functional approach that did not emphasize a deep understanding of self and the use of self. Burghardt's article stresses important aspects of using one's self in both small groups and interpersonal situations.

Community organization, like most other aspects of the social work profession, is usually an organization-based activity. Often, in social agencies, schools, government bureaucracies and the like, the setting inhibits the activity of the worker, forcing him or her into trivial or counterproductive roles. Whatever the reason for this—attempts to control the worker, agency ineptitude, external political pressures, etc.—changes must often be engineered through the sponsoring organization. Pawlak's piece provides some guidelines for maneuvering through the organizational wasteland, particularly to secure at least the minimal level of support required to give an interventive effort a chance for success.

The emphasis on participation in community practice has, in some instances, left us emphasizing process rather than program, and ideology rather than evaluation. Whatever one's particular orientation, an effective programmatic posture is often essential for organizational success. Sooner or later (and probably the sooner the better), a community practitioner needs to craft a program designed to achieve the social action/planning/development goals in question. This formulation is addressed by Hasenfeld.

---

[1] Murray Ross, *Community Organization: Theory and Principles* (New York: Harper & Brothers, 1955).

Possibly no single practice component has proved as irritating to practitioners as evaluation. All too often, they argue, evaluation is used as a weapon to attack or undermine the practitioner, rather than as a tool to enhance his or her (and the agency's) practice. Key, Hudson, and Armstrong take a comprehensive look at evaluation in the context of community work. Especially important is their emphasis on the varying ways of approaching evaluation based upon what one wants to derive from it.

The final article, by Cox, is an attempt to pull together essential components of practice into a general guide to community problem solving. Among other things, it can serve as a checklist to inform any major change effort at the community level. Also pointed up are areas often overlooked in the busy world of everyday practice.

We make no claim that this group of practice elements covers all times and situations. But we do believe that the practitioner avoids these elements at great peril to himself or herself and the people in whose name the struggle for social change is pursued.

3.a.

Shimon E. Spiro

THE KNOWLEDGE BASE OF COMMUNITY ORGANIZATION PRACTICE*

Community organization has been described as a profession evolving "from an avocation or a cause" (Ecklein & Lauffer, 1972, p. 11). The reform origins of community organization are reflected, to this day, in its strong ideological commitment, be it to values of self-determination, participation and consensus which dominated the decade following World War II, or to values of social justice, equality and freedom which were characteristic of the 1960's.

It is difficult to imagine a community organization practice not informed by lofty ideals and causes. However, the claim of an emerging discipline to a specific domain of practice, and to the offices and rewards that go with it, is based neither on revolutionary rhetoric nor on adherence to humanistic values, but on specific expertise, i.e., the mastery of appropriate skills and access to a specialized and relevant body of knowledge. It is the precariousness of this claim which occasionally has raised questions as to the professionalism of social work in general (Toren, 1969), and community organization in particular.

In this paper we shall try to outline the boundaries of the knowledge base of community organization and to draw attention to some problems encountered in attempts to relate knowledge to the realities of practice. In doing so we shall treat community organization as a unique and coherent field

of practice, ignoring on the one hand its relationship to social work or other human service professions, and on the other possible divisions by type of setting (Perlman & Gurin, 1972) or type of practice (Rothman, 1968).

TYPES OF KNOWLEDGE: THE SYSTEMS

Knowledge required for practice in any profession can be seen as having two substantive components: (1) an understanding of the relevant systems, and (2) specification of possible interventions and their expected outcomes.

The units, or systems, relevant to community organization practice include individuals, small groups, social networks, formal organizations, local communities, social groupings, networks of organizations, etc. All of these feature in practice as actors, targets of change or contexts of action. Practitioners require an understanding of their structure and development, the forces which maintain and change them, their potentials and limitations.

Individuals feature in practice as members or officers of organizations, as proponents and opponents of programs, as their victims and beneficiaries. Their needs and motivations, resources and problems, are the stuff community action is made of. Community organizers try to understand why some persons, in some situations, accept new roles or ideas, while others reject them; why some leaders are able to share

*This is a revised version of a paper presented at a seminar jointly sponsored by the International Association of Schools of Social Work and the European Clearing House for Community Work, held at Edinburgh University, March 1975 (Spiro, 1976).

the limelight and others tend to usurp it (and still others shun it altogether), and so forth.

Complex (or formal) organizations, their policies and practices, are both targets of planning and action and the context within which much of community organization practice is carried out. Their ability to mobilize resources and to convert them into relevant programs is affected by attributes such as size, complexity, structure of authority, as well as by the characteristics of their environments (Rothman & Epstein, 1971).

One could go on to discuss the significance of small groups (McCaughan, 1977), social networks (Craven & Wellman, 1974) and other relevant systems. Our point is that the knowledge required for practice is determined by the variety of roles played by the relevant systems.

SOURCES OF KNOWLEDGE AND TYPES OF CONTRIBUTION

Knowledge about the relevant systems and processes can be drawn from all social and behavioral sciences—from psychology and social psychology, sociology and anthropology, political science and economics, etc. Without attempting to list all relevant fields and subfields, we should like to review the types of contribution all of them make to practice. Elaborating on Thomas (1967b), we see the social sciences providing community organization with concepts, theories (or models), hypotheses and bits of information, methodological approaches and a "scientific stance."

Many of the *concepts* informing practice, such as structure and process, community power, conflict and consensus, representation, participation, and others, have been elaborated and clarified (or, occasionally,

obscured) through the work of social and behavioral scientists.

Occasionally practice is guided, or at least informed, by *theories or models* purporting to explain social conditions and to predict the outcomes of social action. Possibly the best-known example of recent decades was Cloward and Ohlin's theory of delinquency (1960) which, for better or worse, served as the theoretical underpinning for "Mobilization for Youth" (Moynihan, 1969). This may be an example of a not-too-common situation, where a complex theory is applied to an ambitious community organization program. More commonly we find simpler models used to make sense of social realities which are of significance to practice. A case in point would be competing theories of participation, striving to explain differentials by social class and especially the low levels of organizational involvement among the poor. On the one hand we have explanations emphasizing the contrast between lower-class life styles and middle-class models of participation (Rainwater, 1968); on the other hand we have Olson's theory of collective action (Olson, 1965), and an explanation of levels of participation derived from it (O'Brien, 1974), emphasizing self-interested rational behavior.

Many specific *hypotheses,* proposed and tested by scientists in a variety of fields, can be of relevance to practice even when not imbedded in more complex theories or models. Some of the more famous ones relate the structure of a community's economy to the shape of its power structure (Clark, 1975) or the atmosphere and effectiveness of groups to their leadership styles (White and Lippitt, 1960).

At a still lower level of abstraction, the social and behavioral sciences provide practitioners with *information* which may or may not be related to theories or hypotheses. Such "mere facts" may, however, shape the working hypotheses guiding professional practice. Studies conducted in various fields produced information about a variety of subjects, including differentials in voluntary organization membership by age, sex, race, class and other variables (Hyman & Wright, 1971), the prevalence of "grassroots" organizations in the U.S. of the early 1970's (Perlman, 1976), and other topics.

Finally, some of the most important contributions of the social sciences to practice are *methodological.* As part of their practice, planners and organizers have to get to know the "power structure" of their communities, to gain entry into hostile groups and subcultures, to evaluate the relative costs and contribution of proposed programs and projects, and to engage in a variety of other activities for which political scientists, social psychologists, anthropologists or economists developed specific methods and tools. No less important is the acquisition of a generalized "scientific stance," namely the willingness and ability to question pat answers and easy explanations, and to search for hard evidence and attempt to evaluate it objectively.

THE PROBLEM OF LINKAGES

In our discussion so far we have pointed to types of knowledge relevant to practice, and to the possible sources of such knowledge in the social (or behavioral) sciences. The link between the two is, however, problematic. Thomas (1967a) has suggested a number of criteria to be used in selecting knowledge for application. These include considerations of validity and predictive potency as well as the identifiability, accessibility and manipulability of empirical referents.

Since much of social science knowledge is not produced with usefulness to practice

as a main motive (Gouldner, 1957), issues of potency, referent accessibility and manipulability have not been the central concern of most scientists. Furthermore, these dimensions are mostly not self-evident, and require specific judgment by potential users. On top of all this, there is the problem of accessibility: how is a practitioner to know of possibly relevant and usable knowledge scattered through hundreds of journals and thousands of new books?

One could suggest a number of different answers to the problem of the practitioner's access to relevant knowledge. First, *professional education* for the human service profession always includes a significant input from the social and behavioral sciences. Thus community organizers trained in schools of social work get, as part of their training, basic or specific courses in sociology, psychology, political science and other disciplines (Gurin, 1970). The form, location and content of such courses have been discussed elsewhere in some detail (Spiro, 1976). The main problem with transmission of social science knowledge to practitioners as part of their basic professional education is its being a one-shot affair. At best the knowledge thus transmitted reflects the "state of the art" in the relevant disciplines at a given point in time. It does not provide the practitioner with continuing access to developments in the social science disciplines. Continuous linkages could theoretically be achieved through appropriate continuing education programs, but, at this stage of development, in most countries, these provide only a partial solution to our problem. This, in itself, does not detract from the importance, for practitioners, of a basic training in the social and behavioral sciences. On the contrary, only through internalization of basic ideas and key concepts, and the acquisition of the "scientific stance" and some basic methodology, can a practitioner understand, evaluate and possibly utilize more specific contributions.

Another possible channel for ongoing transmission of knowledge from the social sciences to the practitioners could be through *current community organization literature.* One would expect the writers of conference papers, journal articles, monographs and texts to acquire, digest and integrate current developments in related fields into their writings. A review of community organization papers by Warren (1967) has shown a rather narrow and unsystematic utilization of knowledge from social science disciplines in current writings on community organization.

Thus there may be a need for specific efforts designed to collect, evaluate and abstract contributions from the social sciences and draw out their major implications for practice. So far the most impressive effort of this sort was the work of Rothman (1974) and his associates. They reviewed close to a thousand studies from the relevant disciplines, drew from them hundreds of key propositions and their corollaries, tried to evaluate the power of the knowledge thus acquired and point to the implications for practice. The value of an undertaking of this sort is not only in the knowledge retrieved and made available to practitioners, but in the systematic examination and evaluation of that knowledge, leading to the identification of gaps, inconsistencies and difficulties in operationalization and application.

So far attempts to collect, codify and digest knowledge from the social and behavioral sciences and present their consequences for practice have been costly and cumbersome, and, consequently, sporadic. The introduction of more flexible mechanisms for the retrieval and codification of social science knowledge relevant to practice remains a task for the future. This again may serve to underline the impor-

tance of a broad education in the basic concepts and ideas of the relevant disciplines.

COMMUNITY ORGANIZATION THEORY

The foregoing discussions might leave the impression that community organization knowledge is derived entirely from other disciplines. This is definitely not the case. Recent years have seen the emergence of a body of knowledge which in some respects is specific to community organization, in others is generic to planned social change. This body of knowledge is still relatively underdeveloped and quite uncrystallized. Much of it goes under the different headings of "planned change" (Mayer, 1972), "agology" (T. T. tenHave, 1972), "community organization" (Perlman & Gurin, 1972), "community development" (Goetschius, 1969; Kramer, 1970), "community work" (Brager & Specht, 1973), etc. Still, there seems to emerge some coherence in terms of questions asked relative to *planned intervention in social organization:*

1. The goals and underlying values of planned change
2. Assumptions about the nature of social organizations which guide planned intervention
3. The roles of change agents
4. The strategies and tactics of planned intervention and their outcomes

Hopefully, much research and theorizing will focus in the coming years on the fourth type of issue, i.e., the relationship between specific actions and their outcomes.

Like other applied disciplines, such as engineering and medicine, social work (and community work) has to draw on the basic social sciences for an understanding of the phenomena with which it deals and the settings in which it operates. It is expected, however, to develop its own body of knowledge when it comes to defining practice and predicting its outcome. The independent development of such a body of knowledge may, in turn, reinforce the links between community organization practice and its knowledge base in the social sciences.

THE DYNAMICS OF THE KNOWLEDGE BASE

Finally, we should like to draw attention to the dynamics of the knowledge base. Community organization practice is constantly in flux. There is little similarity between community organization for social welfare as practiced in the 1950's and the community action movement of the 1960's (Grosser, 1976). Our arguments were, however, presented at a level of generality which made them equally valid (or invalid) for different times and places. Thus we have to remind ourselves that the knowledge base of any profession has to be relevant to practice as it is at any given point in time. This may be more a matter of shifting emphases than of changing boundaries. One would expect conceptions of professional roles, settings of practice and ideological orientation to affect the selection of concepts, hypotheses and methodological approaches. On the other hand, knowledge available for practice is, at any given time, affected by the current "state of the art" in the relevant disciplines. The knowledge base of practice is determined through the interplay between these various factors. An ongoing, free and open interaction between the field, the social work academia, and the relevant social science disciplines may enhance the adaptation between the knowledge base, current practice and the changing social conditions and needs.

REFERENCES

1. Bennis, Warren G., Benne, Kenneth T., and Chin, Robert, eds. *The Planning of Change.* 2d ed. New York: Holt, Rinehart and Winston, 1969.
2. Brager, George, and Specht, Harry. *Community Organizing.* New York: Columbia University Press, 1973.
3. Clark, Terry N. "Community Power" in A. Inkeles, ed., *Annual Review of Sociology,* Vol. I, 1975, pp. 271–296.
4. Cloward, Richard, and Ohlin, Lloyd E. *Delinquency and Opportunity.* New York: Free Press, 1960.
5. Craven, Paul, and Wellman, Barry. "The Network City" in M. P. Effrat, ed., *The Community.* New York: Free Press, 1974, pp. 57–88.
6. Ecklein, Joan Levin, and Lauffer, Armand A. *Community Organizers and Social Planners.* New York: Wiley and Sons, 1972.
7. Goetschius, George W. *Working with Community Groups.* London: Routledge & Kegan Paul, 1969.
8. Gouldner, Alvin W. "Theoretical Requirements of the Applied Social Sciences." *American Sociological Review,* Vol. XXII, 1957, pp. 92–103.
9. Grosser, Charles F. *New Directions in Community Organization.* New York: Praeger, 1976.
10. Gurin, Arnold. *Community Organization Curriculum in Graduate Social Work Education.* New York: Council on Social Work Education, 1970.
11. tenHave, T. T. "On Agology." *New Themes in Social Work Education,* International Assoc. of Schools of Social Work. Proceedings of the 16th International Congress, The Hague, 1972.
12. Hyman, Herbert H., and Wright, Charles. "Trends in Voluntary Association Memberships of American Adults." *American Sociological Review,* Vol. XXXVI, April 1971, pp. 191–206.
13. Kramer, Ralph. *Community Development in Israel and the Netherlands.* Institute of International Studies, University of California, Berkeley, 1970.

14. Leonard, Peter. "The Contribution of the Social Sciences: Ideology and Explanation," in Catherine Briscoe and David N. Thomas, eds., *Community Work: Learning and Supervision,* National Institute of Social Service Library No. 32, George Allen & Unwin, 1977, pp. 69–81.

15. Mayer, Robert R. *Social Planning and Social Change.* Englewood Cliffs, N.J.: Prentice-Hall, 1972.

16. McCaughan, Nano. "Group Behavior: Some Theories for Practice," in Briscoe and Thomas, *op. cit.,* pp. 82–103.

17. Moynihan, Daniel P. *Maximum Feasible Misunderstanding.* New York: Free Press, 1969.

18. O'Brien, David J. "The Public Goods Dilemma and the Apathy of the Poor." *Social Service Review,* Vol. LXVIII, No. 2, June 1974, pp. 229–244.

19. Olson, Mancur, Jr. *The Logic of Collective Action.* Cambridge, Mass.: Harvard University Press, 1965.

20. Perlman, Janice E. "Grassrooting the System." *Social Policy,* Vol. VII, No. 2, Sept.–Oct. 1976, pp. 4–20.

21. Perlman, Robert, and Gurin, Arnold. *Community Organization and Social Planning.* New York: Wiley and Sons, 1972.

22. Rainwater, Lee. "Neighborhood Action and Lower Class Life Style," in John B. Turner, ed., *Neighborhood Organization for Community Action.* New York: National Association of Social Workers, 1968.

23. Rothman, Jack. "Three Models of Community Organization Practice," from National Conference on Social Welfare, *Social Work Practice 1968.* New York: Columbia University Press, 1968, pp. 16–47.

24. ———. *Planning and Organizing for Social Change.* New York: Columbia University Press, 1974.

25. Rothman, Jack, and Epstein, Irwin. "Social Planning and Community Organization: Social Science Foundations." *Encyclopedia of Social Work, 16th Issue.* New York: National Association of Social Workers, 1971, pp. 1351–1361.

26. Spiro, Shimon. "Teaching the Knowledge Base of Community Work," in Thelma Wilson and Eileen Younghusband, eds., *Teaching Community Work: A European Exploration.* New York: International Association of Schools of Social Work, 1976, pp. 21–28.

27. Thomas, Edwin J. "Selecting Knowledge from Behavioral Science," in Edwin J. Thomas, ed., *Behavioral Science for Social Workers.* New York: Free Press, 1967, pp. 417–425 (a).

28. ———. "Types of Contributions Behavioral Science Makes to Social Work." *Ibid.,* pp. 3–13.

29. Toren, Nina. "Semi-Professionalism and Social Work," in Amitai Etzioni, ed., *The Semi-Professions and Their Organization.* New York: Free Press, 1969, pp. 141–195.

30. Warren, Roland L. "Application of Social Science Knowledge to the Community Organization Field." *Journal of Education for Social Work,* Vol. III, No. 3, Spring 1967, pp. 60–72.

31. White, Ralph, and Lippitt, Ronald. "Leader Behavior and Member Reaction in Three Social Climates," in D. Cartwright and A. Zander, eds., *Group Dynamics: Research and Theory.* 2nd ed. Evanston, Ill: Row, Peterson & Co., 1960, pp. 527–553.

3.b.

Roland L. Warren

APPLICATION OF SOCIAL SCIENCE KNOWLEDGE TO COMMUNITY ORGANIZATION

A review of contributions by the social sciences—principally sociology—to community organization indicates that they tend to fall into two principal categories: (1) knowledge about the social context in which community organization is practiced, especially the nature of the community setting; (2) the broad area of social change, and within this, the narrower, more immediately relevant area of purposive social change. Each of these topics has been approached in two ways. The first was to review the literature and develop what seemed to be appropriate categories within which to group the most meaningful or relevant social science contributions. The second was to review all papers in the community organization field in the *Journal of Social Work* and in the *Social Service Review* for a five-year period, 1961–1965, and to note and classify the social science sources that were cited. This paper will describe the results of both procedures, and then offer comment on some of the differences found.

MAJOR AREAS OF SOCIAL SCIENCE CONTRIBUTIONS

Let us look first at a brief review of the topics on which significant work has been done by social scientists and which appear to be directly relevant to the field of community organization. These topics do not constitute a logical outline, but simply a

From Roland L. Warren, "Application of Social Science Knowledge to the Community Organization Field," *Journal of Education of Social Work,* Vol. 3 (Spring 1967), pp. 60–68. Reprinted with permission of the Council on Social Work Education.

convenient group that avoids some, but not all, overlapping.

Values and Value Orientations

Value orientations within the larger society form part of the constraints within which community organization must operate, but they also raise questions as to whether community organization workers have a mandate to try to change those values.[1] On a somewhat different level, differing value configurations provide part of the context within which any specific community organization activity is conducted, and numerous studies point out the way in which these value configurations vary from one community to another, as well as through time.[2] There is a considerable literature on the value structure of American society as well as on variations within this broad configuration in different localities, communities, ethnic groups, and social strata.[3] An important aspect of the value

[1] *An Intercultural Exploration: Universals and Differences in Social Work Values, Functions, and Practice* (New York: Council on Social Work Education, 1967).

[2] Florence R. Kluckhohn, Fred L. Strodtbeck *et al., Variations in Value Orientations* (Evanston, Ill. and Elmsford, N.Y.: Row, Peterson, 1961); Robert S. Lynd and Helen M. Lynd, *Middletown in Transition: A Study in Cultural Conflicts* (New York: Harcourt, Brace & World, 1937); and Irwin T. Sanders, *Making Good Communities Better* (rev. ed.; Lexington: University of Kentucky Press, 1953), pp. 17 ff.

[3] *Ibid.* See also Robin M. Williams, Jr., *American Society: A Sociological Interpretation* (New York: Alfred A. Knopf, 1951); W. Lloyd Warner and Paul S. Lunt, *The Social Life of a Modern Community* (New Haven: Yale University Press, 1941); August B. Hollingshead and Frederick C. Redlich, *Social Class and Mental Illness: A Community Study* (New York: John Wiley & Sons, 1958).

situation is that of value conflicts among different groups in the community, a factual, researchable, and, to some extent, researched area[4] that would seem to be an important knowledge base for the practice decisions that must be made regarding values and the goals derived from them.

Ethnic Group Studies

This is a general rubric for the numerous studies that have been made regarding ethnic and racial group subcultures and the ways in which ethnicity is related to position in society, modes of participation, and the availability or nonavailability of particular types of resources or opportunities. There is a vast literature of research findings and theoretical conceptualizations in this field.[5] Such concepts seem to have two points of special relevance to community organization. The first is perhaps most obvious: the community organization worker will neglect or ignore ethnic group culture and behavior patterns at his peril, if he is engaged in working with different ethnic groups. The second is the growing attention to the social-structural aspects of the life situation of various ethnic groups. We shall turn to the matter of the structural aspects of social problems later.

Voluntary Associations

Community organizers confront voluntary associations in a number of different contexts—the voluntary agency; the numerous voluntary associations related directly to the field of health and welfare; and

the numerous voluntary associations that afford avenues of participation for individuals and that constitute important actors in the community field. A principal contribution of the social scientists has been the large number of studies indicating the direct correlation between socioeconomic status and organizational participation.[6] In this field, small group theory, as well, has made an important contribution on a different level.[7] It is the author's impression that, although numerous social science studies have been made on different aspects of voluntary organizational behavior,[8] they have nowhere been pulled together in the kind of clear and rigorous conceptual framework that would make them directly useful to the community organization worker.

Organizational Theory

The broad field of organizational theory, on the other hand, is a burgeoning one, with great potential usefulness for community organization—a usefulness that is already being exploited.[9] The principal contributions from this field to date seem to lie in the study of bureaucratic organization,[10] as

---

[4]James S. Coleman, *Community Conflict* (Glencoe: The Free Press, 1957).

[5]W. Lloyd Warner and Paul S. Lunt, *op. cit.,* contained an early explicit analysis of ethnic group identification and position in "Yankee City." Since then, various aspects of the question have been reported in numerous publications on the topics of nationality groups, Negroes in the United States, and poverty.

[6]Charles R. Wright and Herbert H. Hyman, "Voluntary Association Memberships of American Adults: Evidence from National Sample Surveys," *American Sociological Review,* 23 (June, 1958), pp. 286–294; and Morris Axelrod, "Urban Structure and Social Participation," *American Sociological Review,* 21 (February, 1956), pp. 13–18.

[7]Robert F. Bales and Philip E. Slater, "Role Differentiation in Small Decision-Making Groups," in Talcott Parsons and Robert F. Bales, *Family, Socialization and Interaction Process* (Glencoe: The Free Press, 1955).

[8]For instance, David L. Sills, *The Volunteers: Means and Ends in a National Organization* (Glencoe: The Free Press, 1957).

[9]An example is the rapid adoption of the work of Levine and others on exchange between organizations. (*See* footnote 15.)

[10]*Cf.,* Robert K. Merton *et al., Reader in Bureaucracy* (Glencoe: The Free Press, 1952).

well as some of its pathologies;[11] the extent to which bureaucratic organization is supplemented by informal social processes;[12] the phenomenon of goal displacement,[13] through which organizations can thrive for long periods while devoting a large portion of their activities to goals other than those explicitly specified in the organizational charter; the relation of organizational structures to different types of function and personnel and different styles of decision making;[14] and the interaction of the organization with its environment, particularly in exchange relationships with other organizations.[15] In all these instances, the mode or level of social science contribution is much the same. It is not that of telling the practitioner how he should go about his business, but rather that of helping the practitioner understand the situation within which he is working—in this case, aspects of the question of why organizations behave as they do.

A related contribution is the more specific one of leadership studies. Perhaps the key issue in this field is the relation between formal positions of leadership and informal leadership processes.[16] Other aspects of leadership are best considered in connection with power structure studies, which will be referred to presently, but one issue merits special attention here. This has to do with the various types of leadership and the dimension of permissiveness or nonpermissiveness. We are lacking systematic knowledge about the circumstances in which the more permissive type of leadership (as opposed to more directive leadership) is most likely to achieve a certain set of goals. This is due, in part, to a lack of sufficiently rigorous research studies. Another reason for our lack of systematic knowledge is, in the author's estimation, a strong ideological investment in the idea of permissive leadership, often resulting in a confusion as to whether we are considering it as a means toward specified task goals or as an end in itself. In any case, although it would be difficult to prove, it appears that the leadership studies that have been done have been a contributing factor in the current trend in community organization toward a more fa-

[11]For example, Robert K. Merton, *Social Theory and Social Structure* (New York: The Free Press of Glencoe, 1957), pp. 195 ff.; Robert A. Dahl and Charles E. Lindblom, *Politics, Economics and Welfare: Planning and Politico-Economic Systems Resolved into Basic Social Processes* (New York: Harper & Brothers, 1953), pp. 247–261.

[12]Fritz J. Roethlisberger and William J. Dickson, *Management and the Worker* (Cambridge: Harvard University Press, 1939); George C. Homans, *The Human Group* (New York: Harcourt, Brace, 1950); and Alvin W. Gouldner, "Organization Analysis," in Leonard S. Kogan, ed., *Social Science Theory and Social Work Research* (New York: National Association of Social Workers, 1960).

[13]Robert K. Merton, *Social Theory and Social Structure* (rev. ed.; Glencoe: The Free Press, 1957), p. 199; and Philip Selznick, "An Approach to a Theory of Bureaucracy," *American Sociological Review,* 8 (February, 1943), p. 48.

[14]*See,* for example, James D. Thompson and Arthur Tuden, "Strategies, Structures, and Process of Organizational Decision," in James D. Thompson *et al., Comparative Studies in Administration* (Pittsburgh: University of Pittsburgh Press, 1959).

[15]James D. Thompson and William J. McEwen, "Organizational Goals and Environment: Goal-Setting as an Interaction Process," *American Sociological Review,* 23 (February, 1958); Eugene Litwak and Lydia F. Hylton, "Interorganizational Analysis: A Hypothesis on Coordinating Agencies," *Administrative Science Quarterly,* 6 (March, 1962); Sol Levine and Paul E. White, "Exchange as a Conceptual Framework for the Study of Interorganizational Relationships," *Administrative Science Quarterly,* 5 (March, 1961); Sol Levine, Paul E. White, and Benjamin D. Paul, "Community Interorganizational Problems in Providing Medical Care and Social Services," *American Journal of Public Health,* 53 (August, 1963).

[16]Two rather differing studies indicate the range of this broad field: William F. Whyte, *Street Corner Society: The Social Structure of an Italian Slum* (Chicago: University of Chicago Press, 1943); and Floyd Hunter, *Community Power Structure: A Study of Decision Makers* (Chapel Hill: University of North Carolina Press, 1953).

vorable predisposition toward directive leadership.[17]

Power Structure Theory

This is likewise a burgeoning field of investigation, particularly among political scientists and sociologists. It has led to a succession of well-documented conclusions, even though there are still many unanswered questions. One of the first big findings was Hunter's conclusion that the people who wield the power over the flow of community events are not necessarily the same people who occupy the official power positions in the organizational structure, governmental or non-governmental.[18] But a rush of more specific findings ensued, namely, that the people who wield power in actual specific community issues are not necessarily those who are reputed to be the power figures; that there are different kinds of power, which may be distributed unevenly among so-called power figures; that communities vary considerably in the extent to which their power wielders tend to be the same people for governmental, economic, educational, and social service matters, or whether these various arenas tend to have relatively discrete power structures; that power cannot be conceived statically, but that at any given time there is "slack" in the power system, and also that, over time, it is possible through organization to add important actors to the power system —an example being the relatively recent rise of civil rights leaders as an important voice in the community dialogue.[19]

In no other area of social science contribution has there been such premature generalization by practitioners (and also, in part, by social scientists) and so much ignoring of the fine print. The banal statement, "We've got to get the power structure behind this if we intend to get anywhere with it," is perhaps a good example of the possible misunderstandings, misinterpretations, and misapplications of the power structure findings, when taken at this naive level of specificity.

Social Stratification

Variation in socioeconomic status has been studied intensively, as have the differences created by such variation in many aspects of living—education, utilization of social services, behavior norms, aspiration level, family living, employment, unemployment, and leisure-time pursuits.[20]

In this field, too, a succession of waves of new knowledge and understanding has emanated from the studies. There was, for example, the early realization that effective social work must be based on an adequate understanding of the total living patterns of people in relation to their position in the socioeconomic hierarchy: middle-class workers must learn how to relate effectively to people of lower socioeconomic status.[21] Then there came a number of research efforts, notably in the fields of delinquency and mental illness, that indicated tremendous differentials in both diagnosis and

---

[17]*See,* for example, Robert Morris and Martin Rein, "Emerging Patterns in Community Planning," *Social Work Practice, 1963* (New York: Columbia University Press, 1963).

[18]Floyd Hunter, *op. cit.*

[19]There is a vast body of literature on the power structure. For bibliographies and for overall depictions, *see* Charles M. Bonjean and David M. Olson, "Community Leadership: Directions of Research,"

Administrative Science Quarterly, 9 (December, 1964); and Nelson W. Polsby, *Community Power and Political Theory* (New Haven: Yale University Press, 1963).

[20]For example, W. Lloyd Warner and Paul S. Lunt, *op. cit.;* August B. Hollingshead, *Elmtown's Youth: The Impact of Social Classes on Adolescents* (New York: John Wiley & Sons, 1949).

[21]Earl L. Koos, *Families in Trouble* (New York: King's Crown Press, 1946).

treatment based on social status differences.[22] More recently, the increasing salience of poverty as a social problem has renewed the interest of both researchers and practitioners in the differences in opportunity structure that social stratification implies, and has focused attention increasingly on the social-structural aspects of such problems as delinquency, unemployment, and dependency, as distinguished from the earlier view, which considered them more or less as aberrations on an otherwise healthy body politic.[23]

Regardless of how one feels about the effectiveness of the total social response to such questions, one is confronted here with a situation in which there has been a richness of relatively competent social science research that has received considerable attention from practitioners.

Community Processes

A number of studies and conceptualizations have been developed concerning processes that have definite relevance to the field of community organization—such as conflict[24] or community reaction to disaster.[25] The relevance of studies such as these to community organization work seems to indicate greater utilization of these types of findings than has apparently been the case so far.

Ecological and Demographic Studies

Numerous studies have been made in the general area of the distribution of people and activities in spatial relation to each other and in the analysis of population structures and rates of change.[26] These have definite relevance to the matter of community and neighborhood analysis in relation to intervention programs of various types. Such studies provide part of the data necessary for informed judgment regarding the differences in possible target neighborhoods, for decisions as to where to intervene, and for decisions as to planning for changing the demographic and ecological configurations of different parts of the city through deliberate policy.

System Theory

System theory has come to be used not only in the analysis of small groups and formal organizations, but also in the analysis of the less cohesive agglomerations called communities, which constitute the area of operations of many community organization workers. Like other approaches to the community, system theory helps in finding an answer to the question "What *is* the community in which I work, and how does my work relate to it?" While system theory affords a means for grasping and analyzing the complex, multistructured network of social relationships involved in the community concept, its principal contribu-

---

[22]August B. Hollingshead, *op. cit.;* August B. Hollingshead and Frederick C. Redlich, *op. cit.;* and Orville R. Gurrslin *et al.,* "Social Class and the Mental Health Movement," in Frank Riessman *et al., Mental Health of the Poor* (New York: The Free Press of Glencoe, 1964).

[23]Harry C. Bredemeier, "The Socially Handicapped and the Agencies: A Market Analysis," in Frank Riessman *et al., op. cit.*

[24]James S. Coleman, *op. cit.;* "Trigger for Community Conflict: The Case of Fluoridation," *The Journal of Social Issues,* 17, No. 4 (1961).

[25]*Cf.,* William H. Form and Sigmund Nosow, "Disaster Strikes the Community," *Community in Disaster* (New York: Harper & Row, 1958).

[26]George A. Theodorson, ed., *Studies in Human Ecology* (Evanston, Ill.: Row, Peterson, 1961); Eshref Shevky and Wendell Bell, *Social Area Analysis* (Stanford: Stanford University Press, 1955); and Wendell Bell, "Social Areas: Typology of Urban Neighborhoods," in Marvin B. Sussman, ed., *Community Structure and Analysis* (New York: Thomas Y. Crowell, 1959). In addition, there have been numerous administrative and planning studies that have used ecological material as a basis for proposed programs.

tion is, perhaps, not that of analyzing communities globally so much as of affording conceptual tools with which to uncover and analyze the particular aspects of the larger community whole in which most community work goes on. Putting this another way, few ventures involve, or even purport to involve, the entire community. System analysis helps to locate and understand those particular networks and constellations that are especially relevant to the venture at hand and to discover and give appropriate consideration to relationships that do not appear on any formal organizational chart. It is particularly helpful in approaching the complex "wheels within wheels" characteristic of the many networks and formal organizational relationships with which the community worker deals, both horizontally: across the structure of the community; and vertically: taking into consideration the relationship of neighborhood to community, to metropolitan region, to state, interstate region, federal, and international organizations and networks.

The increasing importance of these vertical relationships has given added impetus to the use of system analysis. Two aspects of this are particularly noteworthy. One is the increasing need to cope with the metropolitan area as a system, even though it does not coincide with any governmental jurisdiction;[27] and the other is the increase in the activity of federal agencies in providing finances and program stimulation in municipal affairs.[28]

Structural Aspects of Social Problems

The principal interest of sociologists in social problems is in structural aspects, rather than in unique situations of individual cases.[29] In a sense, sociologists take the wholesaler's viewpoint of social problems, rather than the retailer's. They ask questions about the larger context within which individuals come to behave in ways that dominant groups come to define as social problems. They look for orders of data, not so much at the level of the unique individual experience—although that level has its own relevance—as at the level of circumstances in which the adaptive behavior of relatively large numbers of individuals takes such forms as are considered to constitute social problems. This is perhaps best illustrated by the early work of Shaw on delinquency areas, in which he found that certain neighborhoods in Chicago produced high delinquency rates regardless of the country of origin of the people who moved into those areas. There was, in other words, something about the constellation of social processes in and around the neighborhood that produced delinquent behavior.[30]

In a similar sense, but with a whole variety of concepts and analytical techniques, one can ask about the constellation of social processes that produce poverty, racial discrimination, slums, and alienation. This mode of analysis, the most characteristi-

[27] *Cf.,* John E. Bebout and Harry C. Bredemeier, "American Cities as Social Systems," *Journal of the American Institute of Planners,* 29 (May, 1963).

[28] Charles I. Schottland, "Federal Planning for Health and Welfare," in *The Social Welfare Forum, 1963* (New York: Columbia University Press, 1963).

[29] *Cf.,* Robert K. Merton and Robert A. Nisbet, eds., *Contemporary Social Problems* (New York: Harcourt, Brace & World, 1961). Many books of the Chicago school also relate to the structural aspects of social problems. *Cf.,* Walter C. Reckless, *Vice in Chicago;* Clifford R. Shaw, *Delinquency Areas;* and Clifford R. Shaw and H. D. McKay, *Juvenile Delinquency and Urban Areas* (Chicago: University of Chicago Press, 1933, 1929, and 1927, respectively).

[30] Clifford R. Shaw, *op. cit.*

cally sociological one, has little direct relevance to those concerned with the problems of specific individuals. But when one begins to look away from the individual pathology to the context in which that individual and others behave, such sociological studies become more meaningful. As we all know, we are actually in the midst of a sizable shift in emphasis, a shift whose net effect is to place more significance on intervention at the social-structural level and less relative weight on the possibilities of intervention at the individual level. This is the principal reason for the considerable attention the work of sociologists is receiving today, as contrasted with a decade or two ago.

The Structure of Social Services within American Society

A related area of research directly relevant to community organization is the study of social services as an integral part of American society, and as modes of behavior that dovetail with important social values and behavior patterns. We are not referring here to the conflict between the residual and the institutional conceptions of social welfare as depicted by Wilensky and Lebeaux, but rather to the type of analysis their book exemplifies—the attempt to depict and analyze the supply and organization of social welfare services in the United States in relation to their integral connections with important values, processes, and behavior patterns in American society.[31] In a sense, this is an extension of the previous point; it involves not only the consideration of social problems as an integral part of American society—trying to understand them as a deeply rooted part of the whole—but also of social welfare services as an integral part of

American society, taking their form in relation to other parts of the society, and likewise as a deeply rooted part of the whole. Again, as the "wholesale" approach grows relative to the "retail" approach, the relevance of such research grows with it.

Impact-Evaluational Studies

In the past decade, a number of important studies have attempted to assess, through carefully controlled experimental designs, the efficacy, or lack of efficacy, of various types of direct service programs on individual recipients. For the most part, these do not constitute a contribution to behavioral theory. Indeed, most of them are not conceptually related to any specific disciplinary body of knowledge, such as sociology, social psychology, or anthropology. Nevertheless, a number of social scientists have conducted such studies, as have a number of social work researchers.[32] Their importance lies in their affording an alternative method of assessment to the more usual social work type of evaluation based on the following of accepted professional standards. Their relevance to community organization has been, paradoxically, in the generally negative nature of their findings. Hence, the findings of such studies have given added impetus to the "wholesale" approach—to looking at the structural aspects of social problems, and to placing greater importance on intervention in the social structure than on intervention solely with the individuals involved.

[31]Harold L. Wilensky and Charles N. Lebeaux, *Industrial Society and Social Welfare* (New York: Russell Sage Foundation, 1958).

[32]*Cf.,* Edwin J. Thomas, *et al., In-Service Training and Reduced Workloads* (New York: Russell Sage Foundation, 1960); Henry J. Meyer, Edgar F. Borgatta, and Wyatt C. Jones, *Girls at Vocational High: An Experiment in Social Work Intervention* (New York: Russell Sage Foundation, 1965); Roland L. Warren and Jessie Smith, "Casework Service to Chronically Dependent Multiproblem Families: A Research Demonstration," *Social Service Review,* 37 (March, 1963).

Specific Community Studies

The number of careful studies of one community or another in one part of the country or another has grown by leaps and bounds in recent decades. Beginning, perhaps, with the two classical studies of Middletown, such studies have afforded analyses of the interconnected life of a large number of communities, and although each one unfortunately pursues its own conceptual framework, making rigorous comparability impossible, they nevertheless aggregate to a large fund of intensively researched descriptions of social life in various community settings. They offer case studies, as it were, each with a more or less carefully developed set of analytical categories, of the interrelatedness of institutions and activities within American communities; and on this level they afford a rich basis for understanding the setting within which community workers often operate.[33] One should perhaps mention the much smaller number of books that have attempted to organize the rich materials from these studies and from other sources into more or less systematic analyses of American community living.[34]

---

[33]There is a vast number of such community studies. Among the more important are: Robert S. Lynd and Helen Merrell Lynd, *Middletown: A Study in Modern American Culture* (New York: Harcourt, Brace & World, 1929); Robert S. Lynd and Helen Merrell Lynd, *Middletown in Transition* ... ; James West, *Plainville, U.S.A.* (New York: Columbia University Press, 1945); Art Gallaher, Jr., *Plainville Fifteen Years Later* (New York: Columbia University Press, 1961); and Arthur J. Vidich and Joseph Bensman, *Small Town in Mass Society: Class, Power and Religion in a Rural Community* (Princeton: Princeton University Press, 1958).

[34]Irwin T. Sanders, *The Community: An Introduction to a Social System* (New York: The Ronald Press Company, 1958; 2nd ed., 1966); and Roland L. Warren, *The Community in America* (Chicago: Rand, McNally, 1963).

CONTRIBUTIONS IN THE AREA OF SOCIAL CHANGE

Let us turn now to the second large area of social science contribution—the area of social change. Before doing so, brief mention should be made of a controversy regarding theoretical orientation that colors social science work in this field. One can choose two alternative foci as points of departure in analyzing society. One is the question of how individual actions actually aggregate to behavior patterns that are more or less interlocked as well as to larger institutional forms that, likewise, are related in a more or less coherent system of values, roles, behavior patterns, and so on, all of which show remarkable coherence and stability. This theoretical orientation stresses continuity, equilibrium, and system maintenance.[35]

An alternative approach is to note the constant stress and strain, the continual flux and change, the conflict of interest and purpose, and the discontinuity and disorganization. From this view, little is permanent, and a large model of society is not of a system in equilibrium but of a constantly changing set of conditions caused by the constant interplay of shifting forces, interests, and power balances.[36]

This difference in emphasis is noteworthy, not only because it makes more intelligible some of the debates that rage within the social sciences, but also because it has direct relevance for community organization. The relevance lies in the current conflict that prevails around the question of change strategies—particularly as relates to consensus or dissensus, collaboration, or contest—being the practical counterpart of

---

[35]Talcott Parsons, *The Social System* (Glencoe: The Free Press, 1951).

[36]Ralph Dahrendorf, *Class and Class Conflict in Industrial Society* (Stanford: Stanford University Press, 1959).

these two theoretical points of view, the former emphasizing system maintenance, the latter system change.[37]

The observation that systems must change in order to maintain themselves seems so simple as to border on the banal. Yet it helps clarify the theoretical relationship, even if it does not help the practitioner who is asking himself, "Should we give in in order to preserve consensus, or should we fight 'em?"

Generally speaking, social scientists have been concerned primarily with the theoretical difficulties in conceptualizing how systems can change; the relation of values to social change; the question of whether change in some ultimate sense stems primarily from some sector or aspect of society, such as the distribution of economic resources and economic power; or whether technological changes are at the root of most changes in other aspects of society. They have been concerned with change at the macro-level primarily, though, more recently, organizational theory has considered change at the formal organizational level.[38] Most of the emphasis has been on change emerging somehow as a product of social interaction, rather than as the result of deliberate intent on the part of a change agent. There are two exceptions to this statement, both at the macro-level. One is the theory of revolution, and the other is the related theory of social movements.

Both of these are pertinent to the situation within which the community organization worker finds himself, namely, that of seeking to influence change under circumstances where others are likewise seeking to influence change, the others being variously potential allies or potential opponents. But revolutionary theory and social movement theory are understandably directed at the level of the total society rather than at the level where practitioners find themselves trying to influence change in the community, and usually in a relatively narrow field.

Purposive Change

This more confined field, which can be called that of purposive change at the community level, likewise offers a growing body of research findings and pertinent "principles" derived from social science research, though of course these principles are not in any way integrated into a unified theory.

Three particular areas of concentration seem particularly appropriate for the problem of purposive change at the community level:

1. There is a considerable and growing body of literature regarding resistance to change, particularly to types of change goals desired by a change agent who comes in from outside or who represents a different culture or subculture. There are numerous volumes of field studies by sociologists and anthropologists documenting individual cases of trying to bring about changes such as the introduction of new public health practices, of agricultural production technologies, or of social interaction patterns.[39] These studies, from different parts of the

---

[37]Roland L. Warren, *Types of Purposive Social Change at the Community Level,* Brandeis Paper No. 11, The Florence Heller Graduate School for Advanced Studies in Social Welfare, Brandeis University, Waltham, Mass.

[38]*Cf.,* Warren G. Bennis, Kenneth B. Benne, and Robert Chin, *The Planning of Change: Readings in the Applied Behavioral Sciences* (New York: Holt, Rinehart & Winston, 1961); and Ronald Lippitt, Jeanne Watson, and Bruce Westley, *The Dynamics of Planned Change: A Comparative Study of Principles and Techniques* (New York: Harcourt, Brace, 1958). Neither of these books restricts itself exclusively to change in formal organizations.

[39]*Cf.,* Benjamin D. Paul, ed., *Health, Culture, and Community: Case Studies of Public Reactions to Health Programs* (New York: Russell Sage Foundation, 1955).

world, have a much more direct bearing on analogous change attempts within our own society than is usually recognized.
2. A second body of literature is that of carefully researched attempts at community change within our own society. In such instances, the social scientist is not himself seeking to bring about change, but rather, is seeking to study the processes that occur as someone else attempts to bring about change. A decade or so ago, there appeared four outstanding examples of this, one being a study of attempts to accomplish specific objectives—such as hospital construction—in a large number of communities in different parts of the country,[40] and the other three being studies by social scientists of communities that were themselves conducting self-studies with a goal of action, principally in the public health field.[41] Others have studied urban renewal

programs,[42] housing programs,[43] attempts at mental health education,[44] and so on.
3. A third, and closely related, body of literature consists of various attempts, large and small, important and unimportant, based on original field research or on secondary sources, to develop models and other conceptualizations of purposive change at various levels of social interaction, including the community level.[45] As indicated earlier, this effort is not tied in, theoretically, with the large body of social change theory on the macro-level. Nevertheless, the body of social change theory of revolution and of social movements is relevant, especially today, when the overlapping social movements of civil rights and anti-poverty constitute a dynamic component in the changing community situation.

---

[40]Paul A. Miller, *Community Health Action: A Study of Community Contrast* (East Lansing: Michigan State College Press, 1953).

[41]Solon Kimball and Marion B. Pearsall, *The Talladega Story: A Study in Community Process* (University, Ala.: University of Alabama Press, 1954); Christopher Sower *et al., Community Involvement: The Webs of Formal and Informal Ties that Make for Action* (Glencoe: The Free Press, 1957); Floyd Hunter, Ruth Connor Schaffer, and Cecil G. Sheps, *Community Organization: Action and Inaction* (Chapel Hill: University of North Carolina Press, 1956).

[42]Harold Kaplan, *Urban Renewal Politics: Slum Clearance in Newark* (New York: Columbia University Press, 1963); Scott Greer, *Urban Renewal and American Cities* (New York: Bobbs-Merrill, 1965); and Peter H. Rossi and Robert A. Dentler, *The Politics of Urban Renewal: The Chicago Findings* (New York: The Free Press of Glencoe, 1961).

[43]Martin Meyerson and E. C. Banfield, *Politics, Planning and the Public Interest* (Glencoe: The Free Press, 1955).

[44]Elaine Cumming and John Cumming, *Closed Ranks: An Experiment in Mental Health Education* (Cambridge: Harvard University Press, 1957).

[45]Ronald Lippitt *et al., op. cit.;* Warren G. Bennis, Kenneth B. Benne, and Robert Chin, *op. cit.;* Christopher Sower *et al., op. cit.;* Roland L. Warren, *The Community in. . . .,* chapter 10; and Roland L. Warren, *Types of Purposive . . . , op. cit.*

4.

Neil Gilbert and Harry Specht

ADVOCACY AND PROFESSIONAL ETHICS

Advocacy became prominent among social work practitioners in the 1960s. But prominence should not be mistaken for novelty: advocacy was a part of social work practice long before it was labeled as such in the 1960s. Since the beginning of social work practice, as Levy points out, many social agencies have included advocacy among their functions, and, certainly, many individual social workers defended the interests of their clients before such activities were explicitly defined as advocacy functions.[1]

Advocacy, then, was not a new concept in the sixties. On the contrary, social workers throughout this century have discussed and tried to resolve the problematic issue of advocacy's place in social work practice. This issue is, according to Schwartz, the "granddaddy" of social work dilemmas, for it embodies the conflict of the "social" versus the "psychological" and involves "[social work's] responsibility for social reform on the one hand, and individual help to people in trouble on the other."[2] A dilemma for generations of social workers, this problem has been identified anew by each generation in its own terms. In 1909 Richmond defined the issue in terms of the "wholesale" versus the "retail" method of social reform. In 1929 Lee approached it in terms of "cause" versus "function." In 1949 Pray wrote it in terms of "workmanship" versus "statesmanship." In 1962 Chambers spoke of it in terms of "prophets" versus "priests." And in 1963 Schwartz examined the same conflict in terms of providing a service as opposed to participating in a movement.[3]

Although practitioners throughout the century have tried to clarify advocacy's role in social work practice, between 1935 and 1960 concern with this issue was often submerged. During these years the profession's attention was focused more on therapeutic and clinical modes of intervention than on social issues, such as poverty, discrimination, and client rights. In the 1960s however, the civil rights movement and other more general societal pressures for social justice led to the reaffirmation of social work's concern with the client's overall treatment by society and the profession's advocacy functions. That reaffirmation was made explicit and a degree of professional legitimacy lent to advocacy by the publication in *Social Work* in 1969 of a statement framed by the Ad Hoc Committee on Advocacy.[4] The committee, which had been established by the National Association of Social Workers' (NASW) Task Force on the Urban Crisis and Public Welfare Problems, issued a statement that was based on four significant papers on advocacy-related topics written by Grosser, Briar, Miller, and Brager, respectively.[5]

Since the late 1960s and the publication of the Ad Hoc Committee's statement, a rash of papers has appeared on the subject of advocacy. By and large, these papers have used as a starting point the statement of the Ad Hoc Committee and the four papers on which it was based. Because the term *advocacy* has various connotations, those who have written about the subject have actually discussed a wide range of behaviors that, although referred to as advocacy, are considerably different. In the literature, for example, one finds the word used to describe consumer education, civil rights and social protest actions, referral and social brokerage activities, and a big brother program for the developmentally disabled.[6] It would seem, therefore, that *advocacy* has come to mean all things to all workers.

Thus, on one hand, applying the abstract notion of advocacy to the practice of social work has some felicitous results: everyone is free to dream his own dreams and hope his own hopes, most of which are not detrimental to practice. Further, as a symbolic response to the demands that social work become more relevant to the quest for social justice, the call for advocacy has been attractive to the profession. Had the call been merely for sound and ethical social work practice, it would have seemed an old and familiar appeal; advocacy seemed to be something new.

However, the theoretical delineation of advocacy functions has had certain disadvantages. As the authors have noted elsewhere, the expediency of abstraction provides advantages to social welfare policies and social work that are often only short-lived.[7] Abstract ideas such as advocacy contain implicit directives for behavior. As an idea increases in popularity, efforts to specify those directives also increase. Certain problems arise here. For among the illustrations and operational definitions of advocacy there is much mischief and some downright harmful notions concerning how social workers should behave in discharging advocacy functions. In this article the authors examine some of the operational directives for advocacy that they consider to be out of keeping with

sound professional conduct. Their objective is to demonstrate how the concept of advocacy has been subtly transformed to legitimate a form of social work in which the client is relegated to a position that would be highly problematic for any profession.

TWO DEFINITIONS

In its statement, which appeared in *Social Work* in 1969, the Ad Hoc Committee on Advocacy presented two different definitions of advocacy with the observation that they "overlap at many points."[8] The first definition was taken from Briar, who describes the advocate as ". . . his client's supporter, his adviser, his champion, and, if need be, his representative in his dealings with the court, the police, the social agency, and other organizations that [affect] his well-being."[9] Briar further explicitly notes that the social worker's primary allegiance should be to his client, not to the agency that employs him.[10]

Briar's definition reflects a shift in the relationship between social workers and agencies that took place in the 1960s. Up to that time, the majority of social workers had been taught that, as professionals, they were extensions or representatives of their agencies. Many of them modified this view by the early sixties and began to emphasize that adherence to professional, as distinct from agency, standards and ethics was necessary if services that were in the best interests of the client were to be provided. The employing agency was now seen as part of, or only an agent of, a larger system of government. The professional's job was to help his client better utilize the systems around him, which included the client's family, the workers' employing agency, other social service agencies, and the government. Briar expressed this orientation when he wrote of workers and agencies in this way:

... the advocate and social broker function require that caseworkers have much greater *professional* [italics added] autonomy and discretion than now prevail in many, if not most, social agencies. Ninety percent or more of all caseworkers practice in bureaucratic organizations, and the demands of such organizations have a tendency to encroach upon professional autonomy. Every attempt by the agency to routinize some condition or aspect of professional practice amounts to a restriction of professional discretion, and for that reason probably should be resisted, in most instances, by practitioners.[11]

The Ad Hoc Committee's first definition of the advocate was not accepted without reservation by all members of the profession. Certain aspects of the advocate's defined role seemed to raise troublesome issues. Schwartz, for one, was concerned about the perspective voiced by Briar on the relationship between the employing agency and the social worker as advocate. He argued that the "agency-bad, client-good" distinction was oversimplified and that the polarity created by such a distinction encouraged a shallow analysis of client-agency practice. Schwartz pursued his point this way:

[The advocates] subvert their own real identification with the poor and the oppressed by their neglect of the dialectics of the client-agency relationship. An agency is not a static organization with no play of internal forces; and those who insist that it is must cut themselves off from the most progressive elements within it, and take their clients with them....
The basic relationship between an institution and its people is symbiotic; each needs the other for his own survival.... It is a form of social contract; and when the arrangement goes wrong, as it frequently does, those who claim that the contract is broken do no service to the people or to the agency. The arena of need remains the same, and the symbiosis remains intact—merely obscure to the unpracticed eye.[12]

The Ad Hoc Committee did not delve into the troublesome issues about the worker-agency relationship that were raised for some practitioners by its first definition. The second definition presented by the committee pursued the notion that the interests of the client were the first concern of the advocate. This definition was taken from Brager, who stated that the advocate

... identifies with the plight of the disadvantaged. He sees as his primary responsibility the tough-minded and partisan representation of their interests, and this supersedes his fealty to others. This role inevitably requires that the practitioner function as a political tactician.[13]

CODE OF ETHICS

Both the definitions of advocacy put forward by the Ad Hoc Committee are in substantial harmony with the social worker's Code of Ethics. The code was adopted in 1960, nine years before the Ad Hoc Committee's pronouncements on advocacy.[14] Among the code's provisions, which are approximately as general as the Ad Hoc Committee's definitions, is the statement that the social worker's primary obligation is to the welfare of his client, whether that client is an individual or a group. Furthermore, the code indicates the worker's responsibility for modifying agency practices that are unethical or that prevent workers from conducting themselves in keeping with the code.[15] The code's description of the social worker's responsibilities, then, is in several important respects actually echoed by the definitions of the Ad Hoc Committee. In fact, the advocate as defined by the committee appears to be nothing more than a social worker who conducts himself in accord with the standards of behavior set forth in the profession's Code of Ethics.

Beyond symbolically reaffirming ethical practice, what purpose is served, then, by applying the advocacy label to social work functions? Why is the image of the ethical social worker so unappealing that it must be clothed in the guise of advocacy to attract the profession's attention? The latter problem is clearly exemplified in the discussion of the "advocacy challenge" by Wineman and James:

> Imagine the student—caseworker, group worker, or community organization practitioner—who is witness to an act of client dehumanization. *If* [italics added] he wants to enter the lists of advocacy in behalf of a client, only one condition is necessary and sufficient for initiating such action: that his school will regard his action with enthusiasm and support.[16]

Certainly, ethical practice would dictate that no "ifs" be operative regarding instances of client dehumanization. It would also deem a professional to be in violation of the Code of Ethics if he did not support action on behalf of his client in such an instance.[17] Would the advocate social worker and the ethical social worker behave differently in this situation? As described by Wineman and James, there seems to be a choice here between advocacy and some other acceptable form of practice.

The only potentially discordant note between the Code of Ethics and the Ad Hoc Committee's definitions of advocacy involves Brager's reference to the practitioner as "political tactician." This reference is potentially discordant because the phrase "political tactician" has many disturbing connotations. Brager's interpretation of the advocate's role emphasizes "the conscious rearranging of reality to induce a desired attitudinal or behavioral outcome."[18] He claims that the advocate as political tactician is sometimes justified in manipulating others. Schwartz's comments on this aspect of the advocate's role reflect the deeply troublesome issues that such notions present for practitioners. "We find ourselves," he says, "developing a literature of guile, with Machiavelli as the new culture hero."[19] Nevertheless, the Ad Hoc Committee put forward Brager's definition of advocacy without explicitly commenting on this issue. In fact, in a specific example of proper conduct that it cited and that will be examined shortly, the committee apparently condoned Brager's interpretation.

PROFESSIONAL BEHAVIOR

If the levels of discourse on advocacy were all as general as the definitions cited above, this article would not have been written. The authors would have been content to view advocacy as simply another expression of the profession's commitment to the well-being of the people it serves. However, not all efforts to specify advocacy and its behavioral correlates are harmless exercises in drawing superficial distinctions. Indeed, there are a few important exceptions in which attempts to distinguish advocacy behavior are neither superficial nor harmless. These formulations seem to have gained a degree of legitimacy and popular acceptance that far outweighs their merits as guidelines for professional behavior. They are sharply illustrated in the behavioral prescriptions for advocacy put forth by the Ad Hoc Committee.

Recognizing that its general definitions of advocacy raised a number of unresolved issues about specific choices in practice, the Ad Hoc Committee attempted to provide some behavioral guidelines. Two of these guidelines in particular warrant close scrutiny.

First, the committee proposed the following dilemma: What should the advocate do if the promotion of his client's interests in obtaining a scarce resource would deny that resource to someone else? What if this person's need were as great as or greater than the advocate's client? Considering that needy clients and scarce resources are not the exception but the rule in the social services, a dilemma such as that outlined by the committee would arise, in all likelihood, in the majority of situations with which the advocate social worker dealt. And in circumstances involving competing claims on resources between the advocate's client and others in need, the Ad Hoc Committee advised the advocate to weigh the relative urgency of respective claims before deciding to support his client's interest:

> Suppose, for instance, that a child welfare worker has as a client a child who is in need of care that can only be provided by a treatment institution with limited intake. Does he then become a complete partisan in order to gain admission of his client at the expense of other children in need? What of the public assistance worker seeking emergency clothing allowances for his clients when the demand is greater than the supply? Quite clearly, in either case the worker should be seeking to increase the total availability of the scarce resource. But while working toward this end, he faces the dilemma of competing individual claims. In such a situation, professional norms would appear to dictate that the relative urgency of the respective claims be weighed.[20]

This an incredible piece of advice which, if taken seriously, would virtually immobilize all advocacy efforts, if not all direct social work practice. Consider the committee's example of a placement in a child welfare institution. Suppose that the institution serves a medium-sized city and has fifty placements and a waiting list of approximately one hundred and fifty applicants at any given time. Its research staff estimates that there are about four hundred additional children in the population who have never been referred but who would potentially qualify to receive the institution's services. These figures are arbitrary, but they are not exceptionally high: there

are many social service agencies that are larger, serve broader geographic regions, and have higher numbers on waiting lists and greater estimates of undiscovered need.

In the example of the above institution, how would the advocate follow the behavioral guideline of weighing the relative urgency of respective claims before seeking to gain placement for his client? At the least, he would have to compare his client's need to that of one hundred and fifty other applicants. Moreover, a rigorous application of the Ad Hoc Committee's behavioral prescription would require him to seek out the other estimated four hundred children in potential need and make a relative assessment of their claims.

Aside from the prohibitive time and cost factors that make such behavior impractical, certain questions arise. What criteria are social work advocates going to use in weighing the relative urgency of respective claims? Furthermore, who gives an advocate license to decide whether one client is more deserving of service than another? These questions are not intended to imply that mechanisms for mediating among competing claims for social service resources are unnecessary. Such mechanisms are needed, and they exist. The examples given by the Ad Hoc Committee of the child welfare agency and the public welfare department implied that organizations of these types have elaborate sets of rules and policies governing client intake and allocation of scarce resources. These mechanisms may be imperfect and in need of change. But superseding them with the individual judgment of the worker and calling this substitution "advocacy" does not represent an improvement. Imagine a physician telling his patient that he needs an operation. Imagine him then saying that before making a referral to the hospital he must assess, *according to his own criteria,* the relative urgency of all other operations pending at the hospital! Such a professional might be called many things, but surely not an advocate.

SECOND GUIDELINE

The second behavioral prescription offered by the Ad Hoc Committee concerns the situation in which advocacy on behalf of an individual client is incompatible with advocacy on behalf of class interests and institutional change:

> To what extent does one risk injury to his client's interests in the short run on behalf of institutional changes in the long run? It seems clear that there can be no hard-and-fast rules governing such situations. One cannot arbitrarily write off any action that may temporarily cause his clients hardship if he believes the ultimate benefits of his action will outweigh any initial harm.[21]

The community may well be skeptical of a profession's announcement that its members are free to discomfort or disadvantage their clients whenever *they* believe such action will, in the long run, produce beneficial institutional changes. The argument that these changes will ultimately benefit the clients themselves may not mollify the individual client, who may be doubtful about being around "in the long run" to reap the benefits of the hoped-for change.

The issue here is not whether the individual client should or should not suffer temporary hardships for the greater good of institutional change and class interests. An individual's sacrifice for the greater good may be either a noble gesture or enlightened self-interest, depending on whether the greater good redounds to that individual's ultimate benefit. Rather, the issues are these: Who will weigh the potential losses and benefits in a given situation? Who will choose to act out of noble impulse or enlightened self-interest? Who will determine just how long the "long run" will be? And who will decide whether any sacrifice will be made? Contrary to the prescription of the Ad Hoc Committee, the authors believe that a professional understanding, a "hard-and-fast rule," exists that governs situations similar to those the committee described. This rule dictates that the professional *cannot* act on behalf of a client without the client's desire and permission; it is the client, furthermore, not the professional, who decides whether injury to the client's interests in the short run is to be risked to gain institutional changes in the long run.

Generally speaking, the short-term consequences of any given action can be predicted more accurately than its long-term consequences. Therefore, in weighing actions that might produce short-term injury and long-term benefits, the social worker should be mindful that short-term injury is more likely than benefits to be reaped in the long run. Under such circumstances, perhaps, another hard-and-fast rule should be followed: *primum non nocere,* the medical aphorism meaning, "First of all, do no harm." Such a rule would certainly inspire more client confidence in the social work profession than the Ad Hoc Committee's license for advocates to risk injuring their clients' interests on behalf of institutional changes.

Nevertheless, the committee's behavioral prescription seems to have gained a following in the profession. Panitch, in carrying the committee's prescription to greater specificity, first presents a case situation:

> A recent state law eliminated clothing grants. Three children in a family receiving public aid were sent home the first day of school because of inadequate clothing. The presumption is that there was insufficient funding for necessary school clothes. Mismanagement resulted when clothing was not bought because other more pressing bills had to be paid.[22]

He then presents the advocate's stance and considerations in such a situation:

The social worker could arrange a donation of clothing from a local source, help the mother through her presumed depression, and help her with budgeting, which probably kept her from managing her funds from the outset. These are possible solutions, but they are not positions of advocacy. In a position of advocacy, the worker would address questions about children being denied their right to education by the new welfare law. For instance: Is the mother risking a charge of child neglect because of the new state law? The worker might also begin a concerted action to lobby for higher income provisions by referring the mother to a constituent group that deals with welfare rights, while he simultaneously initiates action in a professional association.[23]

Here is a situation in which a worker could have provided concrete assistance to a client. Clothing allotments, interpersonal psychological support, and instruction in budgeting skills would have been of immediate benefit to the client. According to Panitch, however, the advocate would be more concerned with referring the mother to a welfare rights group and pressing for institutional change than with providing her concrete forms of immediate assistance. The short-term injury that presumably will result from the advocate's choice of priorities is that the children will continue to go without clothing and will be unable to attend school, that the mother's state of depression will linger on, and that the financial mismanagement will persist. With advocates like this, who needs adversaries?

SELF-DETERMINATION

Panitch's example is as instructive for what it omits as for what it contains, for what is omitted is any notion of client self-determination. What if the client simply wants clothing for her children to enable them to go to school? Or would like to receive some psychological support and also learn some budgeting skills? Or does not want to be a test case for the new state welfare law? Or is not interested in joining a welfare rights group? The champions of advocacy often forget that it is the right of the client to make these decisions. Perhaps it is easier to endorse professional arrogance when support is called for in the name of "social victims" and "the disadvantaged." But one of the finer aspects of preadvocacy ideas about professional behavior was that the worker was not taught to regard his client as a passive victim of society on whose behalf he, the professional, would act. Instead, the old-fashioned, ethical social worker perceived that his clients, although perhaps social victims, were nevertheless self-determining people who, given appropriate respect, support, and opportunities, could decide what was in their best short-term and long-run interests.

Recent articles on advocacy proclaim the social worker's obligation to act on his client's behalf as the worker sees it; the use of manipulation in such circumstances is also sanctioned. The idea of client self-determination is not much heralded in social work circles these days. Even in the NASW Code of Ethics, which enjoins workers not to practice discrimination in rendering services and pledges them to respect client privacy, the worker's duty to facilitate opportunities for the exercise of client self-determination is not mentioned.

Self-determination may not be an absolute or supreme value, but neither are privacy and nondiscrimination. To be sure, it is as difficult to define self-determination operationally as it is to define advocacy. Keith-Lucas points out that in one respect client self-determination is simply a fact: certain kinds of decisions, such as the decision to seek help, to change, and to grow can be made only by the client.[24] In another respect, client self-determination is an illusion: certain categories of clients, such as infants and the severely retarded, are incapable of making choices. But between the fact and the illusion there is a broad area of social work practice in which clients are capable of making choices but are not always knowledgeable about opportunities available for exercising a choice. Professionals can facilitate client self-determination by maximizing these opportunities. The difficulties involved in drawing boundaries around the elusive concept of client self-determination should not deter the worker from applying this important concept in professional practice. As Bernstein puts it,

> While self-determination is not supreme, it is supremely important. Only through the rich utilization of this concept can we fully honor the human worth value. This is in line with the best in democratic traditions. As we study and diagnose each situation, our concern should be for maximizing the choices for the people we serve. . . . Even with young children, there are appropriate matters about which they should be helped to make decisions.[25]

The NASW is planning within the not-too-distant future to ask the Delegate Assembly to revise the Code of Ethics. Among the issues that should be on the agenda for discussion is whether maximizing opportunities for client self-determination merits more specific recognition than it is currently receiving in the code. At the same time, a determination should be made whether the behavioral prescriptions for the social worker as advocate that are found in the literature adequately reflect the ethical strictures of the profession. The implications for professional behavior that stem from social work's commitment to advocacy and to client self-determination must be examined, and appropriate limits for professional behavior in these areas

must be defined. Specifying these limits and implications is both an intellectual challenge and a professional responsibility. The forthcoming revision of the Code of Ethics will enable the profession to address this challenge and fulfill its responsibility by clarifying, and possibly reordering, the standards of conduct contained in the code. The first step toward dealing with these issues is to recognize that the fervor and good intentions surrounding recent prescriptions for advocacy must be tempered by equally intense concern for client self-determination.

NOTES AND REFERENCES

1. Charles Levy, "Advocacy and the Injustice of Justice," *Social Service Review,* 48 (March 1974), pp. 39–50.
2. William Schwartz, "Private Troubles and Public Issues: One Social Work Job or Two?" *The Social Welfare Forum, 1969,* Proceedings of the 96th Annual Forum of the National Conference on Social Welfare (New York: Columbia University Press, 1969), p. 25.
3. Ibid., pp. 26–27. *See also* Mary Richmond, "The Retail Method of Reform," in Joanna C. Colcord, ed., *The Long View* (New York: Russell Sage Foundation, 1930), pp. 215–216; Porter R. Lee, *Social Work as Cause and Function and Other Papers* (New York: Columbia University Press, 1937), p. 3; Kenneth L. M. Pray, *Social Work in a Revolutionary Age and Other Papers* (Philadelphia: University of Pennsylvania Press, 1949), p. 231; Clarke A. Chambers, "An Historical Perspective on Political Action *vs.* Individualized Treatment," in *Current Issues in Social Work Seen in Historical Perspective* (New York: Council on Social Work Education, 1962), p. 54; and William Schwartz, "Small Group Science and Group Work Practice," *Social Work,* 8 (October 1963), pp. 40–41.
4. The Ad Hoc Committee on Advocacy, "The Social Worker As Advocate: Champion of

Social Victims," *Social Work,* 14 (April 1969), pp. 16–22.

5. Charles F. Grosser, "Community Development Programs Serving the Urban Poor," *Social Work,* 10 (July 1965), pp. 15–21; Scott Briar, "The Current Crisis in Social Casework," *Social Work Practice, 1967* (New York: Columbia University Press, 1967), pp. 19–33; Henry Miller, "Value Dilemmas in Social Casework," *Social Work,* 13 (January 1968), pp. 27–33; and George A. Brager, "Advocacy and Political Behavior," *Social Work,* 13 (April 1968), pp. 5–15.

6. Malinda Orlin, "A Role for Social Workers in the Consumer Movement," *Social Work,* 18 (January 1973), pp. 60–65; Mildred Pratt, "Partisan of the Disadvantaged," *Social Work,* 17 (July 1972), pp. 66–73; Grosser, op. cit.; Briar, op. cit.; Brager, op. cit.; and Charles W. Smiley, "Citizen Advocates for the Mentally Retarded," *Social Work,* 18 (January 1973), pp. 110–112.

7. Neil Gilbert and Harry Specht, *Dimensions of Social Welfare Policy* (Englewood Cliffs, N.J.: Prentice-Hall, 1974), pp. 91–92.

8. The Ad Hoc Committee on Advocacy, op. cit., p. 17.

9. Briar, op. cit., p. 28.

10. Scott Briar, "The Social Worker's Responsibility for the Civil Rights of Clients," *New Perspectives,* 1 (Spring 1968), p. 90.

11. Briar, "The Current Crisis in Social Casework," p. 32.

12. Schwartz, op. cit., p. 34 and p. 38.

13. Brager, op. cit., p. 6.

14. *Code of Ethics,* NASW Policy Statements, No. 1 (rev. ed.; New York: National Association of Social Workers, 1967).

15. Ibid.

16. David Wineman and Adrienne James, "The Advocacy Challenge to Schools of Social Work," *Social Work,* 14 (April 1969), p. 28.

17. *Code of Ethics,* op. cit.

18. Brager, op. cit., p. 8.

19. Schwartz, op. cit., p. 32.

20. The Ad Hoc Committee on Advocacy, op. cit., p. 19.

21. Ibid.

22. Arnold Panitch, "Advocacy in Practice," *Social Work,* 19 (May 1974), p. 329.

23. Ibid.

24. Alan Keith-Lucas, "A Critique of the Principle of Client Self-determination," *Social Work,* 8 (July 1963), pp. 70–71.

25. Saul Bernstein, "Self-determination: King or Citizen in the Realm of Values?" *Social Work* (January 1960), p. 8.

5.

Robert Morris

THE ROLE OF THE AGENT IN LOCAL COMMUNITY WORK

The terms *locality, neighborhood,* and *local community* are often used interchange-

Adapted from "The Role of the Agent in the Community Development Process" in *Community Development as a Process* edited by Lee J. Cary. Used with permission of the editor and the University of Missouri Press. Copyright 1970 by the Curators of the University of Missouri Press.

ably in social welfare literature to identify one end of the social organization continuum which binds individuals to their society. Meeting human needs, and especially their social service needs, in the twentieth century involves the resources and actions of national governments, but effective use of national resources equally depends upon viable and healthy local or grass roots organization to sustain the interface between social services and their consumers.

This rather simple idea is confounded by the various ways in which grass roots organizations came into being and are controlled. Social work owes much of its vigor to its nineteenth-century origins, retaining as it does a faith in individuals' capacities to deal with their own problems, or to create face-to-face social structures for cooperative action on collective needs. As larger units of government, including the nation-state, took on welfare responsibilities, the relationships between the human base and higher levels of organization became more and more complex. For a time, in the 1950s and 1960s, initiative lay with national government and, to a large extent, local welfare organizations seemed limited to passive roles, reacting to national initiatives. By the late 1960s and 1970s, it was again recognized that the heterogeneity of our society demanded more attention be paid to local groups and to the capacity of local organizations to function creatively in the provision of welfare services.

Community organization is that wing of social work which has most consistently sought to deal with such issues. Over time, at least three dimensions of community organization practice evolved to deal with various points of the organization continuum: social planning (usually focused on higher levels of government), locality development, and social action to link the two.

The focus of discussion in this presentation will be on locally based community work or grass roots community organization. This entails, in large measure, models of practice that have been identified in this book as locality development and social action, although elements of social planning will be dealt with as well.

This article is an exploration of the role of the social worker as an agent of local groups which seek to master and to deal with their indigenous social welfare needs through their own efforts. The term agent, rather than professional worker, might well be used to sharply differentiate the worker who is aiding a group of citizens to achieve their collective ends by their own means from the professional employee whose expertise may set him or her apart from the lay citizen.

The term *grass roots community worker or agent* at once introduces a succession of ambiguities in definition. It does not mean every person involved in the process, for this would include the object of change—the resident of the area to be developed—regardless of the nature of his activity. On the other hand, to restrict the term to the temporary professional resident who enters the life of the community as an agent of change would exclude those workers who are recruited from among the permanent residents of the area, and may be called paraprofessional.

It may be best to consider as community work agents all those who are occupationally engaged in helping indigenously defined (or neighborhood-based) groups play an active role in developing any activity to improve their own well-being. As a further qualification, this occupational engagement constitutes the agent's major function over a specified period of time; in other words, employment for the community worker or agent means employment in some full-time capacity. However, such a definition is a convenience flawed by its own limitations, for many individuals who are engaged in the activities to be discussed are, in fact, volunteers whose sources of economic support have little to do with their community activities or whose income as agents is nominal. Workers in R.S.V.P. or the Peace Corps, and some full-time volunteers without pay, are in reality agents of local group development. Nevertheless, the definition by employment is useful in distinguishing the worker from the ordinary citizens who are engaged, as the ancient Greeks and Romans were engaged, in the life of their region.

THE EXPERT VERSUS THE COMMUNITY WORKER

The most troublesome aspect of the subject is whether the community worker has some identifiable set of tasks or skills that distinguish him and separate him from other specialists—the physician, the agronomist, the public health worker, or the teacher—who happen to be working in a development area. In like fashion, how are his skills differentiated from those of the resident population? The answers are equivocal at best, for community work is relatively new and represents an emerging occupation. At the beginning, the community worker was, in fact, a specialist who might have certain scientific skills, such as the physician, or he might have been a more general publicist, organizer, or lobbyist who happened to be working on behalf of a neighborhood or a developing area. With time, the attempt to develop a district or a region became elaborated conceptually, and a close identity between agent and the inhabitants of an area developed. This identity forced the community worker to reconsider the old issue of relationship between the giver and the receiver, the activist and the object of his action. To engage consciously and actively in a social transformation that may be at once social, economic, political, and psychological—and local community work involves all of these— somehow engages all who enter into the action as both givers and receivers.

The primary concern here is to direct attention to the roles, tasks, and dilemmas that confront the individuals who enter into this activity as a career with some new vision of participatory exchange between themselves and others.

At first, the agent has only his special knowledge and sympathy for resources. Building-up of an area involves many aspects of society. The worker may be a builder, economist, agronomist, physician, social worker, nurse, teacher, or other specialist. When the agent's confidence as an expert is tempered by an effective respect for the perceptions, wants, and desires of persons in the area, then he has begun the transformation from expert into community worker. This respect is the foundation of a philosophy that considers meaningful only that change or "development" which is wanted by the residents and in which they can all become actively engaged. To the expert's previously acquired technology or skill have been added new insight, new knowledge, and new skill for the effective engagement between himself and his beneficiary, soon to become a peer or partner.

If the task and role of the community agent are viewed in this light, the addition of new insights to his underlying skill or technique becomes his central concern. He does not interpret it as his function to bring sophisticated techniques to a less-developed area. These insights plus skills combine philosophical orientation as well as explicit content. The aims of this discussion are, therefore, to consider what it is that the community worker adds to his underlying or primary technical skill; to consider the major types of circumstances in which these combinations of skill are applied; and, finally, to review some of the ambiguities and uncertainties that are to be encountered in an evolving occupation. Both the agent's outlook upon the world and the resources he brings to bear in the furtherance of that outlook are here our concern.

The Value Foundations for Locally Oriented Practice Tasks

The value foundations for these emerging roles are fairly easy to identify although difficult to translate operationally. Of the first importance is the recognition that all social groupings, whether communal or societal, are in some stage of development at all times. The natural character of human association and of social organization involves change, whether slow or rapid, whether retrograde or forward-moving into untried forms. As national social change or development has come to be better understood, and as the material benefits of an industrial society (material in the sense of health and goods) have become widely desired, there has evolved a concern that all peoples have an adequate access to these material gains. However, this humane aspiration is coupled with the recognition that social change built around material improvement brings in its wake profound psychological and cultural changes, the direction and benefit of which are often uncertain and unpredictable.

The community worker or agent is, therefore, concerned with inducing change in society but, at the same time, tempering that change by the wishes and pacing of the groups and individuals directly affected. He is inevitably concerned with the responsibility he assumes in trying to bring about change, even though this change is tempered by the deepest humanity. His concern is reinforced by knowledge that national or organizational aims do not necessarily represent complete agreement among the groups or individuals who make up the society. While the community agent may take comfort from the knowledge that someone in a locality has formally invited his help, he is also uneasy because the depth of support for the request is uncertain.

While there are many examples of native or indigenous residents of an area assuming the initiating role of leadership in launching a community process, the more conventional situation is one in which the agent is introduced through some external agency, a government, or a voluntary association. Usually, although not universally, the introduction is from an agency at the next higher level of social organization. Thus, the neighborhood of a city may be the field for agents employed by bodies organized at the level of the city or the state; an entire town may be the object of attention from a region or a nation; a region may be the focus of action from a nation or some international body, and an entire nation may be the center for the efforts of international agencies. It is the higher level of organization that provides the employment base for most community workers.

By the 1970s, this basis for community work was altered through the growing self-confidence of minority neighborhood groups. Many of them, especially in inner-city ghetto areas, were able to demand staff positions and to control selection of persons to fill those positions. But this change seems to strengthen the dependence of local groups on some "outside" organization which at least provides the funds for community workers and has the capacity to negotiate conditions of work. The employment base still depends on external resources, although the nature of community work has been altered by the perceptions of locality groups.

It follows from this circumstance that the agent is usually employed by some formal instrumentality and, to this extent, takes some of his color and some of his approach from the values and purposes of the employing body. These may range from the predominantly self-help–stimulating approaches of certain church organizations to the social and economic development efforts conducted through governments.

The reality of employment by some organizations external to the local area is in sharp contrast to certain concepts about the primacy of attitudes of the ultimate recipient. The community agent is forced to mediate between the larger collective interests and the more personal community desires. This mediating role constitutes the hair shirt of the agent. Lacking objective guides for decision, his own value system must be constantly refined or he must try to frame decisions that will satisfy both sets of demands upon his judgment.

Types of Community Agents

If complete analysis were available, it might well turn out that types of community agents are as various as the employing organizations. However, lacking such analysis, certain major categories of community agents can be identified. It is likely that these categories are not strictly defined, since they are formed without regard to a number of variable circumstances. More likely, these categories of agent types have some close association with types of employing organizations and with certain general philosophies about community development itself. Nonetheless, the categories do serve as a useful framework for analysis.

Various descriptive terms have been applied to the role of the community agent, descriptive terms that seek to reflect the underlying philosophical thrust believed to characterize each. Thus, the widespread use of such terms as *enabler, activist, advocate, community organizer,* etc. has emerged. For each of these terms some description can be identified. However, these terms tend to describe general ways of approach-

ing specific problems. For example, community organization is commonly defined to mean "the art or process of bringing about and maintaining a progressively more effective adjustment between social welfare resources and social welfare needs;"[1] or as "a process by which a community identifies its needs or objectives, orders . . . these needs or objectives, . . . finds the resources . . . to deal with these needs or objectives, takes action with respect to them, and in doing so extends and develops cooperative and collaborative attitudes and practices in the community."[2] Once we move beyond these general definitions, the functions of the staff or workers tend to be described empirically in terms of what various workers do, rather than analytically, so that a wide range of tasks and functions are listed. Thus, the persons responsible for community organization tasks are expected to act, by turn, as administrators, analysts of social problems, fund raisers for programs, legislative activists, aides to enable others to perform responsible civic tasks on their own behalf, and as "creative leaders."[3]

In like manner, community development has been defined as "the process by which the efforts of the people themselves are united with those of governmental authorities to improve the economic, social and cultural conditions of communities, to integrate these communities into the life of the nation, and to enable them to contribute

---

[1] Arthur Dunham, cited by Meyer Schwartz in "Community Organization," in *Encyclopedia of Social Work* (New York: National Assoc. of Social Workers, 1965), p. 179.

[2] Murray G. Ross, *Community Organization: Theory Principles and Practice,* 2d ed. (New York: Harper & Row, 1967), p. 40.

[3] United Nations, Department of Economic and Social Affairs, *Community Development and Related Services* (New York: United Nations, 1960).

fully to national progress."[4] The staff tasks, as described, range from helping (or "enabling") people to improve their own level of living as much as possible by their own initiative, to introducing technical and other services of many kinds.

If general definitions are not yet sufficient, another approach to the subject is that of analyzing the central practical tasks that are to be performed and seeking to categorize these tasks in some coherent and logical but less general fashion. One such effort might lead to main tasks or roles performed by community workers, as follows: (1) the field agent, (2) the advisor or consultant, (3) the advocate, and (4) the local planner. It will be borne in mind that the individuals occupying these roles or performing these tasks seek to combine some expertness with the desire to limit the application of this expertness through some measure of participation and self-motivation of the persons affected.[5]

Deep Social Change and the Value of External Means

As he approaches his tasks, the worker is concerned with two polar considerations that are fused in his philosophy: (1) the conviction that there are needs of a population that can be satisfied by some deep social change; and (2) a belief in the value of some external means that need to be controlled and funneled into localities in order to assist individuals and communities to satisfy their new or enlarged wants.

Application of these considerations is not simple, for the definition of needs is still elusive. At the scientific level, there are certain needs that are assumed to be universal, including the need for minimum adequate diet, suitable shelter, appropriate conditions for the preservation of health and the avoidance of disease, among others. At the most elementary level, this assumption is certainly true, for no individual—unless he is ill—consciously wishes for death, hunger, or lack of shelter. What is difficult to grasp firmly, however, is just what meaning can be given these terms, and at what level health, shelter, and food shall be assured.

As the analysis varies from individual, short-term wants to the social, political, and economic changes that are required to fill these wants, the concept of relative deprivation emerges: measured by former standards, persons may have more food, better health, and shelter; but they may also have become aware that others enjoy wider variety, better health, shelter, and education, and ampler means for the enjoyment of a more meaningful leisure. By contrast, a minimum satisfactory condition that is better when measured only by old criteria becomes outmoded and a sense of relative want and loss results.

For the most part, a community worker begins his assignment with his own vision of the good society, but he seeks to suppress it while he ascertains to the fullest extent possible the wants and desires of the people with whom he is working. Their wants or desires may be expressed at the lowest community level: a better sanitation system, a more steady flow of food, simple health services; or they may be expressed at a more complex level: a modern educational system, suitable for an industrial society, or the training of manpower for technical jobs. The community agent adjusts his vision to

[4]Arthur Dunham, "What is the Job of the Community Organization Worker?" in *Proceedings of the National Conference of Social Work* (New York: Columbia University Press, 1948), pp. 162–172; and Violet Sieder, "The Tasks of the Community Organization Worker," in *The Curriculum Study*, ed. Werner Boehm (New York: Council on Social Work Education, 1959).

[5]See also: Arthur Dunham, *Types of Jobs in Community Development* (Columbia: University of Missouri, Department of Regional and Community Affairs, 1966).

the goals the local area desires and helps them strive toward these goals.

However, this respect cannot remain uncolored by the agent's knowledge and experience. He cannot help but be affected by his own convictions of what programs are best for the area. For example, the local desire to increase the tourist industry or to develop a factory, or increase welfare payments, or to train computer scientists may be less functional for the well-being of that area, as perceived by the agent, than a widely distributed, stable job market or an improved primary educational system. Conversely, a worker's belief in a high-quality maternal health program may not match a neighborhood's wish for an assertive drug program. The tasks of the agent usually involve some open or covert dialogue between the expressed wants of a people and his own externally derived knowledge and insight, although he seeks to discipline his expression to that of a dialogue rather than a dictation.

The other side of this equation consists of the imported means, provided by external agencies, of facilities, supplies, or knowledge that can be coupled with the local talents of the population to achieve the defined goals. Here again, a wide range in the definition of needs becomes apparent. In some places and in some circumstances, it is assumed that all that is required for change is the catalytic presence of the agent in a community. His encouragement and strength will mobilize whatever forces and resources the neighborhood population has within itself to take action and to overcome what may be apathy and resignation to the vagaries of fate. At the other extreme is the recognition that the acquisition of any of the benefits of industrial society—the reduction of poverty, the improvement of health, etc. —requires a capital investment in the form of knowledge and tools. This capital investment might be slowly and painstakingly ac-

quired, or the process of acquisition can be immeasurably stepped up by a benevolent or philanthropic sharing. To the extent that the agent is committed to speeding the process, to that extent he is engaged in securing and providing, from external sources, at least some of the means required for an accelerated tempo of development. These resources may be funds; they may be materials and supplies; or they may be technical knowledge.

If these major elements are considered universal for community tasks, then what can be said of the various types of roles for the community worker?

The Field Agent

The term *field agent* in this usage is closely akin to the concept of the *enabler* commonly cited in the literature, although its meaning is narrower. He is that worker who is in immediate and continuous communication with the individuals of a neighborhood, area, or region. He it is who maintains the essential link between the external world of ideas, values, and resources and the internal situation that is subject to change. He it is who is most sensitive to the pull of tradition, to the values inherent in the culture, and to their painful evolution in some symbolic relationship to the environment. He it is who is sensitive to the particular character of wants and desires expressed by the individuals.

As suggested above, this agent may identify completely with society and grope for those means by which he can stimulate the people to take the steps necessary to achieve that which they desire. Or, he may filter their expressions through his perception of their situation and seek to engage in that dialogue which will lead them to undertake direct action to alter those elements of their situation which they consider to be undesirable.

The concept of the agent as enabler draws intellectual nurture from a number of directions. The agricultural agent has learned how to speak the language of people with whom he works, although it is true that he brings a very explicit knowledge that he does not deny or abandon in the face of differing wants of the people with whom he works. The anthropologist has contributed a major respect for the vitality of any culture and for the fact that each state of social organization represents the achievable balance between the capacities of the people and their environment. The ecological or balance-of-nature concept, which has influenced many community workers, derives much of its strength from anthropological insights into the naturally evolved forms of social organization. The field of social welfare has contributed the concept of local community work, through which the practical aspects of social organization are introduced to enable individuals to capitalize on the benefits of cooperative group action. This concept introduces a familiarity with the varying techniques by which individuals associate in groups, sustain their inner group character, and evolve the means by which they, the group members, can communicate with others for continuity of action. Organizing techniques developed by social workers include such elements as small-group decision-making procedures; location of responsibility for follow-up action; report-back and monitoring devices; and simple organization mechanisms to translate wants into needs.

The Consultant

Another type of community worker is less concerned with the field situation, although he may be "in the field" for varying periods of time. He is the advisor or consultant and is usually responsible to an external employer. The consultant may have traditional expertness in health, education, or economic development, but if he is to function as a community agent, he adds to his expertness the special knowledge of how to link the external operation of the locality.

The advisor may be employed by one of the cabinet departments of a nation—the department of health or of housing—that is seeking to engage the resources of the nation in the aspirations of an economically or socially depressed area; or he may be the employee of a national voluntary association that is seeking to funnel the charitable impulses of a church to a poverty-ridden region. In either case, the community consultant is concerned, as much as anything else, with those modes of behavior which will link the external concern with the realities of the local social organization and with how the interests, impulses, and resources of the external organization can be linked with those of the locality.

The advisor or consultant necessarily requires some knowledge of the local culture as well as of the external culture and acts as a bridge between the two. He may rely on the eyes-and-ears function of the field agent, or he may acquire the equivalent information by periodic forays into the local culture. His advice may take the form of educating the decision makers of the external agency about the desires and circumstances of the area being developed. His sole function may be to identify the situation in the local area in order to organize externally planned education in the area. Or he may be trying to alter the means of communication between the external and the internal culture.

The Advocate

By contrast with both field agent and consultant, the community advocate is committed to the aspirations and desires of residents in the local area. He has identified himself with their needs and wants, regardless of the extent of "mix" between his own perceptions and those of the native population. His main function is to press the views of local needs upon the external agency in order to secure a response, favorable and helpful, if possible. Certain religious groups have functioned—sometimes unconsciously—in this fashion, as have many secular reformers. Danilo Dolci, for example, identified himself so completely with the requirements of the Sicilian village and town that he became spokesman for the culture in trying to force from the external world attention on the needs of Sicily.[6] In the United States, Saul Alinsky and his disciples are prototypes of the locality advocate approach. However, their philosophy contains other dimensions of radical social change.

The advocate is less concerned with bridging than he is with attracting attention to what he considers to be a serious situation. He may be the advocate of particular ways of resolving the dilemma or of simply directing attention to the situation.

The Planner

Finally, there is the local planner, who requires a different combination of technical skills from that of the field agent, the advisor, or the advocate. Planners usually function at the external agent level but are responsible for designing the details of any program that seeks to alter a local situation, whether that locality be defined as a neighborhood of a city, a town, a region, or a nation. True, they are concerned with procuring some sounding of local wants and needs and local attitudes. However, their main concern is to fit local needs into some kind of national or external agency plan. The community planner differs from this model in that he combines technician and advocate skills.

For example, at the national level, the desire of a rural village population for small landholdings and for improved agricultural equipment for family farming may have to be fitted into a national developmental plan that seeks to maximize agricultural production through industrial farming or to develop an industrial economy that will necessarily involve a relocation of population from agricultural to industrial pursuits and from village to town living. Just where each neighborhood, town, and regional want and desire is fitted into the national plan becomes the task of the usual planner. Technically, the planner is concerned with the allocation of external resources in the form of dollars, facilities, supplies, and manpower, and with the relation of these resources to some patterning of development.

By contrast, the community worker acting as a planner reverses these priorities. Instead of fitting local wants into a national plan, he seeks to first develop locally rooted plans and then to assure that national or regional planning fits into the local design, not vice versa. A major example of this reversal has been found in housing and in transportation planning in the past decade, where the plans and views of local groups have forced a change in the routing of interstate highways and have shifted clearance of run-down areas of cities to building restoration.

Since community literature has so long stressed self-help objectives for individuals, groups, and communities, it is necessary to ask whether there exists a task and skill built primarily around the idea of "human development" without being tied to an underlying technical skill as well. Has there

---

[6]Danilo Dolci, an architect and engineer by training, went to Sicily in the early 1950s for a brief visit to study ancient Greek architecture. Because of the poverty he found there, he decided to settle near Palermo and launch a campaign for the economic development of western Sicily. See Danilo Dolci, *Report from Palermo,* translated by P. D. Cummins (New York: Orion Press, 1959).

yet evolved a function for specialists *only* to help others help themselves, without relating this help to a more technically evolved concept about what the modern world requires? Is it likely that a local program for, let us say, improving health will employ health workers to build infant care centers and separately employ persons who will *only* work with the local population to stimulate them to move in any direction they choose as a means of stimulating self-help capacities?

In answering such questions, attention must be given to two quite separate circumstances: the facts of community employment, and the slow emergence of new professional or technical skills. A review of a large number of community programs will reveal that most agents began their employments with some specialized skill, to which they added, often intuitively, the extra talent of arousing self-help responses from the people in the developing area. This extra talent has led to the moderating influence imposed on the expert skill, so that a dialogue has ensued between agent and people, as noted above.

One may expect, over time, that a wholly new and free-standing professional or technical skill will develop that is concerned solely with freeing persons to act on the events in their lives, without being at all concerned *technically* with the content of that on which they are acting. If this does occur, it may take on the value-free character of psychoanalysis, in which the therapist seeks to free the individual from hampering constraints. However, recent research into psychotherapy has revealed the unrecognized extent to which this therapy is heavily influenced by the latent value-biased views and behavior of the therapist.[7] Similar val-

ue-laden handicaps may also emerge in the community organization profession, even though it seeks to dissociate itself from specific ends or goals for the group or community being served.

It may be more fruitful to consider the present reality of community work rather than to speculate on the nature of a future professional form. In this time-shortened view, it is clear that the community agent often (1) combines a technical skill with aspects of working with people or (2) is assigned to a team or to a program or project that has explicit aims and objectives. These explicit aims may be economic development through the introduction of new industry; or training in new patterns of time use as well as training in specific new work skills for the local population; or the improvement of health levels through the introduction of new perspectives and patterns of behavior in sanitation, hygiene, infant care, etc. In such circumstances, the community worker's purposes are to free the people, *but* to free them so they may better achieve the general objectives established by an external development agency itself. He may moderate the tempo of action but not its main direction. If the worker's efforts result in local opposition to the agency objectives (not the timing or means), conflict ensues, for which the literature provides no guidance. The worker must himself find the resolution of such conflicts.

In like manner, local efforts to impose their views on external agencies whose resources are sought may encounter deep conflict about objectives.

The situation of the community worker is succinctly summarized by Dunham in a recent attempt to outline types of community development jobs. He quotes an official as saying, "We look for people with social work training in community organization [persons trained in stimulating and en-

---

[7]See, among others, August B. Hollingshead and Fredrick C. Redlick, *Social Class and Mental Illness* (New York: John Wiley & Sons, 1958).

abling others to act for their own ends]. We find little interest from this group in general. We are therefore forced to look to other sources where people ... seem to have used a 'community development' approach in a more specialized job, such as agriculture, community relations, housing, planning. We thus end up with people educated in a variety of fields. Our young 'generalists' may be recent college graduates in most any field who show an interest and feeling for community development, and they learn on the job."[8]

It is a reasonable conclusion that, for the

[8]See Dunham, *Types of Jobs in Community Development*, 18–19.

present and in fact, the community worker does not yet have a single or "pure" function; rather, he combines some specialized technical skill, or purpose, plus a human development feeling, out of which a new combination of skills is slowly being forged.

As the reader can see, these community work roles entail a range of skills extending across all the models of practice described in this book. Field agent roles are particularly consistent with locality development, the advocate roles with social action, and planner roles with social planning. The consultant is also embraced by the social planning model, particularly those aspects related to interorganizational coordination and linkage.

6.

Steve Burghardt

THE TACTICAL USE OF GROUP STRUCTURE AND PROCESS IN COMMUNITY ORGANIZATION

We community organizers rightfully pride ourselves on our ability to strategically analyze large and often complex phenomena, turning apparent political conundrums into operationally precise programs of action. However, as any experienced organizer eventually comes to realize, our strengths manage to carry certain weaknesses as well. Over time, we learn that political clarity is not the same as personal awareness; our skills in developing a nifty program never seem to guarantee that we can personally carry it all off. What follows here, then, is the "forgotten" side of organizing—that side usually discussed after things go wrong, when we realize that

Manuscript prepared for this volume.

we should have presented ourselves in a quieter, less directed style so as not to have turned off new members (or, or course, the reverse). Two issues are of paramount interest here: first, the organizer's use of self in community practice; second, and in greater detail, the impact of group dynamics and role development on strategy. As we shall see, these issues, while usually secondary to the larger organizational demands of the group, can still be critical determinants in any community organization's success.

THE COMMUNITY ORGANIZER'S "USE OF SELF"

Introspective tools can be used regardless of one's organizing model. But these tools are perhaps most valuable when working with people in a one-to-one relationship. Here the chance for intimacy is greater, and the importance of personal as well as political factors becomes more noticeable. It is not a time of secondary consideration either; after all, most of an organizer's work is done between meetings, conferences, or demonstrations! Certain experiential factors from the past, often subjective, have more than once disrupted an organizer's work in such intimate activity.

Such disruptions most often occur around smaller, less visible prejudices, discomforts, etc. that are often too easily dismissed by organizers as "political differences" or just "irrelevant" personalized factors. For example, a "politically irrelevant" issue that turned out to be personally potent affected a skilled tenant organizer for months. Working in a student community, the organizer had had no success in organizing large numbers of tenants who lived along one particular street in the community. No pattern made sense: less-skilled organizers were doing well in the area, tenants from the neighborhood were voluntarily coming into the office to join the strike, etc. Finally, after much soul-searching and little organizing progress, he realized the problem: almost all the tenants were members of fraternities and sororities. Having had ugly experiences with fraternities a number of years ago, the organizer could not bring himself to believe fraternity and sorority members would now want to do something he supported. Unable to resolve the dissonant situation, he had sought to show their "continued" unwillingness to join the strike: normal questioning on strike procedures was greeted with snarls instead of answers; the first sign of hesitancy, hardly unusual in any tenant, led to a curt withdrawal. Finally seeing the problem as his own, the organizer was reassigned to areas in the community where his unseen

bias had less impact. He also had learned a small lesson in personal humility.

The past can be even more subtly influential with particular individuals. An organizer on the lower East Side of New York found herself consistently impressed by a community member, Mrs. R., whom others found downright boring. While others found Mrs. R. a well-meaning but lonely and overly talkative woman, the organizer had an almost unending desire to seek her out and use her opinions to guide her work. Needless to say, her work had been far more effective before all the advice. Only after she had been confronted by others did she finally tie together the powerful attraction with her past. It seemed that her first-grade teacher, her role model for years, had had the same hand mannerisms as the rather dull community person! Once she recognized this, instead of trying to "promote" her "teacher" into positions of authority she didn't deserve, the organizer was soon able to direct the woman away from her monotonous monologues into less frequent and more effective discussions on her personal problems that might be corrected. As the organizer put it, "I went back to looking at her head and not just her hands—and such a difference!!"

These two examples underline the importance of an organizer's developing introspective skills in his or her work. While they cannot substitute for the galvanizing force of concrete issues in motivating a community, they are nevertheless critical ingredients in an organizer's effectiveness in congealing original group motivation into a cohesive, permanent organization. As community members likewise have their own personal and often highly individualized perceptions of the world, these skills can also help further one's understanding of the day-to-day feelings, attitudes, and ideas of the individuals with whom one is working.

A better use of self may not change the world but certainly can make it more understandable.

ORGANIZING ROLES AND THE TACTICAL USE OF STYLE

While introspective tools are generic to one's work, distinct organizing strategies, as Rothman's model makes clear, tend to emphasize distinct practitioner roles: locality development, the enabler; social planning, the fact-finder and analyst; social action, the activist-advocate.[1] As will be seen later, these role emphases are not only tactically necessary but naturally congruent with particular stages of group development. It is important therefore that the organizer *tactically* understand these distinct stylistic emphases associated with each role, if he or she wishes to maximize *strategic* effectiveness.

However, understanding style must rest on more than just a circular sense of "fit" within the group. In fact each style is reflective of the ideology of the group and its members. Locality development, with its consensual orientation to accommodate the entire community, will necessarily establish norms of collegiality and community sharing. The ensuing legitimating influence for its membership—organizer included—will rest on what French and Raven have called "referent power,"[2] the power to be identified as sharing and incorporating the elements of others' sought-after reference group. For the organizer engaged in long-term community development projects, where there is a strong desire for local leadership development and widespread community involvement, a role that incorporates elements of that reference group is critical. It also must be a role presented in a manner others can understand and share as well. Coming on like gang busters or dripping with technical erudition may have its attractions elsewhere, but not within this organizing model. Being relaxed and more informally directive are critical stylistic innovations in any enabler's role. One organizer wrote about what happens if such considerations are not made:

> (Regarding a new community day-care center) . . . we had directed the group to a point where they were pressured for a decision on the type of action to be pursued. . . . In our need to satisfy our own urgency, we pressed the group to make a decision before they were ready. Rather than utilizing the knowledge of day-care regulations as a time to evaluate the group and its capacity to deal with the problem, we tried to circumvent the group's reluctance by taking an action-oriented posture. . . . It had a detrimental effect on the group.[3]

An organizer's role and style of action must correlate with the group's need to understand itself and its own sense of purpose. As the above suggests, if the organizers had fit their roles to the tactical style of the more reserved day-care members, strategic development itself would have been more effective in the long run. A static conception to role and style can only complicate an active group's rate of participation and growth.

Likewise, a social planning model carries with it the ideological commitment to expertise and technological skill. Such commitments emphasize "expert power" in

---

[1]Jack Rothman, "Three Models of Community Organization Practice," in Fred Cox, John Erlich, Jack Rothman, and John Tropman, eds., *Strategies of Community Organization* (Itasca, Ill.: F. E. Peacock Publishers, 1972), pp. 20–36.

[2]William French and John Raven, "Sources of Power in Groups," in Dorwin Cartwright and Alvin Zander, *Group Dynamics* (New York: Harper and Row, 1963), pp. 218–24.

[3]Irwin Nesoff, "Dynamics in an Alternative Day Care Center," unpublished paper, Hunter College School of Social Work, 1977.

the legitimation of its members.[4] An organizer's role as fact finder must necessarily be directive, clear, and informative to maximize his or her own legitimacy in the group. Social activists, having a mixture of both locality development and social planning goals to achieve, would understandably mix both formal and informal styles in their roles as activists and advocates. (We shall go into greater detail about the complex case of social action later.)

As we move closer to the organizer's actual work with community groups, we can see that the desired style of a particular role and an individual's personal ability to develop that style may be two different things. In fact, Bales has specifically identified two types of leaders in groups: the task leader, who is goal directed and concerned with the achievements of the group; and the socioemotional leader, whose concerns are more with the maintenance of the group itself.[5] While no highly systematic research has been completed yet on organizers' personal styles, informal surveys over the last two years suggest that about two-thirds of all organizers identify themselves as task oriented.

The impact of leadership style on group dynamics will be discussed later on. But a self-identification as either task or socially oriented is important for an organizer to make early in his or her career. There is nothing tactically worse—and at times little that is more embarrassing—than either forcing a hard-driving organizer to take on an extremely social, enabling role, or making a socially able but less directive person chair a volatile, conflictual meeting. Each case creates both organizational turmoil and personal anxiety for everyone. It is far better to become settled in one's style, rec-

ognize its strengths *and* weaknesses, and then, at a more modest personal rate, learn to overcome those limitations in a manner that does not damage the group.[6]

With effort and personal perseverance, a community organizer can add these more subjective skills of introspection and personal awareness of organizer role/leadership styles to his or her organizing kit. Like all other elements of organizing, each is subject to constant revision and updating, but used in perspective, they can help highlight the effective direction of a community group's growth. We shall now analyze in greater detail the role changes and group dynamics of community organizations to see their tactical impact on strategy development.

GROUP STRUCTURE AND PROCESSES

Community groups, just like strategies, go through many changes in their growth and development. Bales and Strodtbeck,[7] among others,[8] located at least three phases of task-oriented group development that have consequences for organizers. Labelled orientation, evaluation, and control, each

---

[4]French and Raven, *op. cit.,* p. 221.

[5]Robert Bales, *Interaction Group Process* (Reading, Mass.: Addison-Wesley, 1950).

[6]For example, the social type would chair small groups and subcommittees before taking on more conflict-ridden assignments; a task-oriented individual might be given *no* assignments at a social function except to circulate and get to know people personally —a "task" harder than one might think!

[7]Robert Bales and Neil Strodtbeck, "Phases in Group Problem-Solving," in Cartwright and Zander, *op. cit.,* pp. 389–400.

[8]Rosemary C. Sarri and Maeda Galinsky, "A Conceptual Framework for Teaching Group Development in Social Group Work," *Faculty Day Conference Proceedings, 1964* (New York: Council on Social Work Education); Warren G. Bennis and Herbert A. Shepherd, "A Theory of Group Development," *Human Relations,* IX (1956), pp. 415–37; Bruce W. Tuckman, "Developmental Sequences in Small Groups," *Psychological Bulletin,* LXIII (1965); and Margaret Hartford, *Groups in Social Work* (New York: Columbia University Press, 1972), chapter three.

stage differentially enhances or impedes three organizing factors: (1) its problem-solving ability; (2) the type of leadership most effectively used; (3) the level of expertise demanded.

Orientation is the initial stage of a problem-solving group's development. It is a time spent less in problem-solving itself than in discovering what the problem really is. Bales and Strodtbeck found group members spend the orientation stage engaged in "directed interaction in the discussion of the problem or potential problem"; people want to know if the problem is worth tackling and if it is possible to deal with effectively.[9] Initial fact-finding activities in social planning or the development of a newsletter for communication in locality development would be the type of short-range task a group might engage in during this phase, as members sought to find out what the group might concern itself with in the coming months. Even those minor tasks may be difficult in the very beginning. One organizer, involved in a community development project, wrote how difficult and amorphous this phase of group life can be:

Committee members ... did not at first understand that "committee" meant a specific group of people, the same people every time. ... Oral announcements were vague and misleading. ... (for a few months) my suggestions were passively accepted. With time they began to pose their own amused cynicism against my professed view that our monthly educational programs were justified if only one person derived some benefit. ... Only later did they actually take over the work.[10]

Clearly, this phase is not always one of dramatic involvement or movement for members or the organizer. While the above case is undoubtedly extreme in its amorphous and passive character, the initial fluidity in group life is natural. It is a phase where efforts must be spent in both membership interaction and modest group activity.

Here the organizer's role will necessarily be made up of complementary parts. The enabler is directive enough to *suggest* purpose to the group, yet not so heavy-handed that the group has little opportunity to identify the group's functions as its own. Likewise, the fact finder in social planning may be informed but not so overwhelmingly direct in all work areas that there is no time for the group's members to define activity and program for themselves.

Evaluation is the second stage of group development. Here Bales and Strodtbeck found that "the problem cannot be an open and shut case. ... (It) involves several different values and interests as criteria by which the facts of the situation and the proposed course of action are to be judged."[11] In short, the group has proceeded from limited understanding of the problem (and thus little understanding of or commitment to the group and its ability to ameliorate the issue) to an intermediate stage where people see the group as having potential value to resolve its problems but disagree on what the problem is and (more likely) on how to correct it. It is not an easy time. (Tuckman called it the "storming" phase of group development.)[12]

For example, a New Left political group had made the strategic decision to enter electoral politics and begin working as an electoral party. It found:

for a few of the organizers, this shift into pragmatic politics was more than a little

---

[9]Bales and Strodtbeck, *op. cit.,* p. 391.

[10]Carla Eugster, "Field Education in West Heights; Equipping a Deprived Community to Help Itself," in Cox et al., *op. cit.,* p. 243.

[11]Bales and Strodtbeck, *op. cit.,* pp. 391–93. See also Hartford, *op. cit.,* pp. 80–85; C. Heinke and Robert Bales, "Developmental Trends in the Structure of Small Groups," *Sociometry,* XVI (1953), p. 7–23.

[12]Tuckman, *op. cit.*

unsettling. Used to activist-advocate roles within strategies demanding little long-term follow-through (e.g., quickly-organized and easily-dissipated demonstrations), a few were unable to change their style. . . . After many fights over what they should be doing, they left. . . .[13]

Clearly in this phase discussion centers more often on the clarifying of procedures and possible actions than on any one set of directed behaviors. The group stage emphasizes a mixture of affective and instrumental behaviors, as members spend time on becoming comfortable with the group and its ability to deal with the now-defined problem at hand.

This stage is often viewed by the organizer as the most talkative—and a quite irritating—stage for the organizer. People in problem-solving groups now know the problem but are not yet acting to resolve it. In short, they are evaluating. What is important, as will be seen below, is that the evaluation is not of the issue but of the group itself.

The organizer who feels he or she can skip this stage because people know what the problem is will be making a mistake. People also have to know the group, and this intermediate stage allows for the group's worth to be clarified and internalized by the membership. The day-care center [in the case cited above] was one example of what can happen if the group passes too quickly through this questioning, anxiety-provoking time. This will be true in even the most task-oriented groups:

The highly task-oriented Hunger Task Force (as a social planning group) passed quickly through the first group phase and went into the evaluation stage, where the members displayed reluctance to (continue work). . . . The work was terminated for a good while. . . . (Later) the conference committee jumped through the orientation and evaluation stages into the control stage. . . . As the group process had been truncated, there was consequent unresolved ambivalence and conflict and frequent motion to return to evaluation (stage 2). . . .[14]

In this stage even the most task-oriented organizer must play a highly process-oriented, enabling role that allows group members to express and work out differences, problems, and questions in as smooth a fashion as possible. While time pressures often interfere with this, an organizer must develop some of this activity for at least minimal on-going effectiveness.[15]

Control is the final stage, where "there is pressure for a group decision and the expectation of group action."[16] The group is at a point of activity in a planned set of behaviors and specified roles; the emphasis is on the task through concerted group effort. The implication of a tight organizational structure with little time spent on socioemotional issues is suggestive of social planning, with its emphasis on expertise to

---

[13]Nancy Romer Burghardt and Stephen Burghardt, "The Changing Dimensions of Social Action: The Case Study of the Ann Arbor Human Rights Party," in Fred Cox, John Erlich, Jack Rothman and John Tropman, eds., *Community Action, Planning, Development: A Casebook,* (Itasca, Ill.: F. E. Peacock Publishers, 1973), pp. 66–67.

[14]Jenny Green Lee, "Group Changes in the Hunger Task Force," unpublished paper, Hunter College, 1977.

[15]The organizer can use the individual, one-to-one interchanges away from the group if necessary. Indeed, the organizer can more easily carry this difficult and time-consuming "group" process into his or her daily, individualized work—answering questions, provoking thought, resolving and respecting individual doubts. This way group time is directed and yet each individual member may experience *all* stages of group development in a congruent manner—through the organizer's daily work!

[16]Bales and Strodtbeck, *op. cit.,* p. 393; Heinke and Bales, *op. cit.,* pp. 301–303; Tuckman, *op. cit.*

achieve clearly stated and well-focussed objectives.[17] This stage, the most obvious for an organizer to identify due to its concrete set of individual and group behaviors (be it writing a detailed health care proposal, coordinating a major fund-raising drive for a block association, or organizing a coordinated set of demonstrations around housing problems), nevertheless, is usually the last stage of a group's development, not its first.

Here we would find the enabler in locality development, having helped prepare new leaders, clarified issues for resolution, and made members cognizant of the group's worth, more removed from the directed activity of the group, letting others assert their new skills and group authority. The social planner would be part of a directed, highly engaged group, facilitating the concrete implementation of a specific program or plan.

As all of the above examples imply, there are strong relations between the dominant group stages of development and the strategy type chosen by a community organization. Locality development, being involved more in communication and education and less in problem solving, would stress the evaluational and, secondarily, the orientation stages of group development. Social planning with its more directed demands and use of specified, expert roles, would function more within the control stages of groups. Social action, which combines elements of both strategies, falls somewhere between the two extremes. But what does each stage actually look like? How does a community organization move from one group stage—or strategy—to another? What is the organizer's job to help facilitate such changes as smoothly as possible?

GROUP DEVELOPMENT AND CHANGING LEADERSHIP STYLES[18]

Strategies, as Rothman makes clear, are not static conceptions; they change and develop to fit the needs and resources of one's organization. Groups, too, develop and change over time, and with them, so do their leadership demands. Hollander has stated that "persons function as (distinct) leaders in a particular time and place and there are both delineating and varying conditions ... to that leadership."[19] These shifts in leadership style and group development are important for the community organizer to note, for correct leadership "by definition facilitates the group's development."[20] By helping emphasize the correct leadership style for a particular period of group development, the organizer may actually heighten the group's strategic effectiveness.

As discussed earlier, Bales specifically identified the two primary types of group leaders as "task-oriented" and "socio-emotional" types.[21] Organizers of course fall into one of these categories. Equally important, an organizer can identify these types within the group itself—be it the friendly fellow in charge of the group's "social hour" or the demanding, well-informed woman specifically involved with consumer affairs for the group.

Organizers also know that each leadership style can be the source of irritation or

---

[17]Rothman, *op. cit.*

[18]Much of what follows here has been adapted from an article appearing in *Sociology and Social Welfare*. See Steve Burghardt, "A Community Organization Typology of Group Development," *Sociology and Social Welfare*, Fall, 1977.

[19]E. P. Hollander, *Leadership, Groups, and Influence* (New York: Oxford University Press, 1964), p. 18.

[20]Cecil A. Cobb, quoted by Hartford, *op. cit.*, p. 214.

[21]Bales, *op. cit.*, chapter two.

admiration—"depending on the situation." However, as Hollander suggests above, it is more likely that each person is appreciated or bypassed for both situational needs and the organizer's need for individual skills to enhance or move beyond a particular stage or group development. Each stage is most closely associated with a particularly effective leadership style; that style is what one wishes to make congruent with the rest of the group's functioning.

Fiedler found that task leaders "function best under conditions that are either very favorable or relatively unfavorable to them."[22] This finding is not as simplistic as it sounds. As one student wrote on her work with a community group,

> Without Mrs. J. I don't know what I'd have done (in the early stages of the group). Mrs. J. was hardly a sweetheart, and she had few friends, but in the beginning she was terrific. Every meeting she'd raise a million ideas for the (senior citizens') club while everyone else just sat there. . . . Finally she hit on a repair program she'd read about and they all started to move—at last! She was a real powerhouse in the program, too. . . .

Tasks that are ill defined are the kind that many find frustrating or too little worthwhile to bother pursuing. An organizer must be aware that it will be a time when those most attracted to the task—and not just the group—will be willing to plow ahead. During this phase—when there is hardly a group at all—such individuals play crucial roles.

Likewise, when community organizations are engaged in concrete and immediate tasks, task leaders would again be expected to play important roles within the

control stage of groups. Indeed, this last stage should be their forte.

We can see that task leaders are of real value in the early stage of group development. But this doesn't seem to apply to locality development, a method that from the start emphasizes process over task, social interaction over concrete goal directions. This makes sense at first glance, but locality development strategies, if they do emphasize process over task, are by definition not problem-solving groups in their beginnings.[23] Eventual action on concerted issues may lie in the far-off future. Therefore, strategies here would not involve an in-depth orientation phase (where problems are specified for relatively quick solution) but would instead truncate this first stage for the interactional benefits and structure of the evaluational stage.[24]

In this second stage, as Fiedler and his associates pointed out, task leaders are much less effective.[25] Still concerned with the tasks ahead and relatively indifferent to the group's membership needs, the task leaders are no longer effective eye-openers who reveal the value of the problem to be attacked; they become overly zealous irritants who bother other members with their constant agenda setting and single-mindedness. See what happened to Mrs. J.:

> After the group had a rough idea of where it was going, they started questioning everything—too much so. Mrs. J. infuriated people by her demands to head up the tenants' group when they still weren't sure how

---

[22]Frederick Fiedler, "Personality and Situational Determinants of Leadership," in Cartwright and Zander, *op. cit., op. cit.,* pp. 362–381.

[23]Rothman, *op. cit.,* pp. 20–21. See also Arthur Dunham, "Some Principles of Community Development," *International Review of Community Development,* No. 11 (1963), pp. 141–51.

[24]Bales and Strodtbeck based most of their research on problem-solving groups of a relatively short duration. There has been little systematic research on community groups and how their stages more precisely develop and change over a much longer period of time.

[25]Fiedler, *op. cit.,* pp. 375–378 ; Cobb, *op. cit.,* p. 220.

they'd operate. . . . I had to smooth a lot of feathers, and spend time socializing more. . . .

But it's not that Mrs. J. had changed; the group had. Seeing that the group may have purposes and yet not fully understanding the responsibilities that group involvement may demand, most members during the evaluational stage need not only to continue clarifying issues but to feel increasingly comfortable with the group. Here is where socio-emotional leaders become so important. Such people, whose skills and interests are more affective than instrumental, perform the crucial roles involved in heightening the attractiveness of the group itself: serving refreshments, making certain new members are comfortable and that older members are kept informed of group events, etc.

These social leaders usually view the group as more important than the task. Where earlier their personalistic orientation appeared slightly irritating (or at least distracting) as the group sought to clarify its mission, here their friendliness and noninstrumentality emerge as highly valued and pleasantly effective. They achieve such high value because groups, like individuals, are resistant to change.[26] Membership needs for understanding both group functions and future tasks can be psychologically unsettling to people. Bales and Strodtbeck found that the move into the second phase of the group was filled with the greatest level of both positive and negative feedback; not surprisingly, it was also the phase with the greatest drop-out rate.[27] Hartford identified groups as either moving forward in this stage or falling

apart with some possibilities for regroupment.[28] In such a stormy period, it is obvious what benefits these socio-emotional leaders can play.

An organizer would naturally appreciate those people who heightened the positive affective functions of group interaction during this phase. By intermingling positive group maintenance functions with the larger issues posed by the group from the earlier stage, the socio-emotional leaders help heighten the group's attractiveness beyond the unsettling work that still lies ahead. New community organizations are often found scheduling a moderately complex fund-raiser in this period. As a task function, it helps raise money for future work on now-clear issues. As a process function, it is still not so demanding in intensity that it discourages people from participation; indeed, the party, festival, or banquet held serves the affective function of heightening the group's value to the membership itself.

The above describes the first two stages of group development in problem-solving groups. Locality development, as mentioned, with its strategy emphasizing process goals, is somewhat different from these more task-oriented groups. It will not originate in manifest form as a problem-solving group but will instead form around, say, a sense of neighborhood pride in a deteriorated section of the community. The orientation period, with its demand for problem clarification and generalized task orientation and leadership, will be truncated, that is, made short so that members do not drop away too easily (as occurred in the day-care center example earlier). Instead, as the group itself will be of value, it will emphasize the evaluational stage of group structure and leadership type. Only after

---

[26]Bernard Bereleson and Gary A. Steiner, *Human Behavior* (New York: Harcourt, Brace, Jovanovich, 1964); Herbert Thelan, *Dynamics of Groups at Work,* (Chicago: University of Chicago Press, 1954).

[27]Bales and Strodtbeck, *op. cit.,* p. 393.

[28]Hartford, *op. cit.,* pp. 80–81.

the process goals have been achieved, with leadership emerging and a sense of group value present, would the organizer move back to the previously truncated orientation stage so that the group and its newly developed leaders could fully begin the tasks of clarifying which problem they would like to solve.

For the organizer engaged in any strategy, this evaluational stage is often extremely difficult. Seeing larger issues ahead and at the same time realizing the need for the membership to value the group, he or she, especially if task oriented, will often squirm with anxiety as the group prepares for the final, more demanding control stage of activity.[29] This is what often makes the process of organizing appear so long, but without it a group often finds itself in serious difficulty—either immediately after the task is completed, when the group falls apart, or during the final activity itself, when there are far too few members to carry on the work successfully.

When the control stage begins, task leaders again come back into prominence and effectiveness. While probably chafing during the previous "motionless" time of the evaluational period, the task leaders are now able to do what they have been waiting to do all along: get the job done. By now, the group's members understand both the problem ahead and the value of the group attempting to ameliorate it. What they must now do is act in a decisive manner, with set behaviors, shared expectations, and formalized assignments.[30] The demands common to social planning, with heavy task leadership style and the group cohesiveness necessary to carry out well-specified tasks, do not make for idle chatter and pleasant socializing.

Here the formerly ingratiating social leader's informal conversation appears out of place on the directed group's work table. Now that the table is set for plans and action, the decisiveness and specificity of the clear task once again makes the task leader the more effective group member.[31] Organizers, recognizing the need for concrete action, can be expected to develop a task leadership style to maximize the congruence between the group's structure and the group's agreed-upon direction toward goal achievement.

"MIXING AND PHASING" IN ACTION: THE APPLICATION OF EXPERTISE TO GROUP DEVELOPMENT

So far in this section we have seen that distinct community organization strategies tend to emphasize a particular stage of group development; in turn, each stage heightens the effectiveness of different leadership styles and organizing roles. We must now analyze what specific types of leadership can be emphasized by organizers if they wish to maintain either a particular stage of development that is most conducive to the overall organizing strategy or, equally likely, mix and phase strategies by moving the group from one stage to another.[32] This issue of structural differentiation is best understood by analyzing the use of formal and informal expertise within the group.

Guetzkow, in his study of group differentiation, delivered a crucial message to organizers. Writing on his findings of group processes, he stated:

> although some explicit understanding of the organization is necessary, understanding per se is not sufficient to induce the development of continuing, differentiated organizations. An analogous state of affairs exists with respect to the existence of roles

---

[29]See Eugster, *op. cit.*
[30]Bales and Strodtbeck, *op. cit.*, p. 392.

[31]Fiedler, *op. cit.*, p. 378; Cobb, *op. cit.*, p. 217.
[32]Rothman, *op. cit.* p. 33.

(in groups): although differentiation of roles is imperative for articulation (of the group), such differentiation is not sufficient in itself to induce an interlocking of the roles.[33]

In organizers' terms, assigning clearly specified roles to members doesn't guarantee the making of a cohesive, permanent group. Developing the cohesiveness necessary to work consistently necessitates the development of expertise, expertise that can be applied to role differentiation in some tactically consistent manner.[34] This expertise will be of two types: (1) the knowledge of one's functional complementarity to others' group tasks; (2) specified planning and other skills.[35]

The more informal expertise is nonspecialized and potentially available to all members of the group. The more formal expertise is specialized and common to particular, trained individuals. For example, knowing to whom and why one is accountable for a group's financial state is learned by any member of a community organization; knowing the principles of accounting is another matter. Both are valuable in helping the organizer move a group beyond the amorphous orientation stage of group development.

Guetzkow's findings clarify an invaluable lesson for organizations—you do not "make" a group by giving people roles like fund-raiser, publicity chief, etc., *if* the roles are not connected so that members see the value inherent in such role complementarity. Indeed, this is much of the knowledge disseminated throughout the early stages of group development. Without it, the common problems bound up in goal displacement are inevitable. Whether community, group, or complex organization, people unknowing of or unconcerned with overarching group goals will invest more of themselves in their own job than in the long-range group task. This holds with small groups, too—the fund-raiser becoming obsessed with raising more and more money, the publicity coordinator dreaming of eight-page newsletters instead of critical, on-going leaflets, etc. Clarifying how each task (and concomitant role) connects to the overall group goals is one easy step for heightening the structural cohesion of the group itself. For the organizer wishing to move from one stage to another, the use of role complementarity heightens structure —the "sense of group"—and obviously speeds up group development.

The value of formal expertise, with its formal training and elements of "bureaucratic intensity,"[36] is understandably suggestive of even more group structure. As Eugene Litwak and Henry Meyer point out in their work on organizational and group structures,

(in comparing qualities of bureaucratic organizations and primary groups as ideal types) it is sufficient to say that professional expertise is maintained in social organizations that stress achievement, instrumental, specialized and impersonal relations, whereas the generalized qualities of the non-expert are maintained in social organizations that share the opposite characteristics. . . .[37]

In a community organization we would thus find the demands of more formalized interaction and direct planning carrying with them expectations for even more heightened role complementarity and

---

[33]George Guetzkow, "Differentiation of Roles in Task-Oriented Groups," Cartwright and Zander, *op. cit.,* pp. 514–31.

[34]*Ibid.,* p. 519.

[35]Eugene Litwak and Henry Meyer have done extensive research on the varying functions of distinct types of expertise. See their *School, Family, and Neighborhood: The Theory and Practice of Community-School Relations* (New York: Columbia University Press, 1973).

[36]*Ibid.,* pp. 2–18.

[37]*Ibid.,* pp. 17.

differentiation that underpin structural cohesion. Just as the organizations discussed by Weber experienced increasing bureaucratization as a result of specialization, so it is with all groups once they use expertise. Any organizer knows that the use of experts—be they lawyers giving legal advice or accountants attending to their books—forces the group to pay attention to the structural demands of the specialized roles. By being so specialized, these experts force the rest of the group to account for what the other group functions are—e.g., a lawyer gives advice on specific property issues confronting tenants, not all law; the accountant tends to fiscal issues only as they lend themselves to the group's present solvency. Such focussed attention on the group itself, the true forte of any specialty, brings into clearer focus what the group is about. It will no longer be possible to open-endedly discuss problems or evaluate group worth. Both the content of the discussion and the group structure will be much tighter when expertise is used.

Role complementarity and the inclusion of group expertise help organizers differentiate group stages and, even more importantly, help the organizer move the group through various stages of group development. Looking first at the orientation stage, with its emphasis on group exploration of a specific problem, we see that it is the stage with the least amount of overall expertise. Only after task leaders push and prod the group to a greater awareness of group purpose—which by definition is an early element of the informal expertise necessary for role differentiation—does the group enter the second, evaluational period.

In this stage, organizing strategies similar to locality development would engage in short-term tasks bound up in the larger process goals of the organization. Indeed, one can see that the "informal expertise" bound up in recognizing the value of the group and its members' ability to perform tasks would be the dominant operational measures used to chart the group's success in achieving its process goals. Regardless of strategic orientation, the evaluation spent in differentiating roles (and thus functions) of the membership would heighten the use of socio-emotional leaders here. As the socio-emotional leaders give attention to group maintenance activities, they are in fact focussing on the inherent worth of nonspecialized knowledge that underpins the developing group's structure. This information, reinforced through affective means, helps others discover and become comfortable with the group and their own role definitions. Tasks such as fund-raising activities that heighten the value of the group are appropriate here. By also assigning people-specific, interrelated tasks of a modest nature, one begins preparing group members for the more demanding control stage that lies ahead.

Finally, the control stage, with its heavy emphasis on planning and goal achievement, will heighten the structure of the group to its greatest intensity. Both group functions and differentiated roles will be the most salient in this period. The organizer will now be less concerned with group maintenance and will instead be heavily task oriented, attempting to implement well-planned and orchestrated activities so suggestive of a cohesive, complex organization.

The paradigm we have developed so far appears in Table 6.1.

An example from locality development will help flesh out the paradigm. As often happens in locality development, a settlement house's year-long program for involving community members in a neighborhood enhancement program did not even begin with a "problem" at all. Instead, the group of seniors first met as a supper and social club. Obviously there was no real problem-solving orientation period, but an extended evaluational stage where people first got to know each other, discover leadership skills through social tasks (organizing dinners, preparing a dance, etc.), and in general started to feel comfortable with the group itself. Only after three or four months, when leaders emerged and people were relatively knowledgeable about the value of the group (informal expertise), did the organizer breach the possibility of getting involved in more task-oriented community problems.

Here the group shifted back to the orientation stage, for now they were an emerging problem-solving group. Social activities and social leaders slipped into the background a bit as recently identified task leaders and the organizer helped encourage the group to decide what specific problem was the most pressing and still manageable for them to handle. Numerous issues were raised—rat control problems, rent strikes, clean-up projects—but the one finally hit upon was a lunch program for their shut-in neighbors. The program was ideal for their members, combining elements of task (providing nourishing food for needy elders) with the already internalized elements of process (consistent interaction with neighbors and other social activities).

Moving back into the evaluational period, the active seniors set out to detail the roles and assignments ahead. Some of the members, particularly those who enjoyed the social benefits of the group, expressed discomfort at the group's "overzealous" direction, but the occasional socials held by

TABLE 6.1
Organizing Strategies, Group Phases, and Organizing Roles and Styles

	Initial Length of Time	Type of Leaders	Level of Expertise		Organizer's Dominant Role	Style of Behavior
			Informal	Formal		
Orientation						
Locality Development	Truncated-Moderate	Very Modified Task	Very Low	Low	Teacher of Problem-Solving Skills	Mildly Directed
Social Planning	Short	Task	Very Mod.	High	Fact Finder	Relaxed but Direct
Social Action	Short	Modified Task	Moderate	Low	Activist	Direct
Evaluation						
Locality Development	Long	Socio-Emotional	Moderate	Low	Enabler	Personable, Engaged
Social Planning	Short	Modified Task	Moderate	High	Facilitator	Explicator of Problems
Social Action	Moderate	Modified Social	Moderate	Moderate	Advocate/Enabler	Direct/Personally Engaged
Control						
Locality Development	Short	Task/Social	High	Moderate	Facilitator/Enabler	Distant yet Available
Social Planning	Long	Task	High	High	Facilitator/Fact Finder	Very Direct
Social Action	Moderate-Long	Modified Task	High	Moderate	Activist/Advocate	Direct/Available

the settlement house kept most of them involved and met their affective needs. This social atmosphere helped move members into more task-oriented roles: collecting information on food programs, finding potential food sources, seeking finances, etc. Such responsibility was gently reinforced by giving reports on each assigned task during every social event.

Finally, after about nine months, the group felt ready to move into a more clearly defined "control" stage. Setting aside its social activities, the group spent all its time on two coordinated efforts: constant fund-raising and proposal writing and, concurrently, a mini–lunch program demonstrating the need for a larger program. This mini-project, giving each group member a potential task to fulfill, served as a demonstration project that the group itself was invaluable for community enhancement—the care and feeding of needy elderly senior citizens. The outcome: a commitment of private and public funds for the group to provide for fifty shut-ins throughout the neighborhood; and, not incidentally, a sense of group pride and strength that they as active, older community members could have an impact on their community.

Mixing and Phasing. This locality development strategy, evolving through all group stages and using different types of leaders and organizing styles to expedite group (and strategic) development, was obviously successful. The group is still going strong—but not just within the "control" stage. The "mixing and phasing" of two desired strategies—planning and development—has led to even greater structural differentiation. It maintains a more structured, control stage that emphasizes relatively high standards of formal, task-oriented expertise through both its nutritional lunch program and local community planning board activities. At the same time, it maintains a commitment to education and community enhancement by using its social leaders, well-steeped in informal expertise of the group, to engage new members. "Mixing and phasing" has thus developed strategically, not by analytic abstraction but by concretely structuring the group to be partially engaged in control stage activities, partially in evaluational ones. The results are a task-oriented but moderately informal community group that enhances both its community and its own membership by its presence.

SOCIAL ACTION: THE SPECIAL CASE OF IDEOLOGICAL COMMITMENT AND GROUP STRUCTURE

Locality development and social planning, by being strategic polarities in many ways, are relatively easy to analyze. But what about social action, the strategy known to mix elements of planning and development in its stated process goals and task orientation?

Social activists wish to educate people to longer-term goals of significant structural change. At the same time, specific tasks similar in intensity and role complementarity to those in social planning (such as in a rent strike) must be carried out. Social action remains the least-used community organization strategy, not only because of the dangers of outside oppression and its potentially conflictual nature. The relative rarity of social action is also due to the organizational difficulty of maintaining such a conflictual stance over a long period of time.

These problems relate in part to the ideological stance of many social action groups. I am not implying that projection of a clearly stated ideology is a mistake, only that those taking strong ideological stands in opposition to established organizations must also prepare themselves so that they can maintain the complex group structures necessary for long-term social action.

Locality development, for example, avoids such problems by attempting to be nonpartisan and open to all groups. This openness does not demand cohesion prematurely; the members themselves are able to slowly develop a program that moves through all stages of group development before opting for a task-oriented strategy. Expertise is used only if it fits the moderately intense task goals. Accordingly, the structure of the group is never so highly complex as to exclude new members or to force people out of the group who may have opposing viewpoints.

Social planning also does not begin with a stated analysis of power relations in the community, although often social planners are obvious in their deference to technocratic authority. Instead, the planning method limits itself to a clearly outlined, concrete problem already agreed upon by most of its membership. The strategy then proceeds rapidly through group development by the legitimacy it gives formal expertise to control the direction of the group.

Most social action strategies have neither the openness of locality development that allows for gradualistic, comfortable group process, nor the willingness to give formal experts the legitimacy to expedite the group's direction. Instead, social action usually begins with the cohesive glue of cleavage due to its members' shared perceptions of some basic problem that separates them from others in the community. The orientation phase will thus be short, for people wouldn't choose a social action strategy immediately if they weren't in common agreement on the seriousness of the problem facing them. They instead will move quickly into the evaluational period as they attempt to determine the group means to achieve their ends. Members of the group who are not certain of the problem cannot remain easily within the group. Wrote one tenant activist about his tenant group's first meeting:

> They were tired of individual attempts to deal with bad housing. . . . At the first large organizational meeting, problems were identified, officers elected, and Block Captains to handle weekly assignments were chosen. . . . Fifteen major grievances were drawn up around which to organize. . . .[38]

This period is often quite agitational (say, for example, as a group prepares for a large rent strike). There will be strong cohesion wrought by the members' shared vision; at the same time, the group's moves toward the control stage will be slowed by at least two factors. First, the group has to have enough members to give it at least the appearance of real clout (e.g., enough tenants must join the rent strike before it is any real economic threat to the landlords). Second, the group's members, many of whom may view formal authority as illegitimate, will often resist the very real moves toward bureaucratization one finds in the use of formalized expertise. (Continuing with the strike example, tenant unions often have profound fears about lawyers dominating tenant strategy.)

This tension between the locality development needs for an increasingly large membership for long-term effectiveness and the planning responsibilities for getting specific and often complex tasks completed is the bane of many social action groups.

---

[38]Tom Jennings, "A Case Study of Tenant Union Legalism," in Steve Burghardt, ed., *Tenants and the Urban Housing Crisis* (Dexter, Mich.: The New Press, 1972), pp. 47–48.

Often they opt for one major goal or the other. For example, some rent strike groups have dropped their analysis for the maintenance of a limited rent strike; others use their ideological perspective in militant, ad hoc settings that attract new members but do little to keep older ones.[39] The first choice leads to lost ideology; the second heightens consciousness but can destroy the organization.

Likewise, organizers find themselves pulled into a variety of roles, often inappropriately. Many social activists have watched or lived through the following scenario more than once: A dynamic, galvanizing orator, accustomed to the excitement of a group's militant beginnings, six months later projects such a strong activist stance that new members in the group become terrified at all the work projected ahead. Trying to recoup, the overly dynamic organizer then becomes so conciliatory that older members are turned off by all the apparent sweet talk. Not wishing to appear a hypocrite, the organizer *then* returns to the former style, only now his or her voice has a quaver in it. In the end, nothing seems effective, and the organizer is left trying to see where his or her group went.

Neither groups nor organizers need opt for such miserable extremes. Both can avoid slipping into such polar options by clearly differentiating the group into "evaluation" and "control" stages, with appropriate roles and behaviors in each. For example, many socialist organizations have a well-developed education program for new members. They are expected to attend and learn about the group's goals and activities at these sessions. This structured "evaluation" stage allows both the new members and the group to evaluate each other before one enters the more demand-

ing "control" tasks of the organization. Here, once the value of the group is understood, formal expertise may relate to ideological training, but the point is the same whether it is a political organization or a well-developed rent strike organization.

The organizer can expect to differentiate his or her roles in an equally appropriate manner. A good example of where that role differentiation can and must take place is in group meetings. By planning the agenda so that different items fall neatly within one group stage (say, evaluation) and another set of agenda items fits into another (perhaps control), the organizer can adapt the correct role to the stage itself.

For example, a Southern Africa Liberation Committee in New York had recently been involved in extensive organizing in the Bronx. Those attending the meeting fell into three distinct groups: very experienced political activists; politically inexperienced committee members active in the work for some time; and numerous new people attending their first meeting. The agenda, prepared by members of the first two subgroups but directed mostly by the experienced members, reflected the divergent membership needs.

The style and role of the organizers reflected those needs. The early agenda items were devoted to introducing new members, explaining the group's work, and going over immediate activity. The organizers, especially the chair, were relaxed, informal, and yet informative. New people were made to feel comfortable, their questions were solicited and answered, etc. Tasks of leadership development were carried out: those with "informal" expertise, the politically inexperienced activists, had been given assignments on explaining the work itself. An "enabling" style fit nicely in the group's evaluation period of the meeting.

As the meeting progressed, a direct political talk was given—again, using a rela-

---

[39] For examples, see the case histories in Steve Burghardt, ed., *Tenants and the Urban Housing Crisis, op. cit.*

tively informal style consistent with the group's goal of increased community involvement. At the same time, much preparation had gone into the talk: political information was complete and precise, so that the political goals related to understanding Southern African Liberation were clear to all. The enabling role projected a style of leadership direct and expertly formed so that both new members and those already active but politically inexperienced would gain from the political analysis. There was plenty of time for questions, but no one belied the seriousness with which members approached the problems in southern Africa and the importance of transmitting the awareness of such problems to the community at large. The "orientation" phase—where problems are specified—had been indirectly but clearly developed in the talk itself.

Finally, moving into a concrete "control" stage that demanded involved activity around a material support campaign (shoes, clothing, Tampax, etc.), the chair and other prepared committee members firmly outlined the tasks ahead, giving assignments, making precise, short pitches to join various committees, etc. Here the emphasis was on crisp facilitation and expertise, with little room for chitchat. Afterwards, when the meeting was formally over, people returned to the more relaxed, personable style of the earlier part of the meeting. But the mixture of group stages,

reflective of differing strategic goals, had been achieved through a nice blending of organizing roles and membership styles of participation. While the effectiveness of the evening was greatly due to the importance of the issue, it was clear that the organizational preparation had smoothed the path to the group's success.

The typology shown in Table 6.2 should help explain the general structural development of groups. It first shows the dominant group stage of their initial development and then presents the structure of each organization once they seek to maintain themselves in the community.

The table outlines the "mixing and phasing" of a group's structure once it has survived its initial period of growth and development. Most groups rarely get beyond their initial attempts at organizing, regardless of strategic orientation. For those who wish to continue their effectiveness, however, the initial goals, tasks, and strategies that propelled them into activity should not be mistaken for having the inherent structural ability of maintaining an on-going community organization.

An organizer, besides concentrating on these more political issues, will gain in effectiveness if he or she is cognizant of how group development can impede or enhance overall strategic success. Likewise, in using his or her introspective skills to individually develop a better understanding of membership needs (including one's own), the orga-

TABLE 6.2
Community Organization Strategy and Long-Term Group Structure

Strategy	Initial Level of Cohesion	Initial Dominant Group Phase	Long-Term Group Stages
Locality Development	Low	Evaluation	1. Evaluation 2. Control
Social Planning	Moderate	1. Control 2. Evaluation	Control
Social Action	High	1. Evaluation 2. Control	Evaluation/Control

nizer may smooth out the group's basic operations. While it must be repeated that nothing can substitute for galvanizing issues, political clout, and a little money, group process skills can make the work a lot more pleasant for all concerned and—with luck—may actually help get the job done.

7.

Edward J. Pawlak

ORGANIZATIONAL MANEUVERING: INTRA-ORGANIZATIONAL CHANGE TACTICS*

To help community organizers improve their skills in dealing with organizations, this chapter identifies tactics they can use to tinker with or maneuver organizational structure, modes of operation, rules, conventions, policy, and programs. The specific tactics discussed treat bureaucratic succession and rules, the white paper or position paper, demonstration projects, modification of board composition, bypassing, influencing grant reviews, leaking information, and protest by resignation. Although the author takes the perspective of agency practitioners, it does not follow that managers are necessarily villains. However, some of the tactics identified here are directed toward those administrators who cause practitioners to harbor severe misgivings about the organization.

The focus of community organization effort extends outward from a change organization toward the community, its people and institutions. Nevertheless, circumstances inside the change agency can constrain or cripple the work of the practitioner–change agent. For this reason practitioners often find it necessary to deal

with internal factors to enhance their capacity to have positive effects on community problems or to provide better service to client groups.

This chapter not only stems from the author's observation of and experience with organizational change, but also draws on contributions of others who have addressed similar themes.[1] It alerts practitioners to

---

[1] See Scott Briar, "The Casework Predicament," Irving Piliavin, "Restructuring the Provision of Social Services," and Harry Specht, "Casework Practice and Social Policy Formulation," *Social Work*, 13 (January 1968), pp. 9–10, 34–36, and 42–43; Archie Hanlan, "Casework Beyond Bureaucracy," *Social Casework*, 52 (April 1971), pp. 195–98; Lawrence Podell and Ronald Miller, *Professionalism in Public Social Services*, Vol. 1, No. 2 "Study Series" (New York: Human Resources Administration, 1974); and Naomi Gottlieb, *The Welfare Bind* (New York: Columbia University Press, 1974), p. 34. Also see Thomas F. Maher, "Freedom of Speech in Public Agencies," *Social Work*, 19 (November 1974), pp. 698–703; Joseph J. Senna, "Changes in Due Process of Law," *Social Work*, 19 (May 1974), pp. 319–24; Irwin Hyman and Karen Schreiber, "The School Psychologist as Child Advocate," *Children Today*, 3 (March–April 1974), pp. 21–33, 36; Rino J. Patti and Herman Resnick, "Changing the Agency from Within," *Social Work*, 17 (July 1972) pp. 48–57; George Brager, "Advocacy and Political Behavior," *Social Work*, 13 (April 1968), pp. 5–15; Carl Martin, "Beyond Bureaucracy," *Child Welfare*, 1 (July 1971) pp. 384–88; Warren G. Bennis, "Post-Bureaucratic Leadership," *Trans-Action*, 6 (July–August 1969), pp. 44–52; and Harold Weissman, *Overcoming Mismanagement in the Human Service Professions* (San Francisco: Jossey-Bass, 1973).

© 1976 National Association of Social Workers, Inc. Reprinted from SOCIAL WORK, Vol. 21, No. 5 (September 1976), pp. 376–380. Revised 1978.

bear in mind the pitfalls and dilemmas of intra-organizational change—that it takes place in a political climate and in a structure of authority, norms, and sanctions.[2]

BUREAUCRATIC SUCCESSION

Bureaucratic succession usually refers to a change in leadership at the highest levels of an organization. Here, however, the author uses the broader concept that includes changes in leadership at all levels in the hierarchy.[3] Bureaucratic succession must be called to the attention of practitioners because it is an opportunity to influence intra-organizational change. For the practitioner to exert influence during this phase of organizational transition, it is essential that he understand certain features of organizational life that frequently accompany succession.

Prior to an administrator's departure, organizations usually go into a period of inaction. Most staff members are aware of the lame-duck character of this phase of organizational life, when any major change is avoided until the new administrator takes office. There are, however, ways in which practitioners take advantage of this period. They can, for example, (1) suggest criteria for the selection of a successor, (2) seek membership on the search committee, (3) prepare a position paper for the new administrator, (4) propose a revision in the governance structure to enhance participatory management, (5) organize fellow subordinates to propose changes that had been unacceptable to the outgoing administrator, or (6) propose the formulation of a task force to facilitate transition.

The "first one hundred days" is another critical phase of bureaucratic succession that should be examined for the opportunities it offers. Although new administrators tend to be conservative about implementing change until they are more familiar with the organization, they still are interested in development and in making their own mark. This three-month period, therefore, provides opportunities to orient and shape the perceptions of the new administrator who, until he acquires his own intelligence about the organization, may be both vulnerable and receptive to influence.

The following case illustrates how practitioners can tinker with organizational hierarchy by taking advantage of a resignation.

> The resignation of the director of staff development in a child welfare agency provided the staff with an opportunity to influence the transformation of the position into that of administrative assistant. The agency had recently undergone rapid growth in staff size, resources, and diversity, without an accompanying increase in the administrative staff. Thus, the resignation became the occasion for examining whether the position should be modified to serve such administrative staff functions as program development and grant management.

Bureaucratic succession, therefore, provides an opportunity for an organization to take pause; to examine its mission, structure, policies, practices, accomplishments,

[2] See Rino J. Patti, "Organizational Resistance and Change: The View from Below," *Social Service Review,* 48 (September 1974), pp. 367–83; Edward Weisband and Thomas M. Franck, *Resignation in Protest* (New York: Grossman Publishers, 1975); Ralph Nader, Peter J. Petkas, and Kate Blackwell, *Whistle-Blowing* (New York: Grossman Publishers, 1972); Irwin Epstein, "Social Workers and Social Action," *Social Work,* 13 (April 1968), pp. 101–8 and "Professional Role Orientations and Conflict Strategies," *Social Work,* 15 (October 1970), pp. 87–92; and A. D. Green, "The Professional Social Worker in the Bureaucracy," *Social Service Review,* 40 (March 1966), pp. 71–83.

[3] For a more detailed discussion of bureaucratic succession, see Bernard Levenson, "Bureaucratic Succession," in Amitai Etzioni, ed., *Complex Organizations* (New York: Holt, Rinehart & Winston, 1961), pp. 362–365; and Alvin Gouldner, *Patterns of Industrial Bureaucracy* (Glencoe, Ill.: Free Press, 1954), pp. 59–104.

and problems; and to decide what it wants to become. Practitioners can use this as an opportunity to participate in these processes and to take advantage of the structure of influence during that vulnerable phase.

RULES

Rules are features of organizations that, by their nature, invite tinkering. They act as mechanisms of social control and standardization, provide guidelines for decision-making, limit discretion, and structure relationships between persons and units within the organizational structure and between separate organizations.[4] There are two types of rules—formal and informal. Formal rules are derived from law or are determined administratively or collectively. Informal rules—which may be as binding as formal ones—are practices that have been routinized so that they have become organizational conventions or traditions. Rules vary in specificity, in their inherent demand for compliance, in the manner in which compliance is monitored, and in their sanctions for a lack of compliance.

Practitioners can tinker with rules either by the kind of interpretations they apply to them or by using their discretion, as is permitted with an ambiguous or general rule. Rules do not necessarily eliminate discretion but they may eliminate alternatives that might otherwise be considered.[5] Gottlieb describes them as follows:

> Rules are not necessarily static. They appear to be a controlling force working impersonally and equally, but they vary both in adherence and enforceability and are

used variously by staff in their adaptation to the "welfare bind."[6]

Hanlan suggests that "in public welfare there exists an informal system that operates without invoking the formal administrative machinery of rules."[7] The author overheard the director of a community action program encourage new workers "to err on the side of generosity in determining eligibility for programs." A vocational rehabilitation counselor reported that many clients received dental care through his liberal interpretation of a rule that allows for the provision of dental services for only those clients whose appearance and dental problems would otherwise have prevented them from being considered for employment involving public contact. These are among many illustrations that show that one can tinker with the manner in which rules are interpreted and enforced.

Another way of tinkering with rules is to avoid what Gottlieb calls "rule interpretations by agents of the system alone."[8] She goes on to report that welfare workers encouraged clients to seek help in interpreting rules enforced by the National Welfare Rights Organization (NWRO). It is generally known that legal-aid clinics have been called on to give a legal interpretation of welfare rules and rules governing commitment to mental hospitals.

A supervisor for public assistance eligibility once reported that a thorough knowledge of all the rules enables the welfare worker to invoke one rule over another in order to help clients get what they need. This observation is supported by Gottlieb, who points out that rules allow for excep-

---

[4]For a detailed discussion, see Charles Perrow, *Complex Organizations: A Critical Essay* (Glenview, Ill.: Scott Foresman & Co.), pp. 23–32.

[5]James D. Thompson, *Organizations in Action* (New York: McGraw-Hill Book Co., 1967), p. 120.

[6]Gottlieb, *op. cit.,* p. 8.

[7]Archie Hanlan, "Counteracting Problems of Bureaucracy in Public Welfare," *Social Work,* 12 (July 1967), p. 63.

[8]Gottlieb, *op. cit.,* p. 8.

tions and that many NWRO members know the rules better than the workers and thus can challenge their interpretations.[9] In his study of regulatory agencies, Nader suggests that rules are both opportunities for action and potential obstacles and that major effort is frequently required to persuade the agency to follow its own rules.[10]

Another way of dealing with rules is to avoid asking for an interpretation. One agency administrator has suggested that personnel should not routinely ask for rulings and urges them to use their own discretion. He commented: "If you invoke authority, you put me in a position where I must exercise it. If I make a decision around here, it becomes a rule."

These ways of tinkering with rules suggest that practitioners should examine the function of rules, discern the latitude they are allowed in interpreting them, and exercise discretion. Although the foregoing examples are primarily taken from welfare settings, the principles outlined can be applied to other settings. In community organization agencies where action takes place in an open, fluid context rather than inside a tightly controlled bureaucracy, there are particular opportunities for practitioner discretion.

WHITE PAPER OR POSITION PAPER

Too often practitioners rely on the anecdotal or case approach to influence change in an organization. Such an approach is too easily countered by the rejoinder that exceptional cases do not require a change in policy but should be handled as exceptions. The white paper, or position paper, is a much ignored means of tinkering with organization.

A white paper is a report on a specific subject that emanates from a recent investigation. A position paper is a statement that sets forth a policy or a perspective. The first is usually more carefully reasoned and documented; the second may be argued instead of reasoned. Both white papers and position papers provide opportunities for social documentation and for formulating a compelling case. Such statements strive for logic and are characterized by their use of both quantitative and qualitative data. As the following example shows, by virtue of their character and quality, both position papers and white papers demand a specific response.

A student social worker wrote a position paper identifying the number of teenage pregnancies, the number of associated medical problems, and the high rate of venereal disease among adolescents. She argued for the redirection of the original planned parenthood proposal from the main office to satellite clinics in public housing developments and schools. The paper was well received and spurred the executive to obtain funding from the housing authority.

DEMONSTRATION PROJECTS

Lindblom has characterized decision-making in organizations as "disjointed incrementalism."[11] Simon indicates that organizations "satisfice"—that is, they make decisions that are "good enough," rather than ideal. Uncertainties in the environment, the inability to scan all alternatives, and the unknown utility of a solution or decision all preclude optimal decision-making. If organizations were to try to comprehend all the information and contingencies necessary before making a rational

---

[9] *Ibid.,* p. 32.
[10] Nader, Petkas, and Blackwell, *op. cit.*

[11] Charles E. Lindblom, "The Science of Muddling Through," in Fred Cox et al., eds. *Strategies of Community Organization* (Itasca, Ill.: F. E. Peacock Publishers, 1970).

decision, the complexity would be over-whelming.[12] Thus, organizations are reluctant to make changes on a large scale because this could lead to large-scale and unpredictable consequences. Resistance to change, therefore, may often be attributed to structure rather than to a malevolent or unsympathetic administrator. This calls attention to organizational structure and processes, but does not mean that the values and roles of administrators are to be ignored.[13]

Given this perspective of organizational behavior, practitioners may consider approaching innovation incrementally and on a small scale by first gaining authorization for a demonstration project.[14] A demonstration project may be bounded by the duration of time or the proportion of the budget or staff time that is devoted to it. The problem with demonstration projects is that the people for whom the demonstration is being carried out are not always specified, nor are they always kept abreast of developments. Often there is a failure to articulate the ramifications and consequences of a successful or unsuccessful demonstration. Practitioners must develop a strategy of demonstration—a means of diffusing innovation throughout the organization or into other organizations and of obtaining commitments from the administration when the demonstration is complete. The following is an example of the commitment one social worker obtained.

---

[12]Herbert A. Simon, *Administrative Behavior* (2d ed., New York: The Macmillan Co., 1957); and Herbert A. Simon, *Models of Man, Social and Rational* (New York: John Wiley & Sons, 1957).

[13]For a useful discussion on organizational resistance to change, see Rino J. Patti, "Organizational Resistance and Change: The View from Below," *op. cit.*

[14]For a negative view of demonstration grants, see George E. Pratt, "The Demonstration Grant is Probably Counterproductive," *Social Work* 19 (July 1974) pp. 486–89.

A community worker in a traditional family service agency was attempting to develop the concept of outreach services. She believed the agency should work directly with clients in a low-income housing project, rather than expecting them—or, more likely, middle-class substitutes—to come to the agency offices. The problem was to convince the agency's board to provide this type of service and the housing manager to clear the way for it to operate within the housing project. The community worker decided to involve a small group of residents living in a court in a low cost housing project. She was able to convince the housing authority that social work intervention could make a difference in the social problems in the housing project; reduce the social causes for eviction. A subgoal was the introduction and sustaining of an out-reach program by the agency to housing project residents. The agency selected one court (five families) out of the entire project as a demonstration; set up a time limit for evaluative purposes; promised progress reports at specific intervals; and met with the residents regularly as well as just "dropping in." This plan was submitted in writing to the board along with periodic progress reports.

The plan worked almost too well in that it was constantly referred to in agency board meetings; the out-reach idea was new but it really impressed the board and the housing director, and was accepted as a legitimate and appropriate agency program. The results with the residents were not as spectacular, but represented at least a beginning. The agency gradually expanded to other courts.

MODIFYING BOARD COMMITTEE COMPOSITION

Agency board committees are typically composed of elected members and the executive director of the agency. In addition, in some agencies, one or two staff members may also serve on committees or occasionally attend meetings to make reports. One strategy of tinkering with the composition of a committee and the kind of information and influence it receives is to promote the idea that nonboard and nonstaff members with certain expertise be included on the committee. For example, a social planner influenced a planning committee to rotate nonvoting professional advisors on and off the committee to provide support to lay members who were hesitant to recommend discontinuance of certain programs.

BYPASSING

Bypassing refers to a process whereby a practitioner avoids taking a proposal for change or a grievance to his immediate superior but seeks instead a hearing or decision from a higher level in the hierarchy. In an enlightened organization, this form of bypassing is acceptable and even encouraged; government workers, in fact, are entitled to it as part of "due process." Bypassing is risky, however, in that it can discredit the judgment of the complainant if the matter is trivial or if it appears that it could have been resolved at a lower level in the hierarchy. Bypassing also places the administration in a vulnerable situation because if the tactic is justified, it reflects poorly on the judgment of the superior and the administrators who hired him. This may lead to questions of nonretention or spur a desired resignation. A successful instance of bypassing is described in the following example:

When an agency worker's complaints concerning the physical plant and security of a youth home went unheeded by the director, he demanded to meet with the executive committee of the board. The director admitted that his own sense of urgency differed from that of his staff, but arranged for the meeting. The executive committee approved some of the recommendations for change and authorized that they be implemented as soon as possible.

INFLUENCING GRANT REVIEWS

Agencies often write grant applications for funds to support their programs. A critical phase of the application process occurs at a public review of the grant application when the funding agency invites comments or letters of support from interested parties. If a practitioner is dissatisfied with a particular program, and if it is an important matter, he can provide the agency issuing the grant with dissenting information, testify at the review of the grant application, or respond from the standpoint of an "expert witness." In any event, the grant-review process may be an opportunity to voice concern about an agency's program and to influence the advisory group to give conditional approval or disapproval. As is shown in the following example, practitioners may attempt to influence the review process indirectly—by encouraging an expert third party to raise questions about the grant application—or directly.

A social worker was asked to serve as a technical reviewer for a volunteer program for young offenders in a regional planning advisory group. The program was modeled after an existing program in another part of the state. The documents supporting the application contained a manual that described the role of the volunteer. It suggested that a volunteer should report any violations of parole to the corrections authority but should not reveal this action to the offender. In seeming contradiction, it emphasized that the volunteer should be a "friend" of the offender. The social worker informed the advisory group of this provision and of his strenuous objection to it. The director of the program had failed to read the manual thoroughly and was unaware of the statement. The advisory group approved the program on the condition that the volunteer not serve as an informer and demanded that the staff codify the conditions under which it may be morally imperative for the volunteer to reveal the offender's behavior.

Social workers are often asked to, and frequently do, endorse a program or a grant application perfunctorily, without having read the proposal. In other instances, programs and grants are endorsed in spite of strong reservations. Notwithstanding the pressures toward reciprocity that exist among agencies, such exchanges of professional courtesy are questionable.

Social workers should take advantage of requests for endorsement or participation in the grant-review process, particularly if they believe that certain aspects of a proposal or program are questionable. The desire for professional endorsement also underlies agency efforts to recruit practitioners for board membership or as paid consultants. Refusal of such offers is a way of "making a statement" about a program.

RADICAL TACTICS

Leaking information, or the covert release of information about an organization, is a tactic that should be used only in grave matters after all other remedies within the organization have been exhausted. The third party to whom the informant gives the information has to verify it and the credibility of the informant, since he is not willing to put his own character and job on the line. However, until "blowing the whistle" becomes an accepted institutionalized value, and until protections are legislated, it is likely that members of organizations engaged in these acts will continue to be viewed as "guerillas in the bureaucracy."[15]

Practitioners who anticipate the need to leak information would be well advised to

seek counsel, for discovery could result in liability damages. They are obliged to have a thorough, accurate, and verifiable account of the objectionable situation. As the ethics of leaking information have not been well formulated, practitioners need to consider carefully the professional, moral, and legal standards that support such action.[16] One way to attack the problem is shown as follows.

> The agency worker in a foregoing example who was concerned about the physical plant and security of a youth home notified the state monitor about the condition of the home. At the next site visit, the monitor raised questions about the residents' access to balconies and the roof and about the staff-client ratio on weekends.

Resignation in protest, or public defection, is another tactic that should be used only when a practitioner experiences unbearable misgivings and finds it both morally and professionally imperative to reveal them publicly. The major problem is that the organization has the financial and operational resources to counter the protest, but the employee has none. Also, with few exceptions, resignation in protest has a history of aversive consequences for the protester.[17]

A resignation in protest may discredit agency administrators who may respond by attempting to repudiate or challenge the claims of the protester. Therefore, prospective protesters must be prepared to have their observations and conclusions verified and their judgment subjected to public review and scrutiny. In addition, the protester must realize that future employers will wonder whether such history of protestation will continue. An example follows.

---

[15]Nader, Petkas and Blackwell, *op. cit.,* pp. 15, 25–33; and Martin L. Needleman and Carolyn Emerson Needleman, *Guerillas in the Bureaucracy* (New York: John Wiley & Sons, 1974).

[16]For some guidelines on this matter, see Nader, Petkas, and Blackwell, *op. cit.,* pp. vii, 1–8, 29–30, 225–30.

[17]See Weisband and Franck, *op. cit.*

When his concerns went unheeded by the board, a social worker resigned in protest. Moreover, he informed the board and the director that he would discourage any professional worker from accepting employment at the agency. He was effective in discouraging local professionals from accepting employment at the agency unless firm commitments were made to modify policies and practices that were detrimental to clients.

The theory of escalation urges the protester to begin by using conventional and formal means to express grievances and influence change. Only after these have been exhausted, and traditional means have encountered failure and resistance, should he engage in a series of escalations to such unconventional or radical forms of protest as boycotting, "palace revolts," picketing, leaking information, and the like. The essential point of this strategy is that the protester should not begin by engaging in the most radical and abrasive strategy. To document the intransigence of the bureaucracy, change must be approached incrementally. If this is not done, the bureaucracy may point to the failure to follow administrative due process. The protester's etiquette and failure to go through channels then become the bone of contention, and the protester becomes the object of protest.[18]

It is likely that practitioners identified with particular models of community organization practice will favor one or another mode of internal manuevering. For example, the social actionist may have an affinity for radical tactics. The social planner would be attracted to the rationality of the white paper. The locality development person might find the demonstration project compatible, with its slow, incremental flow which allows for discussion of results along the way. Other maneuvers might be acceptable to all practitioner groups, such as taking advantage of bureaucratic succession to introduce needed changes. The point here is not advocacy of a particular way of tinkering within the organization, but rather to recognize that internal change effort—by means judged to be effective and ethical on the part of the actor—is an integral part of a community organization practitioner's role.

As a condition of employment and as a professional right and responsibility, practitioners should have the opportunity to bring their insights into the plans and programs of the organization they work for. Such participation requires that practitioners acquire skill in dealing with organizations. It is hoped that the participation of practitioners in organizational activity will promote more responsive service delivery systems and more satisfactory work climates.

At the risk of appearing to be a "double agent," the author plans to write a second article to advise administrators on how to cope with the tinkering of practitioners. After all, organizational power—whether in the hands of practitioners or administrators—"must be insecure to some degree if it is to be more responsible."[19]

---

[18] *Ibid.,* pp. 55–94; Needleman and Needleman, *op. cit.,* 285–289, 335–339; and Nader, Petkas, and Blackwell, *op. cit.,* p. 16–25.

---

[19] Nader, Petkas, and Blackwell, *op. cit.,* p. 15.

8.

Yeheskel Hasenfeld

PROGRAM DEVELOPMENT

INTRODUCTION

Program development and implementation is a common and crucial task of community organization practitioners, yet it has not received adequate attention in practice theory. There seems to be an implicit assumption that, once the community organization practitioner has successfully mobilized action groups or planning task forces to grapple with important community issues, his function is essentially completed. Yet, the most critical element in any community organization activity is the emergence of some idea and design for a *program,* be it a direct service delivery, a training program, a coordination council, a fund-raising program, or the like.

The implementation of such a program, which in almost all instances requires the development of some organizational framework, is in the last analysis the true test of successful community organization, since the program provides in very concrete terms the outputs or services desired and needed by the community. Thus, the overall thesis of this paper is that the community organization practitioner has the dual role of action mobilizer and planner, and of organizer and program implementer. In

this paper, then, I discuss some of the major tasks and skills that the practitioner needs to know and fulfill in order to successfully implement a community-generated program. The term planner-organizer is used to designate the complexity of such a role.

Most frequently, the planner-organizer is asked to develop a program for direct service delivery. Social action groups often develop service programs in order to serve people ignored by existing services, or as a means of gaining community support, or as a device to stimulate existing service providers to change their own programs. Examples include unions instituting information and referral services and recreation programs for retired workers, and the Black Panthers setting up a breakfast meal service and elementary school education program for neighborhood children. Thus, the discussion that follows will focus on program development for direct services. Nevertheless, the tasks and skills involved are clearly applicable to other types of programs.

Development of a new program is by no means an easy undertaking. It often requires a prolonged process of negotiation and planning. Launching a new service inevitably results in some disruption of the delicate balance that exists among various service providers. Some agency representatives may feel they were excluded from participation. Others may see the new program as a challenge to their own domain. While the planner-organizer may find it necessary to disagree with certain groups who oppose

Adapted from "Guide to Agency Development for Area Planners in Aging," Project T.A.P., funded by the Administration on Aging, Grant SRS-HEW 94-P-76007/5-01 to the Institute of Gerontology, University of Michigan/Wayne State University and the University of Michigan School of Social Work Continuing Education Program.

the program, he or she must have enough support and sufficient resources to withstand countervailing pressures.

Every new program requires resources—in particular, money and manpower. Without a fair chance of obtaining these, no effort to develop a new program is likely to succeed. The key to the success of a new venture could be the extent to which the planner-organizer is in a position to control at least some of the funds allocable to the relevant social service programs. Yet money without capable or trainable manpower is of little avail. And without facilities, legitimacy, or some other needed resource, both money and manpower may be expended without benefit to consumers. The planner-organizer must be willing to invest a significant proportion of time to mobilize needed resources and to influence this allocation.

THE SYSTEMS PERSPECTIVE

In considering the establishment of a new program or agency, the planner-organizer may find a "systems" perspective to be particularly useful. Each agency can be viewed as an open "system," composed of a set of interrelated units designed to achieve a common objective or complex of objectives. The activities of these units are aimed at (1) recruiting such *inputs* into the agency as money and credit, manpower, and clients; (2) transforming these inputs into actual services such as medical care, counseling, or community planning; (3) producing *output* in such forms as improved social services coordination, reduction in the incidence of need for protective services, etc.[1]

Service and Maintenance Functions

A second assumption underlying the systems perspective is that the activities of the agency staff are guided by two basic motivations. The first can be termed the goal-seeking motive leading to "service" objectives and the second the self-maintenance motive leading to "survival" objectives. The first motive informs those staff activities designed to achieve the *output* goals of the agency. The self-maintenance motive informs those efforts by staff to maintain the agency through enhancing its access to resources, expanding its services, building a positive climate of public support, etc. Clearly, no agency can achieve its service objectives without consideration of its maintenance needs or survival objectives. Yet if the agency invests all its energies in self-maintenance it will be accused of not accomplishing, indeed of subverting, its service objectives.[2] Both sets of activities are often in tension, causing intraorganizational competition for scarce resources. Improper allocation of these resources reduces the effectiveness of any service provider.

The interplay between the goal-seeking or service function of an agency and its survival needs or maintenance function can be observed in its internal structure. From a systems perspective, five subsystems within an organization are identifiable, each fulfilling an important function without which the agency is likely to experience strain and possible disintegration. Each subsystem is characterized by the function it fulfills in the agency and by a common motivation of those participating in it. The subsystems may be characterized as:

(1) the technical, (2) the environmental support, (3) the institutional, (4) the intelligence, and (5) the managerial subsystems.[3]

---

[1] See for example, D. Katz and R. Kahn, *The Social Psychology of Organizations* (New York: Wiley, 1966); F. Baker ed., *Organizational Systems* (Homewood, Ill.: Richard D. Irwin, 1973).

[2] R. A. Scott, "The Factory as a Social Service Organization," *Social Problems,* 15 (Fall, 1967): 160–75.

[3] D. Katz and R. Kahn, *op. cit.,* Chapter 4.

Subsystems and Their Functions

1. The function of the *technical subsystem* is to provide a service. In a social service agency, it is generally designed to improve or maintain the well-being of a client or client population. The primary motivation of the agency staff providing these services is to achieve proficiency in these assigned tasks. The range of tasks they perform may include assessment of the client's needs; evaluation of the client's resources; counseling or treatment; and referrals to other service providers. The manner in which these tasks are performed is called the agency's service technology.

2. The *environmental support subsystem's* function is to manage or recruit those resources from the environment necessary to the performance of the tasks of the technical subsystems. At least five categories of resources must be brought into the agency: (1) money and credit to cover the costs involved in providing the services and performing other functions; (2) personnel such as administrators, social workers, counselors, clerical staff, and other support staff; (3) clients whose needs or interests can be served by the agency; (4) knowledge and expertise necessary for the successful implementation of the services; and (5) complementary services of other agencies necessary to ensure that the agency's services are effective.

Procurement and management of these resources requires a variety of transactions or exchanges with those external units in the environment (other systems) that control these resources. This requires that certain agency employees perform what systems theorists call "boundary roles": roles that are necessary to develop and facilitate transactions between the organization and its environment. Boundary relationships are generally managed by agency staff with special responsibility for these tasks. For example, when budget staff negotiate with state and national officials for the allocation of fiscal resources, they manage boundary relationships leading to input of fiscal resources. When personnel workers interview or recruit potential staff, intake workers screen potential clients, and various staff members develop relations with other social service agencies, each also performs a boundary role or assumes a boundary function. In most smaller agencies, many of these boundary relationships are likely to be fulfilled by the same person or persons. These activities enable the agency to achieve some mastery over its environment, leading to procurement of needed resources with some degree of certainty or stability.[4]

3. Staff performing *institutional subsystem* functions seek to obtain social support and legitimation for the agency from the environment. Without such support, the agency cannot hope to obtain the resources necessary for other functions. Sometimes, legitimation is in the form of a legal mandate, such as the Housing Act, Medicare, the Social Security Act, or other legislation.

Without understating the importance of these legislative acts, one should not ignore the importance of obtaining social support in the very community in which the program operates. This includes support from potential clients, various civic organizations, governmental agencies, and other social service agencies. Staff activities involve the development of ties with key community influentials, contribution of resources to important community functions, public exposition of the agency's services, etc. Such activities are oriented toward "institutionalizing" the agency in the community,

---

[4]H. Aldrich, "Organizational Boundaries and Inter-organizational Conflict," *Human Relations* 24 (1971): 279–293.

assuring it will be perceived as integral and indispensable to the community's interests.[5]

4. The ability of the agency to develop effective linkages with its external environment as well as an effective service delivery system is dependent on the operation of the agency's *intelligence and feedback mechanisms.* The functions of the intelligence subsystem are: (1) to gather and interpret vital information about the conditions of the target population for which the service is developed and about other potential client populations, about new service opportunities, about the needs and attributes of the clients served, etc.; and (2) to provide feedback to the staff of the agency on the outcomes of their efforts. This may include information about the results of client referrals to various services, evaluation of staff activities in the counseling and treatment of clients, or assessment of the "progress" being made by those clients.

Intelligence activities can help the agency to reduce uncertainty about its efforts and can be used to plan on a more rational basis. Without adequate intelligence, any agency is in danger of finding itself off target or out of the mainstream of client needs.

5. Activities of the *managerial subsystem* cut across all the other subsystems in the agency. Management is in charge of making the key decisions regarding what services get delivered, by whom, and how; relations with the environment; and the use of intelligence. The major tasks of management are: (1) to coordinate the activities of the various subsystems in the agency; (2) to resolve conflicts between the various hierarchical levels, and to elicit the compliance of staff to their work requirements; and (3) to effect coordination between the external demands

on the agency and its own resources and needs. Management acts to achieve control and stability within the agency and to mediate and achieve a compromise between the various needs and demands of the subsystems of which it is composed.

From this rather brief overview, it should be apparent that each subsystem is dependent on inputs from the others in order to fulfill its function. The quality of the performance of each subsystem profoundly affects the quality of work done in other parts of the agency. A change in one subsystem is likely to affect the performance of the others. For example, increased intelligence activities may result in increased capacity to enlist new services for the target population, which in turn influences the ability of those performing the service technology of the agency to help those clients.

Starting a New Service or Program

An understanding of these systemic functions is necessary in any effort to establish a new service or program or to modify and expand an existing one. In choosing whether to work through an existing agency or to establish a new agency, the planner-organizer must consider the costs and advantages of building from what already exists as against building something entirely new.

Developing a new agency to serve certain needs has the clear advantage of freeing the planner from the constraints of existing arrangements. These may include competing objectives of ongoing community agencies as well as tradition, and the custom of following established procedures. Overcoming such obstacles is by no means easy. Consider, for example, the difficulties that might be anticipated in attempting to shift the program focus of a medical clinic serving primarily young mothers and their chil-

[5]C. Perrow, *Organizational Analysis* (Belmont, Calif.: Wadsworth, 1970): 92–132.

dren, to a medical check-up program for the aging, or of getting a citywide planning agency to develop neighborhood planning "outposts."

Adding a new program to an existing agency may result in serious coordination problems between functional units, may lead to conflict with other agency activities, and may ultimately lead to its "benign neglect."

On the other hand, establishing a new agency is often costlier than expanding the services of an existing organization. An established agency is often well recognized and supported in the community. Its staff have the training and experience to run the agency and know how to handle all its administrative details. Moreover, the agency may have all the basic equipment necessary for the new service or program. New agencies often flounder because of the lack of experience and expertise.

PROCEDURES IN ORGANIZING A NEW SERVICE OR PROGRAM

Identifying the Need for Service

No new agency or program should be initiated unless it is propelled by the existence of a concrete and viable need. Self-evident as this may seem, attempts are too often made to develop new services without a clear definition and articulation of the needs to be met. Lack of clarity and specificity of needs is likely to result in two undesirable consequences. First, it makes it far more difficult to mobilize community support for the new program. Second, the actual design of the program may be haphazard, ad hoc, often leading to ineffectiveness and inefficiency. A cardinal principle in program design is that the greater the clarity of the program's objectives, the better its chances for success.

Identifying unmet needs in the community is a complex task that necessitates several steps. The concept of "need" itself often defies adequate definition. What is perceived as a need by one group may not be so considered by another. Nevertheless, there are a number of ways in which planners can get a quick orientation to needs. The following are illustrative strategies:

1. Planners might start by examining available statistical reports such as census data, local Social Security office data, county government surveys, health surveys. While information on the number of potential clients in a given area, their distribution in various neighborhoods, their level of income, housing patterns, health conditions and the like might not indicate what they "need," such information is often suggestive.

2. The planner-organizer might then take a second step: identifying the various agencies in the area that serve the community. This involves finding out whom these agencies serve and what types of services they offer. Statistical reports issued by relevant agencies, the local welfare council and the public social service agencies may be of particular importance. Some communities may have developed information systems for a network of agencies that could provide invaluable data to the planner-organizer.[6]

3. A third step is to explore with the staff of the agencies that are current or potential providers of services to the target population the concerns and problems they have identified regarding gaps or inequities in services.

---

[6]See for example, CHILDATA. Council for Community Services in Metropolitan Chicago.

4. Very early in the process, planners should meet with community groups to discuss their wants, preferences, and interests.
5. A more systematic data-gathering procedure might be developed through a "needs survey" of the neighborhoods in which potential clients are most likely to reside. The facilities of a college or university or a local mental health center, as well as civic groups and volunteers, can be mobilized to conduct the survey. Questions should be designed to elicit information about the problems and unmet needs of those interviewed. A social-indicators–type survey is one of the most useful of the new devices to get at such information.[7]

An important concomitant of the planner's information-gathering activities is his or her effort to increase the community's awareness of the needs of the target population. Involvement of community leaders and representatives of agencies in determination of these needs sensitizes them to existing problems and lays the groundwork for mobilizing them into action. Awareness on the part of key groups and agencies in the community is often fundamental to the initiation of new programs.

Mobilizing Support for the Service

It is extremely difficult to develop a new program without the existence and active support of a group in the community that is highly committed to its development. The planner-organizer must often initiate and organize such an action group. The ac-

tion group then gathers resources and influence, actively representing the new program's objectives, and fights for its support in the community. In short, it assumes an advocate function. Sometimes this group will be the planner's advisory council. At other times it will be a specially organized task force on transportation or protective services or some other need. Again, it may be a purely ad hoc coalition of interested parties.

What persons should the planner-organizer mobilize into such a group? Perhaps more than anything else, participants should share a keen interest in and concern for the welfare of the target population. To be truly responsive, it must include representatives of the clients themselves. Potential for influence is another criterion for inclusion. The greater the individual prestige of the members, the greater their potential for collective influence. Influential members may include representatives of civic organizations, financial institutions, church organizations, and the like.

The higher the level of understanding about the problems of the target population among members of this group and the greater their expertise in the delivery of services to them, the more realistic will be the group's efforts and the greater the credibility of its suggestions to the community. Planners often enlist members of professional associations, physicians, social workers, etc., to assure this expertise. Having representatives of community agencies in the group increases the chances that their support for a new program will be forthcoming.

The function of such a group might be: to formulate the overall objectives of the new program; to identify the target population to be served; to identify sources of financial support for the new program; to present the program objectives to important institutions in the community (such as city coun-

[7]D. Fruin, "Analysis of Need," in M. J. Brown ed., *Social Issues and the Social Services.* (London: Charles Knight, 1974): 27–56.

cil, county government, mental health board, United Fund); or all of these.

This group might also examine in detail the information and ideas developed by the planner-organizer. Although the group itself need not develop a detailed plan for action, consensus regarding the type of program to be developed is helpful. Sometimes, of course, consensus is difficult to reach. Participants must be aware that differences in opinion or in conclusion are possible, and that these experiences can be healthy. An action group should provide the arena where ideas can be exchanged, proposals explored, and creative thinking encouraged. Ultimately, the group should formulate a basic plan for a new program by identifying and agreeing upon its major objectives and the population it should serve.

It is from this action group that a body in charge of defining or reviewing the policies for the new program may ultimately be drawn. This may be formalized as a board of directors, as an advisory council, or as an internal task force within an existing agency. The importance of an action group of this kind cannot be overemphasized. In the founding stages of the new program, the planner-organizer will need to rely heavily on its support, energy, and creativity, and most importantly, on its ability to mobilize necessary resources for the program.[8] The existence of an advocate group is no less crucial when the planner decides to launch the program within an existing agency, than when an entirely new structure is to be developed.

Assigning Responsibilities to a Board or Advisory Council

When the interest group has developed an adequate level of cohesion and formu-

lated a basic statement regarding the mandate of the new program, it may be reconstituted as a formal board or council. It might then be given any of the following charges:

1. Development of a specific plan for the implementation of the new program
2. Responsibility for obtaining the basic resources to get the program started
3. Authority to hire or approve the director of the new program
4. Accountability for the activities of the program director and the disbursement of fiscal resources

The board or council must be helped to develop some internal division of labor to ensure that the necessary tasks will be fulfilled. This may involve designating members as president or chairman, secretary, treasurer, program planning subcommittee and the like. In addition, clear procedures for decision making must be formulated. These steps are of particular importance since the board's decisions are bound to have critical impact on the character and direction of the program.

Defining the Mission of the New Agency or Program

Establishment of a new program requires a carefully planned blueprint that specifies both mission and operational objectives. It requires a thoughtful assessment of the feasibility of achieving each objective and identification of the essential means for implementing it. Identified needs coupled with available resources and means must be translated into a series of program objectives aimed at meeting these needs.

The planner-organizer plays a crucial role at this stage. Possessing critical information regarding needs, as well as knowledge about potential resources, he or she must help the board, advisory council, or

---

[8]M. Zald, "The Power and Function of Boards of Directors: A Theoretical Synthesis," *American Journal of Sociology,* 75 (July, 1969): 97–111.

task force to reach consensus on what the organization's mission will be.

This mission is defined in terms of needs to be met, populations to be served, and services to be given. This mission, however, must be translated into operational terms. This requires first of all, *specification of the needs to be addressed.* These *needs are prioritized* (step no. 1), and *objectives specified* (step no. 2). It is not necessary that the most crucial need be acted on first. Sometimes what is most easily accomplished takes precedence on the planner's timetable. But the ultimate mission must always be kept in mind.

Specifying the Objectives

Specifying the objectives of the program is a process of moving from the general to the specific through careful assessment of alternatives. Assume, for example, that there is a consensus to focus on the needs and problems of aged persons living alone. In the process of identifying the needs of such a population there arises a growing awareness that they are most likely to experience problems in personal management. Such consensus does not lead directly to programs or services. Are these problems expressed in poor household management, in inadequate diet, in poor personal care, in social isolation? Which of these problems are of the greatest urgency? If agreement on the urgency of these problems can be reached, they may be ordered on a chart. In Figure 8.1, four specific problems are identified and ordered in terms of importance.

The next task (step no. 3) is to *specify* the "target" population to determine more exactly what older persons are to be helped by the new or expanded services. A similar process is followed to identify those who manifest the problems most acutely. These may be found in a minority population with low income, residing in a specific neighbor-

hood. Agreements must be reached concerning this target population, as its characteristics will determine the feasibility of various alternatives for responding to the needs.

The choice of the target population should also reflect contingencies regarding the attainment of needed resources. Grants may be earmarked for certain categories of older persons. Certain agencies may be able to provide certain services only to older persons living in their geographical jursidiciton. Also, if it will take two years and $200,000 to develop a service for persons living in neighborhood X, while a similar level of service to persons in neighborhood Y is possible for far less and in only nine months, the choice of initial target population may be clear.

Next comes *exploring alternative program approaches* to dealing with specific problems of the target population (step no. 4). For example, in addressing the problem of nutritional deficiencies the objective may be to provide meals to a given population. Alternatively, the service might be an educational one, in which older persons are taught about proper diet (see Figure 8.2).

Similarly, in response to financial management problems, program objectives may include helping older persons to use their financial resources more efficiently, increasing access and use of banking services, and the like (see Figure 8.3).

Through this process a list of potential agency or program objectives can be developed.

Doing a Feasibility Study

After an inventory of alternative objectives has been formulated, a feasibility study of each (step no. 5) is necessary.

Some of the criteria to be used are as follows:

1. What would be the fiscal cost?

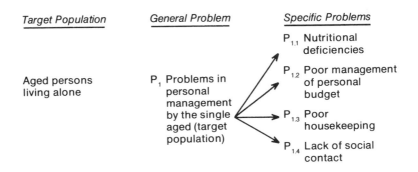

FIGURE 8.1

2. What would be the manpower requirements?

3. What facilities and equipment would be needed?

4. How receptive to the objective could the community be expected to be?

5. What would be the anticipated support of the objective by other community agencies?

With such information on each objective, the planning task force must now shift its focus to the other side of the coin, namely *assessing the potential money and credit* the new program could hope to obtain (step no. 6). Some of the elements in such considerations are:

1. The availability of federal and/or state grants

2. Potential contributions by local government

3. Donations and contributions by local private organizations such as United Fund

4. In-kind contributions by social service agencies and social clubs

5. Availability of volunteers to offset or reduce staffing costs

In considering various sources of support, it is often necessary that the new program be affiliated with, or an integral component of, an existing agency. The auspice-giving or sponsoring agency may be able to allocate a certain portion of its budget for the new program, cut the administrative or overhead costs, or provide the organizational auspices required as qualification for grants.

Following the feasibility study, the board, council, or task force must then, on the basis of all the information on options and constraints, determine which services the new program will provide. This process culminates in a comprehensive policy statement specifying the consented objectives of the new program, the rationale for their adoption, the kinds of services to be provided, the clients to be served, and the individuals and groups who have assumed responsibility for the program and will be accountable for it to the public. Such a statement may serve as a charter, which may be required if the program is to become incorporated. In any event, it is a claim for domain and a statement of intent.

Obtaining Seed Money for Start-up

Some planner-organizers assume that no project should commence unless all the resources needed to ensure its success are secured. This view fails to recognize that the most effective way to obtain needed resources may be to start the project and

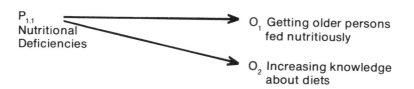

FIGURE 8.2

count on its visibility, demonstrated utility, and receptivity by clients to attract new resources. A program once started often generates its own momentum, attracting supporters unknown prior to the project's initiation and quickly developing spokesmen for itself in the community. This, of course, is not always the case. Many programs have foundered on inadequate funding, regardless of the need for the services. Every beginning necessitates some risk taking. The constraint of inadequate financial resources is a limiting factor, but it need not be an inhibiting one.

Nevertheless, basic "seed" or "start-up" money is often necessary. The planner-organizer with his knowledge of federal and state funds and grants, and through his contacts with local agencies, plays a crucial role in locating and obtaining funds. Together with the sponsoring agency or members of the board, task force, or advisory council, he may initiate or provide technical assistance toward: (1) the submission of grant proposals to federal or state governmental agencies or to private foundations; (2) fund-raising campaigns with the help of local civic associations, fraternal clubs, or churches; (3) solicitation of donations from industrial and commercial organizations; (4) competition for local or revenue-sharing funds; (5) presentations before the United Fund; (6) development of contracts with established community agencies, such as a community mental health board, for the provision of funds for the new program; (7) locating in-kind resources (such as facilities and equipment) through enlistment of the aid of social clubs and the news media; (8) mobilizing volunteers to provide the initial manpower needed to start the program.

The initial resources gathered for the new program must be allocated for two basic purposes: to set up the actual service or program, and to promote the program in the community, attracting additional resources. Often, because of inadequate financing, there is a tendency to ignore the second purpose. Yet if those resources are not allocated to promotion, the program may quickly reach a dead end. While it may be difficult to divert limited dollars from needed services, failure to do so may be shortsighted, ignoring the fact that organizations must survive to be successful. Promotion requires more than money, however. It usually requires the assignment of staff to carry it out.

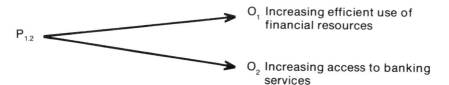

FIGURE 8.3

Specifying the Program Technology

The program objectives formulated in the new program's policy statement do not necessarily define the means to achieve them. The "set of means" by which the objectives are to be accomplished is called the *program technology* of the organization.

As the technology becomes articulated, it provides a series of guidelines for the type of staff and skills needed and the daily tasks to be performed in serving clients.[9]

The components of a program technology can be derived from the program objectives discussed earlier. In the previous example, the problem of nutritional deficiencies led to identification of two objectives—getting older persons fed nutritiously, and increasing their knowledge about diets. In attempting to implement the first of these objectives, the planner-organizer should explore every possible type of service that relates to providing adequate meals for the aging. Schematically, the process can be presented as shown in Figure 8.4.

Thus S_1 may be a meals-on-wheels service, S_2 may represent a cooperative cooking program for small groups of older persons in a given neighborhood, and S_3 might be a hot lunch program at the neighborhood schools. The choice of the specific service may be based on such criteria as: (1) known success of similar programs elsewhere, (2) availability of expertise to implement it, (3) availability of other necessary resources, (4) receptivity by the aged to be served.

Assuming that the meals-on-wheels program has been adopted, the next series of specifications identifies the major tasks required to provide the service. For example, $S_{1.1}$ stands for organizing volunteers with cars; $S_{1.2}$, preparation of weekly visits by a nutritionist; $S_{1.3}$, preparing the meals at the kitchen of the local church, etc.

In short, this process provides a blueprint of all major tasks necessary to make the program operative.

Implementing the Program Technology

Once the choice of technology is made and its components identified, the new program can proceed to obtain the needed personnel. The program technology itself can be used to provide guidelines for the type of personnel required, and to specify the skills required of staff. It can, in fact, be used as the basis for writing job descriptions—although these should not be overly prescriptive or rigid.

Any program, in its initial phase, will require a great deal of flexibility from its staff. Staff may be called upon to switch roles and assume various tasks as the need arises, even though tasks calling for particular skills must be performed by qualified personnel.

The success of the meals-on-wheels-program, for example, may hinge on the skills of a nutritionist needed to plan well-balanced meals. A program in which volunteers cook and deliver meals may only seem to be successful but in fact be missing the objective of getting older people fed nutritiously.

Once personnel are hired they must be given the responsibility to perform those tasks for which they are qualified. A nutritionist, for example, may not be the right person to supervise or organize drivers for the "wheels" part of the meals program. There is often a tendency to assume that a higher level of credentials implies proficiencies in many areas. Yet a nutritionist with an academic degree may know little about

---

[9]On the concept of human service technology see Y. Hasenfeld and R. English, ed., *Human Service Organizations* (Ann Arbor: University of Michigan Press, 1974): 12–14.

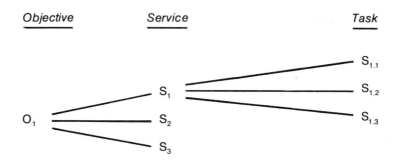

Objective   Service   Task

FIGURE 8.4

counseling or working with volunteers. Often a volunteer is much better qualified.

Developing an Appropriate Delivery Structure

Division of labor, then, is all-important. Effective division of labor requires three critical organizational decisions: Who does what? In what order must various tasks be performed? Who is accountable for what is done? The first decision requires identification of the tasks to be performed and the persons to perform them. The second decision is related to sequence and coordination. Some tasks must be performed before others can be begun. Those that are performed sequentially may be separated among several work units. Other tasks must be performed together and belong to the same work unit.

In every organization there are certain sets of activities for which a supervisory person may be held accountable. The following principles may prove useful in guiding the development of an appropriate set of structural relationships.[10]

1. Those activities which need to be done simultaneously or in close proximity to each other are generally best grouped together. In the example given, the menu planning and the cooking activities should be in the hands of certain staff, while the handling of the delivery of the meals can be in the hands of another group. A set of activities which must be closely coordinated should be conducted or supervised by a single unit supervisor.
2. Activities that have different time and space schedules and contingencies should generally be grouped separately. For example, the meals-on-wheels program should be separated from a group counseling program.
3. Tasks which can be performed through explicit routines should be separated from tasks that are nonroutine. For example, determination of membership, registration, and fee assessment are routine tasks. They should not be performed by those who provide consultation to community groups, a highly nonroutine activity.
4. Activities which require different ways of relating to the clients should be separated. For example, recreational activities for older people should not ordinarily be provided by

---

[10]P. R. Lawrence and J. W. Lorsch, *Organizations and Environment* (Cambridge, Mass.: Harvard University Press, 1967).

the staff who give intensive individual counseling. While the same staff could conceivably do both, there ought to be a clear distinction between their two functions.

5. Staff should not be subjected to multiple supervision if at all possible. If it is necessary for more than one supervisor to relate to a particular staff person because of multiple roles that staff person performs, clear distinction must be made regarding the areas of jurisdiction of each supervisor.

The period of initial implementation of program technology is a period of trial and error. It requires a great deal of flexibility and no little tolerance for failure and for ambiguity. Open-mindedness and willingness to explore alternative routes are essential ingredients. During the early stages of program development, lines of communication with staff and clients must be kept as open as possible. Feedback is essential if the program is to adjust to unexpected exigencies. Staff who work directly with the community can provide invaluable information on the operationalization of the technology and its problems, its failures, and its successes.

It is probably desirable to have a "dry run" of the technology to test its organization and to acquaint the staff with their roles and duties. This can be accomplished through simulation techniques prior to putting the program into the field. Another approach is to select clients who are willing to volunteer for the service, even though the "bugs" in it may not have been fully shaken out.

Developing Inter-Agency Relationships

Concurrent with development of the technology of an agency or program is the development of a "support structure." This structure refers to the organization's patterned relationships to those elements in its environment that provide it with the resources necessary to attain its service and maintenance objectives. These elements include:

1. Clients or *consumers* of its service
2. Fiscal, manpower, technical, and other *resources* essential to the goal-oriented performance
3. *Complementary or supportive services* without which an agency's services would be unattainable, inadequate, or ineffective
4. Support or recognition from regulatory and auspice-providing bodies which give the program its *authority or mandate*

Managing the flow of these elements to and from the program requires establishment of a variety of exchange relationships with other organizations in the environment. This environment is described as an agency's "task environment." It is composed of all those groups and organizations whose actions directly affect the agency's goal attainment. Exchange activities leading to receiving elements from the task environment may take the form of: (1) competition, (2) contractual agreements, (3) cooptation, or (4) coalition formation.[11]

Agencies and programs are frequently in *competition* with each other for needed resources. One agency may compete with another for a federal grant by offering to serve more clients per dollar; it may compete to obtain better-trained staff by offering better benefits.

Human service agencies often make *contractual arrangements,* in which one orga-

---

[11]K. Benson, "The Interorganizational Network as a Political Economy," *Administrative Science Quarterly,* 20 (June, 1975): 229–46.

nization agrees to do something for another (often in return for something). Without such arrangements, many services would be poorly performed or left undone. Examples abound. Agencies may exchange staff with complementary competencies on a temporary basis. One agency may do the mailing and publicity for another. A community group may contract with the Welfare Council to assess the service needs of a particular neighborhood. A county department of social services may purchase services from other agencies for its clients, including recreation, mental health, or protective services it does not have the staff to provide directly.

A new program or agency may also attempt to *coopt* key persons from other agencies whose services it seeks. Cooptation is accomplished through involving others in the design of a service or delivery of a service program. Cooptation strategies are employed when involvement and its rewards are likely to give those who might otherwise oppose a program a greater appreciation for why it is needed and what it is intended to accomplish. Their involvement may not only nullify potential opposition, but may actually increase support.

When agencies pool their resources in a joint venture, they form a coalition. Coalitions differ from contracts in that the latter require explicit agreements about what one party will do for the other. Coalitions, on the other hand, are binding only insofar as working together leads to some mutual goal attainment.

It is not essential for parties in an exchange relationship to benefit equally from the exchange, or to have fully complementary goals. It is only necessary that each party perceive the relationship as being of some benefit to itself.

The choice of each of these strategies depends on numerous conditions, particularly those pertaining to the perceived status and desirability of the new program in the community. The more secure and the greater the importance attached to the agency's services, for example, the more likely it is to employ competitive and contractual strategies.

Enlisting Needed Elements from the Environment

In the discussion that follows, attention will be given to how agencies recruit resources or manage the flow of needed elements from the environment itself.

Clients. Clients can be recruited through referrals by other agencies informed about the new program. Clients may also be informed of a service through the news media. To reach some isolated clients, it is often necessary to launch a door-to-door campaign using volunteers.

Inadequate interpretation of an agency's services or intake policy may result in inappropriate referrals. An agency that turns away many ineligible clients causes a serious and unnecessary hardship to those clients and to its staff as well. It does harm to its own image, often damaging its relationships to other agencies. Thus it is critical for the new program to disseminate accurate and specific information about eligibility, both to the public and to other social agencies. Changes in eligibility criteria should be promptly communicated to all referral sources.

Permanent Sources of Funding. Often a new program must expend some of its initial and temporary resources on activities aimed at securing additional, more permanent sources of funding. Examples of such activities include: (1) entering into negotiations with the United Fund or United Way; (2) preparing grant applications to federal and state governmental agencies; (3) organizing a group of community influentials willing to sponsor an annual fund drive; (4) negotiating with local governmental bodies such as community mental health boards or county commissioners to incorporate the program under its sponsorship.

These and other activities require that certain staff members spend considerable time and energy meeting with potential funding sources, exchanging ideas, and presenting the agency's case.

It is often desirable to designate a specific staff position for such activities and hire a person with considerable experience in mobilization of resources.

Knowledge and Expertise. No new program can function without adequate access to at least the minimal amount of necessary knowledge and expertise. In the long run, the success of an agency may hinge on the quality of services it offers, and that quality may be in direct proportion to the knowledge and expertise of its staff. Inadequate and erroneous information could be disastrous.

The planner-organizer can mobilize expertise through: (1) enlisting the services of experts in the field from nearby institutes and universities; (2) consulting with and visiting programs of similar nature in other communities; (3) arranging information exchanges between the staff of the new agency and those of an established one in another area; (4) exploring the available literature on the problems or needs the program attempts to deal with; (5) obtaining consultation and relevant publications from appropriate state and federal agencies; (6) arranging for training and continuing education seminars.

Complementary Services. The effectiveness of any program is dependent in no small measure on the availability of complementary services for its clients. It is not enough to give one's own service well. No matter how highly specialized a service, the organization providing that service must still assume some responsibility for the general welfare of its clients. It cannot shy away from its obligation to make sure that clients receive other needed services.

This is particularly true when the effectiveness of the very services provided by the agency are dependent on the complementary services of other agencies. For example, if an agency develops a child-care program, it cannot in good conscience ignore the health needs of the children, and it may contract for periodic medical examinations with the local "well baby" clinic. A nutrition program for the aged might not be successful unless it also enlisted cooperation from the outreach staff of the Information and Referral Service, the Visiting Nurses Association, or the Mental Health Crisis Center.

A new program must identify the crucial services it will need to enlist from other agencies and programs in order to meet its own objectives. It is within the planner-organizer's responsibility to see to it that such services are or will be made available. Without them, the new program may fail.

These complementary services can be arranged through several means: (1) actual purchase of such services from another agency; (2) contract of exchange of services between the two agencies; (3) a unilateral decision by the other agency to provide the needed services as a gesture of goodwill; (4) a coalition of several agencies with different services all committed to serve the same clients.

Monitoring and Evaluation. Every program is subject to the monitoring and evaluation of some overseeing agencies. These may be state licensing organizations, other governmental units, local administrative boards, professional associations, citizens groups, or other interested parties. Often these regulatory agencies exert considerable influence. They may impose very specific requirements for the agency to meet.

A state agency, for example, may annually audit the financial transactions of the program, or it may check the extent to which the facilities conform to state regulations. A professional organization may be responsible for accreditation without which outside grants cannot be received.

The planner-organizer must see to it that the program has developed the appropriate mechanisms by which it can meet the requirements of these regulatory agencies. This is not a mere bureaucratic formality. Accrediting bodies and standard-setting organizations are often the key sources of legitimation and support of a new program. For example, an agency approved for internship of urban planners will gain considerable prestige and recognition in the professional community and could, therefore, attract good staff. Similarly, an agency that receives a favorable evaluation by a state agency is more likely to obtain future state grants.

Maintaining appropriate relations with the various agencies and organizations necessitates the establishment of "boundary roles" for program staff. Persons in these roles develop and maintain linkages between the new program and relevant organizations in its environment.[12] A staff person may be designated as the liaison with the state social service agency, county government, local hospital, etc. The duties of boundary personnel include: (1) establishment of the necessary relations with outside groups and organizations; (2) resolution of whatever difficulties may arise in

the course of a relationship; (3) obtaining relevant up-to-date information about the activities of the partner to the relationship; (4) establishment of contacts with key staff in that organization or group who may be favorable toward the agency; (5) alerting the agency to new developments that may alter the relations between the two.

The ability of an agency to seize on new opportunities in the environment, to adapt to new changes, and to be prepared for new constraints depends on the effective job performed by the occupants of these boundary roles. They serve as the ears and eyes of the agency, without which its ability to adapt, grow, and develop would be seriously hampered.

Legitimation and Social Support. Underlying all the inter-agency relations described above is a pervasive need of the program to obtain legitimation and social support. The success of the program in achieving viability is dependent on its ability to become a recognized "institution" in the community. Once the program is perceived by key elements in the community as desirable, indispensable, and an important contributor to the general welfare of the community, it has been "legitimated." Legitimacy implies that the community is willing to accept it as a viable and necessary component of the service structure.[13]

Support and legitimacy do not come easily; neither are they cheap. Concerted efforts to achieve them must be made by program staff. Support generally requires at the very least a satisfied community group or gratified clients. This is the core of an agency's constituent base. This constituency should also include other social service agencies that benefit in some direct way from the services offered by the new pro-

[12]H. Aldrich and D. Herker, "Boundary Spanning Roles and Organization Structure," mimeographed paper (Ithaca, N.Y.: Cornell University, 1974).

[13]P. Selznick, *Leadership in Administration* (New York: Harper, 1957).

gram. The constituent base should also include community influentials and professionals who are committed to the well-being of the target population.

Other mechanisms to promote support for the program include: lectures and presentations by staff to various community groups; establishment of an influential board of directors; public visits to the agency's facilities; reports by the news media of the activities of the agency; etc. But necessary as these are, none is sufficient without solid constituent support.

Getting Staff to Perform Adequately

Persons choose to work in organizations and agencies for a variety of reasons. They often join an agency staff with personal expectations and aspirations. The agency, on the other hand, expects them to perform in accordance with its needs, demands, and schedules. There may be many points of incongruity between personal aspirations of staff and organizational expectations. The larger the discrepancies, the greater the strains and the less likelihood that staff will perform adequately.[14]

Planner-organizers can help a new program determine adequate criteria for staff selection and realistic expectations for performance. Individuals who become employees of an agency make a contractual agreement whereby they accept the role requirements assigned to them in exchange for the various inducements provided by the agency (salary, work satisfactions, good working conditions).

A great deal of misunderstanding can be avoided if the agency specifies its requirements at the point of recruitment. Clearly written requirements can guide the agency

to hire staff who have the needed skills, aptitudes, and attributes. Recruitment, however, is only a limited mechanism to ensure that staff will perform adequately. Socialization is a critical organizational process through which staff internalize agency norms and values and learn specific role obligations. Two important socialization mechanisms are training and staff development.

In the final analysis, however, effective and efficient role performance by staff is predicated on the design of a work unit that is congruent with the tasks it has to perform.[15] Tasks can be categorized by two major variables: (1) *Task difficulty,* which refers to the degree of complexity, amount of knowledge needed, and reliance on non-routine decision making. For example, determination of service eligibility may be a very simple task based on few explicit decision rules, while planning community services necessitates consideration of many factors, reliance on extensive knowledge, and complex decision making. (2) *Task variability,* which refers to the degree of uniformity and predictability of the work to be done. For example, preparation of monthly statistical reports is a relatively uniform and predictable task, while developing ties with various agencies calls for a variety of procedures.

Tasks which are low in complexity and variability call for a work unit structure which is essentially bureaucratic in the classical sense of the word. Tasks which are high in complexity and variability necessitate a work unit structure which is "human relational." In a bureaucratic structure line staff have very limited discretion; there is a clear hierarchy of authority; and coordination of staff is based on an extensive set of rules and operating procedures. In a human relation structure, the discretion of line staff

---

[14]L. W. Porter, E. E. Lawler and J. R. Hackman, *Behavior in Organizations* (New York: McGraw-Hill, 1975).

[15]C. Perrow, *op. cit.,* Chapter 3.

is high; relations with supervisory staff are collegial; and coordination is based on feedback from the other staff.

When the task has both complex and noncomplex components or variable and nonvariable elements which cannot be separated, a "mixed" structure will be most appropriate.[16] Based on the nature of the "mix" such a structure may provide line staff with high discretion in some specific areas and none in others. For example, the task of intake may be of such type. Workers may have high discretion in defining the problem of the client, but none concerning determination of fees, scheduling, and the like.

It can be readily shown that each structure is most efficient if appropriately matched with the characteristics of the tasks to be performed. This is so because the work unit structure is designed to elicit the behavioral and role prescriptions that each task requires.

When conflict arises between two units or among several staff members because of overlapping jurisdictions, lack of coordination, or lack of mutual understanding, an ad hoc task force to deal with the conflict may prove helpful. In a multi-service center, for example, a conflict could arise between the outreach staff and the counseling staff. The former may feel that they do not get any help in scheduling appointments and in coping with problems they encounter in the field. The counseling staff, on the other hand, may feel that they are asked to do the work of the outreach staff and that the outreach staff fail to understand what the counselors are trying to accomplish. To resolve the conflict, an ad hoc task force might be established with representatives of both parties to arrive at an acceptable solution, or an integrator position might be created.

The integrator role requires that a third party become the mediator between parties in the dispute. The integrator is generally a person with adequate knowledge of the activities of the units of persons he or she attempts to bring together, and may be in an authority position in relation to both. In the example above, the integrator might be a person who has expertise in both outreach and counseling, so that his directives to both units will be respected. His function is to identify areas where coordination needs to be established and procedures that can be developed to minimize conflict. He also serves as a mediator, interpreting to each unit the issues and problems the other unit needs to solve.[17]

A further word: conflict is not necessarily dysfunctional to an organization. To the contrary. It can help to effectively identify operational problems, philosophical differences, or staff deficiencies. Properly managed, conflict situations assure a changing and responsive pattern of agency operations. Conflict is often a symptom of healthy adaptation to changing needs and expectations.

Developing an Intelligence and Feedback System

There is a strong correlation between the extent to which an organization can adapt to changes in its environment and the effectiveness of its "intelligence" system. An effective system enables the organization to evaluate its own activities in relation to changes and developments in its environment. Without such a system, the organization may find that its services and modes of operation are rapidly becoming obsolete.

[16]Eugene Litwak, "Models of Organization which Permit Conflict," *American Journal of Sociology*, 67 (Sept. 1961), pp. 177–84.

[17]P. R. Lawrence and J. W. Lorsch, *op. cit.*, Chapter 9.

An effective and efficient intelligence system can provide the program with the new information and knowledge required to adjust to changes from both within and without.

In general, an intelligence system fulfills three interrelated functions: monitoring the external task environment of the agency, internal auditing of staff and client activities, and evaluation of the agency's outputs.

The *monitoring of the agency's external environment* is intended to alert the agency to important changes and developments in the various units upon which it is dependent. These include federal and state programs, the programs of local social service agencies, new legislation, etc. Monitoring activities can also be directed at identifying new developments in service techniques. Finally, external monitoring is required to inform the agency of changes in the character of the population it seeks to serve.

The main purpose of *internal auditing* is to inform the agency of the activities of the staff vis-à-vis the clients. Information generated by internal auditing enables staff to assess the progress of the clients and to determine future courses of action, and enables the agency management to evaluate the operation of the service technology. Without such evaluation, the agency has no way of determining whether it is achieving its service goals at some reasonable level.

Evaluation of agency *outputs* occurs after clients have been served by the agency. The emphasis is on what happened to clients and how many were served.

Fulfillment of each of these intelligence functions requires several steps: (1) collection of the necessary data; (2) analysis of those data so that they are useful and used; (3) transmission of relevant information to appropriate decision makers; and (4) interpretation of the information in order to generate additional knowledge. Since the final step of the intelligence process is the generation of knowledge, malfunction in any of the previous steps is likely to adversely affect the capability of the intelligence system to develop that knowledge.

Effective external monitoring systems are dependent on the performance of boundary personnel who maintain close ties with external units and who actively scan the environment for new resources. Staff members assuming boundary roles may develop specialized working relations with a given set of organizations. The contact person gathers essential information about the availability of given resources and the conditions of their use, and transmits this information to staff members who can use it. This is a necessary function if the agency is to remain up-to-date on changes and developments in its environment.

Personnel who perform boundary roles must develop expert knowledge about the characteristics of the resources in their areas of specialization. They must also be able to develop cooperative and informative relationships with the major suppliers of these resources, and must develop analytic skills necessary to assess and evaluate developments and changes in the nature of the environment. Perhaps most important, they must acquire effective and efficient communication channels to decision makers within their own organization.

Internal auditing enables staff to carry out their activities on an informed and rational basis. Internal auditing is directed at (1) the case or client level, and (2) the operational or departmental level. The function of internal auditing at the case or client level is to provide staff with all the necessary information for decision making at every juncture of the client's career in the agency.

This often requires the use of a client "case record." Each client served by the agency should have a record which includes basic information about him, his own perception of his needs, and the service objectives for him. Actions taken by staff and periodic evaluations of the client's performance in the agency should be systematically recorded and the impact of those services noted. A client record could be organized around topics such as background information, health status, income, housing, nutrition needs, and interpersonal problems. Each action or referral should be recorded in the appropriate topic section.

A scheme must also be developed for the uniform classification and codification of the information items to be used; and procedures for information gathering, update, and retrieval must be planned. This process requires that the basic information the agency plans to collect and use be classified and coded in a system of categories that are explicitly defined, unambiguous, and uniformly applied throughout the entire agency. This process can be used to enable staff to develop an orderly and rational sequence of services aimed at assisting the client to achieve his service goals. It can also be used to monitor the actions taken and to signal staff when new or different decisions need to be made.

Auditing procedures at the "operations" level attempt to answer basic managerial questions about the modes of operation of the agency or units thereof. These could include the analysis of all activities done for clients suffering from visual handicaps; the success of various treatment technologies; analysis of the type of referrals used by the agency; or the responses of staff to clients who drop out. The findings of such auditing enable the agency to evaluate its operating procedures and make necessary adjustments or changes.

Findings may specify such information as (1) the type of clients arriving at the agency, the range of problems they present, and the services they request; (2) assess-

ment of the services given to different cohorts of clients, the consequences of those services, or whether adequate follow-up is done by staff; (3) the performance of various staff regarding size of case load; average number of contacts with clients; (4) type of resources or intervention techniques used.

Perhaps the most important function of an intelligence system is to enable the agency to evaluate its service outcomes. In the final analysis, an agency can justify its existence only if it can show competence in attaining its service objectives. To do so, it must develop reliable procedures to evaluate the use of its services. The problems involved in attempts to measure are extremely complex. They stem from the fact that there is no consensus regarding a norm of "success," nor are there valid and reliable methods to measure success.

There is, however, some risk of developing inappropriate *output measures.* This can be observed when the number of clients seen by staff becomes the measure of success. When this criterion is adopted by staff, they may gear their efforts to obtaining a high ratio of clients per worker while reducing the amount of time they spend with each. There is also a tendency of organizations to adopt "symbolic" criteria when faced with the difficulties of developing substantive criteria. Symbolic criteria are testimonies by staff or clients, display of the "successful" client, self-evaluation, and other approaches that may be highly misleading and in fact could cover up serious failures by the organization.

Any evaluation of an agency may be painful in that it is likely to expose serious gaps between expectations and accomplishments. Such an exposure may undermine the legitimacy of the agency. Yet an agency cannot improve its services if it lacks adequate outcome measures or fears the consequences of such measures. In the long run, lack of adequate outcome measures may lead toward the deterioration of the organization.

An agency's service goals are often multidimensional, with various subgoals and tasks. The design of valid and reliable outcome measures requires recognition of this fact. In general, outcome measures should relate to the goals of each subsystem in the agency. Outcome measures differentiate between the initial state of the client at the point of entry and the terminal state of that client at point of exit from the agency.

In a complex service program, the new client goes through a series of assessments, which are often updated and corrected with the collection of additional information. These assessments may cover a range of attributes and problems, such as personal care, motivation to participate, health status, financial problems, etc. These include the gamut of areas in which the agency activity plans to intervene in order to improve the status of the client. At point of exit, these same attributes are reassessed and the amount of progress shown by the client through actual performance or his own evaluation is recorded. Because an agency may have succeeded more in some areas than in others, one measure cannot summarize the range of activities undertaken by the agency, nor can it reflect the complexity of attributes and problems presented by the client.

Multiple measures are necessary. Each of these should include concrete and precise descriptions of client attributes and behaviors. These measures must become an integral part of the service technology itself. They may serve as assessment devices for the client's progress in every stage of his association with the agency. In fact, they should logically follow the activities that have been specified in the service technology. They should be embedded in the daily work of the staff and not external measures imposed on the agency without direct reference to what it actually does. Needless to say, such measures must be constantly reexamined, updated and refined.[18]

Successful use of measures of service outcome necessitates a comprehensive and effective *follow-up* system. Without one, the information necessary for evaluation could not be obtained. The basic function of follow-up is to gather the necessary information regarding the consequences for the client of services given. It is the basic mechanism by which the agency can find out what has happened to its clients. Unfortunately, few service agencies have established such sophisticated measures. In a number of cases, in fact, output measures of the type described could be overly costly in relation to the sophistication of the services provided.

CONCLUDING NOTE

The process of establishing a new program is highly complex and requires considerations of many inter- and intra-organizational factors. It is not surprising, therefore, to find that while community workers and action groups may conceive of imaginative and innovative service programs, their ability and success in implementing them are at best modest. As was shown in the above discussion, each step in the process of implementation requires a particular set of skills, expertise, and resources. Inability to enlist them at crucial points in the program development may lead to failure or to detrimental consequences in the ability of the program to fulfill its objectives.

Thus, the systems approach used here alerts the planner-organizer to the intricate interrelations among the various building blocks of the program. It identifies the

---

[18]C. Weiss, *Evaluation Research* (Englewood Cliffs, N.J.: Prentice-Hall, 1972).

points at which the establishment of certain subsystems must assume priority over other organizing activities. Nevertheless, it should not be concluded that the model presented here is deterministic, in that each of the steps identified must be so followed. It should not be assumed a priori that an organization is a tightly coupled system in which each component must be closely articulated with all others. There is evidence to suggest that many programs may function quite adequately even if some components or subsystems are not fully developed or are not closely inter-linked. The systems approach advocated here enables the planner-organizer to assess at each point in the program development process the need for the establishment of certain organizational components. For example, he may find that a feasibility study is unnecessary since resources have already been earmarked for certain types of programs, or that whatever service technology will be developed, support of key groups in the environment is assured.

Moreover, it has been stressed throughout that agency or program development involves a great deal of trial and error in the face of many unknown parameters. The approach developed here merely attempts to identify the critical parameters the planner-organizer must consider and thus reduce some of the risks that are inherent in any program implementation.

9.

Michael Key, Peter Hudson, and John Armstrong

EVALUATION THEORY AND COMMUNITY WORK

WHAT IS EVALUATION?

At a rudimentary level, evaluation is an activity answering the general questions: How are we doing? Are we accomplishing what we set out to do? More technically, however, evaluation is seen as the collection of data about outcomes of a programme of action relative to goals and objectives set in advance of the implementation of that programme.

Different writers on evaluation give varying definitions. We concluded that it is more important to understand the different approaches to evaluation than artificially to attempt a universal definition. At the same time we found that many writers developed subtle distinctions of little practical use to us, whilst giving less attention to the basic problems. Accordingly we have not undertaken here a comprehensive review of the literature in the field, but have instead tried to give an overview of the major approaches to evaluation. This means that we have risked oversimplifying complex theories without giving enough specific references. But unless it is clear from the text that a point is our own, readers should assume that they can read deeper in these theories in the books we mention in our Bibliography. [Not reproduced here.]

Source: From Michael Key, Peter Hudson, and John Armstrong, *Evaluation Theory and Community Work,* 1976. Reprinted by permission of Community Projects Foundation and the authors.

Finally, we have understood evaluation to be concerned with studying events that have already happened. We would exclude other usages of evaluation that refer to events that lie in the future on the grounds that such usage probably means something like what we would call "critical choice." For example, arguments for and against staying in the European Economic Community cannot be evaluated until after one has either left or stayed in, although critical discussion and reasoned choice are possible.

APPROACHES TO EVALUATION

From our reading we have constructed a tentative classification of approaches to evaluation.

The approaches can be divided into two main types which are themselves based on a necessarily arbitrary division of an imagined "hard—soft" continuum. The two types are called "hard-line approaches" and "soft-line approaches."

Hard-line approaches are those which assume an exact definition of evaluation and a set of specific procedures to be used, these being procedures and techniques of a rational and objective kind. Those using these types of approaches see evaluation as a substantial and systematic activity.

Soft-line approaches are characterised by a general or vague definition of evaluation with few specific procedures, where such procedures as exist are subjective and allow for opinion, and where evaluation is considered an unsystematic and even marginal activity open to the partial or eclectic application of various techniques.

We do not judge one type of approach to be of itself better than the other. We also see it as possible for one particular technique (e.g., case-study) to be used in several particular approaches and for one evaluation programme to use both hard- and soft-line approaches. However, we feel that simply applying one rigorous technique does not necessarily constitute a hard-line approach to evaluation. It also follows from the characteristics of soft-line approaches that they may be seen mistakenly as merely the use of a technique, rather than as the application of a whole general and unsystematic approach to evaluation. We do not see the use of a soft-line approach necessarily as denoting the failure of a hard-line approach, and we argue that in fact soft-line approaches have virtues absent from hard-line approaches.

We have identified the following divisions within each major type.[1]

Hard-line evaluative approaches
—goal models
—systems models

Soft-line evaluative approaches
—impressionistic enquiry
—opinion survey
—"blue-ribbon" committees
and the "grateful testimonial"
—textbook precepts

Each approach has certain basic elements and the capacity to use certain techniques (see, for example, Appendix I). . . .

A fundamental problem with applying these evaluative approaches to social action programmes—especially the approaches located at the "hard-line" end of the continuum—is that they are informed by con-

---

[1] The division into "hard-line" and "soft-line" was the first stable way to organize the various theories of evaluation that seemed reasonable to us. We have tried to apply it systematically throughout this paper. However, we are now . . . less certain about the allocation of specific types of evaluation to the two main categories. For example, systems models are perhaps "softer" than we have shown, and textbook precepts "harder." Despite such uncertainty, we have left the categories in their original form, both because we cannot guarantee that any change would be better and because we still see the major distinction between "hard-line" and "soft-line," around which later sections of our paper also hinge, as basically valid.

cepts from commerce, industry and science which do not really fit the dynamics of social activism. We will return later to problems associated with the scientific analogy in evaluating community work, but the commercial and industrial analogy deserves mention here. In business enterprises the output of managers and workers can be measured and thus evaluated in terms of the growth or decline of profits. The ideal is that activities which do not generate profits be eliminated. Many aspects of industrial management are concerned with evaluating performances of machines and people against the criterion of profit, and many techniques for "hard-line" evaluation (like those used by Tripodi and mentioned in our next sub-section) were first developed as management techniques in industry. The output of community workers in social programmes, however, proceeds from completely different motives and manifests itself in ways that are difficult to measure and "cost" in the commercial sense. Thus there are bound to be problems with evaluating social action according to conventional approaches that have grown out of industrial and managerial practice.

On the other hand, "soft-line" approaches to evaluation can be seen as developing out of the old tie between social action and philanthropy, where appealing to the opinions and feelings of a few wealthy sponsors was more important than strict scientific accuracy or proof of business-like efficiency. In light of changes in the sponsorship and the whole orientation of community work, these approaches to evaluation must be regarded as being only partially satisfactory.

Hard-line Evaluative Approaches

We identified two sorts of hard-line approach according to the degree to which each focusses on the aims and objectives of a programme to be evaluated. Goal models are highly focussed on aims and objectives; systems models are less so. Both of them, however, assume that aims and objectives are set in advance of programme implementation and fieldwork practice.

Goal Models. The essence of the goal model—the classical model for evaluation—is that a programme of action is planned and later assessed in strict relation to stated general aims and to the objectives that are specified in order to contribute to the achievement of those aims. In so far as aims are narrow, objectives can be turned readily into statements of behaviour that should occur if those objectives have been achieved. This behaviour is then taken as a sign by the evaluator that there has been some progress toward the achievement of the aims. When programme aims are broad, specific objectives are less likely to be meaningful, and the goal model becomes correspondingly more difficult to follow. The basic model is shown in Figure 9.1.

A principal variation is the use of evaluation after each substage in the implementation of a programme (with possible revision of aims and objectives), instead of waiting until the whole programme has been completed.

The most helpful discussion of the goal model that we found was [given] in the book *Social Program Evaluation* by T. Tripodi, P. Fellin and I. Epstein (1), referred to in future as Tripodi. Tripodi spells out a number of phases through which any programme must go and argues that a different evaluative approach is required for each phase. He offers a substantial list of techniques and explains how each one is appropriate to a particular phase of a programme. Since many of these techniques are referred to by other writers on evaluation, fuller details of them are given in Appendix I. A summary of the Tripodi approach [is shown] here as an illustration of the goal model of evaluation [Figure 9.1].

According to Tripodi social programmes, although differing in terms of the nature and multiplicity of their goals, technologies, duration, size, etc., all have to solve similar developmental problems. Workers must get enough human and physical resources to initiate the programme. They must make contact with their clientele. They must supply an effective service to their clientele. These problems give rise to three stages of social programmes, sequential in theory but in reality often overlapping:

1. Programme initiation—getting staff, buildings, identifying needs, identifying target clients, planning the programme, setting objectives.
2. Programme contact—finding a way to contact potential clients and exclude inappropriate ones.
3. Programme implementation—providing the main services or other outcomes of agency activity, including a withdrawal stage if appropriate.

It frequently happens that one agency is operating several different programmes si-multaneously, each at a different developmental stage. Each programme and programme stage needs, therefore, to be recognised and evaluated for what it is. The process of evaluation means going through the following sequence of activities:

1. Recognising both long-range and operational goals for the whole programme.
2. Identifying the current state of programme development (see above).
3. Formulating evaluative objectives appropriate to the current stage of programme development (see below).
4. Selecting and applying relevant techniques of evaluation (see Appendix I).
5. Considering the information produced by these activities.

Tripodi points out that although there can be various evaluative objectives—i.e., criteria for the evaluator to use in his or her work—there are three basic ones:

1. An objective to get descriptive information about the type and quantity of programme activities—programme efforts.

Programme Stages			Evaluation
Planning		Implementation	
General aims	Specific objectives	Actual practice	Measuring practice against objectives
Example	*Example*	*Example*	*Example*
Welfare benefit take-up	Clients know their entitlement, how to claim and take up their entitlement	Welfare Rights Centre Centre operated, advocacy and information offered	Measurement of take-up rates, measurement of knowledge in respect of welfare entitlements
1 ⟶	2 ⟶	3 ⟶	4 ⟶

logical sequence of operation

FIGURE 9.1
Showing Simple Outline of the Goal Model of Evaluation

2. An objective to get information about the achievement of the goals of the current stage of programme development—programme effectiveness.
3. An objective to get information about programme effectiveness relative to programme effort—programme efficiency.

Ten evaluative techniques, grouped as "monitoring techniques," "social research techniques," and "cost analytic techniques" are described by Tripodi (see Appendix I). Each technique is seen as being more or less appropriate for evaluating "efforts," "effectiveness" and "efficiency" at each programme stage. Table 9.1 contains our summary of Tripodi's views as to when each technique is most relevant.

The Tripodi example can be used to illustrate the advantages and the drawbacks of a goal model approach to evaluation. Tripodi spells out clearly and systematically how social programmes are set up and operated and how evaluation relates to their actions. He also has a clear view of what must be done to carry out the specific actions involved in evaluation. His approach accommodates the fact of one agency implementing several programmes and the fact of different programmes being at different stages of development. Having established an overall framework, Tripodi can offer a selection of techniques that will be compatible with different stages in the life of an agency. Of particular value is his separation of programme "efforts," "effectiveness" and "efficiency." Each requires a separate approach by the evaluator. Also of value is the clarity given to the role of the evaluator, and therefore to the task of managing that role.

Evaluation carried out along these lines should produce substantial accounts of the efforts, effectiveness and efficiency of particular programmes. Ideally it can describe whether or not the effects of a programme on people and institutions have been what was intended. Such accounts can be useful to the organisers of social programmes, if those programmes have clearly-defined and narrow initial aims, because the evaluation is tightly focussed on how outcomes compare with initial goals that the organisers have set.

This type of evaluation is also relevant when social programmes that have been set up specifically as experiments are to be evaluated. In such cases, the programme has been based initially on a hypothesis that certain actions will produce certain outcomes. The evaluators use their findings to test the hypothesis. . . .

Against these advantages must be set some substantial drawbacks. There are several difficulties related to the specification of aims or goals. Some goals are fairly explicit in stating what outcomes are to be looked for, as in Figure 9.1. In such cases it may make sense to see if they have been attained. But other goals may be put in such vague or general ways as to give no clue as to what their attainment would consist of. Sometimes these goals are vague because of poor planning. Sometimes these goals are vague because they cannot be converted into anything more explicit, for example, goals concerned with producing a richer cultural atmosphere.

Following a goal model, an evaluator must be able to translate goals into specific objectives which the evaluator then uses. The conversion is easy with explicit, narrow goals—they readily generate objectives of a usable type. With vague goals resulting from poor planning, the evaluator may find it impossible to establish after the fact what, if any, objectives were used by programme staff. He or she will have no objectives to use unless he or she invents them. Even where a programme has genuinely broad goals, attempts by activists or evaluators to

TABLE 9.1
Summary of Tripodi Showing Relevance of Ten Evaluative Techniques to Three Evaluative Objectives within Each of Three Programme Stages

Programme Stages →	Programme Initiation			Programme Contact			Programme Implementation		
Evaluative Techniques ↓ \ **Evaluative Objectives**	Efforts	Effectiveness	Efficiency	Efforts	Effectiveness	Efficiency	Efforts	Effectiveness	Efficiency
Monitoring — Accountability audit	●	●	●	●	●	●	●	●	●
Administrative audit	●	●	●	●	●	●			
Time and motion studies	●		●	●		●	●		●
Social Research — Experiments									
Surveys	●			●	●		●	●	
Case studies	●	●		●	●			●	
Cost Analytic — Cost accounting					●	●			
Cost benefit analysis								●	●
Cost outcome analysis									●
Operation research					●	●		●	●

● Indicates relevance of technique.

Note: many of the techniques can be used more widely than shown: the table indicates only the most relevance. Combinations of techniques are possible too. For further details of the techniques, see Appendix 1.

convert them into specific objectives may fail because there are an enormous number of potential objectives, the exact choice of which will be made opportunistically as the programme develops. Put another way, programme planners may not know in advance of implementation what the achievement of a goal will look like, and they would be wrong to choose objectives arbitrarily in order to satisfy an evaluator when they themselves do not work in this way.

The goal model, then, can only be used when there are fairly clear goals and explicit objectives. In many community work situations these are not the norm. Indeed, in many instances of community work, there could never be specific objectives because general (or "broad-aimed") . . . goals are pursued. Any attempts to develop specific objectives to provide criteria for evaluation would actually misrepresent the nature of these programmes.

To an evaluator seeking to apply the goal model approach a lack of explicit criteria— for whatever reason—represents a major obstacle. A common response is for the evaluator to try to force the fieldworkers to convert their goals into specific objectives. Aside from the practical and ethical issues involved, there is a methodological issue in that the programme, after the evaluator's push for criteria, may be different from what it was before. In particular, the programme being evaluated may receive special attention relative to the other work done, or evaluation may even alter the main focus of the agency. There are different views on the acceptability of these results. Whatever the view adopted, it remains clear that goal model evaluators are limited if they don't have precise objectives, and that such objectives are unusual in community work.

A second type of difficulty related to goals and objectives is that they may change as a programme is implemented. This is

particularly likely to happen to objectives. If the changes are noted, it may be possible for the evaluator to take account of them by altering the evaluation programme. But too much change can leave the evaluator always one jump behind. It also makes it hard for the evaluator to find out if any original long-term goal has been attained, since his information will be related to the specific objectives rather than to the goals. Sometimes goals and/or objectives are changed unconsciously, and the evaluator can end up evaluating outcomes against intentions that programme staff claim they were never pursuing. In an experimental programme, any change of the hypothesis or objectives in the middle is disastrous, since it destroys the possibility of completing the experiment.

The demands facing community workers are likely to cause goals as well as objectives to be constantly reviewed and adapted. A good community worker may need to change direction abruptly in order to take advantage of an altered situation. The logic of the community worker is here quite different from that informing the goal model evaluator, and this represents a significant limitation in the relevance of goal model evaluation for community work.

In particular, there is a risk that the needs of a goal-oriented evaluation will interfere with the necessary alteration of the aims of a social programme as it develops. Misapplication of stringent goal model evaluation can stop much needed elaboration and innovation in community work practice.

A third type of difficulty about the goal model is that by focussing attention on activity related to goals it tends to miss other things. There are two dangers here. One, already mentioned, is that the programmes being evaluated tend to receive special attention at the expense of other work. A second and more important danger is that unanticipated outcomes of a programme, perhaps as important as those looked for, will not be noticed. It is conceivable that a community work programme could fail to attain its goal with respect to take-up of welfare benefits, for example, but could have altered the political climate in the process. A goal model evaluator is likely to miss this last.

All of the arguments above assume some degree of acceptance of the idea of planning programmes in advance of their implementation. But some community workers would reject the idea of setting goals and objectives for their work in this way. Goal model evaluation would be quite unsuitable in such cases. . . . Another problem is that the decision to use a goal model for evaluation ideally should coincide with the decision to provide a programme. If the evaluator is not brought in until the programme is well under way, he or she faces difficulties in establishing current goals and then working back to see if they obtained at the start of the programme.

It is also worth noting that a goal model approach is associated with a high risk of premature evaluation. This means that a newly established programme is too rapidly and rigorously evaluated. What are in fact the early stages of settling down to work (or programme contact in Tripodi's terminology) are mistaken for the mature performance of the programme. Findings from evaluation at that point will bear little relationship to the final outcomes of the programme, although they may be used as if they do. This mistake is mostly caused by misunderstanding on the part of those asking for evaluation. But the mistake can be reinforced by the internal rigour and inherent respectability of the goal model that seems to promise good evaluation without reference to the state of the object to be evaluated. . . .

In conclusion, the goal model of evaluation may be suitable for specific and limited pieces of community work, but in practice it is not suitable for many other pieces of community work.

Systems Models. The basis of this model is that, although a programme tries to achieve goals of its own, its implementation occurs in a wider social context which both receives and influences the programme. Evaluation by this approach is the act of finding out how a programme comes to interact with relevant existing systems to produce new systems, rather than simply establishing which of its planned goals have been achieved.

We found that this model was the least clearly defined in what we read. A particular confusion seemed to be the degree to which "system" refers to the organisational system of an agency ("internal environment") rather than to the system of agency, clients and area of operation ("external environment").

In one view, evaluation itself becomes a sub-system of the organisation, feeding back information on the implementation of each stage of each element of the programme. That can be useful in improving the planning and implementation of programmes, but is weak in giving an overall judgment about the usefulness of one total programme strategy relative to another. This view seems to overlap substantially with the "operations research" method of evaluation described in Appendix I . . . Such a view seems fairly straightforward but less interesting than the other varieties of a systems model.

A second view of a systems model, also focussing on "internal environment," recognizes that organisations or agencies do things apart from achieving their objectives. Factors such as capacity to change, ability to recruit resources, and maintenance of organisational structure are, in systems terms, important as pre-requisites for the organisation to produce outcomes that reflect its objectives. Therefore, it is valuable to investigate the efforts going into organisational maintenance and development, and their effectiveness, as part of the attempt at evaluation. This perspective on the organisation is helpful. It gives a way of rooting a particular programme in the reality of its organisational context. It enables the growth of such an organisation to be identified as something more or less effective in its own right, over and above what it contributes to the achievement of particular programme goals. The evaluative approach, however, is fairly straightforward once organisational sub-systems have been identified, since relatively narrow-aim goals can then be set for each and these can be evaluated in goal-model terms.

A third and distinctive view of the systems model is one that we have elaborated from a number of hints found in writings on evaluation. It identifies the programme as only one element of an immediate system, encompassing other programmes operated by the agency, clients, potential clients, sponsors, and other similar agencies. The system operates within the larger environments of a particular city and nation, as is shown in Figure 9.2. The advantage of this view is that a total programme can be assessed by examining how the programme penetrated its environments rather than by reviewing outcomes against objectives. That is done by looking at how the particular programme functioned within its immediate system (as described above), and how in turn the system, more or less changed by the programme and itself changing the programme, related to the environments of city and nation.

This modified systems model liberates the evaluator from the domination by objectives.[2] Failure to achieve planned goals may actually mean success in another part of the system and, by contrast, the strict achievement of goals may turn out to have been damaging in the social context surrounding an action programme. Implementation of social action programmes may produce unanticipated outcomes that cannot be handled by the goal model of evaluation but which are readily incorporated in the systems model. It also has the advantage of being able to account for actual stages of programme planning, implementation and change by reference to factors in the surrounding environments. It is especially useful for evaluating programmes with either broad or unclear goals which lack the specific objectives required by a goal model approach.

For the model to be successful, the evaluator must conceptualize the programme and its environments adequately in terms of abstract systems, and then relate actual circumstances to these abstractions in order to produce the evaluation itself. The evaluator has to face all the methodological and technical problems that appear in a goal model and also the extra task of understanding and organising the systems with which he or she will work. Further, systems theory as a whole is subject to criticism on the grounds that direct transference to the social sphere of concepts developed in the physical and biological spheres has its limitations, and may distort the perception of social behaviour. However, such criticisms could be applied to any method of pattern-

---

[2]It is possible to see our modified systems model as a sub-type of the "soft-line" approach which we describe below under the title of "textbook precepts." We recognize overlap between "hard" and "soft" approaches but we have included the model here because it seems to have enough substance to count as a major and systematic evaluative method in its own right.

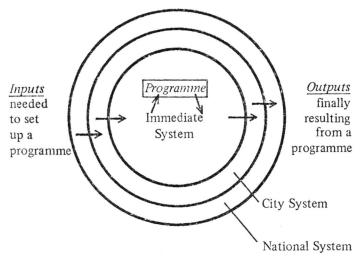

FIGURE 9.2
Showing Highly Simplified Systems Model Perspective
on Programme Implication

ing events, including all of the other approaches to evaluation. A more practical response seems to us to be to consider if the value of insights from a particular evaluative approach outweighs the possible drawbacks of using that approach.

The discussion that we found most relevant to the particular systems model we tried to develop was that of R. S. Weiss and M. Rein in their paper, "The Evaluation of Broad-Aim Programs: Difficulties in Experimental Design and an Alternative" (2, p. 236–49). In this paper the authors do not actually spell out a systems model, but suggest a strategy and techniques of evaluation that certainly correspond to a systems perspective. Their argument is rooted specifically in a strong disagreement with goal models of evaluation that imitate scientific experiments. . . . They also speak to the special problems of evaluating broad-aim programmes, which are characterised by having aims of sufficient abstraction to make it hard to know in advance exactly how changes hoped for in a community will manifest themselves. . . .

For such situations, Weiss and Rein offer as a more appropriate evaluation model one which aims to "develop a coherent and appropriately-near-to-complete [sic] description of the relevant community systems prior to the intervention of a programme, of the nature of the intervention, and of the new system which then develops in which the intervention is a dynamic constituent." (2, p. 243.) The necessary research in this case can emphasise any one of three areas:

1. Process-orientated research emphasising the collection of qualitative data about processes in the community.
2. Historical research emphasising concern with the development of events through time.
3. Case-study or comparative research emphasising the use of a small set of examples as the basis for generalisation.

Weiss and Rein go on to identify three leading issues which their approach raises. These are what conceptual foundations to use, how to handle data, and how to accommodate values.

Conceptual foundations. Any evaluator needs to have some foundation or framework which gives an indication of what an adequate description of the attempted intervention would look like. For example the experimentor in the goal model of evaluation takes the idea of causal determination as a basic framework. Weiss and Rein's evaluator is directed to three conceptual frameworks, although others are not ruled out.

1. Systems theory is useful in suggesting what events or phenomena should be studied, what roles might be played by various people, and how relevant people might interact. Systems should be identified according to particular issues, although correctly defining the boundaries can be difficult. If that can be done, however, it becomes possible to decide whether an unexpected event belongs to the system being investigated, or is an "alien variable" coming from another system, a variable to be noted but not needing further investigation. In this way the evaluator is freed from trying to learn about everything, and is instructed to focus on the interaction between the smallest set of groups and individuals which will account for the greatest part of the dynamic of change.

2. The dramaturgic approach is useful in building up a story of what people did within various settings. It is based on a view of social action as the unfolding of plots and sub-plots, as in a play. In this framework, the evaluator will seek information about what issues bring people into a situation, who the people are, what their commitments are, what action actually occurs, and how the issues were resolved. The approach is especially helpful in describing meetings and other short events in which people interact to resolve an issue.

3. Political process theory is helpful when looking at a connected series of events. The people involved are thought of as belonging to one or other of a number of interest groups, with more or less resources—human and physical. Their behaviour is seen to express strategies of "bargaining with each other, producing and avoiding conflict as each strives to realize its aims, forming alliances, and staking new claims and foregoing old ones." This framework enables the evaluator to assess how groups mobilised their resources in response to a particular intervention, how they committed themselves, and with what success.

Such conceptual frameworks effectively guide the attention of the evaluator. These three in particular help refine the focus on qualitative evaluation of social change urged by Weiss and Rein. Among the three, however, Weiss and Rein give most importance to systems theory: "in the evaluation of an intervention attempt there would seem to be basis for a presumption that the systems outlook, as the more capable of dealing with change, should have primacy...." (2, p. 246).

Data Analysis. Because of the value given by Weiss and Rein to qualitative methods of data collection which tend to generate floods of data that cannot be manipulated in the same way as quantitative data, the authors argue for the evaluator to exert tight control at the report writing stage. They identify three types of report, each on a different level which can contribute an element of control to the evaluative process.

1. Descriptive reports give considerable detail about concrete cases and situations in the area studied.
2. Analytic reports describe the types of systems, structures or processes observed, using concrete detail for illustration only, while still referring to the area studied.
3. Abstract reports describe more general models "for understanding the consequences of introduction of a programme for change of the sort studied into various types of communities" (2, p. 247).

The Roles of Values. In the goal model of evaluation, the only way in which values can be accommodated is by finding those associated with the set goals of a programme. Such values tend to be only those of the programme planners and implementers. Weiss and Rein's approach allows the recognition and inclusion of the values and perspectives of clients, other agencies for social action, local government, and even unrelated sectors of the community. The evaluator can assess the consequences of implementing a programme in terms of the losses and gains each of the groups would perceive. This represents an advance on the goal model because it allows differences in values among groups in the community to be recognised and brought into the open.

We have discussed some of the ways in which a systems model of evaluation improves on the rigidity and other limitations of a goal model. These advantages would also apply to the broadly similar model suggested by Weiss and Rein. But the criticisms of evaluation using systems concepts would also apply. Supporters of the goal model approach might object to the non-scientific methods advocated by Weiss and Rein and their lack of interest in finding direct lines between cause and effect. These objections will be held most strongly by supporters of goal model evaluation using experimental designs, against whom Weiss and Rein were arguing directly.

There has also been another criticism of the Weiss and Rein approach. That approach, although excellent for describing programme implementation, in fact does not permit evaluation in the sense of seeing how far goals were attained—the approach looks at operation, not at outcomes. We feel, however, that this criticism may be premature, both because Weiss and Rein are vague about how they would implement their ideas, and because we have not yet come across an example of an actual evaluation worked by anyone else along the same lines that could show whether or not the criticism is accurate. We do see a modified systems approach as having the potential to describe the effects of social programmes on people and institutions as well as how programmes operate. This potential seems relevant in light of the current state of community work.

Soft-line Evaluative Approaches

The evaluative approaches we have discussed so far are more or less tied to concepts of objectives and outcomes. But there are other ways of answering the general questions: How are we doing? Are we accomplishing what we set out to do? We have already called these others "soft-line" approaches to show that they do not score very well on the test of being scientific, although they may be of great use to sponsors, practitioners or clients.

Impressionistic Enquiry. The enquirer talks to staff and clients, sits in on sessions, reads relevant material, etc. After the collection of information in this way, he or she produces a report on the basis of observations and impressions. The enquirer may be an insider to the programme, but is often an outsider. It is possible for the enquiry to operate in several ways. One way might closely parallel the goal model approach, with the enquirer impressionistically relating his or her observation of practice to the observation of aims. Another way might be an enquiry based on the overall experience and judgment of the enquirer rather than on the stated aims of the project.

There are drawbacks. The method must rely on whatever people are willing to reveal to the enquirer. It also depends on the skills and powers of observation of the enquirer; these may not be good enough to prevent serious bias or to pick up important subtleties. Such an evaluation often amounts to a quick "look-see" exercise which says little about the process of operating or the overall outcomes of the programme. Although using an insider could offset some of these difficulties, it would produce a different set of problems of bias.

We should mention, however, that this method of evaluation is basically the common sense one used by most people most of the time. For example, programme workers are likely to base much of their practice on judgments born out of simple observation. Use of a skilled and experienced observer refines the procedure. Such an observer should be able to produce a report of considerable value for commenting on qualitative (as opposed to quantitative) aspects of fieldwork practice and programme achievements. The method is also quick and cheap relative to more complex evaluative approaches. It may be as effective for decision-making purposes as more sophisticated methods. The special potential of the impressionistic enquiry is that it may be more sensitive than hard-line methods because it gives scope to the intuitive, empathetic and insightful qualities of the observer. If that potential is released, the evaluation may be

better than one produced by other methods, especially better for programmes with broad or unclear aims.

Opinion Surveys. These seek to find out people's views and opinions of a programme by means of questionnaires or interviews. Samples are usual. There are some advantages. An opinion survey reduces the impact of possible bias on the part of the evaluator by putting other people's opinions at the centre of the evaluation. In one sense it gives scope to clients and other interested people to put their views honestly. It also gives clear indications about the perceived strengths and weaknesses of a programme. Such a survey could be valuable as one element of a more thorough research study.

But the opinion survey also has weaknesses. Programmes of social action usually aim to change behavior. Knowing people's current opinions about a programme is unlikely to give the evaluator any insight into the important changes in behaviour that might be related to that programme. Even within its own terms of reference, the opinion survey may prove unreliable. The opinions expressed may be so diverse or contradictory as to make it hard to draw general conclusions. The whole exercise is likely to be as costly in money and time as other research into aspects more central to evaluating the programme. Finally, there is a problem of deciding which people should be surveyed—whose opinions are relevant?

"Blue-ribbon" Committees and "the Grateful Testimonial." These are two varieties of evaluation that can best be used to show if a programme has done well. Logically they could show failures too, but in real life these responses are likely to be identified as "attacks" or "complaints" rather than as "evaluation."

A "blue-ribbon" committee is a group of dignitaries that produces a report or statement praising what a social programme has done. In "grateful testimonials," clients who feel that they have benefitted from the programme say so. If spontaneous testimonials are slow in coming, then the evaluator may solicit them.

These are the most subjective of evaluative methods and therefore they are likely to be repudiated by hard-line evaluators. Yet they should not be too lightly dismissed. Whilst producing conclusions doubtful by scientific canons, the conclusions may be highly pertinent to potential audiences for evaluative material, notably sponsors. Many sponsors have funded social programmes for reasons of politics, conscience or good feeling, rather than on the basis of scientific research; and they may be most open to receive evaluative material that calls up similar feelings. Testimonials from officials and clients may also give a reasonable judgment that a programme has been effective, although the same forms of evaluation may mistakenly describe ineffectiveness as achievement, or fail to cope with lack of achievement.

Because they are open to bias and planned manipulation, testimonials alone would be dubious for an evaluator to use who wished to give an exact and detailed account of the achievements of a programme. However, they may have some part to play in an evaluation making use of a number of different approaches.

By extension, testimonials and statements by committees tend to take the evaluator towards impressionistic enquiries and opinion surveys on the one hand, and towards non-evaluation ... on the other hand. Curiously, hard-line approaches are sometimes treated (or even attacked by people suspicious of evaluation) as if they were no different from these more subjective methods.

Textbook Precepts. With this method a programme is evaluated by the way its implementation relates to the standards or precepts of practice given in textbooks of community work (or to elements of general social theory), rather than by the way its implementation matches initial goals.

The approach may be helpful in giving a perspective on a particular programme where there is a gap in information on goals and local systems. It is also helpful when evaluation covers a controversial topic such as methods of practice, and is particularly relevant if evaluation is intended to establish the degree to which practice was in keeping with academic or professional theory.

A drawback is that community work is still relatively new. Textbook precepts do not exist to the same extent as they do for social work or nursing.

Because of the relative newness of precepts and lack of agreement about them, the precepts themselves inevitably become the subject of evaluation as much as the actual practice. It therefore seems a weak approach to assessing a concrete programme of social action.

Evaluation Programmes

An evaluation programme is a planned series of evaluative activities aimed at finding out how far an action programme has achieved what was intended.

An evaluation programme may be made up of a combination of evaluative techniques. It is also possible for both hard- and soft-line approaches to inform a single programme of evaluation. Planning the programme as a whole is a necessary and separate step from the planning for each particular activity that forms part of the evaluation. . . .

REFERENCES

1. Tripodi, T., Fellin, P., and Epstein, I., *Social Program Evaluation* (Itasca, Ill.: F. E. Peacock Publishers, 1971).
2. Weiss, R. S., and Rein, M., "The Evaluation of Broad Aim Programs: Difficulties in Experimental Design and an Alternative," in C. H. Weiss (ed.), *Evaluating Action Programs* (Boston: Allyn and Bacon, 1972).

APPENDIX I

Ten Evaluation Techniques from Tripodi

These techniques are described as they would be used in evaluating an agency's programme. Obviously they could also be used to evaluate, say, a client group's programme. The techniques are only outlined; further reading would be needed to operate any specific technique.

Monitoring Techniques. These give a direct review of programme operations.

1. Accountability audit methods amount to reviewing records kept for purposes of programme accountability. There are two main types of record involved: general accounting records (keeping track of programme financial costs), and social accounting records (keeping track of programme beneficiaries).

The auditor (i.e. the evaluator) first establishes if the records exist and are accurate, and then uses the information gained from this investigation to report whether or not the recording systems are appropriate and satisfactory in terms of the aims and objectives of the programme. Recommendations can be made about which kinds of information pertinent to programme goals and evaluation objectives should be collected.

The evaluative purpose is to check how certain primary tasks are being done.

2. Administrative audit methods compare what staff do with performance standards set down as policies, organisational patterns, and job descriptions. Information is collected from policy documents, organisation charts, correspondence and other written records, and from interviews with staff. Each piece of information is checked for internal consistency, and then for consistency with other pieces of information. Specific methods such as critical path analysis may be used.

The auditor (i.e. the evaluator) may be able to make recommendations about both standards and performance.

The evaluative purpose is to check how the management and administration of the programme are being done in the light of the programme's aims and objectives.

Note: Compare this with the 'textbook precept'. . . .

3. Time-and-motion studies relate the use of time by programme staff to the activities in which they are involved. Information is collected by methods such as time sheets kept by staff, observation and interviews, all using time as the unit of measurement.

The evaluative purpose is to check how time is being spent by staff in relation to the aims and objectives of the programme.

Social Research Techniques. These develop, modify and expand knowledge about the programme which can be communicated to, and verified by, independent investigators.

4. Experiments seek evidence as to whether or not programme efforts "cause" the accomplishment of programme aims. How and what evidence is collected is determined by the experimental design chosen ... and then the use of data collection methods such as questionnaires, observation, interviews, tests, etc. ... Experiments are difficult, but may produce information not obtainable in other ways.

The evaluative purpose is to see how far programme efforts produce the changes required by programme aims.

5. Surveys, at their simplest, get facts which describe a social programme. In an experiment they may also have an explanatory use. They often deal with some kind of sampling from a population (e.g. the intended beneficiaries). Data can be collected by various methods. ... Surveys collect descriptive facts quickly and cheaply, especially if sampling is used.

The evaluative purpose is the production of descriptive facts which can be used to endorse or adapt programme aims, objectives and efforts.

6. Case studies provide full and detailed descriptions of what happens as a programme develops. Whereas experiments and surveys tend to collect quantitative data, case studies give much weight to sensitive, qualitative data, collected by methods such as participant observation, group analysis and content analysis. The student may apply particular conceptual schemes (e.g. "group dynamics") to the extensive data collected.

Case studies take time, but are especially useful for developing programmes where "there is difficulty in specifying objectives and in selecting programmatic means to accomplish those objectives" (1, p. 93). They

are also useful to pinpoint potential problems in implementing a programme.

The main evaluative purpose is to find out in detail how staff activities and staff perceptions of programme goals contribute to overall programme efforts.

Cost-analytic Techniques. These estimate the relative value of a programme in relation to programme costs.

7. Cost accounting is similar to general accounting, but goes on to convert programme outputs into measurable units of activity, such as the number of young people counselled. The cost of each unit of output is calculated. For broad-aim programmes, it is difficult to arrive at unit costs. For other types of programme, the more specific method of "programme budgeting" may be useful.

The principal evaluative purpose is to find out how programme resources are allocated relative to actual programme outputs, with a view to improving programme budgeting.

8. Cost-benefit analysis is a more complex method used to find out the "benefits" (i.e. whether or not programme objectives have been achieved, and the monetary value that such achievement represents) as well as the costs of a programme. The value of the benefits is compared with the value of the costs —this is expressed as 'benefit-to-cost ratio.' The greater the benefit-to-cost ratio, the more effective the programme.

Clearly, this method is irrelevant when it is not possible to give benefits any meaningful monetary value.

The principal evaluative purpose is to get a measure of the effectiveness and efficiency of a programme that is being implemented. It also can be used to compare alternative programmes.

9. Cost-outcome analysis relates the costs of a programme, as expressed in monetary terms, to the outcome of the programme, without translating outcomes into monetary terms. The information produced is descriptive, and usually compares the costs of alternative programmes that achieve the same objectives. The technique can show the minimum costs that are necessary to produce a given outcome.

The evaluative purpose is to assess the relative efficiency of alternative programmes, or aspects of programmes, in the implementation stage.

10. Operations research is a sophisticated application of many methods to study different organisational solutions to providing programmes. Objectives are identified, and the organisational system is described in an effort to relate it to the objectives. A mathematical model of the organisational system and its objectives is developed. This model gives mathematical solutions to various programme problems, which can be put into operation. Its high cost makes operations research useful only for large-scale programmes, assuming that significant programme variables can be translated into valid mathematical expressions.

The evaluative purpose is to show how effective and efficient programmes are during the contact and implementation stages.

10.

Fred M. Cox

COMMUNITY PROBLEM SOLVING: A GUIDE TO PRACTICE WITH COMMENTS

This problem-solving guide was developed by the editors and their students. Community practitioners will find that the guide directs their attention to a number of factors central to assessing community problems and developing a course of action for attacking them.

There have been a number of efforts to provide a model to guide community organization practice. Murray G. Ross developed a set of principles to guide community organization and a discussion of the roles of the organizer. (16, pp. 155–228; 17, pp. 157–231) Ronald Lippitt and his collaborators studied a wide range of planned change efforts, which include efforts at the community level. From this study, they formulated a discussion of the phases of planned change, the role of the change agent, an approach to diagnosis in planned change, and an analysis of the forces operating for and against change. (9) Roland Warren provides a five-stage model of the "development and change of community action systems." (25, p. 315 and pp. 303–39) Robert Perlman and Arnold Gurin offer a "problem solving model" in their study of community organization, prepared under the auspices of the Council of Social Work Education. (12, pp. 61–75) This list is by no means comprehensive, (19, pp. 504 ff.) but it includes those that have been most influential in shaping the present effort.

The guide is ordered sequentially as the factors considered are likely to be encountered in practice. The guide should be used flexibly. The experienced practitioner may not need to explore each point as carefully as one new to a situation. Few will have the opportunity to employ it systematically in every practice context. Nevertheless, we believe the practitioner will find it useful as a reminder of issues that may otherwise be overlooked or questions that provoke thought that may have an important bearing on practice decisions and outcomes. Some practitioners will be confronted with more "givens" and fewer choices than others. A clear understanding of the "givens" as well as the options is crucial for effective practice.

Like most general models, this one may fail to call attention to certain questions of importance in specific situations. Many practitioners will want to refine and elaborate the guide to suit the particulars of the practice situation in which they are involved. In general, however, we believe that the guide can contribute to a more logical and coherent approach to confronting problems in the multiple pressures and confusions of community practice.

THE GUIDE

I. Preliminary Considerations
  A. *Summary of Assignment.* Brief description of the worker's assignment and developments leading to it, designed to introduce and make intelligible what follows
  B. *Agency* (organization employing the practitioner)
    1. Type
      a. Based on primary beneficiary (2, pp. 45–57), mutual benefit, commonweal, service, and business.
      b. Based on locus of control at the top or base (13), corporate or federated
      c. Representative, collegial, bureaucratic, or anomic (23)
    2. Constitution and goal orientation (formal statement and informal "understandings" of purposes, *modus operandi*)

      a. Domain and extent of community consensus on domain (8)
      b. Narrowly defined and specific or broad and general (13)
      c. Change or service orientation (Reading #13)
      d. Member or nonmember targets (Reading #13)
      e. Institutional or individual targets (Reading #13)
    3. Constituency (those who control the agency) and resource base (funds, clients, and personnel and their sources) (Reading #13)
      a. Homogeneous or heterogeneous on various dimensions—social class, ethnic characteristics, sex, interests, etc.
      b. Organizations or individuals
      c. Extent of agency dependence on constituency and resource base.
    4. Internal structure (Reading #14)
      a. Authority—hierarchical or collegial
      b. Division of labor—specialist or generalist
      c. Rules—predetermined and imposed on functionaries, based on internalization of goals by functionaries, ad hoc, etc.
      d. Interpersonal relations—impersonal or personal
      e. Personnel assigned on basis of merit or on criteria irrelevant to organization's goals
    5. Programs and functions of agency and their relation to worker's assignment
  C. *Practitioner* (person employed by agency who is working on given problem)
    1. Motivation, capacity, and opportunity to perform assigned tasks (14)
    2. Role ambiguity, conflict, discontinuity, and strain in the situation and their management (22)

II. Problems (15)
  A. *Problem Analysis* (as perceived by the practitioner)
    1. Nature: What specific kind of problem are you concerned about?
    2. Location: Where is the problem? (geographically, socially, psychologically, institutionally)
    3. Scope: Who (kinds of people, groups) are affected?
    4. Degree: How much are they affected?

B. *Past Change Efforts*
1. By whom?
2. How effective?
3. Reasons for successes or failures
C. *Perceptions of the Problem by Significant Others* (individuals, groups and organizations) (15)
1. Who perceives the problem as the practitioner does?
2. Who perceives it differently—as nonexistent or insignificant, or as qualitatively different?

III. Social Context of the Problem
A. *Origins of the Problem* (where relevant) (4)
B. *Theory of the Problem*
1. Why this rather than some alternative explanation?
2. Empirical and ideological justification
C. *Structural-Functional Analysis of the Problem*
1. Social structures that maintain, increase, or reduce the problem
   a. Societal, regional, state, local, neighborhood
   b. Formal organizations, voluntary associations, primary groups
   c. Power alignments, social/demographic factors, ecological/economic relations, cultural/technological factors
2. Consequences of the problem for significant elements of the social structure—who gains, who loses. In what ways is the problem situation functional or dysfunctional for the maintenance of the groups having a stake in the problem?

IV. The Client (the population segments or groups that are the primary beneficiary of the practitioner's efforts) (2, pp. 45–57)
A. *Physical Location,* boundaries, size
B. *Social, Economic, Political, and Demographic Characteristics*
C. *Formal Organization of the Client*
D. *Divisions and Cleavages* within the client
E. *Significant Relations* with other parts of the social structure
F. *Significant Changes* in the above, over time

V. Goals (11; 18)
A. *Goals in Their Approximate Order of Priority* for dealing with the problem as identified by:

1. Agency
2. Client
3. Significant others
B. *Practitioner's Preferred Goals and Priorities,* in the light of the above, including:
1. Task goals (goals related to task attainment regarding a substantive community problem)
2. Process goals (system maintenance and enhancement goals—social relationships, problem-solving structures, and processes)

VI. Strategy. In the light of preferred goals and priorities, consider two or three feasible strategies, in the following terms: (9, pp. 71–89)
A. *Minimum Tasks Required for Success*
B. *The Action System.* Identify the resources and supporting groups from within the agency, the client and significant others required to carry out strategy under consideration
C. *Resistance* (opposition) *and Interference* (inertia, distraction) *Forces*
1. Review functional analysis (III.C. 2., above)
2. Identify opposing groups, their probable actions and impersonal difficulties which might be encountered
3. Indicate how the strategy under consideration would cope with these
D. *Evaluation of Practitioner's Ability To Utilize Strategy*
1. Can minimum tasks be carried out and sustained?
2. Can needed resources and supporting groups be mobilized, and their cohesion and goal-directed behavior maintained?
3. Can resistance and interference forces be managed?
E. *Preferred Strategy.* Of the strategies considered, select one and give the rationale for this choice

VII. Tactics (9)
A. *Gaining Initial Support*
1. Entry—where does one start and with whom?
2. Leverage—what initial actions give one the best chance for sustaining one's strategy?
B. *Involving and Organizing* (or Reorganizing) *the Action System*

1. Clarification of the problem, including gathering and interpretation of relevant data
2. Clarification of goals and preferred strategy
3. Clarification of role expectations of change agent, agency, and various parts of the action system
4. Establishing a "contract" (or basic agreement between the practitioner and those making up the action system)
   C. *Implementation of Action*
   1. Training and offering organizational and psychological support to the action system
   2. Scheduling actions over time
   3. Utilizing available resources
   4. Utilizing "Action-Reaction-Action" patterns (designing a sequence of actions to take advantage of anticipated responses) (1)
   5. Dealing with opposition, as necessary (confrontation, neutralization, questioning legitimacy, bargaining, etc.)

VIII. Evaluation (Reading #9)
   A. *Success of Strategy in Problem Solution*
   B. *Effectiveness of Tactics*

IX. Modification, Termination or Transfer of Action
   A. *Designing New Goals, Strategy, or Tactics*
   B. *Facilitating Termination or Modification of Practitioner's Activity*
   1. Disengaging practitioners from action system
   2. Transferring relations to new practitioner
   3. Maintaining or institutionalizing change effort
   4. Moving action system toward terminal goal(s)

COMMENTS[1]

As part of the effort to increase the professional character of community organization practice, we need to develop guidelines

for decision making that are grounded upon tested generalities. As our knowledge base expands, it should be possible to rely more heavily on insights drawn from the social and behavioral sciences. The problem in basing decisions on tested knowledge is to find a way to join the hodgepodge which is the reality of community practice and the generalizations derived from research, which necessarily oversimplify, and select a few factors believed to be of overriding importance.

This problem is a difficult one for at least two reasons. First, our knowledge of what factors are most influential and their effects upon matters of importance to the practitioner, together with the various conditions that affect such cause and effect relationships, is very limited. Typically, we must be content with a combination of practice wisdom and partially tested theory validated under conditions quite different than those faced by each practitioner. For example, conclusions about group behavior are often based on laboratory data rather than field studies.

Second, even when knowledge is very full and based on rigorous study, there are serious problems in applying it. Scientific knowledge is the knowledge of probabilities, of the chances that certain actions or events are likely to be followed by particular consequences. But even a high probability of B being followed by A leaves room for the possibility, in some minority of instances, that A will not produce B. And there are always newly emerging contingencies, the effects of which are unknown, and relatively unique configurations of events and conditions that were not anticipated in the research studies. Thus, even under the best conditions, we must guard against expecting too much from scientific knowledge in guiding practice decisions.

What does the problem-solving guide contribute to this process? First, it suggests

---

[1]The author acknowledges the contributions made by his colleagues John L. Erlich and Jack Rothman, whose critical comments and suggestions were used extensively in preparing this supplement to the preceding guide.

the major types of information that must be obtained by the practitioner if he or she is to reach informed decisions. Second, it offers the outline of an interconnected set of frameworks within which to collect this information. It does not, however, provide propositions or generalizations to which decisions must be referred; these comments will suggest some additional sources we have found useful for this purpose. The comments are organized in the same order and under the same headings as the guide above. Wherever possible we relate these comments to the three models of community organization around which this book is organized.

I. PRELIMINARY CONSIDERATIONS

A. Summary of Assignment

The practitioner provides a brief orientation to the nature of the assignment. If the guide is used for training purposes, the instructor may find this summary particularly useful.

B. Agency

The organization that sponsors the practitioner's work is the agency referred to. Its primary significance is in the possibilities it opens and the constraints it places upon practice.

Social action is typically sponsored by groups of like-minded people who feel generally oppressed by the wider society, are offended by particular governmental decisions or social norms, or share common interests they believe can be achieved more effectively through collective action. The group is held together by some common identity (ethnic or racial characteristics, ideological or cultural similarities, goals, a piece of turf, a shared sense of being op-

pressed by the larger society). While the sponsor is likely to be homogeneous in some respects, necessary funds may be generated by the group itself or may come from outside sources which may not fully identify with the sponsor, its goals, or, particularly, its methods. This constitutes a problem for some social action groups because, as they engage in controversial activities, they may jeopardize their financial support. On the other hand, to the extent they are homogeneous they are able to pursue their objectives single-mindedly, without undue debate over ends and means.

Locality development may be sponsored by a national government, as in the case of many community development programs in developing countries or in industrialized countries with groups of people isolated from modernization. In such cases there may be conflict between the aims and values of the national government and the people toward whom locality development is directed. Governmental sponsorship, however, may bring otherwise unavailable resources to bear upon problems of underdevelopment. In other cases, locality development is sponsored by groups who seek self-development, often at the initiative and with the continued assistance of some outside group (American Friends Service Committee, a community development program in a land-grant college). Under these conditions, considerable emphasis is placed upon representing various segments of local people and upon their voluntary choice of aims and activities. Given the diversity of people within a locality, problems often arise in finding consensus and in sustaining motivation to work on common problems, but, because these are necessary, the programs chosen represent what local people really want and may be more permanent than those imposed from outside.

Social planning may be sponsored by government at various levels or by private organizations. Backed by constituted authorities or the socially or politically elite, these agencies tend to view their mandate as deriving from the established political process or from democratic procedures in which all citizens are at least nominally free to participate. They typically focus on bringing technical skills to bear upon social problems and are dependent upon the sources of legitimacy, so that they often overlook the views of those who are the presumed beneficiaries or targets of their planning efforts. Insistent demands for wider participation may create operating problems for social planning agencies. If the agencies can secure substantial support, both financial and political, and highly qualified specialists, however, they may be able to resolve social problems to a greater degree than if support from those affected by the plans were required or fewer resources were available.

The extent to which organizations are bureaucratized has a major impact upon the kinds of tasks they can undertake and the strategies and tactics available to the practitioner. (Reading #14) Organizations vary not only in internal structure but in relations with the social environment. They emerge out of the needs of particular constituents, with whom they have a variety of understandings about goals and methods. As noted in the text above, social action agencies are oriented toward their members, while social planning agencies are created by elites to control social problems experienced by nonelites. Zald discusses this with special reference to factors affecting the autonomy of the strategies available to the community organization agency. (Reading #13) Rein and Morris discuss the effects of the planning organization's goals and structure upon the strategies it employs. (13, pp. 127–45)

Parenthetically, it should be noted that formal organizations may be important to the practitioner not only as sponsors of action but as allies in a joint effort or as targets of strategy. Litwak and Rothman's article, which discusses linkages between formal organizations and primary groups (Reading #14), and Hasenfeld and Tropman's, which summarizes the literature on interorganizational relations (Reading #15), are useful guides to working with organizations as allies or targets.

The work of the authors mentioned in parentheses in the guide is discussed more fully in the Introduction to "ARENAS" and in the selections included in "STRATEGIES."

C. Practitioner

The practitioner's activities can be analyzed from two perspectives. The first, which examines the practitioner's motivation, capacity, and opportunity, was developed by faculty members at the University of Chicago's School of Social Service Administration. (14) This perspective raises three general questions: (1) To what extent do the personal and professional goals of the practitioner coincide, reinforce, compete, or conflict with the goals of those he is trying to help and with those of the sponsoring agency? (2) Does the practitioner have the basic qualities of intelligence, ability to empathize with others, a sense of personal identity, and the special skills and knowledge necessary to operate effectively in a particular community organization assignment? (3) Does the practitioner have the support of the agency, the human and financial resources that are necessary for him to do the job with a reasonable expectation of effective performance? If there are impediments in the situation, what, if anything, can be done to correct them? Ronald Lippitt and his collaborators give attention to some of these questions. (9, pp. 92–99)

The motivation, capacity, and opportunity required will vary with the type of practice and the nature of the sponsoring agency. For example, the practitioner's ideological predilections and world view will affect the motivation to work for various types of agencies and the willingness to use different strategies and tactics. Skills in working with different kinds of people (poor people, local elite) and in using various techniques (making population projections, teaching people how to handle unfamiliar situations) affect the capacity to work in different settings. The types and amounts of resources needed for effective practice vary for agencies with various scopes, goals, and strategies.

Role theory provides perhaps an even more useful perspective for analyzing the practitioner's work. The ambiguity and conflict in role definitions by various persons with whom the practitioner interacts, the discontinuity between the various roles one plays currently and between past and present roles, and the personal strain involved in learning a new role and coping with the problems inherent in role ambiguity, conflict, and discontinuity must be taken into account in understanding the practitioner's behavior and decisions. (22, pp. 17–50; 9, pp. 91–126)

II. PROBLEMS

This section of the guide directs the community organization practitioner's attention to an analysis of the difficulties he or she is trying to remedy. The problems of concern are usually social rather than personal, affecting a substantial portion of the people served and out of harmony with their preferences. They may be substantive in character, i.e., problems such as mental illness, insufficient housing or delinquency, or they may involve process, affecting the

way the society, the community, and its institutions are organized, formally or informally, for dealing with social problems. Often the two are closely connected as, for example, when it is assumed that the negative reaction to the mentally ill stems from the lack of community-based institutions for dealing with them—well-organized family care homes, recreation programs, emergency services for coping with personal life crises, etc. Community practitioners are typically concerned with problems of both substance and process.

At this point the guide calls for careful observation and description. Explaining the problem is reserved for the next section. The practitioner describes the kind of problem dealt with as clearly as possible, where it is located, how widely it is distributed among different kinds of people, and the degree to which one group is affected in comparison to another. The practitioner looks at past efforts to improve conditions, who made them, the extent of their successes or failures, and the probable reasons for these outcomes. He or she gives particular attention to differences in perceptions of the problem among the affected groups.

The varying ways in which the problem is perceived will be of particular importance. The agency, various subgroups of the client, and the practitioner may all see the problem a little differently and thus favor different solutions.

In the context of social action, the problem will be viewed as one of social injustice —an oppressed minority not receiving its fair share of political, economic, and educational resources, a group that has been deprived of some benefit or has had some social cost inflicted upon it, or a group seeking some benefit for itself at the expense of others for reasons it considers justified. Of increasing importance recently, many negatively regarded groups seek improved status and respect.

In a locality development context, the problem will often be defined as a failure to modernize, to develop the necessary capital and skills to facilitate industrialization at an appropriate rate or to build the necessary services ("infrastructure") needed to support an urbanizing population. The problem may be regarded as opposition to change (strong traditional or new but counterproductive forms of social organization), anomie (languishing social organization), or loss of local autonomy (an organized community losing control to national business, philanthropic, and governmental institutions). A normative view held by some community developers is that the problem stems from the failure of local democracy, the lack of concern about and a sense of responsibility for local problems.

Social planning agencies tend to define the problem as one or more fairly discrete social problems (mental illness, crime and delinquency, poverty, poorly organized services) for which they seek various technical solutions. The problems with which social planners deal are seen as forms of deviant behavior or social disorganization. Deviant behavior, such as mental illness, delinquency, or child abuse, is at variance with prescriptions for particular social roles. Merton makes a useful distinction between two types of deviant behavior, nonconformist and aberrant, which is particularly appropriate in the light of unrest among women minority groups, gays and students. (10, pp. 808–11) The nonconformist announces his or her deviant behavior, challenges the legitimacy of rejected social norms, tries to change norms regarded as illegitimate, and calls upon higher social values as justification for actions. Conventional members of society recognize that the nonconformist is dissenting for disinterested reasons. In contrast, the aberrant individual hides his or her acts from public view, does not challenge the legitimacy of broken norms, tries to escape detection and punishment, and serves personal interests through aberrant behavior.

Social action groups of oppressed people may define their behavior as nonconformist and seek responses from the rest of society that first confirm this definition and ultimately redefine the behavior, prompting the nonconformity as acceptable rather than deviant. For example, those seeking abortion law reform, acceptance of homosexual preferences, or equality in job opportunities may use nonconformist means to secure redefinitions of abortion, homosexual behavior, and equal employment opportunities as nondeviant. Social planners may assist them through legitimate ("conformist") means that are possible within the context of their work—drafting legislation, taking matters to court, enlisting the support of community leaders, and so forth. Social planners may also participate in efforts to redefine the behavior of some deviants who, by this definition, are aberrant but whose crimes are trivial and are not regarded as morally reprehensible, or as victimless. The smoking of marijuana in moderation may increasingly be regarded as a trivial offense at best or a victimless crime at worse. Those who engage in drug abuse, prostitution, gambling, and homosexuality are often hurting no one but themselves. Even where behavior cannot be redefined as acceptable, social planners may assist in relieving exacerbating responses, through plans for bail reform and community care for the mentally ill, for example. Finally, planning services to modify the behavior of deviants, using new techniques such as behavioral modification, will continue to be useful for a number of forms of deviant behavior.

Other social problems are regarded as symptoms of social disorganization, not necessarily involving deviations from pre-scribed norms but rather reflecting incom-patibilities between various parts of a social system, such as different rates of change (for example, technology changes more rapidly than social values). Poverty, hous-ing shortages, water pollution, unemploy-ment, and racial discrimination are often regarded as examples of social disorganiza-tion that constitute social problems social planners seek to solve.

Locality development practitioners typi-cally view social problems from this stand-point, focussing on those that retard the maintenance or enhancement of a society or community (sharply increasing birth rates, general apathy, lack of entrepreneurial skills, or a failure of leadership). They are also concerned with the inability of a local-ity to obtain resources or achieve results from self-help efforts.

Another way of looking at social prob-lems is offered by Arnold Rose, (15, pp. 189–99) who defines two perspectives. One, which we will call "disjunctive theory," re-gards social problems as arising from differ-ent meanings being attached to objects that form the context of social interaction or from different values being assigned to the behaviors displayed in relation to those ob-jects. Marijuana (an object) is regarded by some as a potentially dangerous mind-alter-ing drug and by others as a means to a pleasant "high." The smoking of marijuana (behavior in relation to the object) is dis-valued by some and enjoyed by others. Pov-erty in the United States today (a set of objects or conditions) is regarded by some as an unfortunate but inevitable by-product of the free enterprise system and by others as a needless hardship inflicted upon sub-stantial (though decreasing) numbers of people by the economic system. Living in poverty (behavior in relation to that condi-tion) is regarded as avoidable and remedia-ble by individual effort or as essentially ir-remediable "tough luck" by some and as unnecessary deprivation remediable by col-lective effort by others. In each case, the problem is regarded as arising from lack of agreement on meanings, values, or both.

The disjunctive theory is often held, at least implicitly, by those practicing locality development and leads to emphasis upon the socialization process, education, and communication. If meanings attached to the same objects differ, efforts can be made to give people "the facts" so that increas-ingly meanings can be shared. If values as-sociated with particular behaviors conflict, communication between those who dis-agree may ultimately lead to a greater de-gree of consensus.

The other perspective Rose calls "con-flict theory." From this point of view, social problems are the product of competition for scarce resources (wealth, prestige, power) which results in painful struggles over their distribution, with some being dissatisfied at the outcome.

Conflict theory assumes that values are held in common, that is, most people want the same things and will fight over their distribution, while disjunctive theory as-sumes that social problems arise from want-ing different things or defining the same things in different ways. Those engaged in social action tend to regard social problems from the perspective of conflict theory. Al-though these practitioners may agree that some secondary grounds for conflict may arise from different meanings being at-tached to the same events (for example, the lack of a common understanding about the "facts" of poverty), they argue that the ba-sic problem is one of maldistribution (of jobs or income). Social action practitioners try to solve social problems by mobilizing power to induce a redistribution of the valued objects in favor of their clients.

III. SOCIAL CONTEXT OF THE PROBLEM

A. Origins

The practitioner must take care to interpret the origins of a problem. He or she may understand how a problem came to be by examining its origins, but cannot thereby explain its persistence. Conditions that brought about a problem originally often fade, so that present conditions can only be explained by reference to factors currently operating. The practitioner must search for contemporary conditions that are causally connected with the problem and try to change them.

An effort should be made to understand the historical roots of the problem, particularly if there is a long or significant history affecting the present state of affairs. Coleman discusses what he calls residues of organization and sentiment that build up as people interact in community life and may take the form of collaborative patterns, expressed in latent or manifest forms of social organization or in organized cleavages such as those between rival political parties or ethnic groups. They may also be expressed in sentiments of liking and respect or of hostility. (4, pp. 670–95)

B. Theory of the Problem

It is at this point in the analysis that attention is directed toward a search for controlling factors. Assuming that most problems are sustained by a wide variety of factors and that some are more influential than others, the practitioner's task is twofold: First, one must locate factors that have a major effect on the problem to be corrected. Second, one must choose problems one can reasonably expect to influence, given the time, money, personnel and other resources at one's disposal.

In many social action contexts, the problem will be understood as some form of conflict between "haves" and "have-nots." But greater specificity is required. Which particular interests are pitted against one another? What are the dynamics of the conflict? Are there any aspects of the problem or any facts that do not seem to fit into a conflict perspective? What are the implications for intervention? In many cases of locality development, the problem will be regarded as arising from barriers to communication or different rates of change, i.e., some form of disjunction or social disorganization. But it is important which specific theory or set of theories is selected, for this will exercise an important influence on strategies and tactics chosen. Most practitioners engaged in social planning will consider alternative theories explaining various social problems they are charged with ameliorating. But, again, the specific theory chosen is of great importance in shaping the action taken. If, for example, lower-class male delinquency is conceived of as arising from a lack of legitimate opportunities for success in American society, efforts will be made to expand those opportunities. If, on the other hand, delinquency is thought to arise from psychological problems or parental rejection, efforts will be directed toward various forms of counseling or the strengthening or substitution of parental relations. Or, if the labeling of youngsters as delinquent and the consequent processing through the criminal justice system are thought to be responsible for the perpetuation of delinquent behavior, efforts will be made to decriminalize certain behavior and handle young people who transgress social norms outside the criminal justice system.

Unfortunately, the explanation of the problem chosen by (or more typically implicit in the behavior of) the practitioner is usually limited by the ideology and values of the employing organization or the practitioner. The practitioner should explore his or her own preconceptions and those of the employer to determine what limits such preconceptions place on the choice of an explanation for the problem. However the theory of the problem arises, whether it is implicit in various predisposing values or is more rationally developed, it will have a major influence on the goals and strategies chosen for dealing with the problem.

C. Structural-Functional Analysis of the Problem

The practitioner begins with an assessment of available "theories of the problem." He selects the most reliable theories, and within them the factors that are both potent and potentially controllable. The next step is careful observation of the particular social problem in its context, collecting information within the framework of the theories and hypotheses selected earlier. The outline suggests that both the impact of various factors on the social problem in question and the effect of the problem on these factors be assessed. For example, we might identify particular social structures (schools, employers) that systematically deny opportunities to persons of lower socioeconomic or ethnic minority status, thus creating discontent, delinquent behavior, and so forth. We might then show the impact of such behavior on schools, ethnic minorities, and so forth, emphasizing the differential effects on various groups. This, of course, has implications for which groups, individuals, or organizations may be recruited into organized efforts to alleviate the problems.

Two terms used in this section of the outline are functional and dysfunctional: The functional consequences of action strengthen and unify social systems; dysfunctional consequences produce conflict or threaten disruption of existing social patterns. However, these terms should not be confused with "good" and "bad." Functional consequences can perpetuate what is, from the practitioner's perspective, an undesirable system, such as patterns of racial discrimination in housing and employment. Likewise, dysfunctional consequences may be exactly what the practitioner desires. For example, the early sit-ins, in addition to disrupting preexisting patterns of race relations, tended to enhance the self-esteem of black people and provide experience in contentious organized action.

IV. THE CLIENT

The client is defined as the primary beneficiary of the practitioner's activities. It may be a group of people, a formal organization, or a population category. The client can be analyzed in terms similar to other forms of social organization. Some of the factors that may be most important are outlined in the guide. The major implication of this section is that the client must be identified and understood both in its context, i.e., its relations to other social phenomena, and in its internal structure. We must also be sensitive to changes that have taken place in the client and the reasons for them.

The definition of the client forces the practitioner to be clear about whom he or she is trying to help and to differentiate them from others who are regarded in more instrumental terms. There was a time when it was conventional for the community organizer to say that the client is the community. This rhetoric tends to hide the fact that particular actions may benefit some, harm others, and have little effect on still others. The suggested definition makes the practitioner consider whose interests will be sacrificed last if decisions must be made requiring that someone pay a price. It also demands that the practitioner consider how much to expect others to "pay" for the sake of the clients and decide whether the price is justifiable.

If the clientele is a group of individuals with strongly held common interests that can be rather precisely defined, the practitioner will have little difficulty in knowing what benefits to work for on their behalf. On the other hand, one is likely to have difficulty in gaining allies and support for the group. If the clientele is a heterogeneous group with common interests that can be defined only at the most general level, the practitioner probably will have trouble in defining precisely what to aim for. The chances of alienating some faction of the clientele are increased, but the group is likely to be much more inclusive, and thus the practitioner will have less difficulty in gaining needed outside support.

As Rothman notes (Reading #1), the client is viewed differently in the several contexts of practice. In locality development, clients are citizens and participants in local problem solving. In social planning, they are consumers and recipients of services. In social action they are victims of oppression and employers or constituents of the practitioner.

The kind of client one is able to serve is limited, in important ways, by the type of organization that employs one. That is, it is most difficult for a practitioner to give primacy to the interests of a group that is not the primary beneficiary of his or her employer. Blau and Scott have developed a typology of organizations based on the identity of the groups that are the primary beneficiaries of organizations. (2, pp. 42–57) The main implication for practice is that the practitioner experiences grave difficulties in making clients out of groups other than those that are naturally the primary beneficiaries of the type of organization employing him. For example, the primary beneficiary of a mutual benefit association is its members. If the practitioner employed by,

say, a labor union defines some nonmembers as the client—perhaps the people living in an impoverished neighborhood—he is likely to run into difficulties with members who resent the diversion of their dues for purposes not directly related to their welfare. Community practitioners employed by such agencies as public assistance bureaus sometimes experience difficulties when they select client-serving goals with which the public is out of sympathy. Part of the reason for these difficulties is a failure to recognize the true character of such social service agencies as commonweal organizations whose prime beneficiary is the general citizens instead of, as commonly believed, service organizations whose primary beneficiary is the clientele.

V. GOALS

At some point in his or her work, the practitioner must define as clearly as possible the particular goals to be achieved with the client. Lack of clarity may lead to goal displacement, i.e., the unintended replacement of goals by new, often unrecognized objectives. Under some conditions—when the situation is very unstable, when there is little experience to guide action, or when knowledge of aims would help those opposed to them—it may be necessary to be vague in public statements or to move toward goal definition through a process of successive approximation. Many other factors also lead to goal displacement—insufficient resources to pursue multiple goals, factional differences in interests, procedures which come to be valued by those who benefit from them, and so forth. Precise goal definition is one defense against goal displacement, however, and provides some criteria against which results can be measured. Resistance to goal displacement should not be used as an excuse to avoid adopting new goals when old ones have been achieved or are no longer appropriate, or new resources make it possible to add goals.

The practitioner must take into account not only his or her personal objective but also the views of the sponsoring organization, the clientele, and other groups whose support is needed or whose resistance or objections must be anticipated. It is not necessary to accommodate the interests of the opposition or of those who are largely indifferent to or unaffected by the action, but one must do so for those whose cooperation, whether as active collaboration or passive awareness and the absence of hindering responses, one must have. Those whose interests must be taken into account if the practitioner is to achieve his or her objectives are called the "action system." (This term is used in the guide under the heading "Strategy.")

As suggested above, various groups have different *goals,* attach varying *importance* to particular goals, and have contrasting sets of *priorities.* Factions within groups may also differ in these ways. In taking these differences into account, the practitioner may decide on a strategy of "something for everyone," or may begin with one easily achieved goal of fairly high importance to all elements in order to build confidence in the organization's capability. One may develop some other rationale for selecting goals, but information about the relative priorities and salience of the goals of different factions is essential to a reasoned decision. (11, pp. 25–31)

Social problems may reside in a group's relations with its environment (inadequate police protection or unresponsive public officials) or among its members (uncoordinated activities, low morale, lack of commitment). Goals are of two parallel kinds. For example, a welfare council may appeal for additional public funds for a child care center or try to develop support for a human relations commission. These are commonly referred to in the literature as "task goals." Other goals affect the maintenance and enhancement of the organization (resolving destructive factional rivalry or transforming member apathy into involvement and commitment). These are called "process goals." In general, both types of goals must be served, but at particular times one type may be more important than another. At one time it was generally believed that the community practitioner should pursue only process goals, that is, be concerned exclusively with facilitating or "enabling" clients to achieve self-defined goals. Rothman argues persuasively that the practitioner need not be limited in this manner. (18, pp. 24–31)

VI. STRATEGY

Perfect rationality (or anything approaching it) is unattainable in most practice situations. Computer technology may enable some to come a bit closer. But most of us must, as Herbert Simon puts it, "satisfice" rather than "maximize" the efficiency and effectiveness of our decisions. (20, p. xxv.)

However, some practitioners approach questions of strategy with predetermined formulas, agency traditions, and little imagination. While it is not feasible to consider every possibility and identify the single best way to achieve objectives, it does not follow that one strategy is as good as the next. The practitioner is asked to consider at least two good possibilities and exercise judgment in choosing the best one.

Perhaps more than any other activity, strategy development offers the practitioner an opportunity for creativity. In applying the guide, he or she sketches each strategy, outlining the minimum tasks required to achieve success; the necessary elements of the action system; the resistance (opposition), interdependence (entanglements), and interference (competition and indifference) forces that may be encountered; and the plans to handle them. (9, pp. 71–89) Finally, the practitioner evaluates his or her ability to carry them out and develops a rationale for choosing between the various strategies being considered. As a general approach to decision making this applies to all types of practice. However, the relative emphasis given to various tactics (research, client participation, confrontation with organizations and their leaders) will vary with the model of practice used.

To the extent that success depends upon a correct theory of the problem and an effective strategy, success may be limited by the choices permitted by the elites or the political process. Because social planning strategies normally depend upon the effective manipulation of large-scale bureaucracies, success may also depend heavily on whether the strategy chosen can be effectively administered. And finally, because those whose actions are required for success —the functionaries and the targets—are not ciphers but people with interests and values that guide what they will respond to and what they will do, strategies that assume values about which there is little consensus or which assume a nonexistent community of interests are likely to enjoy limited success.

Some recent analyses suggest that strategies that operate as much as possible in a way analogous to a competitive market situation are most likely to succeed. They maximize individual choices and allow for individual differences. They require a minimum of bureaucratic complexity, especially detailed rules and numerous functionaries to enforce or monitor compliance. It has been suggested that this is the reason for the failure of such programs as the War on Poverty, the success of Social Security, and the promise of income maintenance programs based on negative income tax principles. (7)

VII. TACTICS

Strategy shades imperceptibly into tactics. The inspiration for much of this part of the guide comes from Lippitt and his colleagues. (9) Among the questions the practitioner is asked to consider are: Where is it possible to gain a foothold in the targets? At what point are efforts likely to be most effective? For example, the practitioner may have access to other practitioners working in low- or middle-echelon positions in a target organization. His or her analysis, however, may lead to the conclusion that, to achieve the objective, the practitioner must gain access to the top executive. One may, therefore, bypass colleagues in the target organization and approach a member of one's board with the necessary social and political contacts to gain the ear of the target agency executive.

In order to avoid misunderstandings, it is important for the practitioner to communicate with key people in the action system (those whose cooperation is needed to carry out the strategy) so that they may develop common ideas about such things as definition of the problem, objectives, approaches, roles each participant will perform, and amount of time each participant will commit to the endeavor. The resulting set of agreements is referred to as the contract. Although the concept is borrowed from the law, it does not imply legal or even written form. The expectations must be as clear and unambiguous as possible, and all necessary participants must understand and commit themselves to the terms of the contract.

In carrying the plan into action, it may be necessary to train and support participants who feel more or less uncertain about what they are doing. This is particularly relevant for those who are inexperienced in the sort of activities required by the contract. The timing of various actions must be carefully planned. Resources of several kinds may require difficult coordination—it may be necessary to induce competing professionals to work together or to provide the press with newsworthy events involving large numbers of people so that politicians will take the action system's demands seriously.

The idea of an "action-reaction-action pattern" is borrowed from Alinsky. (1) We refer to these patterns when one group makes a move which is intended to elicit a response from an adversary that makes possible further action to achieve objectives that could not have been otherwise undertaken. For example, a group might leak information to an adversary that it plans a massive disruption of the adversary's business. The expected response is an offer to negotiate which, in turn, makes it possible to obtain concessions favorable to the group that would not have been secured by an initial request for negotiations. Such tactics depend on credibility; if the adversary does not believe that there is a genuine threat, it is not likely to negotiate.

The practitioner should anticipate that some form of opposition to the program undertaken by the action system may emerge and make plans to handle it. Under some circumstances, no such opposition will develop—organizing a council on aging or applying for funds from the federal government to mount programs for the aging should arouse no controversy or opposition. If insurmountable opposition can be expected, however, plans should be changed unless the practitioner is deliberately trying to heighten awareness of impotence and stimulate anger as a prelude to other, perhaps stronger forms of action. If opposition is inevitable, a variety of approaches is available to cope with it in ways that may further the action system's objectives. In particular, Walton discusses methods for dealing with two types of opposition, negative attitudes and countervailing power.

VIII. EVALUATION (21; 5; 3; 6; 24; Reading #9)

Evaluation should be an ongoing process. Plans must be worked out for the collection of information from participants in the action system regarding effectiveness with respect to both task and process goals. This may be quite informal (setting aside a portion of a meeting to discuss "how we're doing") or much more rigorous (standardized data collection, written reports) depending upon the size, complexity, and other requirements of the effort in which the practitioner is engaged. The important thing is that assessment not be overlooked, for the process allows the practitioner and the organization to revise their program if activities are found to be less than satisfactory.

Practitioners often find annual or semi-annual meetings good opportunities for taking stock. The results may be set forth in a periodic report. There is a tendency at such meetings to "put the best foot forward" and overlook difficulties in order to maintain or enhance morale, build financial resources, and avoid offending those who have been active in the organization. Ordinarily it is best to find ways to say what may be the unpleasant truth in a manner that minimizes problems. For example, it is possible to express gratitude for individual contributions while calling attention to persistent difficulties that exist "in spite of the best efforts of everyone involved."

IX. MODIFICATION, TERMINATION OR TRANSFER OF ACTION

Evaluation of program and organizational effectiveness may lead to any one of several conclusions. First, the practitioner may conclude that the program is operating much as expected, is achieving its intended purposes, and should be continued. Second, he or she may find that some aspects are faulty, because of an erroneous analysis of the situation, a poor strategy, or particular actions that were inappropriate or poorly carried out. This conclusion should lead to necessary revisions. Third, the practitioner and those he or she is working with may conclude that the program has served its purpose or, alternatively, is hopelessly inept. In either case, the conclusion should be to discontinue operations and the practitioner must plan carefully for this. Finally, for a variety of reasons the practitioner may be leaving the job. Under these conditions, it is necessary to arrange either the transfer of professional responsibilities to another practitioner or the termination of the program.

CONCLUSION

These comments suggest how the guide may be used and offer some additional references which are intended to give it a broader scope and greater utility. We hope that practitioners will use the guide to remind themselves of some of the more important factors they need to take into account in planning their work.

Obviously the busy community practitioner will be unable to utilize fully the analysis suggested here in daily work. However, many of the steps in the problem-solving process will become part of the professional "equipment" he or she may apply, perhaps less formally and less rigorously but nonetheless effectively, in making day-to-day practice decisions. This is the hope we have had in preparing the guide and using it in teaching community organization practice.

BIBLIOGRAPHY

1. Alinsky, Saul D. *Reveille for Radicals.* Chicago: University of Chicago Press, 1946; and *Rules for Radicals.* New York: Random House, 1971.

2. Blau, Peter, M., and Scott, W. Richard. *Formal Organizations.* San Francisco: Chandler Publishing Co., 1962.

3. Campbell, Donald T. "Reforms as Experiments." *American Psychologist* 24 (April 1969): 409–29.

4. Coleman, James S. "Community Disorganization," in Merton and Nisbet, op. cit., pp. 670–95.

5. Herzog, Elizabeth. *Some Guidelines for Evaluative Research.* Children's Bureau Publication No. 375. Washington, D.C.: U.S. Dept. of Health, Education, and Welfare, 1959.

6. Hyman, Herbert H., and Wright, Charles R. "Evaluating Social Action Programs," in *The Uses of Sociology,* edited by Paul F. Lazarfeld, William H. Sewell, and Harold Wilensky. New York: Basic Books, 1967. pp. 741–82.

7. Levine, Robert A. *Public Planning: Failure and Redirection.* New York: Basic Books, 1972.

8. Levine, Sol; White, Paul E.; and Paul, Benjamin D. "Community Interorganizational Problems in Providing Medical Care and Social Services," *American Journal of Public Health* 53 (August 1963): 1183–95.

9. Lippitt, Ronald; Watson, Jeanne; and Westley, Bruce. *The Dynamics of Planned Change: A Comparative Study of Principles and Techniques.* New York: Harcourt, Brace and World, 1958.

10. Merton, Robert K. "Epilogue: Social Problems and Sociological Theory," in *Contemporary Social Problems,* 2d ed., edited by Robert K. Merton and Robert A. Nisbet. New York: Harcourt, Brace and World, 1966.

11. Morris, Robert, and Binstock, Robert H. *Feasible Planning for Social Change.* New York: Columbia University Press, 1966.

12. Perlman, Robert, and Gurin, Arnold. *Community Organization and Social Planning.* New York: John Wiley and Council on Social Work Education, 1972.

13. Rein, Martin, and Morris, Robert. "Goals, Structures and Strategies for Community

Change." In *Social Work Practice 1962.* New York: Columbia University Press, 1962.

14. Ripple, Lillian. "Motivation, Capacity and Opportunity as Related to the Use of Casework Services: Theoretical Base and Plan of Study," *Social Service Review* 29 (June 1955): 172–93.

15. Rose, Arnold. "Theory for the Study of Social Problems," *Social Problems* 4 (January 1957): 189–99.

16. Ross, Murray G. *Community Organization: Theory, Principles and Practice.* New York: Harper & Bros., 1955.

17. Ross, Murray G., with Lappin, B. W. *Community Organization: Theory, Principles and Practice.* 2d ed. New York: Harper & Row, 1967.

18. Rothman, Jack. "An Analysis of Goals and Roles in Community Organization Practice," *Social Work* 9 (April 1964): 24–31.

19. Sanders, Irwin T. *The Community: An Introduction to a Social System,* 2d ed. New York: The Roland Press, 1966.

20. Simon, Herbert A. *Administrative Behavior,* 2d ed. New York: The Macmillan Co., 1957.

21. Suchman, Edward A. *Evaluative Research: Principles and Practice in Public Service and Social Action Programs.* New York: Russell Sage Foundation, 1967.

22. Thomas, Edwin J., and Feldman, Ronald A. with Kamm, Jane. "Concepts of Role Theory," in *Behavioral Science for Social Workers,* edited by Edwin J. Thomas. New York: The Free Press, 1967.

23. Thompson, James D., and Tuden, Arthur. "Strategies, Structures and Processes of Organizational Decision," *Comparative Studies in Administration,* edited by J. D. Thompson et al., pp. 195–216. Pittsburgh: Pittsburgh University Press, 1959.

24. Tripodi, Tony; Fellin, Phillip; and Epstein, Irwin. *Social Program Evaluation: Guidelines for Health, Education and Welfare Administrators.* Itasca, Ill.: F. E. Peacock Publishers, 1971.

25. Warren, Roland L. *The Community in America.* Chicago: Rand McNally, 1963.

PART TWO:
ARENAS

Introduction

In the past few years, the social sciences have added a great deal to our understanding of the realities which confront community organizers. These contributions have been both conceptual and empirical. We have been greatly assisted by some of the ways they have conceived of the "booming, buzzing confusion" which confronts us as we go into action. We have found a social systems perspective on communities, organizations, and the relations among them to be particularly helpful. In addition, we are beginning to get some glimmerings of the regularities in social phenomena that enable us to make a few tenuous predictions and thus exercise some control over our field of action.

Arenas of Community Practice

One major contribution of the social sciences to the practice of community organization has been in understanding the context in which we work, what we call the arenas of community practice. These arenas include interpersonal relations, small groups, formal organizations, neighborhoods, communities, and societies. We have chosen two of these arenas—the community and the formal organization—for special attention in this volume. We believe they are particularly salient for community organization practice.[1]

---

[1]Other works are available for those who wish to examine the other arenas more closely. On interpersonal relations see: Bruce J. Biddle and Edwin J. Thomas (eds.), *Role Theory: Concepts and Research* (New York: John Wiley & Sons, Inc., 1966); Arthur W. Staats and Carolyn K. Staats, *Complex Human Behavior: A Systematic Extension of Learning Principles* (New York: Holt, Rinehart & Winston, Inc., 1963); on small group: Dorwin Cartwright and Alvin Zander (eds.), *Group Dynamics: Research and Theory* (2d ed.; Evanston, Ill.: Row, Peterson, 1960); Barry E. Collins and Harold Guetzkow, *A Social Psychology of Group Processes for Decision-Making* (New York: John Wiley & Sons, Inc., 1964); on society: Robin M. Williams, Jr., *American Society* (2d ed.; New York: Alfred A. Knopf, Inc., 1960).

To view communities and formal organizations as arenas, instead of as means or ends as others have done, lends a special perspective. As arenas, they are viewed as the context within which action occurs, conditions of the practitioner's work to be understood and, largely, taken as given in doing community work. The reaction of some will be that this is altogether too passive, too accepting of the status quo and quite reactionary from a political point of view. But most of the conditions one finds as one begins to work must be accepted as they are even though a few may be changed. Time and resources—people, influence, etc.—are limited. What is selected for change must be chosen very carefully, calibrated not only to the hopes and aspirations of the clientele and those who serve them but also to available resources. To argue for regarding communities and formal organizations as arenas, then, is to argue for understanding, analysis, and the assessment of objectives and possibilities, not to counsel despair or the inevitability of existing conditions. Only then can one choose wisely what is to be changed. That may well be some aspect of community, some organizations, or some set of relations among them. The decision will be the product of observation and analysis rather than the a priori end of all community organization practice. Murray G. Ross, the author of a widely used text in community organization, assumes that the sense of community has been weakened, if not destroyed, by industrialization and urbanization, and that the major objective of our practice is to build or strengthen community integration.[2] This might well be the outcome of observation and analysis in particular instances. But to take community integration as the goal of all community organization practice, without regard to the circumstances of particular situations, as Ross does, seems inappropriate.

Others will object to viewing community as the context of practice on the grounds that it fails to take hold of possibilities, the dynamics of local life that provide the leverage and power needed to bring about change. But understanding must precede action if success is to be more than accidental. To know what opportunities there are for change is not given in advance or in some formula. The rush to act may prove fruitless unless observation, diagnosis, and understanding come first. Thus, careful observation and analysis of a particular community may lead to the selection of appropriate means to change what needs changing. In contrast, Saul Alinsky, perhaps the best-known practitioner in the field of community organization, regarded the development of powerful local "people's organizations" as the basic means for achieving his clients' objectives, and disparaged other approaches to change.[3] Under certain conditions—intensely felt grievances for which specified persons or organizations may be held responsible, relative powerlessness in the local community, willingness to engage in conflict strategies, resources to ensure persistence through disappointments, requisite skill and leadership, etc.—Alinsky's strategy may prove best. But one cannot know all this in advance without a careful study of the situation at hand.

---

[2]Murray G. Ross, *Community Organization: Theory and Principles* (New York: Harper & Bros., 1955), pp. 52, 78–81.

[3]Saul D. Alinsky, *Reveille for Radicals* (Chicago: University of Chicago Press, 1946).

Defining the Arenas of Community Practice

Individuals may be understood as persons occupying a variety of social positions. A person, for example, may be a family member, an employee, and a member of a political party. Within each position, a person is expected to play one or more roles. As a member of a political party, a person may be asked to campaign for certain candidates, study and report on political issues, and vote in the party's primary elections. An individual may be subjected to ambiguous or conflicting expectations, arising from the different positions he occupies or the different roles he performs in a given position. He searches for ways of extricating himself from those uncertainties and conflicts.[4]

George C. Homans defines a group as follows:

> We mean by a group, a number of persons who communicate with one another often over a span of time, and who are few enough so that each person is able to communicate with all the others, not at secondhand, through other people, but face to face.[5]

Groups are composed of individuals, and formal organizations contain groups but are not merely "groups writ large."

Formal organizations are patterns of social interaction and shared perspectives "that have been deliberately established for certain purposes."[6] The fact that formal organizations are planned for the achievement of explicit objectives should not be taken to imply that all of its activities occur according to plan. As Peter M. Blau and W. Richard Scott put it:

> It is impossible to understand the nature of a formal organization without investigating the networks of informal relations and the unofficial norms as well as the formal hierarchy of authority and the official body of rules, since the formally instituted and the informally emerging patterns are inextricably intertwined.[7]

Groups are among the most important informal relations found in formal organizations, but such relations also include friendships, common interests such as politics and religion outside the formal organization, etc.

Roland L. Warren defines a community as:

> ... that combination of social units and systems which perform the major social functions having locality relevance. This is another way of saying that by "community" we mean the organization of social activities to afford people daily local access to those broad areas of activity which are necessary in day-to-day living.[8]

Each of these functions, e.g., production, distribution and consumption of goods and services, social control, education of the young, etc., is carried out by conger-

---

[4]Robert K. Merton, *Social Theory and Social Structure* (rev. and enlarged ed.; Glencoe, Ill.: The Free Press, 1957), pp. 368–84; Edwin J. Thomas and Ronald A. Feldman, "Concepts of Role Theory," in E. J. Thomas, *Behavioral Science for Social Workers* (New York: The Free Press, 1967), pp. 15–50.

[5]George C. Homans, *The Human Group* (New York: Harcourt, Brace & Co., 1950), p. 1.

[6]Peter M. Blau and W. Richard Scott, *Formal Organizations* (San Francisco: Chandler Publishing Co., 1962), p. 5.

[7]*Ibid.*, p. 6.

[8]Roland L. Warren, *The Community in America* (Chicago: Rand McNally & Co., 1963), p. 9.

ies of groups and formal organizations, partly dependent on one another but in no way centrally controlled.

This is what Edward O. Moe implies when he suggests that a community may be thought of as a "system of systems." In the same vein, Norton E. Long described the local community as an "ecology of games." Unlike the formal organization, a community is not planned but implicit or emergent. It is not centrally directed, like parts of a formal organization. Rather its parts run themselves and articulate with one another, conflicting, competing, and exchanging resources in unplanned ways.[9]

From the perspective of these arenas, community organization practice may be defined as the deliberate effort of a practitioner to influence the ties that bind individuals into small groups, relate two or more groups, connect two or more formal organizations, relate groups to organizations. His or her purpose may be to improve the relations between individuals, groups and organizations, to assist them in collaborating to achieve some tangible goal, or both. Influence may be directed within the community in an effort to change local attitudes, administrative practices, etc. or toward the larger society in attempts to effect national opinion, legislation, etc. The practitioner may do this directly by working with the individuals in groups and organizations, and indirectly by influencing the characteristics of the groups and organizations themselves such as size, representativeness, operating procedures, etc., as well as by intervening in the relations between individuals, groups and organizations, i.e., bringing them into closer communication or cooperation, increasing their autonomy, facilitating confrontation and contention, etc. More detail is given in Part Three. Here we must be content merely with indicating the relation between the arenas and the strategies of community organization practice, and focusing attention on the arenas selected for detailed analysis and some of their important features.

Salient Characteristics of Groups and Organizations

Groups and organizations differ in a number of important respects. Although it is traditional to define primary groups and bureaucracies as "ideal types" representing polar extremes of organizational characteristics, it is more useful to identify continua along which groups and organizations may be placed.[10] Certain features are universal characteristics of organizations, and we discuss these first.

Functions

All social systems must satisfy certain requirements to maintain themselves. Talcott Parsons offers one useful classification of the functions of social systems

---

[9]Edward O. Moe, "Consulting with a Community System: A Case Study," *Journal of Social Issues,* Vol. 15, No. 2 (1959), p. 29; Norton E. Long, "The Local Community as an Ecology of Games," *American Journal of Sociology,* Vol. 64 (November, 1958), pp. 251–61.

[10]Part of the following is discussed in the selection by Eugene Litwak and Jack Rothman in Chapter 4.

which we paraphrase as follows: (1) *adaptation to the social environment,* particularly obtaining resources necessary for operation such as money, personnel, and material; (2) *goal attainment,* securing the gratifications desired by the units of the system, such as profit or better housing, usually in response to external units on which the system depends; (3) *integration* or organization of the units of the system and their functioning; and (4) *tension management and pattern maintenance,* developing positive sentiments, including mechanisms for resolving disputes, training of new recruits, etc.[11] Adaptation and goal attainment are called *task* functions. These activities take place across the boundaries of social systems. Integration and tension management are called *maintenance* functions and occur within systems.

Parsons also pointed out that adaptive and tension management functions are *instrumental,* the *means* for attaining the system's objectives. Obviously obtaining resources (adaptation) is a necessary means for securing the system's objectives; perhaps less obviously, maintaining respect for authority, resolving internal disagreements, and training new recruits (tension management and pattern maintenance) are also means for keeping the organization together and moving forward to achieve its objectives.

Goal attainment and integration are consummatory, the ends or objectives of the system's activity. Again, goal attainment is obviously connected with achieving a system's objectives; less obviously, dividing and sequencing a system's work, assigning various roles to be performed, communicating between various elements of the system (integration) are necessary for achieving the system's ends and are, in effect, among the system's intermediate ends, necessary for goal attainment. The ends may be achieved by interaction among the members of the system, such as those engaged in some joint recreational pursuit, or through exchange with those outside, as when a business earns profits through transactions with its customers or a community organization practitioner helps his clients obtain a piece of legislation.

These ideas may be summarized in a diagram, adapted from Parsons[12] as follows:

	INSTRUMENTAL FUNCTIONS (MEANS)	CONSUMMATORY FUNCTIONS (ENDS)
EXTERNALLY ORIENTED TASK FUNCTIONS	Adaptation	Goal Attainment
INTERNALLY ORIENTED MAINTENANCE FUNCTIONS	Pattern Maintenance Tension Management	Integration

---

[11]Talcott Parsons, "General Theory in Sociology," in Robert K. Merton, Leonard Broom, and Leonard S. Cottrell, Jr. (eds.), *Sociology Today* (New York: Basic Books, Inc., Publishers, 1959), pp. 4–7.

[12]*Ibid.* p. 7.

As suggested above, these functions are universals. They are activities in which all social systems must engage. But organizations may differ on which of these functions are their primary *raison d'être.* For example, the community chest is engaged in collecting funds for private welfare agencies, that is, it serves an adaptive function. Welfare agencies help people resolve interpersonal difficulties, overcome physical handicaps, adapt to the demands of social institutions, etc., that is, they help manage tensions that arise in the course of social relations. Councils of social agencies, in the past, brought together representatives of welfare agencies so that they might work together effectively, serving mainly an integration function.

Some groups are largely consummatory in nature, providing direct gratifications for their members. Families, friends, churches, and recreation groups are primarily of this sort. Others are mostly instrumental tools for achieving other purposes. Most social welfare agencies, schools, block clubs, and neighborhood associations are aimed at achieving some external goals rather than providing intrinsic satisfactions for their members.

An organization's primary function may differ for its various units. For example, a local property owners' association may be regarded by some members as instrumental to the protection of property values and the exclusion of "undesirable elements," while it offers other members a sense of participation and belonging. Organizations typically function in several ways for their members. A women's rights group may serve a consummatory function by providing an acceptable outlet for personal frustrations at the same time that it is instrumental in improving women's access to jobs, etc.

The functions served by an organization for its members will often differ from the roles it plays for organizations outside its boundaries. For example, a family may find its interrelations inherently gratifying, while the state regards the family as instrumental to its population policy. A civil rights organization may achieve more equal opportunities for its members (a task function) and serve the community by reducing racial tensions (a maintenance function).

Variables

There are a number of organizational variables which are important in understanding the special capabilities of organizations with which community practitioners must deal. (See Reading #14) These include (1) authority structure which may be hierarchical or collegial, (2) division of labor which may be on the basis of specialized or generalized role definitions, (3) performance guides which may be in the form of predetermined rules, the internalization of the organization's goals by the work force, or unplanned *laissez faire* determination of duties, (4) goal and policy setting which may be done by a separate cadre of policy makers or by those who administer programs, and (5) assignment of personnel on the basis of merit or such ascribed characteristics as race, sex or family status which are essentially irrelevant or detrimental to the achievement of organizational goals.

In addition, there are a number of other significant organizational variables which include the following:

Breadth of Function. Some groups and organizations are very *narrow* in the spectrum of participant interests they encompass, others are very *broad*. A community council may concern itself simultaneously or serially with any of the various interests people who live in a contiguous area may share, while a voluntary association with the same geographic base may confine its interests to the eradication or treatment of a particular disease, the resolution of interpersonal problems in families, or the removal of discriminatory practices based on race.

Characteristics of Participants. Some groups and organizations include persons whose social characteristics are quite similar. Others bring together people of a widely varied sort. Significant characteristics on which participants may vary include socioeconomic status, age, sex, race, political sympathies, perspective on organizational goals and methods of work, membership in other groups and organizations, etc. The significant factors will vary. Thus, members of the National Association of Social Workers are quite similar with respect to professional training, skills and socioeconomic status, while they vary as to age, sex, race and perhaps political affiliation. A voluntary association with which a community organization practitioner works may be quite homogeneous in many respects, or may be deliberately composed to include a sampling of the variety of social characteristics and opinions to be found in the community.

We have sketched some of the important structural features which differentiate organizations. It remains to show how these are related to distinct organizational abilities. First we indicate the variables associated with two "ideal types"; bureaucracies and primary groups. Quickly abandoning these types, we proceed to summarize conclusions drawn from some of the literature which relates these structural variables to particular organizational capabilities.

Organizational Structure and Capabilities

The traditional view of bureaucracy[13] is that it consists of the following pattern of characteristics: a hierarchical authority structure, a division of labor among technically competent specialists, strictly delimited functions, impersonal relations, and laws or rules as the basis for decisions. Primary groups fall, in several respects, at the other extreme: personal, face-to-face relations; lack of specialized training and competence; largely consummatory rather than instrumental in function; and serving broad, ill-defined functions.

Eugene Litwak and Henry J. Meyer[14] point out two very important facts: First, some formal organizations and parts of many are much closer to primary groups in their characteristics than they are to bureaucracies. These primary group–like

---

[13]H. H. Gerth and C. Wright Mills (trans. and eds.), from *Max Weber: Essays in Sociology* (New York: Oxford University Press, Inc., 1947), pp. 196 ff.; A. M. Henderson and Talcott Parsons (trans. and eds.), *Max Weber: The Theory of Social and Economic Organization* (New York: Oxford University Press, Inc., 1947), pp. 324 ff.

[14]Eugene Litwak and Henry J. Meyer, "A Balance Theory of Coordination Between Bureaucratic Organizations and Community Primary Groups." *Administrative Science Quarterly,* 2:1:31–58 (June 1966).

organizations called "human relations" organizations are more capable of dealing with highly complex and idiosyncratic situations than traditional bureaucracies.

Second, bureaucracies and primary groups are not merely antithetical in their characteristics. Rather than viewing them as alternative modes for achieving social objectives, these authors find that, in many respects, they are complementary.

James D. Thompson and Arthur Tuden[15] found that organizational structure affects the kinds of problems an organization can tackle effectively. They pose four types of problems, based on differences in two variables. One variable is the extent of agreement on the causes of a problem, that is, whether or not knowledge is available or thought to be available for dealing effectively with it. The second is the extent of agreement on objectives for dealing with a problem.

A bureaucratic structure is most effective in dealing with problems where there is agreement on both objectives and causation. A collegial body—a group of peers with similar training in whom authority resides—is best for handling problems where there is an agreement on objectives, but knowledge of causes or effective means of intervention is uncertain or a matter of judgment. A collegium is charged with the responsibility for what must be done in the face of uncertainty not about the desired outcome but about what action will be most effective. A *representative body,* bringing together various interests, is best in reaching a compromise on preferred outcomes or in settling differences on the order of priorities when knowledge is available for achieving any of the outcomes under consideration. Finally, an *anomic collectivity,* operating without rules and encouraging inspiration, creativity, and "experimentation," is indicated when there is neither agreement on goals nor the means for their attainment.

In several respects, the conclusions reached by Thompson and Tuden and by Litwak and Meyer converge and complement one another. Litwak and Meyer conclude that uniform events, that is, ones of moderate complexity, which can be mastered through disciplined study and occur with some regularity, can best be managed by a bureaucracy. Thompson and Tuden find that matters on which there is agreement on ends and knowledge of appropriate means are handled most efficiently by a bureaucracy.

These conclusions appear to be related, for uniformity in a phenomenon is required if knowledge of suitable means for mastery is to be developed. Litwak and Meyer fail to take into account the extent of agreement on goals and values. Their analysis assumes agreement on basic objectives. Thompson and Tuden, in effect, specify that nonuniform events of high complexity require a representative structure when agreement on major issues is lacking, but can be resolved by a collegial body if there is agreement on ends. Nonuniform events which are both highly complex and of infrequent occurrence, Thompson and Tuden might have said, can best be handled by an anomic collectivity that can search for and try out various ends and means. On the other hand, Litwak and Meyer suggest that

---

[15]James D. Thompson and Arthur Tuden, "Strategies, Structures and Processes of Organizational Decision," in J. D. Thompson *et al.* (eds.), *Comparative Studies in Administration* (Pittsburgh: Pittsburgh University Press, 1959), pp. 195–216.

nonuniform events that require only simple, widely distributed skills can best be handled by primary groups, a contingency ignored by Thompson and Tuden.

Martin Rein and Robert Morris have suggested that there is a close connection between the goals and structures of organizations engaged in community organization practice.[16]

Community organization practitioners may work with organizations engaged in promoting the interests of some faction or segment of the community, such as the poor, Puerto Ricans, or the mentally ill, or some particular set of objectives, such as birth control or civil rights. In contrast, they may work with organizations which try to harmonize, reconcile, or compromise various goals and interests in the community. In the first instance, the organization's goal orientation may be referred to as the pursuit of *factional interests,* [17] while in the second, *community integration* is the goal orientation.

Corporate organizations consist of a small, relatively homogeneous leadership cadre which is in basic agreement on the goals and means of the organization. In such an organization, others may be invited to join in order to assist in the achievement of this preestablished program. In contrast, *federated* organizations are collections of the diversity in the community. They endeavor to be representative of a wide range of groups, interests, or types of people. Others may be invited to join not because they agree with the specific program of the organization but because they represent otherwise unrepresented groups.

Rein and Morris' basic hypothesis is that a corporate structure is most appropriate in pursuing factional interests, while a federated structure is best adapted to the search for community integration. In the long run, achievement of factional interests may relieve strains in the social fabric and contribute to community integration. Likewise, the promotion of community integration, particularly in the reinforcement of norms which set wide limits on the pursuit of special interests, aid factions in achieving their interests. Nevertheless, an organization should select a structure appropriate to its particular goal orientation and allow the long-range effects to work themselves out. If an organization is saddled with a particular structure it should select an appropriate goal orientation. Otherwise, it is likely to fail.

A representative structure and what Rein and Morris call a federated structure appear similar in the diversity of interests which they bring together. Rein and Morris conclude that a federated structure is best adapted to achieving community integration, while Thompson and Tuden believe that a representative structure is useful for achieving compromise in the event of conflicting preferences. These assertions seem quite similar.

Blau and Scott, from their review of the empirical literature, reached related conclusions. Their focus is on situations that require "efficient coordination" in

---

[16]Martin Rein and Robert Morris, "Goals, Structures and Strategies for Community Change," *Social Work Practice 1962* (New York: Columbia University Press, 1962), pp. 127–45.

[17]Rein and Morris prefer to call this goal "change." But this is so ambiguous a term that we have adopted "pursuit of factional interests" in its place. For example, change can and does occur as practitioners pursue community integration, bringing social values into a better adjustment with one another or, more frequently, bringing action into a closer approximation of the values we espouse.

comparison to those that need "a single correct or best answer." Where there is agreement on both outcomes and causes, the main problem is to coordinate the necessary means to achieve the desired results. When there is disagreement on either objectives or appropriate methods, the problem is one of deciding which of various possible objectives or methods ought to be sought or employed. While Thompson and Tuden's conclusions are somewhat more refined than Blau and Scott's the latter support the former:

> In sum, groups are superior to individuals, and groups in which there is a free flow of communication are superior to groups in which differentiation impedes communication, in solving problems which call for a single correct or best answer; but individuals are superior to groups, and hierarchically differentiated groups are superior to undifferentiated groups, in performing tasks that primarily depend on efficient coordination.[18]

Seldom does an organization deal with but one type of problem or face but one kind of circumstance. In short, organizations must develop a variety of capabilities, and one way they can do this is by incorporating various types of substructures appropriate for dealing with the problems they most typically confront. Thus, a large-scale bureaucracy which must deal with some nonuniform events may create special departments structured along collegial or "human relations" lines to deal with those events. A second way groups, particularly small ones, can deal with this problem is by changing structure over time as the kind of problems confronted shifts. Thus, a community council (representative structure) may meet as a committee of the whole to decide on a program and establish priorities. Once this has been agreed upon, the council may divide into "working committees" and subdivide the job further among subcommittees and individual members, all of whom are responsible to the chairman (bureaucratic structure).

Factors Influencing Linkages between Arenas

Community organization practice, as suggested above, involves bringing influence to bear on the relations among groups and organizations. As the practitioner comes to understand what affects these linkages, he is in a better position to exercise control over them—or to know when to avoid wasting resources on attempting to change what he can do little about.

Groups, organizations, and communities are bound together by two major sets of ties: *cultural* and *social. Cultural ties* consist of shared tools and technology; common sentiments, that is, beliefs about the nature of reality, attitudes toward various institutions and roles within and outside the system, ideas about right and wrong, good and bad, etc. *Social ties* are interactions between people, their nature, pattern, and frequency. Some interactions are direct, face to face; others are mediated by third parties or by various forms of communication, including the mass media. Litwak and Meyer[19] offer us an analysis of the relations between

---

[18]Blau and Scott, *op. cit.,* pp. 125–26.
[19]Litwak and Meyer, *op. cit.*

external primary groups such as families and formal organizations like schools or neighborhoods. Basically, they suggest that there is a balance in the social distance between these antithetical structures that maximizes the achievement of social goals, for example, education of the young. The community organization practitioner serves as the link between the two types of structures and employs four principles in deciding how to bring them closer, move them farther apart, or maintain the existing social distance between them. Drawing conclusions from studies of mass communication, Litwak and Meyer point out four barriers to communications or linkages between formal organizations and external primary groups: (1) selective listening to those messages with which one agrees; (2) selective interpretation, perceiving messages that are heard in ways that are consistent with personal attitudes or group characteristics; (3) complexity of messages, varying from simple to complicated; and (4) scope or numbers of people the message must reach.

These authors offer some general guidelines for the practitioner in choosing appropriate methods for overcoming the barriers noted above: (1) In overcoming selective listening, i.e., a predilection not to listen to messages, the practitioner can choose a method which permits a high degree of organizational initiative. Thus, instead of inserting a notice in a local newspaper or distributing handbills, the practitioner may knock on doors or stop people on a busy street corner and engage them in conversation so that the message gets through. (2) In dealing with selective interpretation, i.e., message distortion, one can choose communicators who have the trust of the persons receiving the message or persons who have the time and training to develop positive relationships with message recipients. (3) In coping with complexity, one may use experts or specially trained persons to get the message across, using face-to-face communication to allow message recipients to ask questions and seek clarification. (4) To assure maximum scope, one may use various forms of mass communications designed to reach the targeted audiences.

The practitioner's first task is to determine the nature of the communication problems with which he or she is faced, and then select one or a set of interrelated methods that are likely to be most effective in dealing with the problems or barriers, diagnosed at the least cost. Obviously, if the practitioner is dealing with people who are ready to listen (e.g., other middle-class people with goals and motives similar to those of the practitioner, or groups of people who must cope with a common disaster) selective listening will not be a problem and a high degree of organizational initiative will not be required. Similarly, if the senders and receivers of messages are much alike in status, age, sex, attitudes and opinions, or are in regular and sympathetic interaction, there will be little problem with selective interpretation. Simple messages can be carried by ordinary people without special expertise, and a few people can be reached without use of the mass media. But if the targets are not predisposed to listen, some degree of organizational initiative will be necessary; if messages are likely to be interpreted selectively, some form of intensive relations between practitioners and targets will be required; if messages are complex, experts must be relied upon and available to answer questions; and if many people must be reached, some form of mass media must be chosen.

Clearly, methods that resolve one problem are not necessarily suitable for handling others, especially as the practitioner must take account of costs. Thus it is difficult to maximize both scope and organizational initiative or intensity of relations. The practitioner's task is to diagnose the problem accurately and then select a set of approaches and activities, often phased over time and otherwise interrelated, that will solve the problem at the least possible cost.

As James D. Thompson and William J. McEwen[20] have suggested, organizations vary in the extent to which they are dependent upon their environments, ranging from something approaching complete control over the environment (e.g. giant cartels and trusts) to total dependence upon the environment (e.g. many service enterprises). Thus they may relate to their environment in a number of different ways, depending upon their strength and independence of the environment.

In descending order of power, organizations relate to their surroundings by (1) absorption of competitors and suppliers; (2) competition; (3) cooperation in the form of *(a)* bargaining and exchange, *(b)* co-optation, *(c)* coalition, alliance, and merger; and (4) conflict in the form of harassment.

Giant corporations often buy up smaller competitors rather than forcing them out of business through competition because their managerial know-how and markets add to the parent corporation's strength, although antitrust legislation puts some brakes on such activity in this country. In the welfare field, the large and well-endowed hospital may buy up nursing homes.

When two or more organizations vie for the resources of third parties, they are engaged in competition. The business example is clear enough. In the health field, the independent health agencies—heart, cancer, etc.—compete for the contributor's dollar. One may find a rehabilitation agency with a wealthy constituency constructing a fine facility in a prime location which reduces the demand for existing services. However, given the paucity of treatment resources, two rehabilitation programs may be able to coexist if trained personnel and income are available in sufficient quantity. Contributions to one organization do not necessarily detract from those received by another; the total amount contributed may be larger.[21]

When two organizations are approximately equal in power and produce goods and services needed by each other, they may negotiate or bargain with one another to settle the terms of their cooperation. Sol Levine, Paul E. White, and Benjamin D. Paul have made an important contribution to our understanding of the conditions affecting exchanges between health and welfare organizations.[22]

[20]James D. Thompson and William J. McEwen, "Organizational Goals and Environment: Goal-Setting as an Interaction Process," *American Sociology Review,* Vol. 23 (February, 1958), pp. 23–31.

[21]John R. Seeley, *et al., Community Chest* (Toronto: University of Toronto Press, 1957), pp. 365–66, 408–11.

[22]Sol Levine, Paul E. White and Benjamin D. Paul, "Community Interorganizational Problems in Providing Medical Care and Social Services," *American Journal of Public Health,* Vol. 53, No. 8 (August, 1963), pp. 1183–95.

Based on their research, these authors show that exchanges between organizations depend upon (1) the functions they perform, which, in turn, determine their needs, (2) their access to needed resources from outside the system of health and welfare agencies or, conversely, their dependence on such agencies, and (3) the extent to which there is consensus among health and welfare agencies about their respective domains.

Robert Morris has also studied the conditions affecting cooperation between agencies concerned with chronic illness under Jewish auspices in seven cities in the United States. He found six factors of importance in fostering cooperative relations, in descending order of importance: (1) a simultaneous crisis in the organizations that ultimately engaged in cooperative activities, (2) informal interaction among trustees, (3) availability of a planning organization perceived as objective, neutral, and nonthreatening, (4) leaders possessing qualities of statesmanship, that is, trusted by all parties, skilled in negotiation techniques, and capable of creating formulas for cooperation that alter organizational autonomy without destroying it, (5) expert studies which confirm and legitimate conclusions reached by local leaders, rather than providing blueprints for action, and (6) a discriminating use of incentives.[23] One cannot help but wonder what conclusions Morris would have reached if he had examined relations between agencies that have differing capacities to sustain themselves in their environments.

One organization may absorb or co-opt into its decision-making structures representatives of another to head off potential threats to its stability or integrity. At the same time, it may pay the price of adapting its program in the interests of those so absorbed. Philip Selznick found two types of co-optation in the organization he studied. The first he called informal co-optation. In this type, the co-opted party is not actually found on the boards or committees of the organization, but its interests are considered or informal consultations are held with its leaders before major decisions are reached. Those co-opted exercise real influence in the organization, although they are not formally a part of it. The second type he called formal co-optation. Groups are formally co-opted by bringing representatives into the decision-making bodies of the organization. But real influence on basic decisions is not shared because it doesn't need to be. When formal co-optation takes place, it is not because the co-opted parties represent a potential threat to the organization but because bringing them in provides assistance in administering programs or adds to the legitimacy of the organization in its social context.[24] Co-optation is often the substance of various moves toward "democratic administration," such as those engaged in by local community action agencies under the Economic Opportunity Act of 1964. There is little evidence that formal co-optation of the poor by the War on Poverty was parlayed into control or substantial influence by the poor over funds, programs, content, job opportunities, etc.[25]

---

[23]Robert Morris, "New Concepts in Community Organization," in *The Social Welfare Forum* (New York: Columbia University Press, 1961), pp. 128–45.

[24]Philip Selznick, *TVA and the Grass Roots* (Berkeley and Los Angeles: University of California Press, 1949), pp. 13–16.

[25]Lillian Rubin, "Maximum Feasible Participation: The Origins, Implications and Present Status," *Poverty and Human Resources Abstracts*, Vol. 2, No. 6 (November–December, 1967), pp. 5–18.

When an organization is so powerless in relation to its environment that it is unable to carry out an effective program, it may seek other organizations with which to form coalitions. Coalitions are often short-term agreements to achieve specific purposes but may begin or develop into relatively permanent alliances. For example, coalitions may form to elect a candidate or pass a school bond issue. Most community chests began as alliances of local businessmen and wealthy philanthropists who, working separately, were unable to evaluate the character of the numerous requests for charitable contributions they received. Neither were they able to increase the efficiency of fund-raising efforts. The community chest enabled them to pursue both objectives. When organizations agree to cooperate but give up their separate identity, one speaks of merger.

Eugene Litwak and Lydia F. Hylton found that alliances in the form of coordinating agencies arise when organizations are interdependent, perceive their interdependence, and can define their transactions in standardized units. They concluded that very high levels of interdependence lead to merger, and low levels may be handled by *ad hoc* coordination (for example, a telephone call). Only moderate levels give rise to coordinating agencies such as a council of social agencies. Highly standardized units of action are handled by rules or laws (such as those governing eligibility for public assistance) while low levels of standardization result in *ad hoc* coordination (such as case conferences between agencies making and receiving referrals). Only moderate amounts result in coordinating agencies. Finally, they found that a small number of organizations requiring coordination does not warrant a coordinating agency, but can be handled on an *ad hoc* basis, while a very large number of organizations can only be coordinated through laws, directories of organizations, a competitive market system, etc.[26] The implications for practice are clear. With some knowledge of the presence and magnitude of the factors identified by Litwak and Hylton, the practitioner can select and promote a suitable approach to coordination, ranging from merger to *ad hoc* communications.

A very weak group that is grossly dissatisfied with its social environment, perhaps convinced that it is the victim of great injustice, may relate to other organizations by attack and harassment. Contenders having a major power advantage (for example, an illegal syndicate, state and local governments) may engage in overpowering conflict when it is required. But those at the opposite end of the power hierarchy may be able to create considerable inconvenience, disruption, embarrassment, annoyance, etc., without being able to overpower. By so doing, they put themselves in a position closer to parity with their adversary so that they can bargain effectively for their interests in exchange for ceasing their harassment. Some of the tactics of the civil rights movement may be understood in these terms. The lunch-counter sit-ins, the bus boycotts, and the Poor People's Campaign of the summer of 1968 reflect this type of conflict relations. Saul Alinsky has created and applied such tactics with great skill.

---

[26]Eugene Litwak and Lydia F. Hylton, "Interorganizational Analysis," *Administrative Science Quarterly,* Vol. 6, No. 4 (March, 1962), pp. 395–420.

James Coleman has made a major contribution to understanding the way individuals, groups, and organizations relate to one another. He notes that *activities which are independent of one another,* such as the meeting of a welfare agency's board of directors and a family's evening meal, have no effects on the relations between the two groups involved. The directors develop an interest in the social agency, and the family in its dining activity and conversation, and the actions taken are independent of one another. The cultural and social residues created thereby are an attitude of indifference between the meal-takers and the meeting-attenders, and a pattern of noninteraction or mass.

If, on the other hand, people are engaged in *similar activities dependent on the same events,* such as traveling to work on the same set of roads or sending their children to the same schools, then their activities intersect in such a way that all benefit or suffer together. If the roads are bad or the schools poor, all are harmed. In this way, they develop common interests in improving their roads and schools and are likely to take collective action to that end. The residues that are produced include sentiments of identification with one another and patterns of interaction that take the form of communitywide organization.

A more complicated set of results occurs when people engage in *dissimilar but interdependent activities.* For example, one set of families sends their children to the public schools, and another group of people teaches them. In one respect, all benefit from these activities. These families and others pay school taxes, for which they receive, in exchange, educated children. Others contribute their working hours to the education of those children, for which they receive their livelihood. The results are the same as when people engage in similar activities dependent on the same events, discussed above.

But the same situation may produce benefits for some and costs for others which do not balance out. Some parents may prefer to send their children to private schools and resent paying school taxes. Some must pay school taxes even though they have no children in school. Teachers may not be paid adequately for their work and demand higher salaries which the taxpayers find it difficult to meet. Thus, interests are opposed, resulting in *conflict, unilateral action,* or *inaction.* The residues produced include sentiments of hostility and organized cleavages.[27]

What determines whether activities which hurt some and benefit others will result in conflict, unilateral action, or inaction? At this point, several additional concepts must be introduced. *Density* refers to the number of organizations per unit of population or the proportion of the population who are members of organizations. *Distribution* refers to the proportion of organizations in different sectors of society. For example, in our society, there are proportionately more organizations among middle-class people than lower class people. *Interlocking* refers to the extent to which the same individuals belong to two or more organiza-

---

[27]James S. Coleman, "Community Disorganization," in Robert K. Merton and Robert A. Nisbet (eds.), *Contemporary Social Problems* (2d ed., New York: Harcourt, Brace & World, Inc., 1966), pp. 670–95.

tions. *Cross pressures* are felt by individuals when they belong to several organizations which hold conflicting expectations for their behavior.

High density is likely to draw many people into controversies. Organizations are the vehicles for the articulation of interests. The more interests that find organized expression, the greater the chances for the emergence of opposed interests. As high density means large numbers of people in organizations, the higher the density, the more people are likely to be involved in controversy.

The greater the degree of interlocking membership, the more likely that controversies, when they do arise, will be compromised or stalemated. The greater the degree of interlocking, the more likely it is that people will be subjected to cross pressures. If they cannot win others over to their point of view or work out the basis for a compromise, they are likely to withdraw from the organizations with which they disagree or urge their organizations to take no action.

If there is a narrow distribution of organization in the community, involving, for example, the middle but not the lower classes, and there is a fair degree of common interests among those who are organized, by virtue of their similar class position, then unilateral action may be expected. For example, the dental and medical societies and the public health department may urge the city council to fluoridate the water supply and, with little discussion, the necessary ordinances are passed. But if the lower classes are mobilized, conflict of an extreme variety is likely to occur, such as the spreading of initial disagreement on one issue to many issues, and from a disagreement on policies to attacks upon individuals. Organizers have frequently entered communities that have instituted fluoridation to mobilize the opposition and appeal to normally apathetic lower class voters through various scare tactics.

In general, a high degree of density plus a low amount of interlocking is conducive to conflict. When Martin Luther King organized the Montgomery bus boycott, he deprived the organized white community of the opportunity for unilateral action and created the conditions necessary for conflict—a Negro organization relatively free from interlocking membership in white organizations. (He also overcame the reluctance to act springing from dependence on the white community.) In contrast, as organized labor has developed increasing ties with management through profit-sharing plans, informal interaction of union leaders with management, upward mobility of working men into management positions, etc., conflict between labor and management has been limited to "bread and butter" issues, and virulent labor-management conflict has all but disappeared.[28]

Summary and Comments

The arenas within which community organization is practiced are important determinants of the nature and effectiveness of the practitioner's interventions. We have given major attention to two of those arenas—groups and organizations —recognizing that others are of at least equal importance. Chapter III provides the reader with further understanding of the community apart from its organiza-

[28]James S. Coleman, *Community Conflict* (Glencoe, Ill.: The Free Press, 1957), pp. 20–23.

tional components, and we have referred to a few sources for information about other arenas.

Our first argument is that the structure of groups and organizations varies in ways that influence their capabilities and, thereby, their utility for practitioners. Our second is that differences in patterns of communication, perception, power and dependency have significant implications for the selection or prediction of linkages between groups and organizations.

We are a very long way from being able to exercise significant control over the complex phenomena with which community practitioners are concerned. But if we are ever to achieve this—and success is by no means assured—it will come, in part, through careful examination and classification of the phenomena with which we deal. Many social scientists are interested in applied problems and are sure to give us a hand. But practitioners, with their intimate knowledge of practice arenas, must take responsibility for selecting and mastering relevant theoretical and empirical work from the social sciences and determine whether the factors identified are, for all practical purposes, unalterable, or are subject to a measure of control. This path is both uncertain and tedious, but it holds much promise. It is in this spirit that we offer the selections in Part Two of this volume, and the reader may well ask whether they meet the tests of relevance and control.

FRED M. COX

CHAPTER III

Communities

The community is one of two arenas upon which we have chosen to focus in Part Two. Community, as used here, is the territorial organization of people, goods, services, and commitments. It is an important subsystem of the society, and one in which many "locality relevant" functions are carried on.

Communities are in serious trouble at this point in American history. Although the sense of imminent disaster that characterized the protests and riots of the late 1960s and early 1970s has dissipated, serious problems remain. Pollution; traffic congestion; flight from the cities to the suburbs, exurbs, and rural communities, and more recently from the "frostbelt" to the "sunbelt"; energy shortages; disinvestment in the central cities; and serious unemployment coupled with double-digit inflation which has led to great caution in government expenditures to help the cities have confronted citizens and community organizers alike. If there is to be any hope for American society, the problems of the cities (and affecting the cities) must be solved.

It is now painfully clear, to community practitioners and laymen alike, that the problems of the urban community will not yield quickly to solution. Part of the reason for this intractability lies in the fact that the community is one of the weakest competitors for the time and attention of the contemporary citizen. The family, the work place, the church, and the school have all been able to attract long-time commitments from able citizens. People are fleeing urban places, moving to the suburbs, and, if they commute to jobs in the cities, leaving as soon as possible at the end of the work day. Large cities lack stable populations with which to plan.

This inability of the community to claim the commitment of its citizens is in itself a serious problem and symptomatic of deeper ills as well. Fundamentally, the modern urban community contains goods and services, but controls very few of them. Hence, it is increasingly unable to assemble resources to address its important concerns. Community organizers should function, then, not only to point out problems in the community, but to develop community competence in local problem solving.

Clearly, the community is more than a series of problems confronted by the practitioner. The major perspective of this book is to view the community as arena or context within which, in general, people carry out their daily lives and, in specific, community organizers and planners do their work. The community and its various elements both limit possible actions and present opportunities for action. The practitioner's task is to accept the former and seize upon the latter. From another perspective, the community and its various elements provide the means for action. Both of these conceptions of community plus the view of community as problem receive attention in Fred M. Cox's selection which surveys the various approaches taken by scholars toward the community and their implications for community practice.

The chapter begins with Harold R. Johnson and John E. Tropman's discussion of the settings in which community organizers apply their skills. Using the concept of the triple community—subculture, territory, and organization—they classify and describe the settings and the way each type of setting shapes practice.

11.

Harold R. Johnson and John E. Tropman

THE SETTINGS OF COMMUNITY ORGANIZATION PRACTICE

The concept of community organization is rather confused when one considers its settings, the organizations and environments where the knowledge and skill of organizers are put into practice. There is no index of community organization agencies, no commonly accepted classification of settings. Who sponsors community organization activities? Where is community organization done, and what are the roles that community practitioners play?

There are many ways one could approach such a discussion. Historically, con-

cepts of public, or governmental, settings and private voluntary ones have been used with community organization usually conducted in the private sector. Today, with private agencies heavily supported by public funds and public agencies often engaged in community work, that distinction is less powerful than it once was.

Similarly, one could distinguish between sectarian and nonsectarian settings (religious versus secular auspices) or between primary and secondary settings (in which community organizers play a major versus a supporting role). Other distinctions include the scope or level of the setting (i.e., national, state, and local) or the various fields of practice or social problems ad-

Source: From Harold R. Johnson and John Tropman, "Settings for Community Organization Practice." Unpublished. Reprinted by permission of the authors.

dressed by different agencies. Another way of describing settings is in terms of their relationship to the three models of community organization practice. As many settings involve a mixture of practice modes, this may not be the most useful way of distinguishing among settings.

Perhaps the most ambitious attempt at analyzing practice settings is the work of Robert Perlman and Arnold Gurin.[1] They developed an entire theory of community organization practice based on variations in setting.

> We have found three kinds of organizations that are distinguished by the central function associated with each, by their structure or form, and by the typical problems and tasks they present to practitioners in community organization and social planning. The three contexts of practice that constitute our framework are (1) working with voluntary associations, (2) community work with service agencies, and (3) interorganizational planning.
>
> *Voluntary associations* cover a wide variety of groups and organizations based on a membership whose common interest is in achieving some change or improvement in social arrangements, institutions, or relationships. A *service agency* is a formal bureaucratic organization that has as its central purpose the provision of a service to a designated target population. *Planning and allocating organizations* are networks of formal organizations whose function is the determination of how to organize and deploy resources to deal with social problems.[2]

Among other things, these authors relate the essential characteristics of each type of setting, as well as variations in those characteristics, to the functions of each setting and the roles of the community practitioners working in them.

Our objective is quite different. We provide a framework for classifying the types of settings in which community work is performed and the major roles of practitioners in the various settings. Our framework—the triple community—serves as a way of classifying practice settings and suggesting examples beyond those listed. In addition, it has the advantage of highlighting the focal concerns and the bases for common ties among the members of each type of community.

THE TRIPLE COMMUNITY

It is important to consider the nature of the community in which the practitioner is working, and the extent to which it shapes the strategy selected in a particular instance. In *Tactics of Community Practice* one of us proposed the concept of the triple community and the three types of community to which it refers: the *subcultural community,* in which the key communal element is a set of common beliefs, origins, backgrounds or experiences; the *territorial community,* in which the common element is identification and commitment through residence or other use of a particular area; and the *organizational community* in which the workplace is the common element.[3]

A subcultural community may be centered around such groups as racial and ethnic groups, supporters of particular ideologies, people who band together because of similar age, health problems, etc. Territorial communities are those where a shared turf plays a key role. Usually these are particular neighborhoods defined by function—middle-class residential, skid row, etc.—or by natural or man-made barriers—expressways, rivers, hills, railroad tracks, etc. With widespread access to per-

---

[1]Robert Perlman and Arnold Gurin, *Community Organization and Social Planning* (New York: John Wiley and the Council on Social Work Education, 1972).

[2]*Ibid.,* p. 76.

[3]Fred M. Cox, John L. Erlich, Jack Rothman, and John E. Tropman, eds., *Tactics of Community Practice* (Itasca, Ill.: F. E. Peacock Publishers, 1977), pp. 9–11.

sonal transportation and the development of extensive road systems, geographic boundaries are becoming larger. Metropolitan and other multicounty regions, often similar to ones the U.S. Bureau of the Census calls Standard Metropolitan Statistical Areas (SMSA's), have become increasingly important in social planning. The workplace is the setting least thought of as a community, although a majority of Americans spend a good part of the day there, derive most of their income from it, and build their social lives around it. Much organizing goes on there, including that undertaken by industrial unions, trade unions, professional associations, and trade associations.

One example of an organization with a membership base drawn from any one of the three types of communities is the credit union. Usually, credit unions are organized on the basis of workplace affiliation, and can only be used by people in a given employment. Sometimes the geographic area is the locus of organization. Occasionally, participation is limited to members of some group, such as a racial, ethnic, or religious group. For example, there are several feminist credit unions. There are times, of course, when two or three types of community might provide the membership base for a credit union as, for example, one that serves predominantly black labor unions in a large city.

The triple community concept suggests several locations in which community organizing is done. These include (1) intra-community, (2) intercommunity (interorganizational) and (3) trans-community organization. In the first, the function of the organizer is to enhance the operation of one of the communities. In the second, the attempt is to bring two or more communities closer together, and provide for a greater articulation of activities. For example, one may find labor and management groups joining with the residents of a school dis-

trict to pass a millage [tax increase] proposal. At the level of trans-community organization, there are two directions: *upward,* toward associations of state and national agencies, and *downward,* toward families and neighborhood associations, block clubs, etc. Communities are affected by both external-national and internal-local events, and need to be linked to them. See Figure 11.1.

To continue our example of credit unions for a moment, one can see that they need to make each set of links. On the upward side, they must relate to various state and national credit union interests, regulatory agencies, etc. On the downward side, they must be aware of the nature and habits of the primary groups they serve. Different groups may have different spending and saving habits, patterns of borrowing, and needs for loans, etc. For organizations to be successful and effective, they must design procedures that are related to the special needs of their clients and customers.

SETTINGS

We begin our discussion of settings with an outline, using the triple community concept, of practice settings in each type of community. Then we turn to a discussion of each setting, with special reference to the roles played by community organizers in each setting.

Territorial Communities
    State Government and Quasi-Public Bodies
        Legislative Branch (legislative bodies, staff assistance organizations)
        Executive Branch (*ad hoc* commissions, governor's office, regular departments)
        Land-grant College Extension Programs
        State Welfare Planning Organizations
    Regional Public or Quasi-Public Bodies
        General Purpose Organizations
        Councils of Governments
        United Way Organizations

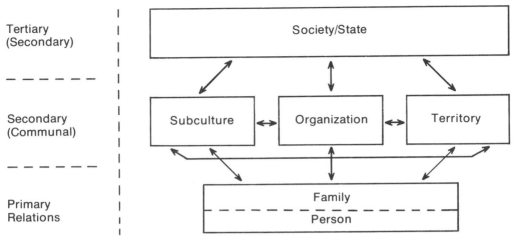

FIGURE 11.1
The Triple Community

Specialized Organizations Focused on Particular—
Problems (mental illness or retardation, juvenile delinquency)
Programs (hospitals and health care, public assistance)
Population Categories (children, families, the aged)
Local Government
Legislative Branch (city councils, county commissions, school boards)
Executive Branch (neighborhood city halls, planning agencies, school-community relations agencies, libraries)
Local Quasi-Public Agencies
Settlement Houses and Neighborhood Centers
Community Improvement Associations
Social and Health Agencies (hospitals, family counseling agencies)

Subcultural Communities
Racial and Ethnic Organizations
Religious Organizations, Schools
Disadvantaged Groups
Various Groups of the Handicapped (mentally retarded, deaf, blind)
Various Groups Labeled Delinquent (juvenile delinquents, ex-convicts, drug addicts)
Various Groups with Other Bases for Low Status (gays, women, the unemployed)
Various Groups Suffering Role Deprivation (the aged, parents without partners)

Organizational Communities
Labor Unions (industrial, trade, marginal workers)
Professional Organizations
Trade Associations
Chambers of Commerce

In the list above, we have not attempted to be exhaustive but only to illustrate each of the types of communities. In the discussion that follows, we shall not try to deal with each of the examples in the outlines above, but shall focus, instead, on the functions of the settings and the roles performed by community organizers working in them.

TERRITORIAL COMMUNITIES AND PRACTITIONER ROLES

State Government

State government is an important setting. The legislative arena is a critical subsetting. While election to public office should be open to all citizens, community organizers are well qualified to run for office by virtue of their professional training. State government is becoming increasingly important, and elected positions are commanding more adequate salaries. Someone with a community organization background might well prepare for a career as a legislator or other elected official, at the local as well as the state and national levels. In addition to elective offices, there are a number of related positions. These include staffing legislative committees, serving as aides to legislators in working with their constituents, preparing legislation, etc.

In the executive branch, from the office of the governor through various bureaus and departments, there are positions for one with the skills of the community organizer. Ad hoc, time-limited study commissions may be formed to study a variety of social problems and programs and bring the governor recommendations for action. Regular departments of state government—social service, mental health, corrections, public health, education, etc.—need staff to fill a number of roles for which community organizers and planners are admirably suited. For example, they need people to help plan, evaluate, and improve on-going and new programs, meet with legislators and legislative committees to interpret agency needs and views or assist in the preparation of legislative testimony, and deal with citizens or more specialized constituency groups who wish to or perhaps have a legislatively mandated right to be heard in the formulation of policy, programs, and regulations.

The land-grant colleges, with their programs of agricultural and now often more broadly defined community extension work, serve every county. While tasks are often specific and technical, there are also roles for those in community organization, linking the college and its expertise with the community, assisting the community in defining its needs and making effective use of the college, and serving as a technical expert in areas for which the organizer may have special skills—housing, social services, public health, etc.

Regional Bodies

There are, between the state and the local levels of government, a range of public and private organizations that span several counties, and occasionally states, with a range of purposes. Sometimes a problem area, like aging or mental health, is a focal concern. At other times, such bodies have responsibilities that cut across a variety of social problems or programs. These responsibilities may include fund raising, allocating funds, and planning and coordinating services. We cannot discuss all of these bodies, but some of the most salient are as follows:

United Way Organizations. These are usually regional agencies covering one or more counties. In some instances they parallel SMSAs. They are the successor agencies to community chests, united funds, and councils of social agencies. They seek to assess needs within their service area and mobilize public and voluntary resources to meet these needs. There are many hundred United Way organizations in the country. Most raise and distribute funds and plan and coordinate services. In some of the larger cities there are separate but related organizations carrying out the fund raising, allocating and budgeting, and planning and coordinating functions. In a few places, United Way agencies engage in community development and facilitate citizen participation and lobbying for community improvements. Community organizers may serve United Way and related agencies as fund raisers, planners, and community developers, largely facilitating the work of volunteers in carrying out each of the United Way functions.

Other Regional Planning Organizations. In addition to the United Way organizations, most regions have a multiplicity of planning bodies. These include councils of local governments concerned with planning and organizing transportation, solid waste disposal, housing and economic development, crime control, social services, etc. More specialized planning agencies include community mental health boards, and councils devoted to planning and coordinating hospitals and other health services, law enforcement, recreation and parks, etc. Councils of government are voluntary associations of cities, counties, school districts, etc. Other bodies generally represent a collectivity of individuals and organizations around some specific interest, and have a variety of bases of authority. Often they are mandated by law, but in some instances are established as voluntary groups. They seek to determine needs, coordinate community services, and plan for future needs.

The roles community planners and organizers may play in such organizations include (1) studying problems and services and planning policies or programs for dealing with them, (2) involving citizens and constituents in decision-making processes of such organizations, (3) influencing legislation or administrative regulations, and (4) fund raising, including grant writing, budget preparation, and justification.

We offer two examples of specialized regional planning organizations, area agencies on aging and community mental health boards:

Area Agencies on Aging. Well over five hundred regional communities have such agencies. Their primary responsibility is to represent the interests of the aging in their respective regions and to advocate improved service programs. This mandate results in a number of planning, coordinating, and funding activities on behalf of older Americans. It is less likely that they will organize the aged. Many communities have a range of groups that serve to unite the aged for educational, recreational, and social action purposes.

Community Mental Health Boards. Operating under federal and state legislation, most regions have mental health planning and service agencies in which several forms of organizing go on. In the more populous counties, mental health boards conduct planning and budgeting functions and oversee the direct services offered by affiliated agencies in their catchment areas. In less populous areas, mental health boards usually provide direct services as well as carrying out planning functions. Sociological theory suggests that community disorganization leads to mental health problems. This prompts these agencies to assign staff to tasks designed to increase community cohesion and thus improve the mental health of the community. In addition, the agency often works to strengthen the local network of services, helping to link organizations within a geographic area and to strengthen ties between primary groups and mental health agencies.

City and County Government

Increasingly, city and county government are important settings for community practitioners. The alleged unresponsiveness of local government has compelled many to establish neighborhood city halls, consumer protection agencies, police-community committees, etc. Such agencies of government are logically staffed by persons with community organization training. Also, an increasing number of community-oriented social workers are finding positions in local government analogous to positions in the legislative arena in state government, mentioned above.

The developing ecological arena is one that is of importance, and the need is to work with citizens' groups around waste water and solid waste disposal, recycling, and related concerns. Energy conservation and use is another issue in which citizens frequently demand a voice. In many instances—including housing assistance and community development, equal employment opportunity, zoning and zoning variances—local government is required to seek advice from citizens before taking action. These requirements create new opportunities for community practitioners.

Libraries, Businesses, Schools, and Hospitals

There are many other local organizations in which community practitioners might serve. Branch libraries, for example, frequently need help in developing strong linkages with the population of their service areas. Helping groups who make little use of library resources take an interest and express their needs for library services, suggest policies and practices that would make libraries more useful to them, etc. is a role a community practitioner could play. Business firms, particularly quasi-public ones such as utility companies, provide another setting for community practice. Insofar as their planning is for public service, they can benefit by public input into rate structures, expansion plans, development of new resources and services, etc., to which the community practitioner can make a contribution. The need is particularly strong in states where regulatory agencies are insisting on a stronger voice for the public in utility rate decisions.

Schools and hospitals are typically public service oriented. Both routinely employ social workers with clinical skills. Some hospitals and schools, however, as they relate to the range of subcultures they serve, or as problems of service delivery become increasingly complex, are using community practitioners to help with these tasks.

Neighborhood Planning Agencies

In many communities there are model neighborhood, school district, and urban renewal district councils. These official neighborhood planning groups tend to take a community development and social action approach, developing their own resources on the one hand, and seeking through negotiation and pressure to secure additional resources from the broader political jurisdictions on the other. Practitioners serve to develop and encourage citizen participation and focus action on larger units of government—the city, county, state, etc.

It is worth noting that with the various forms of revenue sharing now available, city and county administrations have a greater range of discretion in allocating available resources. This may make the work of the local organizer more rewarding. There is stiff competition for funds, but in most communities a well-organized group has a good chance of securing some funding.

Community Improvement Associations

Community associations and neighborhood improvement groups are similar to neighborhood planning agencies. They focus on the general well-being of a geographic area. However, they are entirely voluntary in nature and operate on their own initiative, not pursuant to any legislation. Such groups may engage in development, planning, or action strategies, but development is the preferred mode, followed by action. They rarely have the technical expertise to do planning. They are particularly useful in enhancing grass-roots participation, mobilizing discontent, and protecting local interests against broader ones.

Settlement Houses and Community Centers

One of the oldest community-oriented social services in the country is the settlement house. From Hull House in Chicago and the University Settlement in New York to community centers around the country, these organizations provide facilities for community activities and sponsor various social services for the local neighborhoods, particularly neighborhoods of the economically deprived. The very best programs have a pattern of constant interaction with the community and serve to enhance community development. The more limited programs are "building bound," expecting their clientele to seek out their facilities and services rather than reaching out to the neighborhood.

SUBCULTURAL COMMUNITIES AND PRACTITIONER ROLES

One base for organizing is, as we have mentioned, the geographic area. In that case, shared location is the common bond, but other links may be missing, important among them a shared identification or belief. In the subcultural community, the reverse is true. People may live in disparate locations but share beliefs or identity. Frequently, this needs to be strengthened, made more salient vis-à-vis competing identities, more acceptable to the outside world, and so on. When the basis for a group is shared identification or belief, the practitioner is working with a subcultural community. Common identity and belief, while often occurring together, do not always do so. Minorities may have minority status in common but, within the group, antagonistic class levels. In some cases, identification with the group needs to be enhanced; in others, especially religious organizations, it is shared beliefs that need enhancement.

Racial and Ethnic Organizations

Organizations representing people of color, such as the Urban League, the National Association for the Advancement of Colored People, and Hispanic, Native American, and Asian-American organizations, all represent loci for community organizing. In some cases, strengthening group ties and working out internal differences is the primary assignment. In other cases, these organizations pursue a range of tasks that improve the well-being of their members in some tangible way, while recognizing that the process of accomplishing these goals may be used to enhance group solidarity. Assisting the group in making plans for future development is often involved. Helping group members make their aspirations known to external authorities and, at times, organizing protests and other social action activities are often included among the responsibilities of community practitioners working with such organizations.

An awareness of common ethnic identity may cut across racial or color identity. Puerto Ricans, for example, may be black or white or brown. Native Americans are of many different tribes. In a given case, racial or ethnic identity may predominate. Depending on the organization's purposes, the practitioner's task may be to enhance one source of identity over another. Many ethnic groups have organizations that serve to embody and enhance their common identity. Often such groups, like their racially based counterparts, undertake specific tasks in the process of which the group is strengthened.

Religious Groups

Historically, organizations and activities based upon religious identification have been important in the United States and are a basic type of subcultural community. While racial and ethnic groupings have recently become more acceptable, it was not always so. As Glazer and Moynihan comment,

New York organizational life is in large measure lived within ethnic bounds. These organizations generally have religious names, for it is more acceptable that welfare and health institutions should cater to religious than ethnic communities.[4]

Religious groupings are fundamental subcultural communities in America, as Glazer and Moynihan indicate. Within the social welfare field, religious groups play, and have played, a crucial role.[5] They form special purpose groups including social agencies, plan programs, raise and allocate money, and provide services. In the fundraising, allocating, planning, and action phases of these activities, as well as in the many activities designed to enhance group cohesion, there are important roles for community practitioners. The religious auspice of such community work does raise an issue for practitioners. Should a practitioner be of the same religious persuasion as the group? While discrimination against a nonmember may be a violation of the law, practitioners need to consider the impact of nonmembership on their functioning in such a setting.

Communities of the Disadvantaged

Persons who are disadvantaged often organize into groups in a way that cuts across other subcultural lines, mentioned above. Their shared problem or condition is the common bond. It should be noted that an inherent attraction of such groups is the support derived from sharing problems and helping others. In such groups, community development principles are dominant. Rather than seek help from the "outside,"

these groups band together to provide help for themselves. Examples include groups of parents without partners; parents with emotionally impaired or mentally impaired children; associations of people with certain diseases, handicaps, or common institutional experiences such as ex-convicts or welfare recipients; associations of people of a certain age, sex, or sexual preference; organizations of the workless such as the unemployed, those seeking sheltered work, and those hoping to return to work after an extended absence. They band together for mutual support and friendship and to pursue common interests such as resources for help of various kinds and increased public awareness of their situation. In such settings the role of the community organizer is to provide assistance in strengthening the organization and achieving its purposes.

Some self-help groups emphasize individual therapeutic change, rather than community development, as their goal. Alcoholics Anonymous is one such group; a variety of marathon weekend encounter and personal growth groups are other examples. In these settings the role of the community worker is minimal, as the goals are not communal. However, community workers may assist in initiating such groups.

Community Creation

In some instances, the main task of the community practitioner is to help create the community. In the 1960s, this process was called "radicalizing"; the women's movement calls it "raising consciousness." This arises when a group of people are in a similar situation that entails having common experiences, and a small cadre of would-be leaders believe others of their kind do not recognize their plight. The role of the worker here is to work with this cadre and

---

[4]Nathan Glazer and Daniel P. Moynihan, *Beyond the Melting Pot* (Cambridge, Mass.: M.I.T. and Harvard University Presses, 1963), p. 228.

[5]W. J. Reid, "Sectarian Agencies," in *The Encyclopedia of Social Work,* ed. J. Turner et al. (New York: National Association of Social Workers, 1977), pp. 1154–63.

create conditions that will spread and intensify awareness of their common plight.

To some extent, this practitioner has a built-in conflict, as this work raises questions about the extent to which the professional's role is to assist the community in self-determination or to lead. If a group decides that it is not disadvantaged, however erroneous this judgment may be, then the practitioner must decide whether to abide by the group's wishes or take some other actions such as resigning or forming a new group. The conflict is particularly poignant for the practitioner who shares the group identity and seeks to combine personal and professional commitments.

ORGANIZATIONAL COMMUNITIES AND PRACTITIONER ROLES

In addition to common geographic locations and common identity and beliefs, the shared workplace or work experience is an important practice context. Occupational linkage is the key factor identified by Marx as salient for identification and intervention purposes. The growth of labor unions and professional associations is indicative. Much time is spent in the workplace, and many close ties are developed there.

Unions

The development and maintenance of union organizations is a very important setting for community practice, and one that has been less emphasized in schools of social work than one might expect. Not only is the organizing process central to union activity, but the ideological orientation is harmonious with that espoused by many practitioners.

Within the union framework, there are several settings that are appropriate for community practice. One is organizing employees of particular trades or firms. A second lies in the central office operation, assisting with the development of social welfare programs and the use of community resources, linking the union to national and international activities, developing and conducting training activities for union leaders, and assisting with social planning and social action including lobbying for social welfare legislation favored by labor organizations.

Local union organizing and contract negotiation provide opportunities for those who enjoy social action. For those students of community practice who are interested, local union organizing is one of the few places to make a contribution, gain experience, and plan a career in social action.

Professions

Professional organizations have much in common with unions, including their interest in salaries and fringe benefits. On the other hand, professions have accepted social responsibilities for self-policing and protection of clientele against malpractice not placed on unions. They, too, are a fertile setting for community practice. A few social workers have been attracted to positions in their own professional organizations, such as the National Association of Social Workers and the National Association of Black Social Workers. Each has roles for community organizers, ranging from the development of professional communities to social action on behalf of the profession as well as planning, interorganizational, and management tasks. Although it is not surprising that other professions would turn to their own members as employees of their professional organizations, many could benefit from staff assistance by community organization practitioners. In the future we should explore other professional organizations, particularly those with similar goals and values, as settings for community practitioners graduating from schools of social work.

Trade Associations

Within the field of social welfare, there are organizations very similar to trade associations in private industry. These include the Council on Social Work Education (among social work educators), the National Assembly (among private, nonprofit national voluntary health and welfare associations), and the National Conference on Social Welfare (drawing together a very wide spectrum of those interested in social welfare). Similar organizations are to be found in the fields of public health, education, recreation, etc. These organizations, collectively, are devoted to the advancement of their field of activity by developing knowledge, coordinating the work of separate organizations, sharing experience, promoting legislation and administrative rules that benefit organizations in their field, etc.

JOB AND WORK IN COMMUNITY

Community workers may work within a community, link communities to each other, and tie communities on a vertical dimension to state and national agencies above, and to family and other primary groups below. In undertaking these activities, they employ a variety of strategies and tactics. This activity is the *work* or professional commitment of community organizers, and represents the largest conception of the role of the community workers. The *job* or assigned duties, however, may appear somewhat more mundane.[6] Spending night after night in meetings, passing out handbills, and the routine aspects of organizing may not appear to have the importance of the organizer's real work. Putting them in this context may help practitioners see some of the larger implications of the tasks they must perform.

In addition, the job may appear more diffuse in other ways, and may include administrative and other aspects not directly linked to community practice. However, if the setting lends itself to community practice, then in time the worker may develop a more focused community orientation in the job and close the gap between the job and the larger work of community practice.

---

[6]The distinction between job and work is one made by Henry J. Meyer, Professor Emeritus of the University of Michigan School of Social Work. However, he cannot be held responsible for the way it is used here.

12.

Fred M. Cox

ALTERNATIVE CONCEPTIONS OF COMMUNITY: IMPLICATIONS FOR COMMUNITY ORGANIZATION PRACTICE

INTRODUCTION

Students of communities, urban and rural, large and small, have approached their subject from very different perspectives. Following Warren[1] this paper explores these various conceptions, extending Warren's analysis by drawing out their several implications for community organization practice. For the practitioner, as Kramer and Specht have noted,[2] community is context, the arena within which the practitioner operates; target, the source of problems or harmful conditions the practitioner tries to change; and vehicle, or the means by which change is effected. In this discussion I explore community from all of these perspectives with emphasis on community as context and vehicle. The next chapter offers one contemporary analysis of the metropolitan area in general and the central city in particular as problem and target of change.

Warren defines community as "that combination of social units and systems which perform the major social functions having locality relevance." He goes on to explain that "this is another way of saying that by 'community' we mean the organization of social activities to afford people daily local access to those broad areas of activity which are necessary in day-to-day living."[3] He identifies five such functions: (1) production-distribution-consumption, (2) socialization—"a process by which society . . . transmits prevailing knowledge, social values, and behavior patterns to its individual members";[4] (3) social control—"The process through which a group influences the behavior of its members toward conformity with its norms";[5] (4) social participation; and (5) mutual support—which may take "the form of care in time of sickness, the exchange of labor, or the helping out of a local family in economic distress."[6]

In the following discussion I have divided Warren's categories of approaches to the study of community into three major subgroups: context, vehicle, and problem. The division is based on judgments about the central utility of each approach for the community practitioner.

COMMUNITY AS CONTEXT

The Community as the Locus of Daily Activity (Site or Place)

Max Weber defined the city as a settlement with a market.[7] The early rural sociologists were interested in identifying the

---

Source: This article was written for this volume.

[1] Roland L. Warren, *The Community in America,* 2d ed. (Chicago: Rand McNally Co., 1972), pp. 21–51.

[2] Ralph M. Kramer and Harry Specht, eds., *Readings in Community Organization Practice,* 2d ed. (Englewood Cliffs, N.J.: Prentice-Hall, 1975), p. 17.

[3] Warren, *op. cit.,* p. 9.
[4] *Ibid.,* p. 10.
[5] *Ibid.,* p. 11.
[6] *Ibid.,* p. 11.
[7] Roland L. Warren, ed. *Perspectives on the American Community: A Book of Readings,* 2d ed. (Chicago: Rand McNally College Publishing Co., 1973), p. 2.

boundaries within which people traded. By extension, the community may be conceived of as a place where a group of people live and conduct various activities of daily living: earn a living, buy the goods and services they are unable to produce for themselves, school their children, transact their civic and governmental affairs, etc. The early human ecologists of the Chicago school took an interest in identifying urban zones (central business district, transitional zones, workingmen's homes, etc.) and smaller natural areas (apartment house districts, slums, transient areas, etc.) and in examining the processes that established and changed such zones and areas (cooperation, competition, and conflict; concentration and dispersion of people; centralization and decentralization of functions; segregation, invasion, and succession of activities and people; etc.)

The community practitioner will find a number of uses for this concept of community. As one asks, Who shall be organized? the question of community boundaries arises. Is the significant area one that shares a common public school or set of schools? Is it the people who use a particular neighborhood shopping area or the downtown shopping area? Or is it the political boundaries of the city or county that are significant for a particular set of interests around which organization is to occur?[8] In modern urban communities these questions become very complex indeed. How does one measure frequency and intensity of interaction that may serve to establish a community boundary? Assuming that a detailed survey is not feasible, what surrogate measures may be applied? May it be assumed that major roads, highways or freeways bound a

neighborhood or community? Or, given the ubiquity of the automobile or public transportation, do such barriers really limit interaction or identification with place? Perhaps there is very little identification with the locality. Has it been replaced by union, occupation, profession, ethnic group, political party, or some other intense interest? Or is there, in fact, very little in the way of any identification with anything that might be called "community?"

Put somewhat differently, this perspective raises the following questions of importance to the practitioner: (1) Who interacts and shares a common identity with whom? These people might well provide a base for collective action. (2) Who has little interaction with whom? These people may be relatively indifferent to one another. While the parties seem apathetic to one another, they may interact intensely in other arenas (e.g., occupational) or may interact only in secondary relations, characteristic of a mass society. (3) Who competes with whom for the business or resources of third parties? Competitors have an interest in gaining an advantage over one another and may organize internally for this purpose (as when a group of social agencies forms an alliance to increase their chances for obtaining a grant); at the same time, they will come together if there is a threat to their resources (as when trade associations including professions and groups of social agencies organize to resist unfavorable legislation). (4) Who is in conflict with whom over fundamental values (as with racial segregationists and integrationists or with radical and liberal politicians)? Opponents are interested in overwhelming or subduing one another or in protecting vested interests or obtaining a "just" distribution of scarce resources, and each side will organize to these ends.

The dynamic processes identified by the Chicago school of human ecologists are useful in understanding such phenomena as

---

[8]It is not uncommon to find that the place itself is irrelevant to organizing unless it also identifies people who share a particular social class or racial, ethnic or religious identity, i.e. institutions and values, discussed below.

racial "block busting," attempts at residential racial integration, the reactions to returning large numbers of mentally ill persons to the communities from the relative isolation of mental hospitals (and similar programs for juvenile delinquents, adult offenders and the mentally retarded), drives to "get rid" of red-light or skid row districts, and urban renewal that involves major displacement of low-income people. Although it is not possible to give detailed analyses of these phenomena here, the perspectives of the Chicago school lead to asking questions of the following sort: (1) What social, economic and political factors lead to shifts in population groups? (2) What happens to those displaced? To those moving into a new area? (3) Why are efforts to mix people of differing social identification (class, life-style, ethnic group) so often ineffective? Under what conditions can integration (or dispersion) succeed? (4) Which community functions (activities, businesses, etc.) are spatially compatible with one another? Which are incompatible, and why?

The Community as Described by the Demographic Characteristics of Its People

The census provides data on the composition of the population broken down by age, sex, income, occupation, education, race and ethnic identity, etc., some of the data being available for areas as small as a city block, others aggregated by census tracts, cities, counties, and states. Other surveys of the population provide information about birth, death, marriage, divorce, illness, disability, delinquency, and crime. These data are very useful to the community organization practitioner in a number of different ways.

First, by looking for clusters of characteristics and their distribution geograph-ically, it is possible, following Shevky and Bell,[9] to identify the various social areas of cities and use these analyses to plan patterns of services appropriate to the several types of social areas identified. For example, it is clear that areas that include large numbers of young families with school-age children will require a different pattern of services than areas that house mostly older people whose children are grown and out of the family. Depending upon the cluster of characteristics used, social areas may be defined for a variety of social planning purposes. Data on health conditions may be used to plan the location of public health programs of various types, mental health programs, etc. Data on the frequency of delinquency and crime will suggest areas in which efforts should be concentrated.

Second, many sets of demographic data are available in time series, showing trends and developments. Using various forms of projection, plans may be created for developing services to meet anticipated needs in growing or declining areas, areas of increasing health problems, or whatever.

The Community as Shared Institutions (Values, Norms, Traditions)

Differences in the ecological relations between communities and neighborhoods, urban zones and natural areas, and differences in the population characteristics found in urban social areas do not explain all of the differences between communities of significance to the community practitioner. Studies cited by Warren[10] demonstrate that communities that are very like one another in these respects may, nevertheless, respond to problems in very different ways that can only be understood as differences in values

[9]Eshref Shevky and Wendell Bell, *Social Area Analysis* (Stanford, Calif.: Stanford University Press, 1955).
[10]*The Community in America,* pp. 32–36.

and the importance attached to and the quality of their institutions. For example, the importance of the public schools and, therefore, the willingness of people to increase school taxes or endorse school bonds will depend, in part, on the proportion of people who send their children to parochial and other private schools and, by implication, value various forms of private education more than the public schools. Reactions to proposals for the fluoridation of the water supply or to campaigns to provide physical examinations for all school-age children will depend in part on the value attached to health, trust in public officials and the medical profession vs. dependence on home remedies and folk medicine.

The study of a community's values and institutions will be particularly important when the social identity of the practitioner and the community served are quite different. Ignorance of indigenous values may even exist among those with a surface resemblance to those served. For example, Spanish-speaking South Americans may have little appreciation for the folkways and values of Mexican-American farm workers or Puerto Ricans living in New York City. Likewise, black social workers raised in middle-class families may have been shielded by their parents from learning the street language and mores of the black inner city ghetto.

Plans and proposals for community action or social services may be formulated with little understanding of the values of the population served and the failure of such efforts may be misinterpreted. For example, Gans's study of the working-class Italian population of North Boston suggests that the residents would have been a very poor vehicle for united community action to protect their interests against encroaching urban renewal, in part because of their very strong extended family and friendship ties and their distrust of outsiders, even including other Italian-Americans faced with the same threat of destruction to their community.[11]

Beginning organizing efforts or planning services that are grounded in the basic values and institutions of the people to be served provides a point of entry that may, as trust develops between practitioner and community, lead to possibilities for action not as central to or even at some variance with local traditions. "Beginning where the client is" applies to community work as well as casework. Alinsky insisted his organizers do so, i.e., (1) identify concerns and interests widely held in the community as a basis for mobilization and organizing people and (2) build an organization consisting of an alliance of preexisting indigenous organizations, which means appealing to their interests and values.[12] His work illustrates very well how a "people's organization" can move from issue to issue and transcend parochial interests as the members begin working together.

The Community as a Social System

For the community practitioner, the analysis of communities as social systems serves two primary functions. First, it permits a comparison of communities with other social systems to arrive at what is unique about community in contrast to other social systems. For example, like other social systems, as Moe points out,[13] particularly large ones, the community is a system of systems, with many different organizations, institutions, and groups as components. Unlike a formal organization,

---

[11]Herbert J. Gans, *The Urban Villagers* (New York: Free Press, 1962).

[12]Saul D. Alinsky, *Reveille for Radicals* (Chicago: University of Chicago Press, 1946).

[13]Edward O. Moe, "Consulting with a Community System: A Case Study," *Journal of Social Issues,* 15:2:29 (1959).

e.g., a city welfare department, the community is not centralized. That is, there is no planned hierachy of authority and command in a community as there is, say, in city government, but rather a collection of parts that are often relatively autonomous in relation to other subsystems in the community. Finally, Moe points out that the community is implicit in nature rather than explicit in comparison with the formal organization. Put somewhat differently, the community is emergent rather than contrived.

The second value of the social system perspective on the community for the community practitioner is that it permits systematic analysis, using concepts that have been developed and applied to other social systems. It helps the practitioner avoid overlooking some aspect of the community that might otherwise be forgotten. There are a large number of social systems concepts that may be used for this purpose. Three examples: (1) If a community is to be understood as, in some sense, a separate entity, it must have some boundaries, geographic or conceptual. Social systems analysis forces one to identify those boundaries and ask how they are maintained and changed. (2) All systems have vertical and horizontal interactions, that is, relations among various subunits (i.e., Red Cross and Travelers Aid) and between subunits within and units outside the system (i.e., local and national Red Cross and Travelers Aid). One may examine the nature and functions of such interactions (e.g., between families and the public schools or social services, and between local social services and their counterparts in other communities). Warren has concluded that a pervasive feature of American communities is the weakening of horizontal patterns and the strengthening of vertical ones,[14] with the result that the autonomy of American com-

munities is diminishing. (3) Finally, there are various schemes for analyzing the functions of social systems. Parsons' scheme, described in the Introduction to Arenas,[15] is illustrative. This scheme leads one to ask the following questions: With respect to each of the community's subsystems, what functions do they serve for the community? How do they attain their goals and adapt to the environment? How are the various subsystems integrated or coordinated? How do they manage the tensions that arise within and between them?

THE COMMUNITY AS VEHICLE

The Community as Exchanges among People and Institutions (Interaction)

The sociologists who have studied communities from this perspective have concentrated on the action that takes place within them. Some of them, notably Harold F. Kaufman,[16] have carefully distinguished between community action and action involving other social institutions and organizations that takes place within the community. For example, much of the action that occurs in families takes place within localities, but that is not to be mistaken for community action. Rather it is action at the subcommunity level. Certain fund-raising efforts of national health organizations likewise take place within communities but are directed and controlled at the state or national level and may best be thought of as extra-community action.

The special contribution of this perspective to community organization practice is the attention given to the natural process of interaction, the stages through which com-

---

[14] *The Community in America,* pp. 161 ff.

[15] See the Introduction to Arenas (Part 2, this volume).

[16] Harold J. Kaufman, "Toward an Interactional Conception of Community," *Social Forces,* 38:1:9–17 (October 1959).

munity action or community development efforts move, and the implications for practice. If various types of community action or development can be identified, and if stages of interaction can be described through which a given type of community action passes, we are on our way to understanding the relation between action and result and therefore to prescribing what the practitioner must do to achieve desired results through planned intervention. Beyond types of action and stages, it is important to understand how one action leads to another, the reactions that occur, and therefore the possibilities for failure and reversal as well as success.

At this point, we are very far from a prescriptive science of community action, development, and planning. Such a science would involve the careful observation of such interaction across a wide range of communities under varying conditions. But it is possible to use such studies suggestively to guide practice. There are, for example, a substantial number of such studies of urban renewal and community action to block the destruction of local communities through the urban renewal process. If one were embarking upon social planning in an urban renewal or related context, one would do well to review a number of these studies.

It should also be pointed out that this is one way in which the community practitioner can make a contribution to the development of practice knowledge. Keeping detailed records of community actions engaged in, particularly if they are related to studies that have similar categories of information collected and reported, can contribute to inductively developed theories of various types of planned community action.[17]

The Community as a Distribution of Power

This perspective has been so central to the interests of community practitioners that it has been given a special place in the literature of community organization practice. Arising out of the frustration with traditional community organization (we would call it community or locality development) practice principles, these studies, perhaps most notably those by Floyd Hunter and his colleagues, gave the community practitioner new insights and direction. Instead of counseling participation by those affected by community decisions and urging plans based on the felt needs of grass-roots people, this literature directed the practitioner to locate those who exercised major influence in the community and bring pressure to bear upon them if one desires to achieve professional objectives. Participation is regarded as secondary to gaining the support of local power figures. Because this point of view is so important to community organization practitioners—because it treats community as vehicle and target, and not merely context—we include an extended excerpt from Warren[18] that summarizes the literature very briefly.

The Community as a Distribution of Power

Few developments in the field of community studies in recent years have made such a vast impact on community theory, research, and practice as the growth of *community power-structure* analysis. This has been a means of coming to grips with the observable fact that certain individuals in the community exercise much more influence on what goes on than do others. Recent study has been concerned with ascertaining the extent to which this is true, just how much influence is wielded, by

---

[17]See also: Ronald Lippitt *et al., The Dynamics of Planned Change* (New York: Harcourt, Brace and World, 1958); and Warren's *Community in America,* pp. 303–39.

[18]Roland L. Warren, *The Community in America,* Third Edition, © 1978 Rand McNally College Publishing Company, pp. 40–46. Reprinted by permission of the publisher and the author.

whom, how, on what issues, and with what results.

The concept of differential ability to influence social behavior is not itself a new one. Thrasymachus, in Plato's *Republic*, gives a vivid description of how members of a ruling group are able to utilize the state and political institutions for their purposes, and a "ruling class" theory has developed through such classic works as those of Machiavelli, Marx, Mosca, and Pareto. The concept of social power is related to this special degree in which some people influence the actions of others. A classical definition of such power was given by Max Weber, who wrote, "In general, we understand by 'power' the chance of a man or of a number of men to realize their own will in a communal action even against the resistance of others who are participating in the action."[19] For centuries it has been realized that such influence over collective action is not confined to the prerogatives of a formal office, such as king, president, general, and so on, but that it can be of other types, as well.

In the second Middletown study the Lynds devoted an entire chapter to "The X Family: A Pattern of Business-Class Control" and pointed out the inordinate influence that members of this leading industrial family exerted in various aspects of the institutional life of that city and the channels through which this influence was exercised.[20] Likewise, in the Yankee City study Warner and his associates described the manner in which concentrated power was wielded by the upper classes in that community, and Hollingshead, in his social class analysis of the youth of a small midwestern city, showed specifically how the school system was controlled by a small number of upper-class people and made to function for their own interests.[21]

The more recent interest and activity in the field of the exercise of social power at the community level was largely set in motion by a study of community power structure by Floyd Hunter. Defining power as "a word that will be used to describe the acts of men going about the business of moving other men to act in relation to themselves or in relation to organic or inorganic things," he studied community power in a southeastern city that is a regional center of finance, commerce, and industry.[22] The book focused its attention on the 40 persons who were found to be the top power leaders in the community. He located these 40 people essentially by canvassing those in a position to know within business, government, civic associations, and "society" activities. From a list of 175 suggested names, 40 were chosen as the top leaders as follows: 11 from large commercial enterprises, 7 from banking and investment, 6 from the professions, 5 from industry, 4 from government, 2 from labor, and 5 classified as "leisure personnel." Although the method of selection was more complex than is indicated above, it nevertheless constituted a relatively simple method that apparently yielded good results and could easily be emulated and refined.

Through carefully planned interviews with these leading power figures and through other community-study methods, Hunter was able to gain a picture of the influence that these individuals wielded, the channels through which they wielded it, the relation of these power figures to each other, and the patterns through which community action in Regional City took place.

Hunter found that these power leaders generally not only knew each other personally but were in frequent interaction with each other, much more so than chance would allow. Their frequent interaction often involved joint efforts in community affairs. This group of leaders was at the top of the power pyramid, and its influence was found to be exerted through organizational positions and through formal and informal connections with a whole group of subordi-

---

[19]From *Max Weber: Essays in Sociology*, trans. and ed. H. H. Gerth and C. Wright Mills (New York: Oxford University Press, 1946), p. 180.

[20]Robert S. Lynd and Helen Merrell Lynd, *Middletown in Transition: A Study in Cultural Conflicts* (New York: Harcourt Brace, 1937), chap. 3.

[21]W. Lloyd Warner and Paul S. Lunt, *The Social Life of a Modern Community* (New Haven, Conn.: Yale University Press. 1941); August B. Hollingshead, *Elmtown's Youth: The Impact of Social Classes on Adolescents* (New York: John Wiley & Sons, 1949).

[22]Floyd Hunter, *Community Power Structure: A Study of Decision Makers* (Chapel Hill: University of North Carolina Press, 1953), pp. 2–3.

nate leaders who usually did not participate in making major community policy decisions but were active in implementing such decisions. "This pattern of a relatively small decision-making group working through a larger under-structure is a reality, and if data were available, the total personnel involved in a major community project might possibly form a pyramid of power, but the constituency of the pyramid would change according to the project being acted upon."[23] Thus, though major power was exercised by this group of leaders, they were not all necessarily involved in any single action at the same time.

Hunter emphasized two important characteristics of the power system in Regional City. The first was that economic interests tended to dominate it. The second was that the formal leaders of community organizations and institutions were not necessarily the top people.

In the general social structure of community life social scientists are prone to look upon the institutions and formal associations as powerful forces, and it is easy to be in basic agreement with this view. Most institutions and associations are subordinate, however, to the interest of the policy-makers who operate in the economic sphere of community life in Regional City.

The organizations are not a sure route to sustained community prominence. Membership in the top brackets of one of the stable economic bureaucracies is the surest road to power, and this road is entered by only a few. Organizational leaders are prone to get the publicity; the upper echelon economic leaders, the power.[24]

Hunter found that the understructure of leadership through which top power leaders operate is not a rigid bureaucracy but a flexible system, including people described by top power leaders as first-, second-, third-, and fourth-rate. The first-raters are industrial, commercial, and financial owners and top executives of large enterprises. Second-raters include bank vice-presidents, people in public relations, owners of small businesses, top-ranking public officials, and so on. Third-raters are civic organization

personnel, petty public officials, selected organizational executives, and so on, while fourth-raters are ministers, teachers, social workers, small-business managers, and the like.[25] Thus, people who hold office in one or another important civic activity may not be those who actually wield power but may be third- or fourth-raters among their lieutenants.

On community decisions of major importance, actions are considered and developed by top leaders and their immediate followers, or "crowds," and then spread out to a wider group of top leaders and crowds for further support and basic decision-making. Only much later, at the carrying-out stage, are the usual civic organization leaders, the press, and interested citizens' groups brought into the picture.

One of the reasons Hunter's book received so much attention was that it challenged much current thinking in the field of community organization and development, which tended to follow such procedures as "encouraging participation in policy-making by the people who will be affected by the policy," "letting plans arise from the felt needs of community people," "basing programs on grass-roots decisions," and so on. If basic community decisions are not made primarily at city hall or at the community welfare council but at the country club and even more exclusive clubs as well as in informal conferences among a small group of top leaders, then important community actions must be supported and approved by these top groups. Community planning agencies and professional leaders in such fields as public welfare and public health recognize this situation.

Actually, however, like other significant books, Hunter's left a number of important questions unresolved. Their resolution has led to a lot of research activity in the community field, and some of the answers are now beginning to appear in research reports.

One question that can be raised with regard to the concept of community power structure as developed by Hunter is, If the power structure is so important, how does it happen that it so often loses in the contest

---

[23] *Ibid.*, p. 65.
[24] *Ibid.*, pp. 82, 86–87.

[25] *Ibid.*, p. 109.

to determine a public issue? For example, in controversies involving the decision to fluoridate a community's water supply, the "power structure" is usually on the side of fluoridation, yet it often loses. Does the power configuration surrounding any particular community issue invariably take the form that Hunter describes, with top policy being determined by members of essentially the same small power group? Or is it not possible that on some community issues, decisive power is exercised by organizations and minor officials as prime movers, rather than merely as the henchmen of a small power group? There are actually two issues here. One relates to the possible multiplicity of power pyramids, depending on the area of the community activity involved in the issue. The other has to do with the extent to which power on specific issues may fluctuate according to specific organizational campaigns, as against the more or less permanent structure of power wielding that Hunter described.

Turning to the first, a number of studies have been made bearing more or less directly on the question of one versus a number of power structures.[26] With few exceptions, these studies indicate that the picture is much more complex than the one Hunter described, and they indicate a multiplicity of power structures with the power pyramids being much less a tightly knit group of leaders in close interaction than was found in Regional City.

Regarding the more or less flexible aspects of power, as opposed to the concept of a fixed structure, the question would seem to be, To what extent is any particular community issue open to genuine contest, and to what extent is it already determined by the structure of existing power leadership and the attitudes of these leaders with relation to it? Many students of the community are willing to assign much more potential effectiveness to citizen campaigns, organizations promoting particular civic actions, newspaper opinion, and so on, than Hunter would allow. Putting this another way, the power situation surrounding a particular community decision is believed to be influenceable by the organizational activities of various citizens' groups. As Kornhauser asserted, regarding fluoridation controversies, "The anti-fluoridation forces often win in spite of their general lack of power and prestige, because in many cases they are able to mobilize people who, like themselves, are only poorly attached to the community."[27]

Investigators have also explored other aspects of power than just the making of decisions and obtaining of consent. These other important leadership activities might include initiating formal community proposals, supporting or fighting proposals through such visible means as fund raising, endorsing, public speaking in behalf of an issue, mobilizing extracommunity pressures, articulating, defining, and suppressing issues, and actually making decisions as a community official.[28]

Another question often raised regarding community power structure relates to the "conspiracy" dimension, that is, to what extent the power structure represents a self-consciously functioning group of people in league with each other to control the community and to manipulate subordinates and formal organizations in their own narrow interests. Most community sociologists who have investigated the question do not believe that such a conspirational dimension is operative to any considerable extent. Hunter himself seems to be somewhat ambivalent on this question, but in a later work on which he collaborated there was an ex-

---

[26]See Alexander Fanelli, "A Typology of Community Leadership Based on Influence and Interaction within the Leader Subsystem," *Social Forces,* 34: 4 (May 1956); Roland J. Pellegrin and Charles H. Coates, "Absentee-Owned Corporations and Community Power Structure," *American Journal of Sociology,* 61: 5 (March 1956); Robert O. Schulze and Leonard U. Blumberg, "The Determination of Local Power Elites," *American Journal of Sociology,* 63: 3 (November 1957); Robert O. Schulze, "The Role of Economic Dominants in Community Power Structure," *American Sociological Review,* 23: 1 (February 1958); Nelson W. Polsby, "The Sociology of Community Power: A Reassessment," *Social Forces,* 37: 3 (March 1959); and "Three Problems in the Analysis of Community Power," *American Sociological Review,* 24: 6 (December 1959). The literature is, of course, too voluminous to list exhaustively here. Several of the above contain additional references to other studies.

[27]William Kornhauser, *Power and Participation in the Local Community,* Health Education Monographs, no. 6 (Oakland, Calif.: Society of Public Health Educators, 1950), p. 33.

[28]Polsby, "Sociology of Community Power," 233.

cellent example of such cold, self-conscious manipulation. The issue involved the transfer of title of some public playground land from the city of Salem to a power company, a proposal that had generated considerable popular opposition. In the words of a leading attorney,

In the electric plant situation the city council was on the spot because they had to stand up and be counted before a large group of citizens. To many of them it seemed like political suicide to vote for the land transfer, but the big brass in the community had been working on the city councilmen individually, *"reasoning"* with them, and they voted for the measure in spite of the fact that most of the civic associations, the veterans organizations, and a good many individual and substantial citizens were against it. One by one they voted as they were told to vote. It isn't very often that we have to have such a test of strength as this, but when the chips are down the interests that I am talking about will throw their weight around.[29]

A final question appropriate to the present discussion is that of the deliberate development and coming prominence of new sources of power through formal organization of such interest groups as organized labor, Blacks, and other racial or ethnic groups. There is considerable indication that officials of these and other voluntary organizations, whether representing special interests or promoting broad planning or health and welfare goals, are exerting increasing power by virtue of their official positions and the strength of the organizations that they represent.[30]

THE COMMUNITY AS PROBLEM

As Kramer and Specht have noted, the community may be understood, from the practitioner's point of view, as the context within which practice takes place, affecting that practice in various ways, and as vehicle or the means through which action is taken. The discussions, above, of community as place, people, shared values and social system are useful largely for their insights on the community as context. In contrast, the discussion of the community as a process of interaction and a distribution of power provide insights into ways the practitioner may use the community or various parts of it to achieve practice objectives.

In this section, we consider briefly Kramer and Specht's third perspective: the community as the problem that must be solved or ameliorated by the practitioner, the target of change efforts. Warren,[31] after setting aside problems of the larger society that affect the community, such as unemployment, delinquency, or family breakdown, but which are not problems of the

---

[29]Floyd Hunter, Ruth Connor Schaffer, and Cecil G. Sheps, *Community Organization: Action and Inaction* (Chapel Hill: University of North Carolina Press, 1956), pp. 104–5.

[30]More recent explorations of the "power" concept have taken three important emphases. The first is the continued pursuit of many of the questions raised by the earlier studies. Claire W. Gilbert made a systematic attempt to summarize the numerous findings in "Community Power and Decision-Making: A Quantitative Examination of Previous Research," in Terry N. Clark, ed., *Community Structure and Decision-Making: Comparative Analyses* (San Francisco: Chandler Publishing Co., 1968). Willis Hawley and Frederick M. Wirt, eds., provide a valuable collection of important articles in this field in *The Search for*

Community Power (Englewood Cliffs, N.J.: Prentice-Hall, 1968, 1974), which also contains an extensive bibliography. There is also recent emphasis on multicity studies of community power configurations, expecially as they affect decision-making. Clark, *Community Structure,* has this emphasis. A more recent example is Michael Aiken and Robert R. Alford, "Comparative Urban Research and Community Decision-Making," *The Atlantis,* 1: 2 (Winter 1970). See also Clark's *Community Power and Policy Outputs: A Review of Urban Research* (Beverly Hills: Sage Publications, 1973). A third vein of elaboration has been associated with social action for a transfer of power from existing structures to sectors of the population who exercise little power. A popular example is Stokely Carmichael and Charles V. Hamilton, *Black Power: The Politics of Liberation in America* (New York: Vintage Books, 1967). John Walton has reviewed the development of community power studies since Hunter with a critical eye. See his "Community Power and the Retreat from Politics: Full Circle After Twenty Years?," *Social Problems,* 23: 3 (February 1976). . . .

[31]*The Community in America,* pp. 14–20.

TABLE 12.1
Selected Characteristics of Moral Communities and Mass Societies

Moral Communities	Mass Societies
Identification Members of the moral community have a deep sense of belonging to a significant, meaningful group.	*Alienation* Members of mass society have a deep sense of being "cut off" from meaningful group associations.
Moral Unity Members of the moral community have a sense of pursuing common goals and feel a oneness with other community members.	*Moral Fragmentation* Members of mass society pursue divergent goals and feel no sense of oneness with other members of the mass society.
Involvement Members of the moral community are submerged in various groups and have a compelling need to participate in these groups.	*Disengagement* Members of mass society have no meaningful group memberships and feel no compulsion to participate in the collective activities of various groups.
Wholeness Members of the moral community regard each other as whole persons who are of intrinsic significance and worth.	*Segmentation* Members of mass society regard each other as means to ends and assign no intrinsic worth or significance to the individual.

community, identifies two types of problems: (1) loss of community autonomy over decisions in the community (e.g., when national or multinational corporations decide to locate a plant or close down, the local community has little to say), and (2) lack of identification with the community which takes the form of (a) citizen apathy regarding community affairs and (b) loss of useful roles in the community (e.g., the social consequences of aging) and of belief in the community's dominant values (e.g., manifested in delinquent behavior and legitimate social protest).

Poplin[32] points out that the term community may be used in a moral or spiritual sense epitomized in such terms as the quest or yearning for a sense of community or sharing. The absence of this sense has been defined as problematic. He provides the analysis shown in Table 12.1, contrasting the sense of community, which he refers to as "moral communities," with mass society.

---

[32]Dennis E. Poplin, *Communities: A Survey of Theories and Methods of Research* © 1972. Reprinted by permission of Macmillan Publishing Company.

CHAPTER IV

Organizations and their Linkages

Most community organizers, unlike many professionals, are salaried employees of organizations, often large and complex ones—schools, community mental health and public health agencies, United Way organizations, public assistance agencies, hospitals, city planning departments, human relations commissions, etc. The major exceptions are university-based community organization consultants and a few organizers who work on a free-lance, fee-for-service basis. Even those who work outside the professions—the movement organizers endeavoring to mobilize the latent discontent of oppressed minority groups, exploited workers such as farm laborers, domestic workers, etc.—typically work through some form of organization. Sponsoring organizations, or "change agencies" as we refer to them, exert a profound influence on the practitioner's work.

Community organizers of all stripes frequently are engaged in influencing these organizations and others whose activities affect their clientele. Thus formal organizations are often the context within which organizers work, the targets of their efforts to bring about change, and the means used for changing undesirable conditions.

In modern industrial society, complex organizations are essential tools for achieving collective purposes. They can contribute in significant ways to realizing the kinds of lives people want. But too often organizations are neither positive nor benign in their impact upon clients. Organizers not only need to know how to get organizations to deliver services but often they must have the skills necessary to change the way organizations operate and the kinds of services they deliver to a clientele defined as worthless, helpless, or degenerate.

Thus, an understanding of formal organizations is essential for community organizers. Practitioners sometimes become discouraged by the limitations organizations impose. Although these limitations are often very real, the organizer may be able to discover paths around organizational obstacles and find potentialities for action or change. Such discovery may begin with a detailed understanding of the factors affecting organizational behavior. This chapter is designed to help the practitioner develop such insight.

In formal terms, two sets of factors affecting organizations are (1) the structure and functioning of the organization, and (2) the social environment of the organization. The selection from Eugene Litwak and Jack Rothman's work focuses upon the first, and Mayer N. Zald's paper discusses the second.

The first part of the Litwak and Rothman paper discusses two ways of understanding formal organizations—the single model and the multimodel approaches, the latter growing out of dissatisfaction with the explanatory power of the first. They link various features of organizations with their capabilities for handling different kinds of problems. The reader may find it helpful to review "Organizational Structure and Capabilities" in the Introduction to ARENAS in conjunction with Litwak and Rothman's piece.

Zald analyzes the community organization agency as a sociopolitical entity. He explains the agency's constitution—its "basic zones of activity, goals and norms of procedure and relationships"—as a response to the nature of its constituency, resource base, target groups, and external relations. A series of propositions is offered that answers questions of great importance to practitioners: Under various conditions, what kinds of goals and activities can one expect of the agencies with which one works? What kinds of roles and what styles of action are likely to be both possible and effective in response to these external forces?

In an increasingly complex and differentiated environment, a vital question that confronts all practitioners at one time or another is how to affect a successful "connection" between themselves (and the organizations by which they are sponsored) and potential allies or targets in the change process. At least five patterns of linkage seem to bear special relevance for the community practitioner. In the first place, he must be aware of those processes by which individuals and small groups seek out and join with other individuals and small groups. (Clearly, it is often through the primary group that the individual member is most effectively reached.) This we refer to as linking of primary groups with other primary groups. Secondly, with the rising militance of the low-income and minority group populations, the processes by which community-based groups have an impact on institutional bureaucracies have become an issue of critical importance. We refer to this as linking primary groups to formal organizations. Third, looking at the reverse of this procedure, most efforts initiated by social welfare organizations proceed from them to individuals and groups in need. This involves affecting linkages from formal organizations to primary groups. Fourth, more traditional social welfare interventions often involve organizations or groups of organizations (i.e., the welfare council) in trying to change, coordinate, or renew the actions of other organizations. This pattern we call linking formal organizations with one another. Finally, more and more efforts in the planning area require contact between welfare agencies and municipal government, county governments, state legislatures, and the like. This process may be referred to as linking formal organizations and larger aggregates.

Surely, the relative importance of each of these units—primary groups, formal organizations, and larger aggregates—will vary from situation to situation and community to community. Considering the primacy of linkage between the systems described above as a precondition for community-based change, this area has received all too little attention in the social welfare literature.

Portions of the Litwak and Rothman paper deal with certain aspects of linkages, especially linkage among formal organizations and between formal organizations and primary groups. The complementary roles of formal organizations and primary groups in achieving social goals are noted, and a "balance theory" of the appropriate social distance put forward—neither too close (leading to nepotism or favoritism) nor too distant (leading to failure to communicate and cooperate in the achievement of common purposes) is considered appropriate. In the relations between formal organizations, the question of organizational autonomy (to assure the freedom to pursue the special purposes of the organization) and cooperation among organizations (to achieve purposes beyond the capability of a single organization) present similar problems of appropriate social distance. In both cases, the factors predisposing to stronger or more attenuated linkages are explored. The reader may find it helpful to read "Factors Influencing Linkages between Arenas" in the Introduction to ARENAS in conjunction with the Litwak and Rothman article.

Yeheskel Hasenfeld and John E. Tropman have identified three types of action engaged in by the practitioner in interorganizational relations: (1) developing new programs or strengthening existing ones, (2) mediating among various organizations and changing their patterns of interrelations, and (3) affecting the organization or distribution of social services in a community. They review the literature bearing on each of these classes of action. They also deal with the problem of helping organizations establish a niche in their environment—what others have called turf or domain.

13.

Mayer N. Zald

ORGANIZATIONS AS POLITIES: AN ANALYSIS OF COMMUNITY ORGANIZATION AGENCIES

The interdependence of subject matter in the fields of community organization and sociology has long been recognized by teachers and practitioners. Possibly to a greater extent than with any other segment of social work, the problems of this field of practice are grist for the mill of the student of society and the community. And yet there is no systematic sociology of community organization (hereinafter referred to as "CO"). Such a sociology would include a social history of the emergence and growth of the field of practice, an analysis of its ongoing social system, and diagnostic categories and criteria for investigating community problems and structure.

This paper focuses on one aspect of the social system of the field, presenting, in particular, a set of concepts and propositions about the structure and operation of CO agencies. These concepts and propositions are designed to explain some of the determinants of agency processes and, consequently, the styles and problems of professional practice.

Indeed, much more of the variability of practice in CO is determined by its organizational context, as compared with many professional fields. The needs and problems of the community are not funneled and defined directly between the practitioner and the community segment to which he is related; instead, needs are defined and shaped by the constitution and goals of the employ-ing agency. Furthermore, the means selected to deal with community problems depend on organizational requirements, stances, and definitions. Whatever the practitioner's activity, he is guided by the structure, aims, and operating procedures of the organization that pays the bills.

Therefore, any useful theory of CO practice must include concepts and propositions about how CO agencies shape practice and how such organizations are themselves constrained. The question then becomes: *How are we to analyze community organization agencies?*

ORGANIZATIONAL ANALYSIS

The general approach used here is that of organizational analysis.[1] It is a form of analysis that takes the total organization,

Source: © 1966 National Association of Social Workers, Inc. Reprinted from SOCIAL WORK, Vol. 11, No. 4 (October 1966), pp. 56–65.

[1]Organizational analysis has been developed most explicitly by Philip Selznick and his students. For example, see Philip Selznick, *T.V.A. and the Grass Roots* (Berkeley; University of California Press, 1949); Selznick, *Leadership in Administration: A Sociological Interpretation* (Evanston, Ill.: Row, Peterson & Co., 1957); and Selznick, *The Organizational Weapon* (New York: Rand Corporation, 1952). See also Burton Clark, *The Open Door College* (New York: McGraw-Hill Book Co., 1960); and Charles B. Perrow, "The Analysis of Goals in Complex Organizations," *American Sociological Review,* Vol. 66, No. 6 (March, 1961), pp. 854–866. The following works also are informed by this perspective: David L. Sills, *The Volunteers* (Glencoe, Ill.: Free Press, 1957); Martin Rein and Robert Morris, "Goals, Structures and Strategies for Community Change," *Social Work Practice, 1962* (New York: Columbia University Press, 1962), pp. 127–145; and Robert D. Vinter and Morris Janowitz, "Effective Institutions for Juvenile Delinquents: A Research Statement," *Social Service Review,* Vol. 33, No. 2 (June, 1959), pp. 118–130.

not some subpart, as its object. Typically, studies using this approach focus on the relation of goals to structure and the pressures to change goals arising from both the environment and the internal arrangements of the organization. A common focus is the allocation of power to different groups and the manner in which subgroup loyalties and power affect the operation of organizations. Furthermore, organizations are seen as developing distinctive characters—styles and strategies of coping with recurring problematic dilemmas of the organization.

Central to organizational analysis, but often only implicitly treated, is an analysis of the polity of organizations—the patterned distribution and utilization of authority and influence. The frame of reference taken in this paper is explicitly quasi-political. CO agencies are among a class of organizations in which goals are often in flux; in which the patterns of power of influence ebb and flow, but are central to understanding the problems of the organization; in which conflict is sometimes subterranean, sometimes overt, but almost always there; and in which organizations are in unstable relations to their environments. Thus, it seems warranted to give explicit attention to problems of power and the modes of binding people together for collective action. CO agencies can be analyzed as miniature polities.

Four interrelated concepts form the core of this analysis:

1. Organizations have *constitutions,* that is, they have basic zones of activity, goals, and norms of procedure and relationships that are more or less institutionalized in the organization and that are changed only with great effort and cost.

2. Constitutions are linked to the *constituency and resource base* of the organization. The constituency is not the clientele; rather, the term refers to the groups and individuals who control the organization

and to whom the agency executive or executive core is most immediately responsible—the board of directors, key legislators, officeholders, major fund-raisers or grantors.

3. CO agencies wish to affect *target populations,* organizations, or decision centers.

4. Finally, CO agencies exist among a welter of other agencies; they have foreign or *external relations* that can facilitate, impede, or be neutral to the accomplishment of their goals.

These concepts are not mutually exclusive, yet each focuses on somewhat different observations. For purposes of exposition they can be treated separately.

ANALYSIS OF CONSTITUTIONS

In a sense, the constitution of an organization represents its social contract—the basic purposes and modes of procedure to which the major supporters and staff of the organization adhere.[2] When attempts are made to change the constitution of an organization, the agency can expect conflict and disaffection, unless clear benefits adhere to the major supporters. The constitution of an organization is made up of the agency's commitments to major programs and modes of proceeding (goals and means). This is, of course, more than just the formal or written statement of goals and procedures, for these may have little to do with the organization's actual constitution. On the other hand, many patterned aspects of agency operation may not be part of the constitution, for these patterns may not

---

[2]Not much attention has been paid to organizational constitutions by sociologists because they often work in organizations whose constitutions are not problematic. E. Wright Bakke uses a conception of constitution or "charter" that is even broader than the author's, but has the same intent. See *Bonds of Organization: An Appraisal of Corporate Human Relations* (New York: Harper & Bros., 1950), especially chap. 6, "Organizational Charter," pp. 152–179.

deal with basic agreements about goals and means.

Analysis of constitution and goals is important for a sociology of CO practice because it clarifies several important aspects of it—the problems agencies confront when they attempt to change goals and structure, the possibilities of effectiveness vis-à-vis specific goals, and the styles of the professional's work. To be fruitful, analysis of constitutions must be broken down into more specific analytic problems. This paper will treat two: analysis of agency goals and constituency and agency autonomy.

DIMENSIONS OF GOALS

Organizations come into being to pursue collective ends. A central part of the constitution of any organization is the sets of agreements about goals that are understood by major constituents. Not only do goals represent a set of constituting agreements, they focus organizational resources on a problem field. That is, organizational goals along with beliefs about how to attain them set tasks and problems for agency personnel.

Although there are several conceptual and methodological approaches to the study of goals, two aspects are especially crucial here.[3] First, the goals of the organization determine some of the basic types of CO work. Second, attempts to shift the objectives of the organization can threaten its body politic. The goals of CO agencies can be classified along three analytically distinct dimensions: (1) change or service orientation (that is, according to whether

the goal is to give the recipient of service essentially what he or his representative wants—information, program, and the like —or whether the community or individual is changed regardless of whether it or he initially wanted to be changed); (2) institution or individual and group orientation; (3) member (internal) or nonmember (external) orientation. The dichotomous cross-classification of these three dimensions yields the typology shown in Figure 13.1.

Of course, it is clear that some of these organizations are more likely to be sites for group work than for CO practice. But community organizers can be found in all of them.

The typology classifies organizations by their target and the ends they wish to achieve with each group. For instance, a community center (Cell D) usually offers services to individuals, rather than attempting to change them; it is oriented to groups and individuals who are members rather than to institutions (other large-scale organizations). On the other hand, in Cell B are agencies that attempt to mobilize people to change the society and its institutions.

The typology brings to the fore regularities of practice problems shared by agencies "located" in the same cell and differences among agencies in different cells. For instance, typically CO organizations aimed externally, at change, and at institutions (e.g., to change the school system) have to be able to mobilize sanctions against the target. On the other hand, those aimed at providing services to individual members (e.g., community centers) have the problem of finding attractive programs to bring people in the door—no question of conflict or of mobilizing sanctions arises in such cases.

In general, *the more change oriented the goals are, the greater the incentives needed by the practitioner and his agency to accom-*

---

[3]See Mayer N. Zald, "Comparative Analysis and Measurement of Organizational Goals: The Case of Correctional Institutions for Delinquents," *Sociological Quarterly,* Vol. 4, No. 3 (Summer, 1963), pp. 206–230.

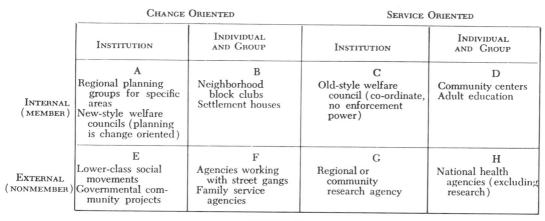

FIGURE 13.1
Goal Dimensions of Community Organization Agencies

plish these goals. (Of course, incentives can come from within the target or client group, e.g., an alcoholic may strongly desire to be cured of his alcoholism.) Furthermore, *the more member oriented an organization is, the greater the likelihood of a consensus on action,* because the act of joining implies some agreement about goals. Member-oriented agencies are more likely to use persuasive techniques than non-member-oriented organizations (who must use appeals to self-interest or sanctions). Finally, *the more institution oriented the target is, the more likely the bonds of organization are not solidaristic—based on the emotional attachments between agent and client—and the more likely they are based on exchange relations, on criteria of institutional rationality.*

These dimensions also relate to the problems of organizational maintenance in the face of attempts to attain specific goals or to change goals. The constitution of the organization consists of a set of expectations that, if violated, threaten the maintenance and stability of the organization. For example, Peter Clark has discussed the case of a local voluntary organization com-posed of businessmen interested in taxation and governmental efficiency.[4] The standard activity of the organization was information-gathering and education on different tax and governmental programs. Clark found that when any specific tax legislation or assessment was proposed it was difficult to get the organization to take a definite stand on the proposal. Instead, often a group of businessmen who favored or opposed the tax would form a specific ad hoc committee to lobby for or against the issue. Clark concluded that although the organization was concerned with taxation, any specific piece of legislation tended to have differential effects on members and internal conflict would result if any attempt were made to take a definite stand. Instead of fighting an issue through and creating dissension, members took action outside the organization. Clark's case represents a situation in which the constitution did not allow for change attempts. Similar problems occur in other organizations. The general

---

[4]See "The Chicago Big Businessman as Civic Leader." Unpublished doctoral dissertation, University of Chicago, 1959.

point is that *as an organization begins to change its basic goals, constitutional problems emerge.*[5]

The foregoing discussion of dimensions of goal analysis will also be of relevance in the discussion of constituency and target groups that follows.

CONSTITUENCY AND AGENCY AUTONOMY

Some CO agencies have the goals of integrating and co-ordinating major constituents. However, even when agencies have other goals, the question of constituency-agency relations is a focus of organizational constitutions. A pattern of normative expectations develops about consultation, discretion, and the locus of initiation of agency goals and programs. This pattern is largely a function of the resource dependency of the agency.[6] *To the extent that an agency is heavily dependent on its constituency it is likely to develop a constitution giving little room for discretion.*[7]

Constituency-agency relations are crucial to understanding executive roles. Professional CO role-taking varies in terms of how much and how often the executive must report to the constituency. Professional roles may vary from a situation in which the executive does little more than facilitate constituency decision-making to one in which the constituency is consulted seldom, if at all.[8] What determines these roles?

Three factors (excluding personality style) appear to be important in affecting the level of executive decision-making—the fund-raising base, the role of the constituency in accomplishing organizational goals, and the knowledge base differential between constituency and staff.

1. *The more routinized and relatively independent of the constituency the agency's fund-raising base is, the less likely the staff is to consult with and involve the constituency systematically in decision-making.* Thus, agencies that have an immediate and vital appeal to the public (such as the national voluntary health organizations) or have legal and routinized access to funds are less likely than others to have broad participation by their constituencies in decision-making.

2. *When the agency is directly dependent on its constituency for achieving organizational goals, greater attention will be paid to constituency wishes and participation.* An agency is dependent on the constituency for achieving goals when its prestige and influence must be utilized to mobilize other segments of the community. After all, the only moderate prestige and influence of CO professionals is usually insufficient to generate widespread community support. An agency is also dependent on the constituency when it is their change that is sought (when the constituency and the target group are the

---

[5]On the succession of goals in organizations, see David L. Sills, "The Succession of Goals," in Amitai Etzioni, ed., *Complex Organizations* (New York: Holt, Rinehart & Winston, 1954), pp. 146–158. See also Mayer N. Zald and Patricia Denton, "From Evangelism to General Service: On the Transformation of the Y.M.C.A.," *Administrative Science Quarterly,* Vol. 8, No. 2 (September 1963), pp. 214–234.

[6]For one treatment of the problem of organizational autonomy see Charles Perrow, "Organizational Prestige: Some Functions and Dysfunctions," *American Journal of Sociology,* Vol. 66, No. 4 (January 1961), pp. 854–866. See also, Selznick, *Leadership in Administration,* pp. 120–133.

[7]Note that the proposition does not apply to the formal or stated charter of the organization alone, but rather to the expectations that develop out of the actual dependency bases of the organization. The point is important, for many organizations, notably business corporations, formally "decentralize" and on paper sometimes resemble what are called "federated" systems. Yet through the judicious, and sometimes injudicious, use of central power these corporations never really build up a constitution of federalism.

---

[8]See Rein and Morris, *op. cit.;* and Sills, *op. cit.*

same).[9] Attention to the constituency may be only formal or surface; nevertheless it affects the conduct of office.

3. *The greater the knowledge differential between staff and constituency, the more likely the staff will be given autonomy in the exercise of their work and the more likely the constituency will be consulted only on "boundary" conditions—changes that affect the relation of the agency to the community.* In general, the more decisions are defined as "professional" problems, the less likely are constituencies to be involved.

It would be wrong, however, to assume that an executive cannot influence agency-constituency relations. Constitutions are not immutable! Furthermore, the executive might not want autonomy; the constituency might represent a resource that can be cultivated usefully.

CONSTITUENCY CHARACTERISTICS AND AGENCY OPERATION

The constitution of an organization emerges and is maintained partly to satisfy the constituency. At the same time that they give the organization its continuing mandate, the characteristics of the constituency may lead to a limit on goals and means.

Class Basis of Constituency. A large body of literature testifies to the greater difficulty of involving working-class individuals in voluntary organizations as com-

pared to middle- or upper-class persons.[10] Extending these findings to CO agencies, the following proposition emerges: *the lower the socioeconomic status of the constituency, the more difficult it is likely to be to maintain their interest and participation.* In other words, the CO practitioner with a lower socioeconomic class constituency will devote more of his energies to motivating the constituency than he would in other organizations.

Not only is level of participation affected by the socioeconomic basis of the constituency, but there is some reason to think that the style of participation is also likely to differ. In general one would expect that *when a CO agency aimed at changing some aspect of the community has a middle- and upper-class constituency it will be more likely to attempt to gain its ends through persuasion, informal negotiation, and long-range harmonizing of interests.* On the other hand, *the more an organization has an essentially lower-class basis, the more it will resort to direct action, open propaganda, and agitation* (when it takes action at all).[11] First, the higher up one goes in the stratification system, the more likely it is that the constituency has easy access to office-holders, can command respect from them, and can threaten use of sanctions that the target person will recognize. Thus, the more élite the constituency the more likely it is that informal negotiations will take place and can be fruitful.

---

[9]It should be clear, however, that there is an analytic difference between a target group and a constituency. A target group or institution is the change object of the organization. The target group is not directly involved in the choosing of means, the personnel, or the goals of the agency. Target groups become part of the constituency when they become part of the decision-making apparatus of the agency.

[10]For a careful summary of much of this literature and an attempt to understand the dynamics of the phenomenon, see William Erbe, "Social Involvement and Political Activity," *American Sociological Review,* Vol. 29, No. 2 (April 1964), pp. 198–215.

[11]See the discussion in Herbert J. Gans, *The Urban Villagers: Group and Class in the Life of Italian-Americans* (New York: Free Press of Glencoe, 1962), especially chap. 5, pp. 104–120. The necessity of active and direct modes of expression in the appeal to lower socioeconomic groups is one of the essential elements in Saul Alinsky's approach to CO.

Second, people from higher socioeconomic groups begin having organizational experiences from an earlier age. The higher up in the status system, the more likely the constituency will have had experience in organizational negotiation, the more time they can comfortably spend in organizational participation, and the more rewarding to them is such participation.[12]

Obviously, the CO practitioner must take these factors into account. The attempt to get concrete results, the amount of time spent in agitational versus more neutral activities, and the mechanisms of involving the constituency will each differ depending on the class base of the constituency.

Organizational versus Individual Constituencies. For many CO agencies the crucial characteristic of the constituency is not so much that of its class base but whether its basis is individual or organizational. All else being equal, *the more an agency has a constituency made up of agencies, the harder it is to get commitment to an action program that does not have widespread societal consensus and the more likely the agency is to serve as a clearinghouse for information and co-ordination.* [13]

One of the advantages to a CO agency of having a constituency comprised of organizations is that it then has a built-in multiplier effect. That is, those programs that are agreed to can be disseminated through a wide range of other organizations—the population that can be reached is greater. On the other hand, a constituency made up of organizations requires the agency to work through the problem of new and extreme programs with all constituent agencies. If the new program threatens the autonomy of the organizations or challenges *their* constituencies, there will be little incentive for commitment. Because of the desire to protect organizational autonomy, agencies comprised of organizations are more likely to have a structure similar to a representative assembly, which permits veto powers, while agencies comprised of individuals are more likely to have either straight majority rule or an oligarchic structure.[14]

The "all else being equal" clause in this proposition is especially important. If the organizations have joined the CO agency with the expectation that extreme programs would be proposed, then such an agency might be as likely as one comprised of individuals to initiate new and extreme programs rapidly. Thus, some community councils organized for purposes of neighborhood protection and development have been constituted out of organizations and still have initiated "radical" action programs.

TARGET GROUPS AND CO PRACTICE

The purpose of the professional and his agency is to improve the functioning of

---

[12]Catherine V. Richards and Norman A. Polansky have shown that among adult women, those who participated in organizations as adolescents and whose parents also participated were more likely to participate in voluntary associations than those who did not have either of these characteristics in their background. The over-all rate of parent and adolescent participation is, of course, directly related to socioeconomic status. See "Reaching Working-class Youth Leaders," *Social Work,* Vol. 4, No. 4 (October 1959), pp. 31–39.

[13]The author has less confidence in this proposition than in the previous one. For one thing, it may cause comparison of disparate organizations, for instance, neighborhood block clubs with welfare councils. Ideally, to test such a proposition one would take CO agencies in similar types of communities with similar types of goals and see if variation in their constituencies did in fact lead to different types of action programs. Such a design might be difficult to realize.

[14]See Rein and Morris, *op. cit.,* for a discussion of the problems of agencies whose constituencies are made up of organizations.

groups, individuals, and communities. To do this he attempts to change individuals and the relationships among individuals and groups. His goal may be reached not only by changing relationships and attitudes, but by changing the facilities—hospitals, schools, trading associations—used by people in carrying out their daily lives. Thus, he may be attempting to mobilize the community for a relatively specific substantive proposal and the target group may only be changed insofar as it has reached a fairly specific decision. Values, norms, and social relations may not be changed; only questions of efficiency may be involved. Differential diagnosis of target problems has important organizational implications. Let us examine two aspects of agency-target relations—the role definitions of line workers and the tactics of institutional penetration.

Role Definitions of Line Workers

The problem can be posed as a question: Should line workers be substantive specialists or should they be "multipurpose" workers coached by substantive specialists? Should the worker be a technical specialist, knowledgeable in the specific problems of the community, or should he be a generalist, knowledgeable about how to relate to communities?

At least partly the answer depends on the extent to which the target group accepts and is committed to the purposes of the agency. *To the extent that an organization's goals are accepted and its functions in a community understood, a specialist organization can most efficiently communicate information and methods that can then be utilized by a target group.* However, *to the extent that members of a target group are suspicious of an agency, communication channels will be blocked.* In such a situation a generalist will be required whose main job is to establish an organization-target group linkage. As that linkage is established, it then becomes possible to reintroduce specialists, now trading on the generalist's relations.[15]

But what of the qualifications of such multipurpose workers? Who should they be? To the extent that the target group is difficult to penetrate because of problems of distrust, and to the extent that major sanctions are not controlled by the organization, the most effective generalist is likely to be one who minimizes social distance at the same time that he represents the "ego ideal" of target group members. "Personalistic" as opposed to "professional" criteria become crucial.

As many field workers have noted in working with lower-income ethnic groups and delinquent gangs, and as Katz and Eisenstadt have suggested for Israeli administrative agencies, the overcoming of distrust may require the worker to appear to identify more with the problems and perspective of the target group than with the agency. As the level of distrust decreases, however, the target group becomes amenable to the norms and procedures of the agency and more normal agency-client relations can be established. Thus, in order to be effective, CO agencies must evaluate the extent to which target groups are receptive to their policies. Staff role definitions must be fitted to this diagnosis. Sometimes, however, CO diagnosis involves the question of how one makes specific decisions, not how one reaches a group. When the target question switches to penetrating institutional deci-

---

[15]See Albert Mayer and associates in collaboration with McKin Marriott and Richard Park, *Pilot Project India: The Story of Rural Development in Etawah, Uttar Pradesh* (Berkeley: University of California Press, 1958). See also Elihu Katz and S. N. Eisenstadt, "Some Sociological Observations on the Response of Israeli Organizations to New Immigrants," *Administrative Science Quarterly*, Vol. 5, No. 1 (June 1960), pp. 113–133; and Gans, *op. cit.*, chap. 7, pp. 142–162.

sion centers, a new set of diagnostic criteria becomes relevant.

Tactics of Institutional Penetration

The legacy of Floyd Hunter and C. Wright Mills to the practice field can be summed up as "to the power structure!" Many CO workers, civil rights workers, and others who are trying to change communities seem to be saying: "If you want something done you must get the power structure behind you." If community organizers followed this dictate, they would find themselves pursuing a chimera. If they tried to mobilize the same élite on every decision, they would fail both to mobilize them and to attain their objectives.

Furthermore, the power structure is often relatively irrelevant to many decisions, for it is often isolated and in an official decision center or is most sharply affected by the sentiments of that most diffuse of all decision centers, the voting populace. Thus, the job of analyzing decision centers requires the most precise diagnosis of the chain of influence and mechanism of decision-making for each specific decision.

If the decision involves a referendum, different kinds of issues appeal to different groups. Machiavellian advice to a community organizer interested in promoting school bonds is to see that the middle class is overrepresented (as it is when the turnout is low), since they tend to vote for school funds. On the other hand, when, as in some states, referenda are held on welfare matters, the lower class should be motivated to vote, for they tend to vote "yes" on these measures.[16]

[16]For a study that looks at the relation of income and ethnicity to "public" and "self-interest" voting on referenda see James Q. Wilson and Edward C. Banfield, "Public Regardingness as a Value Premise in Voting Behavior," *American Political Science Review,* Vol. 58, No. 4 (December 1964), pp. 876–887.

In mobilizing a target group, the CO practitioner and agency must face squarely the dilemma of their relative commitment to "the democratic process" versus their commitment to specific social values. The advice given above obviously conflicts with faith in the democratic process. This is a dilemma not only for CO practitioners, but for all advocates of social welfare. However, in part the problem of whether to pursue specific goals regardless of an idealized conception of the democratic process resolves itself according to agency goals and mandates. For instance, the more specific and concrete an organization's objectives and the greater the demands on the organization by the constituency, the more likely it is that workers' concerns about "process" will be relegated to the background.

EXTERNAL RELATIONS

In attempting to mobilize a target group, reach a specific objective, or integrate services, CO agencies must deal with other agencies. The CO agency may be but one among many and it may be without a mandate to guide, direct, or lead the other agencies. Often a CO agency has as part of its mandate the integration of the disparate institutions, but the mandate may be honored more in the breach.

One of the basic premises of organizational analysis is that only under very special conditions do organizations purposely attempt to decrease their scope, actually admit that they are ineffective, or willingly give up "turf." These special conditions involve low ideological or career commitment to the organization on the part of staff, an increasingly difficult fund-raising problem, and a constituency that increasingly finds better alternative uses of time and money. As a working assumption it is reasonable to assert that most organizations will attempt to maintain autonomy and increase their scope.[17] Even when it is obvious that one agency is more capable of achieving a shared goal than another, it would be rare indeed for the latter to donate its income for the expansion of the former. And it is rarely obvious that one agency has such superiority over another.

Given the assumption that agencies generally wish to increase autonomy and scope, the integration and co-ordination of agency policy and programs depends on the enlightened self-interest of the treaty signers —the independent agencies. As a general postulate, co-ordination, sharing of facilities, and proper integration are likely to take place only when both of the autonomous agencies stand to gain. Specific conditions follow:[18]

1. *If two agencies are essentially in a competitive relation to each other for funds, constituency, and staff, full-scale co-ordination and merger of programs would indeed be unlikely.* (Nor, given the nature of funding processes in which multiple appeals increase the total amount of funds available for the welfare sector, would a merger of identities necessarily lead to a more effective welfare economy.)

2. *The greater the marginal cost of co-ordination and integration or the lower the* *marginal profit, the less chance of integration and co-ordination of programs.* (Cost and profit do not necessarily refer to money; there can be costs of time and energy, for instance.) It follows that co-ordination will most easily be achieved on problems that are least expensive to both parties. Co-ordination is more easily achieved on a specific case than on over-all programs.

3. *The greater the organizational commitment to a fixed program or style of operation, the less likely the co-ordination and integration.* Agencies develop commitment to programs on ideological grounds and, because the programs help the agency to solve problems of identity, they thereby become part of the organizational character.[19] To the extent that a program must be changed by a merger, the costs mount.

These three propositions state the conditions that impede co-ordination and integration. Stated somewhat differently, they indicate conditions contributing to co-ordination, co-operation, and integration:

1. *The greater the symbiotic relation between agencies, the more likely the co-ordination.* For instance, interestingly enough, the police and an agency working with delinquent gangs have more to gain from co-operating than a family service agency and a street work agency. The latter agency can actually contribute only occasionally to aiding the family service agency in its work with its case load and, at best, the family service agency can help "cool out" an offender. On the other hand, the police and the street worker have a strong symbiotic relation. The street worker gains status with the boys with whom he is working by being able to negotiate with the police,

---

[17]In addition to Perrow, *op. cit.,* see Norton E. Long, "The Local Community as an Ecology of Games," *American Journal of Sociology,* Vol. 64, No. 3 (November 1958), pp. 251–261.

[18]This discussion draws on the following articles, which have recently discussed problems of co-ordination and interorganizational relations: William J. Reid, "Interagency Co-ordination in Delinquency Prevention and Control," *Social Service Review,* Vol. 38, No. 4 (December 1964), pp. 418–428; Eugene Litwak and Lydia Hylton, "Inter-Organizational Analysis: A Hypothesis on Coordinating Agencies," *Administrative Science Quarterly,* Vol. 6, No. 4 (March 1962); Sol Levine and Paul E. White, "Exchange as a Conceptual Framework for the Study of Inter-Organizational Relationships," *Administrative Science Quarterly,* Vol. 5, No. 4 (March 1961), pp. 583–601.

---

[19]On the concept of organizational character see Selznick, *Leadership in Administration.*

while the police have fewer problems with the gang. The same principle applies to the relation of membership groups to the "Y's," of mental hospitals to general hospitals, and so on.

2. *The greater the marginal profits, the more likely the co-ordination.* Sometimes funds are granted only to co-operating agencies. If the funds are great enough they overcome the costs of integrating or joint planning. Marginal profits of co-ordination may be seen in the face of a crisis in facilities. When programs become overburdened, when facilities are inadequate and multiple expansion funds are not available, a negotiated settlement may allow specialization between agencies, reducing overall financial needs and making co-ordination profitable.[20]

There is also some evidence to suggest that overlapping constituencies contribute to such co-ordination.[21] *The less constituencies overlap, the more likely it is that the constituencies are either neutral to or distrust each other and thus the longer it will take and the more difficult it will be to gain co-operation.*

---

[20]See Robert Morris, "New Concepts in Community Organization Practice," *Social Welfare Forum, 1961* (New York: Columbia University Press, 1961), pp. 128–146.

[21]*Ibid.*

This last point suggests that external relations may also be related to the concepts discussed earlier; that is, costs and profits are defined in the context of and affected by organizational constitutions and goals, constituency, and target groups.

CONCLUSIONS

In this paper one part of a sociology of CO practice has been developed—the organizational analysis of CO agencies. In each section several testable propositions were presented about the conditions under which different kinds of CO agency problems and processes arise. However, this paper has not presented a complete analysis of CO agencies. First, there are not enough empirical studies of these agencies to permit this. Second, the internal role structure of agencies has not been dealt with. Nevertheless, the writer is convinced that analysis along these lines will be valuable for both sociology and CO practice. For sociology the reward will be rich in that studies of sets of organizations will permit an examination of problems of mobilizing support and community consensus; for community organization the reward will be rich in that an analytic and differential basis will be developed by which to assess CO agencies and evaluate practice roles.

14.

Eugene Litwak and Jack Rothman*

THE IMPACT OF ORGANIZATIONAL STRUCTURE AND LINKAGE ON AGENCY PROGRAMS AND SERVICES

THEORETICAL APPROACHES TO ORGANIZATIONAL ANALYSIS

The theoretical framework we will use includes two general avenues of investigation that appear fruitful for the analysis of social welfare agencies: (1) internal structure, emphasizing a multimodel conception of organizational behavior; and (2) linkage theory, concerned with how organizations deal with units in their environments, especially clients and other agencies. Linkage theory offers a useful conceptual tool for analyzing service delivery problems.

INTERNAL STRUCTURE ANALYSIS

Single Model Approach

There have been two basic approaches to the study of the effects of organizational structure on the work situation. The first may be called a "single model" theory of organizational structure. It assumes that there is one ideal organizational structure which is optimal for all tasks undertaken by formal organizations. Several such ideal models have been selected, each one implying a conceptual dimension along which organizations can be arrayed, with the various positions along the dimensions hypothesized to be related to specific effects on the work to be done by the organization.

---

*Excerpted from *Working Papers No. 1: National Study of Social Welfare and Rehabilitation Workers, Work and Organizational Contexts* (U.S. Department of Health, Education and Welfare, Social and Rehabilitation Service, May 1971).

One of the earliest of such single model theories is that which Weber called the monocratic model (34), but also referred to as a rationalistic or a rules-oriented model. Though investigators have used different languages in discussing this model and differentially stress various aspects of it, they are all responding to the same basic set of dimensions or variables. Following Weber's formulations, these dimensions may be described as: (1) appointment and promotion by merit; (2) delimited specialization of work roles; (3) specified rules for carrying out organizational functions; (4) hierarchical authority; (5) impersonal relations among organizational members; (6) a priori specification of duties and tasks; (7) separation of administrative and policy decisions; and (8) requirement that personnel be full-time employees of the organization.

These various elements or characteristics were said to provide the most effective form of organizational structure because they presumably concentrate the maximum amount of knowledge and resources on the tasks which the organization must perform. Thus the demand for appointment and promotion on merit functions to assure that the most knowledgeable persons are being hired to perform the work. The stress on specialization assures that workers have maximum experience regarding the tasks they perform and thus are able to handle them most propitiously. The use of rules assures speedy and consistent coordination between people and task segments so that the right person is at the right job at the right time. When rules are insufficient to achieve coordination, the hierarchical authority assures that consistent and informed decisions will permeate the entire organization.

The impersonality of staff relations and a priori delimitation of duties and rights decrease the chances for personnel to substitute their own personal goals for those of the organization. Thus formal relations limit the ability of interpersonal likes and dislikes to intrude on task functions. They also limit the power of the superordinate and prevent forcing subordinates to work on his private projects as the price of getting ahead in the organization.

The separation of policy and administrative decisions permits the rapid introduction of policy changes without requiring the discharge of all the organizational members and a new cycle of recruitment and training of new staff.

This model of organizational milieu was pervasive in most kinds of organizations through the 1940's. In the world of business it ultimately manifested itself in scientific management and management by objectives, which especially concern themselves with certain components of the monocratic model, e.g., hierarchy, specialization, and span of control. In hospitals and schools there was concentration on staff-centered, professionalized, rule-oriented bureaucracies, while in prisons there was emphasis on custodial regimes.

A series of pioneering studies in the field of business in the 1930's and 1940's began to question the efficacy of this model and led to the creation of an alternative single model formulation. Mayo and his colleagues began to demonstrate in a series of studies that positive affect and peer group solidarity were extremely important dimensions in business productivity (26;1). Somewhat independently, the work of Lewin and his co-workers in group dynamics suggested that collegial decisions might be more productive than hierarchical ones (4). Other studies of the American and German armies during World War II suggested that peer group decision making and solidarity were important to military effectiveness (28). Given that an army is the quintessence of the classical model of a rationalistic, formal bureaucratic structure, these studies were highly significant and damaging to the model.

During the 1950's and 1960's a series of studies in hospitals and prisons suggested the validity of a therapeutic patient-centered approach (8, 36, 29). These studies further implied a move away from hierarchical structure and intense specialization by placing more emphasis on positive affect and generalist work roles.

At the same time, school systems began to show increasing concern for a pupil-centered approach which included curriculum designs capable of matching individual children's needs. Unlike some of the other kinds of organizations mentioned, schools had already gone through a number of transformations in educational philosophy. While these transformations were not often translated into organizational terms, they were in fact associated with structural changes (16). The progressive approach of John Dewey and later pupil-centered and open-classroom developments demanded collegial, decentralized administrative systems in order to function well, whereas the earlier standardized subject matter content emphases could be managed through rationalistic bureaucracies.

The kind of organizational structure implied by these developments is a more open one. It has been given various names—human relations, therapeutic, treatment-oriented, goal-oriented, democratic, participatory, and others. Despite differences in labels, there is a core of structural features which differentiates these organizations from those described by the older rationalistic model: (1) general specialist rather than detailed specialist; (2) committee meetings rather than rules; (3) collegial rather than hierarchical relations; (4) positive affect rather than impersonal relations; (5) general specification of duties and privileges rather than precisely defined statements; and (6) merger of policy and administrative decisions rather than separation. They also leave open the possibility of including within their administrative staffs people who are not full-time or professionalized employees, such as patients, students, indigenous nonprofessionals, etc. In our previous work in the area of organizational analysis, we have referred to this kind of structure as a human relations type of organization. The point to be made here is that this model identifies alternate poles of dimensions or variables which are anchored at the other end in the rationalistic model, thus expanding the list of constructs by which organizations can be described and analyzed.

Multimodel Approach

The multimodel approach is a more recent development. The human relations model blossomed in the mid-1960's and the bulk of organizational theorists still view it as the ideal alternative to the Weber model. However, since the mid-1960's a series of studies has suggested that the human relations model is not, by itself, adequate to account for the ways in which organizations structure themselves (35; 25; 31). Consequently, some theorists have searched for a new single model of organizational behavior which will be applicable to all problems with which organizations deal. Others have branched off and suggested that there may be multiple models of organizational behavior, depending on the kinds of problems with which organizations deal, in effect adding a classification of problems as another

set of variables necessary for describing and analyzing organizational structure. These "multiple model" theorists do not abandon the practitioner to uncertainty and confusion; rather, they suggest that within their conceptual frameworks there may be a set of rules for relating organizational variables to specific organizational tasks. Once one arrives at the position that different organizational tasks demand different kinds of organizational structures, then the classification of tasks and the linkage of structure with function become important conceptual and empirical problems.

One group of theorists have proceeded by taking as their major focus the degree of uncertainty about organizational tasks. They have given this uncertainty different names, and they have often treated different dimensions of uncertainty. But their work has an important commonality because of the emphasis on task variability or unpredictability (14, 25, 31, 12). In brief, these theorists suggest that the more uncertain or unpredictable the task, the more effective are elements of the human relations model, while the more certain the task, the more effective is a rationalistic structure for the organization.

These writers also speak of organizations with multiple tasks, each requiring a somewhat different structure. As a result of investigating ways in which organizations operate with two or more different substructures based on different principles, these theorists have developed a conceptual scheme which includes a variety of types of organizational structure. However, because these various types are evolved from a limited set of underlying concepts, it is possible for the practitioner to locate his particular structure through application of the underlying dimensions.

Let us illustrate the multimodel approach in another way. This model would suggest that different modes of influence are associated with different tasks and organizational circumstances. No single mode of organizational control meets all situations. Thus they point out that organizations may gain compliance by coercion, by instrumental expediency, by utilization of reference power, or by legitimation (5). Different modes of influence may be associated with different structures, as well as with different organizational goals. Basically this approach takes one dimension of organizational structure, form of motivation, and suggests it be given causal priority. However, it more or less comes to the same conclusions as the above multimodel theorists. For example, instrumental forms of power are most compatible with rationalistic organizations and use of referent or legitimation power is most compatible with the human relations structure (5).

From our point of view, it is probably an exaggeration to give this special emphasis to modes of motivation. At first blush it would seem this approach defines tasks differently. It defines them by their relations to modes of influence rather than certainty or uncertainty. However, others have pointed out that mode of influence is strongly related to the visibility of task performance, and, we suggest, to the degree of standardization of the task (32). The more visible the task, the more subject to monitoring, then the more the organization can utilize coercive modes of influence. The less visible the tasks, the more the organization must rely on legitimation, referent power, or internalized modes of compliance. These notions supplement the multimodel theories by suggesting additional dimensions of tasks which may be related to organizational structure and by refining the multiple ways in which organizations obtain compliance. Further, it can be shown that the more common-sense classification of organization types (e.g., democratic, laissez faire, autocratic, paternalistic) are essen-

tially variations of the same dimensions discussed in connection with the multimodels (16). Finally, the multimodel approach generates numerous points of contact between concepts of task analysis (e.g., time span of discretion, locus of performance of evaluation, nature of performance standards), which permits an integration of analyses at several different levels. For example, use of this framework should make it possible to link studies of organizational characteristics directly with job and task analyses and with modes of control and influence, through interfacing variables common to varying levels of analysis.

ANALYSIS OF ORGANIZATIONAL LINKAGE

Associated with the progression from single to multiple models for organizational analysis has been the development of systematic analyses of the linkages between organizations and their environments. Some investigators deal with the environment in generalized terms such as heterogeneous vs. homogeneous (31), competitive vs. facilitative (23), turbulent vs. nonturbulent (30). Discriminations may be made between an organization's relations with other formal organizations and its relations with primary groups (17, 27).

Such discriminations have clear implications for certain policy questions. One set of policy considerations has to do with the circumstances under which one organization should relate to another in order to increase the contributions of both through cooperation. Another set of policy considerations has to do with how an organization reaches into communities to clients who need their services, as well as how clients affect agencies to insure that they do the jobs they are supposed to do (2). The development of community mental health centers, outreach programs, and concepts regarding indigenous workers and participation of the poor are manifestations of official efforts to develop linkages with communities and to include clients in service delivery patterns.

Organization—Community Linkages

Previous work in this area (17, 10, 31) suggests some leads to manipulating linkages for practice and policy ends. Because we are restricting our analysis to organizational components, we shall put our major emphasis on how organizational structures permit or prevent certain kinds of linkages to the outer community. Such an analysis and conceptualization should have relevance to such questions as the kinds of structures which facilitate or inhibit the effectiveness of a detached gang worker program, the kinds of probation department structures conducive to the development of a stress on community intervention, and manpower service structures which influence the extent to which manpower agencies attempt to ferret out and deal with the unique community problems of the hard-to-employ.

Analysis of the linkages between bureaucratic organizations and community primary groups centers on mutual needs for each other's help in order to achieve goals in a context of great differences in organizational atmospheres. For example, delinquency control agencies, educational institutions, and mental health agencies seek and need community resources (clients, neighborhood groups, community leaders, etc.). Nevertheless, it is clear that community groups stress positive affect and generalized rather than specialized relations (i.e., a human relations kind of organizational structure) while the bureaucracies of agencies such as those mentioned stress contractual impersonalized relations and specialized agencies and

functions (i.e., a rules-oriented type of structure). When the two kinds of organizations become too closely mixed, the result is often charges of nepotism or favoritism (11), while too great a distance between the two leads to charges of irrelevance, autocracy, and welfare colonialism. In other words, criteria for evaluating one type of structure are applied to the different, but linked, organization with negative consequences.

In our work we have evolved what we call a balance theory to conceptualize events such as these. Balance theory consists of some modifications and adaptations of communication theory and organizational theory (17, 19). Theoretical speculations and empirical evidence suggest that there is a range of possible matches or consistencies between organizational structure and the type of linkage it uses to relate to the community (31, 10).

Linkages between Formal Organizations

Basically, the same set of balance theory hypotheses may be applied to linkages between formal organizations. However, whereas distance between organizations is the most relevant factor in the organization-community linkages, the maintenance of autonomy of the linked organizations is the crucial feature of linkages between formal organizations (3, 7, 13, 15). Considerations of autonomy influence the types of linkages which can be developed between formal organizations. Our multifactor theory of organizational linkages (18) suggests that the effectiveness of various kinds of linkages depends on such factors as the volume of exchanges between organizations, the number of linked organizations, whether they are engaged in competitive or facilitative interdependence, whether the element to be exchanged between the organizations is highly standardized or not, and the extent to which the organizations are in symmetrical or asymmetrical power relations.

ILLUSTRATIVE APPLICATIONS OF CONCEPTUAL FRAMEWORK TO SOCIAL WELFARE ORGANIZATIONS

Illustrative Multimodel Analyses

The dimensions of organization described above can be used to classify and describe most formal organizations. For example, Miller (23) describes a series of organizations in a large city which were temporarily allied to deal with problems of delinquency. According to this account, the social work agency which was specially set up to deal with hard-core delinquents comes very close to fulfilling the requirements for classification as a human relations organization. He points out that it had a small staff which was completely devoted to the task (i.e., missionary zeal). This is another way of describing the concept of internalized organization policy. The agency he describes had as its primary task the treatment of hard-core delinquents through group therapy. We would classify this task as relatively nonstandardized, compared to the county youth board in the same community and the recreational department, whose jobs can be defined in standardized ways. The county youth board defined its job in terms of loose supervision to insure that the law was not publicly violated; the recreation department defined its job as providing relatively standardized facilities and housekeeping functions. In contrast to the small social work agency, the personnel of the youth board and the recreation department were governed more by rules and regulations than by individual discretion. Workers in these two agencies had not internalized the values of their or-organizations but rather viewed their jobs

as opportunities for personal advancement. They had a much more specified hierarchical system and less use for collegial meetings.

Thus we have a series of agencies ostensibly similar in that they were involved in problems of adolescence and delinquency. However, they defined their tasks differently, as far as degrees of uncertainty are concerned. The social work agency used a definition of greatest uncertainty (i.e., the complexity of group therapy); the probation officers and recreation department defined their tasks with most certainty (i.e., reporting public violations of probation and maintaining standardized recreational facilities). As expected from the theory described earlier, they thus vary in structure from an extreme form of human relations type to a very rationalistic merit organization.

If we examine the public welfare organizations, we can again classify their tasks in terms of the degree of uncertainty. The most certain task is the distribution of funds in the income maintenance programs. Next in line is the establishment of eligibility for these funds. Next in degree of uncertainty is the task of providing welfare recipients with relatively standardized information about services available to them when some common needs arise (e.g., medical or dental care, employment, and housing). Still less certain is the supportive treatment, therapeutic casework, and psychotherapy. According to our theory, the rationalistic structure would be most effective for handling the standardized tasks. Thus the distribution of funds can be handled according to explicit rules, by people and machines with highly specialized skills, in an atmosphere of impersonality, with great separation between policy and administration, and with great ability to specify duties and privileges. The Social Security Administration exemplifies this approach in many ways. All this would be even more obvious if public welfare moves in the direction of a negative income tax or family allowance.

By contrast, the provision of psychotherapy requires a far different kind of job activity. Here there is a demand for internalization of policy, activities cannot be specified ahead of time, and therefore there can be no highly specified rules detailing all aspects of the job. Professionals must be free to talk to colleagues and clients in an atmosphere of positive trust to handle problems in such uncertain situations, and they must be given much discretion rather than having decisions handed down by a hierarchy. In other words, the job pressures in therapy are very different from those in income maintenance.

This illustration raises one of the key problems which some multimodel theorists highlight: How does an organization survive when it must deal with two tasks requiring different administrative styles? Typical welfare departments survive by isolating or departmentalizing the two kinds of tasks, so that different people handle the different tasks. The isolation not only involves physical separation but also role differentiation (e.g., different job statuses) and often time separation as well. Similarly, unemployment compensation staffs have recently been physically separated from vocational counseling and job placement staffs in employment service offices.

To illustrate this point further and at the same time make clear that the solution of departmentalization is limited, let us look at the educational system. As stated above, Litwak and Meyer (16) have pointed out that two opposing philosophies of education imply different degrees of uncertainty about the educational tasks as well as different administrative styles. The "drill" (sometimes called the Three R's) approach assumes that the transfer of knowledge is a very standardized event (i.e., repeat infor-

mation often enough and have a rigorous testing procedure). By contrast, in the pupil-centered approach, the educational task is highly unique to each pupil and therefore, in terms of our analysis, highly uncertain. The first approach calls for a rationalistic structure, while the second approach is more consistent with a human relations structure. Thus the school in the first instance can detail ahead of time the lesson plans, what the teacher is to cover, the kinds of teaching material which shall be used, the hours the teacher will be in the school, etc. All of this can be laid down from a hierarchical level, and there is a minimum need of positive affective interaction between teachers, who are encouraged to become specialists within their fields. By contrast, in the pupil-centered approach there are no fixed curriculum or teaching materials which can be laid out ahead of time or from above. Rather, each teacher must have the discretion to pick her materials in consultation with the pupils. Projects may be extended into the community, and the hours of schooling are not so firmly fixed. Teachers are encouraged to engage in positive affective relations with both colleagues and students.

A combination of these two extremes is contained in the position that, although the task of motivating students to learn requires almost artistic creativity and in this sense has much uncertainty, there are a whole series of jobs which are certain and can be clearly programmed: keeping grade and attendance records, insuring that proper teaching materials are at hand, keeping the rooms clean, etc. Furthermore, both the uncertain tasks of motivation and the certain tasks of keeping track of students' academic progress and attendance are crucial to the system. As in the welfare and employment service illustrations, this situation requires one organization to perform two different tasks which have somewhat contradictory elements. However, unlike the earlier examples, this particular structure cannot readily isolate the tasks by departments and by people. The teacher typically performs both kinds of tasks. If there is a need for a mechanism of isolation, it must be some form of internalized role segregation. Thus the teacher must recognize that there are two roles with contradictory demands which she is being asked to perform. The potential friction between these roles can be minimized if the teacher realizes that the two roles relate to different tasks. However, if she has not properly internalized the roles as well as the legitimation for their separation, there will be considerable confusion on her part over the assignment of priority to one set of the organizational goals over the other (e.g., keep good records at the expense of good teaching, or stress good teaching at the expense of keeping good records).

If one turns to the field of closed institutions and correctional institutions, one finds very similar problems. Zald (36), for instance, points out that correctional institutions may stress either custodial goals or treatment goals. According to our analytic framework, custodial goals permit much more certainty than treatment goals. Custody involves the assurance that inmates do not escape from the institution; this can be accomplished by creating maximum security institutions and keeping the inmates in cells as much of the day as possible. It is a relatively straightforward solution as compared with treatment goals. In the latter case there is much more uncertainty and art. Zald demonstrates that the more the institution defines its goals as custody, the more likely its structure is to resemble what we have called a rationalistic organization. There is a sharper hierarchical structure, there are more detailed rules, relationships among staff and between staff and inmates are much more impersonal, rights and du-

ties can be more clearly defined, and the staff do not have to internalize policy. By contrast, when treatment goals are stressed, just the opposite relation occurs. Authority is spread throughout the institutions, it is more difficult to design rules which can detail the job requirements, there is much greater need for the staff to internalize the values of the organization, and there is a much greater stress on positive affect among staff members and between staff and clients.

Zald also describes the situations in which the correctional institution stressed both custody and treatment goals. He points out the tendency for bifurcation of staff in such institutions. However, lacking our multimodel theory, Zald could not deal with the mechanisms of isolation and the problem of two different systems which must be simultaneously maintained. Perrow (25), dealing with these same data, suggests in retrospect that he would have analyzed them differently in order to take account of this problem.

This analysis of correctional institutions has an exact parallel in prisons which also deal with custodial and rehabilitation goals. For an excellent description of the way in which these tasks pressure an organization in two different directions, see the discussion by McCleery (21). McCleery and those administering the changes in prison had no clear idea of a multimodel approach and thus missed a solution to the organizational problem through two different administrative structures which would have to be in communication while being kept in isolation from each other. However, the reader who examines the description of what took place when a prison sought to move from a rationalistic structure with emphasis on custodial tasks to a human relations structure with emphasis on rehabilitation tasks can easily understand the consequent problems. The human relations structure was ineffective for custodial goals. What the "reformers" should have recognized was the need to maintain both goals and the consequent structural demands.

Another area in which the problems of organizational structure and certainty of tasks become central is that of mental health. The problem arose first in hospitals where the concept of a therapeutic milieu was used to describe both the structure of the organization and its goals. Hamburg (8) has one of the best descriptions of what happens when one conceives of therapy as involving uncertainty and therefore attempts to change the structure of the mental health ward from a rationalistic one to a human relations one. He points out that the ward psychiatrist moves toward giving greater decision-making freedom to the ward attendants, nurses, janitors, and patients. Furthermore, there is a systematic attempt to internalize the policy of the therapeutic process among all staff members including nurses, attendants, janitors, etc. There is a stress on positive affect among staff, there is less detailed specification of jobs in terms of rules, and in general there is less specialization as each person devotes some time to the therapeutic process. Hamburg argues that this shift in administrative structure (i.e., from a rationalistic to a human relations basis) produces better therapeutic results (e.g., patients are released more quickly, there is less violence among the patients, staff turnover is reduced). We would argue that insofar as Hamburg is talking about a ward which is part of a larger hospital, it must also deal with the other tasks the hospital faces which are defined as having more certainty; e.g., billing, records of the patients' progress and status, feeding of patients, visiting hours, etc. A close look at some of these areas would indicate that in fact the hospital described by Hamburg had multiple tasks and that the purely human relations structure which

Hamburg rightly stresses is not an adequate picture of the structure of the hospital.

One of the earliest approaches to a multi-model analysis of closed mental health institutions was provided by Henry (9). His descriptions of various closed institutions and their treatment of the mentally ill runs the full range of organizational types. Thus his description of the very small private treatment home for disturbed children places it very close to a true human relations structure, with great emphasis on treatment procedures derived from psychotherapeutic principles and involving much uncertainty. The staff emphasizes positive affective relations; there are few if any rules for defining tasks; heavy reliance is placed on internalized values and diffused tasks. In contrast to such settings, his descriptions of large state hospitals for the mentally ill suggest that they are rationalistic structures which either have largely custodial goals or define the treatment process as one involving far more certainty than does psychotherapy (e.g., electroshock and drug treatments which can be routinely administered).

We shall conclude our illustrations with some discussion of employment programs. Ferman (6) describes employment agencies which were set up to find jobs and develop training programs for the hard-to-employ. He contrasts these with the traditional state employment agencies. From his description it is clear that the traditional employment service agencies define their jobs in routine terms. They have more or less standardized processes of listing available jobs and similar standardized qualifications for such jobs, such as education, prior job experience, and health. By contrast, the newer agencies have a much looser and uncertain definition of qualifications. They try to look at work motivation; they seek to determine the family conditions which produce or reduce such motivation; they attempt to determine the client's psychological state and how it must be altered to produce work motivation, etc. Characteristic of this kind of eligibility assessment is the extreme complexity and uncertainty involved. Precise and objective criteria are avoided. They define job procurement in a less standardized way. Instead of waiting for the employers to come to them, they actively go out and seek jobs. In addition, they do not accept the employer's definition of the job and its recruitment but try to persuade him to tailor the job to the needs of the client. They may ask employers to modify their attendance requirements, so that the new employee will not be fired if he does not come to work regularly, at least during an initial period of adjustment to the job.

This concept of job development involves much more uncertainty than the traditional employment agency, which accepts the employer's definition of the conditions. These programs thus require a human relations structure, while the regular employment agencies can operate with a more rationalistic structure. When both are put in the same organization without mechanisms of isolation to keep them apart, then one or the other goal will suffer, as is clear from the experience of Concentrated Employment Programs which attempted to wed employment service agencies with community action agencies. Historically, it has been the goal of finding jobs for the hard-to-employ which has suffered. Although finding jobs for such people has always been within the mandate of the traditional employment agencies, they have never given emphasis to it. This lack of emphasis in part occurs because the task performances required by such a goal demand a very different structure than their rationalistic one. Not recognizing the need for multiple structures, agency personnel choose one (the rationalistic) over the other (human relations) and as a consequence make it impossible to

fulfill those tasks which involve high uncertainty.

Illustrative Linkage Theory Analyses

In a similar fashion one can illustrate the problems of linkages between the organization and its environment. We will provide some pertinent illustrations and refer the reader to previous work by the investigators for much more illustrative material.

One of the important problems of linkages involves the ways in which formal organizations relate to each other. This problem has been most clearly illustrated in the field of welfare by the series of government and foundation attempts to produce more explicit coordination between welfare agencies within cities. In general, the move in the recent past has been toward a formal overall coordinating agency (e.g., Community Action Programs, Model Cities programs, earlier delinquency programs) such as described by Marris and Rein (20), and Kramer (11).

One of the central questions which has arisen as a result of these attempts at more formal coordination is exactly how much explicit authority such coordinating agencies command. For instance, Marris and Rein seem to feel that one formal coordinating agency for handling the multitudinous problems results in too much inflexibility. They also point out that establishment of formal coordinating structures is unrealistic because coordinating agencies do not have the financial or legal power to enforce their will. Mott, in his description of a New York Health Council (14), goes further in suggesting that, even where such authority exists, the single autonomous coordinating agency tends to be inflexible. Both authors suggest that a more decentralized procedure would be more effective, given the circumstances of the multiplicity of tasks and power bases. Marris and Rein go further than Mott in suggesting models of coordination which involve much more ad hoc, incremental kinds of planning. In other words, one of the key practical questions which face people in welfare planning is how formal the linkages with other organizations should be, how much autonomy should be given to the linking structure, and how much should be retained by the member organizations.

We would in addition suggest several other dimensions of linkages to be considered. Ferman (6), in speaking about the relationship between traditional employment agencies and the newer ones established to deal with hard-to-employ people, and Miller (23), in his analysis of the relationships between social work agencies and county youth boards dealing with delinquents, point out that the structural differences between the organizations frequently lead to friction between personnel who serve as linkage agents between them. These linkage agents have radically different definitions of work which tend to be translated into interpersonal disputes when they have to work together. Miller also suggests that many of the coordinating efforts are made on the assumption that there is no real intrinsic conflict between the needs of the various organizations. As a result, it is often assumed that further information would iron out any differences. However, as Miller and Riessman (22), Kramer (16) and Miller (23) suggest, there may be some basic conflicts between segments of the community. Thus it is not clear that the demands of the poor for a greater voice in the running of the OEO programs were consistent with the needs of the professionals, the middle class, or the politicians. Miller points out that the secular approach of the social work delinquency agency was not at all consistent with the demands of the church groups that all treatment take place within a religious moral context. Neverthe-less, the social work agency and the religious organization were tied into a common coordinating network.

Our balance theory suggests that one of the key things to look for in the linkages is whether or not there are modes for adjudicating disputes. Thus in situations where agencies involved in competitive interdependence are also coordinating with each other, they need adjudicating devices or they tend quickly to split up. This happened in the case described by Miller as well as several described by Marris and Rein. By contrast, where organizations are linked in facilitative interdependence, we would hypothesize that there is no need for adjudicatory devices in the linkages. The traditional stress on communication would be sufficiently effective. In any case, these preliminary analyses suggest the need to classify linkages on the basis of their adjudicatory devices.

The problems of linkages between formal organizations and community primary groups are somewhat different from those of linkages between formal organizations. One of the major bases for this difference is the extent to which their structures are antithetical to each other. Thus, as Litwak and Meyer (17) point out, there are two kinds of dangers involved in this kind of linkage. One danger is that the bureaucracy and the community are so far apart that neither can achieve its goals. It was this kind of consideration which led some social workers to move toward an aggressive casework technique. It also led to the detached gang worker program as social workers realized that they could not deal with the problem of delinquency until they were able to get closer to the gang which played such a key role in the maintenance of delinquency. This movement also caused some of the schools to introduce community agents and a "lighted" school (i.e., a school building kept open for community use after school hours) in order to bring the school and community closer together. In part, the legislative mandate that required the OEO programs to have local community participants was an effort to insure that the distance between bureaucracies and people would not be too great; as a consequence, the programs of the bureaucracies were expected to have a greater chance of meeting their stated goals.

Similarly, the development of community mental health programs has as one of its components the need to decentralize the treatment of the mentally ill and bring services closer to the people who most need services, especially the very poor. Thus some community health programs have sought to develop "storefront" services in ghetto areas. Finally, the demands of community groups for a greater say in the bureaucracies, such as the demand for decentralized schools, civilian review boards for the police, and greater participation of local groups in agency programs have been efforts on the part of the community to close the distance between it and bureaucratic organizations, despite the disparities between community structure and formal agency structure.

These illustrations have suggested only one issue in the linkage problem between bureaucracies and community groups. Another problem is that of community groups that are too close to bureaucratic organizations. Family, friendship, and neighborhood groups are not run on the basis of merit. Love, unlimited commitment, and noninstrumental relations, which are essential to family relations, become destructive when introduced into formal organizations, where they are described as favoritism, nepotism, and corruption. Balance theory suggests that too much closeness between formal organizations and primary groups will lead to the destruction of both, because their structures are incompatible. On the

other hand, if they are kept too far apart from each other, they will not serve each other's needs. Thus our theoretical structure suggests that they must meet at some middle point.

Up to very recently, the problem has been that welfare and social service bureaucracies have been too distant from community primary groups. However, as society has begun to correct this defect, we can see some of the problems of too much closeness beginning to emerge. Kramer illustrates the problem of too much closeness by pointing out that, in various settings, community action agencies had to deal with charges of nepotism, favoritism, and corruption because primary group standards were applied to professional situations. He also illustrates the problems of too much distance when he points out that officials of organizations did not sufficiently have the needs of local communities in mind.

From this analysis we suggest that a key problem in studying linkages between bureaucratic organizations and primary groups is the analysis of the properties of linkages which permit primary groups and bureaucracies to increase or decrease social distance.

REFERENCES

1. Bendix, R., and Fisher, L. "Perspectives of Elton Mayo." In A. Etzioni, ed., *Complex Organizations.* New York: Holt, Rinehart, and Winston, 1964.
2. Brager, G., and Purcell, F. *Community Action against Poverty.* New Haven: College and University Press, 1967.
3. Clark, B. "Interorganizational Patterns in Education." *Administrative Science Quarterly,* 1965, 10, 224–37.
4. Coch, L., and French, J. R. P. "Overcoming Resistance to Change." In D. Cartwright and A. Zander, eds., *Group Dynamics.* Evanston, Ill.: Row, Peterson, 1953.

5. Etzioni, A. "Organizational Control Structure." In J. March, ed., *Handbook of Organizations*. Chicago: Rand McNally, 1965.

6. Ferman, L. *Job Development for the Hard-to Employ*. Ann Arbor, Mich.: Institute of Labor and Industrial Relations, 1968.

7. Guetzkow, H. "Relations among Organizations." In R. Bowers, ed., *Studies in Behavior in Organizations: A Research Symposium*. Athens, Ga.: University of Georgia Press, 1966.

8. Hamburg, D. "Therapeutic Aspects of Communication and Administration Policy in the Psychiatric Section of a General Hospital." In N. Greenblatt, et al., *The Patient and the Mental Hospital*. Glencoe, Ill.: Free Press, 1957.

9. Henry, J. "Types of Organizational Structure." In N. Greenblatt, *op. cit.*

10. Hollister, C. *Bureaucratic Structure and School-Parent Communication in Eighteen Detroit Elementary Schools*. Doctoral Dissertation, University of Michigan, 1966.

11. Kramer, R. *Participation of the Poor*. Englewood Cliffs, N. J.: Prentice-Hall, 1969.

12. Lawrence, P., and Lorsch, J. *Organization and Environment*. Boston: Harvard University Graduate School of Business, 1967.

13. Levine, S., and White, P. "Exchange as a Conceptual Framework for the Study of Interorganizational Relationships." *Administrative Science Quarterly*, 1961, 5, 583–601.

14. Litwak, E. "Models of Bureaucracy That Permit Conflict." *American Journal of Sociology*, 1961, 57, 173–83.

15. Litwak, E., and Hylton, L. "Interorganizational Analysis: A Hypothesis on Coordination." *Administrative Science Quarterly*, 1962, 58, 395–420.

16. Litwak, E., and Meyer, H. "Administrative Styles and Community Linkages in Public Schools." In A. Reiss, ed., *Schools in a Changing Society*. Glencoe, Ill.: Free Press, 1965.

17. ———. "A Balance Theory of Coordination between Bureaucratic Organizations and Community Primary Groups." *Administrative Science Quarterly*, 1966, 11, 31–58.

18. Litwak, E., and Rothman, J. *Towards the Theory and Practice of Coordination between Formal Organizations*. Ann Arbor, Mich.: Mimeographed, 1969.

19. Litwak, E.; Shiroi, E.; Zimmerman, L.; and Bernstein, J. *The Theoretical Basis for Community Participation in Bureaucratic Organizations*. Ann Arbor, Mich.: Mimeographed, 1970.

20. Marris, P., and Rein, M. *Dilemmas of Social Reform*. New York: Atherton, 1969.

21. McCleery, R. "Policy Change in Prison Management." In A. Etzioni, ed., *Complex Organizations*. New York: Holt, Rinehart and Winston, 1964.

22. Miller, S., and Riessman, F. *Social Class and Social Policy*. New York: Basic Books, 1968.

23. Miller, W. "Delinquency Prevention and Organizational Relations." In S. Wheeler, ed., *Controlling Delinquents*. New York: Wiley, 1968.

24. Mott, J. *Anatomy of a Coordinating Council*. Pittsburgh: University of Pittsburgh Press, 1968.

25. Perrow, C. "A Framework for the Comparative Analysis of Organizations." *American Sociological Review*, 1967, 32, 194–208.

26. Roethlisberger, F., and Dickson, W. *Management and the Worker*. Cambridge, Mass.: Harvard University Press, 1939.

27. Rosengren, W., and Lifton, M. "Organization and Clients: Lateral and Longitudinal Dimensions." *American Sociological Review*, 1966, 31, 802–10.

28. Shils, E., and Janowitz, M. "Cohesion and Disintegration in the Wehrmacht in World War II." In D. Katz, et al., *Public Opinion and Propaganda*. New York: Dryden, 1954.

29. Street, D.; Vinter, R.; and Perrow, C. *Organization for Treatment*. New York: Free Press, 1966.

30. Terryberry, S. "The Evolution of Organizational Environments." *Administrative Science Quarterly*, 1968, 12, 590–613.

31. Thompson, J. *Organizations in Action*. New York: McGraw-Hill, 1967.

32. Warren, D. "Modes of Conformity and the Character of Formal and Informal Organization Structure: A Comparative Study of Public Schools." Doctoral Dissertation, University of Michigan, 1964.

33. Warren, R. "The Interaction of Community Decision Organization: Some Basic Concepts and Needed Research." *Social Service Review,* 1967, 41, 261–70.

34. Weber, M. *The Theory of Social and Economic Organization.* Tr. & rep. Glencoe, Ill.: Free Press, 1947.

35. Whyte, W. "Human Relations—A Progress Report." In A. Etzioni, ed., *Complex Organizations.* New York: Holt, Rinehart and Winston, 1964.

36. Zald, M. "Organizational Control Structures in Five Correctional Institutions." In M. Zald, ed., *Social Welfare Institutions.* New York: Wiley, 1965.

15.

Yeheskel Hasenfeld and John E. Tropman

INTERORGANIZATIONAL RELATIONS: IMPLICATIONS FOR COMMUNITY ORGANIZERS AND COMMUNITY ORGANIZATION

INTRODUCTION

The theme of interorganizational relations which focuses on patterns of interaction among purposefully designed social units is central to community study and practice. Social scientists interested in understanding and explaining the structure and processes of the contemporary urban community tend to visualize it as a network of formal organizations and other social units dependent on each other for their self-maintenance and survival. Hence, they are likely to address themselves to such issues as the number, type and size of organizations in a given community; patterns of interdependence; exchange and reciprocity among them; conditions that elicit competition, conflict or cooperation; and processes that promote integration vs. fragmentation in the community.

Social practitioners—community organizers, policy developers, social agency managers, community extension agents, and the like—have at least two reasons for their interest in interorganizational problems and issues. First, the social problems with which such practitioners deal are often interorganizational in nature and are seen by society as such. Juvenile delinquency as caused by poor relationships between school and court would be one example. Community deterioration as caused by a lack of "cohesion" among neighborhood organizations, and clients who fall through uncoordinated "cracks" in the service system would be two others.

The second reason interorganizational issues are of interest to social practitioners is that interorganizational change strategies may be used as a practice technique in trying to develop better relationships between home and school, better neighborhood cohesion, or mechanisms that will prevent clients from becoming lost in the service network. To the extent, then, that practitioners are able to diagnose problems as

Source: From Yeheskel Hasenfeld and John E. Tropman, "Interorganizational Relations: Implications for Community Organizers and Community Organization." Unpublished. Reprinted by permission of the authors.

interorganizational and develop and implement interorganizational strategies will they be more effective.

For both social scientists and practitioners, interorganizational relations hold primary importance in understanding and effecting change at any part of the triple community, namely the territorial, subcultural, and organizational (Tropman et al. 1977). At the level of the territorial community, the major foci are: (1) the effective utilization of geographically bounded resources such as water, energy, raw material, people, and land; and (2) the management of the distribution of people and organizations in a geographic area, and the integration and coordination of resource exploitation by them. These include concerns with such issues as transportation, land use, municipal government, housing, and the like.

The concerns and issues generated by the territorial community give rise to numerous organizational forms such as industrial organizations, municipalities, transportation authorities, and public utilities. The relations among them and to other levels of the community have immense consequences for the quality of life in the territorial community.

At the level of the cultural community, the critical concern is in the development, maintenance, and enhancement of collective identities, be it through ethnic, religious, or ideological affiliations. The mechanisms developed in the community to facilitate these objectives include educational institutions, religious organizations, voluntary associations, and a multitude of organizations promoting various cultural activities. For both social scientist and practitioner there are several important issues in reference to the cultural community: First, what processes promote or hamper harmony in the community?; Second, what conditions enable or constrain

various social groups in the community to develop culturally enhancing organizations?; Third, how do the other levels of the community affect social processes in the cultural community? It is quite apparent that an interorganizational perspective is essential in any systematic attempt to address these issues.

Finally, at the level of the organizational community, one is primarily concerned with the distribution of power among the organizations that share a common pool of resources, be they industrial organizations or human service organizations. Put differently, the polity of any given community can be conceptualized as patterned relations among organizations with differential access and control over power which in turn determine how power is mobilized and used. This is a "political-economy" perspective on the community which concentrates on the problem of governance and the regulation of various political and economic interests among social units sharing and competing for the same resources. Many of the activities of political, legislative, and regulatory units, such as city government, board of education, welfare council, reflect the characteristics of the organizational community. Hence, interorganizational relations are the main vehicle by which the various organizations attempt to influence and control each other. These must be of particular interest to the community worker who has to effect changes in the polity in order to achieve many of the community objectives he is mandated to pursue.

In this essay, we focus upon four major areas of concern to the community organization practitioner: (1) providing a conceptual framework that the practitioner can use in thinking about interorganizational problems; (2) showing how interorganizational factors, especially power, resources, and organizational status, are important determinants of community organization practice; (3) offering a theory that suggests that interorganizational structure is heavily dependent upon the extent of articulation the organization has with its environment, and notes that the role of the community organization practitioner is often aimed at improving that articulation; and finally (4) mentioning some "proper" and "maladaptive" organizational/environment interactions, illustrating with some archetypical models of each organizational response.

CONCEPTUAL FRAMEWORK FOR INTERORGANIZATIONAL RELATIONS

The perspective that this social practitioner adopts in reference to the interorganizational field is largely a function of his target of change and intervention objectives. In each instance his choice of orientation must be grounded in an empirically validated social science theory of the field. We will show that each class of action the community practitioner might undertake can be anchored in an appropriate social science model of interorganizational relations.

One class of action the practitioner may be asked to undertake is to develop a new program or strengthen an existing organization, both necessitating manipulation of the organizational environment. Such activities should be guided by the accumulating knowledge on organization-environment relations.

A second class of actions involves mediation among various organizations, changing the patterns by which they may relate to each other. Efforts to enhance cooperation among social agencies, form coalitions, and enhance coordination are examples of such actions. Here the social science perspective is based on the study of interorganizational relations between two or more agencies.

Finally, the practitioner may be asked to affect the way social services are organized or distributed in a given community for a particular social need or population. The referent point for such activities is a network of organizations as an action system. Examples of such networks may be all the youth-serving agencies in a given community, the mental health network, and the social service organizations serving low-income clients in the inner city.

Organization-Environment Relations

Viewing the organization as an open system, the maintenance of its viability and effectiveness necessitates consideration of the following issues: (1) mobilizing resources from the environment; (2) establishing a viable niche in the environment, and (3) adapting to changing environmental exigencies.

The environment itself, following Hall (1977), is conceptualized as composed of the "general environment" and the "specific environment." The former denotes environmental conditions that affect all organizations such as technological, economic, legal, demographic, and cultural.

The "specific environment" refers to the set of organizations and social units that control critical resources needed by the organization and thus are in interaction with it.

In many respects, the character of the organization is shaped by the nature of the environment in which it is located. The environment may be characterized by: (1) degree of stability, (2) heterogeneity of its units, (3) richness of resources, (4) concentration or dispersion of resources, and (5) degree of turbulence (Aldrich, 1976). An environment heterogeneous and rich in resources which are dispersed among social units provides for a greater potential for the emergence of new organizations and attainment of organizational autonomy. In contrast, an environment lean in resources which are concentrated in a few organizations forces a high degree of organizational dependency and discourages innovation. Thus, in general, the success of the organization depends on its ability to produce outputs that are desirable in its environment, ensuring as a result a steady flow of resources to the organization. Specifically, the organization must make strategic choices as to the particular segments of the environment it chooses to interact with that will optimize its control over resources (Child, 1972). For the social service agency, this implies critical decisions concerning the population to be served, needs to be addressed, and services to provide. Decisions along these dimensions simultaneously involve interaction commitments with other organizations such as funding sources.

A critical factor in maintaining organizational viability is the ability of the organization to engage in boundary-spanning activities aimed at reducing environmental uncertainty. The greater the boundary-spanning capabilities of the organization, the greater its ability to adapt to changing environmental conditions. As Lawrence and Lorsch (1967) suggest, the effective organization develops an internal division of labor reflecting the various environmental exigencies it must respond to. For example, units in the organization that face an unstable environment, with unpredictable frequency of feedback, are likely to be characterized by a highly flexible structure and horizontal rather than hierarchical relations.

Interorganizational Relations

The organizational strategic choices of environmental elements with which to interact in order to mobilize needed resources generate a network of relations between the organization and critical elements in the environment. The resource dependencies among organizations are therefore the primary force that leads organizations into exchange relations among them (Jacobs, 1974) whereby each organization attempts to obtain resources controlled by the others. Each relationship can be characterized by a power-dependence dimension which measures the amount of influence each organization exercises over the other in the relationship. Following Thompson (1967), an organization is dependent on a given element in the environment (1) in direct proportion to its need for the resource controlled by the element, and (2) in inverse proportion to the availability of the resource elsewhere. Clearly, the greater the dependence of the organization on any given element in the environment, the greater the power of the element, and the greater its potential control over critical activities of the organization. To quote Benson (1975: 234), "Power permits one organization to reach across agency boundaries and determine policies or practices in a weaker organization. Failure or refusal of the weaker organization to accede to the demands of the stronger can have serious repercussions for the resource procurement of the weaker organization."

It is for these reasons that nonprofit organizations are more likely to become captives of their donors than organizations that sell their products on the market. This further suggests that when the critical resources needed by the organization are concentrated in the hands of few external units, the organization will have hardly any autonomy in defining its mission, as the case may be for public correctional institutions, the department of welfare and the like. Of course, to the extent to which these organizations provide a critical service not available elsewhere, they are able to countervail some of that dependency. Thus, the amount of control over resources by each organization is the major determinant of the power differential among organizations.

From this perspective, the dynamic that shapes interorganizational relations is the aim of each organization to maintain or enhance its autonomy and thus stabilize the inflow of resources. There are several strategies that organizations may employ to change the balance of power in the interorganizational field (Benson, 1975; Thompson, 1967): (1) Cooperative strategies in which change is sought through bargain, coalition, or cooptation. In each instance, each organization makes a commitment of future resources to the other cooperating organizations. Such strategies are likely to be used when each organization has some critical resources needed by the others. (2) Disruptive strategies in which change is sought through threats on the availability of resources to the target organization. These may involve efforts to divert funds away from the organization; to undermine its social legitimation; or to develop competing services. Benson (1975) suggests that these strategies are likely to be used when there is a substantial power imbalance and low level of integration among the organizations. (3) Manipulative strategies that attempt to alter the conditions affecting the flow of resources. These may include changing the regulations by which agencies may receive funds, modifying the formula by which funds are distributed, and the like. (4) Authoritative strategies that change relations among organizations via authoritative directives by a very powerful organization such as federal and state government. These directives may force an agency to give up part of its autonomy, share resources with other agencies, or submit to some form of collective planning.

The use of these and other strategies generates the "rules of the game" by which resources are allocated among organizations. Moreover, they establish a "domain consensus," which defines for each organization the set of actions that it can pursue without threatening other organizations (Levine and White, 1961).

Network of Organizations

From a macrosocial perspective, the community—be it territorial, subcultural, or organizational—can be conceptualized as a network of interacting organizations that are partially interdependent on each other. To use the description offered by Turk (1977:3),

Any city, society, or other macrosocial unit . . . consists of constellations of organizations. It is logically possible for such constellations to range from loose aggregates of autonomous associations that in no way respond to one another, through interorganizational systems of economic or ecological conflict, competition, or cooperation to actual sociocultural *unions* of organizations, which may themselves range from loose federations and solidarities to legally sanctioned and politically coordinated networks.

In the human services, examples of networks of organizations may range from the constellation of health service providers to the association of mental health agencies and the United Fund. The object of analysis, hence, is the network itself, its structural characteristics, patterns of internal organization, and its outputs as a macrosocial unit. The importance of the network structure in shaping and distributing human services cannot be underestimated. Warren, Rose, and Bergunder (1974:20) argue that any network of human service organizations is likely to develop a "common institutionalized thought structure" which they define as "the framework of thought and social structure through which the behavior of these organizations takes place and within which it is interpreted."

Put differently, the network of human service organizations develops a normative consensus regarding how each organization is to define social problems and is to respond to them. This consensus may arise from an implicit understanding of how resources are to be allocated in the network. Deviation from the institutionalized thought structure is likely to draw sanctions from the other organizations, endangering the domain of the deviating organization.

It can be posited that the level of normative consensus in the network is a function of its internal organization. That is, when the organizations in the network have minimal interaction with each other, and mostly in the form of competition, limited consensus, if any, is likely to arise. In contrast, when the organizations in the network are legally or politically coordinated, normative consensus will be strong. The structure of the network is, in turn, a function of a complex set of variables. For example, Turk (1977) proposes that with increased organizational complexity and external linkages of the organizations, the network is likely to develop large and multiple regulating and coordinating mechanisms. Yet, the plurality of interests represented by the organizational complexity will resist centralization of decisions in the network. On the other hand, when the distribution of power among the organizations in the network results in a distinct organizational stratification and dominance, one is likely to expect greater centralization of decisions in the network (Aldrich, forthcoming). In the human services, the existence of organizational hierarchy in the network is likely to result from governmental policies and regulations, which, for example, may designate a specific agency as the chief coordinator of all mental health or youth services.

There are intriguing implications from the structure of organizational networks to social change. Turk (1977) demonstrates that the ability of the network to mobilize for joint action such as the initiation of antipoverty programs is in part a function of its organizational complexity, external linkages, the multiplicity of internal coordinating mechanisms, and the existence of consensual solidarity. Warren, Rose, and Bergunder (1974), on the other hand, argue that this consensual solidarity, while it may enable the network to act collectively, is the major barrier for social reform. In the same vein, Aldrich (forthcoming) hypothesizes that social change will occur only if it is compatible with the existing patterns of relations and dominance among the organizations in the network.

INTERORGANIZATIONAL FACTORS AS DETERMINANTS OF COMMUNITY PRACTICE

The various approaches to interorganizational relations discussed in the previous section suggest that there are at least three critical factors that influence the nature of these relations and, therefore, shape community practice as well: (1) organizational resources and power, (2) organizational status, (3) organizational/community relations.

Organizational Resources and Power

The position and activities of the organization in the interorganizational field are largely determined by the amount of resources and power it controls or is able to mobilize. The resources-rich organization is in a position to "shape" its environment and control it in such a manner that its dominant position is maintained and enhanced (Benson, 1975). It has the autonomy to decide with which other organizations to interact, what should be the basis for such interaction, and what should be the essential characteristics of the service delivery patterns of the network. For example, Alford (1975) in his study of the health care system points out that the exclusive control over medical resources by private physicians, voluntary hospitals, and medical insurance companies has created a medical care system that is least concerned with quality, distribution, accessibility, and reasonable cost to the consumer. Moreover, dominant organizations can more readily neutralize challenges for change through such tactics as preventing, blunting, and repelling the challenging organizations (Warren, Rose, and Bergunder, 1974).

It is abundantly clear that organizational resources are a critical determinant of community practice in the sense that the success or failure of community intervention strategies is often largely a function of the power of the organization in which the community practitioner is anchored. Here lies one of the inevitable paradoxes of community practice: changing patterns of community processes necessitate a challenge of dominant organizations in the community, and yet, the community practitioner must typically operate from an organizational base that is lean in resources and power.

Organizational Status

Closely related to the resources controlled by the organization is its relative status and prestige in the interorganizational field. Control over resources and power is a necessary but not sufficient condition for organizational status, since the latter is also determined by the amount of legitimation accorded to the organization in the community, and the congruency between organizational goals and dominant community values. Thus, for example, the police could control a great deal of power in the community but have low status and prestige. Having a high degree of status and

prestige enables the organization to have a strong and influential voice in the articulation of the social service network in the community. The prestige of the American Psychiatric Association and the National Association for Mental Health was a key factor in shaping the structure and substance of community mental health programs (Connery et al., 1969). Gockel (1966) points out in his monograph *Silk Stockings and Blue Collars* the differential recruitment base by sex, of persons into social work school. The women tend to come from middle class backgrounds, while the men tend to have working class origins. Meyer comments, "As a 'female profession' social work shares the generally lower prestige of women in the occupational world. . . ." (Meyer 1966:496). It is for this reason, perhaps, that much organizing that has gone on within the occupational world, in unions and the like, has maintained a distance from social work community organization.

Hence, the effectiveness of the community practitioner is significantly affected by the status of his organization. Such status is influenced in no small way by the social position of the clients served by the organization. An organization that is committed to serve the poor cannot prevent the adverse impact this effort will have on its own status in the community.[1] This generates a second paradox and dilemma for community practitioners. When community prac-

---

[1] In a sense, the proportion of women in the profession may be one way of providing some protection. Organizations generally secure prestige from the clients they have; prestige law firms have prestige clients, and the like. Women, however, are somewhat exempt from this rule of status-by-association; rather, they receive their status from the men with whom they are associated—usually their fathers or their husbands. (This statement is a descriptive one; it is not the opinion of the authors!) While this pattern may be changing, society might well have "assigned" women to work with the poor so that they would not be affected by the lower status of their clients.

titioners are committed to improve the social and economic position of socially disfranchised constituencies who have very low status in the community, the prestige of their own organization is likely to be adversely affected. As a result, the effectiveness of the community practitioner in influencing community decisions on behalf of the disfranchised is reduced, and considerable efforts must be made to mobilize for the cause other prestigious organizations and individuals.[2]

Organization-Environment Articulation

Most studies of interorganizational relations point to the central proposition that the survival and effectiveness of the organization is predicated on its ability to articulate with its environment and occupy a vital niche in it. Finding such a niche implies that the organization can *seize* upon opportunities that arise in the environment, adapt itself to changing environmental conditions, and develop mechanisms to effectively interact with critical elements in that environment. A great deal of organizational failure can be attributed to lack of such articulation (Aldrich and Pfeffer, 1976). In contrast, organizations that articulate effectively with the environment are more efficient and effective (Lawrence and Lorsch, 1967) and can improve their position in the organizational network.

The effectiveness of a community practice organization is equally determined by its ability to articulate with its environment. A community practitioner whose organizational base lacks adequate linkages and boundary-spanning mechanisms with

the environment is likely to experience serious barriers in carrying out his role. He may find, as a result, that he lacks critical information about the environment, that there are no units in his organization that can process the information that is received from the environment, or that there is no sufficient expertise in the organization to deal with various components of the environment. In fact, it can be proposed that an important function of the community practitioner is to assist his organization in developing such articulation. It is to explore this point that we devote the remainder of this paper.

THE INTERORGANIZATIONAL THEORY OF DIFFERENTIATION

As suggested earlier, the environment can be conceived both as a pool of resources and as a flow of information. The distribution of resources in the environment and the conditions of their mobilization and exploitation must be closely considered by the organization as it determines its own internal structure and activities. Simultaneously, the ability of the organization to do so is also a function of its capacity to process information from the environment as input for strategic choices. That is, to be effective the organization must first of all be able to "read" the environment correctly by obtaining information about potential resources, clients, competing and complementary services, sources of threat to it, and the like. It must develop internal mechanisms to process such information by the establishment of various units and roles that collect, process, and interpret such information. When an organization cannot secure relevant environmental information, or that information is insufficiently discriminate, or it cannot process what it gets, that organization is likely to fail, whether it is a

---

[2]Some community organizations are involved in seeking to mobilize the elite on behalf of the nonelite. Often, they are accused of too much fraternization, and, as Cloward and Epstein (1965) point out, some social work agencies actually leave the poorer clientele behind.

profit-making or a non-profit-making operation, a public utility, or a human service agency.

Secondly, once such information is received, the organization must develop its internal work structure and select activities that optimize the flow of resources into the organization. It is through these processes that the organization can achieve a better articulation with its environment.

This line of thinking implies that the environment will have significant impact on the internal structure and activities of the organization, and that there is probably some optimal correspondence between the characteristics of the environment and the division of labor in the organization. This process by which the interaction between the environment and the organization creates a pressure upon the organization to adjust its internal structure to more effectively link to that environment we call the interorganizational theory of differentiation.

Environments, of course, are certainly not all of a piece, and identifying them, and their salient characteristics, is a task in and of itself. For our purposes here, we identify complexity, heterogeneity, and instability as crucial to the organizations, and especially to community organization agencies and community organization practitioners. As the complexity, heterogeneity, and instability of the environment increase, the difficulties experienced by the organization in processing information become greater. The organization therefore must develop a highly differentiated yet flexible internal system to effectively process information from such an environment. There must be multiple boundary-spanning roles sensing the various elements of the complex environment; there must be multiple levels of communication within the organization so that diverse sources of information can be processed and evaluated effectively; and there must be a flexible and decentralized structure that can rapidly respond to changing flows of information in the environment. Thus, for example, a community planning agency that faces an environment that is composed of many highly diverse social agencies, multiple sources of funding, and large and changing populations cannot hope to begin to engage in effective planning unless it develops many boundary-spanning roles that can process information for all of these external units; acquires internal flexibility so that it can rapidly respond to changing needs in the community; and provides mechanisms for the various staff to share information and assess the meaning of multiple information inputs. Dluhy (1975), for example, found that planning units in small city governments were usually overwhelmed and, finally, lost when confronted with the wishes of developers and their highly sophisticated planning departments. In other words, the organization has to develop information-processing mechanisms that correspond to the flow of information in the environment.

In addition, the organization must also respond to the structure and distribution of resources in the environment. It must develop internal units whose function is to respond to the contingencies and constraints prescribed by these resources, and select activities that can optimize the mobilization of resources. Thus, the environment that has a complex and heterogeneous distribution of resources will necessitate that the organization develop a highly differentiated internal structure in which various units specialize in relating to specific segments of the environment. In contrast, organizations that function in a simple, undifferentiated, and stable environment are likely to have a simple, undifferentiated internal structure, with limited specialization of functions.[3] Thus, for example, a social service agency that must respond to multiple client needs, relate to different funding sources, and enlist the cooperation of many other agencies is likely to develop internally units and roles that specialize in serving specific types of clients, designate certain executive and managerial positions to deal with each of the funding sources, and establish specialized liaison roles with each key complementary agency.

Moreover, as new opportunities arise in the environment, such as new sources of funds and new service needs, the effective organization is likely to respond by adding functions and activities. In fact, there is evidence to suggest that an organization that is internally complex and diverse and engaged in multiple activities is more likely to seize new opportunities in the environment (Friedman, 1973).

In sum, we expect that, as the environment becomes more complex, organizations will be pressed to become more internally differentiated. In addition, organizations will be uniquely differentiated, in part because the nature of their specific environments is different, and in part because their style and habit of internal differentiation creates a slightly different niche for them than for other "similar" organizations in different environments.

Optimal Styles of Organizational Action

The interorganizational theory of differentiation suggests that an undifferen-

tiated organization would be found in a simple, homogeneous and stable system, and a differentiated organization would be found in a complex, heterogeneous, uncertain system. However, optimal matches between organization and environment are not always found. In some cases, organizations are overdifferentiated with respect to their environment, while in other cases they are underdifferentiated with respect to their environment. These possibilities are displayed in Figure 15.1. In essence, two "proper" relationships are implied, proper in the sense that the organization and the environment have a structural fit. Two "off-diagonal" relationships are also proposed, one in which the organization is underdifferentiated with respect to the environment (cell B) and another (cell C) in which the organization is overdifferentiated with respect to the environment. Each of these positions calls forth a specific pattern of style of organizational action, and we shall turn to this point momentarily. First, though, we need to explain how it happens that there is a "poor fit" in some cases.

Overdifferentiation

Overdifferentiation occurs when there is a complex, specialized organization existing in a relatively simple environment. National organizations interacting with local environments, organizations with fast development spans and extramural resources fall into this category. Such resources can include cash, personnel, prestige, technology, and the like, which are possessed by the organization in an overabundance with respect to its environment.

Alternatively, the organization can be in possession of superior information about environmental exigencies and be able to capitalize on that information in terms of its own structure and resources faster than the rest of the interorganizational network.

---

[3]One should not confuse size with simplicity, defined here as lack of differentiation. A simple agency is one with few departments, divisions, or units. All the employees do pretty much the same thing. Such an organization can be quite sizeable. Conversely, a small organization can have many assignments, roles, divisions, and, in fact, be quite complex. While size might be an indicator for complexity, it is not, itself, the definition of complexity (Tropman, 1976).

FIGURE 15.1

Differentiation and Specialization of the Organization	Interorganizational Complexity, Heterogeneity, Uncertainty	
	Low	High
Low	A Optimal	B Organization is Underdifferentiated
High	C Organization is Overdifferentiated	D Optimal

Its intelligence system may bring it information faster and more accurately than those of other network members, and internally, it may be able to use that information more rapidly and more efficiently.

On the other hand, in juxtaposition to the organizational growth model, one can posit an environmental shrinkage model as well. If, for example the resources supplying the entire organizational network dry up, as when an oil well goes dry or a mine runs out of ore, then the organization may find itself in a situation of having more complex machinery because the environment has suddenly simplified itself—in the cases mentioned, one is the only store in a ghost town!

Time, too, needs to be taken into account. Environments and organizations may both mature, but they may do so at importantly different rates, rates that may depend more upon technological developments than anything else. In this case, the speed of an organization's growth, for example, might exceed that of its environment.

For at least these reasons, and perhaps others as well, the organization/environment fit may be less than perfect, resulting in organizational enhancement relative to the environment.

Organizational Underdifferentiation

The converse may also be true. An organization may be new, or grow at a slower rate than the environment, or have a paucity of resources. If organizations are in this situation, they are likely to be underdifferentiated with respect to the environment. The lack of differentiation may lead to, or result from, a faulty system of organizational intelligence, which fails to bring relevant information into the organization. Even if an organization is getting information, the range of complexity of information from complex environments requires a complex refining apparatus and an additional internal structure that processes and acts upon that information. The underdifferentiated organization may not have such an internal system. For example, a social service agency that relies traditionally on a single source of funding may find itself facing dramatic new developments in its field of service, including new multiple sources of funds. Lack of an elaborate internal structure may hamper its ability to capitalize on the new opportunities, and it may lose out to other more internally differentiated agencies.

OPTIMAL STYLES OF ORGANIZATION RELATIONSHIPS TO ENVIRONMENT

These different modes of organizational/environmental articulation suggest some optimal styles of organizational action, vis-à-vis their environment. They are indicated in Figure 15.2.

FIGURE 15.2

Differentiation and Specialization of the Organization	Interorganizational Complexity, Heterogeneity, Uncertainty	
	Low	High
Low	Limited Cooperation	Coalition
	+	
High	Domination Cooptation	Competition Coordination Bargaining

Limited Cooperation: Occurs when an undifferentiated organization exists in a relatively undifferentiated environment. Cooperation is used when it seems to benefit the organization using a narrow conception of benefit. The simplicity of the organizational structure means that cooperative arrangements can be established and severed quickly and with a minimum of fuss.

Coalition: Occurs when an organization is relatively undifferentiated with respect to a complex environment. Coalition can be considered a sort of "crafted complexity" in which a number of organizations, banding together, seek to approximate the structure of a more differentiated opponent. Usually in this situation organizations take on special differentiated roles during the coalition period and for purposes of the coalition; one becomes an "executive" section; another becomes an information section, and so on.

Domination, Cooptation: Occurs when an organization is very differentiated with respect to its environment. In this case, the organization dominates its environment, and brings it into its own purview.

Competition, Bargaining, Coordination: Occurs when organizations and environments are evenly differentiated. In such a case organizations are specialized, and so different from, rather than similar to, each other. For this reason, they will bargain for those shares of the domain in which they overlap; some competition may occur also. Although the very process of interorganizational differentiation and specialization should produce some coordination, additional coordination may also occur on an organization-initiated basis.

ARCHETYPICAL ORGANIZATIONS

All organizations that one could locate in one or another box would not be characterized by the optimal style, for a variety of reasons. Some do not have the staff, or the staff they have may not perceive the nature of the situation they confront. Others may have historical factors that make them embrace or avoid an organizational style regardless of its appropriateness for them. We would like to suggest some organizations that are characterized by the optimal style for their position.

Limited Cooperation

Perhaps organizations in small towns are more characteristic of this style. While the system is somewhat complex, it is certainly less so than the larger urban area (Vidich and Bensman, 1968). The spirit of cooperation historically associated with the small town church and school reflects the limited cooperation style to which we refer. Each organization has its job to do, but each has, as well, an interest in cooperating. Little will be lost through a cooperative posture.

Coalition

As the system becomes more complex, organizations need to either band together for mutual support or to create, collectively, what they do not have singly. Neighborhood organizations are a good example of this trend, as are councils of governments and civil rights coalitions (Baker and Jansiewicz, 1970).

Sometimes, coalitions, or the executive functions of coalitions, take on an organizational structure of their own. This process occurred with federated fund raising in the welfare field, and there is now an organization called the United Way (usually) in most cities.

Domination

Domination occurs when the organization becomes sufficiently specialized and differentiated to overcome the community. A company town is one example. The expertise of high-price land developers in contrast to the more limited expertise of town planners may be another. In college towns, universities often assume this role. While the domination can be intentional, it can also be inadvertent but is real in both cases.

There are other examples. Colonial regimes are a case of a resource-laden, technologically expert external power dominating whole peoples. And on a different level, many is the advisory council or committee that has been dominated and coopted by those whom it advises, because the full-time, highly focused expertise of the regular employees is not matched by the occasional outside expert, meeting in a loosely structured committee.

It was, perhaps, fear of this situation occurring with the Office of Economic Opportunity that led the planners of that enterprise to formulate the doctrine of "maximum feasible participation of the poor." It was thought that if the people affected by the local activities could be involved in the directorate of the organization, then cooptation would be prevented, or at least blunted.

Competition, Bargaining, Coordination

There is a sort of progression that suggests the range and level of possible relationships involved when a differentiated, specialized organization interacts with a complex environment. Our theoretical position suggests that these organizations will be relatively unique, each having worked out some special niche in the organization set.[4] But this specialization often means that each has a resource base, each has some clients, customers, each has some areas that serve to support it. To whatever extent possible, each will seek to enlarge that domain somewhat, and, perhaps most importantly, each has the resources for some competition.

Often though, competition will be seen as a costly and resource-consuming activity by the executive cadre, and other mechanisms for interrelationship will be developed. Sometimes bargaining is one such mechanism, in which the various organizations agree in negotiation to a "domain consensus" that removes the problem somewhat. Within the bargaining framework, competition is just a "moment" away and can return at any moment. Bargaining does, however, imply that the organizational units themselves are the key actors.

More complex still is the mechanism of coordination. Coordination occurs, from our perspective, when an external agent, such as a council, central bureau, interagency committee, or the like is set up to facilitate organizational interaction and activity. In a coordinated framework, more

---

[4]This uniqueness does not necessarily mean a unique service. Two organizations may provide the same service, but to different religious or racial groups; there may be enough volume of service for different geographic areas to be involved. Or, there may be unique strengths in relating to family or national communities. The important element is that the organization has some specialized role within the interorganizational setting.

than just the interests of the "bargainers" are present; the interests of the entire interorganizational network are involved and represented by the central group. The use of a coordinative mechanism implies that all organizations may not be willing to come into the interorganizational framework. For this reason, the central committee or "coordinating organization" has the job of encouraging, threatening, cajoling, and otherwise seeking to involve the member organizations.[5] One example of such a coordinating council is the organization that used to be called, in community organization, the Council of Social Agencies and is now often called the Welfare Council or Welfare Planning Council (Tropman, 1972). Founded originally as a manifestation of the coalition strategy in the early years of this century, it came to be an organization focused on coordinating for the private social agencies. To some extent, however, it has not been able to continue its own specialized role, and many are now merging with the United Way organizations (Tropman and Tropman, 1977). The human service situation became so complex that a single agency could not provide that coordination, and in many cases conditions of competition and bargaining are the essential mechanisms for interrelationship.

There are other organizations that could be located under each of the strategies. General Motors, for example, often tends to be influential in towns where it has major plants. This situation often leads to cooptation. The important element here is to analyze the internal structure of the organization with respect to the nature of its environment, and to assess the extent to which the organization is able to process the information coming in from the environment and make use of that information in developing its own structure.

CONCLUSION

The role of the community practitioner is one that is heavily concerned with interorganizational relationships. That practitioner and his or her efficacy are heavily dependent upon the position of the community organization agency in the interorganizational network within a given community. In addition, the task for the practitioner is often one of assisting, facilitating, enabling, or encouraging more productive relationships between some client organization or group and the environment of that group. The suggestions made in this paper are but a beginning effort in laying out some of the considerations involved, and they should be regarded as sensitizing and illustrative ideas, rather than complete formulations in any sense. Yet sensitivity to such interorganizational matters as we do mention here can improve practice, and as theory improves, we are sure that more information will be forthcoming.

BIBLIOGRAPHY

Aldrich, H. "Resource Dependence and Interorganizational Relations: Local Employment Service Offices and Social Services Sector Organizations." *Administration and Society* 7 (February 1976): 419–54.

———. "Organization Sets, Action Sets and Networks: Making the Most of Simplicity." In P. Nystrom and W. Starbuck, eds. *Handbook of Organization Design.* Amsterdam: Elsevier. Forthcoming.

---

[5]In a complex system, it is not likely that all organizations in a given interorganizational network are at the same level of differentiation and specialization, for the reasons mentioned previously. Therefore, simple, overspecialized, and underspecialized organizations, as well as ones appropriately specialized, are likely to be present. One of the reasons for the development of coordinating councils or coordinating organizations is to process and deal with this heterogeneity of differentiation. Some community organization techniques such as the "community study" have been developed in part to respond to this heterogeneity.

Aldrich, H. and Pfeffer, T. "Environments of Organizations." In A. Inkeles, ed. *Annual Review of Sociology,* vol. 2, pp. 79–106. Palo Alto, Calif.: Annual Review, 1975.

Alford, R. R. *Health Care Politics.* Chicago: University of Chicago Press, 1975.

Baker, L. and Jansiewicz, D. "Coalitions in the Civil Rights Movement." In S. Groennings, E. W. Kelley and M. Leiserson, eds. *The Study of Coalition Behavior.* New York: Holt, Rinehart and Winston, 1970.

Benson, T. K. "The Interorganizational Network as a Political Economy." *Administrative Science Quarterly,* 1975, 20: 229–49.

Child, T. "Organization Structure, Environment and Performance—The Role of Strategic Theories." *Sociology,* 1972, 6: 1–22.

Cloward, R. A. and Epstein, I. "Private Social Welfare's Disengagement from the Poor: The Case of Family Adjustment Agencies." In M. Zald, ed. *Social Welfare Institutions: A Sociological Reader.* Pp. 623–43. New York: Wiley, 1965.

Connery, R. H., et al. *The Politics of Mental Health.* New York: Columbia University Press, 1969.

Dluhy, M. J. "The Dynamics of Suburban Community Development in the Detroit Metropolitan Area." Ph.D. Dissertation, University of Michigan, 1975.

Friedman, T. "Structural Constraints on Community Action: The Case of Infant Mortality Rates." *Social Problems,* 1973, 21: 230–45.

Gockel, G. *Silk Stockings and Blue Collars.* Chicago: Natl. Op. Res. Center, 1966.

Hall, R. H. *Organizations: Structure and Process.* 2d ed. Englewood Cliffs, N.J.: Prentice-Hall, 1977.

Jacobs, D. "Dependency and Vulnerability: An Exchange Approach to the Control of Organizations." *Administrative Science Quarterly,* 1974, 19: 45–49.

Lawrence, P. R. and Lorsch, J. W. *Organization and Environment.* Cambridge, Mass.: Harvard University Press, 1967.

Levine, S. and White, P. E. "Exchange As A Conceptual Framework for the Study of Interorganizational Relations," *Administrative Science Quarterly,* 1961, 5: 583–610.

Meyer, H. "Social Work," in D. L. Sills, ed. *International Encyclopedia of the Social Sciences* New York: Free Press, Vol. 13 and 14, 1966.

Thompson, J. D. *Organizations in Action.* New York: McGraw-Hill, 1967.

Tropman, J. E. "A Comparative Analysis of Community Organization Agencies," in I. Spergel, ed. *Community Organization: Studies in Constraint.* Beverly Hills: Sage Publications, 1972.

———. "The Social Meaning of Social Indicators." *Social Indicators Research,* 3 (1976).

Tropman, J. E., Erlich, J. L. and Cox, F. M. "Introduction," in F. M. Cox, *et. al.,* eds. *Tactics and Techniques of Community Practice.* Itasca, Ill.: F. E. Peacock, Publishers, 1977.

Tropman, J. E. and Tropman, E. J. "Community Welfare Councils," in J. Turner ed. *Encyclopedia of Social Work.* New York: National Association of Social Workers, 1977.

Turk, M. *Organizations in Modern Life: Cities and Other Large Networks.* San Francisco: Jossey Bass, 1977.

Vidich, A. J. and Bensman, J. *Small Town and Mass Society; Class, Power and Religion in a Rural Community.* Rev. ed. Princeton, N.J.: Princeton University Press, 1968.

Warren, R., Rose, S. and Bergunder, A. *The Structure of Urban Reform.* Lexington, Mass.: D.C. Heath, 1974.

PART THREE:
STRATEGIES

Introduction

A fundamental problem for nations, for organizations, and for individuals is that of getting from where they are now to where they would like to go. The planned process by which nations and individuals (and everything in between) arrive at chosen objectives may be referred to as strategy. This sense of the word "strategy" is derived from game theory, which distinguishes games of individual skill, games of chance, and games of strategy—the last being those in which the most effective course of action for each player depends upon the actions of other players and the players' anticipation and assessment of those moves. As such, the term emphasizes the interdependence of allies' and adversaries' decisions and their various expectations about each others' behavior.

The centrality of strategy for the community practitioner is undeniable. Without it, ideology and commitment are reduced to empty rhetoric. Used by themselves, interventive actions tend to become merely forays against *ad hoc* "targets of opportunity" without any sense of how they may fit into some larger plan. The vigor with which problems of strategy are endlessly debated is but one example of their critical importance to community practice. Some have even gone so far as to suggest that strategists are born rather than made. In any case, a solid grounding in strategic thinking is a requisite for effective community practice. Only through a thoughtful and pragmatic consideration of alternatives can a reasonable evaluation of various plans of action and their respective strengths and weaknesses be made.

Just what is strategy? How may it be distinguished from tactics? When and how should one change strategies? What tools, what action "rules of thumb" are available to guide practitioner actions?

These are the questions faced by community practitioners every day. However, efforts to pose these issues sharply, or explicate them fully, are few and far between in the literature. Part Three is an attempt to do this. The articles cover a broad range of strategic approaches. Separate chapters are devoted to each of three main strategic orientations—planning, development, and action. A preliminary statement introduces this material, and a final section suggests ways in which strategic approaches may be mixed and phased.

The purpose of this introduction is to present a theoretical consideration of the problem of strategy as it relates to community practice. We discuss critical contextual problems in the selection of strategies and offer a scheme to help community change agents organize their own thinking about strategy choice, implementation, and mixing.

A Conceptualization of Strategy

Basically we regard strategy as an orchestrated attempt to influence a person or a system in relation to some goal which an actor desires. It is "orchestrated" in the sense that an effort is made to take into account the actions and the reactions of key allies and adversaries as they bear upon the achievement of the proposed goal. That goal may be something which relates directly to an individual actor (like a supplementary welfare check for winter clothing), or it may be much more general, such as a particular "state of the system" desired by the change agent. For example, exorcizing white racism from a big city educational bureaucracy may be a state-of-the-system goal. While most practitioners are well acquainted with thinking about strategy as influence, the notion of orchestration probably bears further attention. In a sense, it is intended to convey a dramatic "arrangement"—with different performers, each with various skills and roles, each of whom may enter and leave the scene according to some action plan. Solos articulate with the movement of the whole piece. The change agent's roles include prompter and producer-conductor. He lays out a "score" for the performance and attempts to integrate its diverse elements as the performance goes forward. In all likelihood the score itself will have to be changed—in response to shifting conditions—one or more times during any given performance.

But more is implied here than the interplay of many persons, or persons and institutions, at any given moment. There is a progression over time—as each phase of the action scheme is completed. Indeed, it suggests the notion of a "means-ends chain," where all of the simultaneous performances are at once ends in themselves, and means to a more general end. A familiar example to practitioners is the community clean-up campaign. The project is an end in itself, as well as a means to the more general goal of community cohesion and pride. Thus community strategy often involves a complex and dynamic pattern of performances within performances. However, in this general framework there are several critical issues which need to be explored in more detail.

Conflict Strategies and Consensus Strategies

The problem of strategy in the contemporary literature is often dichotomized into a choice between conflict and consensus approaches. This trend toward polarization has led some contemporary writers to offer the illusion of choice between "masculine" and "feminine" strategies, of "brave" and "cowardly" ones, or "radical" versus "establishment" modes. While, in the terminology of the Left, this polarization may facilitate the "radicalization" of uninitiated or oppressed minorities, it also creates a new level of confusion for the practitioner. Nevertheless, these dimensions are a real and common part of everyone's daily life. As Weber points out, "Conflict cannot be excluded from social life . . . 'peace' is nothing more than a change in the form of conflict or in the antagonists or in the objects of the conflict, or finally in the chances of selection."[1]

Yet consensus is, paradoxically, a part of conflict, as much as the converse is true. Without subsequent negotiation, agreement and some form of reconciliation, the fruits of conflict are likely to be very meager indeed. Even when total revolution or the transfer of substantial power is effected (or attempted), the "outs" who are now "in" must move to consolidate their gains through at least a modicum of consensus and reconciliation. At the same time, the current powerful thrust toward "conflict management" is also to be closely scrutinized. Any attempt to move everything by consensus and agreement, to keep everything "nice," may be used to mask significant problems and avoid the possibility of arriving at decisions on critical issues.

The inevitable coexistence of conflict and consensus has received strong support from the social science literature. Work relating to small groups is replete with comments on the task and maintenance functions which must be performed by their members. The literature which discusses task and process goals in community organization offers similar intelligence. Task goals refer to "hard" production-oriented functions in which decisions are made, individual interests neglected, feelings disregarded. Process goals involve the repair of ruptures caused by task activities and an attempt to create a higher level of group solidarity through which task business can proceed more effectively.

It has been previously pointed out that the use of conflict or consensus may be predominant in a given model of practice—such as social action in the former mode or consensus in community development. Seen more broadly, conflict and consensus are viewed as the Siamese twins of social process. If both these task and maintenance functions are not attended to, progress toward social goals may be sharply truncated, if not halted, as William Gamson points out in his article on "Rancorous Conflict in Community Politics."[2]

Ideological Commitment as Goal

Most practitioners are well aware that long-term agency goals are often so vague as to be unapproachable in the real world. This problem, along with the lack of specificity about short-term or intermediate goals, is sometimes solved through goal idealization. Practitioners become "true believers" in the sense in which Eric Hoffer has suggested.[3] Since progress toward the desired goal cannot be accu-

---

[1] Lewis Coser, *Functions of Social Conflict* (New York: The Free Press, 1956), p. 21.

[2] William Gamson, "Rancorous Conflict in Community Politics," *American Sociological Review,* Vol. 31, No. 1 (February, 1966), pp. 71–81.

[3] Eric Hoffer, *The True Believer* (New York: The New American Library, Inc., 1958).

rately assessed, the "purity" or motivation of the practitioner becomes the foremost consideration. While not more typical of community organizers than any other group of change agents, this solution tends to move the goal out of the realm of the "practical" or empirically concrete and to develop a series of personalistic assessments. From this perspective, "commitment" becomes a culmination for the believer; without it, progress becomes impossible.

Specification of Ends and Means: A Strategy of Problem Definition

The battle over the specification of ends and means, clearly propounded by the Greeks, has been vigorously waged ever since. We believe that Saul Alinsky has handled the matter admirably in his piece "Of Means and Ends" (Reading 27), and we make no attempt to deal with it further here. However, this debate has tended to obscure a perhaps more fundamental issue—that of defining the problem in such a way that means and ends may be fully articulated in designing a strategy aimed at solving or ameliorating it. Wherever possible, practitioners should attempt to select public, rather than private, means and ends. That is, the worker should choose as a means something which is concrete and subject to open verification, rather than something which is private and covert. The same can be said of ends. For example, a worker who sets as a goal the global aim of eliminating racism in a particular community is bound to be disappointed. This is not to say that the elimination of racism should not be one of his goals, but rather that it should not be *the* goal. On the other hand, if the goal is one of bringing integration to a suburban housing area, or providing new job or educational opportunities for blacks, then the results can be monitored more effectively. Without intermediate and feasible proximate goals, the worker's interventions cannot be evaluated to any significant degree and progress cannot be assessed.

The problem of means/ends specification is not limited to ends. Deciding which means and monitoring the means is also difficult. All too often it is solved by means of ritualism. Here we find, for example, the agency which relies heavily on a continuing series of meetings from which nothing ever seems to emerge. The operations of some welfare councils and race relations organizations provide excellent illustrations of this process.

The Means-Ends Spiral

Despite some tendencies in community organization toward goal idealization and ritualistic means, most practitioners recognize both the alternation of conflict and consensus approaches and the operation of means-ends chains as common practice experiences. Putting the two notions together, strategy can be redefined as an outward means-ends spiral, alternatively emphasizing task and process, conflict and consensus modes.

The concept of strategy as an orchestrated means-ends spiral has a number of important consequences for community organization. For one thing, it suggests that total reliance on a strategy of either consensus or conflict will in most circumstances be unsuccessful. It anticipates the skill of the organizer in moving with the community or group between task and process phases. And it offers the idea of progression toward intermediate objectives as a measure of strategic success. Now let us turn to an examination of the contexts in which strategic successes must be achieved.

Contextual Variables in Strategic Assessment

Strategy is not devised in a vacuum. The strategic thinker works in some specific community, with specific groups and probably for some organization. As he develops his plan, there are a number of factors which he needs to take into account.

Strategic thinking and development must begin with a consideration of the agency resources in people, money, and equipment which the agent has at his disposal. Often there are intra-agency fights over the allocation of these resources. And, whatever the level, we know that in community practice there are never sufficient amounts of any one of the resources to meet the demand. Since they are scarce, competition for them becomes intense. The more scarce the resources (and thus, the more intense the competition), the more a strategy of power-building self-help is indicated.

The resources of the broader system in which the organizer must act are another consideration. Such resources may be the availability of money, on the one hand, and that amorphous but all-important resource, public support and understanding on the other. Sometimes the agency and the system have resources differentially available to them. In some developing countries, community agents have access to expensive and sophisticated equipment which the indigenous population does not know how to use. Thus, even the presence of resources does the worker no good if they cannot be used. More frequent, and characteristic of many urban change programs in America, is the target system that has more resources than the change agency. Hence, from a strategic point of view, the system (or particular elements within that system) can "hold out" much longer than any agency-backed client organization and win most struggles. In general, when the target has more resources than those available to the change agent or agency, a social action strategy is indicated.

The amount of resistance to change objectives is a third factor of critical importance. Generally, we assume some resistance to change proposals as a matter of course. Sometimes, however, the complexity of the problem itself gives the appearance of resistance. We must be careful to distinguish between a situation where a social problem is complex, but there is no substantial resistance (for example, many public health problems fall into this category) and one where many solutions are known but there is strong resistance (for example, income maintenance). Then, too, areas where important gains can be made, and where the system is neutral to mildly opposed (for example, tutorial programs), should be considered.

In modern urban America, class variables are a very strong predictor of behavior and institutional preferences, from sex habits to styles of child rearing, from religion to responses to pain.⁴ It is thus with some concern that we note the absence of literature which substantially attempts to exploit these differences in the conceptualization of strategic alternatives.

Generally speaking, the change agent can represent a constituency which is of higher, equal, or lower social class than the change target. For the community practitioner this situation offers certain strategic "hints." They devolve upon the fact that change strategies are "handicapped" by their class of origin—particularly as viewed by the recipient of the change proposal. For example, a change proposal coming from a high-status change agency (or agent) to a low-status community has a good likelihood of "success," particularly if the agency is willing to utilize its prestige in achieving the desired goal over the objections of community residents. On the other hand, a change proposal coming from a lower-class constituency directed toward a middle-class formal organization is likely to be stalled, sidetracked, and indefinitely tabled or ultimately defeated. It is all too easy for the class "handicap" (either positive or negative) to obfuscate the merits of any given change proposal. Many of the demands for "power" of various sorts —as enunciated by the poor, racial and ethnic minorities, and women—can be understood as a demand for a new set of handicapping arrangements in the system. Welfare mothers, for example, suffer from the stigma of poverty and recipient status. Welfare rights organizations attempt to redress this balance and place recipient mothers on a more equal basis for negotiation with middle-class welfare bureaucrats. Problems of lower-class constituencies may be handled by developing social action strategies to build a new handicapping system (that is, causing shifts in power and/or resource allocations), followed by appropriate strategies of development and planning.

Finally, variability in problem complexity is a relevant issue and poses questions of problem "tractability." Community problems are comprised of many unique and interrelated elements. Sometimes even the simplest technical problems—garbage collections, for example—are confounded by political complexities of great magnitude. On the other hand, problems which have substantial support across a wide range of publics—job-training projects—may falter on technical insufficiencies. Other complexities—from agency staff changes to national upheavals—also may enter the picture. Fundamentally, the change agent, taking the problem in all its ramifications, must be able to assess the degree of complexity involved, and how amenable to solution it may be. Different degrees of complexity require different kinds, timing, and sequencing of strategies.

Four substantive problems—resources, resistance, class, complexity—in the development of a successful community intervention strategy have been discussed.⁵ There is no implication that these four are the only important factors; nevertheless they seem significant in that they cut across any functional area of

---

⁴Reinhard Bendix and Seymour M. Lipset (eds.), *Class, Status and Power* (New York: The Free Press, 1966).

⁵For a useful consideration of some others, see Neil Gilbert and Harry Specht (eds.), *Planning for Social Welfare* (Englewood Cliffs, N.J.: Prentice-Hall, 1977).

community action and are common to most social change situations. How can they be dealt with conceptually in an interrelated way? One source of help is social science.

Strategy and Means of Influence

Often we become confounded by the variety of styles of influence (as well as current vogues) and fail to recognize that there are fundamentally three, and only three, core modes of influence. To get another person, group or organization to do what is desired, force, inducement, and agreement may be used.[6] These three modes occur not only on the individual level as strategies of influence, but they are main change initiators at the societal level as well. Let us consider each in some detail.

Force, or coercive power, has been a vital concept in the analysis of human events. The possession of force, or control over the means of force, gives the change agent an important weapon. Often it is not necessary to actually use available force, but simply to make a *credible threat.* At other times, the actual application of force is necessary (for example, to establish credibility through a "show of strength"). Modes of force may range from physical violence and war on one end of a continuum, to sit-ins, confrontations, and personal harassment at the other end. Drawing on our previous distinction, force constitutes a conflict strategy, and its use typically creates resentment. The use of force also suggests the existence of resistance. Indeed, there are strong moral sanctions against using force when resistance is absent, as in the case of "shooting an unarmed man" or attacking a "defenseless" nation.

In all well-integrated social systems, the subsystem which has primary responsibility for control over the use of force is the polity, or governmental structure. Agents of force, such as the police, the army, etc., are under this kind of political control. Access to certain positions in the polity are sought because of the relationship they have to the potential mobilization of force, even though the notion of force may be obscured or veiled. The second means by which social goals may be achieved is inducement. Often, goals can be purchased or traded. Force need not be used, although value consensus may not be present. For example, people who argue that integrated housing is a "good investment" are using an inducement strategy. On a more fundamental level, the entire economic system is an inducement system. People contribute to the system and receive differential payments in return. This pay can be traded for many other goods in the system. The purchase of goods is, in turn, an inducement to the manufacturer to create new and more profitable goods.

In using coercive power, one has to control the means of force. To use an inducement strategy, one needs to manipulate the goods by which people may be induced. Money is one such "good." Interestingly, power is another. (This sug-

---

[6]These dimensions are similar to the modes of compliance used by Etzioni. See Amitai Etzioni, *A Comparative Analysis of Complex Organizations* (New York: The Free Press, 1961).

gests an interaction between the three main modes which we shall discuss momentarily.) Status positions, prestigeful associations, jobs, symbols of recognition, access to personnel and equipment are also among the most desired goods. In earlier times, salvation and indulgences were coin of the realm. Increasingly, control over information is coming to be an important and negotiable commodity. As society comes to be more and more complex, more and more specialized, more and more technological, detailed information is required to solve even apparently simple problems. Hence, it becomes a desired good, and a most significant one.

Perhaps the most subtle and sophisticated method for achieving social goals is through value consensus or agreement. A consensus mode proceeds through the development of an agreement between the actors that a course of action should be followed. Typically, the consensus is based upon fundamental agreements on underlying values in the social system. Then the parties attempt to demonstrate that the position they wish to take is closely attuned with that value or operates according to it. One simple example deals with the vote. In the United States, it is common and widely accepted practice to settle matters in dispute with a vote of those present. This procedure requires a plurality achieved through the rule of one-man-one-vote. However, the strong biases inherent in this procedure are often ignored. The intensity of preference on an issue, the fact that some people may feel very strongly while others take the matter rather lightly, is simply neglected in this procedure. Similarly, with each member having a single vote, differences in knowledge, experience and analytical ability are not accorded any special weight. The presumption is made that somehow the most desirable alternatives possible will receive a full hearing.

Value consensus usually emerges through some kind of socialization process. In the most obvious case, of course, it is the socialization of infants and children to the norms and mores of the dominant culture or their own ethnic group. Less explicit, but socialization nonetheless, is a host of processes which go on in adult life—the peer group of friends, the informal "clique" at the work place or factory. Then too, many of us have a broader and more undefined group which we use as a reference point to assess our own attitudes and progress (political parties, a profession, the church, etc.).

Means of Influence and Modes of Intervention

These three types of influence have some very interesting additional properties. For one thing, each may be a goal as well as a means to the others. Thus, inducements can be used to secure power and the control over force. Force can be used to secure agreement, although in perhaps a more limited fashion. Inducements, when applied over time, tend to produce value agreement. This is the time-honored process of "cooptation."

Second, each is the basis for an important part of the stratification system in society. Certainly people possess different amounts of power and can be located somewhere on a power continuum ranging from most to least. People also have differential control over various inducements, such as money and information. A rank ordering can be done of those "commanding" salient inducements. Finally, people are closer to, or further from, valued positions in society. This is often referred to as "status." For this reason, each of these means of influence is an important "good" in the system. One might conceptualize the task of the community worker in terms of equalizing the distribution of these "goods," or improving the position of his constituency on one or more ranking scales. Often he will attempt to capitalize on the properties of one system to produce increments in another.

Third, none of these influence means can exist without the others. Not only do they interpenetrate on a goals-means basis, but they also are mutually supportive. Hence, the use of force generally exists within some context of agreement about the conditions under which force may be used and the amount of force necessary to produce certain results, etc. On the other hand, the use of force often produces a new situation with which the existing web of value agreements must cope. Both are supported by a framework of inducements. Without inducements, the potential user of force cannot often muster the necessary elements of force.

Finally, force, inducements, and value agreement are the means by which society at large insures order and stability in the social system, and the means by which the society is changed. Force, for example, can be a means by which order is maintained, or disrupted. Inducements are used to develop commitments to the system, or to lure people to other competing systems. Values are at once sources of common bonds and of great divisiveness in the society.

It might be useful at this time to relate these three means of influence to the earlier discussion of three models or modes of community intervention (Reading 1). On the intervention level, social action is most closely related to the force variable. Police, courts, and the military are typical examples of force used to maintain the system. As a change variable civil disobedience and other forms of disruptive militance are typical. Social action usually attempts to build up the pressure of cumulative force through massing large numbers of people in united and often dramatic activity.

Planning as an intervention technique articulates best with the inducement means of influence. Planning involves a complex of processes (which may include, as elements, development and action). Fundamentally, the planner attempts to induce the system to adopt a proposed plan through a variety of techniques. Typically, the situation is one of high complexity, and the planner brings to bear significant expertise on the location and extent of the problem, past attempts to deal with it, and the most desirable alternatives in view of current circumstances.

The value means of influence best articulates with the locality development mode of intervention. In both cases, the achievement of value agreement and common orientations is a central focus of either change or system maintenance objectives.

The development of these two sets of terms—one set pertaining to means of influence and the other to modes of intervention—permits us to develop a framework for considering the types of styles of strategies available to the change agent. This framework is displayed in Figure 1.

Figure 1 suggests that there are at least nine basic strategic themes that may be employed. While, as we pointed out, each mode of intervention is characterized by a particular means of influence (as indicated by its location on the diagonal in Figure 1), in actuality other means of influence are also typically utilized. Thus, while militance often is expressed in social action interactional schemes, inducement through negotiation takes place, as well as value consensus through moral exhortation.

In addition each mode of intervention offers special leverage on a key contextual variable or general problem situation. Thus social action is concerned especially with unequal distribution of goods and resources in the society as reflected in class stratification; planning deals with matters of high complexity; and locality development is particularly useful with a situation of limited communal resources.[7]

Strategy Confrontation: The Mixing and Phasing of Strategies

It is often the case, as we have suggested in the means-ends spiral notion, that the practitioner must move from one strategy to another as shifts occur in the conditions affecting his overall objectives. Figure 1 suggests a possible scheme for mixing and phasing the strategies under two fundamental problem conditions.

The first set of problematic situations requires moving horizontally across the chart. It assumes that society or some target system is using one of the means of influence to maintain a problem condition. If the change agency, for example, is dealing with a problem defined by the system as one of force and power, one begins with a militant action strategy (1A) to build power and influence, and then moves to a planning strategy to consolidate the acquired influence and build a power block (2B), and finally to a development strategy for building value consensus and establishing channels for negotiating the allocation of scarce resources (3C). In contrast, where inducement is the main mode of maintaining the status quo, one begins with a planning strategy, bringing expertise to bear on a detailed analysis of the problem (1E). Then, one can move to an illustration of the plan through small projects (2F), and subsequently to a position of hard bargaining and negotiation (3D). In the case where values form the main vehicle of conservative influence, value "liberation" needs to take place (often in small groups) (1I), followed by a more action-oriented strategy of moral confrontations and radicalization (2G), and then to a planning framework in which a number of interests are represented as negotiations take place (3H).

The second problem orientation begins not with the mode through which society maintains the status quo, but rather with the mode of intervention to which some change agent or agency is committed. This orientation helps to illustrate the type of strategic configuration which remains within one interven-

---

[7]Furthermore, as suggested in Chapter IV, each intervention mode is often associated with particular patterns of linkage. Thus social action typically involves local primary groups banding together to make demands upon (or link up with) formal organizations. Planning often includes a number of cross-linkages among formal organizations, as well as formal organizations tying in with neighborhood groups to improve, for example, service delivery. Finally, locality development usually requires the establishment of good working relationships among primary groups and, at a later stage, cooperative arrangements with appropriate formal organizations.

MODES OF INTERVENTION

Basic Means of Influence	Action	Planning	Development
Force (Power)	*Militance* (1A) Disruption, sit-in, "liberation" of institutions, para-military activities	*Power Elite* (2B) Involve influential elites	*Reconciliation* (3C) (Client system with power groups)
Inducement	*Negotiation* (3D) Bargain, confrontation with "facts"	*Expertise* (1E)	*Pilot Projects* (2F) (Illustrative of potential gains build to larger tasks)
Value Consensus	*Moral Exhortation* (2G) Expose, "Radical thought"	*Representation* (3H) "Federation" of interests	*Group Development* (1I)

CRITICAL CONTEXTUAL PROBLEMS

	Low social class High resistance	High complexity	Low resources

FIGURE 1
A Matrix of Intervention Strategies,
Means of Influence and Contextual Variables

tion mode. If an agency is committed to a social action mode, its scenario begins with militance (1A). After a militant demonstration, one moves to a position of bringing values in line with action (2G), and then to a negotiating position (3D). On the other hand, a development-oriented agency, because of its limited resources, usually begins in a group organization phase (1I) and moves through an inducement phase (2F) before coming to an action phase (3C). Planning starts with the calling together of experts (1E), moves to building a power block (2B), and concludes with some representation of all significant interests (3H).

The main point is that one can use either the characteristics of the problem or the type of change agency (action, planning, or development) as a point of departure. In either case, to achieve closure on particular problems, a differential set of strategies needs to be used, perhaps relying on different agencies and different persons at different phases of action. Two elements remain constant in either departure perspective: one is the notion of the means-ends spiral, and the other is that the *beginning* strategy should be articulated with the primary maintenance means (and this initial target of change) in the system.

JOHN E. TROPMAN

JOHN L. ERLICH

CHAPTER V

Social Planning

Social planning is at once the most articulated and most tumultuous change approach we are considering. New technology has made it possible to predict and project social trends that a few short years ago would have been regarded as almost complete guesswork. As goals and objectives are more often specific and public than they are in social action or locality development, measures of success and failure are usually readily available. On the other hand, as planning and policy formulation have merged increasingly into national, state, and local political processes (i.e., revenue-sharing allocations), vigorous disputes seem to emerge at almost all planning levels.

At the community level, many people associate planning with some sort of "foreign" political ideology or assume that it will require unacceptable levels of constraint. Some simply equate it with governmental control. Caught between the conflicting pressures of increasing complexity and the tradition of self-determination (coupled with a society-wide distrust of authorities), the community response to planning is often profoundly ambivalent.

Conceptually, two themes run through the planning literature. One views planning as a rational-technical skill, requiring special training and often a professional jargon unintelligible to the uninitiated. Rhetoric here emphasizes neutrality, impartiality, "the facts," and "the public interest." The other theme describes planning as a political process, in which the planner pursues goals that are often not widely shared. Part of the planner's task is to persuade the community to accept these goals. His job is to "engineer consent." Planning is regarded as more an art than a profession. Furthermore, it is the art of the possible rather than the profession of the desirable. The contributions in this chapter demonstrate both approaches and some attempts to amalgamate the two.

In the first article, Armand Lauffer offers a broad perspective on social planning. He reviews the varied definitions of planning, the types of problems addressed by planners, and the settings and structures through which planning is carried out. The significance of the planner's view of the community is also addressed. In looking toward the future, he considers possible effects of planning on emerging social policy.

Looking at planning from a low-income community's perspective, Alan Guskin and Robert Ross argue for a much more extensive use of advocacy planners. They also trace the historical development of the advocacy role in terms of "the myth of political pluralism." Throughout, special attention is given the value orientation of planners, and the way that constraints under which they operate impinge on values.

Planning for the aging has become a major preoccupation of governmental offices and community agencies. Sheldon Tobin offers some projections about the development of the aging population—in both age and numbers. The emergence of community-based noninstitutional care, smaller long-term care institutions, and terminal care centers are predicted as the three major structural forms of service delivery over the next twenty years. What are the possibilities for each to fulfill its potential?

The fourth article offers a very different perspective on planning and the development of social policy. In it, the California League of Cities suggests guidelines for a comprehensive social needs assessment. A step-by-step process of moving from needs assessment to policy development, program development, implementation, and monitoring and evaluation is detailed and strongly recommended.

Neil Gilbert and Harry Specht tackle one of the most central problems in social planning and policy formulation: Who plans? They address the planner's role, major conceptions of the public interest, and competing values that are integral to the planning process in relation to major social planning efforts of the recent past. The relationship between the planner and those for whom he or she plans is carefully considered.

We believe these articles capture both the excitement of a rapidly expanding practice area, and the danger of looking to planning as a panacea for our most intransigent social ills.

16.

Armand Lauffer

SOCIAL PLANNING IN THE UNITED STATES: AN OVERVIEW AND SOME PREDICTIONS[1]

A chicken is just an egg's way of making another egg.   Samuel Butler
A difference that makes no difference is no difference.   Josiah Royce
The dogmas of a quiet past are inadequate to the stormy present. Let us disenthrall ourselves.   Abraham Lincoln

A chicken is an egg's way of making another egg. Some critics have claimed that social planning is just a way in which planners find jobs and increase demand for other planners. The accusation is unfair. One might better claim that social planning is society's way of making another society. An overclaim, perhaps, in light of today's realities, but not necessarily an overclaim for the future.

Professional social planners work under a variety of auspices. Their training may have been in any of several dozen professional schools or academic disciplines. Their ideological commitments may vary from conservative to radical. Despite this heterogeneity, their work shows considerable similarity when broken down into its operational components.

Nearly all social planners are engaged in such activities as (1) fact-finding and problem definition, (2) building communication networks or operating structures, (3) selecting and determining social goals as reflected in the policies and designs of action strate-
gies, (4) some aspect of plan implementation, or (5) monitoring the resultant change, assessing feedback information, and evaluating impact or process. Together, these activities may be considered the stages of a planning process. The planner may not be engaged in each.[2] To the extent he is not, however, his influence and power to influence change may be diminished.

Planners are not free agents. They are employed on a regular or consultation basis by organizations and groups. What they actually do, and the problems they attune themselves towards, are very much the function of the auspices under which they work. Planners are found in direct-service agencies, in coordinating and allocating organizations, and in planning units at the local, state, regional, or national levels. Their social-planning concerns may be comprehensive or limited to a particular social or functional sector.

DEFINITIONS OF SOCIAL PLANNING

The literature on planning betrays overly self-conscious attempts to define the planning process. The planner's social position, and the frequently ambivalent nature of his occupational role, puts pressure on him to justify his reasons for being. Playing

---

[1] Parts of this article were abstracted from Chapter 8, "Social Planners in Service, Coordinating and Planning Settings" in Joan Levin Ecklein and Armand Lauffer, *Community Organizers and Social Planners* (New York: John Wiley and Sons, Inc. and the Council on Social Work Education, 1972).

[2] Robert Perlman and Arnold Gurin, *Community Organization and Social Planning* (New York: Council on Social Work Education and John Wiley & Sons, Inc., 1972).

new and uncertain roles in well-established institutions or representing organizational interests in an interorganizational arena, the planner may have much work to do to establish his position. To be considered seriously, his organizational roles must be clearly defined and the domains well staked out.

A planner's objectives may vary according to the setting in which he finds himself, the auspices under which his work is supported, the time span he takes into consideration, the geographic scope his efforts encompass, the problems to which he is attuned, and the organizational structure within which his activities take place.

Within these constraints, the planner may be further influenced by the nature of his ideological positions and value preferences, by his characteristic manner of looking at or defining problems, and by his political, interactional, technical, and analytic skills. These in turn may affect his definition of the planning process.

Some planners define their work as:

1. A way of *concerting community influence* towards achievement of a common goal.
2. A *rational method of problem solving.*
3. A process in which *policy*, determined by a separate political process, *is translated into a set of operational orders* for the execution of that policy.
4. A *systematic ordering* of the near future; a designing of the future.
5. Rational, goal-directed behavior seeking the *optimum adaption of means and ends* as guided by a limiting set of social values.
6. A process whereby the planner feeds more *information into the decision-making system.*
7. *Program development* based on a process of goal selection and the progressive overcoming of resistances to goal attainment.

8. A means of directing social change through some form of *coordinated program* in order to further social well-being by attacking social and community problems.

None of these definitions is fully satisfactory. They tend to express values or preferences. Emphases differ according to whether the focus of planning is on "process" or on "end," or "consensus" or "rationality," on "goals" or "means" selection, on "development" or "change," and finally on "policy determination" or "design of action."

While definitions may include such elements as future orientation, problem solving, policy or goal determination, strategy formation, and means selection (plan-making), most definitions tend to be either incomplete for certain settings or overly ambitious for others.[3] Despite a body of planning skills, what planners do is still very much related to the settings in which they do it. A way out of this bind is to stress the phases or stages in a planning process, the levels or locus of planning intervention, or the analytic and interactional components in the planner's task in a definition. Normative in nature, however, such definitions tend to be prescriptive rather than descriptive.

At this juncture, it may be wiser to describe social planning than to attempt an all-encompassing definition. Certainly, only description will be time bound and limited to the author's own observations. In the absence of any satisfactory theory of social planning, such descriptions and the accompanying analysis may be a helpful prelimi-

---

[3]Alfred Kahn, *Theory and Practice of Social Planning* (New York: Russell Sage Foundation, 1969); Charles I. Schottland, "The Future of State Planning for Public Welfare Programs," in David G. French (ed.), *Planning Responsibilities of State Departments of Public Welfare* (Waltham, Mass.: Brandeis University, 1966).

nary to understanding the nature of the planning process.

ANALYTIC AND INTERACTIONAL ACTIVITIES IN THE SOCIAL PLANNING PROCESS

Some observers note that social planning is differentiated from community organization because of the planner's greater respect for rational means and careful analysis. There is little empirical justification for such a conclusion. While many community organizers, under the press of action situations, may not be sufficiently analytic or self-conscious about their practice, the same is true of many planners. Planners do, however, tend to use a number of analytic tools, such as program budgeting and information systems, PERT, evaluative research, etc., to inform their practice, making it appear that their practice is rationally based. While these planning tools contribute to rational analysis, they do not obviate the necessity for the planner to undertake interactional tasks. Similarly, the fact that these tools are somewhat less useful to the organizer does not obviate the necessity for his being analytic. Social planners and community organizers share many similar ties in that they must both use a variety of analytic as well as interactional skills in their practice.

At the point of *defining a problem* to be acted on, or on choosing an objective or intervention, for example, the planner will have to choose from among a number of competing goals. Such a choice will not be made on the basis of information about the problem or considerations of cause-effect relationships alone. The actual processes of problem definition and tentative goal selection are influenced by all those individuals with whom the planner interacts as he gathers information about the problem, as he

elicits interpretations about it, and as he assesses the influence of those individuals and groups that maintain different perspectives on the problem situation.

The process of problem identification flows directly into *the establishment of a working structure* to deal with the problem. Planning, at this stage, is essentially an art of choosing and guiding coalition partners. The planner must concern himself with the establishment of communication and interactional patterns that will extend over time, long enough to establish some desired end.

Policy formulation and goal selection, too, is as much an interactional as an analytic process. The planner may bring to bear his insights based on former experience. He may utilize his understanding of the political process to assure selection of a feasible objective. He may allow situational logic to dictate the specifics of his plan and its objectives. He may also engage in an interactional process in which he elicits and examines the interests and preferences of fellow staff members, constituents, powerful community figures, target populations or organizations, and members of a sponsoring or auspice-providing organization.

Planning implementation may require a variety of organizational and interactional tasks. It also requires careful specification and detailing of the tasks to be performed at every step in the process. It may be particularly important for the planner, at this stage, to utilize his relationships with relevant actors so as to influence them towards actions that will not result in goal displacement. This too requires a careful reading of the consequences of every act.

The design of a *monitoring, feedback, and evaluation* system requires the receiving and elicitation of information based on the experiences of relevant actors, and the analysis of the consequences of plan implementation. The use of information systems is detailed in the final chapter of this section.

It should be clear from this discussion that planning is not social engineering; it is not simply a technical activity. While it involves the application of "know-how" within the limits of organizational and community capacities, planning is just as much a question of interest. The question is, *who gets what, when, and how?*

What differentiates planning from community organizing, therefore, is not the relative weights given to analysis or interactions, to rationality or politics, or to technical or relationships skills. It is rather the target at which the practitioner's activities are directed. Planners concern themselves with the modification, elimination, or creation of policies, services, programs, or resources in service systems. Organizers direct their activities towards modifying the behavior of people in their roles as citizens, constituents, consumers, clients, members of organizations, or functionaries. Both organizers and planners, of course, may be concerned ultimately with similar structural changes. Certainly, the line between organizing and planning is a fine one. The practitioner may become engaged in both planning and organizing activities sequentially, or at the same time. Similarly, practitioners whose major organizational roles may be administrative or in the provision of a direct service may also engage in planning or organizing activities so as to complement or enhance their primary functions.

PLANNING AS A CORRECTIVE IN THE SERVICE-DELIVERY SYSTEM

Most American social planning activities are directed towards creating changes in service organizations and in service systems. In general, they do not aim their efforts directly at the amelioration or eradication of social problems and social ills. Instead, they attempt to deal with the effects of social problems by altering the processes of resource allocation, service delivery, and program development in those systems currently or potentially charged with supplying appropriate social provisions.

In practice, American planners have neither the mandate nor the tools to influence or direct basic changes in the fabric of society. Their planning activities are generally aimed at (1) reexamination of the linkages between service agencies and between service systems and relevant community groups such as resource allocators, clients, and consumers, and (2) provision of new or extended services to populations that have been rejected for service or that have never been appropriately served.

Social planning in the United States generally proceeds from the assumption that a service network is somehow deficient in its capability to serve the needs of an identifiable population. Four types of deficiencies may be acted on:

1. *A quantitative lack of services or resources.* (This assumes that the means for dealing with actual or potential social problems are known.)
2. *Ineffective or inappropriate services or programs.*
3. *Inappropriate structuring of services and resources.* (This assumes that services are present but are either too splintered or too centralized or are offered under inappropriate auspices.)
4. *Lack of responsiveness to needs and wishes of some actual or potential consumer group or ineffective outreach to consumers.*

Without distinguishing between these deficiencies, otherwise competent planners may apply unsuitable tactics in their efforts to produce changes in target organizations. An effective strategy aimed at a service organization that is inappropriately structured to deliver its services would be quite different from a strategy aimed at an unresponsive organization. Careful analysis of the presenting problem and its contextual elements is called for.

GOALS AND OBJECTIVES

While the planner attempts to bring rational means to play in the improvement of the conditions he finds at the outset of a planning process, this is not to suggest that planning is fully rational. In all probability it will never be so. A planner, his constituents, and his sponsoring organization must make choices at every stage in the planning process. These choices are frequently made on the basis of preferences, value commitments, and available information. Preferences are expressions of wants. They can never be fully ordered. They are never fully satisfied. Values are by their nature too general to ever be fully realized. Information is rarely adequate. Successful accomplishment of planning goals may result in the recognition of new wants, the identification of different value commitments, and the reordering or uncovering of new information.[4]

Whatever its limitations, rationality in social planning aims at producing the greatest return for the efforts expended. It chooses a middle ground between effectiveness, efficiency, and feasibility. It aims at what Herbert Simon and other administration theorists have termed "optimization" rather than "maximization." Much of a planner's success may be due to his ability to calculate a middle ground between goal attainment, reduction of costs, and the string of credit for future projects.

The social planner's emphasis on planned change gives order to the otherwise purely technical or essentially political processes of attempting to influence social change. A new birth-control device, a new fuel, a surgical technique, or a new data-processing system are examples of technological innovations that create social change. Quid pro quo agreements, the use of coercive power, or an appeal to public opinion are examples of political efforts to influence the direction of change. Planners certainly utilize technological innovations and political tactics. What distinguishes planning from other processes, however, is its attempt at a balanced ordering of feasible objectives and/or the use of analytic tools to determine the efficacy of various means to overcome resistance to desired change—that is, to replace the irrational forces of the market with rational, calculated change strategies.

Planning is not an entirely new or modern phenomenon. History is replete with attempts by men to concert their decision-making powers through cooperative efforts to deal with the consequences of social problems or to anticipate the future and prepare for it. What distinguishes contemporary social-planning efforts from earlier models is the recognition that planning can encompass conflicts of interest and differences of opinion. Planners may engage in either collaborative or conflictful strategies. They may attempt to coordinate the activities of numerous parties, or they may attempt to negotiate between or on behalf of parties to a conflict. In contemporary social planning, cooperation and conflict are not mutually exclusive or antagonistic strategies. Elements of conflict and cooperation are combined with the planner's technical expertise to guide the process of change.

A number of critics as well as a number of proponents of social planning have equated planning with social harmony. But differences of opinion are rarely resolved at the beginning of a planning process. There

---

[4]Paul Davidoff and Thomas A. Reiner, "A Choice Theory of Planning," *Journal of the American Institute of Planners,* Vol. 28 (May, 1962), pp. 103–15.

should be no notion of perfectibility in the process of social planning. Planners do not aim their efforts at the achievement of some perfect and harmonious end-state. Planning activities may themselves create new sources of social conflict, even as plan targets are reached. The greatest source of problems, Eric Sevareid once commented, is solutions.

NATIONAL AND COMMUNITY PLANNING IN THE UNITED STATES

The American brand of social planning is as much a spin-off of the crises born of governmental intervention as a method to direct that intervention. There are many social programs in this country. There is too little societal planning. Planners are not the ones to be blamed. National planning would entail the selection and ranking of social goals, and the assessment of both their cost and feasibility.

In the absence of a clear set of national social goals, planners have had to engage in remedial action.[5] Planners frequently evidence a caretaker orientation, creating programs to serve those individuals who cannot meet their own needs or who have been structurally or psychologically alienated and disenfranchised. The American planner's orientation towards creation or modification of service programs has been described as a "vacuum-filling" process. Unfortunately, most service programs operate within a context of very limited resources. The vacuums remain large. While

planning, by its very definition, is the opposite of laissez-faire, it has frequently degenerated, as Alvin Schorr has pointed out, into a national program of "évitez faire" in which inadequate funds are poured into demonstration programs rather than into comprehensive, structurally oriented change efforts.

American social planning is by its very nature an attempt at ad hoc solutions to specific problems. Suffering from a lack of comprehensiveness, it serves primarily as a corrective device for a complex of welfare services. These services, in turn, evolved in order to compensate for the wastage and breakage of a competitive, industrial, urban society in which individuals and groups are frequently cut adrift or left behind.

Planning is based on the assumptions that the aggregate of individual and group activities does not adequately distribute resources or opportunities, and that preferable conditions may be brought about. Planners further assume that the absence of planning deprives man of freedom of choice.

In the United States, planning has been largely an attempt to introduce order at the local or community level and in the midst of generally uncoordinated efforts to influence the direction of economic growth, physical and urban development, and income and power redistribution. Although a tendency towards centralized decision making at the extracommunity level is increasingly evident, for the moment the location of authority for goal determination and resource allocation in the United States has been obscured. Despite a myth as to the countervailing power of the federal government, there is little evidence that federal power is adequate to redistribute goods, control that distribution, and guarantee adequate welfare for the citizenry.

National planning in this country is still more a myth and a mystique than an actual

[5]Harold B. Chetkow, "The Planning of Social-Service Changes," *Public Administration Review,* Vol. 28 (May–June 1968), pp. 256–63. John W. Dyckman, "Social Planning, Social Planners, and Planned Societies," *Journal of the American Institute of Planners,* Vol. 32 (March, 1966) pp. 66–76. Bertram M. Gross, "National Planning: Findings and Fallacies," *Public Administration Review,* Vol. 25 (December, 1965), pp. 263–73.

fact or serious endeavor. This stems only partially from the historic evolutionary and ideological commitments of the country. Our inability is also based on the inadequacies of planning theories and planning instruments. This is, itself, an accident of history. Scientific technology and physical engineering have progressed much more rapidly than knowledge in the social sciences or technology in social policy determination.

In part, however, the problem lies in our unwillingness to specify national social priorities and in our reliance on the counterbalance of vested interests. This unwillingness is not accidental. It is the effect of these vested interests. It has been possible for the nation to harness scientific and technological know-how of gigantic proportions to reach the moon. Hundreds of professional specializations and scientific disciplines were coordinated in one of mankind's most spectacular collective achievements. It seems unlikely that similar resources or concentration of efforts will be directed at the resolution of urban problems. There is no project comparable to NASA in the fields of urban problems, social welfare, and social policy. The dogmas of a quiet past still prevail upon us, inadequate as they may be to the stormy present.

Until recently, central or national planning, if it existed at all in this country, was relegated to such instrumentalities as White House Conferences, Presidential task forces, and congressional investigatory and legislative committees. In the 1960s, civil rights, mental health, housing, and antipoverty and social security legislation gave some evidence of a shift towards national planning. Increasingly, too, pressures for the development of a national system of social accounts, for a Presidential Social State of the Union message, and for policy recommendations from federal bureaucracies may shift the balance from the local to the national level and from resource acquisition to resource utilization in accordance with national priorities.

Presently, however, most planners are employed by organizations with limited mandates and limited power to affect the course of social change and the arrangements of social institutions. Even venturesome organizations and social movements become institutionalized at the point at which they settle on the provision and maintenance of a service perspective. Planning organizations, like all other organizations, are dependent on exchanges with what Roland Warren calls "input" and "output" constituencies.[6] Input constituencies provide them with legitimation, community support, staff, financial revenue, knowledge, and other resources. Output constituencies are those that are the recipients or beneficiaries of the planner's or planning organization's interventions.

Input constituencies generally exercise more control over the planner or the planning organization than do output constituencies. For this reason, planning efforts may be biased towards the provision of services and the establishment of programs aimed at changing individuals rather than changing the basic structural arrangements of society. It is easier to develop a job-training program to experiment with new educational technologies than to attempt to intervene at the causal level of structural unemployment. It is also less risky.

The planner directing his efforts at more basic structural changes will threaten some of his more powerful input constituencies. Even apparently secure and independent sources of funding may dry up, if the planner appears to threaten entrenched and

---

[6]Roland Warren, "Interaction of Community Decision Organizations: Some Basic Concepts and Needed Research," *Social Service Review,* Vol. 41, No. 3 (September 1967), pp. 261–70.

powerful institutions. The dismantling of the antipoverty program provides evidence of this fact, as do recent pressures put on the National Council of Churches following its support of Alinsky organizing efforts, or on the Ford Foundation following its support of controversial school decentralization in Ocean Hill—Brownsville. All too frequently, efforts aimed at changing the system or structure of institutional relationships shift so in orientation that the end result of a planning effort may be the provision of new or expanded services aimed at changing individuals.

This is the basic contradiction in most planning efforts. In the absence of clearly defined social objectives or a priority of national goals, even planning efforts aimed at reducing the fragmentation of social services and at restructuring the service network frequently end up with fragmented and palliative additions or correctives to the existent system. A *difference that makes no difference is no difference.*

Planners, then, may act neither on the primary causes of social problems, nor on the primary consequences of social change. Many planning interventions may be said to be at the tertiary level. Planners intervene in the workings of those institutions that themselves act on the secondary consequences of social change (that is, inadequate housing, poor schooling, inaccessible medical services, unemployment, and the like) and accompanying social problems.

PLANNING SETTINGS AND STRUCTURES

Planning settings and structures in the United States vary according to whether they are under governmental or voluntary auspices, according to geographic scope, and according to the area of programmatic concern. The best approximation of a fully comprehensive planning effort may be found at the regional level in the Tennessee Valley Authority (TVA), where economic, ecological, social, and other concerns were all included. Other than the TVA, however, social-planning units generally can be distinguished on the basis of whether their concerns are: (1) limited to certain sectors of the welfare system (for example, education, aging, delinquency, dependency, and child welfare), in which case they may practice within (*a*) a particular service agency or (*b*) a specialized coordinating or planning unit; or (2) intersectorial or more comprehensive either (*a*) at the local level or (*b*) beyond the local level.

Sectorial Planning

Sectorial planning takes place within a specialized problem or program arena. Such planning involves promotion of the interests of some target population, a service agency, or a service network organized on behalf of that population. Sectorial planning is frequently spurred by federal or voluntary appropriations or by the existing agencies to expand their domains, extend their effectiveness, or increase their efficiency. Much of the planning in this area, while nominally directed at expansion of resource allocation, is in reality engaged in resource acquisition.

The planning that goes on within or on behalf of direct-service agencies is a case in point. Whether in social welfare, education, health or other sectors, these agencies grew in response to societal dysfunctions engendered by industrialization, urbanization, and bureaucratization. They deal with those individuals or groups that are the casualties of social and economic change. Their services, however useful and important, tend to be splintered, fragmentary, and limited in scope.

Direct-service agencies are dependent on external sources of financial support and goodwill. An agency's effectiveness is based in part on the skill and expertise of its practitioners and on the appropriateness of its services. Planners employed by direct-service agencies generally perform three functions: (1) they mobilize support for the agency's ideology, program, or financial needs; (2) they guide the process of interorganizational exchange of such resources as personnel, specialized expertise, facilities, funds, and influence; and (3) they direct their efforts at changes in community resources and programs outside the direct jurisdiction of their agencies but necessary to the welfare of their clients and constituencies.[7]

Mobilization of community support assures that the agency can maintain viable programs through (1) the winning of public acceptance, (2) the recruitment of clientele, and (3) the securing of adequate financing. If there is a lack of adequate support, the planner may seek to isolate or nullify external threats or to reexamine the very nature of the agency's services with the view of rectifying inadequacies.

Just as agencies are dependent on external services, so are they looked upon for support by other organizations. Frequently, the planner in the direct service agency enters into (1) collaborative exchanges with other organizations through the coordination of services or responsibilities for mutual client systems or (2) joint-action efforts aimed at community education, the passage of new legislation, or the securing of new resources to be shared. Such exchanges depend on mutual (although not necessarily equal) sharing of benefits.

Agency planners may also attempt to change the directions of other service systems or influence the general direction of community resource allocation. Their efforts may result in the creation of new services that are autonomous, jointly sponsored with other agencies, or, some cases, developed within their own agencies.

The planner's success will depend on the values attached to his efforts by his own and other existing service agencies. It will also depend on the administrative and other supports he receives within his own agency.

The press of ongoing administrative and maintenance responsibilities makes it unlikely that direct-service agencies can adequately plan for sectorial needs apart from their immediate clientele. Accordingly, a variety of other sectorial planning bodies has been developed. In government, urban-renewal authorities and city-planning commissions, statewide health, mental health, or retardation planning councils, and commissions on human resources and human rights are examples of centralized planning bodies. Private foundations for the blind, for the handicapped, for the aged, and for the extension of family services play similar roles, although generally without official public (governmental) sanction.

Intersectorial or Comprehensive Planning

The proliferation of sectorial planning bodies and programs aimed at specific populations poses the problem of coordination and the need for more comprehensive approaches. Accordingly, a number of coordinating, allocating, and intersectorial planning bodies have grown up during the first two thirds of the 20th century. At the local level, these have included welfare councils, sectarian federations, community-

---

[7]James R. Dumpson, "Planning by Social Agencies," *Social Progress through Social Planning,* Proceedings of the 12th International Conference of Social Work, Athens, 1964; Violet Seider, "Organization of the State Welfare Department for Community Planning," in French, *op. cit.*

action agencies, model-cities boards, community mental health boards, and human resources commissions.

Welfare councils have had the longest standing relationship to social work and social welfare agencies. Their major contributions have been to further cooperative relationships between voluntary social agencies, to raise the standards of professional practice, and to stimulate the planning and coordination of new services.

Sectarian federations have played similar roles within ethnic or religious communities, notably among Catholics and Jews. In addition, "functional" federations, limited to particular fields, have coordinated and planned for other services. Examples are hospital associations, the National Federation of Settlements, the National Urban League, and nursery school associations. Community-action agencies, funded by the Office of Economic Opportunity, were organized with the objective of stimulating existing agencies and councils to attempt innovative and necessary new programs, while providing a voice to the disenfranchised poor. CAAs also spawned a number of new direct-service programs, particularly in the area of youth services and job training. Community mental health boards have undertaken to stimulate the growth of county- or region-wide, community-based, comprehensive care to populations with mental health needs. The human-resource commission (HRC) is still another form of service-coordinating agency that emerged in the late 1960s. Generally under local governmental auspices, the typical mayor's HRC is concerned with integration of governmental and private service networks.

Attempts at comprehensive planning beyond the local community are still rare. Most recent attempts at comprehensive planning have been largely ad hoc in nature. Nevertheless, evidence abounds of new attempts to coordinate planning efforts at state and regional levels. State planning bodies and regional counterparts have developed in some 36 states. Their form may be that of the interdepartmental commission or the superdepartment of human services. While these are still in their infancy, it is likely that a new governmental emphasis on creative federalism, bringing together planners from federal, state, and local levels, may spawn new and effective forms during the 1970s.

THE PLANNER'S PERSPECTIVE AND ITS EFFECT ON HIS ROLE PERFORMANCE

Much of the planning literature evidences concern with man's current inability to predict, shape, or control the effects of technological changes and its repercussions for social values, social customs, and patterns of social interaction. Questions of consumer control or citizenship involvement vary according to whether the location of the planning unit is at the locality level or extracommunity in locus and scope. The planner at the community level, close to his clients or to the populations affected by his intervention, may give high priority to consumer choice and the problems of individual liberty. Planners at the extracommunity level may be more concerned with the establishment of overall goals and the "greatest good for the greatest number." In both situations, however, regardless of the planner's democratic ideal, there is in practice a tendency to short-cut processes, an impatience with delays, and an emphasis on efficiency.

While almost all planners adhere to the principle of citizen involvement, one is not hard put to identify at least two contradictory perspectives. Some planners envision planned change as emerging from the bottom and moving upwards. In their work, the general citizenry or a specific population may be involved in the process of both goal formation and task accomplishment. Planners of this persuasion may play advocacy roles or may concern themselves with the processes of community involvement more than with specific goal attainment. They may be found representing grass-roots organizations or acting in coordinating capacities on welfare councils representing social agencies. In each case, their definitions of relevant constituencies may vary somewhat, but their conviction of the need to involve representatives of affected organizations and populations is shared.

Other planners may place greater emphasis on specific goal attainment, on "objective" central planning. Change emerging from the bottom up, they argue, is limited in perspective, fragmentary in objective, and divisive in effect. Comprehensive planning can only be done from a centralist position. Freedom, they argue, can best be guaranteed by planning for it, rather than by allowing the competition of the marketplace to distribute liberties inequitably. Planners who represent the interests of particular constituencies, they argue, may actually jeopardize the interests of the community as a whole.

This points up the central dilemma in planning. Opposition to planning in the name of freedom is self-defeating.[8] Social change continues at an ever-accelerating rate regardless of planned intervention. Man's freedom of choice can only be preserved by choice. Without control over the direction of change, man is at the mercy of his social environment, much as in an earlier day he was the victim of a harsh physical environment. Nevertheless, complete centralization would undermine effective

participation and remove from the citizenry control over the directions of their own lives.

The unanswerable or perhaps multianswerable, question is, how much and what planning is desirable? The question becomes somewhat less intolerable when we accept the fact that the outcome of planning is not known. Planning is still a system of interaction and adaptations whose outcome is never fully predictable. In practice, planning goals are rarely fully fixed, are never completely calculable, and are ever moving and changing.

Planning efforts may vary in accordance to the value placed on mutuality of goals and cooperative strategies, as against the utilization of contest and conflict strategies. This, however, may be neither a political nor an ideological consideration. Warren has observed that the successful utilization of various strategies may be more the effect of the social environment surrounding a planning effort than the planner's personal preferences of strategy. In an environment of consensus on goals and means, collaborative and cooperative strategies may be the most effective and efficient. In an issue environment where differences of opinion or plain indifference exists, the more effective strategy may be one of persuasion. Where differences of opinion are strong and where dissension as to either goals or means is present, contest or conflict strategies may be the most effective. The planner's analytic skills may determine both his understanding of the situation in which he finds himself and his selection of strategies.

Despite the influence of setting and environment and the constraints imposed by funding sources and other constituencies, much of what a planner chooses to do and how he goes about his work may be influenced by his characteristic manner of looking at problems. Cognitive styles may be as influential as ideological perspectives.

---

[8]Robert Morris (ed.), *Centrally Planned Change: Prospects and Concepts* (New York: National Association of Social Workers, 1964).

A number of planners function in much the same manner that the "operationalist" does in the social sciences. In examining a presenting problem, the planner may begin with the following observations. "These are the skills I possess (for example, negotiating skills or the use of cost-benefit analysis), and these are the problems I observe that are within the scope or domain of my agency." He then asks himself, "Which of the problems I observe are amenable to intervention and what goals can I accomplish within the constraints of my organization and with the skills I have at my disposal?" Taken to the extreme, this position may suffer from what Abraham Kaplan calls "the law of the instrument." Give a small boy a hammer, and he may find that everything in sight needs pounding.

Other planners put implicit faith in the utilization of data and theory for the formation of goals. The gathering of relevant data and the analysis of facts become the guiding criteria for action. In positivist tradition, they may begin the planning process by asking themselves, "If this were so, what must I do?" They gauge the distance between some normative ideal and the observation and measurement of conditions as they perceive them to exist. There is a tendency for these planners to state objectives in terms of ideal goals and to assume implicitly that by pursuing some immediate and measurable objective, movement towards the more distant objective has been demonstrated.

For still other planners, the meaning of current situations and observed social problems lies in their implications. In pragmatist fashion, they ask, "What difference does it make if this is so, and what difference would it make if it were altered in this manner or that?" Planners of this persuasion tend to be less selective about ends and more apt to see the interconnectedness of ends and means. They aim toward optimization and let their actions be dictated by their interpretations of what is and what is not feasible.

Planners also differ to the extent that they are willing to take risks. The planner who does not take risks may face a secure if dull future. Many good planners do take risks. An experienced city planner confides that to be effective he stirs up so much trouble that he must move on every few years. "It's my job to open up the community. Other people can then come in to consolidate actions." Another planner calls himself a "social-work bum," and still another decries his position at the end of an "occupational yo-yo." Students who graduate from schools of social work and other graduate professional programs in which planning is taught report that they are not always able to find a job that is initially defined as planning, but that they soon find themselves engaged in planning activities or helping to professionalize others in their agencies or within placements who perform planning functions. Staking a claim and defining one's mandate is of critical importance.

There is another side of this picture. Although planning in this country is a relatively new field and the economy is tight, there is, nevertheless, always a trickle of new money coming down the pike—not enough to really "solve" our massive social problems, but enough so that some people will make a good deal of money and others can consolidate political power. All kinds of people are attracted to planning, many of them opportunists whose hidden agenda is their own political future. In such a freewheeling situation, planners with a social work or other professional background may suddenly find themselves working with people who play by different rules. This poses a serious problem and is of concern to all those practitioners who want to see their occupation legitimized and fully recognized.

PLANNING OF THE FUTURE

Where does planning go from here? Will planning take us into the future, or will we drift aimlessly forward, allowing the currents of time and the uncontrolled forces of change to take us in directions over which we have no control? Will planners assume greater responsibility in steering a course for society?

Despite the haze that obscures every planner's crystal ball, some trends emerge relatively clearly. First, as unplanned or partially planned service systems become increasingly more complex and as new types of services are developed, planning will continue to be an important corrective device. One can expect that planners will be employed in larger numbers by a greater variety of service systems in many evolving and newly developing welfare sectors. Social planners will undoubtedly be involved with population control, will work in environmental protection agencies, and will be concerned with segments of the population not currently being served or being underserved. At this writing, legislation is being readied for the development of 600 new area planning councils for the aging throughout the country. Planners in these agencies will soon find themselves in constant interaction with planners and service personnel in health settings, in the field of nutrition, in the field of housing and architectural design, in recreation and education, and so forth.

The intersectorial nature of planning will increase in importance in direct proportion to the increasing importance of the sectorial aspects of planning. Changes in one sector will increasingly be felt in others. Social issues and social problems will become more and more intricately related to one another. Planning in one part of the system will result in the necessity for planning in another part of the system. The move towards intersectorial or comprehensive planning will put more and more onus on the public sector to assume more responsibility for the direction and the consequences of change. As the public sector gains in importance and planners assume more and more responsibility for public policy formation, increases in the centralization of government will require new social forms for public participation in decision making.

Planners may be expected to take responsibility for shaping and directing those new forms and for advocating on behalf of populations that have neither the sophistication for effective participation nor access to participatory mechanisms. The increasing complexity of bureaucratic structures will require advocate planners on the behalf of individuals and groups who might otherwise be ignored, misprocessed, or stripped of their dignity as they attempt to maneuver through the intricate maze of services, requirements, and regulations.

Planners can expect increasing tension between cultural forms and the social structure of society. Many cultures exist simultaneously in our society, a number of them sensate, permissive, expressive, and hedonistic. Structural forms do not change as rapidly as cultural forms, behavioral norms, and personal styles. For this reason, the social structure may increasingly be accused of irrelevancy and unresponsiveness. Social planners can be expected to take new responsibilities for bureaucratic and organizational structural reorganization. To cope with the need to change systems and structural forms, planners will use their growing arsenal of hardware and software technologies—systems analysis, costs-benefits analysis, Delphi and other forecasting techniques, and so forth.

The growth and rapid development of newer technologies will become an increasingly powerful tool for social planners. It will enable them to gather, process, and disseminate information in ways not available to laymen. It will enable them to engage more fully in the political arena. It will enable them to predict the consequences of alternative actions, to argue for the efficacy of certain strategies, and to build and maintain constituencies which will enlarge their power base.

Perhaps the *dogmas* of the *stormy present* will no longer be adequate to the future.

17.

Alan E. Guskin and Robert Ross

ADVOCACY AND DEMOCRACY: THE LONG VIEW

The last few years of urban crisis have generated a new concern about the citizen's role in the planning process. Given the complexity of the issues and the growing sophistication of techniques in urban and social planning, many writers have argued that community groups, especially in low income neighborhoods, need the expertise of professionals to defend their interests in the policy process. From this perspective, the idea of planners who are advocates for low income communities has generated interest within the planning and health professions, and a great deal of commentary on the part of social scientists, policy makers and others concerned with the inner city. The phrase *advocate planner* has become current in discussing the role of a professional acting as advisor and sometimes spokesman for poor people's organizations in the inner city policy process.

The justification and argument for advocacy is typified in a fund-raising document by one of the most experienced advocate groups in the country—Urban Planning Aid[23] in Boston:

> Government planning without community participation helps to destroy democratic values. It can produce feelings of impotence and fierce struggles for power and self-determination by those at the bottom of the urban system.
>
> The groups with power and those able to present their case forcefully are the ones reckoned with, while the needs of the poor and the black community are rather easily neglected.
>
> One way to correct this is through the processes which planners are beginning to talk about as *advocacy planning*. The advocate planner tries to make public planning less one-sided by providing special help to the groups which tend to get passed over.

The setting for these assertions is a contemporary urbanism and urban government notable for the extreme complexity of factors, layers of organization, and the specialized knowledge needed to make the system operate. The scale and scope of government responsibility alone is huge. From air pollution to rat control, the poli-

Alan E. Guskin and Robert Ross, "Advocacy and Democracy; The Long View," *American Journal of Orthopsychiatry*, Vol. 41, No. 1 (January 1971), pp. 43–57. Copyright © 1971, the American Orthopsychiatric Association, Inc. Reproduced by permission.

cy-making apparatus is a maze of bureaucracy and data; the specialists who are able to make their way through this maze are very few, and the demand for their skills very high.

The scope of the problems facing municipal (and other) governments creates, in turn, an objective necessity for advance planning. Correspondingly, a decision-making process emerges that takes into account as much of the relevant data as possible. Dependence on computers, various kinds of social data collection, and the ability to project into the near future (when the policy or program under consideration actually becomes operative) generates very esoteric specialties. And, the length of lead-times stretches further and further into the future.[19]

In the face of these developments, the ordinary citizen finds the details of the city planning processes beyond his ken. Passive acquiescence serves as consent for many whose basic interests are more or less served; apathy or frustrated rage (its near relative) is the response of those who do not comprehend the processes and who feel their interests are excluded from the process of tacit representation.

The advocate's role responds, then, to two major themes in contemporary community development and reform. On the one hand it seems to accept the idea of a pluralism of contesting interest groups in American society as a defective, but more or less adequate, way of understanding the political process in America: it asserts, though, that poor, black, and minority ethnic groups are left out of the process by which other groups contend, generally successfully, in order to advance or defend their vital interests. The title of the key document in the discussion of advocacy, for example, is "Advocacy and Pluralism in Planning," an article by Paul Davidoff.[6]

On the other hand, addressed as it is to planning and the provision of service in the inner city, the movement for advocacy intimates another aspect of American political life besides that of interest group contests: namely, the increasing importance of technical expertise in the management of the policymaking apparatus of an advanced industrial capitalism.

In this context the demands for community participation in black communities and elsewhere and the rise of the notion of advocacy take on their important historical meaning. The black community is attempting to gain, from the affluent capitalism that surrounds it, fundamental changes—especially those concerning land development, housing and, of course, schools. The demand for participation in planning—for whatever service or project is underway—is a reflex of its sense that only the black community or its direct agents can be trusted to represent itself.

But black citizens, like all of us, confront some key problems. Until recently, for example, average time for the development of one type of nonprofit subsidized housing was forty-four months. In order to make that work, literally countless layers of governmental and financial negotiation must be encountered; full time work of sophisticated corporate managers is required.[12] Estimation of traffic potential on newly routed streets, to take another example, is not likely to be in the repertoire of skills of most community activists—especially in areas where schools do not generate high numbers of trained personnel in residence. So the need to put technical ability at the service of what are called "client" populations has emerged from the social and technological trends of the '60s.

In the last five or six years, the concept of community control, linked historically to community action, has become associated with advocacy. It was thought that by decentralizing power and authority, in some cases to the neighborhood level, citizens' interest would be weighed in the decision-making process. A number of obstacles have made clear that, by itself, this is an inadequate strategy for reallocating power alignments and the representation of interests. Two of them are relevant here: once on various committees or boards, residents of low income communities were often manipulable, for the issues were presented to them by experts or political professionals, and it was beyond their ability to deal with the technical terms; second, community control is a relatively undifferentiated concept, especially in the black community where, because of residential segregation, there are frequently conflicting class interests internal to the black community as a whole.

From these insights into inadequacies of community control and community action ideas, then, came the notion of advocacy *for* the community on the part of professionals responsible to the community, not to an agency of the city government or other groups. But in order to respond fully to the need to redistribute power, the advocate must address himself to the nontechnical as well as technical problems faced by his community client: community organization is one; education about what he, the advocate, can actually offer is another. We shall return later to problems that arise in the course of meeting these needs. At this point it is necessary to indicate what this implies for American democracy.

THE MYTH OF POLITICAL PLURALISM

Through the '50s, the most widely accepted view of American power political processes was, as we noted, that of "plural-ism."[5] That argument may be briefly summarized: While town-meeting democracy was both mythic and inadequate to the tasks of governing a highly complex society, there developed, by a process of virtual representation through a variety of interest groups, a vehicle for the advancement of individual citizen's interests by the interplay of more or less equally powerful groups. Such groups were at least able to exercise vetoes over each other and over government actions that threatened the individual's ability to survive or prosper.

Of course, this view of American politics came under attack from a variety of perspectives, some of which have been discussed by William Gamson.[11] C. W. Mills, for example, argued that this horse-trading of interest-lobbyists took place only at the "middle levels" of (Congressional) power, whereas real priorities, such as the Cold War, or monopoly expansion, took place among "power elite." E. E. Schattschneider, a political scientist, argued that the process of lobbying in Washington was very much a process of settling disputes between the already affluent and established —effectively leaving out the working class and the economic strata below it. And Gabriel Kolko[16] has shown the persistence over time of inequalities in wealth and power, despite various reforms.

In the '60s, it became clear that government processes were not in fact inclusive in their pluralism. Groups like the poor, black and third world minorities did not have the resources to compete successfully in the influence process. It also became clear that as a regulator of other basic processes of an advanced technological state, the political capitalism* of the post-War era did not protect the white middle class consumer of

---

*See, Kolko[17] for an explanation of the term "political capitalism."

drugs, food, mass media, or, for that matter, air. Advocacy, seen in this light, is a way to compensate for an imperfect pluralism.

As the theories of pluralism were blooming, another generation of political theory appeared that justified existing power. This family of perspectives had as its institutional and intellectual base the reform-minded liberalism of the late '50s and early '60s. It was in these years that the theory of the democratic Chief Executive, who should be unencumbered by a stalemated or conservative Congress, was elaborated and celebrated. Building on the traditions of the New Deal and the charismatic leftovers of FDR, reforming liberalism associated itself with a political style best understood as "deference to the executive" (e.g., Burns[3]). The Bricker amendment, Congressional opposition to trade with Communist nations, and even the highly questionable basis upon which the Gulf of Tonkin resolution was passed, all were defeated or passed in the cause of giving the President "freedom of action."

The development of this deference to society's executives seems to emerge as the social order becomes more highly technological, and the sophistication—technical, scientific and political—needed to run it becomes an ever more demanding prerequisite for those who would guide the destiny of cities, states, regions and nations. A commonplace truism, this, but in it is hidden a whole process of ideological and political developments that form the guiding precepts of the managers of the society and their academic colleagues.

Commanding the heights of the public and private organs that make social policy are men who are talented in management—or trained in it—if we are to believe their apologists and academic theorists. Peter Drucker[8] asserts:

The professional manager has emerged as a new focus of social order, or social mores, and of individual aspirations. The manager is the agent of economic and social development. . . . For the manager is the carrier of our new capacity to organize. [p. 57]

Among the key functions of these managers is the judicious use of technical, scientific and professional advice bearing upon the problems facing political leadership. The managerial perspective may be seen as another way to "patch up" pluralism. By manipulation of groups from the top of executive hierarchies, groups or interests not served or defended by "normal" political processes may be linked to power. "Experts" within the hierarchy come to stand as surrogates for the contending groups themselves. Daniel Moynihan[20] has discussed the workings of this process in the War on Poverty.

The War on Poverty, and even before that, urban renewal, did much to create a sense that these professionals—sometimes called planners, sometimes called advisors or researchers—are the key factors in what is called "innovation." Given the complexity of the task of simply maintaining livable conditions in the cities, the expert's perspective becomes increasingly visible and valued.

Therefore, another force in the manager's attempt to "provide" for the people by using professional advice is the advent of "social engineering" perspectives. Hauser[14] states that social engineering is neither "liberal" nor conservative. Rather,

. . . the social engineer, as yet represented by a pathetically few professions—e.g., the public administrator, the city manager, the social workers, the educator, the criminologist, the planner, the professional businessman—is emerging to apply the knowledge of social-science to the solution of social problems, in the same manner as the electronics engineer applies the knowledge of physics to electronics problems, or the biological engineer, the physician, applies the knowledge of the life sciences to problems of ill health. [p. 14]

Hauser, mindful that we live in a nominally democratic society, qualified the implicit authoritarianism in his doctor-patient analogy with the following:

Although a majority of the people must fix the goals of a society, the social scientist and the social engineer are in a strategic position to participate in goal formation. *They must work closely with political and other leaders* to help develop a broad spectrum of choices. . . . [p. 15, emphasis added]

Quoting sociologist Hauser should not imply that this sort of perspective is limited to his discipline, or even his particular role in his discipline. As the ideology of pluralism and democratically elected bodies waned in effectiveness in the '60s, similar perspectives began to emerge rapidly and universally.

Allen Schick[22] of the Brookings Institution characterizes the emerging "cybernetic state;" the cybernetic state, he says, is one that *succeeds* first the administrative and then the bureaucratic state. It is cybernated in that it responds automatically, he projects, to categorical situations: Politics "withers away." For example, if you haven't adequate income, then there are preprogrammed steps for that money (or services in kind) to be delivered unto you. One might reasonably ask of this programmed state of affairs: who writes the program?

Brzezinski[2] seems to provide us with an answer.

. . . the rapid pace of change will put a premium on anticipating events and planning for them. Power will gravitate into the hands of those who control the informa-

tion, and can correlate it most rapidly. [In] pre-crisis management institutions the tasks . . . will be to identify in advance likely social crises and to develop programs to cope with them. This could encourage tendencies during the next several decades towards a technocratic dictatorship, leaving less and less room for political procedures as we know them. [p. 16]

American innovation is most strikingly seen in the manner which the meritocratic elite is taking over American life, utilizing the universities, exploiting the latest techniques of communications, harnessing as rapidly as possible the recent technological devices. [p. 23; for another aspect of this perspective see Galbraith,[10] *passim,* especially Chapter XXV.]

Our analysis thus far has brought us to this point: pluralism as a reigning perspective on American society was weakened significantly in the course of the attacks even while at the height of its success; emerging in its place is the notion of social engineering, a notion, of course, that takes us to the very outer boundaries of political thinking that could be called democratic. What has this all to do with advocacy, in planning or elsewhere?

RECENT REFORMS

A new generation of social programs succeeded the urban renewal and public housing reforms of the first wave of post-War concern with the slums of the inner city. Spurred by the militant civil rights movement and the black liberation radicalism succeeding it, "Community Action" of various forms, followed by Model Cities, and now by black capitalism have been the reforming vehicles of the last few years. These programs were generated by professionals and social scientist-engineers who dwell in the middle layers of formal and informal government. Of course such plans are delivered into the hands of the publicly celebrated executives upon whom the media focus political attention: but their genesis indicates the nature of the transformation occurring in what we increasingly see as post-democratic America.[20]

Basically, these developments presume that solutions to social problems can be engineered through the application of management techniques—which, to be sure, may be participatory—to the objectives that applied social scientists have identified as "strategic"—that is, objectives with decisive impact on a broad range of what is defined by various policy elites as deviant behavior. However, the reality of experience tends to dampen the glowing hope in these words.

As Marris and Rein[18] and Moynihan[20] have demonstrated, rather than consensus between community and political and business leadership that the Ford Foundation social scientists envisioned in its "gray areas" programs, poor people who get control of some organizational resources have tended to oppose what they saw as an Establishment, despite its protestations of benevolence. Similarly, it is becoming increasingly evident that many of the Model Cities programs will result in little more than the creation of model plans with little commitment to them on the part of community residents, and almost no hope at all of implementation through a public sector that is financially committed to subsidizing other apparently deserving public needs—like highways, airports, and, through the ABM, defense electronics firms.

And here we have the crux of the matter. Pluralism cannot be considered outside of the context of class inequality. Some will compete more successfully, more powerfully, over time than others. A combination of wealth and bureaucratic access appear to be the chief components of success in the competition for the resources of the public

sector. The same holds true for competition for the scarce resources of technical skills and planning capacity in the society: If knowledge is power, than it tends to flow to the already powerful, and to be defined and utilized in the ways most expeditious to their purposes. This is the political conclusion of processes that have as their base an oligarchic economy; it is the reality facing all reform effort.

Thus, the movement towards advocacy in a number of professions is not merely concerned with the delivery of more or better service to disadvantaged populations in an unequal society. Rather, the *need* that calls forth the phenomenon reflects deepseated trends in the development of the social system—trends we have come to conceive of as post-democratic. We have felt compelled to raise these matters in the context of advocacy programs, for too often such projects are seen as subjects for the so-called "nitty-gritty" practical problems of the practicing professional. Yet, these general trends in our social system place great restrictions on the efficacy of advocacy programs. As we turn now to some of these problems—of role conflict, of professional identity, of relations with community clients, and so forth—these trends should be kept in mind. In the latter part of this paper we shall return to them, for our understanding of the problems faced by advocates—be they in medicine, mental health, planning, architecture, law, media, etc.—is intimately associated with our sense of the strategic directions needed by those who would redress the inegalitarian distribution of resource and amenity in social life.

ROLES OF ADVOCATE PLANNERS

Actions of the advocate planners reflect their view that it is mainly by means of political and technical advocacy that past and present abuses can be attacked. Also evident to these planners has been the lack of success of past planning efforts to effect equitable change on a city-wide or specific community basis.[13]

Advocate planning can best be defined in terms of the work or roles the advocate planners perform. What they do differs in many respects from the work of traditional planners and professionals, but the advocate professionals still utilize their skills as physical planners or architects, health planners or psychologists. Along with community members, advocate planners attempt to develop program alternatives to those being pursued by the city planners or politicians and attempt to assess the differential costs and benefits of each of these programs for the poor. This might involve developing plans for alternate highway routes, or indicating the type of rehabilitation program that can be an alternative to building demolition. Given the nature of the city-wide policy process, this frequently means the advocate is not merely creating "alternatives," but also is *oppositional* to the existing municipal administration or its agencies.

But one of the basic problems for a planner who attempts to advocate ghetto community interest through alternative plans is that in many communities the poor *are unorganized,* and often unable to articulate issues in ways amenable to the formulation of actual proposals. As a result, some advocate planners have seen their major task as creating organizations of the poor capable of articulating and supporting the community's concern. These advocates[9] raise such questions as: How do you get people to be involved as model city program representatives? How do you effectively involve poor people on decision-making boards for planning urban renewal sites? This community organization frequently leads to a confrontation strategy, by which the

community attempts to fight the plans laid down by city agencies. The oppositional tone of this activity reflects both the substantive inequities perceived by the organizations, and a sense of formal impotence. It is also symptomatic of the defensive nature of much of this work; "they" initiate a proposal, for example, a school location, "the community" and its advocates "oppose" it.

The problems of the community organization role of the advocate planner are similar to those experienced generally by organizers: the uncertain boundaries of the community, the lack of participation of certain community groups, the community leaders' fear of visibility and increased vulnerability, and the fact that the community's experience has taught it to reject the plans of others rather than to develop alternatives.

Related to the advocate planner's role as community organizer is his function as a liaison-spokesman for his client with city planners or political-bureaucratic decision makers. This role naturally develops as the next step after unilateral and effective political protest and after communities are better able to present a somewhat unified voice. Often, such a role brings the advocate planner into direct confrontation with conventional planning concerned with city-wide issues.

The liaison role may be seen by the establishment-oriented city planners as "constructive" when there is some concern by the city government for developing the ghetto areas. In such situations the liaison-spokesman role of the advocate planner becomes an important middleman function between the poor and the city's planning department. Provided the advocate is a trained planner, he may be able to talk the "language" of the city planner while being committed to the interests of the poor. This role may be particularly difficult for the advocate planner, who may be seen by the poor as an undercover agent of the city agencies. This may be acute when the advocate himself is from a different ethnic background or the community is not well organized. A great difficulty related to his being suspect is that in the non-homogeneous black communities there may not be a consensus community interest to represent.

Moreover, the problem of the role of advocate as liaison-contact person is not merely one of perception or trust by the community with which he is working. The process of negotiation, the discussion of "feasibility," the exchange of notes and memos, all these may, in fact, result in a *pacification of discontent,* grounded not merely in perception but in objective conditions of life. Thus, the advocate may find himself torn between two realities: that of bureaucratic and technical detail which is necessary, and that of anger and anguish which is just.

Another role that has been performed by some advocate planners is that of the social scientist who collects data to support protests (e.g., abusive policies and actions of government agencies or private groups, census information, surveys of facilities, conditions and opinion). The particular effectiveness of this role is that it deals with city agencies on their own terms. Thus, respectable social scientists become advocates for the poor (i.e., their clients) with the agencies that are affecting them and use their data for purposes of changing proposed plans. A peculiar problem for the social scientist in this role is that he may believe he is representing the poor by his collection of data about and from the poor (this is especially true when he's working for an agency that is a nominal advocate for the poor—e.g., OEO, Model Cities) but in actuality he may be seen by the poor as not advocating for them and surely not part of them.[15] This problem has some similarity

to the more general advocate planner problem, in which the poor perceive him as an establishment agent or manipulator.

Here, too, the advocate as researcher faces two realities. The official processes need (or sometimes merely want) certain data for the sake of budgets, proposals to Washington, etc. But the poor and black community has had experience with these studies; they want action, not questionnaires. The result is frequently quite mechanical: a survey is done which, predictably enough, indicates that "the people" want good housing, better transportation, protection from criminal violence, and, always, decent schools and jobs. Occasionally, of course, such work will be an important guide to policy that is beneficial to a community: problems unrecognized may be found (for example, infant lead poisoning from peeling paint); densities may be found to be higher than realized because of undetected illegal subdivisions and conversions; or surface quiescence may be found to hide deep anger. Nevertheless, even the sincere advocate researcher has most typically had to face the quandary of giving trivial information to elites about the poor, rather than, for example, getting significant intelligence back to the community. This latter function has most often been performed by activist students who have occasionally done situationally valuable investigation of land-holding, political corruption, etc. (The flow of information is thus usually *upwards,* enabling elites to plan for *their* objectives with more accurate data than otherwise available. Communities thus served are planned *for;* the opposite of this "surrogate pluralism" would be for detailed data and reconnaissance about the elites and their plans to flow *down,* enabling communities to plan for themselves.)

So far, the advocate planner role has been viewed as that of a physical planner or architect, a community organizer, a liaison-advocate (spokesman) for the poor with government agencies, and a social scientist. Because of the necessity for performing more than one of these roles, advocacy planning often is practiced by a team of people who have all or most of the skills needed to carry out these functions. One of the best examples of this team effort is the Urban Planning Aid (UPA) group of Boston. It includes faculty members in architecture, city planning, and sociology, an urban anthropologist, and such practicing professionals as a civil engineer-architect, community organizer-sociologist, lawyer and transportation planner.

These roles, however, create some potential problems for the advocate planners. Probably the single most important problem is that of trust by the client group. The relationship reaches its greatest test when the planner begins negotiating with the target agency. Since the client usually is a minority group and the advocate usually a white upper-middle-class professional, the suspicion can be considerable—especially if any compromise is proposed.

The client's fears of being manipulated by the advocate planners are further stimulated by existing funding arrangements. If the target of protest is a city agency (e.g. Redevelopment) and the advocate planner's salary is paid by another city/federal agency (e.g. OEO or Model Cities), the client group may feel its interests will be compromised in favor of the "establishment." This role ambiguity has required some advocate planners to prove themselves through a heightened *verbal militancy* in an attempt to show commitment to the client. The implications of this for relationships between advocate planners and convention planners or city-wide and region-wide planners are considerable. The need to be militant on an issue could lead advocates to reject long range issues in order to fulfill the organizational requisites of immediate ac-

tion and success, even if such action does not adequately resolve the structural problems facing the community.

This need constantly to prove oneself could take a large psychological toll on full-time advocate planners. This stress, in conjunction with the limited financial rewards available in this area, may lead some who are interested in advocate planning to do it on a part-time or even voluntary basis, thereby enabling them to maintain their professional status in the eyes of other planners without totally compromising what they see as the dictates of their conscience. On the other hand, less thick-skinned and more role-oriented planners might choose to work on long range issues less directly related to the immediate demands of poor communities. It seems logical that advocate planners would tend to be among the more risk-oriented, less professionally integrated, younger and less technically trained planners; there is some indication that this is, at present, the case.[1]

IDEOLOGY OF ADVOCATE PLANNERS

The key factor in determining a professional's choice to become an advocate planner is likely to be his ideological orientation and commitment. In a role that is so highly politicized, the planner's values become most critical—especially from the point of view of the poor, his main client group.

The most salient value-orientation common to *all* advocate planners and the communities they serve is a strong belief in the participation of the poor—and citizens generally—in decisions (i.e. plans) that directly affect their lives. This participation is seen by some as a right, an end state in itself, and only secondarily as an instrumental act in making plans more effective. It reflects a commitment to perfect pluralism. Much of the activity of the advocate planner is based on the implementation of this value. Hatch,[13] the founder of ARCH, states this "participation ethic" most strongly when he says that

> We must recognize that the salvation of the ghetto and of the nation lies not so much in the provision of a little more goods and services . . . but in the new sense of manhood which comes out of controlling the institutions which now make decisions on behalf of black people. . . . A respect for these special psychological needs and a sense of guilt at the disservice which the architectural and planning professions have done to the poor underlie the new profession of advocacy—and *it* must be sensitive to the need for black leadership. [p. 73]

The priority placed on a "participation ethic" by advocate planners clearly separates them from all other types of planners. It thus has important implications for the type of people who will become advocate planners and the type of plans around which they will attempt to organize the poor: that is, if the poor are to be involved as key decision makers then all plans must deal with what the poor consider most important. Given the defensive and oppositional setting of the inner city communities, their desires for immediate payoffs will be primary. They have critical needs that must be filled if they are to think about broader community-wide issues. Those who, like James Q. Wilson,[25] identify the citywide elite as the bearers of progressive change will see this as "obstructionist."

A second major value orientation of many advocate planners is a belief in the necessity of some short range payoffs. While some advocate planners have longer range perspectives, the nature of the overwhelming needs and conditions of the poor lead the planners and the communities they serve to seek as many immediate victories as possible. These victories, in turn, strengthen the cohesiveness of the community. Rather than representing a faulty analysis of the ultimate needs of the society, this seems to reflect a major concern for an immediate reorientation of the present urban decision making processes that fail to take into account the poor. It also reflects a need of the advocate planner to prove his worth to the poor.

A third critical value orientation that most advocate planners hold is a distrust of the established decision makers in public and private bureaucracies.[21] This distrust is probably most evident in matters relating to urban renewal. It is also prominent in their clients' targets of protest. Most advocacy planning groups spend a good deal of time in fights with such agencies. If they were not distrustful before they began their work they quickly get that way from an identification with their clients' problems or through recognition of the reality of establishment "repression." The egalitarian ideological underpinning of these planners' attitudes is, of course, an implicit base for this distrust.

Advocate planners also seem to distrust government bureaucracies because they have been and are relatively resistant to change, because they often place major emphasis on organizational efficiency rather than on analysis of the client's problems and because of the irrelevancy of traditional planning, embedded in these bureaucracies, in dealing with the present social crises. Finally, the high saliency of the participation ethic makes the advocate planner suspicious of decisions emanating from the top.

Advocate planners seem to believe strongly that there is no separation between planning and politics or planning and values. They correctly understand planning decisions as being made within a context of competing vested interests and value orientations, albeit among only certain sectors of society. The recognition of this and the frequent use of conflict or contest strategies to deal with it clearly distinguishes advocate planners from other types of planners.

Thus, the primary goal of the advocate planners' clients, and therefore their own commitment, is to improve the quality of community and individual life. This leads the advocate planner to propose, organize, plan, and fight for the interests of a particular community as against those of other interests or communities in the city. This is based on a belief by the clients and the advocate planner that there are limited resources in the city that are being denied them and that they need. The strategies of change that the advocate planner and his clients utilize revolve around the inherent conflict in the interests of different community groups in the city and the need to organize in their own community to attain their own interests. There is also the implicit assumption that the resources they need can be attained in the particular community through the assertion of their power. Hence there is a strong behavioral commitment to the belief that democratic strategies inherent in the advocate planner/community relationship can achieve the resources that the community needs. The problem with this commitment to a democratic strategy at the community level is that many of the most critical needs of the poor are not related to their immediate community but reflect city-wide, regional and national power centers. Hence, the advocate planners are attempting to perfect a political pluralism in a government that is increasingly centralized and has limited its pluralism to only certain sectors of society.

THE LIMITS OF COMMUNITY REFORM

An unequal pluralism, technocratic trends, and certain inherent strains in the role and training of planners: these are the problems this paper has delineated thus far. But the concept of professional advocacy for the poor, or any other group seeking redress, must address itself to still other structural realities of contemporary society. Chief among these is that the strategic levers of power for many service-oriented objectives are not located at the neighborhood level. This should not need lengthy explication after a generation of "Big Government," but brief illustration of some key variables will indicate the nature of the problem faced by community planners.

Resource availability in the public sector under present taxation and fiscal policies does not in any way depend on the direct actions of an affected neighborhood. Obviously this applies to the budgetary and legislative process in Washington. The corporate economy entails the proposition that, though government will grow, the kinds of public allocations, or the kinds of programs so subsidized, are subject to a political process in which national elites, not locally mobilized citizens, are the most important actors. As illustration, take the Federal Reserve Board. Its action in raising or lowering prime interest rates, for example, is more decisive on employment and unemployment than any Model Cities proposal could be, as long as one does not envision advocates as speaking for one set of deprived contestants against another within a single city system. Similarly, welfare service and renewal programs all compete with one another in the budgeting process, and they compete as well with health programs, farm subsidies, etc.; that is, they compete within the . . . federal budget "left over" from defense allocations. In turn, defense allocations are the least amenable to public reaction, debate, etc. of all the contestants in the federal arena. Community planners have come up against the symptoms of this problem again and again: they design programs that cannot be funded.

Of course the relevant arena is not only federal: the city-wide fiscal situation is bleak. A basically regressive real property tax base is being eroded rapidly, and the bonded indebtedness alternatives are limited, and lead to further regressive budgetary practices. Thus, the alternatives which are practically open to even the most progressive or liberal city administration are relatively limited. The two pincers, policy set nationally and limited resources locally, are illuminated and exacerbated by the suburbanization of industry and the way the governments involved have sought to deal with this basic trend.

As industry and middle class whites have moved out of the inner city, the basic governmental response of the last fifteen years has been to build high speed highways to give commuters access to their downtown jobs, and to give industry needed transport facility. But the poor family without a car, or the working class family with more than one wage earner and only one car, has not been serviced with the public transport to take them to jobs or to other sections of the city in a cheap, attractive, efficient mass transit system. In the course of building these highways, housing for the poor has been eliminated, the objective impact of the outlay of public monies has been redistributive, favoring the affluent, and industry has been further encouraged to move out of reach of inner city job seekers. Meanwhile, federal housing programs encouraged segregated suburbs, and public housing intensified inner city segregation. In this complex mix of policy and basic social trends any given community has had little leverage—even if mobilized and adequately equipped with technical advice.

Marris and Rein[18] summarized the failure of community organizations they studied in this way:

Since the promotion of a national policy to reallocate services and jobs to benefit the poor lay beyond their scope, the projects naturally emphasized other aspects of poverty that lay more within their means. Any approach to reform must accept some practical limit to its aims, and work within a setting that partly frustrates its ideals. But by ignoring the wider issue, the projects risked deceiving both themselves and others as to what they could achieve, and provoking a corresponding disillusionment. The difficulties of younger people from the ghettos in mastering the demands of employment, or the insensitivity of schools and social agencies, only became crucial as the resources to provide decent jobs and training were assured. Forced to apply their remedies without the backing of complementary national reforms on which any widespread success depended, the projects could only act as pioneers, exploring the means to implement a policy that had to be undertaken. And even as pioneers, they were handicapped by lack of any foreseeable funds adequate to the need. The competition for scarce resources accentuated institutional rivalries; unemployment and the impoverishment of social services embittered relations between poor neighborhoods and any official source of help. Thus the search for an enlightened, rational plan to promote change, endorsed by the whole community, set out to confront problems aggravated by a vacuum of national policy it could do nothing to fill. [p. 91–92]

Thus, the role of advocacy planning or any community oriented strategy must face the reality of its limited resources to change policies and decision making structures at state, regional, and national levels.

ADVOCATES AND PARTISANS

The literature on the problems of the inner city and poverty, and of advocacy in various professions, is remarkable in that almost nowhere is the realistic scope of the political and social structures facing the advocate analytically delineated. A counter-trend among young planners loosely associated with the New Left has led to a reconceptualization of their initial attraction to advocacy and community planning. The response has been political. The Urban Underground in New York, for example, is a group of planners who have taken to surfacing their accusations of corruption and maldistribution of public favors at public hearings.[24] Radical caucuses are beginning to appear at meetings of professional planners, and at meetings of social workers and other involved groups (e.g. the caucus of Radicals in Mental Health that first appeared at the American Orthopsychiatric Association annual meeting in 1969).

These seem to us predictable responses to the dilemmas of reform we have been discussing. A "national" nation requires national bases of power to mobilize the energy necessary to redistribute resources. To the extent that conditions of life in neighborhoods and communities are at stake, of course, community organizations and the technical help they need are important components in a general social movement that is still developing. But one prediction is that more and more professionals who identify as advocates will move towards identifying themselves as partisans in an ideological sense. The categories of thought that create such self-identification are apt to be diverse at first. Some will think in terms of capitalism and socialism; others will think in terms of national welfare rights organizations and the mobilization of clients on a national, not just city or state level. Finally though, that which created the ferment—the struggle for equality and social justice as seen by both the participants and their advocates—seems to be recovering from the centrifugal tendencies of intense neighborhood preoccupation that has been the case until recently.

What does this portend? First, the professionals so engaged may very well find that in order to do work in the *general interests* that motivate them, the *particular* neighborhood focus of their work will be deserted, modified, or transformed into the notion of national political movements. Besides the indications mentioned earlier, Paul Davidoff's latest contribution to the discussion of advocacy in planning is a symptom of this shift.[7] From the beginning, he asserts, ideological advocacy was seen as part of the conception of the advocate: the general interest is the client, the planner's idea of what serves it is the program, the theaters of operations are the relevant legislative, community, or media arenas. Similarly, the Student Health Organization is a national group of liberal-to-radical medical students and health services students who are organized nationally as professionals, even though many of their best programs are designed to bring services to local communities. Ronald Caines,[4] Director of Advocacy Programs of the American Institute of Planners, has written an article putting "national" programs at the "top of a ladder of advocacy."

As citizens and as social analysts, then, we are predicting and suggesting that advocates begin to see themselves as a national movement; this implies the creation of national organizations—both of clients and themselves. Eventually, in fact, it implies a new partnership in a new partisanship. There is not evidence now to say whether this will be liberal or radical, reformist or socialist; but there is strong evidence that it will, one way or the other, have to overcome the weak theory it started with in terms of the possibilities of a perfected pluralism in a class society, and will have to deal with the scope of the power needed to solve problems in a nationally engineered society.

REFERENCES

1. American Institute of Planners. 1968. AIP Newsletter, September, vol. 3.
2. Brzezinski, Z. 1967. America in the Technetronic Age. School of International Affairs, Columbia University, New York.
3. Burns, J. 1963. The Deadlock of Democracy. Prentice-Hall, Englewood Cliffs, N.J.
4. Caines, R. 1970. Advocacy for the seventies will aim at public policies. AIP Newsletter (January 1970). American Institute of Planners.
5. Dahl, R. 1967. Pluralist Democracy in the United States: Conflict and Consent. Rand-McNally, Chicago.
6. Davidoff, P. 1965. Advocacy and pluralism in planning. Amer. Inst. of Planners 31(4): 331–337.
7. Davidoff, P., Davidoff L., and Gold, N. 1970. Suburban action advocate planning for an open society. J. Amer. Inst. of Planners 36(1):12–21.
8. Drucker, P. 1959. The Landmarks of Tomorrow. Harper and Row, New York.
9. Edelston, H. and Kolodner, F. 1969. Are the poor capable of planning for themselves? *In* Spiegel, H. (ed.), Citizen Participation in Urban Development, vol. I. National Institute for Applied Behavioral Science, Washington, D.C.
10. Galbraith, J. 1967. The New Industrial State. Houghton Mifflin, Boston.
11. Gamson, W. 1968. Stable unrepresentation in American society. Amer. Behav. Scient. 12(2):15–21.
12. Goldston, E. 1969. Burp and make money. Harvard Bus. Rev. 47(5):84–99.
13. Hatch, C. 1968. Some thoughts on advocacy planning. Forum. 128(5):72, 73, 103, 109.
14. Hauser, P. 1969. The chaotic society: product of the social morphological revolution. Amer. Sociol. Rev. 34(1):1–18.
15. Kaplan, M. 1969. The role of the planner in urban areas. *In* Spiegel, H. (ed.), Citizen Participation in Urban Development, vol. II. National Institute for Applied Behavioral Science, Washington, D.C.
16. Kolko, G. 1962. Wealth and Power in the U.S. Praeger, New York.
17. Kolko, G. 1970. Power in America in the twentieth century. *In* Colfax, J. and Roach, J. (eds.), Radical Sociology. Basic Books, New York.
18. Marris, P. and Rein, M. 1967. Dilemmas of Social Reform. Atherton Press, New York.
19. Michael, D. 1968. The Unprepared Society. Basic Books, New York.
20. Moynihan, D. 1969. Maximum Feasible Misunderstanding. The Free Press, New York.
21. Peattie, L. 1968. Reflections on advocacy planning. J. Amer. Inst. of Planners 34: 80–88.
22. Schick, A. 1970. The cybernetic state. Transaction. 7(4):14–26.
23. Urban Planning Aid. 1968. Fund-raising proposal: Development of Advocacy Planning (July 1968).
24. Urban underground resurfaces: Testimony at New York City Planning Commission, February 1969. Available from MDS, 225 Lafayette Street, New York, N.Y. 10012.
25. Wilson, J. 1968. Planning and politics: citizen participation in urban renewal. *In* Spiegel, H. (ed.), Citizen Participation in Urban Development, vol. I. National Institute for Applied Behavioral Science, Washington, D.C.

18.

Sheldon S. Tobin

SOCIAL AND HEALTH SERVICES FOR THE FUTURE AGED*

It is anticipated that future cohorts of older persons will not only live about 5 years longer than the present cohorts but they will also stay healthier to a more advanced age. There is no evidence to suggest, however, that they will be less incapacitated in the final phase preceding their death, nor that the length of a pre-terminal phase will be shorter. Thus, it can be anticipated that about 1 of every 5 Americans aged 65 and over will need a combination of intensive and extensive social and health services.

This amount of need is reflected in current survey data: about 5% of older Americans currently reside in institutions, and for every older person in an institution there are at least 2 others who are homebound, 1 of 4 of whom are bedridden (Shanas, Townsend, Wedderburn, Friis, Milhoj, & Stehouwer, 1968). Corroboration for this amount of need for social and health services comes from the planners of protective service programs for the elderly, who have estimated that about 1 of 6 older Americans who are not institutionalized are so impaired as to necessitate one or more types of direct social and health services (see, for example, Hall, Mathiasen, & Ross, 1973). When this 15% to 16% of community-dwelling elderly who need services are added to the 5% who reside in institutions, the total again is about 20%—or about 1 of 5 older Americans. Most of these 20% are among the old-old, those ages 75+, who, in

successive decades, will be increasingly older when they need social and health services.

It is impossible to forecast how well the needs will be met of these very old impaired individuals. The *effectiveness* of future social and health services are obviously more speculative questions than the characteristics of the future aged population—characteristics such as their number, sex distribution, family structure, and residential location. It is possible, however, to make some educated inferences on the *form* of future social and health services. To be explicit, three current trends will, in all likelihood, be translated into structural forms in the next decade or two. First is the community-based, local or neighborhood organization that is now being developed to deliver and to integrate a wide range of social, health and other services in order to prevent premature institutionalization. Second is the smaller long-term care institution for those aged persons who must have custodial care; institutions that will be an inextricable part of community based service organizations. Third is the terminal care center or the hospice, for persons who are in the terminal phase of life, centers that will be visible and important components of hospitals. These three forms of social and health services will, on the surface, remarkably change the topography of organizations and institutions devoted to long-term care for elderly individuals, but their effectiveness may not be any greater than that of the current *nonsystem* of social and health care.

*The editors thank John Colen for suggesting this article to them. Copyright © 1975 by the Gerontological Society. Reprinted by permission from THE GERONTOLOGIST, Vol. 15, No. 1, February 1975.

Actually, within the current *nonsystem,* the components for a system are already in evidence. These components, as listed in Table 18.1, however, are not effectively linked one to another and they are not so organized that they are readily available either simultaneously or sequentially. The integration that is now lacking will be achieved only if sufficient funds are allocated for that purpose.

COMMUNITY-BASED ORGANIZATIONS

The possibility for realizing the first form of social-health services—the community-based organization that under one auspice attempts to integrate a range of services—is reflected in legislation that was proposed by Kennedy and Mills (in HR 13870, 93rd Congress, 2nd Session, 1974). This legislation included a modification of Medicare that would cover the costs of providing those social and health services that would help older persons avoid institutionalization for as long as possible, and that would also cover institutional care when such care becomes necessary. The proposed legislation incorporated the Morris (1971) proposal for local Personal Care Organizations to be developed and funded through nonprofit corporations that would purchase care for all beneficiaries within a substate area. The intent of the Morris proposal was to create for each beneficiary a package of social and health services that would be tailor-made to meet his particular needs.

This particular proposed legislation reflects the political pressures of various types that led prestigious legislators such as Kennedy and Mills to endorse what, if passed by the Congress, would surely eventuate in far-reaching changes in social and health services, ones that would be costly as well. Foremost is the pervasive discontent with the quality of institutional care, care that ultimately is being paid for by the taxpayer. Recent cutbacks in federal and state allocations for institutional care have only raised further public concerns that institutional care is not available for those persons who need it, nor are alternatives available for those persons who might otherwise be institutionalized prematurely (see, for example, Church, 1971). The development of viable alternatives to institutionalization has also been urged by voluntary service agencies and by not-for-profit provider groups, primarily by administrators of not-for-profit institutions—especially administrators of sectarian homes for the aged. Although these groups have not been as effective in arguing their cause with Congress as have the lobbyists for the proprietary nursing home industry, their voices have nevertheless begun to be heard. Their cause is strengthened by the increasing pressures from families of older people and from older people themselves—from families who would prefer not to institutionalize their aged member and older people who are increasingly trying to avoid entering what they perceive to be a "death house."

Although the present cohort of the elderly may have strong feelings against entering an institution, they are more likely to passively accept their adverse circumstances than will future cohorts. Aged persons in the future will be more inclined to see their personal problems as being remediable either by informal or by professional help from others; and to a greater extent, they will have already used professional help in meeting earlier personal problems. These changed attitudes are likely to occur regardless of educational level. At the same time, the use of professionals is more frequent among persons with higher educational levels, and the fact that future cohorts of the aged will be more highly educated—the average educational level for those 65 years of age and over will

TABLE 18.1

Some Current Services for the Elderly

A continuum of services:
From services for the comparatively well elderly through services that provide alternatives for preventing premature institutionalization to services for those who need institutional care.

Home-Delivered (Service delivered to the home)	Congregate Organized (Person travels to the service)	Congregate-Delivered	
		Congregate Residence	
Outreach	Adult education	Senior housing	
Information and referral	Recreational senior center	(includes retirement hotels)	
Telephone reassurance		Senior housing with recreation	
Friendly visiting		Senior housing with recreation and social	
Work at home	Nutrition sites	services	
Senior wheels to	(wheels to meals)		
shopping			
doctor			
dentist		Sheltered care	
social functions	Multipurpose senior center	Half-way houses	
Escort service	(all of the above plus outreach,		
Homemaker service	health and social follow-up)		
(housekeeping, handyman, etc.)		Mental hospital	
Meals-on-wheels		Institutional care	
Home health care		(nursing homes and homes for the aged)	
(visiting nurse, rehabilitation, speech	Day care	Intermediate nursing care	
therapy, dentist and doctor)	(day and night hospital)	Skilled nursing care	
Foster home care		Short-term crisis care	
(complete social and health care for		Vacation plan	
bedridden person at home)		Terminal care	

rise in the next 20 years from an 8th-grade to a 12th-grade level—is likely to lead to the increased use of professional care-givers.

In addition to the heightened expectations of future cohorts, the results of current social experiments in the delivery of social health care to the impaired elderly may also influence the shape of future legislation. Local personal care organizations are now being developed which may prove to be financially feasible. A singular effort, for example, is that represented in the Greater Hartford Process (1972), where public and private monies have been pooled in Hartford for setting up a city-wide Community Life Association. In this experiment, the locus of service integration is within the Neighborhood Life Center. Beyond offering services to persons of all ages, these Centers provide special programs for maternal and infant care, for adolescents, and for personal care services for the impaired elderly. If data on benefits become available—especially, if favorable cost/benefit ratios can be demonstrated—the data may supply decision-makers with a clear rationale for developing local, and specifically neighborhood, systems of integrated social-health services.

Data such as those presented by Golant (1975) will also be important, data that suggest persistence of neighborhoods with high concentrations of elderly people, where such local service systems will be welcomed, if not demanded.

It is only, however, if such local systems make a prior commitment to the very old—and specifically to the prevention of premature institutionalization—that they will be effective. This problem is well recognized by all those who developed and are now implementing Title III of the 1973 amendments to the Older Americans Act. This legislation mandates the development of linkage networks by mobilizing and coordinating services so that there can be maxi-mum "independence and dignity in a home environment for older persons capable of self-care with appropriate supportive services" (Section 301). Unless there are adequate resources—not only for the linkage function but also for the actual services that are to be coordinated—a viable service system for the very old cannot be developed by the Area Agencies on Aging (see, for example, the discussion by Hudson, 1974, of the problems inherent in implementing the intent of this legislation).

THE LOCAL INSTITUTION

The second future form of social and health care, the small local institution, is not now a reality. Although small institutions are potentially less dehumanizing for their residents than are large institutions, they are not perceived as economically feasible. Professionals have not yet been able to mobilize sentiment for constructing more humane but possibly more costly institutional facilities. If, however, local care *systems* are developed, the developers and managers might play an important role in developing local institutions that provide more desirable environments for those elderly people who need them. If a continuum of care is created that includes both community and institutional components, older people who reside in a local institution might be regarded as being the continued responsibility of the local provider organization. Once having delivered services to an older person with the intent of maintaining him in the community, the local system might well assume a larger responsibility for assuring him optimal institutional care if and when he needs it.

What type of institution is likely to become available? Will there be no choice but to send the older person to a "warehouse for the deteriorated and infirm?" Many argue (see, for example, Anderson,

1974) that our society will not allocate sufficient funds for therapeutic institutional care for the very old, saying among other things, that it is very costly to hire personnel for the unpleasant task of caring for the chronically-ill aged. Yet it may become feasible to limit costs, if small institutions can make use of new technologies and can then use para-professionals in implementing modern theories of human service organizations.

If, for example, the local primary care system is effectively linked to secondary general hospitals and to the specialized services in tertiary medical care centers, it would be more possible to design feasible local, prosthetic environments for the impaired older person. Such prosthetic environments could make use of computerized systems in helping the person with the tasks of everyday living. Architectural design could facilitate independence. New technologies and new attitudes on the part of older persons toward using technological devices may make these innovations more feasible. The future aged, who will have experienced the increased benefits of science and technology, are likely to become increasingly more comfortable with sophisticated medical technology and advanced electronic gadgetry.

Many devices and systems are now being developed that will be helpful for the impaired elderly person within an institutional setting, as well as in his own home. For example, in a recent issue of *Aging,* Culclasure (1974) discusses several ways in which NASA space research led to technology that can be adopted for the elderly. One picture showing a patient in a hospital bed has the caption: "Above, an immobilized patient, by merely moving her eyes, can dial a telephone, turn pages of a book or magazine, or change TV channels." Using computers, as in this case, for supporting and enhancing life functions, seems to

offer unlimited possibilities (see, for example, Gordon, 1969).

Another type of technological advance that will be useful for the future impaired elderly is that of telemetric monitoring. The impaired person can be monitored for changes in various physiological parameters if he wears a simple unobtrusive device (see, for example, Milsum, 1970). Through this monitoring device, the person in an institutional setting, or in his own home, could be assured that a marked change in physiological function would be responded to at once by human service personnel. The efficient use of monitoring obviously necessitates various combinations of paramedical personnel, biomedical instrumentation, transportation, and communication technology. One example of this technology is that now used in Nebraska in emergency care for highway accident victims (Stratbucker & Chambers, 1971). Vital function telemetry permits monitoring of the accident victim as he is being transported to the hospital, at the same time that the physician in the hospital transmits instructions to prepare for receiving the patient in the emergency room. Telemetry and computers, in turn, can be incorporated into architectural designs that enhance security and mobility. Housekeeping could be made easier by employing devices now in use in modern hotels such as suction-cleaning systems that are built into the floor. Various writers (see, for example, Fozard & Thomas, 1973) have suggested other ways of redesigning the environment to optimize the functioning of an older person.

Given, then, new attitudes in elderly persons and rapid advances in technology, the local small institution becomes more possible for the future aged. This type of institution, a free-standing congregate housing facility for even as few as 20 to 50 impaired elderly persons—architecturally designed to assure maximum mobility and social interaction, telemetrically equipped so that the individual could control food preparation, room cleaning, and other tasks of daily living—need not lack the all-important human component. Social service personnel could be available, but the personnel would also include architects and engineers as well as physicians, nurses and therapists. A critical factor in controlling costs would be to maximize the use of paraprofessionals.

The "decentralized" institutional facility could be articulated with other components of the long-term care system. In addition to linkages with other medical facilities, a major linkage would be with the social-provision system.

This type of institution appears unrealistic in terms of our present orientation and our present economic realities. Current thinking is that about 180 beds is the efficient size for a long-term care institution, given the costs of operating a combination hotel, hospital, and social community. Once the basic costs are established, the effort then turns to humanizing the environment. Less, however, may be more: an optimal size, from the perspective of the resident, is much smaller than 180. Small institutions could be efficient if professional expertise of a wide variety of types was used to develop and coordinate the delivery of diverse, high-quality services. The "decentralized" long-term care facility would also appear more realistic if the Kennedy-Mills proposal or similar legislation were passed. Indeed if the small institution were embedded in a community social-provision organization that was directed at preventing premature institutionalization, then there could be a more cogent argument for adequate reimbursement to the institution.

Given current social and health practices it is more economical to deliver social and health services in the community than in long-term care institutions. But this may not be so if these community services were to become more widely available and if they were coordinated. They would then be very different from the "hit and miss" programs that are now operating. More costly still would be the delivery of services to the homebound and to the bedridden who now all too often suffer in silence and who receive no services. Thus, gearing-up to offer extensive services to all who could benefit from them would be costly, indeed; but in the long run, such services might cost less because they would prevent or delay the individual's deterioration. At present, because of the absence of preventive care, more older persons are being placed in total institutions than is warranted. If, therefore, the social and health system were efficient, institutional care could be prevented for many and, for others, could be used more selectively. Examples of *selective* use of institutions include post-hospital stays where realistic efforts are made at once to return the person to a less institutional environment; and brief stays during crises, or when family members who care for the older person wish to have a vacation.

In sum, the local institution could become a flexible resource for the community provision system. In the long run, if effectively linked to the secondary and tertiary components of the health system, it could be less costly than other forms of care, possibly less costly than our present reliance on the proprietary nursing home industry which articulates with neither other community providers nor hospitals.

TERMINAL CARE

The third form of social-health service that may emerge in the near future is the terminal care center, the hospice modeled after Saunders's (1972) center in England where terminal patients are helped through the dying process by the careful management of pain and the maintenance of maximal social supports. Because Saunders's hospice is embedded in a hospital complex it becomes a legitimate and specialized service, much like a surgical service. The hospice helps both the dying person and the family at the "bedside." The staff of the hospice, much in the English tradition, could also go into the community to help the dying patient and his family at home.

Hospices are beginning to be developed in this country, some in hospitals where a fixed number of beds is designated for terminal care. The development of these centers is possibly a reaction to the increasing preoccupation in our society with euthanasia, as well as to the growing awareness that current hospital practices do not ease the crisis for the patient nor for the patient's family. At present it is in these very hospital and other institutional settings that over 60% of all deaths occur. Furthermore, deaths are increasingly concentrated in old age rather than being spread more evenly across the life-span. Three of four deaths in 1967 (77%) occurred in the 55+ age group (Vital Statistics of the United States, 1969). Given the present situation, as more people live longer, they are also more likely to die in settings that are least conducive to easing the dying process for themselves and their families.

The development of terminal-care centers may be hastened by the evidence that is being amassed that the process of dying can indeed be eased for the person himself as well as for close family members. Students of thanatology believe that sensitive and trained personnel can be helpful to both the dying patient and the family. The work of Kubler-Ross (1969) and others emphasizes the importance to the dying person of completing a series of psychological stages in preparation for death. These stages, if worked through, eventuate in a final resolution in which there is an evalu-

ation of one's own life as meaningful and in which death becomes more acceptable. However we may conceptualize the "best death," or even the "successful death," the aged of the future will, in all likelihood, manifest a different set of attitudes and expectations regarding societal responsibilities for easing the dying process. The demand will grow for a wider range of options for the family in maintaining some degree of control over the management of death. Indeed these issues are already under discussion in various voluntary organizations that are now developing hospices.

The trend toward establishing hospices is also related to the current misuse of institutional settings. Some mental hospitals, for example, have been admitting increasing numbers of terminal patients who are simply identified as mentally ill (Markson & Hard, 1970). If the patients so misclassified were treated as "dying," it might be possible to improve their terminal experience. In other institutional settings patients are labeled terminal, and then ignored. Efforts to reach these patients have at times proved successful. Kastenbaum (1972), for example, used a "reach out" procedure for mental hospital patients who were treated by staff as if they were already dead, and he identified half such patients as capable of sentient experiences and responses. Efforts such as these have illuminated the possibilities for more humane practices in the care of the dying patient.

The creation of specialized terminal care institutions within the hospital system would make it possible not only to provide better care for patients in the center itself, but also throughout the hospital system. Professionals and paraprofessionals from the center could be mobilized to provide terminal care and counseling in the same way that other therapies are now ordered for patients in the hospital. With these personnel being used throughout the hospital, practices in caring for the medical and psychological needs of the elderly patient would be modified. At present, efforts to change practices for the terminal patient in hospitals—usually limited to offering seminars to change the attitudes of service personnel—have not been very successful. The presence of a terminal care *service* may, however, have much better outcomes.

In addition to being articulated with the total hospital system, the hospice could also make a needed contribution to the efforts of other community agencies if personnel could also go into people's homes to facilitate the dying process. Thus, the terminal care center draws attention again to the need for coordinated *systems* of social and health services.

OVERVIEW

The forms of social and health services discussed here are likely to become more visible in future years. Currently there is a broad array of services for the elderly, but they lack articulation. Fortunately these issues are now being seriously confronted by service providers and legislators alike. The problems inherent in developing services that can be delivered both simultaneously and sequentially—currently referred to as the issue of "continuity of care," "service integration," "unnecessary duplication of services," and "appropriate level of institutional care"—are becoming better understood. As older people age their needs shift —from general life-enhancing services, to services that maintain the individual as a viable member of the community, to survival needs that often necessitate institutional care. As self-care capacity deteriorates among the heterogeneous cohort of the old-old, a *wide variety* of services is helpful, including home delivered

services, congregate organized services, and congregate residential services. It is recognized that only through efficient linkages will there be a fit between changing needs and services.

The local provision system that has as one task the prevention of premature institutionalization, the community institution that has the task of humanizing custodial care for those severely debilitated elderly who need institutional care, and the terminal care center that has the task of helping the dying person—these may indeed be the emerging service forms of the future. The question remains whether they will accomplish the lofty tasks for which they will have been developed.

REFERENCES

Anderson, O. W. The sick aged and society: Some dismal implications for public policy. Paper presented at the Annual Meetings of American Public Health Assn., New Orleans, 1974.

Church, F. *Alternatives to nursing home care: A proposal.* USGPO, Washington, 1971.

Culclasure, D. T. NASA space research aids civilians, including the elderly. *Aging,* No. 239–240, Sept.–Oct., 1974, 14–17.

Fozard, J. L., & Thomas, J. C. Why aging psychologists ought to get interested in aging. Paper presented to the Symposium on Human Aging and Engineering Psychology, American Psychological Assn., Montreal, Aug., 1973.

Golant, S. M. Residential concentrations of the future elderly. *Gerontologist,* 1975, *15,* 1:2, 16–23.

Gordon, T. J. The feedback between technology and values. In K. Baier & N. Escher (Eds.), *Values and the future.* Free Press, New York, 1969.

Greater Hartford Process, Inc. A new system of social services for 1980. Hartford, CT, March, 1972. (mimeo)

Hall, G. H., Mathiasen, G., & Ross, H. A. *Guide to development of protective services for older people*. National Council on the Aging. Charles C. Thomas, Springfield, IL, 1973.

Hudson, R. B. Rational planning and organizational imperatives: prospects for area planning in aging. *Annals of the American Academy of Political & Social Science,* 1974, *415,* 41–54.

Kastenbaum, R. While the old man dies: Our conflicting attitudes toward the elderly. In B. Schoenberg (Ed.), *Psychosocial aspects of terminal care*. Columbia Univ. Press, New York, 1972.

Kubler-Ross, E. *On death and dying*. Macmillan, New York, 1969.

Markson, E. W., & Hard, J. Referral for death: Low status of the aged and referral for psychiatric hospitalization. *Aging & Human Development,* 1970, I, 261–272.

Milsum, J. H. Biological engineering. In A. B. Bronwell (Ed.), *Science and technology in the world of the future*. Wiley Inter-Science, New York, 1970.

Morris, R. *Alternatives to nursing home care: A proposal*. Printed for use of the Special Committee on Aging. USGPO, Washington, Oct., 1971.

Saunders, C. A therapeutic community: St. Christopher's Hospice. In B. Schoenberg (Ed.), *Psychosocial aspects of terminal care*. Columbia Univ. Press, New York, 1972.

Shanas, E., Townsend, P., Wedderburn, D., Friis, H., Milhoj, P., & Stenhouwer, J. *Old people in three industrial societies*. Atherton, New York, 1968.

Stratbucker, R. A., & Chambers, W. A. Vital function telemetry as part of a mobile emerging medical care system. Paper presented to the Biomedical Science Instrumentation Symposium, Milwaukee, Aug.–Sept., 1971.

Vital Statistics of the United States, *1967,* Vol. II, *Mortality,* Part B. National Center for Health Statistics, Washington, 1969.

19.

League of California Cities

SOCIAL NEEDS ASSESSMENT: A SCIENTIFIC OR POLITICAL PROCESS?

The difficulty inherent in carrying out an assessment of social needs is that the ultimate decision as to what social needs are—along with any conclusion as to the extent of their presence in the community—is *political.* If the citizens who experience the needs, the professionals and workers who provide, and the electorate which pays for

them do not accept either the definition or the conclusions, the assessment is meaningless. No matter how finely honed its tools of analysis, no matter how carefully its data are collected, a needs assessment will be no more than an empty exercise if steps are not taken to build into it acceptance, understanding and significant input from all relevant segments of the community.

The current debate concerning social priorities and programs has a sufficient number of participants. Adding to it the

Source: From League of California Cities, *Assessing Human Needs,* "Social Needs Assessment: A Scientific or Political Process?," pp. 13–24, 1975. Reprinted by permission of the League of California Cities.

individual conclusions of an urban social planner, a human resources administrator, or even an entire city government without the appropriate process to resolve differences and plan priorities would only serve to intensify the existing pattern of fragmentation and discontinuity. The role of a city social needs assessment should be to assist in translating these disparate, fragmented attitudes and directions into a common set of understandings and conclusions. The point of a city social needs assessment is not to add a new voice to the chorus of viewpoints but to assist in the development of a basic harmony within the community regarding social problems and goals.

. . . Social needs assessment is, in the final analysis, a political art. It requires political sensitivity as well as technical expertise.

Cities can and should develop more sophisticated methods for measuring problems. They should have a greater capacity for collecting and analyzing census and other statistical data. Needed are more rational, orderly processes for analyzing and evaluating information on city conditions and problems. Of equal importance is a clearer picture of the service resources that exist and function in their communities. City governments should develop more orderly and systematic approaches to identifying priorities, setting objectives, and developing plans. Nonetheless, these new approaches must be politically, as well as technically, sound.

The basic assumption . . . is that needs assessment is an art, not a numerical system which produces scientifically certain conclusions. Its outcome is as much the product of judgment as of computation; of discussion as of rank order; of public involvement as of data collection; of community consensus as of statistical summary. It includes computation, rank order, data collection, statistical techniques and indicators; but it does so only in the context of the political process—in the best sense of the word *political*. If the political process in a democracy means providing the opportunity for citizens to participate in the decisions that will affect the conditions of their lives, then the needs assessment process is a tool with which citizens together with public officials may make decisions about their social environment on a more informed, rational, and comprehensive basis. . . .

WHAT ARE SOCIAL NEEDS?

Traditionally, social needs have been discussed in dramatically negative terms such as racism, poverty, alienation, and alcoholism. These phrases—indicative of personal suffering, deprivation, and frustration—are effective means for generating action and eliciting commitment. They are not always effective guides to action, however. Their very emotional impact may cloud potential approaches to their resolution. A more fruitful approach is to define social needs in a broader, comprehensive and positive framework. Social needs are those requirements in mankind for conditions that will allow survival, existence, growth, and fulfillment. Transcending distinctions between physical, personal, and collective social needs are requirements affecting all individuals. They include needs for adequate shelter, nourishment, health, knowledge, income, personal development, social involvement, political organization, and personal liberty. Basic needs—such as adequate income, optimum health, sufficient safety, etc.—may then be translated by individual communities into goals and serve as benchmarks against which to measure local conditions and progress. *Social needs are always present. Social problems exist when minimum benchmarks are not achieved.* The purpose of the social needs assessment process is to identify those social needs which are not being met.

Such a broad statement of basic human needs has significant implications for cities which are already dealing with such needs as safety, housing, waste removal, recreation, etc. It does not mean that all existing city functions be incorporated in the social but, rather, that traditional city functions be carried out with respect to their implications for the health, employment, educational, cultural needs of the citizenry. A broad statement of human needs upon which to base the social needs assessment implies a recognition of the fact that policies and programs may not easily be separated into the personal, social, or physical. For example, the absence of physical shelter becomes poverty, loneliness, crime—all social rather than physical problems. Similarly, the absence of safety translates rapidly into confusion, fear, crime, violence, and hostility. The differences between social and personal needs are only distinctions in degree. The personal needs for food, shelter, or safety, when present in sufficient numbers, become social phenomena of mass hunger, strikes, unrest, etc.

This does not mean that every area of concern to cities must be included in the social element. What it does require is that consideration of land use, public safety, and housing policies and activities be included in the social element.

The "state of the art" in human resources planning is not advanced. Consequently, calling for a broad approach is easier than adopting one. Planners operate with a variety of mismatched terms, overlapping concepts and imprecise definitions. There are an infinite number of categories of social concerns and numerous "systematic" efforts to combine them into a coherent system. No one system—widely accepted and used—has yet to emerge. However, an approach developed by a nationwide task force representing United Way agencies, called UWASIS,[1] may be a useful starting point. While there is no reason to assume that their approach is "correct" in any absolute sense, it does exhibit important characteristics—simplicity, flexibility, and comprehensiveness—that recommend it to cities beginning to look at social problems.

The UWASIS describes six basic social needs or goals and the services available to meet them:

Goal I   ADEQUATE INCOME AND ECONOMIC OPPORTUNITY including employment, income maintenance and consumer protection

Goal II   OPTIMAL ENVIRONMENTAL CONDITIONS FOR PROVISION OF BASIC MATERIAL NEEDS: food, nutrition, clothing, housing, transportation, safety, justice

Goal III   OPTIMAL HEALTH: public health, medical care, mental health, rehabilitation

Goal IV   ADEQUATE KNOWLEDGE AND SKILLS: education, libraries, special education

Goal V   OPTIMAL PERSONAL AND SOCIAL ADJUSTMENT AND DEVELOPMENT: family counseling and support, child care and family planning, crisis intervention, recreation, group and intergroup services, cultural and spiritual development services

Goal VI   ADEQUATELY ORGANIZED SOCIAL INSTRUMENTALITIES: community and political organization, human and economic development, administration, communication and research and equal opportunity programs.[2]

---

[1]United Way of America, *United Way of America Services Identification System* [UWASIS], Alexandria, 1972.

[2]UWASIS, pp. 7–14.

In addition to understanding the scope of social needs in a functional framework, e.g. health, income, etc., it is also useful to consider such needs in relation to one another. The eminent late psychologist, Abraham Maslow, suggested that a hierarchy of needs existed and that unless the more fundamental needs were met, those further along the scale could never be satisfied. Although the questions of priority must be left, as has been suggested, to political processes, it is important that such concepts as Maslow's be considered as needs assessment efforts are undertaken. Maslow's view permits decision makers to select the most fundamental needs. It permits a distinction to be made between resources allocated to survival, subsistence, developmental and fulfillment needs. Maslow's hierarchy includes five levels.

Level 1   PHYSIOLOGICAL
           Hunger, thirst, rest, shelter, protection from enemies
Level 2   SAFETY
           Protection against danger, or threat of deprivation
Level 3   SOCIAL
           Belonging, associations with others, friendship, love
Level 4   EGO
           Self-confidence, recognition, appreciation, respect, status
Level 5   SELF-FULFILLMENT
           Realization of one's potential, self-development, creativity, volunteering ...[3]

IDENTIFYING AND MEASURING SOCIAL NEEDS

There are three basic approaches to detecting the existence of social needs: through the use of statistical indicators; through the judgments of competent human service professionals and workers; and through the expressed needs of citizens

[3]Abraham Maslow, *Motivation and Personality.* Harper and Row, New York, 1970.

themselves. There is no fixed body of technique—universally accepted and scientifically proven—that may be automatically applied in any given situation. The state of this art is still severely underdeveloped; and individual cities will have to apply the approaches which in their judgment are most appropriate given the nature of the problem, the skills of those making the study, and the resources available to carry it out. Some combination of each of the three approaches—statistical, professional, and citizen—should be considered.

The most widely used approach—yet most inadequate if used alone—is the collection of statistical data. Statistical figures indicating the existence of unemployment, divorce rate, incidence of drug abuse, burglary arrests and a variety of other human problem phenomena are excellent "indicators" of potential problems. The emphasis is on the word *potential.* Statistics must always be examined carefully, not merely for the way they were collected and analyzed, *but for the actual conditions that lie behind them.* For example, a venereal disease rate that is twice as high in one neighborhood as in another *may not* mean epidemic in that area. It is possible that such patterns are equally high in other neighborhoods but that victims or doctors are not reporting. Similarly, if unemployment is equally high in two separate neighborhoods, it does not necessarily mean that the services offered be identical. One may be a middle income neighborhood suffering unemployment because of the closing of a factory or business from which the workers will move on to other employment. The other may be a traditionally poverty stricken, minority neighborhood whose unemployment may be among low-skilled individuals perennially out of work with little chance to find—much less hold—stable, well-paying jobs. The services needed are different in the two cases. Not only is it necessary to get additional statistical data (e.g. changes in indicators over time; changes in indicators related to factory closings, health services available, etc.) but to make direct contact with potential service recipients and on-the-scene providers to gain an insight as to what conclusions are to be drawn and action to be proposed.

A second approach in the detection of social problems is to observe their effects on people. Competent practitioners in human services occupations—given their training and experience—may make judgments regarding the nature of the problem, its severity and—given broad professional contact with a given population—its extent and location within the community. Professional[4] service providers who deal daily with such problems as drug abuse, alcoholism, child care, recreation, school counseling, crime prevention, unemployment, and charges of discrimination (to name a few) are especially well able to provide information with respect to such difficulties. While necessitating a wider range of more complex contributions than statistical indicators, such professional judgments offer two benefits not present in statistical approaches. One, their analyses are generally able to see potential causes behind social needs phenomena. Drug abuse counselors, unemployment office employees, and high school counselors may be in a position to point out from first hand experience factors contributing to drug abuse, the needs of unemployment insurance recipients and the interpersonal problems of high school students. Two, their judgments are more likely to imply possible solutions as well. The drawback of this method is that these judgments are still

subjective and generally reflective of that segment of the population usually in professional positions: white, middle class, and generally male.

A third approach to detection is described generally by the term *citizen participation*. This approach goes directly to the recipient of services or potential client for information. This approach comes closest to the political realities of the needs assessment process. It assumes that decision making must be determined through the conscious communication and recognition of problems by all those involved. Consequently it seeks information by those who might need the services or be affected by the problem. This information gathering may be formal—such as in an interview or questionnaire; or it may be in the form of a community meeting in which citizens are invited to share their experiences and problems. This method, like the professional approach, has the benefit of going behind statistics for explanations, but adds the broad involvement of those affected to validate and support any conclusions that are drawn or decisions made. At the same time, the process is subject to both political manipulation and a lack of the tools of analysis which may be present in professional analysis.

The suggestion here is that each of these approaches must be used to balance, verify, and correct one another. Explanation for statistical phenomena should be sought through professional analyses and community feedback. Professional and community observations should be confirmed by statistical measurements. . . .

WHY A "PLANNING" EMPHASIS?

It has been suggested that recent "cuts" in categorical social programs together with the enactment of General Revenue Sharing and block grant bills such as

_____

[4]The term *professional* as used here is not restricted to individuals traditionally classified "professional" such as social workers, psychologists, etc. It includes community aides, intake workers, counselor assistants, etc., any of whose experience, training, or skills enable them to assist in the provision of human services.

Manpower and Community Development account for the new attention placed by cities upon social problems. . . .

These factors alone, however, do not explain the particular planning orientation that this attention is taking. They are insufficient to explain the particular emphasis on planning capabilities, citizen participation processes and intergovernmental decision making structures that are called for in the League [of California Cities'] Action Plan and are emerging throughout the state.

These developments have come about for four basic reasons:

1. In the absence of any other factors, they represent good management techniques.
2. Declining revenues, already high taxes and increased public scrutiny requires rational and defensible decision making processes.
3. Suspicion on the part of the U. S. Congress regarding the intentions and capabilities of local officials has spurred the creation of effective social policy making and management capacities at the city and county level.
4. The myriad of social program planning and service agencies—both public and private—demand a higher level of rationality and coordination.

1. It Is Good Management. Although cities have developed planning processes for physical development, they have not, by and large, approached community social development in the same way. Nor have they looked at the social impact of the physical developments and other services they do plan and provide. It makes sense for cities to bring techniques of systematic decision making to the social realm. In the draft copy of Pasadena's Interim Social Element, these two management goals were stated:

The development of a planning process that includes human factors as an integral component, and which provides for a whole approach to the prevention or minimization of human problems.

The development of an overall human service planning and service delivery mechanism which can effectively provide those services necessary to meet the total needs of the residents of the city.[5]

2. The Competition for Scarce Resources and Active Public Scrutiny Demand It. What would ordinarily be considered an important management need becomes an absolute imperative, given the intense political pressures which emerge around social program funding. When general revenue sharing funds first became available, many cities had no "accepted priorities" or identified needs to guide the apportionment of resources. Given time deadlines and severe political pressures, some cities were able to set priorities through ad hoc mechanisms too often hurriedly developed and not fully representative of a community decision making process. By and large, however, cities could only announce the availability of funds for social purposes and then had to make individual decisions about the relevance, usefulness or competence of those programs needing funding. Of course, these efforts did not produce coordinated programming activities nor did they offer adequate answers to the supporters of non-funded projects.

A process which assesses needs on the basis of a systematic and realistic set of standards and considerations, establishing priorities through a broadly participatory decision making process, will provide the basis for more acceptable, coordinated approaches to social programing.

---

[5]City of Pasadena, Interim Social Element (Draft Copy), July 12, 1974, p. 5.

Improved evaluation techniques are equally significant. If cities are to establish a foundation for basic changes in resource allocation of their own as well as other programs, it is essential that they have the ability to assess the effectiveness of current and prior efforts. The existence of clear evaluation statements, especially if based upon mutually agreed upon criteria, is an effective means for generating service improvement and building public support for city initiatives.

3. Federal Oversight and Congressional Suspicion of Revenue Sharing and Block Grants Require It.

As emphasized above, the Congress, along with many in the federal bureaucracy, needs little excuse for curtailing or discontinuing the initiatives commenced in the past several years. They will be very critical of the uses to which federal revenues are put. In particular, they are concerned that all segments of the community—particularly the disadvantaged—be involved in the decisions leading to the allocation of funds. They will also be looking closely at the social impact of programs funded with federal resources.

In addition, cities are constrained to perform effectively in the light of their own criticisms of the centralized categorical approach. Having argued that they needed decentralization to rise above the inadequacies of direct federal program administration, cities must make good on the claim that their proximity to the services-recipient contact point makes them the most logical decision maker in the social realm. Cities are closest to citizens and should be more in tune with their needs and aspirations. They are in a position to monitor and evaluate the success of existing services. But to make this potential a reality, the tools for more effective, sensitive, and responsive decisions must be established and used.

4. The Vast Number of Social Service Organizations Requires Improved Planning Capabilities.

A chief problem already present in the human service resources system is the vast number of uncoordinated participants already active. Unquestionably the system needs additional services and increased capabilities. A fundamental need, however, is for the myriad of actors to work together to coordinate existing services, priorities, and strategies. In fact, the most important role that cities can play may well be to provide the leadership and the initiative to build an increasingly rationalized approach. As the unit of local government closest and most accessible to citizens, cities are best able to assist others in the system to assess priority social needs, develop program strategies, and evaluate progress and problems. Consequently, to maximize their own efforts and to ensure that citizens receive the services they need, cities must begin to evolve their own social planning capabilities in conjunction with the comparable efforts of counties, community action agencies and private social service providers. . . .

THE COMPREHENSIVE SOCIAL PLANNING PROCESS

The overall planning activity of which a Social Needs Assessment is but one step is described as THE COMPREHENSIVE SOCIAL PLANNING PROCESS [shown in Table 19.1]. Simply stated, the COMPREHENSIVE SOCIAL PLANNING PROCESS is a series of activities involving city officials, private citizens, and the representatives of other organizations and jurisdictions designed to identify the existence of community social problems, inventory the resources available to resolve those needs, analyze their relationships with physical factors and develop solutions

TABLE 19.1
The Comprehensive Social Planning and Decision Making Process
Summary of Stages, Steps and Outcomes

Stage/Process	Steps	Possible Work Products/Outputs[1]
Preparation	1. Staff, structure and management decisions	Citywide human resources advisory commission/department
	2. Cooperative involvement with public/private service providers and planners	Countywide human resources advisory council
		Citizen input mechanisms
	3. Collecting preliminary information and developing tools of analysis	Technical advisory committee
		COMMON FRAMEWORK OF NEEDS/SERVICES
		COMMON DATA COLLECTION AGREEMENTS
		DEFINING DATA NEEDS/ RESOURCES
Needs Assessment	1. Identifying needs and problems	SOCIAL PROFILE AND SUBJECTIVE ANALYSIS
	2. Inventorying services and resources	SERVICES INVENTORY
	3. Analyzing problems	BROAD STATEMENTS AND ANALYSES OF SOCIAL CONCERN
Policy Development	1. Analyzing interrelationships among social, economic, environmental and physical factors	SOCIAL ELEMENT
	2. Establishing goals, policies and objectives	
Program Development	1. Identification of special areas of concern	COMMUNITY SERVICES OR HUMAN RESOURCES PLAN
	2. Inventory of available resources and services	PROGRAM DESIGNS
	3. Identification of services gaps, overlaps and deficiencies	
	4. Assessment of service needs	
	5. Specific strategies, approaches, services to be employed	
Implementation	1. Service providing	City services
	2. Service obtaining	Contracted services
	3. Budget allocations	Coordination/cooperation with private/public agencies
	4. Use of regulatory powers	Service center
		Information and referral services
		Participation in regional, county, local planning/service activities
Monitoring and Evaluation	1. Identifying measurable goals	Annual update of SOCIAL PROFILE
	2. Monitoring monthly/semi-annual performance	INDIVIDUAL PROGRAM EVALUATIONS
	3. Analyzing deficiencies	
	4. Continuing feedback and updating to initial stages	

[1]Capitalized work outputs represent written documents.
*Inventory created in NEEDS ASSESSMENT stage may serve as the basis for this more detailed look at services.

based upon the available resources. The process may be considered to consist of six basic stages: PREPARATION, NEEDS ASSESSMENT, POLICY DEVELOPMENT, PROGRAM DEVELOPMENT, IMPLEMENTATION AND MONITORING AND EVALUATION.

The term *comprehensive* emphasizes two facets of the process: (1) that as many [as possible] of the actors affecting human needs be included in the process, and (2) that the process attempt to integrate physical, environmental and economic factors with social problems. In short, this comprehensive planning seeks to bring together as many of the human services resources as possible and, in addition, tie the solution of social problems to the existence of physical and other developments and problems.

The term *social* is used in its broadest connotation. It refers not only to the services and problems associated with welfare programs but, depending upon circumstances, usually extends as well to such areas as education, health, mental health, employment, recreation, safety, and environment.

The term *process* implies that the activities we are describing do not limit themselves to the development of a particular service or program—or even the generation of an overall plan or set of articulated social goals. Rather, it is an on-going set of activities and pattern of relationships used to assess needs, set goals, establish programs, and evaluate results in a variety of areas employing a number of different resources and strategies. The initial stage of the *process* is a preparatory one.

In the *preparation* stage, the city will seek to establish cooperative relationships with other jurisdictions and organizations to assist in forming common planning ventures. This stage should also see city staff defining data needs and resources, and the development of conceptual tools to use in subsequent stages. Cities will make basic human resources staffing, organizational, and management decisions during this period.

The second stage is *needs assessment* which lays the groundwork for the development of policy and the planning of programs. *Needs assessment* involves a process of identifying needs and services and discerning problem areas not served by existing resources and services. Out of this process may come a Social Profile, a Services Inventory, and a Basic Statement of Social Concerns, to serve as guides to policymakers in defining where and what action should be taken.

The third stage is *policy development* which is the expression of particular policies and goals set out by the city to resolve the problems and needs identified in the *needs assessment.* These basic statements of policy and direction are best articulated in the city's General Plan. A Social Element, containing these policies, can be used as the basis for reviewing and evaluating existing city policies and programs for their impact upon social conditions. It can also serve as the mechanism by which the city may guide its relationships with other organizations and jurisdictions, such as the county, the school district, and private school agencies. Finally, the city's Social Element principles can guide the allocation of city resources, the selection of appropriate program priorities, and the development of appropriate city policy and legislation.

The fourth stage of the process is *program development.* This stage involves the adoption of specific areas for city attention and the development of particular techniques, strategies and approaches. Out of this stage can emerge a Community Services or Human Resources Plan, as well as specific Program Designs. Cities will decide here whether to use their regulatory powers, their influence with other jurisdictions or their own capacity to establish and provide services.

The fifth stage is *implementation* in which specific action is taken. It should be emphasized again that, while the outcome of this stage may include the delivery of services by the city, it may also include the passage of legislation, the alteration of existing city regulations (codes, permit processes, or zoning guidelines), participation in joint problem solving ventures with other entities—either public or private—or the informal use of city resources and influence. These actions should result in the achievement of the social goals specified in the city's Social Element or Human Resources Plan.

The *monitoring and evaluation* stage measures whether in fact these accomplishments have taken place. Monitoring—a continuous collection of program and activity data—keeps periodic check on the achievement of specific objectives and the progress of specific program efforts. Evaluation, a more thorough examination of the relationship between program efforts and ultimate goals, provides the basis for decisions about continued policies and programs. It answers the question—in the light of our current efforts and present conditions—what changes should be made for the future? It is in fact the first step in a new needs assessment stage as the decision making process begins again. . . .

PRACTICAL CONSIDERATIONS

The vast majority of cities will probably find at the outset that the implementation of this complete comprehensive social planning process may be beyond their immediate needs and capabilities. It is expected that staff limitations, inexperience, and political constraints may make it impossible initially for cities to embrace *all* the concepts of comprehensive social planning and the broadest spectrum of social needs. It may be necessary to start with a less sophisticated planning process with concentration in only one or two areas of human needs. In subsequent years the planning process can be refined to encompass additional problem areas, to include increased application to other city activities, and to involve more sophisticated planning and intergovernmental decision making techniques. There is no reason to believe that the process should (or could) emerge full blown the first time around. It is important, however, that cities keep in view the larger role they can play through a comprehensive social planning process and work toward it.

It is possible to initiate social concerns in only one or two areas—social services and health, or manpower and social services, for example. It may be best to start with a more focused effort and expand into other areas later. A number of cities, for example, have begun their experience in the social realm by allocating revenue sharing funds to a limited number of programs addressed to specific outstanding problems. This has earned them important experience and credibility as well as the recognition of the need for a broader perspective. Others have bypassed certain areas initially because of political factors involved. An uncooperative private agency or school district may make a particular problem area too difficult to tackle at the outset. In some cases available resources and staff may provide the impetus for efforts in a particular sphere—such as unemployment through the resources of the Comprehensive Employment and Training Act. Similarly, it may be necessary to await the application of social considerations to traditional city physical and safety activities until after some success in the social arena has been clearly established.

The most important consideration, however, is that social planning and needs assessment efforts should be directed in the long run at the larger picture. Ultimate efforts should be sufficiently broad to encompass the various social effects of existing city plans and policies as well as the direction of the various social services pro-grams funded and operated by non-city entities. The reason for this is that the city's greatest potential impact lies not in the provision of the few social services its limited resources can support, but in its ability to serve as spokesman of the community's priority needs and mobilizer of its already existing resources. Consequently, initial efforts should be launched toward basic understanding of the broad field of human service needs, services, and actors.

20.

Neil Gilbert and Harry Specht

WHO PLANS?

The dispute between the modern planners and their opponents is not *a dispute on whether we ought to choose intelligently between the various possible organizations of society; it is not a dispute on whether we ought to employ foresight and systematic thinking in planning our common affairs. It is a dispute about what is the best way of so doing. The question is whether for this purpose it is better that the holder of coercive power should confine himself in general to creating conditions under which the knowledge and initiative of individuals are given the best scope so that* they *can plan most successfully; or whether a rational utilization of our resources requires* central *direction and organization of all our activities according to some consciously constructed "blueprint."*

FRIEDRICH A. HAYEK,
The Road to Serfdom

Source: Neil Gilbert, Harry Specht, DIMENSIONS OF SOCIAL WELFARE POLICY, © 1974, pp. 178–199. Adapted by permission of Prentice-Hall, Inc., Englewood Cliffs, New Jersey and the authors.

. . . In this chapter our attention shifts to a dimension of choice that is found, not in the design of the product, but in the process of policy formulation. While we have emphasized policy issues that relate to the product, it is important for the beginning student not to lose sight of the point that the arrangements governing how decisions are made are as significant a policy issue as questions pertaining to the substantive content of the decisions.

Hayek, writing in 1944, claimed that the dispute between "modern planners and their opponents" is not around the desirability of planning per se, but about the merits of alternative planning arrangements and the degree to which they allow for expression of individual interests as opposed to the collective will. This issue may be expressed in the question, Who plans? Specifically, the question is whether smaller units of society—individuals and groups—are directly involved in planning for their own interest or whether plans in the public interest are centrally determined. It was the latter course that Hayek perceived as the "road to serfdom."[1]

In recent years this dispute appears to have lost some of its edge. There are a number of modern planners who (along with Hayek) would critically question the desirability of unitary, centrally determined plans. As Paul Davidoff, an influential member of the professional planning community, puts it:

> A practice that has discouraged full participation by citizens in plan making in the past has been based on what might be called the *"unitary plan."* This is the idea that only one agency in a community should prepare a comprehensive plan; that agency is the city planning commission or department. Why is it that no other organization within a community prepares a plan? Why is only one agency concerned with establishing both general and specific goals for community development, and with proposing the strategies and costs required to effect goals? Why are there not plural plans?[2]

Pluralistic planning occupies a middle-range position somewhere between the laissez-faire, highly individualistic approach to planning that Hayek advocates and the highly collectivist approach of the centralized unitary plan. The pluralistic approach conceives of planning as a contentious process involving the clash of different interests in the community but emphasizes the group (or micro-collective) rather than the individualistic nature of these competing interests.

There is considerable distance on the spectrum of political thought between the nineteenth century laissez-faire liberalism of Hayek and the twentieth century liberalism of Davidoff. And, to be sure, their positions contain disparate views on various aspects of the social planning enterprise. Yet their convergence of thought on two fundamental points is interesting. First, as indicated above, they favor diversity in planning arrangements in place of the centrally produced unitary plan. On this point Hayek's views are stronger and more extreme in the sense that they are inclined towards laissez-faire and the diversity of individual choices. Davidoff's position favors pluralistic planning and the diversity of group choices. Second, they tend to emphasize similar conceptions as to the nature of the public interest. That is, both Hayek and Davidoff hold the view that the common good is arrived at out of contending individual and group interests.[3]

THE PLANNER'S ROLE

There are other conceptions of the public interest that call for different answers to the question of who plans. Before discussing these relationships, however, we would like to clarify the planner's role in the planning enterprise. The policy issue might be put to rest simply by saying that the planner plans. But in so doing he is more or less influenced and directed by his own values, knowledge, and inclinations as well as by the values, knowledge, and inclinations of other relevant parties in the planning environment. The issue with which we are concerned turns on the degree to which planning decisions are more or less influenced by the

---

[1]Friedrich A. Hayek, *The Road to Serfdom* (Chicago: University of Chicago Press, 1944), pp. 32–42.

[2]Paul Davidoff, "Advocacy and Pluralism in Planning," in *Community Organization Practice,* ed. Ralph M. Kramer and Harry Specht (Englewood Cliffs, N.J.: Prentice-Hall, 1969), p. 440.

[3]Hayek, *The Road to Serfdom,* pp. 56–65; and Davidoff, "Advocacy and Pluralism in Planning," pp. 438–50.

planner in comparison to the influence exerted by the influence exerted by other relevant parties. Thus, "who plans?" is a relative matter that depends upon the organizational arrangements among planners, political and bureaucratic leaders, and consumer publics. To whom is the planner primarily accountable? Whose values and interests guide the planning choices that are made? Efforts to answer these questions confront policy planners with major policy choices that govern the planning process and the development of organizational arrangements for how to decide what is to be done.

Role refers to the ways in which responsibilities, expectations, and commitments are structured in regard to the planner's job. There is some body of knowledge, skill, and expertise that all planners who claim "professional" status are supposed to have mastered. But obviously, in any given professional position there are specific tasks the worker must do, there are expected ways in which he must behave and there are people to whom he must be accountable. And these vary from job to job. The policy-planning professional is not an independent operator. In addition to a guiding set of professional ethics there is some sponsor, usually an agency, to whom he is accountable, and clients and/or constituents to whom he is also accountable. The competing claims of his profession, his sponsor, and his client frequently constitute a great source of strain and sometimes conflict for the planner since their demands upon and expectations of him may be contradictory.

The profession may place great importance on "professional standards" of practice and award recognition, as well as status to practitioners who observe and defend these standards (e.g., seeing that only properly credentialed people perform professional tasks). The sponsor may have more interest in economy and efficiency than in standards and therefore constrain the planner to find the least expensive way of doing things. Clients or constituents will tend to evaluate the planner in terms of what he produces for them and are not likely to have as great an interest in maintenance of professional standards or in economy. (This is not to say, of course, that professional standards, economy, and effectiveness are necessarily contradictory.)

The social context of the planner's role, then, is one of the factors that determines the kind of process he can engage in successfully. His relationships with these other actors, his sponsors and clients, play an important part in determining the values and interests that will be uppermost in his work. To a large extent he is both committed to and limited to working in certain ways by the nature of these relationships. The professional who is involved in policy planning should be cognizant of the features of the social context that bear upon his work.

The planner's role requires the integration of knowledge and skill to deal with both interactional and analytic functions. . . . The planning process is frequently discussed and analyzed according to two perspectives: planning as a sociopolitical process and planning as a technomethodological process. Perlman and Gurin and Kramer and Specht suggest that these perspectives are different sides of the planning coin—both equally required to bring the process to fruition. These authors use the notions of "analytic" and "interactional" tasks to describe the technomethodological and socio-political aspects of the planning process.[4] Analytic tasks (or

---

[4]Robert Perlman and Arnold Gurin, *Community Organization and Social Planning* (New York: John Wiley & Sons, 1971), pp. 52–75; and Ralph M. Kramer and Harry Specht, *Readings in Community Organization Practice* (Englewood Cliffs, N.J.: Prentice-Hall, 1969), pp. 8–9.

techno-methodological considerations) involve data collection, quantification of problems and analysis in light of these data, ranking priorities, specification of objectives, program design, and the like. The interactional tasks (or socio-political considerations) involve the development of an organizational network. This requires the structuring of a planning system within which communication and exchange of information among relevant actors takes place and planning decisions are made. The ways in which these interactional tasks are completed are the means of resolving the question of who plans. The distinction between techno-methodological and socio-political aspects of the planning process may be illustrated by examining the planning requirements for the Model Cities Program.

AN EXAMPLE: PLANNING IN THE MODEL CITIES PROGRAM

Briefly, the Model Cities Program was run as follows: All cities were invited by the Department of Housing and Urban Development (HUD) to submit applications for planning grants. In these applications the cities described their characteristics, social problems, and their "plan for planning." In the first application period, which ended May 1, 1967, 193 cities had sent in applications. After a careful and complex scrutiny of the applications and the applicants, 75 cities were selected to receive planning grants.[5] Announcements of the grants were made on November 16, 1967. A similar process was used in the following year to select another 73 cities bringing the total to

148 cities given grants over the two-year period.[6] The Model Cities experience for any given city was planned to last approximately six years (the first for planning and the next five for implementation).

With regard to the analytic and interactional sides of the planning coin, the HUD guidelines for the Model Cities Program participants were quite clear and firm on techno-methodological approaches and rather vague and loose on the socio-political aspects of planning.

Techno-Methodological Approaches

The HUD planning model stipulated that cities follow a predefined, rational, analytic process in developing their Comprehensive Demonstration Plans (CDPs). Initially, this entailed a three part CDP framework:

Part I was to describe and analyze problems and their causes, to rank these problems in order of local priorities, and to indicate objectives, strategies, and program approaches to solving these problems. This document was to be submitted to HUD two-thirds of the way through the planning year. Based on these documents HUD was to provide appropriate feedback to the City Demonstration Agencies (CDA's) that would be useful for the completion of Parts II and III.

---

[5]For a detailed description of this process see Neil Gilbert and Harry Specht, *Planning for Model Cities: Process, Product, Performance, and Predictions* (Washington, D.C.: Dept. of Housing and Urban Development, Government Printing Office, forthcoming).

[6]For further details on the Model Cities Program legislation, guidelines, and operational procedures, see the following: Gilbert and Specht, *Planning for Model Cities: Improving the Quality of Urban Life: A Program Guide to Model Neighborhoods in Demonstration Cities,* U.S. Department of Housing and Urban Development, HUD PG-47, December 1966, and HUD PG-47, December 1967 (Washington, D.C.: Government Printing Office); Marshall Kaplan, *Model Cities and National Urban Policy* (Chicago: American Society of Planning Officials, 1971); Marshall Kaplan, Gans, and Kahn, *The Model Cities Program: A Comparative Analysis of the Planning Process in Eleven Cities* (Washington, D.C.: Dept. of Housing and Urban Development, Government Printing Office, 1970); and Roland L. Warren, "Model Cities' First Round: Politics, Planning, and Participation," *Journal of the American Institute of Planners,* Vol. 35, No. 4 (July 1969), 245–52.

Part II was to be a statement of projected five-year objectives and cost estimates to achieve these objectives. This document was to be submitted at the end of the planning year with Part III.

Part III was to be a detailed statement of program plans for the first action year, the costs involved, and administrative arrangements for implementation. This document was to be a logical extension of the analysis, strategies, and priorities outlined in Part I.[7]

. . . The extent to which cities were able to satisfy the methodological requirements of the planning process is detailed in some of the studies we have cited.[8] In general, . . . the cities made considerable effort to follow the guidelines, but few were able to do more than approximate the ideal process prescribed by HUD. In part this is because the demands were strenuous even for those cities that could command the required technical expertise. Their causal analyses of problems had a tendency toward infinite regress, and the problem analysis approach often proved to be a frustrating and unilluminating exercise to the participants in the planning systems. Given the limited planning resources that were available, five-year projection plans could hardly demand the investment of time, effort, and commitment that planning for the following year's programs received; and in fact, the Part II CDP submission was often the most superficial document prepared by the cities. Moreover, many cities simply did not have the staff expertise to do comprehensive planning according to HUD's model. This is strongly suggested by data from a nationwide study which indicates that 64 percent of the cities used private consulting firms to provide technical assistance during the planning period.[9]

Socio-Political Approaches

While the technical requirements of the planning process for the Model Cities Program were spelled out in detail, the socio-political aspects of the process were left largely to the determination of local groups. The major prescription HUD offered was that ultimate administrative and fiscal responsibility for the program be vested in the local chief executive. Beyond this, the guidelines left considerable latitude for the types of linkages and relationships among groups that might develop to imbue the decision making around CDPs with an element of social choice as well as technical procedure. The first Program Guide states it as follows:

> [The CDA] should be closely related to the governmental decision-making process in a way that permits the exercise of leadership by responsible elected officials in the establishment of policies. . . . It should have sufficient powers, authority, and structure to achieve the coordinated administration of all aspects of the program. . . . It should provide a meaningful role in policy making to area residents and to the major agencies expected to contribute to the program.[10]

While "a meaningful role in policy-making to area residents" is an innocent enough statement, the HUD administrative staff responsible for the Model Cities Program were philosophically inclined to favor substantive citizen participation and vigorously sought the realization of citizen influence in the decision-making process. (The Model Cities Administration was staffed largely from outside of HUD. A number of Office of Economic Opportunity [OEO] personnel had transferred to the Model Cities Program anticipating that this program was where the Administration would concentrate its urban thrust.) Vari-

---

[7]Summarized from *Improving the Quality of Urban Life.*

[8]See footnote 6.

[9]Gilbert and Specht, *Planning for Model Cities.*

[10]*Improving the Quality of Urban Life,* p. 11.

ous case studies indicate that first-round planning grant awards were often accompanied by stipulations that the city spell out or strengthen its provisions for resident participation in Model Cities planning.[11] Further evidence of this is found in data from a study of the Planning Grant Review Project. The Planning Grant Review Project was the means used by HUD to select the cities that were to be funded for first-round planning grants. In the Project, federal staff rated each city's success potential based upon information provided in their applications. Results of the study of the Project indicate that the federal staff gave highest ratings to those cities that later proved to be most successful at achieving high degrees of citizen participation. However, there were either no correlations or negative correlations between these ratings of success potential and other measures of performance.[12]

Though citizen influence in the planning process was emphasized, the guidelines for its achievement and the structure of relationships between professional planners, political leadership, and citizen groups were relatively vague compared to guidelines for the technical aspects of the planning process. Overall, a number of planning arrangements emerged in which planners were accountable, in varying degrees, to different parties.[13] In general terms these different patterns of relationships among planners, political leadership, and citizen

groups are associated with the ways in which the "public interest" is defined.

CONCEPTIONS OF THE PUBLIC INTEREST

One justification for any form of social planning is that the decisions arrived at and the choices made will serve the common good or the ends of the whole public. This is true whether the planner is primarily accountable to himself, to political or bureaucratic leaders, or to the consumer public. It is true whether planning is done under public auspices or by private agencies. Take, for instance, the United Community Funds and Councils of America. This private organization explicitly disclaims that the community planning activities under its direction reflect the special interests of its member agencies. Thus, the Council literature prescribes:

> There are valid and compelling reasons why policy decisions and program determination of a Council should be vested basically in the hands of lay citizens. A true planning body should be a citizens' organization. It should not be a creature of agencies nor a federation of agencies. *The board of directors of a Council should view health and welfare needs from a total community point of view; they must be able to look beyond agency structure and issues of agency territorial rights or aspirations.*[14] [Emphasis added.]

But the problem with claims that planning activities serve the public interest is that there are different conceptions of precisely what constitutes the common good and the means by which it is served. It is a matter of opinion whether, for practical planning purposes, "a total community point of view" is attainable or for that mat-

---

[11]See, for example, Marshall Kaplan, Gans, and Kahn, *The Model Cities Program* and Warren, "Model Cities' First Round."

[12]Gilbert and Specht, *Planning for Model Cities.*

[13]For example, in the Marshall Kaplan, Gans, and Kahn study, *The Model Cities Program,* five types of planning systems are identified: staff dominant, staff influence, parity, resident influence, and resident dominant. Each of these systems is characterized by different sets of relationships among planners, political leadership, and citizen groups.

[14]*Essentials for Effective Planning* (New York: United Community Councils of America, 1962), p. 4.

ter even desirable as a means for defining the public interest. Depending upon how the idiom is interpreted, planning *pro bono publico* may be expressed through several socio-political processes, each of which involves different relationships between planners and relevant parties in the planning environment. To illustrate let us examine three conventional meanings of the "public interest" as described by Banfield: these are the *organismic, communalist,* and *individualistic* conceptions.[15]

The Organismic View

According to this conception there is an ideal public interest that transcends the specific preferences and interests of the individuals of which the public body is composed. The public body is viewed as a unitary organism whose interests are greater or different than the sum of its parts. Thus, for example, in community planning the community is believed to have certain anthropomorphic needs and interests that are essential to its health: its arteries must be able to sustain a sufficient flow of goods and services; its tax base must be sufficient to nourish growth and maintenance costs; and police are needed to protect, social services to mend, and sanitation agencies to cleanse its parts. To stretch the analogy a bit further, given this view, the planner's relationship to the community is akin to that of doctor to patient. In diagnosing the community's interests the planner is guided primarily by his own values and technical expertise. While he may be working out of a public or a private agency, the planner's

primary accountability is to the profession. In essence this conception of the public interest in its purest form gives rise to *technocracy.*

The Communalist View

According to this conception there is a unitary public interest composed of the interests that all members of the public share in common. This single set of common ends is viewed as more valuable in calculating the public interest than are the unshared ends that individuals and groups may hold. The public's common ends are embodied in political leaders and community institutions. This view of the public interest is associated with a planning process that includes, as Rothman notes, "legislators or administrators who are presumed to know the ends of the body politic as a whole and to strive in some central decision-making locus to assert the unitary interests of the whole over competing lesser interests."[16] In this context the planner is accountable primarily to political or bureaucratic leadership. Planning choices are guided by the values and interests these leaders express.

The Individualist View

According to this conception, there is no unitary public interest, only different publics with different interests. The unshared ends that are held by individuals and groups are seen as of more consequence than shared ends in determining the common good. In this view the public interest is a momentary compromise arising out of the interplay among competing interests; it is constantly shifting as new groups are able to make their interests known and re-

---

[15]Martin Meyerson and Edward Banfield, *Politics, Planning, and the Public Interest* (New York: Free Press, 1955), pp. 322–29. These conceptions are similar, respectively, to the idealist view, the rationalist view, and the realist view of the public interest as analyzed by Glendon A. Schubert, *The Public Interest* (New York: Free Press, 1960).

[16]Jack Rothman, "Three Models of Community Organization Practice," in *Social Work Practice, 1968* (New York: Columbia University Press, 1968), p. 38.

spected. Individualistic conceptions of the public interest are associated with *advocacy planning,* an arrangement in which the planner is accountable to a specific group whose values and interests guide planning choices. The objective is to increase this group's participation and influence in the competitive process through which definitions of the public interest are achieved.

Each of the conceptions of the public interest implies socio-political processes that involve different planning roles and different relationships among planners, political and administrative leaders, and consumer publics. Along the continuum of possibilities three modal types emerge that may be summarized as follows:

1. The planner as a *technocrat* accountable primarily to the profession and operating with a view of the public interest derived from the special skills and knowledge in his possession
2. The planner as a *bureaucrat* accountable primarily to the political and administrative hierarchy and operating with a view of the public interest derived from institutional leadership
3. The planner as an *advocate* accountable primarily to the consumer group that purchases his services and operating with a view of the public interest derived from consumer group preferences

These modal types represent the logically consistent planning arrangements corresponding to organismic, communal, and individualistic conceptions of the public interest. We indicate that they range along a continuum because reality sometimes intrudes upon conceptual distinctions such as these in a disconcerting manner.[17] And students of social planning will find that incon-

sistencies are incorporated in the operations of individuals and organizations engaged in the social planning enterprise. As Banfield explains:

> An institution may function as a mechanism which asserts at the same time different, and perhaps logically opposed, conceptions of the structure of the public interest. The members of a citizen board, for example, may endeavor to explicate the meaning of some very general ends which pertain to the body politic or *ethos* while at the same time—and perhaps inconsistently—seeking to find that compromise among the ends of individuals which will represent the greatest "total" satisfaction.[18]

Alternative views of the public interest are sometimes held simultaneously because of the dynamic interplay of competing social values that are associated with these views.

THREE COMPETING VALUES: PARTICIPATION, LEADERSHIP, AND EXPERTISE

There is a continuing cycle of competition among three values that govern the management of community affairs, and that affect the degree to which different conceptions of the public interest are emphasized. These are the values of participation, leadership, and expertise. All three are prized values that compete for ascendancy in community life. These values and their significance for social planning have been noted and described in the literature.[19]

---

[17]For an excellent analysis of the complexities and some variations in these planning relationships see Francine F. Rabinovitz, *City Politics and Planning* (New York: Atherton, 1969), pp. 79–117.

[18]Meyerson and Banfield, *Politics, Planning, and the Public Interest,* p. 329.

[19]For example, see Herbert Kaufman, *Politics and Policies in State and Local Government* (Englewood Cliffs, N.J.: Prentice-Hall, 1964); Martin Rein, "Social Planning: The Search for Legitimacy," *Journal of the American Institute of Planners,* Vol. 35, No. 4 (July 1967), 233–44; and George A. Brager and Harry Specht, *Community Organizing* (New York: Columbia University Press, 1973).

Our particular interest here is to point out the dialectical relationship among these values and how it affects the community planning process. Each value, when it is maximized, contains the seed of its own undoing and generates conditions which will, in turn, encourage another of the values to emerge. While policy planners have relatively little control over these dynamics, there is benefit in understanding the dialectical process.

Participation is a value that extols the virtue of each and every man joining meaningfully and directly in making decisions that affect his welfare. In the extreme it supports the vision of a participatory democracy and vigorously champions schemes for community control and decentralization. It is celebrated in the slogans "Power to the people" and "One man—one vote." Theoretically, this value is supported by findings from small group experiments and industrial psychology which indicate that when people participate directly in the decisions that impinge upon their lives, they are more likely to feel a part of their community. Decisions arrived at by participation are more likely to be binding, and alienation and apathy are reduced.[20]

Countervailing theory contends that an urban industrialized society is too large and complex to allow the value of participation to operate in the extreme. Rather, participation must be organized and expressed through a representative system. The New England Town Meeting might have been an appropriate decision-making device for eighteenth century small-town America,

---

[20]For example, see Eric Fromm, *The Same Society* (New York: Holt, Rinehart and Winston, 1955); Ralph White and Ronald Lippitt, "Leader Behavior and Member Reaction in Three Social Climates," in *Group Dynamics,* ed. Dorwin Cartwright et al. (Evanston, Ill.: Row, Peterson and Company, 1953); Jacob Levine and John Butler, "Lecture vs. Group Decision in Changing Behavior," *Journal of Applied Psychology,* Vol. 36 (February 1952), 29–33.

but modern society needs electoral machinery for selecting representative leaders of organized interests.

The value of participation in the management of community affairs always exists, though at some times and places it is more prominent than at others. For example, the Jacksonian era, which followed the Revolutionary War, and the Populist period of the late 1880s were times when issues of participation were paramount. In terms of governmental forms, the value of participation finds expression most directly in county government which, because of its rural, small-town heritage, has been disposed to value neither leadership nor expertise. County government is the personification of Emerson's view on the general functions of government—"the less, the better."

Participation becomes the primary value in governing community affairs when leadership or expertise are perceived as unresponsive to those being led or served. Under these circumstances, movements for change will grow around dissatisfactions with the ways community institutions are run by their custodians. Decentralization, localism, and constituency satisfaction are likely to be the major programmatic goals of planning. Major evaluative concerns about programs will derive from the central question: Do the people like it?

Leadership as a value is the antithesis of participation. Because complex decisions must be made continuously and in great number, and authority must somehow extend to their implementation, leadership becomes important in any organized collectivity. In a heterogeneous society like ours where a swarm of competing claims to the public interest descend upon a complex framework of levels and types of government, community decision-making is bound to generate a hopeless drone of discussion and debate unless citizens can find leaders whom they trust, whom they can hold responsible, and who have the ability to mitigate conflict and regulate competition with equity and dispatch. Unless the executive committee, the board of directors, the officers—in short, leadership—undertake these tasks for the community, chaos will reign. The extreme example of leadership in government is the boss system and the political machine. Historically, both the nineteenth century movement against the "long ballot" and the twentieth century charter reform movement aimed to strengthen the power of governors and mayors.

When leadership emerges as the prime value in community life, centralization and growth become the major programmatic goals of planning. The major evaluative question is: Does it work? But the capacity to rule and lead does not ensure the capacity to plan and implement. Leaders searching for ideas, concerned and constrained to rule with economy and efficiency, eventually turn to the repository of another set of values—the experts—for assistance.

Expertise is a value that makes rationality the supreme criterion for decision-making. Theoretically, experts choose among programmatic alternatives on the basis of merit rather than politics. Expertise is an antidote to corruption and waste in government. Historically, expertise in government, whether in the form of civil service, the merit system, or the city manager, often appears on the scene to undo or restrain the ravages of leadership. Because he is presumably insulated from the vagaries of politics, the expert is free to bring knowledge and skill to bear on the problem-solving process, enabling leaders to make the most sensible decisions for the community.

As the expert's role gains primacy, the major concern in the planning enterprise moves to the touchstone of professionalism —technique. Refinement of professional skill, experimentation, coordination, and the attainment of improved methods of executive intervention become the major planning interests. Evaluative concerns deriving from this perspective focus on information about how and why different programs operate.

However, experts often succumb to their own ambitions. They may be inclined to preserve the status quo and to protect their privileged positions, whether as *eminences grises* to the ruling coalition, as the vanguard of an emergent technocracy, or entrenched administrators of planning "empires." In time, experts may suffer from "hardening of the categories" and become a major obstacle to innovation and change. The synthesis then transforms to a new thesis in the dialectic process. Technocracy may be challenged and community renewal brought about by new efforts to mobilize the dissatisfied public, to organize the disadvantaged and from their ranks to draw fresh leadership. Sooner or later, these leaders will call upon the experts for advice— and the cycle recurs.

The Cycle of Values

The political scientist Robert Michels saw this dialectic in the great European socialist political parties earlier in this century. His "Iron Law of Oligarchy" was based on the doctrine that history is a record of a continuous series of struggles over values, all of which culminate in the creation of new oligarchies that eventually fuse with the old, "representing an uninterrupted series of oppositions . . . attaining one after another to power and passing from the sphere of envy to the sphere of avarice."[21] His insights into this process are timely.

The democratic currents of history resemble successive waves. They break ever on

---

[21]Robert Michels, *Political Parties* (New York: Dover Publications, Inc., 1915), p. 319.

the same shoal. They are ever renewed. This enduring spectacle is simultaneously encouraging and depressing ... Now new accusers arise to denounce the traitors; after an era of glorious combats and inglorious power, they end by fusing with the old dominant class; whereupon once more they are in their turn attacked by fresh opponents who appeal to the name of democracy. It is probable that this cruel game will continue without end.[22]

Contemporary experience suggests the ways in which the dialectic of social planning operates. In the years following World War II, the technician emerged as the central figure in community welfare planning. The notion of a community "master plan" developed by professionals achieved broad support. In the 1950s dissatisfaction grew with this process of planning and its effects. Citizen participation, as a check on the professional planners, was a significant ingredient of the Seven-Point Workable Program for urban renewal contained in the Housing Act of 1954. Initially, this participation involved the appointment of a city-wide advisory committee, generally composed of civic leaders, to work with planners; representation of the poor, who were usually most affected by renewal activities, was neither mandatory nor commonplace. As experience with resident opposition to renewal increased, agencies began to give greater consideration to the involvement of neighborhood residents, although as various studies and observations indicate citizen participation in urban renewal was modest.[23]

Other efforts in the late 1950s and early 1960s gave citizens an increasingly active role. These included the Grey Area Projects, the planning programs spawned by the President's Committee on Juvenile Delinquency, and the War on Poverty. All gave increasing emphasis to the value of participation vis-à-vis leadership and expertise. (It is interesting to note that at their inception, *all* community planning programs seem to invoke all three values, though this kind of *tout ensemble* never comes off very well. One of the values is sooner or later elevated above the rest.) By the mid-1960s the value of participation reigned; the expertise of professionals was rejected or disrated in favor of the direct visceral experiences of neighborhood residents who were called upon to "tell it like it really is."[24] Meanwhile, leadership fretted, floundered, and failed to achieve consensus.

AN EXAMPLE: PLANNED VARIATIONS AS A BLUEPRINT FOR LEADERSHIP

The Model Cities Program followed the direction set by the earlier Economic Opportunity Act and other federal legislation in calling for a rapprochement among the three values. As suggested by the Program Guide, elected officials were to exercise leadership, area residents were to have a meaningful role, and the planning agency was to exercise powers and authority in the planning process. In the early stages of this program, community participation was emphasized as the guiding value. Federal, regional, and local interests and energies were

---

[22]*Ibid.,* p. 408.

[23]Peter Rossi and Robert Dentler, *The Politics of Urban Renewal* (New York: Free Press, 1961); James Q. Wilson, " Planning and Politics: Citizen Participation in Urban Renewal," in *Urban Renewal: People, Politics and Planning,* eds. Jewel Bellush *et al.* (New York: Anchor Books, 1967); and Scott Greer, *Urban Renewal and American Cities* (Indianapolis: Bobbs-Merrill, 1965).

[24]Neil Gilbert and Joseph Eaton, "Research Report: Who Speaks for the Poor?" *Journal of the American Institute of Planners,* Vol. 36 (November 1970), 411–16.

almost completely occupied with questions about resident organizations, proportions of resident representatives, and the allocation of funds to facilitate participation. That technicism and expertise received short shrift is evident in early reports on the program.[25] However, by mid-1970 interest in participation had begun to subside on all levels. As the federal investments in efforts to achieve widespread citizen participation were retrenched, a new era opened in which concerns for building the capacities of local executive leadership became prominent.

From the early 1970s the federal government drifted from fostering community participation toward supporting and building local political leadership. The drift, though most evident in policies developed in Washington, D.C., reflected some of the changing currents in all of American society. We shall explore this change by examining Planned Variations, a HUD program designed to enhance the authority of local executive leadership.

Planned Variations is one program among several that reflects a policy emphasis on strengthening local competence which began to develop in the late 1960s and early 1970s. Others include the Office of Management and Budget's "A-95" project notification and review system, the Office of Economic Opportunity's policy governing local checkpoint procedures, and the Department of Health, Education and Welfare's arrangement for certification sign-off by CDA directors on grants for programs impacting on Model Cities neighborhoods. Each of these mechanisms allow local political leaders varying degrees of influence on independent agency applications

for federal grants.[26] On a broader scale these mechanisms may be viewed as pilot efforts in the national administration's strategy to enhance local leadership and autonomy through revenue sharing.[27]

In 1973, the "drift" became a tiderace. The abandonment of community action programs like OEO and Model Cities was announced as official federal policy with the publication of the 1974 federal Budget.[28]

Announced in 1970, Planned Variations was a pilot effort to shift the locus of allocative decision-making within the federal urban grant system. Combined into one package, the Variations offered a preview of the Nixon administration's "new federalism" by breaking ground for revenue sharing via what approaches a system of block grants to Model Cities Programs at the local level. Later on in 1973, revenue sharing was touted as the Nixon administration's method for communities to fill the gaps left by the 1974 budget cuts.[29]

In early statements on the program the HUD secretary, George Romney, announced that the major Variations would (1) eliminate all but statutorily defined federal reviews concerning the use of supplemental and categorical funds in cities; (2)

---

[25]Marshall Kaplan, Gans, and Kahn, *The Model Cities Program,* 1970; Warren, " 'Model Cities' First Round."

[26]A cogent analysis of these and other policies that have implications for the exertion of local leadership may be found in a study by Marshall Kaplan, *et al., Local Government Leadership in Federal Assistance Programs: Some Experience with Existing Planning and Coordination Mechanisms* (San Francisco: Marshall Kaplan, Gans and Kahn, 1971); and Melvin Mogulof, "Regional Planning, Clearance and Evaluation: A Look at the A-95 Process," *Journal of the American Institute of Planners,* Vol. 37, No. 6 (November 1971), 418–22.

[27]Marshall Kaplan, *et al., Local Government Leadership.*

[28]"Savings Expected to Be Made through Reductions and Terminations in Federal Programs in 3 Fiscal Years," *New York Times,* January 30, 1973, p. 20.

[29]"Excerpts from President Nixon's Budget Message as Presented to Congress," *New York Times,* January 30, 1973, p. 21.

permit development of Model Cities plans and programs for entire cities rather than just specific neighborhoods; and (3) grant local chief executives the right to review, comment, and sign-off on all federal agency categorical programs prior to use in their cities.[30]

Fifteen months later, the program's objectives had expanded from three to eight, as follows:

Planned Variation Program Objectives

1. Develop comprehensive plans for the entire city, not just the original and new Model Neighborhood Areas (MNAs), by using administrative, planning, and evaluation funds on a citywide basis.
2. Coordinate the planning of federal programs through the local chief executive by utilizing the Chief Executive Review and Comment (CERC) procedure on major federal program activities.
3. Build the capacity of the local chief executive to budget resources and determine priority needs on a city-wide basis by using administrative, planning, and evaluation funds on a city-wide basis.
4. Extend the impact of the Planned Variations funds to New Target Areas.
5. Increase local control of federal programs by reducing federal reviews and requirements and encouraging cities to request waivers.
6. Improve procedure for applying state resources and technical expertise to local needs by establishing State-Local Task Forces.
7. Develop a comprehensive and coordinated federal response to local needs by encouraging use of Regional Councils for coordinating technical assistance and project funding.
8. Coordinate the delivery of HUD categorical programs to the locality in accordance with local priorities by negotiating

an Annual Arrangement with each Planned Variation city.[31]

Of these eight objectives, the two principal ones are clearly Chief Executive Review and Comment (CERC) and city-wide planning. The intention of eliminating all federal review had dwindled to a more or less hortatory statement that reviews would be limited. In any case, the limited review concept applied to all Planned Variation cities; there were no cities for which *all* federal review of plans and projects had been eliminated, even experimentally.

The major import of the Variations is to shift the locus of allocative decision-making along two dimensions of the federal grant system, as indicated in Figure 20.1. On the horizontal plane the changes designated are *within* the levels and on the vertical plane they are *between* levels.

Limited federal review reduced the number of agency criteria used to assess grant applications and reduced the number of reviews to which an application is subject. Typically, an application is reviewed six to ten times as it moves through local, regional, and federal layers of agency and interagency review committees. This cumbersome, extended system involves extensive coordination. Clearly, since coordination had proven less effective than was hoped, the federal government was ready to experiment with new forms of centralized decision making in CERC and city-wide planning.

If the multiplicity of federal reviews was to be replaced by the one overall decision of whether to fund or not to fund ("go—no go," in bureaucratic parlance), then allocative decision-making would be contracted

---

[30]Department of Housing and Urban Development, *HUD News,* #70——723, "Statement by Secretary George Romney, September 30" (Washington, D.C.: Government Printing Office, 1970).

[31]Department of Housing and Urban Development, Office of Community Development, *Planned Variations Evaluation Report* (Washington, D.C.: Government Printing Office, 1971).

FEDERAL LEVEL   Contraction
                                      |
                          (delegation of authority)
                                      ↓
CITY LEVEL   Centralization
                                      ↑
                          (delegation of authority)
                                      |
NEIGHBORHOOD LEVEL   Dispersal

FIGURE 20.1
Planned Variations Impact on Allocative Decision Making

at the federal level with more discretion and authority over detailed reviews channeled down toward the local level. But in the meanwhile, the thrust of Planned Variations was upon strengthening the mayor.

On the city level, increased centralization is brought about by the mayor's sign-off Variation which requires the chief executive's review of local applications for federal assistance. The mayor could make written comments on each application prior to its submission. Before this shift the procedure was such that numerous local private and public organizations received federal grants over which local chief executives had no control and little influence.

There are now over 500 federal categorical grant programs.[32] Most large city mayors find it a formidable task just to keep abreast of the amounts, locations, and purposes of these grants. As the mayor's sign-off becomes a requirement for an increasing number of federal grants, the mayor's office is transformed into a clearinghouse for local applications for federal funds. While the mayor's review and comment do not constitute a formal veto power, it does have that effect in practice. The intent of this procedure is both to give the mayor an opportunity to influence and regulate the flow of funds into his city and to have the grantee agency take the mayor's priorities into account when drawing its application. With skillful operation, a mayor can employ this mechanism to adjust the flow of federal funds to coincide with local needs.

Aside from substantially increasing the administrative workload of the mayor's office, the implementation of this Variation requires special staff competence to review and assess projects within a broad planning framework, to create a modus operandi for planning between the mayor's office and local agencies (a delicate matter, as agency autonomy is compromised under these new arrangements), and to initiate project applications when a need exists that is not currently being met. Most cities now lack the staff capacity to effectively use the mayor's sign-off as a central planning mechanism. Larger, more competent staffs are likely to be established in the mayors' offices to vitalize the nascent central planning functions inherent in mayoral sign-off.

As suggested earlier, the exercise of leadership tends to generate a demand for sup-

[32]See William Lilley, "Urban Report: Both Parties Ready to Scrap Grant Programs in Favor of 'City Strategy' Package of Aid," *National Journal,* Vol. 3, No. 6 (July 1971), 1391–97; and Advisory Commission on Intergovernmental Relations, *Special Revenue Sharing: An Analysis of the Administration's Joint Consolidation Proposals* (Washington, D.C.: Government Printing Office, December 1971), pp. 19–20.

portive expertise. A model that is put forth to fulfill this demand is the kind of structure that evolved in Butte, Montana, one of the twenty Model Cities participants selected to take part in the Planned Variations. With HUD's full approval, the Butte City Demonstration Agency, renamed "Office of Programming and Management," serves a staff function in the mayor's office.

This evolution is not unique to the urban scene. Over the last decade cities have used urban renewal programs not only to secure federal funds for themselves but also to create, outside the city's regular departmental structure, a cadre of professional talent that could be employed in various capacities. "The best local renewal authorities," Wilson observes, "became generalized sources of innovation and policy staffing and their directors became in effect deputy mayor (and sometimes more than that)."[33] The move, as in Butte, to incorporate these functions under the formal jurisdiction of the mayor's office has the effect of centralizing planning under the chief executive's leadership.

On the neighborhood level, the impact of Planned Variations is to experiment with the relegation of allocative decision-making to city hall. This relegation is inherent in the "City-Wide Variation" which encourages Model Cities plans and programs to be developed on a city-wide basis instead of for a subarea (i.e., Model Neighborhood Area) as under the original Model Cities requirements. This Variation also increases the number and variety of groups who may claim a stake and seek a voice in the program's outcome. As the program opens to the whole city, there are more opportunities for planning on functional bases that transcend neighborhood boundaries. One would expect the emergence of new interest

groups and a dispersal of resident influence on Model Cities Program development.

This dispersal of influence is likely to result in decreased resident cohesion and increased competition among would-be beneficiaries. Thus the overall impact of Planned Variations is to centralize authority in city hall. As indicated above, this is accomplished by limiting discretionary review at the federal level and by dispersing citizen inputs at the neighborhood level. While allocative decision-making authority is siphoned off at these two levels, the mayor is provided with power in the form of the "mayor's sign-off" variation to encourage the exercise of his authority.

There are, of course, certain obstacles to the realization of these objectives. As Banfield points out, organized beneficiaries of the categorical grant system are prone to be unenthusiastic about any changes that deprive them of their special status, such as dissolving their identities in a mass of supplicants through grant consolidation.[34] Congressmen, too, have a special affinity for categorical grants that can be tailored to suit particular groups of constituents. Moreover, the rhetoric of local control notwithstanding, it is unclear exactly how anxious mayors are to assume authority and responsibilities that may prove politically awkward when the foil of federal control is removed.

However, the blueprints of Planned Variations, executed even on a moderate scale (and the message of the 1974 federal budget suggests that the scale is more likely to be quite grand) will distinguish urban planning in the seventies from urban planning in the sixties in at least two ways. First, mayors will be held increasingly accountable by their constituencies for plans and programs

---

[33]James Q. Wilson, "The Mayors vs. the Cities," *Public Interest,* Vol. 23, No. 3 (Summer 1969), 30.

[34]Edward Banfield, "Revenue Sharing in Theory and Practice," *Public Interest,* Vol. 23, No. 2 (Spring 1971), 33–45.

in their cities. Mayors often claim that they cannot keep track of all federally assisted programs coming into their cities, or that they have no authority over the agencies receiving federal funds, or that if they do have authority over the local agencies, they must comply with federally designed program guidelines. In each case, accountability that is impaired by the exigencies of the categorical grant system would be enlarged under Planned Variations.

Second, citizen participation characterized by grass-roots organizations, created in Community Action and Model Cities neighborhoods to assist in planning and implementing these programs, will be emphasized less in federal requirements for grant assistance. As programs are designed for a broader urban constituency, the influence of neighborhood groups will diminish. Instead, the focus of political activity on the neighborhood level is likely to shift from elected neighborhood councils to the formal city-wide political apparatus—perhaps injecting a new vitality into urban politics.

SOCIAL WELFARE PLANNING: BY DRIFT OR DESIGN

Where does the policy planner fit into all this? Does he conveniently gravitate towards executive leadership for the authority to plan when leadership is in the saddle, and "back to the people" when the impulse for participation arises? Is there any meaning for professional planners in what we describe as the dialectical relationship among the values of participation, leadership, and expertise beyond, perhaps, the recognition that planning is an awfully complex business?

In response to the last question, Rein suggests that conflicting values such as participation, leadership, and expertise invest the planning enterprise with insoluble dilemmas.[35] From the dialectical perspective, however, the competition among participation, leadership, and expertise is not a dilemma but a dynamic, necessary, and continuously unfolding process that sustains the pulse of democracy in the planning endeavor. Policy planners should encourage rather than avoid the dialectical relationship among these values, so that no single value becomes the professional's polestar. This implies that the planner regard the contradictions among these values as a healthy stimulant to his profession and be prepared to keep each value salient as emphases in the community change.

To conclude, we should like to emphasize our own view about the values described in this discussion. Shifts in the values that guide social planning bear careful scrutiny. In the short run, a change from participation to leadership will be welcomed by many members of the planning profession who experienced some of the turbulence and frustration of citizen participation in the Community Action and Model Cities Programs. They may be inclined to embrace the value of leadership warmly. And as leadership perpetually looks to expertise, planners in general may expect to be well received.

But planners should be mindful that as local executives extend their spheres of authority and the numbers of planners on their staffs increase, the executive's ability to control his planners is reduced, laying the ground for technocracy. Instead of being an advocacy planner for the poor as he was in the sixties, the planner-technocrat of the seventies could become exceedingly remote from the would-be beneficiaries of his enterprise. Only by continuing to work with

---

[35]Rein, "Social Planning."

representatives of different groups, including consumer publics, can this estrangement be avoided.

A central challenge to social planners at any time is to avoid drifting on the currents of change towards whatever value happens to be in favor; rather they must chart an independent course of action—one designed to facilitate the dialectical process and enliven the clash of values that seems fundamental both to democracy and to social welfare.

CHAPTER VI

Locality
Development

The crux of locality development is citizens from all walks of life learning new skills and engaging in a cooperative self-help process to achieve a wide variety of community improvements. It implies a condition of limited resources and an effort to increase and expand such resources for mutual benefit. As Arthur Dunham puts it, this approach involves—

> ... helping people to deal more effectively with their problems and objectives, by helping them develop, strengthen and maintain qualities of participation, self-direction and cooperation. . . .[1]

Moreover, this strategic orientation is optimistic and positive about people's ability to work with each other around common concerns.

What range of problems might be successfully attacked using a community development approach? What are the major weaknesses of the orientation? S. K. Khinduka addresses himself to these and other questions central to utilizing this interventive style, including the perspective of the Third World. The interweaving of interpersonal processes and program objectives is given special attention.

The second piece in this chapter articulates the dominant value position of locality development. There is a decided philosophical point of view that is often alluded to in a rather fragmentary way in the literature. The special contribution of the article by William and Loureide Biddle is that it offers a coherent, philosophical perspective on locality development. Such concepts as cooperation, self-help, reconciliation, and communication are organized in a framework of operational assumptions, hypotheses, and generalizations drawn from field experience.

---

[1]Arthur Dunham, *The New Community Organization* (New York: Thomas Crowell, 1970), p.4.

Health education is a major area in which the locality development approach has been utilized. The work of Virginia Wang and her colleagues in a one-year demonstration project in Maryland is reported in the third article. The program emphasized learning experiences that aided health services consumers—individually and as part of groups—to make more informed decisions about health-related matters. How consumers, agency providers, and community leaders were mobilized to cooperate in the effort is carefully described.

Perhaps no single aspect of locality development is more vital than participation. Without significant participation of the population in question, the approach becomes an empty shell of rhetoric and value preferences. And as most practitioners know from personal experience, getting people to participate on their own behalf is no easy task. The article by Jack Rothman, John Erlich, and Joseph Teresa lays out a tactical guideline for workers to follow in trying to foster participation, with illustrations from a wide variety of situations in which it was used.

We conclude with an article on locality development in a special context, neighborhood work for the prevention and control of delinquency. Irving Spergel calls locality development the "social-stability approach." He discusses several attributes of the approach and gives illustrations from practice that vividly depict these characteristics as they emerge in action. The attributes receiving attention include: establishing relationships, communication, providing support, developing group and individual competence, developing leadership, and facilitating intervention by indigenous leadership. All of these features of the "social-stability approach" are consistent with the concept of locality development articulated in this book.

In the crosscurrents of the turbulent sixties, social change approaches with modest objectives and consensus-based means were attacked and belittled. However, unlike some of the more radical departures supported by its critics, locality development has stood the test of time. Accepted for what it is—a modest means of social reform—locality development can make an important contribution to improving community life.

21.

S. K. Khinduka

COMMUNITY DEVELOPMENT: POTENTIALS AND LIMITATIONS

Despite numerous definitions by conferences, international bodies, and writers, the concept of community development remains vague. This vagueness has evoked two entirely different reactions. Some social scientists tend to dismiss community development as a totally "knowledge-free" area, remarkable for "the murky banalities, half-truths and sententious nonsense that abound" in its literature.[1] Other writers maintain that community development is the only key to the modernization of traditional societies.[2]

Community development includes a composite process and program objectives. As a process, it aims to educate and motivate people for self-help; to develop responsible local leadership; to inculcate among the members of rural communities a sense of citizenship and among the residents of urban areas a spirit of civic consciousness; to introduce and strengthen democracy at the grass-roots level through the creation and/or revitalization of institutions designed to serve as instruments of local participation; to initiate a self-generative, self-sustaining, and enduring process of growth; to enable people to establish and maintain cooperative and harmonious relationships; and to bring about gradual and self-chosen changes in the community's life with a minimum of stress and disruption.

The multipurpose, intersectoral character of its program is the other major feature of community development. In rural areas, agriculture, irrigation, rural industries, education, health, housing, social welfare, youth and women's programs, employment, cooperatives, and training of village leaders constitute important components of community development. In the urban areas, community development covers a wide array of similar activities.

It is inevitable that such a gigantic international movement, which has received official sanction and support from governments in Asia, Africa, and Latin America and which is viewed by many as a cure for the riot-torn cities of this country, should encounter difficulties in achieving its goals. Problems of manpower, training and organization have proved formidable barriers to the realization of its objectives in some nations. Inadequate staff, indifference in national bureaucracies, and lack of coordination and communication among specialists at the local level have often combined to create bottlenecks in the implementation of programs. Some governments have paid lip service to community development, but have not earmarked adequate funds for the projects. In a number of instances, community development programs have created adverse side effects which were neither intended nor antici-

Source: Reprinted from S. K. Khinduka, "Community Development: Potentials and Limitations," in *Social Work Practice, 1969,* © National Conference on Social Welfare, New York: Columbia University Press, 1969, by permission of the publisher and the author.

[1]David Brokensha, "Comments," *Human Organization,* XXVII, No. 1 (1968), 78. See also Charles J. Erasmus, "Community Development and the *Encogido Syndrome," ibid.,* pp. 65–74.

[2]See, for example, B. Mukerjee, *Community Development in India* (Calcutta: Orient Longmans, Ltd., 1961), p. vii.

pated. Moreover, accentuation of inter-group tensions instead of a strengthened community solidarity and the rise of an op-portunistic type of party politics instead of a widespread consciousness of people's rights and responsibilities have not been al-together absent. In some situations, the equalitarian rhetoric of community devel-opment has infuriated the rich, while the unequal distribution of its benefits has frus-trated the poor.

However serious these may be, neither the flaws in implementation nor the possi-bility of undesirable consequences reflects the real weakness of community devel-opment. With a better trained cadre of workers, a stronger commitment by governments, and a more efficient pooling of international experience, many of these deficiencies can be substantially rectified. What is more difficult—and more impor-tant—to change, is the basic ideology of community development; for, more than anything else, the ideology of community development has definite assumptions and biases in favor of citizen involvement, con-sensus, localism, and gradualism. In its ex-treme form, this ideology prefers non-material goals to tangible ones. It holds that change in the individual's values, moti-vation, attitudes, and aspirations is a neces-sary precondition for any worthwhile alteration in the society. Although some theorists recognize the significance of ac-complishing physical tasks,[3] the commu-nity development approach to social change, by and large, is still dominated by a process orientation which evaluates the actual outcome of a community project pri-marily in terms of what happens in the minds of men rather than in terms of its impact on the social structure.

It is the thesis of this paper that commu-nity development is a rather soft strategy for *social change.* As a method of *social service,* however, its contribution can be very significant.

Community development has a latent propensity for delaying structural changes in the basic institutions of a society. No-where does this become clearer than in the familiar strain for precedence between its process and task-accomplishment goals.[4] In such a conflict, the community developer typically upholds the process aspect, which stresses citizen involvement, consensus, lo-calism, and change in the attitudes and val-ues of people as a necessary condition for effecting institutional changes.

There is no doubt a great deal to com-mend in community development's concern with human values and aspirations. As an antidote to some experts' penchant for ex-plaining all industrial backwardness in purely economic terms, and to the equally unwise preoccupation of some governments with narrow models of economic growth, community development's wholesome at-tempt to underline the human factor and to plead for balanced social and economic progress has indeed had a salutary effect. No wonder that recent approaches to na-tional development have turned away from exclusively economic models.[5] An increas-ing number of economists now appreciate the significance of noneconomic variables in economic development. "Economic devel-opment," two economists observe, "is much too serious a topic to be left to econo-mists."[6]

---

[3]Arthur Dunham, "Community Development—Whither Bound?" *Social Work Practice, 1968* (New York: Columbia University Press, 1968), pp. 48–61.

[4]Melvin M. Tumin, "Some Social Requirements for Effective Community Development," *Community Development Review,* No. 11 (1958), pp. 3–4.

[5]See, for example, Gunnar Myrdal, *An Asian Drama: An Inquiry into the Poverty of Nations* (New York: Twentieth Century Fund, 1968).

[6]G. M. Meier and R. E. Baldwin, *Economic Development* (New York: John Wiley & Sons, Inc., 1957), p. 119.

While community development and social welfare workers have been among the first to recognize the lopsidedness of many prevailing models of economic growth, they have made the reverse error of overstressing the culturally and psychologically propitious preconditions for development. Ever since Max Weber suggested a positive correlation between a people's value system and their economic development,[7] it has become commonplace in many circles to attribute the poverty of a people to their otherworldliness, fatalism, lack of thrift, industry, and entrepreneurial aptitude, and, more recently, to their low achievement motivation. Weber's thesis is now being used not only as counterpoint to the Marxian theory of economic production and social classes, but also as spurious anthropology that overlooks internal and external exploitative economic relationships and explains economic backwardness as if its causative factors were located entirely within the individuals who suffer from it. In embracing this theory, community development, like much of professional social work, leaves itself vulnerable on scientific as well as on strategic grounds.

Attitudinal and value modifications do not necessarily precede behavioral or structural changes; they may often follow them. It is not necessary, for example, to wipe out prejudice (an attitude) in order to eradicate segregation (a behavioral practice). Modifications in individual and group behavior can be brought about by a change in the social situation in which people function.[8]

Festinger's theory of cognitive dissonance holds that, under certain conditions, behavior can produce cognitive and attitudinal realignments in the person. When a person commits an act which is contrary to his beliefs, he is in a state of dissonance, which is unpleasant to him. Reduction of this dissonance is achieved mainly by changing his beliefs, since the "discrepant behavior" has already taken place and cannot be undone.[9] Epstein's study of two Indian villages showed that it was economic development that led to behavioral changes, not vice versa. She reports:

> Whenever there was ... economic change we also found corresponding changes in political and ritual roles and relations as well as in the principles of social organization. Thus we have established a positive correlation between economic, political, ritual, and organizational change, with economic change being the determining variable.[10]

It is an oversimplification to attribute all or most of the difficulties in development to people's mental outlook. It will not do to invoke values to explain economic underdevelopment without referring back to the social structure and economic processes which permit some values to persist and others to change.

One might add that even if modification of attitudes and values is considered a necessary precondition for structural social change, community development has chosen an incomplete, if not an inappropriate, target group. Although it may be important to change the attitudes of the victims of social and economic injustice, it may be more useful to bring about a shift in the attitudes and values of those sections of the population who are its principal beneficiaries. That is why concentration of commu-

---

[7]Max Weber, *The Protestant Ethic and the Spirit of Capitalism,* H. Talcott Parsons (London: George Allen & Unwin, Ltd., 1930).

[8]Kenneth B. Clark, "Some Implications for a Theory of Social Change," *Journal of Social Issues,* IX, No. 4 (1953), 72.

[9]Leon Festinger, *A Theory of Cognitive Dissonance* (Evanston, Ill.: Row, Peterson & Co., 1957). See also Albert O. Hirschman, "Obstacles to Development: a Classification and a Quasi-vanishing Act," *Economic Development and Cultural Change,* XIII (1965), 391.

[10]T. Scarlett Epstein, *Economic Development and Social Change in South India* (Calcutta: Oxford University Press, 1962), p. 334.

nity development programs among blacks, Puerto Ricans, Mexicans, and Indians will not be enough unless they are accompanied by a similar educational effort to resocialize the privileged, affluent, and suburban segments of the society.

Once it is recognized that values, beliefs, and aspirations are not in every circumstance the optimum locus of professional intervention for social change, the strategic weakness of the community development approach becomes clear. The strategy of concentrating on a group's outmoded attitudes which are assumed to constitute the principal obstacle to its growth does not recognize that there may be legitimate reasons for people not to take the initiative or the necessary risks in the adoption of new practices. Where benefits are apt to be absorbed by middlemen or moneylenders, for example, it would be unrealistic to expect the villagers to venture the investments or muster the enthusiasm for a new project.[11]

Since a change in value systems of tradition-haunted societies is a matter of generations, such an emphasis on changing the value system may have a pessimistic and despairing implication for the rapid socioeconomic development of the "third world." The assumption that a man's activities cannot be changed without altering his values may result in neglect of the appropriate targets of intervention. A psychologist observes:

> An effective strategy for inducing social change would consist of bringing about change in the societal system—and its reinforcing mechanisms—and the development of the appropriate patterns of motivation—and expectancy—through suitable programmes. For any social change, the pri-

mary condition is a change in the societal system without which appropriate changes cannot be introduced or, if introduced, cannot be sustained.[12]

If the planners and policy-makers wait for attitudes to change and do not intervene at the structural level with social policy and legislation, then achievement of economic development in the third world and of social justice in the "first world" is likely to take a hopelessly long time.

Another dimension of the inadequacy of community development as a strategy for large-scale social change is concerned with the time and rate of change. In the belief that far-reaching social change produces tensions and maladjustments—which are to be avoided at all cost—community development has put great emphasis on moving at a slow pace. Time, it is suggested, should not be allowed to become a major factor in the process of community growth.[13] Here, again, community development has aligned itself with only one school of thought in the social sciences. Heilbroner, however, states that the world political situation enjoins the speediest possible time table for development.[14] Under some circumstances, notes Margaret Mead, the least dislocating change is one which is introduced rapidly.[15] A social scientist from the third world, Guillermo Bonfil Batalla, of Mexico, makes another point clear:

> Sometimes it looks as if those who work along the road of slow evolution intend to achieve only minimal changes, so that the situation continues to be substantially the

[11]United Nations, Department of Economic and Social Affairs, *Local Participation in Development Planning: A Preliminary Study of the Relationship of Community Development to National Planning* (New York: United Nations, 1967), p. 27.

[12]Udai Pareek, "Motivational Patterns and Planned Social Change," *International Social Science Journal,* XX (1968), 465–66.

[13]Murray G. Ross, *Community Organization: Theory and Practice* (New York: Harper & Brothers, 1955), p. 22.

[14]Robert L. Heilbroner, "Counterrevolutionary America," *Commentary,* XLIII, No. 4 (1967), 33.

[15]Margaret Mead, *New Lives for Old* (New York: William Morrow & Co., 1956), pp. 445–47.

same; this is, in other words, *to change what is necessary so that things remain the same.* Those who act according to such a point of view may honestly believe that their work is useful and transforming; however, they have in fact aligned themselves with the conservative elements who oppose the structural transformations that cannot be postponed in our (Latin American) countries.[16]

Community development's insistence on consensus as the only satisfactory basis for major community decisions provides another example of its limitations. It is, of course, more pleasant to work in an atmosphere of consensus than in one of contest, controversy, or conflict. However, it is easier to obtain near-unanimity on superficial and innocuous matters; issues of substance, which affect the diverse subgroups of the community in different ways, often generate controversy as well as a clash of interests.

Major structural reforms have rarely been instituted with the enthusiastic consent of those who are most likely to lose as a result of those reforms. A certain modicum of legal coercion is a necessary component of any effective strategy of social change. Community development has been rather slow to appreciate this elementary principle. This may in part account for the more or less peripheral role that it has played in movements for rural land reform in most Asian nations.

Its fondness for consensus, however, is only an extension of community development's faith in the desirability and efficacy of citizen involvement. Here, it seems, an essentially instrumental value has been converted into an ultimate value. Citizen participation takes various forms; each form,

in turn, rests upon certain assumptions and conditions peculiar to itself. It cannot be assumed that all types of citizen participation are appropriate for all occasions or for all organizations.[17] Excellent participation is not sufficient to introduce major changes into a community,[18] nor is voluntary participation always a prerequisite for rapid, extensive cultural change.[19] The principle of citizen participation has been advanced on ethical grounds: people are intrinsically good; given an opportunity, they will do the "right thing." As a technique, it is not backed up by unequivocal evidence that it is indeed as crucial a mechanism for the success of a community development project as has been so frequently suggested.[20]

A noteworthy feature of community development is that it seeks to promote an identification with, and a loyalty to, the local community. The locality is the key unit around which people are to be mobilized for community development projects, and a locality-centered strategy for social change has to face certain problems.

In the first place, the local community no longer exercises decisive control over the lives of an increasingly mobile population. Due largely to the population explosion, implosion, and diversification, and the accelerated tempo of social and technological change—factors which constitute the

---

[16]Quoted in Gerald D. Berreman, "The Peace Corps: a Dream Betrayed," *The Nation,* February 26, 1968, p. 266.

[17]Edmund M. Burke, "Citizen Participation Strategies," *Journal of the American Institute of Planners,* XXXIV (1968), 293.

[18]See Peter H. Rossi, "Theory, Research and Practice in Community Organization," in Charles R. Adrian *et al.,* eds., *Social Science and Community Action* (East Lansing, Mich.: Michigan State University, 1960), pp. 9–24.

[19]Alex Weingrod, *Reluctant Pioneers: Village Development in Israel* (Ithaca, N.Y.: Cornell University Press, 1966), pp. 197–203.

[20]Gilbert Kushner, "Indians in Israel: Guided Change in a New-Immigrant Village," *Human Organization,* XXVII (1968), 359–60.

"morphological revolution"[21]—the local community does not offer any realistic possibilities of a genuine *Gemeinschaft* environment dictated by natural will and characterized by intimate, spontaneous, inclusive, and enduring personal relationships. Even if the morphological revolution could be halted, it would require all the power and resolution of a sovereign world organization; local communities are too feeble to effect such a reversal.

Local institutions can no longer remain unaffected by the extra-community system. Local destinies, for the most part, cannot be decided locally. Nor can the major problems of a locality—poverty, unemployment, housing, and discrimination—be solved merely or mainly by mobilizing local efforts.

History is replete with examples showing that some of the most progressive policies have emanated from the legislative, executive, and judicial branches of a national government. Untouchability would never have been proscribed in India if each local community had been allowed to fashion its own rules. Nor would much progress be made in the United States in establishing racial equality if the decision-making power were vested entirely in the local political institutions. Paradoxically, an indiscriminate application of the seemingly sound principle of local self-determination is at times incompatible with the tenets on which a democracy rests. The fact that it is not possible today to preserve total local autonomy is thus a cause for optimism, not for alarm.

A complicating factor is that the idea of local autonomy is used for two quite conflicting purposes. On the one hand, there are champions of local rights who oppose federal intervention so that they can perpetuate the injustice of the local political and economic arrangement. The principle of local rights is thus invoked mainly to defeat, delay, or dilute national policies designed to correct the inequities of the local system. An entirely different and socially much more justifiable demand is also couched in the idiom of local self-determination. When the blacks in the ghettos ask for control over local institutions, they are, in effect, saying that they no longer want white domination of their lives and institutions. This is a demand for self-determination, *not* local self-determination. Despite their superficial and deceptive similarity, these demands represent two diametrically divergent objectives: the latter seeks to restore respect for a group often subjected to conscious and unconscious indignities; the former is calculated to deny precisely this egalitarian end.

It has often been assumed that local development and national development always proceed hand in hand. However, community development may inadvertently reinforce economically inefficient customs and practices which prolong the hold of growth-resisting tradition. The desire for local autonomy may create distrust of the national government, its central bureaucracy, and those federal laws which curb a locality's power to manage its own affairs. Recognition of this dilemma has led some community development advocates into an even less tenable position: they will have nothing to do with national development and focus all their efforts on the local community.[22]

---

[21]Philip M. Hauser, "The Chaotic Society: Product of the Social Morphological Revolution," *American Sociological Review,* XXXIV (1969), 1–19.

[22]William W. Biddle, "Deflating the Community Developer," *Community Development Journal,* III (1968), 191–94.

The besetting limitation of community development as a strategy for social change is its psychological rather than socioeconomic approach to social problems. Community development programs aim at revolutionary change in the people's psychology without bringing about an actual revolution in their socioeconomic relations.[23] They are concerned with people's psychological capacity to make decisions, not with their economic power to do so. By encouraging them to participate in community activities, community development seeks to give them a feeling that they count and they are competent, but it stops there. Community development will do practically everything to improve the psychological lives of the poor: it will create among them a sense of self-respect and confidence, of civic pride, and identification with their locality—which may be an uninhabitable slum; it will provide recreational programs; it will even organize courses and encourage handicrafts to increase their earning capacity. But it will not usually question the economic system which permits the coexistence of poverty and plenty. And when poverty is at least as much a function of social injustice as it is of individual ineptitude, it is questionable if psychological repair of an individual can accomplish what requires a fundamental rearrangement of economic and social institutions.[24]

Some community developers are really caseworkers practicing in a community setting. They use the community development method for expediting the personality growth of the members of the community.

According to William and Loureide J. Biddle, personality growth, through responsibility for the local common good, is the focus of all community development.[25] No wonder economic improvement is dismissed as a "materialistic measure" not quite fit to become a community development goal. "If economic betterment is not an extravagant hope, it is an inappropriate one," writes William Biddle.[26] It is just this preoccupation with process and with personality that keeps community development from becoming an effective instrument for large-scale institutional change.

We do not deny the value of community development as a program of social service or its validity as a response to specific local situations. By stressing the crucial role of the human factor in national development, community development has done a great service to mankind. Its integrated and holistic concept of development is, similarly, a refreshing improvement over the narrow, sectoral approaches to national planning.

For certain types of goals and within a certain sphere, community development can be a very effective strategy. Community development is a gentleman's approach to the world. It brings people together; it helps them live and reason together. By involving them in the local decision-making process in the community, it aims to strengthen participatory democracy. If some values and attitudes are detrimental to social progress, it attempts to modify them gradually, with the least disruption and maximum voluntary cooperation, without conflict or contest, shunning bitter controversy, seeking better consensus. Perhaps it

[23]Charles Madge, "A Sociologist Looks at Social Education," *Community Development Bulletin,* XII, No. 1 (1960), 23.

[24]Simon Slavin, "Community Action and Institutional Change," in *The Social Welfare Forum, 1965* (New York: Columbia University Press, 1965), pp. 155–57.

[25]William W. Biddle and Loureide J. Biddle, *The Community Development Process: the Rediscovery of Local Initiative* (New York: Holt, Rinehart & Winston, 1965), p. 78.

[26]William W. Biddle, "Deflating the Community Developer," p. 192.

does not recognize the existence of classes; it sees only a community. Where this community has "eclipsed," it seeks to resuscitate it. Where it is disintegrated, it reorganizes it. When passions run high and factions grow intolerant of one another, it applies the healing touch of understanding and empathy. In this sense, community development is an extension of group work to the community setting; both processes are dedicated to helping people live harmoniously with fellow human beings.

Essentially, community development is a humanistic and humanizing method. The promise and potentials of such a method are almost self-evident in an age when much of what we call "progress" conceals widespread alienation, apathy, antagonism, cynicism, impersonal bureaucratization, and self-centered pursuit of purely hedonistic ends. The only problem is that community development's relative neglect of such equally humanizing principles as equality, justice, and material well-being are apt to create an uncomfortable gap between its intent and its effect.

Community development can be a potent program for mental health. Students of urban life have noted with dismay the strong feelings of anomie, dependency, and personal worthlessness among the residents of urban slums. Many of these people feel uprooted and marginal; they do not identify with, or belong to, communal organizations. Community development programs can meet the socialization needs of such people.[27] These programs can also be used, as they have been in many countries, to educate people in the art and intricacies of the democratic processes of participation and persuasion. Community projects can likewise strengthen the spirit of unity in a community. Community development activities, which create linkages between various communities, can, similarly, be helpful in improving intercommunity relations. By successfully completing even relatively inconsequential community projects, the participants may develop a sense of competence, a new faith in their ability to overcome forces of nature. This faith in their capacity may be very important for people who live in small, rural areas of traditional societies.

Community development stands for cooperation between public and private effort. Problems sometimes arise in working out arrangements between governmental and voluntary agencies. The idea of "maximum feasible participation" of the local people, for example, may at times result in "maximum feasible misunderstanding." Nevertheless, community development presents a fairly workable model for combining outside technical assistance with indigenous enterprise. As a strategy for mobilizing voluntary efforts at the local level, it is particularly applicable in those communities where people have become excessively dependent on government and community initiative has more or less atrophied.

Although community development is generally viewed as a program designed to strengthen the horizontal pattern of a community,[28] its great potential consists, especially for the third world, in its ability to help weld numerous small localities into a large national polity. Community development can make a significant contribution to the political development of the third-world nations if it puts greater emphasis on inculcating a sense of national purpose and national identification than on merely identifying with the local community. Equally valuable is its potential as a feed-

---

[27]Lloyd E. Ohlin and Martin Rein, "Social Planning for Institutional Change," in *The Social Welfare Forum, 1964* (New York: Columbia University Press, 1964), p. 87.

[28]Roland L. Warren, *The Community in America* (Chicago: Rand McNally & Co., 1963), p. 324.

back mechanism. In many countries community development programs have resulted in a better understanding of local problems by higher government officials.[29] Community development can thus provide two-way communication between the local community and the state or national government. Such channels are particularly important in newly independent countries where long periods of foreign rule have created a hiatus between the people and their governments.

Even at the local level, community development is capable of making a more significant contribution if it deemphasizes its earlier self-help orientation and boldly but discriminately incorporates in the mainstream of its ideology some of the features of recent attempts to organize the urban poor. The main objectives of the former model are: creation of community feeling, self-reliance, local leadership, and cooperation between the government and the people in the use of services.[30] The latter model extends the goals of community development to include economic and political objectives, such as the realignment of power resources in the community.[31] The community developer following this model does not fight shy of using negotiation, bargaining, advocacy, protest, noncooperation, and other forms of nonviolent social action[32] in order to help the community attain a composite of social, psychological, and political-economic objectives.

Community development is no substitute for centrally planned changes in the institutional structure of a society. However, one should not downgrade the services of the thousands of dedicated community development workers who quietly help bring about slow, incremental adaptations in the social system. Within this less ambitious sphere, community development is potentially quite a powerful social invention. Its effectiveness will perhaps increase if it modifies the locality-oriented, enabling model and recognizes the legitimacy of other nonviolent approaches to organizing people for redressing their grievances.

[29]Irwin T. Sanders, "Community Development," in David L. Sills, ed., *International Encyclopedia of the Social Sciences* (New York: Macmillan Co. & Free Press, 1968), III, 172.

[30]For an example of this model, see Marshall B. Clinard, *Slums and Community Development* (New York: Free Press, 1966).

[31]Charles Grosser, "Community Development Programs Serving the Urban Poor," *Social Work*, X, No. 3 (1965), 15–21. Reprinted this volume pp. 300–12.

[32]See George Brager, "Organizing the Unaffiliated in a Low-Income Area," *Social Work*, VIII, No. 2 (1963), 34–40; George Brager and Harry Specht, "Mobilizing the Poor for Social Action," in *The Social Welfare Forum, 1965* (New York: Columbia University Press, 1965), pp. 197–209.

22.

William W. Biddle and Loureide J. Biddle

INTENTION AND OUTCOME

Most community developers are optimistic about people. The belief in human potential for favorable growth is necessary to the process they hope to inspire. But despite their hopefulness, many may not realize the extent to which they have yielded to a popular cynicism, which is one of the sophisticated clichés of our time.

The attitudes that a worker with people has toward them contributes substantially to their development or lack of development. People respond to their perception of attitudes as these are expressed in gesture, word, and deed. If the worker acts as though he believes people are unworthy, not to be trusted, or selfishly motivated, his influence is not likely to awaken generous initiative. If he acts as though he believes people have constructive ideas (often despite evidence to the contrary) and potentialities for development beyond their present limitations, he is likely to prove more encouraging. The beliefs he holds about human beings and his intentions, stated or implied, are important to the outcome in people's lives.

What beliefs about people and consequent intentions guided the encouragers in the two case studies reported? Those operating assumptions that trusted the participants' ability to make ethically wise choices were selected.

If the basic intention of the encouragers was the observation of participant-guided growth, this expectation rested upon optimistic assumptions (general hypotheses) about the people involved. The community workers believed that the people were at least potentially capable of self-guidance. But the belief had to be genuine. It was not a mere verbal assurance that could be given or withdrawn. It had to represent a sustaining philosophy of life that gave warmth to the relationship between the encouragers and the citizens. Psychiatrists refer to this warmth of relationship as "rapport." Theologians call it "love." Whatever the term used, it is very real and very necessary in the starting and sustaining of a process of growth toward community responsibility.

Intentions (toward people) affect outcomes (in their lives).

DIFFICULTIES OF COMMUNICATION

Among the reasons why the literature of community development is so inadequate is the difficulty of communicating richly meaningful experience through the medium of words. The words can convey meaning only if the reader has passed through similar experiences. But if his point of view has been such as to limit his contacts with people to responses that support distrust, then the account will lack persuasiveness.

If the reader has known people only in situations that call for an acquiescent or even subservient behavior, he will scarcely be able to convince himself that such people can have original ideas, or initiative. If, because he has assumed them to be self-seeking, and they prove to be just that in situations where no other response is appropriate, then generous behavior will seem well-nigh impossible.

Community development processes, resting upon optimistic assumptions about people, tend to bring forth behavior that the worldly-wise doubt is possible. The reader may be called upon to understand and believe human responses that contradict his previous experiences and belief.

The reader is asked further to understand a method of influencing people that neither seeks to control them nor waits for them to ask for help; it is neither directive nor permissive. The first approach demands a pre-chosen response; the second abdicates responsibility. The method based on optimism about people's potential for development takes the initiative to awaken initiative in others. It seeks to help them discover their own abilities and good impulses, which they often have not realized they possessed.

Participants in the process of development are not urged to seek control over others, not even over those who have dominated them. They are urged rather to share ideas, points of view, and control, because even the power of figures of a community ought also to be afforded an opportunity to develop. Development for people of low status frequently means an increase in their influence. For those who already exercise control over others, it often means the humbling discovery that they are happier and more human when they share the decision making.

Further discomforts of understanding are asked of the reader—to realize that an important process has been going on, even though it was not housed in an impressive institutional headquarters, and did not make use of much technical equipment or illustrate high-sounding methods of procedure. Hopefully, a well-trained community developer has an institutional connection and knows about the equipment and techniques. But he reaches the people where they are, away from headquarters. And he holds the technical methods in abeyance while he concentrates upon the people and their perceived need for growth. He plays up the institution and introduces technical equipment and methods only when they will expedite the development process.

OPERATIONAL ASSUMPTIONS

Intention can be made explicit by listing the operational assumptions that we as community developers attempted to illustrate in the case studies.[1]

1. Each person is valuable, unique, and capable of growth toward greater social sensitivity and responsibility.
   a. Each person has underdeveloped abilities in initiative, originality, and leadership. These qualities can be cultivated and strengthened.
   b. These abilities tend to emerge and grow stronger when people work together in small groups that serve the common (community) good.
   c. There will always be conflicts between persons and factions. Properly handled, the conflicts can be used creatively.
   d. Agreement can be reached on specific next steps of improvement, without destroying philosophic or religious differences.

[1]Editor's note: The two case studies on projects referred to here and in the rest of this article are reported on in the original work from which this is taken. See William W. Biddle and Loureide J. Biddle, *The Community Development Process: The Rediscovery of Local Initiative* (New York: Holt, Rinehart and Winston, Inc., 1965).

e. Although the people may express their differences freely, when they become responsible they often choose to refrain in order to further the interest of the whole group and of their idea of community.

f. People will respond to an appeal to altruism as well as to an appeal to selfishness.

g. These generous motivations may be used to form groups that serve an inclusive welfare of all people in a community.

h. Groups are capable of growth toward self-direction when the members assume responsibility for group growth and for an inclusive local welfare.

2. Human beings and groups have both good and bad impulses.

a. Under wise encouragement they can strengthen the better in themselves and help others to do likewise.

b. When the people are free of coercive pressures, and can then examine a wide range of alternatives, they tend to choose the ethically better and the intelligently wiser course of action.

c. There is satisfaction in serving the common welfare, even as in serving self-interest.

d. A concept of the common good can grow out of group experience that serves the welfare of all in some local area. This sense of responsibility and belonging can be strengthened even for those to whom community is least meaningful.

3. Satisfaction and self-confidence gained from small accomplishments can lead to the contending with more and more difficult problems, in a process of continuing growth.

4. Within the broad role of community developer, there are several subroles to be chosen, depending upon the developer's judgment of the people's needs:

a. Encourager, friend, source of inspiration, and believer in the good in people.

b. Objective observer, analyst, truth seeker, and kindly commentator.

c. Participant in discussion, to clarify alternatives and the values these serve.

d. Participant in some actions—not all.

e. Process expert, adviser, conciliator, expediter of on-going development.

f. The prominence of the community developer is likely to be greater in the early stages, then taper off toward a termination date, but it may increase temporarily at any time.

Finally, in summary:

5. When community developers work on a friendly basis with people, in activities that serve the common good;

When they persist patiently in this;

When their actions affirm a belief in the good in people;

When the process continues, even in the face of discouragement;

Then people tend to develop themselves to become more ethically competent persons;

Then they may become involved in a process of self-guided growth that continues indefinitely.

The list contains much more than the pious slogans to which "proper" people give lip service. It represents a compilation of the operating principles that were followed by the community developers, to the best of their abilities, in the two projects.

The list is meant to include the basic assumptions of developmental good will. It stands in contrast, for example, to the assumptions that people will move into action only to serve selfish interest or only to gain power. It places faith in the unrealized potentials for good to be found in even the least promising of human beings. But it tries to avoid straying off into a pollyanna cheerfulness. The encouragement of the community development process seeks to minimize the antisocial and strengthen the prosocial impulses that people discover when they search for a common good.

HYPOTHESES

Operational assumptions can be tested in reality of the developmental process upon the local scene. They are hypotheses-in-action. Are they subject to scientific proof or disproof?

Hypotheses about human beings and the ways in which they may be expected to change may be classified in many ways. At one extreme is the generalized attitude of trust or distrust, of friendship or antagonism, and so on. Such attitudes (seldom stated in a form that can be tested) contribute importantly to human behavior.

In the middle of the scale are broad hypotheses (which may or may not be stated in words). Evidence to support or contradict such broad hypotheses can be accumulated over long periods of experience, especially if these have been reduced to a verbal statement and a record of development has been kept.

At the precise end of the scale of exactness are specific hypotheses, stated accurately and subject to proof or disproof in the limited time span of a traditional social scientific research.

The operational assumptions we have given are located from the general to the midpoint of the scale of exactness. They are stated in a form that allows an accumulation of experimental evidence to support or to contradict them. Developmental experiences will modify the generalized attitudes of the participants, and hopefully, might do something similar for a few nonparticipants who read about the experience. Toward the precise end of the scale, some of the assumptions could be restated more explicitly

as specific hypotheses for short-time testing.

Many workers with human beings, including numerous social scientists, allow generalized attitudes and broad but unstated hypotheses to govern their contacts with people—because "everybody knows" about "human nature." These unexamined generalized attitudes and conclusions, in our age of disillusion, are more likely to be uncomplimentary than complimentary. One modest virtue we can claim, in stating our operational assumptions, is that we have tried to make more explicit our underlying attitudes and governing conclusions, so that these may be subjected to some critical testing in experience.

INTENTIONS OF PARTICIPANTS

What of the intentions of the people who entered into the two projects? They did not subscribe to, were not even aware of, our operating assumptions about them or about people in general—except as these were expressed in our behavior. The participants' intentions were probably more specific, although they had to be inferred from the responses to the problems that brought the people together in cooperative action. As their experience with the process continued, it was our hope (and intention) that the developing citizens would become more aware of our operational assumptions (and similar value judgments that might govern conduct).

SELF-FULFILLING PROPHECIES

Wise sociologists draw attention to self-fulfilling prophecies. In research upon human beings, a social scientist will predict the probable response people will make. This is refined into his hypothesis for experiment. His hypothesis will reflect his conscious or unconscious attitudes toward and assumptions about the people. Then he will set up a test, but so organize the experiment as to make easy or even inevitable a response of most people that will "prove" his prediction was correct. Pollers of opinion and makers of questionnaires have concluded that they are more likely to find a majority giving the "right" answer if the question is phrased to invite that answer. In certain community studies, the citizens will be asked "Who are the members of the power elite in this city?" or "List the powerful people who make the real decisions in this town." Responders will name the people they believe fit the description, thereby "proving" that the city or town is run by a powerful minority. But the scientific "finding" was implicit in the question that was asked.

If our hypotheses about people are carried into the treatment they receive, do these operational assumptions become self-fulfilling prophecies? If they do, so much the better. If we can prove that all kinds of people tend to become more ethically intelligent and responsible when dealt with in a manner that invites such development, then that is all we ask.

RE-EXAMINATION OF OPERATIONAL ASSUMPTIONS

What preliminary conclusions can be drawn from the two case studies?
1. Each person is valuable, unique, and capable of growth toward greater social sensitivity and responsibility.

This broad statement of faith is inherent in the democratic tradition. It affirms the possibility of encouraging growth. This statement is not subject to specific test. Experience noted under the subheads that follow might or might not corroborate the faith.

1a. Each person has underdeveloped abilities in initiative, originality, and leadership. These qualities can be cultivated and strengthened.
1b. These abilities tend to emerge and grow stronger when people work together in small groups that serve the common (community) good.

In both projects, local people emerged as leaders with initiative, originality, ideas of their own. These emergent leaders acquired the ability to carry some of their ideas into action, but not without episodes of fumbling and discouragement. The abilities appeared in certain participants, but not in all, and certainly not in all residents of the areas involved. On the other hand, leadership did emerge which had not been discernible before the projects began and which certain knowledgeable onlookers had predicted would not be found. And it emerged among some whom the community developers had not considered likely candidates.

A reasonable anticipation would seem to be that leadership ability can be expected to arise in community development projects when proper steps of encouragement are taken. It did in these two populations. Furthermore, when certain emergent leaders proved inadequate or had to step aside, other leaders developed out of and were refined by the process.

1c. There will always be conflicts between persons and factions. Properly handled, the conflicts can be used creatively.
1d. Agreement can be reached on specific next steps of improvement, without destroying philosophic or religious differences.

The first part of the first statement is another broad generality which is unprovable except as one reads history to predict the future. The second part of the statement is subject to test in group behavior that is focused upon a growing concept of the common good. The creativity was found in decisions for cooperative actions that led to greater group responsibility to continue to make problem-solving decisions.

The second statement points out that conflict can be resolved with mutual respect for differences. In both projects conflicts occurred. In both instances, after some struggle, the controversies were sufficiently resolved to allow the process to go on. The choosing of such cooperative activities as the building of the flood wall and the preserving of the park gave the participants the self-confidence to seek for further cooperation. The people found that they could plan more and more complex activities, yet could respect the fact that other participants belonged to religious faiths other than their own, to other races, to other political movements, or took opposing positions in matters under debate.

1e. Although the people may express their differences freely, when they become responsible they often choose to refrain in order to further the interest of the whole group and of their idea of community.

The experimental results are not too clear on this point. Some individuals in both projects came eventually to discipline themselves to serve the larger group and the community good. Others were unable to do so. Some who found such self-discipline irksome dropped out, but there were also other reasons for their discontinuing participation. Some others who found self-discipline difficult were asked by the groups as a whole, or by responsible individuals, to give greater heed to the common purpose than to their own eloquence.

An interesting example of the learning of self-discipline is found in the urban project, in the meetings that followed the factional split. It was apparently clear to responsible participants that the overfree expression of

antagonisms had destroyed the group, at least temporarily. In re-establishing the council, those who felt the greatest responsibility held their tongues and drew attention to the challenges that lay before the reconstituted association. Since that time, those who hold first loyalty to the group's service to its neighborhood have determined the atmosphere of the meetings.

1f. People will respond to an appeal to altruism as well as an appeal to selfishness.

1g. These generous motivations may be used to form groups that serve an inclusive welfare of all people in a community.

Here the empirical evidence is much clearer. In both situations, invitations to start group activities were couched in terms of service to all the people in an area—to the folks who live around here (in the mountains), to the people of "our" neighborhood (in the city). The responses of those who were to become participants were given as proposed services to the people in yet-to-be defined areas (in both instances). One could argue that selfish impulses were still present. (They always are. Which of us is motivated by pure altruism?) But as far as the community developers and the responding future participants were concerned, the conscious motivation was service to some concept of the general good.

When a beginning generous motivation was sought among the rural, mountain people, their response opened up a new experience of initiative. These people had long been the recipients of charity, but had been largely unaware of the self-help that cooperation for a wider good would make possible. Altruistic motivation became the key to development.

1h. Groups are capable of growth toward self-direction when the members assume responsibility for group growth and for an inclusive local welfare.

This assumption draws attention to the development of the group in addition to the development of the individuals who comprise it. (The group progress is viewed as being more than the sum of the individual parts—following the thinking of Gestalt psychologists.[2]) The evidence is clear that the central groups in both projects achieved a stability and responsibility, in spite of changes in personnel and rotation of leadership. In fact, both were sufficiently successful to call for imitation on the part of nearby people who wished to form similar self-directing groups.

In totality, the subheads 1a through 1h seem to offer experience that supports faith in human potential for development, both as individuals and as community-serving small groups. One can infer from all this that each person is capable of prosocial growth and therefore is valuable and unique.

2. Human beings and groups have both good and bad impulses.

2a. Under wise encouragement they can strengthen the better in themselves and help others to do likewise.

As given, the assumption presupposes that standards of good and bad exist. It does not presuppose that the members of a group will agree with one another or with the community developer. But human beings, and the group, as they mature in responsibility, will arrive at ethical judgments about proposed actions.

Again and again in group discussions, moral considerations were matters of controversy. The participants (including the community developers) were aware that doubtful and antisocial impulses were being expressed (at least by other people) as well as the prosocial. In the normal process of making a decision, acting on that decision, and criticizing both the decision and the action, the prosocial suggestions that could be put into action, and that seemed feasible, tended to prevail. It was possible for the community developers to raise questions, to inquire about the principles that a proposed decision was to serve, to suggest other alternatives for consideration and trial. Out of the participants' own experience and increasing sensitivity, the more cooperative and kindly impulses tended to be strengthened. The rural people decided to become friends and to work together with the members of churches that they had originally condemned. The city people came to accept some real estate dealers they had originally attacked as enemies.

2b. When the people are free of coercive pressures, and can then examine a wide range of alternatives, they tend to choose the ethically better and the intelligently wiser course of action.

2c. There is satisfaction in serving the common welfare, even as in serving self-interest.

The first assumption is given as an assurance by psychotherapist Carl R. Rogers, who has had many years of clinical practice with disturbed people.[3] He was able to remove many of the pressures of hectic living in the quieter atmosphere of his client-centered counseling. The problem for the community developer was to achieve a comparable freedom from pressures upon individuals in groups that met to contend with local controversies.

Often the participants came to group meetings to act as obvious spokesmen for their churches, race (or fraction of a race),

---

[2]See Peter F. Drucker, *Landmarks of Tomorrow* (New York: Harper and Row, 1957), Chap. 1. Kurt Lewin, *Field Theory in Social Science,* Dorwin Cartwright, ed. (New York: Harper and Row, 1951), Chap. 4.

[3]Carl R. Rogers, "A Therapist's View of the Good Life," *Humanist,* No. 5 (1957), pp. 299–300.

occupational classification, geographic area or total community. They reflected a coercion from the faction for which they spoke and, as a consequence, they found difficult an examination of the merits of proposals before the groups. How, then, to reduce the sense of coercion?

Various initiatives were open to the community developer: He could seek to multiply the alternatives from which the group could choose, beyond the usual opposed pair presented by contending factions. He could appeal to the unity of the group or of the total community. He could work to create an atmosphere of friendliness and confidence in persons, despite their vigorous differences of opinion. He could urge individuals to express their points of view openly but kindly to strengthen the unity of the group. Such steps require of the community developer a skill in human relations, a flexibility in varying the approach as needed, and a firm belief in the ultimate good intentions of those to be helped.

When these steps had reduced the pressures upon group members, there was a tendency for a more intelligently ethical choice to be made spontaneously. The community worker then had to accept the choice as a better one from the point of view of the participant choosers, not necessarily from his point of view. The choice was more likely to be made in the form of a consensus of the meeting, after much discussion and criticism of previous action, than in the form of a majority vote.

The choice, once made and acted upon, carried its own reward. Seldom was there self-congratulation or a pious sense of righteousness. Instead, the participants expressed quiet satisfaction at a good decision and at a job well done. And then they often inquired, "What do we do next?"

2d. A concept of the common good can grow out of group experience that serves the welfare of all in some local area. This sense of responsibility and belonging can be strengthened even for those to whom community is least meaningful.

In the rural project, there was little sense of any community at the beginning of the work. People were more identified with the "holler" in which they lived, and were suspicious of people up the stream or over the ridge. During the years of the project they clearly gained a sense of community larger than the loyalty to the "holler" that preceded it. Apparently, this consciousness grew out of cooperative planning and work together. It has extended also to contacts with cities some distance away in the county and with state offices and functions as well. A sense of their own dignity to meet with these other people and their identifications was a part of the growth achieved.

In the urban project, the older residents of the area already had an identification with the neighborhood (although its limits were ill defined). Newcomers had little or none; some even were new to city dwelling and to the proper behavior expected of good city neighbors. As far as we could determine, the sense of neighborhood became more sharply defined for the old-timers, with an increasing loyalty that held them and induced some to move back into the area. For the newcomers, a sense of neighborhood loyalty tended to grow, aided by committees of welcome, attendance at meetings, hearing about the activities of the neighborhood council and perhaps other such events.

3. Satisfaction and self-confidence gained from small accomplishments can lead to the undertaking of more and more difficult problems, in a process of continuing growth.

Both projects depended upon immediate activities to establish the groups and to start the process. In one, it was the construction of a flood wall. This moved on rapidly to include such additional interests as the construction of playgrounds for children and the rehabilitation of churches. In the other, it was the saving of a park. This was followed by efforts to provide equipment and supervision for the park, then by steps to survey the neighborhood to see who needed recreation and other social welfare services. In both instances, the immediate first activity was accepted as the initial step in a long-range improvement purpose.

This operational assumption, and the supporting experience, stand in contrast to those community development formulas that call for a self-survey as the necessary first recommended step.[4] In both projects, such self-surveys came later, and continue to be conducted in an ongoing process. But when we encouraged local people to follow the logic of their own good motivations, they proceeded through immediate, simple activities to other more complex interests (with greater opportunity for controversy).

Although these two groups of people moved from simpler to more complex activities, there is no guarantee that such well-modulated progress will always occur. May not inexperienced groups choose an early activity that is so far beyond their present capabilities that it threatens to halt the process in immediate failure? Yes, the ups and downs of human learning experience suggest the need for warning, as well as for encouragement. This necessity makes the function of the community developer doubly important.

4. Within the broad role of community developer there are several subroles to be chosen, depending upon the developer's judgment of the people's needs:

4a. Encourager, friend

4b. Objective observer, analyst

4c. Participant in discussion

4d. Participant in some action

4e. Process expert, adviser

4f. Flexible adjuster to varying needs for prominence

To expedite the process for both projects, community developers took all these subroles at one time or another. Since there were several persons fulfilling the broad role, it was possible to ask different persons to carry different subroles from time to time. But the chief community encourager himself had to emphasize one contribution to process at a time, then be prepared to shift emphasis as the need changed.

From the outset, the community developers let it be known that they hoped the process would have no termination, but that their contact with it, and with the people involved, would. These encouragers planned to stay with the projects for approximately three years (an arbitrary time span decided upon for reasons other than awareness of process). But in that time they hoped the process would have gained a sufficient momentum of its own. Their changing subroles were related to this expectation.

The summary assumption follows (Number 5) with emphasis upon patient belief in the good in people, which is expressed in action over a period that includes discouragements. Then, it is assumed, they tend to develop themselves into more ethically competent persons as a result of their involvement in the self-guided process. In general, this is a summary of the events that took place in the two projects. The people involved did improve themselves while working upon the task of improving their concept of their community.

Such projects give support to a belief in the dignity of man. But the support given is much more than a verbal proclamation; community development activity seeks to make that dignity real. It seeks to enhance and utilize that dignity, so that it can be

---

[4]Richard W. Poston, *Democracy Is You* (New York: Harper and Row, 1953).

rediscovered and strengthened even in the impersonal modern world.

These case studies (and other accounts of community development projects) present empirical evidence to support a belief in man's improvability. This belief stands in contrast to many philosophies of gloom—theological, scientific, and governmental. There is this difference, however: The optimism growing out of community development experience is a dynamic one, directed toward the realization of favorable potential in man, not resting upon a cheerful assertion. Community development seeks to strengthen the dignified ethical motivation of man in the face of his present inadequacies and antisocial motivations.

Every community developer knows about antisocial motives in man. He contends with them daily, in his contacts with other people—and in himself. The optimism about man's dignity and probability of growth is achieved in actual experience of facing and overcoming evil. In contending with and transcending antisocial impulses in dozens of decisions, actions, and evaluations, he observes people improving. There is, as yet, no known limit to the growth that may occur.

TENTATIVE GENERALIZATIONS

Out of these case studies, but also out of familiarity with many programs of community development, it becomes possible to formulate some tentative generalizations. These are offered as preliminary to an outline of a typical community development process.

The process seems to depend upon the formation of a community-serving small group—or the utilization of one already in existence. It frequently starts with a single group, but may proliferate into subassociations of many similar groups. But the intimate relationship of participants in small groups is important for the development of personal competence.

An encourager who takes responsibility (frequently professionally employed) is usually necessary for the activation of the process.

The encourager can influence growth toward self-direction; he cannot direct it. The learning of self-direction is learner-motivated. There are many other influences affecting the learning of citizens. The community developer's is but one of many.

The number of people from any population who become actively involved in a community project will be small at any one time. Those who give time to the planning and to the making of responsible decisions will usually be less than 5 percent of the total residents of an area, at any one time. The number participating in the planned activity will be larger (in work periods, in circulation of petitions, in parades or mass meetings, and so on). The number whose lives will be affected by the activities or by the changes in the community will be even larger. Over a period of several years, the number who have had responsible experience will increase, if steps are taken to rotate individuals into and out of office within the small groups.

Some people never become active participants. Some become active for a time and then drop out, with little or no evidence of favorable development—even though the process continues.

The development of persons, groups, and communities seldom occurs smoothly. It comes in the midst of heartache, worry, disappointment, and at irregular rates of progress. Human achievement is uneven. There are periods of enthusiasm and discouragement, activity and apathy, as the process moves on.

In a free-flowing process of community development, there is little of the crusade of all righteous people, on one side, against the forces of evil, all bad, on the other. Instead, people of good will are seen to be human, ambivalent, suffering from mixed motives, and developing by irregular increments of learning.

On the other hand, the process often works in the midst of controversy within the group and within the wider community. At best, it becomes a means for helping people to conciliate controversy by honestly facing the issues in contention.

Though the process starts with a few people and continues through the actions of small groups, it is holistic. That is, it seeks a local wholeness that includes all people, all factions.

Leaders can be expected to emerge from almost any population when the skill of the community developer is great enough.

Democratic responsibility and initiative are more readily acquired in the active meeting and solving of problems together than in verbal learning alone. Interpretive discussion can speed this learning from experience.

Learning is reciprocal between the citizen participant and the community developer.

The major skills for the community developer grow out of a friendship that encourages self-respect and self-confidence. Friendship means several things—a lack of

domination, a willingness to suffer with the group, and to work cooperatively on the activities chosen by the group, and a willingness to share ideas in the expectation that these will be examined on their merits, not on the prestige of the suggester.

Progress occurs most rapidly when a collaborative effort invites the work of all institutions, agencies, class levels, and helping professions. The community approach seeks to be locally all-inclusive, focusing the efforts of many contributions upon the problem of human development, seeking no aggrandizement of any one individual or agency or faction or association.

GUIDES FOR PROCESS

We present these tentative generalizations as broad hypotheses to be checked against further experience, our own and other investigators'. . . .

There is a need for much more experience with the development of people on the local scene. There is a need for more enterprises of this kind, to be set up carefully and recorded as events occur. There is a need for a greater awareness of the processes through which these enterprises go and for an understanding of how development can work in the complicated contemporary world.

23.

Virginia Li Wang, Hayden Reiter, George A. Lentz, Jr., and Gene C. Whaples

AN APPROACH TO CONSUMER-PATIENT ACTIVATION IN HEALTH MAINTENANCE*

Medical care is only one aspect of health care—there is a need for a broader health focus that emphasizes health maintenance and disease prevention. It has been suggested that the greatest single untapped manpower resource is the individual consumer who can take the initiative to preserve personal health. When sufficiently motivated or "activated," the educated consumer will take positive steps to prevent the occurrence of illness, the progression of minor illnesses, or the onset of personal dependency. This consumer will understand the changing delivery system and to gain entry to it. Moreover, he will learn what he can accomplish by self-help before calling on the formal health care delivery system. Thus, consumer-patient activation can help to alleviate the pressures bearing on service delivery, scarce manpower resources, and health facilities (1, 2).

As the demand for health education increases, new configurations in the delivery of health education services become essential. The Maryland Consumer Health Education Demonstration Project, carried out in 1972, was a major effort to unite the resources of the Extension Service of the University of Maryland and the university medical center. State universities and land grant colleges have a system of service delivery through their extension services. Traditionally, the Maryland Extension Service has employed educational outreach to bring the resources of the university to the local community. Its strength lies in the ability to identify problems and needs, organize groups, and work with and through existing local resources and power structures in generating programs that meet the recognized needs of the people.

The Maryland demonstration program sought to transfer and adapt extension education methods and processes in community development to an urban health center in order to support health services delivery. In this paper we describe the program, present the objectives in nine functional areas that were identified for consumer-patient activation, and discuss some general observations on the question of partnership between the extension service and the health center and between providers and consumers.

THE MARYLAND PROGRAM

Community Pediatric Center and Target Population. The Community Pediatric Center of the University of Maryland is an outpatient, walk-in facility that provides free, comprehensive medical and dental ser-

*The editors are indebted to Doman Lum who brought this article to our attention.

Source: "An Approach to Consumer-Patient Activation in Health Maintenance," in *Public Health Reports,* Sept.–Oct. 1975, Vol. 90, No. 5, pp. 449–54 by Virginia Li Wang, Hayden Reiter, George A. Lentz, Jr., and Gene C. Whaples. Reprinted by permission.

vices to approximately 10,000 inner-city, newborn to age 19, patients in southwest Baltimore. The center also provides training for students in the health professions and hospital staffs, and it conducts research in health care delivery.

The center's services are organized to blanket the target population with a wide range of preventive services; to screen the target population for treatable, common illness in its early stages; and to provide facilities for curative and episodic care that are geared to the needs of preschool, school age, and adolescent patients.

For the demonstration program, youth ages 10–19 were selected as the target population because this was the age group that was the least affected by the existing services at the center. Because an obvious communication gap existed between the center and the adolescent community, there was a need to develop mechanisms to reach and influence this group to use the center's services. Furthermore, this age group constituted a most promising population because health-maintenance knowledge, attitudes, and behavior acquired during adolescence tend to have a positive effect later in life.

Of the major health problems identified by the Community Pediatric Center, teenage pregnancy, premature births, venereal disease, drug use, dental caries, and malnutrition were found to be particularly prevalent among adolescents. Poverty and lack of knowledge, coupled with a lack of role models for achievement and career goals, added to identity problems for these youth. The health problems of adolescence reflect a combination of stresses resulting from rapid social and physical development in a sometimes turbulent and unsympathetic society.

The total population within the area is approximately 55 percent black and 45 per-

cent white. Generally, the families are in the lowest 10th of the economic level. The educational level of the heads of households is 8 or 9 years. Many homes have only one parent and are matriarchal. The majority live in cramped rowhouses or walkup tenements that often are poorly heated, without adequate bathroom facilities, and infested with roaches and rats.

Objectives. The overall objective of the demonstration program was to influence the adolescents toward preventive health behavior through positive individual and group experiences. It was hypothesized that a modified program in 4-H and youth work and home economics under the urban Maryland Cooperative Extension Service would favorably affect health knowledge, attitudes, and behavior in relation to the services provided by the Community Pediatric Center. The parents of the adolescents constituted a subtarget population, because inherent in the 4-H philosophy is leadership training and development which involves both youth and adults. The program was therefore aimed at enabling the youth to *(a)* engage in decision making for healthful individual, family, and community living, *(b)* practice healthful living, including constructive use of leisure time, *(c)* strengthen personal standards and citizenship ideals, *(d)* cultivate desire and ability to cooperate with others, *(e)* develop leadership talents, and *(f)* explore career opportunities and continue needed education. A related objective was to develop a closer relationship between health professionals and consumers, while sensitizing the professionals to community needs and the planning of programs to meet those needs.

Conceptual Base

It has been shown that efficiency of delivery, although very important, is not the only essential to assure full medical use of the clinic. In a community where food, housing, employment, and education are more pressing needs than medical care, a broad, social approach to health must be adopted. As Hilleboe *(3)* pointed out, "Health no longer is an end in itself . . . but a means for attaining optimum social well-being within the constraints of the physical, social and biological environment in which man finds himself. Health care can no longer be viewed out of context of the social and economic aspects of daily living."

Health education is concerned with people and their health behavior. It is an educational process through which people increase their understanding or change their ways of thinking or actions as a result of exposure to new experiences. Obviously, health education cannot attempt to refashion the society by imposing the values of those originating the program. Decisions must be reached in collaboration with informed consumers, who should have a major voice in decisions of how and what to change. In a clinic where the socioeconomic gap between providers and consumers is wide, the gap can be narrowed by engaging people in such learning experiences and decision making as defining the relationship between a center and the community it serves.

The rationale has been that through learning by doing, in skill development and in learning responsible actions through involvement with others, people in the community can be guided to launch an aggressive attack on a host of health problems. Program emphasis was on learning experiences which led to greater individual and group effectiveness in decision making in health-related matters. A program may begin with recreation and craft skills, but it will lead ultimately to learning experiences in, for example, clinic utilization, the use of prophylactics, nutrition, or hygiene.

Project Team Development

The demonstration team included a health educator, a home economist, a 4-H agent, and five program assistants who served as outreach workers. The program assistants were selected from more than 60 applicants from the community. After an initial interview, 30 applicants were invited to the group-interview phase of the selection process. By means of a modified nominal-group approach *(4)*, candidates were brought together in one sitting at which each applicant, functioning as a member of a group, responded to the study question: "What are the physical, mental, and social problems confronting the youth in the community?" Self-selection listings, obtained by peer ratings and ratings by the professionals present, were compiled. Initial interview records and references were also considered in the screening process. An important byproduct of the nominal-group process was the documentation of perceived needs by the 30 applicants. The most frequently listed needs were health (for example, drugs, venereal disease, and alcoholism), lack of education and motivation, unemployment, crime, racism, school drop out, and family problems (for example, child abuse), broken homes, and the generation gap. A further examination of the southwest Baltimore area revealed that polarization existed between blacks and whites, and that youth socialization was largely confined to one city block.

A focus of the demonstration was the retraining of extension personnel in health education methods and processes. Inservice training for the professional staff consisted of consultation with the project co-directors, extension service personnel, service chiefs of the Community Pediatric Center, visits to community agencies, and consumer interviews. Community resource assessment further served the staff in determining needs and problems of the target area and building baseline data.

The program assistants participated in a five-week intensive induction training program immediately following their employment. The training was oriented to enable the staff to acquire understanding and skills in identifying community needs, community organization, interpersonal relationship and communication, and health service organization.

Center staff provided information about their respective service areas and assisted in staff development. Their participation as resource persons during training also facilitated communication and coordination of services. Cooperation in planning efforts during the initial period further helped the center staff to become acquainted with health education methods and processes and extension outreach education.

Community Contacts

At the community level, nearly 60 social, educational service, and consumer action agencies were contacted. Contacts were also made with community leaders and lay groups to seek their support in problem identification, program planning, and implementation.

Active entry into the community began for the program assistants during induction training. Goals for the team included acquiring knowledge of the community and designating target areas. The staff concentrated on facilitating cooperative efforts with other agencies in the area and determining consumer needs and interests in program coordination. In addition to the Community Pediatric Center, the project obtained the use of three area facilities in which to conduct educational programs.

The staff went into the neighborhoods and contacted teenagers on street corners,

in homes, and at popular gathering places. Teenagers and parents were included in planning and developmental activities that focused on the expressed needs of adolescents. During the first eight months, more than 3,500 persons participated in the program. Group activities featured discussions on sex education, drug abuse, nutrition, home economics, recreation, and community improvement.

Program assistants worked across the board in community organization and in support of the services provided by the Community Pediatric Center. Flexibility in scheduling was an important element in programing. Many activities were held in the evening and on weekends at hours convenient to the clientele. While the initial contact was usually on a person-to-person basis, all outreach activities and program efforts were organized into group work.

The following brief descriptions of several activities illustrate extension outreach in health education in the Maryland program.

The game concept of health carnivals was introduced at a community fair. Games were devised to promote Community Pediatric Center services and encourage audience involvement. Staffing of health carnival booths by center employees helped to advance community relations.

Through a roller skating program, youths learned to work together, planned their schedules, organized transportation and raised the fare, and mingled socially on an interracial basis. Parents and older teenagers functioned as leaders and supervised the younger children. A first-aid course was introduced as a precaution against possible accidents at the rink, as well as to provide a lesson in access and entry to the health care system.

In a 6-week drug education series, professionals in health and community services, neighborhood leaders, and rehabilitated addicts were used as instructors. The final meeting featured a fashion show—complete with orchestra comprised of rehabilitated addicts—that was attended by families and friends of the participants.

"Tot Lot" for preschool children was one result of organized community efforts. Through person-to-person contact, a group was organized to convert a garbage dump on a vacant block into a playground. Guided by a program assistant, concerned citizens organized a task force and negotiated with city agencies for funds to construct the playground. Residents agreed to supervise the park when playground equipment is installed. The lighting of a 20-foot Christmas tree, donated by merchants, brought out 200 local residents for a holiday festival. The decorated tree stood on the site for 2 weeks; no vandalism occurred.

In an effort to develop a dental education program for primary school children, 40 sixth graders were recruited and trained as "minidentists" to conduct dental screening in schools and in the Community Pediatric Center for 500 first- and second-grade pupils.

As program outreach expanded, the project demonstrated that health education is a process of people involvement and community organization. Program planning and coordination, as well as training professions, aides, volunteers, and related workers in health education methods and processes were included.

The project services were integrated into the Community Pediatric Center's program. These services included recruitment of staff for a nutrition program, referrals ranging from psychological assistance to vocational rehabilitation, project staff working with social workers to strengthen the citizens council, and home visit followup. Volunteer teenagers were recruited and trained as tutors in a patient-education program for adolescents at the university hospital.

CONCEPTUAL OBJECTIVES

After a six-month testing period, the demonstration project staff designated nine

main program components—referral, patient education, advocacy, community organization, recreation, resource management, skill development, staff development, and consultation—as salient features of extension educational work that complement and support the delivery and use of health services. The nine components and the conceptual objectives of the program (see Table 23.1) can be combined in any manner to meet the needs of a specific population. Although referral, advocacy, patient education, community organization, training, and consultation should be inherent in any health education program for any audience, recreation, resource management, and skill development are essential for a disadvantaged clientele or teenage groups. Conceptually, the functional objectives are defined as follows:

REFERRALS OF CONSUMERS will be conducted to maximize exposure to and visibility by as many direct-service facilities as possible within the legitimate bounds of the project service area. Increased referrals will encourage providers to (a) use the team approach when dealing with consumers either as groups or individually, (b) maintain open avenues of communication for effective and efficient delivery of services, (c) use resources outside the direct medical service sphere where necessary—for example, food stamps, social services, and schooling counseling, and (d) explore existing support systems for the widest range of assistance available. Consumers will gain from the referral process by learning of the most appropriate and effective sources of assistance in both the medical care delivery system and the community at large.

PATIENT EDUCATION will be conducted to provide experience in determining personal and family health care, medical care needs, and appropriate behavior for better physical, mental, and social well-being. Activities in this area will be designed so that consumers can develop skills to (a) identify their specific health needs, (b) become aware of the different roles of practitioners within the delivery

TABLE 23.1
Schema for Maryland Consumer Health Education Demonstration Project

	Program components	Programs	Intermediate objectives	Objective
	Referral	Consumer health education	Specific behavior	Health
	Patient education			
	Advocacy		Aroused consumer	Well-being
	Community organization			
Activities	Recreation		Medical care organization staff behavior & organizational change	Awareness of self-worth
	Resource management	Medical program		
	Skill development			Decrease of problem areas
	Staff development		Family habilitation	Upward mobility
	Consultation			
		Social service Mental health Schools		
	Medical center			

system and to seek out appropriate medical care services at proper times in the most efficient manner, *(c)* practice preventive health care, *(d)* relate to the professional needs of staff delivering care so that a more efficient system can evolve, and *(e)* use the telephone as the first line of inquiry about minor symptoms.

ADVOCACY OF CONSUMER DIRECTION in planning, modifying, and maintaining the medical and social service delivery systems will be conducted in light of developing the "activated consumer." Providers will *(a)* increase parent involvement in determination of optimum delivery of services, *(b)* improve use of present systems, *(c)* maintain avenues for feedback as a "check" on present systems of delivery and interaction with them, and *(d)* recruit and train consumers to become legitimate workers or volunteers within present service systems.

COMMUNITY ORGANIZATION ACTIVITIES will be conducted to maximize support from community groups and engagement of parents in project activities,

development, and utilization. Staff will conduct activities to achieve a unified community of consumers and providers toward bridging service gaps. Further, consumers will develop skills to *(a)* develop leadership within their own neighborhood and social groups and *(b)* delegate tasks and responsibilities to other residents of the area toward achieving community improvement.

RECREATIONAL PURSUITS will be offered in an effort to organize youth and parents and to provide structured experiences. Experience in structured recreational pursuits will enable parents and children to *(a)* recognize their status as members of their respective social groups, *(b)* develop leadership skills in planning individual and group activities, and *(c)* determine optimum use of leisure time based on resources available in the community.

RESOURCE MANAGEMENT will be reflected through skill development in the determination of day-to-day living habits and household organization. As an educational function, the project will prepare consumers to *(a)* assess their quality of living in relation to available personal resources, *(b)* practice decision making to alleviate frustration in conducting activities of daily living, and *(c)* plan use of time in regard to the use of existing medical, social, and community services.

SKILL DEVELOPMENT PROGRAMS will focus on individual development as consumers. Determination of programing in this area will be largely in response to the expressed needs of the consumers. Training programs will afford participants the skills to *(a)* recognize their present skill levels and assess potential through self-growth, *(b)* develop a sense of self-worth through accomplishment of tasks, *(c)* determine social as well as vocational opportunities relative to personal ability, and *(d)* plan for and seek improvement of personal skills by exploration and use of community resources.

STAFF DEVELOPMENT OF PROVIDERS will increase their potential to *(a)* understand the consumer's orientation toward the medical care organization system, *(b)* seek out consumer input to planning and decision making, *(c)* develop efficient mechanisms in meeting the consumer needs, *(d)* deal with change while minimizing conflict, *(e)* become involved in an increasing number of community activities, external to the medical center and established delivery system, and *(f)* decrease "emergent" and crisis-oriented delivery of medical care.

CONSULTATION will be provided to both providers and consumers to enhance their abilities in program planning and decision making. Consultants will be drawn from the Community Pediatric Center, the university and the community at large in order to *(a)* provide solutions to problem areas, *(b)* bridge possible communication gaps between providers and consumers, and *(c)* draw out the potentials already existing within providers and consumer groups.

DISCUSSION AND CONCLUSION

Mobilization of resources of community, school, health, and other services is essential if a project is to meet its stated objectives and relate to health education of the citizenry. Eventually, professionals and lay leaders—regardless of their specialties and interests—must recognize that they share vital functions in disease prevention and health maintenance and the promotion of physical, social, and mental well-being.

The one-year demonstration did not allow sufficient time to conduct a systematic evaluation. While we cannot claim with certainty that the project achieved its objectives, there are manifestations that information transferred by the change agents has affected *(a)* development of understanding of the Community Pediatric Center by consumers, *(b)* development of skills for movement through that system by consumers, and *(c)* establishment of behavior patterns necessary to maintain optimum health by consumers.

The joining of the Cooperative Extension Service and the Community Pediatric Center in outreach health education probably would not have occurred had it not been stimulated by Federal financial support. The extension service's staff specialist, who had been trained in public health, and its program base for health education provided a bridge to the health center and facilitated the formation of a partnership.

If organizations are to work effectively together, all parties must respect the competencies and understand the needs and limitations of each other. In our demonstration program, the extension service and the Community Pediatric Center personnel had diverse backgrounds and capabilities; however, dedicated people committed to the project overcame what could have been insurmountable obstacles. A basic problem lies with the common notion that health care is a domain of the health professionals. Undoubtedly, this is related to the disease concept of health care. That health is often a byproduct of the quality of life strongly influenced by lifestyle is frequently overlooked.

When it is essential for persons to assume responsibility for their own health care, extension outreach in health education can enhance medical service delivery and complement health care. The thrust of this program has been to influence consumers to understand and react positively to medical care delivery and other social factors infringing on their health and lifestyles.

While the extension service has long professed a commitment to better health, and the pediatrics center has been committed to patient care, neither has regarded health education as a priority in the allocation of resources. To unite permanently the resources of both facilities, incentives must be provided continuously in order to cultivate that kind of partnership. A change in organizational behavior requires time for redirection.

Consumer participation in decision making attracted nationwide attention in the mid-1960s with the Office of Economic Opportunity's pronouncement of "maximum feasible participation." After a decade of steadily mounting appropriations and increased attention to comprehensive health planning, there is little evidence today that mandated consumer participation has been truly achieved *(5)*. It has been observed that one reason for the inability to achieve results is that consumer participation has grown out of political rather than educational concerns *(6)*.

Much has been said about the relevance or irrelevance of education. Unless health education is made relevant to people's needs, they are not likely to be motivated to learn more about health care. Health and sickness are relative concepts that vary among cultures and groups. There is a tremendous gap between what the consumer knows and what the professional knows

about health and disease. Most consumers are not concerned about health unless stricken with illness. But they are concerned with living and the amenities in life. The Maryland Consumer Health Education Demonstration Project was made attractive to people by relating it to their activities of daily living. Thus, the people in the community responded quickly and enthusiastically with their support.

We were willing to seek out the clientele, help them identify felt and unfelt needs, and then expose them to experiences that satisfied those needs through active participation. This called for sensitivity and keen observation on the part of providers. Response of the people in the community went beyond acceptance of the services they desired. They generated program activities as well as learning experiences for themselves and for their community.

Involvement of volunteers in program services deserves emphasis. It is often said that the poor seldom volunteer their services, and that the concept of volunteerism is almost nonexistent in poverty areas. We found that this hypothesis is not tenable. The Consumer Health Education Demonstration included more than 300 adult and teenage volunteers who worked in many capacities to serve some 3,500 teenagers. The project's commitment to volunteer leadership development was an important factor. In keeping with the philosophy of extension education, the staff was trained to identify, recruit, support, and provide training for volunteers.

The project demonstrated that a concerted health education effort in support of a medical delivery unit can effectively promote a bona fide provider-consumer partnership in health care. By assimilating the project into the center staffing, the providers developed a greater appreciation of the multi-dimensional factors influencing consumer reaction to service delivery. The demonstration brought together consumers and providers on a mutual plane and made them more sensitive to each other's needs. It enabled each group to understand better the other's role in the partnership for health, as well as their mutual responsibilities.

We wish to emphasize that outreach is a task usually assigned a second- or third-order priority to primary medical care delivery. If health education is merely an adjunct to service rather than a specific program effort, it will fall short of accomplishing the objective of educating consumers in self-help. When a program does not receive strong endorsement and fiscal support, there is a spontaneous lack of commitment by the staff. Health education as practiced in the Maryland Consumer Health Education Demonstration served the double role of consumer-patient activation and provider sensitization. It holds the potential to serve as a model for the broader development of true consumer participation in comprehensive health planning.

REFERENCES

1. The University of Wisconsin: Interim report of project-planning proposal for consumer health education. University Extension, Professional and Human Development Division, Health Science Unit. Madison, 1971, mimeographed.
2. Wilson, V. E.: Rural health care systems. JAMA 216:1623–1626, June 1971.
3. Hilleboe, H. E.: Public health in the United States in the 1970's. *Am J Public Health* 58:1588–1610 (1589), September 1968.
4. Van de Ven, A. H., and Delbecq, A. L.: The nominal group process as a research instrument for exploratory health studies. *Am J Public Health* 62:337–342, March 1972.
5. Galiher, C. B., Needleman, J., and Rolfe, A. J.: Consumer participation. HSMHA Health Rep 86:99–106, February 1971.
6. Hochbaum, G. M.: Consumer participation in health planning: toward conceptual clarification. *Am J Public Health* 59:1698–1705, September 1969.

24.

Jack Rothman, John L. Erlich, and Joseph G. Teresa

FOSTERING PARTICIPATION

The importance of participation in community practice is self-evident. There remains, however, the vital question of how to get people to attend, join up, speak out, work on a committee, or lend support.

A school social worker faced this kind of practical problem:

> The mothers' program began in October and ultimately involved nine mothers—seven tutoring and two helping with the materials center. In April, the teacher in charge of the program sought my assistance. Two mothers had recently dropped out of the program, and only three mothers were attending their general meetings.

CONCLUSIONS OF RESEARCH

Findings of recent research on participation can be summarized in this generalization:

> The amount of voluntary participation in an organization depends on the benefits gained from participation, and the degree to which the benefits are shown to result directly from participation.

THE ACTION GUIDELINE

The concept of benefit provision suggests the following Action Guideline:

> To foster participation in organizations, programs, or task groups, practitioners should provide or increase relevant benefits.

From Jack Rothman, John L. Erlich and Joseph G. Teresa "Fostering Participation," pp. 7–25. Reprinted by permission of the authors.

The term "participation" in the guideline should be interpreted in a broad sense. The term is meant to include not only the recruitment of new members, but also changes in the patterns of existing members' participation. For example, an individual who had merely attended an activity might shoulder responsibilities or become an officer.

Many professionals intuitively use benefits as a tool in their work, and the guideline may seem an obvious statement. However, we are trying to make this common approach more explicit and more systematic so that it may have a greater impact on participation in programs and services. Though derived from an independent literature source, the guideline is related to certain learning theory or behavior modification concepts, as we will discuss shortly.

TYPES OF BENEFITS

Benefits may be described as either *instrumental* or *expressive.* Instrumental benefits provide material, tangible, task-oriented returns, such as getting an increased welfare allotment or new equipment for the agency. Expressive benefits are intangible and psychological in character, such as increased friendships, personal satisfaction, or pride. Further distinctions may be made within the two categories.

(1) *Instrumental benefits* may be:
  (a) *material*—obtaining a loan or grant, securing needed information or authorization, etc.

(b) *Anticipatory*—setting up an action structure, or obtaining a verbal commitment as a partial achievement toward the material gain.

(2) *Expressive benefits* may be:

(a) *interpersonal*—making new friends, having an enjoyable social experience, etc.

(b) *symbolic*—receiving an award which represents public approval or recognition of an individual's participatory activities, being mentioned in a newspaper article, etc.

In practice, these approaches are often used in combination; sometimes one is given special emphasis and supplemented by others.

ILLUSTRATIONS OF BENEFITS FROM PRACTICE

Here are descriptions of how professionals used the four different types of relevant benefits with different groups:

(1) Instrumental Benefits: Material

Our community mental health program in the housing project was floundering. I had been working with a few residents in the project to develop a self-help group. When our efforts faltered, I decided to use the guideline with the goal of increasing participation in group meetings.

We elected to increase benefits by resolving specific problems for each family; for example, getting free roach spray from the manager (he usually charged residents), getting a toilet repaired, obtaining special educational attention for certain children, and transporting families to the dentist. At the same time we saw the families individually and informally, and decreased the number of group meetings from weekly to bi-weekly to "on call." In a sense, elimination of unnecessary meetings was another reward. On a group level, when tenants ran into rent disagreements with the management, we set up contacts with Legal Aid.

Eventually we called the group together, and then personally visited those who did not come suggesting that we could not con-

tinue to help them unless they attended the group sessions! It worked. By providing concrete benefits and by making them depend upon participation, the group began to function again.

(2) Instrumental Benefits: Anticipatory

I used this guideline to help organize the Black Student Union at the junior high school. The kids had come to me for help because of my role as program director at the local community center.

We called a meeting in which the students identified the areas for union concern, and set up appropriate committees supervised by my staff. The organization devised plans for a Black History Week. This effort enabled the student union to develop a program with a large number of black students participating.

This satisfying action structure achieved, the group proceeded to establish broader goals and I was able to withdraw my staff.

(3) Expressive Benefits: Interpersonal

By employing the guideline, I was able to increase participation in our district-wide organization of secondary students. Meeting with their steering committee, I suggested that the group might enjoy a weekend "retreat." When the school agreed to cover part of the expenses, I proceeded to plan the excursion. The event was a definite success: the students interacted socially and looked forward to meeting one another again.

The eventual effect was that our regular attendance nearly doubled, and previously inactive members became more vital participants.

(4) Expressive Benefits: Symbolic

As a school-community agent, I desired to increase community participation in the school and to improve services to children through volunteer help. Special classes were decided upon according to the interests of the students and volunteers. These included: arts and crafts, cooking, crochet, dramatics, modern dance, and sewing.

The participation guideline gave continuity to the program. I provided recognition for the volunteers by working toward a presentation of activity "products" at the end of the program, offering service awards, and providing publicity. I requested that a regular PTO meeting be rescheduled for the final presentation, in order to reach a large number of community people. The program met with great success: the volunteers and students both wanted to repeat it for another six-week session.

THE PATTERN OF IMPLEMENTATION

We have found that one general pattern was followed in all the cases in our field tests. This pattern consists of five steps:

1. goal determination
2. selection of benefits to be used
3. initial contact with potential participants
4. follow-up contact with potential participants
5. delivery of benefits, or operation of the event

We will consider each of these steps in turn.

(1) Goal Determination

The first step is to select the goal of participation. In our experience, the guideline was used to form new groups or to maintain or increase participation in existing groups. Here are illustrations of these objectives, as stated by participants in the field study:

My goal is to increase the number of participants in the Mental Health Association's annual chapter leadership workshop.

My goal is to get the Welfare Rights Organization groups in the area to participate in securing an Early Preventive Screening, Diagnosis, and Treatment program for their local communities.

My goal is to maintain the current level of participation in the mothers' tutoring program in the school, and to increase the number who attend the group meetings.

(2) Selection of Relevant Benefits

The selection of relevant benefits for increasing participation is apparently a two-stage process. First, the practitioner must identify the benefits available; second, the benefits must be matched to the target population. (If the practitioner has access to ample resources, it may be possible to reverse the order of these steps.)

In our experience, the majority of the practitioners who used the participation guideline provided multiple benefits. Most chose a combination of instrumental and expressive benefits, frequently combining material and interpersonal rewards.

(3) Initial Contact with Potential Participants

The method used for the initial contact varied according to the nature of the target system. The major difference in approach lay in the ease with which the potential membership could be identified and located, and in the degree to which the practitioner was in day-to-day contact with that membership. The types of initial contacts varied, ranging from direct personal conversations and telephone discussions, to flyers, mailing, and notices in the newspapers.

(4) Follow-up Contact with Potential Participants

Practitioners in our study tended to use a different medium for the recontact than was used for the initial contact. When the potential membership was individually identifiable, the contact and follow-up were usually by formal letter or memo in alternation with an informal conversation, either face to face or by telephone. When the potential membership was diffusive or broadly defined, practitioners tended to use a different form of mass media for the recontact stage than they had used for the initial contact. The value of newspapers, radio, or television in supplementing handbills and posters should be considered. Note that a variation in the follow-up medium is not a necessity; it is simply a common practice.

(5) Delivery of Benefits

The actual delivery of the promised benefits is particularly important. When the benefits are in the form of a social event, the practitioner should oversee the proper operation of the event.

Several professionals in our study developed contingency plans, so that if one benefit turned out to be unavailable, another could be substituted. If the benefits were interpersonal, the worker had to expend more energy during an event. Other types of benefits, particularly material, required greater effort prior to an event. Generally speaking, the less control workers had over the delivery of the rewards, the more active the workers were, often using multiple and contingency approaches.

IDEAS FROM BEHAVIOR MODIFICATION

Readers may have recognized this reward (or reinforcement) principle as an element of behavior modification. Although behaviorist concepts have not been generally directed to systems intervention, a few ideas and terms are relevant to community and organizational work. While the concepts may be familiar to some readers, their application to social systems will be new. We believe that these behaviorist ideas can be used without any coercion to foster voluntary participation.

Behavior Specification

It is essential that the user specify the exact nature of the behavior to be changed. In the case of participation, we may be attempting to increase:

1. *rate:* the frequency with which an individual attends meetings, programs, etc.
2. *form:* the type or quality of participation, that is, attendance, committee chairmanship, making financial or other material contributions, speaking up at meetings, etc.
3. *duration:* the extent of participation over a period of time
4. *variability:* the stability or regularity of participation

The assumption is that different types of benefits may be effective in encouraging different aspects of participation behavior.

Positive Reinforcement

This refers to benefits contingent upon the performance of some desired behavior. The clinician or caseworker has certain direct reinforcers available in relationships with clients. These include approval, attention, and affection. In a group or community context, these rewards may be offered to one individual through other individuals. . . . In human service community work the agency's resources offer varied reinforcement possibilities, as do those external community resources with which the agency has operating ties. The trick is to locate these, recognize their reward potentials and make them available.

Contracting

There has been increasing use of this concept in settings such as schools and community mental health programs. A practitioner might come to an agreement about a level of participation, which, if followed for a designated time, could result in a desired outcome. For example, contracting was used in the issuance of a certificate to leaders who completed the six-week volunteer service session in the school-community example cited earlier.

Shaping

This involves a series of sequential goals leading up to a long-range objective. In an organizational context, one might speak of "interim goals." As a hypothetical example, a community worker wants a woman to take on an appointive office; the worker starts by asking her to attend a committee, then later asks her to chair a committee, and finally to hold an office.

Group Contingencies

Benefits may be offered to groups as well as to individuals. The United Fund offers a great number of social and symbolic rewards to volunteers who achieve their goals, often using graphs and charts to dramatize the group objective. A committee or organization might set certain goals or standards for participation, and foster group satisfactions for successful attainment.

PROBLEMS OF EXECUTING THE GUIDELINE STRATEGY

Our field staff encountered some difficulties implementing the guideline, and they made a variety of suggestions.

First of all, they pointed out that the benefits selected must have real significance for the target group. One worker stated:

I had to be sure that the benefits were really viewed as worthy by the group members. Without this, the whole thing would have failed.

Another noted that:

The benefits must be perceived as important by participants. The benefits could be potential as well as actual.

The need for interim, short-range benefits to sustain motivation was also stressed.

I often feel that a long-range goal is achievable but a group may not be able to keep that goal in sight—or even to agree with it at that stage of the game.

Because of existing power relationships in society, low-income persons lack the clout to make rapid gains or to resolve their pressing problems. This means that their participation must be sustained while they struggle with those problems. The structuring of participation to provide expressive experiences and immediate social gratification permits this. Those of us who are highly issue oriented tend to forget or neglect that. We dare not!

Many workers highlighted the difficulties of choosing appropriate benefits.

Since instrumental or expressive rewards vary by individual and by situation, the determination of rewards was a problem. Also, it was not within my power to assure delivery of all the benefits which might have reinforced participation.

Guaranteeing the benefits was the most difficult aspect of this approach.

I think that a practitioner who promises only expressive benefits, without any instrumental rewards, is fighting an uphill battle.

GETTING STARTED

(1) Think of some existing . . . problem in your agency situation that could be aided through increased or improved participation (by clients, other agencies, staff members, etc.). . . .

(2) Specify the nature of participation behavior that you will be dealing with in

your intervention and the direction in which you would like to change it. For example, will you be dealing with:

recruitment

retention or maintenance

increasing the rate of participation

changing the form of participation
(attendance, membership, committee participation, volunteer work, officership, contributions)

stabilizing or varying the pattern of participation

(3) Try to select relevant benefits which are both attractive to target groups and available for you to deliver.

What types of benefits would be effective in stimulating the desired participation? Consider:

Instrumental:

material

anticipatory

Expressive:

interpersonal

symbolic

Consider multiple rewards. Get to know your group. Observe them; ask them about their likes; ask other experienced professionals.

What types of benefits are available to you? Consider such sources as:

your personal relations

agency resources and good will (the board, volunteers)

agency links with external resources

the group itself

(4) Decide whether some special reinforcement technique may be applied, such as:

shaping

contracting

group contingency

Don't let these get in your way, however. Use them only if they are applicable and potentially useful in your situation.

(5) Consider ways of making benefits known and available to the relevant target group.

(6) Carry out the guideline. Don't forget follow-up contact.

(7) Try to assess the results of your work. Specify real indicators of change in participation. These may include such factors as:

change in specific number of persons at meetings

changes in number and/or percentage of dropouts from programs

increase or decrease in the number of individuals who collaborate by taking responsibility

PRACTICAL ADVICE DERIVED FROM THE FIELD STUDY

The personal resources of the practitioner are his most effective tools. These include: selecting appropriate benefits, announcing them, motivating people, and delivering both interpersonal and material rewards.

It is advisable to choose a goal and a strategy that are consistent with (or which can be enhanced by) your experience and position in the agency. Choose a goal about which you have conviction and enthusiasm.

With regard to your agency situation, seek a goal that will fit in with your other assignments, and attempt to gain whatever support you can from fellow staff members and agency administrators. Try to locate suitable physical facilities, or plan a program that fits the available facilities.

Choose a program that will be of specific interest to clients, or work hard at developing their interests. It helps if you choose a group of clients who are receptive to your agency and the program; attempt to build this kind of receptivity as you proceed.

Try to clarify your personal goals and assignments in the agency, so that you are free to concentrate on this task without heavy pressure from other demands or without the neglect of other assignments. Lack of staff and resources may impede you; selection of a feasible objective is an important strategic consideration.

Several field workers warned that the intervention cannot be carried out in a mechanical, ritualistic manner. The art of practice has to shape the science of any intervention strategy. This involves the practitioner's attitudes, interpersonal skills, sense of timing, etc. As two of them advised us:

There is a need to develop trust and a decent relationship with client groups. This takes time and demonstrated proof that you can deliver.

There is the consideration of the personal qualities of members, as well as the level of enthusiasm conveyed by the practitioners.

More specific observations were offered:

I found little difficulty in using this guideline. The only problem was self-imposed: a limited time in which to develop the offered benefits.

One difficulty was my lack of information about the community I was working in. Insufficient time forced me to form a group before I had adequate community information.

Do not burden the staff or clientele by trying to solve the problem in one day.

The phone conversations proved to be crucial to the success of this guideline. Through these personal contacts, we were able to respond to the needs and concerns of those to whom we spoke.

I ran into the usual organizational interferences. Too many complicated chains of communication hindered the application of a simple idea.

Realize also that clients and community people will have other activities that compete for their time and interests. The benefits you offer must be strong enough to gain their attention and capture their motivation. Clients and residents may lack knowledge of the organization or may not possess certain skills for adequate participation. You may need to make up these deficits as you continue. . . .

25.

Irving A. Spergel

ORGANIZING THE LOCAL COMMUNITY: THE SOCIAL-STABILITY APPROACH

The community worker engages in both organizing and interorganizing activities.

From Irving A. Spergel, *Community Problem Solving* (Chicago: University of Chicago Press, 1969), pp. 128–42. © by The University of Chicago. All rights reserved. Published 1969. Reprinted with permission of the author and the publisher.

The geographical scope and functional complexity of the organization, as well as its strategic commitment, determine which method he emphasizes. Thus, the worker with a neighborhood organization is concerned primarily with organizing; the worker with a metropolitan welfare council, with interorganizing.

THE SIGNIFICANCE OF LOCAL ORGANIZATIONS

Since at least the time of Tocqueville, the institutions of local self-government and voluntary associations have been regarded as integral to the success of the American democratic system. Local organizations

inhibit the state or any single source of private power from dominating all political resources; they are a source of new opinions; they can be the means of communicating new ideas to a large section of the citizenry. They train men in political skills and so help to increase the level of interest and participation in politics.[1]

Tocqueville and others feared certain trends of modern society—industrialization, bureaucratization, nationalism, apathy, the absence of meaningful citizen participation, and especially the lack of organized opposition to the power of the central government. Local and voluntary organizations were viewed as countering the negative consequences of the mass society. Centralized power was regarded as fundamentally evil, and the ideal society was predicated on the diversity of organized interests. The expression of local interests was expected to lead, through competition and conflict, to basic cultural and political unity.

In every community, no matter how apathetic or problem-ridden, there are untapped leadership, positive human resources, and institutions which can contribute to the well-being of both the local and the larger community. Any local community organization effort may, therefore, be designed to reach even the most disorderly and disorganized community and seek out its constructive human resources. The reference here is to the islands of orderliness and normality which survive in even the most unfavorable social settings, and which are presented by self-sustaining social groups and by integrated persons of high morale. The forms taken by these groups differ from neighborhood to neighborhood. In some, they are found in the religious institutions; in others, in mutual aid societies, or clubs set up to promote the recreational sports, or socializing interests of its members. . . .

Generally, these groups and persons are groping toward the goal of upward mobility, that is, the improvement of status in the wider social order. It is this activity together with sentiments of protectiveness toward their children which represent the social forces to be harnessed to the service of delinquency prevention. . . .[2]

A case has also been made *against* the value of local organizations in the solution of local problems, the charge being that most existing organizations, even indigenous associations in slum areas, are generally not concerned with the welfare of its most needy inhabitants. While the membership of a block club or neighborhood organization is lower class in many of its characteristics, its identification may be primarily with middle-class norms and values. A self-selective membership process rules out the problematic members of the ghetto community; home owners, white collar workers, business people, representatives of the stable, upwardly aspiring groups gravitate to such local associations, and they look down upon those persons who are deviant and especially upon families which produce delinquent children, regarding them as immoral, shiftless, and worthless.

[1]Seymour Martin Lipset, *Political Man* (New York: Doubleday & Company, Anchor Books, 1963), p. 52.

[2]Henry D. McKay (Statement), Committee on the Judiciary, U.S. Senate, 86th Cong., 1st sess., S. res. 54, pt. 5, *Juvenile Delinquency,* p. 172.

Another criticism is that many of the organizations, albeit labeled grass-roots, tend to be undemocratic.

> ... Very few of them regularly afford their members an opportunity to vote on the stands the group will take. Very often the leader will speak for the group without having consulted the membership. Many of the organizations consist of small cores of local activists who have no significant following and little status in the local community. . . .[3]

Further, it is argued that local organizations are inherently limited and usually exaggerate their influence.[4]

Nevertheless, despite serious questions about the viability and value of local organization, sufficient evidence has accumulated which indicates that local community organizations under certain conditions can be effective social instruments.[5] They can dissolve apathy and stimulate interest in local problem solving; they can provide low-income membership with new perspectives about their own capabilities; they can afford significant experiences in self-help, develop political leadership, and provide important social services.[6]

THE INTERPERSONAL ORIENTATION

The main purpose of the interpersonal orientation is to initiate a set of attitudes and activities by which members or representatives of a local community seek to identify, and to take action to solve, community problems—not, as in the change orientation, to take action to secure particular reforms or achieve organizational power.

Establishing Relationships

A fundamental ingredient of organizing is establishing relationships with many different persons and representatives of groups who are concerned with a problem like delinquency. The enabler is likely to give special attention to meeting representatives of the formal structure—probation officer, youth worker, teacher, and minister; the developer, representatives of indigenous groups—block club leader, head of the ladies' auxiliary of the church, and especially parents of delinquent youths.

The worker uses every opportunity and device possible to elicit interest and draw people together to do something about a serious problem. He must be articulate and persuasive.

> I first went to the churches and talked to the ministers. If any were interested, I asked him to set up a meeting with members of his congregation. I would talk with these people about different possibilities and usually suggest that all these little groups get together to really do something about the problem.
>
> Often it was one key person from a group who was especially interested, who might have had previous organizational experience, and whom I could count on to bring people down to the next meeting.

The professional enabler systematically approaches the establishing of community relationships.

> The first thing I do is talk to the heads of the various agencies, especially the schools, the churches, and the police department. I also go to some of the storekeepers, and the places where kids hang out. I make contact as well with the organizations that seem to play an important role in the lives of adults,

[3]J. Clarence Davies, III, *Neighborhood Groups and Urban Renewal* (New York: Columbia University Press, 1966) pp. 206–7.

[4]Muzafer Sherif and Carolyn W. Sherif, *Reference Group,* (New York: Harper and Row, 1964), p. 292.

[5]Saul D. Alinsky, *Reveille for Radicals* (Chicago: University of Chicago Press, 1945).

[6]Marshal B. Clinard, *Slums and Community Development* (New York: Free Press of Glencoe, 1966).

Kiwanis, or the Lions' Club. The people who are most helpful to me are often the school personnel and the police. I find out what the main problems of the kids are, what the schools are doing about them. I find out who the main people in the community are, who are the most active. Then I talk with them and get their ideas and feelings. I begin to probe the agencies as to what they see as the direction of their programs and how they plan to meet the problem. I get a line on people who should be invited to a first meeting to consider the particular delinquency problem. This is my first step.

Communication

The process of communication is extremely important in any effort to organize individual groups and agencies. The enabler must state his purpose with clarity and conviction as he makes his contacts. In low-income areas, failures in communication may constitute a major barrier to any community problem-solving endeavor. Indeed, the problem of communication itself may need to be solved before any others are attempted. For example, one grass-roots organization gave first priority to its communication problem:

1. To assist our probation department in communications with our delinquent youth.
2. To aid and assist our delinquent brothers and sisters in their communication problems with various probation and law enforcement officers.
3. To aid and assist store and property owners and their communication with people of the community.
4. To aid and assist our teachers in their communication problems with delinquent students.
5. To seek a line of communication with various departments of public service. . . .

There are two key aspects to the worker's job of communication: he must facilitate the flow of information about community problems to the community group, and he must make certain that the role of the group is understood by other significant sectors of the community. The community group may need to discuss various aspects of the problem. They have to understand what their objective should or can be, and whether and how they can manage the resources to carry out a proposed plan. This internal group discussion phase serves to involve people in giving opinions, making decisions, and developing relationships with each other, and it may take a great deal of time. But preliminary discussion of the problem must at some point come to an end and a plan of action finally set and carried out.

The solution of any given problem, however, is never in the hands of the community group itself, not at least in the complex urban areas. Support for the purpose and program of the community group must be enlisted. "Selling" key groups in the community on the value of a particular project depends on communicating how the solution will directly affect the contributors.

> After four years, the committee people are beginning to sell the little businessmen such as the grocers, the pharmacist, the cleaning establishment on the idea of a recreation center so the kids won't be on the streets and in their stores causing them all kinds of headaches.

The scope of community concern about a problem is widened through an active process of communication. Communication is thus both an important prelude to, and a critical means of action for, solving a community problem.

Enlarging the Scope of Concern

Getting people to a meeting may be fairly simple, but involving them in a series of constructive actions toward solving a problem is very difficult. One of the first things to be done is to enlarge the scope of people's concern about a given problem—no small task when their resources of hope, aspiration, experience, and educational background are limited.

> These people are looking for some way of expressing their interests in young people and doing ... something in a direct and immediate way about them. You can hardly blame them for picking up the first likely thing that comes along. Now, for example, it is quite characteristic, you know, that they say it's a law enforcement problem. Where the heck are the police, they say. They start hollering that they need more police protection.

The task of the worker is to help the group engage in a problem-coping experience that has meaningful scope and depth. The problem needs to be examined within the limits of the understanding and resources of the participants. The emphasis may be on the development of new ideas and possibilities for action.

> Maybe the answer is not alone increased police protection, and recreation, but getting teachers to be innovative of school programs and to accept lower-class kids better. The problem may be how to influence key people in the school system to do any number of feasible things for which they have not taken enough responsibility, such as counseling, remedial help, job referral.

Focusing, Partializing, and Progressing

Members of community groups in lower-income areas may have special difficulty in determining precisely how to achieve their objectives. They may, after considerable discussion, know what they want but not how to get it. The objectives, which may have seemed fairly clear at first, have become complex and elusive. The members seem suddenly to lack focus—they tend to confuse means and ends. The larger picture may be clear, but its comprising elements are hard to see. The worker may need to propose alternative actions and to assist the group in detailing particular tasks. Certain data may be needed. Membership responsibilities may have to be assigned. Subsequent activities may need to be anticipated.

The entire organizing process must be progressive in its stages. Limited goals must be set and relatively smaller efforts undertaken before larger goals and major projects are attempted.

> This is the whole idea of the smaller projects. When I first met with these people they wanted a mammoth recreation center for their kids. They had been after this center for fifteen years. The group met sporadically every few months, but there was no real organization or build-up and preparation for this major and expensive undertaking. The people would get together and call four or five meetings in succession, but the project idea would fall by the wayside.
>
> What I did when I came to the group was to get them to focus on the things that they could do fairly quickly and which would pay off with success. It was extremely important that they meet regularly, develop a sense of involvement and organization, and, of course, develop skill in organizational matters. We had projects on clean-up and fix-up of streets and houses. Then we invited speakers on health and sanitation. We set up a cooperative baby sitting service. From there we moved to sponsoring a project of day care services for working mothers. We may not get to the recreation center thing until next year or the year after, when the situation is ripe for it. Meanwhile, we're also planning a teenage beauty pageant and an adult fashion show.
>
> All these things will provide useful organizational experiences. Success will build on success and we will tackle only the problems we can handle at any given time. My job is to keep these people involved and carrying out more and more important tasks.

Providing Support

Grass-roots persons and agencies may be uncertain and ambivalent about their participation in problem-solving activities. They may develop resistance because they lack confidence about the value of their contributions. In such circumstances, a great deal of support is required, especially by persons of limited education and organizational experience:

> They will say they don't know anything and I'll say, "You can describe the problem as you see it. You have ideas as to what should be done."
>
> Then they'll say, "But suppose we decide to do something I can't do. Suppose we decide to talk to the principal or the police captain."
>
> Then I'll say, if it's a woman, "You know how to talk to your child. You can tell your husband what to do. The school belongs to all the people. You have a right to talk to persons who are doing the job of education for you."
>
> Then they have this pitch, "You're getting paid to bring us together. It's your job. You do it."
>
> Agencies will give you basically the same pitch. Their representatives will come to one or two meetings just to see what's happening. But they say they are too busy with their own programs. I tell them, "Your recreation and casework programs aren't going to be worth a damn. They're too little and too distant from the problem. You got to hit the problem more directly, maybe in the schools or the homes. It takes extra effort, but it makes their programs more meaningful."

Such supportive comments help encourage and stimulate people to participate, to take the first steps toward organized involvement in community problem solving. Emphasis must be on their ability to solve the problem as well as on the serious nature of the problem itself.

The interpersonal approach to organizing assumes that people must first meet their own personal needs before they can solve the problems of others and of the community. Community activity may serve primarily as a means for certain low-income persons to project their own personal anxieties, hostilities, and distorted perceptions and to interfere with the realistic solution of social problems. Such problem-ridden individuals must therefore be helped themselves before—or even as—they attempt to assist others. Social, educational, and cultural enrichment services may be needed to widen their horizons and to develop their self-confidence.

A service program tied in with community action assumes that there are persons who want to receive personal gratification as well as give energy and time to other people's problems. People expect a *quid pro quo,* one way or the other, for efforts expended. The return to the low-income person is personal and social development.

> We consider delinquency prevention and neighborhood improvement as part of the same process. We try to get people naturally involved in issues that are coming up. Now this is a nonpolitical and nondenominational approach. We don't as a rule have politicians coming down to sway our people or take over our meetings. We encourage our people to read and to become involved in every way they want.
>
> We have adult education classes. Speakers come down to discuss general subjects. There are also classes of specific interest, for example, to parents about raising their kids. We have had psychiatrists, heads of social agencies. We had some one come down to speak on Social Security. The public aid commissioner of the county discussed the kinds of problems his agency faces.
>
> We also have a crafts and recreational program for adults and their children as well. All these things are kind of interrelated. For example, we had one woman who came down for a lecture on child care. The concern and the enthusiasm that was generated resulted in organizing a tot lot. Some of the men in our classes go to court

to represent our organization's interest in kids who appear before the judge.

Youth programs are often leverage points for developing contacts with parents and others who may themselves be recruited into both recreation program and community solving projects.

We have a game room and the adolescents come down two or three nights a week. We have a weekly dance. Adults in the community do most of the supervision and teaching of the kids. When a kid gets into trouble in the program, that gives us an opportunity to go to his home and meet his parents or go to his school. You get to know what's going on with the youngsters and what the problems in the community are. You begin to involve teachers and parents in the organization's larger concern about poor housing, poor facilities, poor curricula. We can then call a meeting of all these people and develop some kind of joint project to see what we can do to solve not just the one youngster's problem, but the problem of a lot of kids.

Finally, the worker may be in a position to supply a supportive service to another agency, usually less well developed in its problem-solving skills. The worker may provide experience, facilities, or simply stimulation to another group to initiate a program or do a better job with a problematic sector of the youth population.

The Sisters of St. Mary were wondering about setting up a program serving delinquent girls in the community. We consulted with them and urged them to go ahead. They had obtained a group of volunteer young women from the local colleges to assist in the program, but they needed help in orienting these volunteers to serve the needs of the girls and in recruiting the delinquent girls.
The community worker was assigned to meet with the group of volunteer college students. At the first meeting general information about the community and the needs of delinquent girls was given. The commu-

nity worker arranged for a female detached worker to lead a discussion about the dynamics of girl street gangs. At another meeting, the volunteers discussed the forthcoming program. They decided they wanted to work with the girls in the area of music, art, homemaking, physical education, and beauty culture. It was very successful. In a short time, by virtue of additional word of mouth contacts, 72 girls were registered in the program.

Developing Group and Individual Competence

Organizing the community at the local level is fundamentally a group process. The community group or organization represents—or *is*—the community to all intents and purposes for the worker. As an enabler or developer, his primary job is not to get this group to solve particular community problems, but to learn to use an appropriate interactional process for attacking these problems. The sense of community and the success of the organization depends chiefly on the quality and quantity of interaction of the members among themselves and with others.

Unlike the development worker, the enabler, especially if he is a professional, tends to give very careful attention to recruiting those persons and representatives of local agencies who are leaders, have influence, and can make a significant contribution to community problem solving. Depending on the purpose and structure of his sponsoring organization, he will attempt to involve mainly key people in the initial meeting of the community group. (This does not deny the responsibility of the worker to assist a great variety of persons, with and without leadership qualifications, to participate in the group once it is under way.)

Community groups appear to go through a life cycle. The members may have difficulty in forming at the beginning, and their membership may be quite passive, inept, and fearful. Then suddenly a few of the members seem to take over and provide drive and energy for the entire group, and a superabundance of energy may be released. In low-income communities this may be an over-reaction to past inertia; the group moves from being highly dependent on the ideas and direction of the worker to a kind of rebellious independence. It is only at a later stage that consistent, substantive, and steady movement is made by the group with decreasing assistance from the worker. However, with elections and the departure of key members, with unanticipated failures in group projects, the community group may have to form again and the cycle begin anew. An organization may be fixated or set at any one of these stages for an indefinite period of time. Then, too, many local community groups are paper organizations. A handful of people meet irregularly to conduct business and plan events of limited problem-solving utility. The organizational process here may be highly ritualistic.

One of the early pitfalls the worker has to avoid is over-structuring or over-formalizing the group before it develops the sense that it is a group. Low-income groups tend to move too rapidly into a formal organizational phase, for example, election of officers, drawing up a constitution or bylaws, and dues collection. The group needs to have the experience of interaction and shared experience in limited problem solving before it is really a functioning organism and is aware of its own potential.

Some people think they have an organization when they really don't have one. A couple of people with grandiose ideas go off and work on an idea of their own. It is only when you have a series of activities in which a fairly large number of people are participating that the idea of organization begins to develop.

If you have, for example, six consecutive meetings, fifteen to thirty people meeting once a week, you begin to have an organization. People begin to want to come to meetings and feel part of it. Habits begin to form. If you start collecting dues and formalizing the structure too soon, then it's somebody else's organization, and they don't really identify with it.

Of paramount importance, especially to the social-work trained staff, is the meaning and quality of involvement of individual participants in the community program. The worker should be highly sensitive to the need for as many selected individuals as possible to participate in making decisions and implementing them. He may devote an inordinate amount of time in discussions with people outside of meetings to support their participation in meetings and projects. He tries to tailor jobs to meet specific interests. He is constantly aware of blocks in communication and relationship among members, and if he can't solve them, he will try to work around them. For example, two ladies on a committee may be constantly at each other's throats, vying for leadership. The decision for the worker may have to be support of a third person for a particular office or responsibility, but at the same time, he will attempt to keep the other two ladies as much involved as possible, taking time, if necessary even during the meetings, to smooth ruffled feelings.

This trained sensitivity to the interacting process is the mark of the professional social worker. He may even decide to sacrifice a program in order to preserve harmony among group members, since the capacity of the group and its individual members to develop and keep functioning is his major objective. Consequently, the organization's task objective in terms of solving a particular community problem may in the short run take on secondary importance.

There is a tendency in local neighborhood organizations to focus too highly on particular needs of individuals and indeed indiscriminately to select service problems which are readily available. Funds to send individual youths to college may be raised, special training and work experiences for a few promising youths may be developed—and the notion of a planned approach to a major problem of educational reform or job development is easily subverted. More concrete and immediate service types of programs tend to be given preference. Also, programs which have less immediate payoff require a delay in organizational gratification of which the membership may not be readily capable. The worker needs to steer carefully between the Scylla of social and personal development programming and the Charybdis of more significant but difficult community problem solving. The group may founder either in its development toward a social club orientation or in trying to solve a problem for which sufficient resources of interest, concern, expertise, and time are not available.

Developing Leadership

Leadership development, or more precisely the guidance of the process of leadership development, is of extreme importance in organizing the community group. The life style, the mission, and the accomplishment of the organization hinge largely on the type of leadership it develops. It is assumed that every organizational and group situation serves to develop certain opportunities for leadership. The worker, particularly the enabler, tends to exercise a great deal of influence over the leader selection process.

> The staff has to exercise a certain amount of control over the selection of leadership. It sounds like a very undemocratic thing, but the fact is, in many situations, the prospect of getting erratic leadership is very great.

This is not so great a problem at higher echelons of organization, because the competitive process tends to weed out poor leadership, but the possibilities at the local level are considerable.

Frequently in grass-roots organizations, individuals who have great personality needs for domination, attention, and status but who are without demonstrated competence—in areas of living such as family, job, peer group—assume leadership roles. Such persons may be highly conscientious and invest a great deal of time, effort, and even their own limited funds in the organization, but—unfortunately—their leadership may be manipulative, erratic, authoritarian, or paternalistic and their participation may short-circuit the interactive process. Weak or obviously incompetent leadership can also be a problem, but it may in some respects be easier to solve than domineering leadership because the group is more likely to express its dissatisfactions openly and to accept the need for change.

Both domineering and weak leadership tend to retard the development of the community group, and particularly to thwart the objective of shared leadership. Various devices need to be employed by the worker to guide the leadership process. Facilitation of the group process encourages democratic decision making in the group, is a major warranty against poor individual leadership, and creates opportunities for new leaders to arise.

> Right away when a group meets for the first time they want to elect leaders. I prevent this as best I can. Sometimes we compromise with the election or appointment of a short-term chairman or president. It's important that people really get to know each other and especially what each can do in the organization. In fact, I try to delay the election process as long as possible. Meanwhile, we get a number of projects going. Each project will have its own chairman; this

gives a number of people a chance to demonstrate and develop leadership capacities. Then later, say six months to a year after the first meeting, if they want to elect officers they can do it. By that time, though, they really don't have to elect because they know who the real leader or leaders are, and who is constructively putting out for the organization.

The worker must be ever alert to evidence of leadership ability as it arises in the course of ongoing organizational affairs or business. For the development worker, it is generally less important to select persons who have relatively high formal status in the community—such as a doctor, lawyer, or businessman—than to encourage the selection of persons who are motivated to work for the good of the organization, are fairly articulate, have community contacts, and can use these contacts appropriately.

In attempting to encourage the development of leadership, the enabler or the developer may take over the leadership role himself, at least temporarily. While the worker attempts generally to assist others to exercise critical decision-making power and seeks continually to help the group become self-sustaining and independent, there are times when he must step in and exercise clear and forceful leadership. The worker, particularly the developer, may allow himself to be elected to a position such as secretary or vice president for a limited period of time. More likely, if he is a professional social worker, he will provide advice and consultation which affect the direction the organization takes. The danger here, of course, is that freedom for new leadership to arise may be hindered.

The worker, however, cannot avoid influencing the development of leadership, and he therefore needs to know why, when, and how to provide support, how to make clear whose point of view or position he supports and whose he does not. He can, for example, focus the group's attention on the utility of an idea or suggestion by a group member, thereby enhancing that person's status and providing an opportunity for that person to exercise additional initiative and leadership. The worker may also be drawn into a political game of aiding this or that organizational faction. If he is he must decide deliberately which subgroup or leader he will aid and what the consequences for his own relationship and the development of the organization will be as a result of his action. Ideally, the growing strength of the organization and the development of competent leadership will permit gradual but steady withdrawal of the worker's influence.

CHAPTER **VII**

Social Action

Observe the smallest action, seeming simple,
with mistrust.
Inquire if a thing be necessary
especially if it is common.
We particularly ask you—
when a thing continually occurs—
not on that account to find it natural.
Let nothing be called natural
in an age of bloody confusion,
ordered disorder, planned caprice
and dehumanized humanity, lest all things
be held unalterable.

Bertolt Brecht
The Exception and the Rule

To believe that social action is dead is to be badly deceived. The provocative rhetoric and mass confrontations of the late 1960s and early 1970s may be gone, but the quest of America's poor and oppressed minorities for social and political justice continues. As established action organizations have dug in for protracted struggle, so new groups have emerged to champion the rights of other disenfranchised peoples—gays, the aging, the handicapped, ex-offenders, low wage workers, and the like. Substantial revision in our systems of resource allocation, more open and responsive institutional decision-making practices, and a more equitable distribution of power are being sought. The skills of those originally "trained" in the civil rights, student, antiwar and other mass movements of the past twenty years have become widely dispersed in America.

Recently a strong emphasis in social action technology has been on the components and configurations of power—particularly political power. The strategic, technological and theoretical underpinnings to support the rhetoric of social protest and the fly-by-the-seat-of-the-pants radical style have evolved, broadened, and deepened since the early 1970s. The articles in this chapter offer a perspective on these changes. For the practitioner, they suggest some varied, but often quite specific, guides for seeking change through social action.

Janice Perlman provides a comprehensive review of sixty grass-roots groups, both urban and nonmetropolitan, in sixteen states across the country. Special attention is given to such basic components as origins, organizational structure, goals and issues encompassed, membership, funding and tactics. The strengths and weaknesses of the groups are pointed out as their attempts to take advantage of "cracks in the system to win victories and demonstrate that authority can be challenged" are described.

"The real and only question regarding the ethics of means and ends is, and always has been, 'Does this *particular* end justify this *particular* means?' " Saul Alinsky suggests this fundamental perspective in dealing with ends and means in the context of social change. Contrasting the ethics of action with the ethics of inaction, he goes on to outline eleven rules for dealing with the fundamental problems of means and ends. Illustrations of the ways in which these principles may be applied to action are drawn from a wide variety of sources, ranging from the American Revolution to the context of black power organizations. He gives particular attention to the achievement of moral support and justification for social action efforts.

Many social action efforts are developing in cities and towns where there had previously been little in the way of grass-roots organizing. The article by the Bois d'Arc Patriots describes one such mobilization in the inner city of Dallas, Texas. From a small but concrete beginning in free pest exterminations, the tactics and roles of the organizers are followed.

Perhaps nothing has been so lacking in the social action literature, nor more desired by practitioners on the firing line, than general guidelines for building organizations of poor and oppressed people. Warren Haggstrom's article offered here is based on his long years as an organizer, and draws extensively on his knowledge of Saul Alinsky's Industrial Areas Foundation. Day-to-day and week-to-week requirements are delineated. Emphasis is also laid on the hard political and moral choices that confront almost every social action organizer.

The concluding contribution is a Studs Terkel interview with a man whose adult life has been devoted to social change and social action. Perhaps it helps to explain why some people choose to become organizers and what it takes to keep from burning out. Maybe, too, it's about trying to live your life the way you want to.

Taken together, these articles suggest a series of possible value stances regarding social action for the community practitioner. In addition, a range of potential intervention roles is clearly delineated. While the emphasis is on conflict-based strategies, the authors do not neglect the fact that these strategies must often give way to those involving bargaining and negotiation. A careful reading will also suggest the kinds of agency auspices under which various social action modes might be most effectively utilized.

Because these articles touch on some of the central substantive problems faced by community practitioners around the country—housing, employment, medical care, police-community relations and the like—they also provide specific interventive techniques geared particularly to these problems. No final "answers" are offered and this is as it should be. As Haggstrom notes, the world of the social actionist is a place where ". . . complex structures constantly dissolve and re-form before him," a world ". . . of possibility in which he takes a hand to reshape the future."

26.

Janice E. Perlman

GRASSROOTING THE SYSTEM

Whereas in the 1930s struggles for social change took place for the most part at the point of production, with the lines of conflict drawn between workers and management, and the union movement playing a prominent progressive role, today's progressive struggles are often waged at the point of consumption. Given the greatly expanded role of the state, more and more such conflicts are between individuals or groups of individuals and the state or some part of its regulatory or delivery apparatus. The seventies are spawning a plethora of grassroots associations involving local people mobilized on their own behalf around concrete issues of importance in their communities. An outgrowth of the social movements of the past 15 years, yet vastly different in organization and style from the media-attracting demonstrations and protests of the sixties, the new grassroots activ-

ity is emerging at a time when the fundamental values and institutions of this country have been severely undermined and their legitimacy called into question. . . . Let us look at some examples of grassroots activity:

- A network of neighborhood organizations from over 100 urban areas called National Peoples' Action successfully lobbied for federal legislation forcing metropolitan savings and loan associations to disclose the locations of the mortgages they held and loans they made. The same group staged simultaneous actions in 12 cities protesting unjust federal housing policies for low-income familes.
- ACORN, a group based in Arkansas, supported a generic drug bill which passed the state legislature, obtained $6 million in refunds for Arkansas and Louisiana gas customers through the regulatory commissions, and successfully pressured a huge power plant (projected to be the largest coal-fired electric generating plant in the United States) into cutting down its size by

Source: From Janice E. Perlman "Grassrooting the System" in SOCIAL POLICY (September/October 1976) Vol. 7, No. 2, pp. 4–20. Reprinted by permission of SOCIAL POLICY published by Social Policy Corporation, New York, New York 10036. Copyright © 1976 by Social Policy Corporation and the author.

approximately one-half and installing sulfur controls before going into operation. At the same time, it elected 194 of its members to the Quorum Court, the county legislature which includes the capital city of Little Rock.

- In rural Virginia, 45,000 poor Blacks organized for the first time, forming into conferences of 50 people each and countywide assemblies made up of representatives from each conference. These Virginia assemblies deal with everything from individual grievances to racial discrimination in schools and jobs to the economics of tobacco acreage allotments.
- In California the Citizens Action League got a lifeline utility bill into state law setting a low flat rate for the basic electricity and gas needs of an average family and making all rates progressive, thus reversing the prevailing system of charging less per unit cost for the large industrial customers.
- Massachusetts Fair Share, a group which started in the city of Chelsea, after two years had grown into eight chapters with the largest grassroots organization in the state. The group succeeded in collecting enough signatures to put the utility rate reform issue on the ballot in the forthcoming elections.
- In Chicago a group called Citizens Action Program successfully thwarted Mayor Daley and his powerful political machine by stopping the construction of the massive Crosstown Corridor Expressway which would have destroyed numerous multiracial neighborhoods from the inner city to the suburbs. It also succeeded in getting tax reassessments for industrial and residential properties and in forcing banks and savings and loan associations to make loans in the neighborhoods where their investors live.

- Three women worker organizations—in Chicago (Women Employed), in Boston (Nine-to-Five), and in San Francisco (Women Organized for Employment)—are waging a coordinated campaign against Marsh and McLennan, the world's largest insurance brokerage house, for its discriminatory hiring and promotion policies. They demand compensatory affirmative action programs and back pay. Women Employed has already won a $500,000 settlement in back wages from another major insurance company—C.N.A.
- In the Mississippi delta Black lawyers working with a 14-county group called MACE (Mississippi Action for Community Education) won a successful ruling from the U.S. Fifth Circuit Court of Appeals declaring it unconstitutional for a municipality to provide unequal service delivery in different sections of the city. Brigades of citizens counted the fire hydrants, street lights, sewers, and paved roads in a number of delta towns in order to bring cases of service discrimination to court. . . .
- Well-organized senior citizens in Rhode Island won a struggle for free bus service from 10:00 A.M. to 3:00 P.M.; the Chicago Senior Senate won demands for half-fares anytime; and in Hot Springs, Arkansas, seniors in an ACORN chapter pressured the city council into taking over the failing private bus company.
- A group called SOCM (Save Our Cumberland Mountains) spanning five counties of stripmining area in East Tennessee succeeded in getting state legislation stipulating that land be taxed according to its mineral worth, not merely its surface acreage. Coal producers will now put millions into the public treasury. SOCM is now lobbying to have the tax money earmarked

for services in the same counties from which the wealth is extracted.

- The Rhode Island Workers in Action forced hospitals to provide free medical care ($50,000 so far) for unemployed workers and impoverished families. Using the same precedent (the Hill-Burton Act), a group in Philadelphia has already pressured one hospital into doing the same.
- In South Texas the radical La Raza Unida party won control of Crystal City (pop. 10,000) and Zavala County, in which it is located. . . . Similar Raza electoral takeovers are now being planned for other counties in South Texas.
- The Carolina Brown Lung Association, located in the textile towns of North and South Carolina, is fighting on the occupational health and safety issue. It is demanding and beginning to get retroactive health compensation and strict air quality standards within the mills.
- Thirty thousand families, primarily Black and low income, have organized in some 150 cooperatives in rural communities throughout the South struggling to survive against large "agribusiness." Most are associated with the Federation of Southern Cooperatives and/or the Southern Cooperative Development Fund. The latter is presently planning to create rural alternative life-styles according to the Israeli *moshav* model with dense villages of 60 families living and farming collectively.

The lack of available information on grassroots associations and activities in this country prompted me in early 1976 to undertake a study which included 60 such groups at some 30 sites, both urban and outside of metropolitan areas, in 16 states across the country. Those associations se-

lected for the study had one or more of the following characteristics: they were mobilizing large numbers of people, having a significant impact, and/or using a particularly innovative approach. . . .

LESSONS OF THE SIXTIES

The social movements of the sixties set the stage for the newly emerging grassroots activity by raising questions and mobilizing people around a great variety of national issues. The civil rights movement called into question this country's commitment to equality; the welfare rights movement revealed the dehumanizing effects of public policy and showed how the welfare system was designed to maintain dependency rather than foster autonomy; the antiwar movement questioned American foreign policy and political priorities; the women's movement challenged the structure of the family, the division of labor at home and at the workplace, the elitism and dominance of leadership (including that of the left), and the fundamental nature of human relations; and the consumer and ecology movements brought to light the proprofit, antipeople nature of corporate behavior and the interlocking interests of government and business.

But the problem with the protest movements of the sixties was that when the smoke and commotion cleared and the TV cameras went away, people were left as anomic individuals relating symbolically to a national-level thrust. Yet the lessons of the sixties have served the seventies in good stead; to begin with, it has become obvious, as Richard Flacks says, that most people are less concerned with "making history than making life." They may, if sufficiently aroused over an issue, drop their routines temporarily to devote their time to a cause, but for the most part people do not remain mobilized, especially if they focus on issues that are remote. Thus, the thrust of the seventies is on local organizations and on issues which are more rooted in people's daily lives, have a longer-term perspective, and raise people's consciousness through involvement at a concrete level in their communities.

Another clear lesson of the sixties is the need for a *mass base* rather than a minority base. One of the insuperable problems of the welfare rights movement, for example, was that no matter how many welfare mothers were organized, they were still a small minority—mostly Black and very poor women. What organizers have consequently sought in the seventies are issues which will unite low- and moderate-income people and people of different racial groups, including whites, on the same side of the fence, and pit them against their common enemies rather than against each other.

In terms of *ideology* there were still other lessons. The radical rhetoric of the sixties has been toned down and deintellectualized considerably so as to start from where the "people's heads are." The isolation of the Black Panthers, even from their own community (which was largely alienated by their militant style and upfront socialism), and the widespread disaffection of working-class people from the student movement, taught patience over preaching. The groups now are for the most part strongly anticorporate, though not altogether anticapitalist. They are reformist more than revolutionary. Many in fact are dogmatically anti-ideological. Others consider themselves pluralist, populist, or progressive. Many of the leaders consider themselves radical, independent left, or even socialist, but they are so committed to consciousness through experience that they are often unwilling even to discuss their own ideology in the abstract.

It was striking to see how little grassroots activity the new left of the sixties had spawned. The new left networks (the New American Movement and vestiges of Students for a Democratic Society) not only have no involvement with grassroots organizing, but those interviewed were virtually unaware of the extent of this activity. The few grassroots groups that are explicitly leftist (Cut Cane in Georgia, the Gulf Pulpwood Association in Mississippi, and the Fight Back groups in the larger cities) are generally so absorbed in sectarian infighting that they do little else. On the other hand, many of the leading organizers and staff of the new breed of successful grassroots groups were formed through the radical movements of the sixties. They often had experience in SDS (Students for a Democratic Society) or NWRO (National Welfare Rights Organization) leadership and are now applying what they learned from their mistakes. As Tom Hayden (one of the founders of SDS) . . . says: "The radicalism of the sixties has become the common sense of the seventies."

In short, what most of the contemporary grassroots groups do is take advantage of the cracks in the system to win victories and demonstrate that authority can be challenged and that the people can generate power through their numbers. They do not rely on the media for their credibility and they often do rely on full-time, trained, paid organizers. They draw on the type of organizing that Saul Alinsky was doing as far back as the fifties and up until his recent death, but are different in their variety and eclecticism. . . . They draw on union models, Cesar Chavez boycott models, welfare rights models, civil rights models, service provision, economic development, electoral involvement, etc. and invent new approaches as well as adopt pieces of others. What they all have in common is that they are independent community-based membership organizations (or coalitions of such organizations) composed of people acting on their own behalf. They focus collective action on their own social, economic, and physical welfare through (1) demands directed at the public and private institutions controlling selected goods and services, (2) electoral strategies to take over the institutions, and/or (3) initiating alternative arrangements to cope with the needs of the population that those institutions fail to meet. By definition then, these are not governmentally initiated and controlled programs such as Community Action Program, Model Cities, etc. They are not nationally based organizations with community chapters such as the NAACP or League of Women Voters; nor are they advocacy organizations such as Nader groups, legal aid, or advocacy planners which act on the behalf of others. They deal in collective rather than individual activities and are typically both multi-issue and multistrategy groups.

CHANGING CONSCIOUSNESS OF THE SEVENTIES

These grassroots associations have found particularly fertile soil for growth in the seventies, for a new era of disillusionment has dawned in U.S. history and grassroots activity is providing an outlet for many people's sense of impotence and rage.

A series of international and internal events have had the effect of delegitimizing our institutions of power: the empire was defeated by a people's struggle in Vietnam; American economic hegemony is being challenged by Japan, West Germany, and the oil-producing nations; the most venerated of public offices, the presidency, has been severely undermined by the humiliations of Watergate; and one by one, institutions of the government, especially the intelligence agencies, have been exposed and discredited. Simultaneously we . . . entered the most severe recession since the 1930s. This . . . meant rampant unemployment, inflation, and the first decline in real wages in 25 years (putting us back to the

1966 level). The fiscal crisis of the state and of the cities has meant a decline in the quality and quantity of public services coupled with an increase in taxes. People watch their neighborhoods deteriorate from lack of funds for services and scarcity of mortgage and loan money. They see their county hospitals, local fire stations, and neighborhood libraries being closed, and transportation systems cut back. The "energy crisis" has skyrocketed fuel prices for consumers so that in the winters of 1974, 1975, and 1976 thousands of families had inadequate heat. . . .

The mood in the country is not only one of anger and frustration, but also one of growing anticorporate and antigovernment sentiment. The thrust is toward decentralization, "small is beautiful," and local self-reliance in everything from neighborhood government to intermediate technologies. Even the national public opinion polls have begun to reflect these trends for the first time. According to the Quarterly National Survey done by Yankelovich, Shelly, and White in fall 1975, 65 percent said they felt things were going poorly in the country, and that they felt pessimistic about inflation and national trends. Over a third said that they were being seriously hurt by the economy—having trouble paying bills, meeting mortgage payments, losing their jobs, etc. Still more striking is the finding of a nationwide Hart Public Opinion Survey done at about the same time that people have begun to blame big business, not themselves or "the times," for the country's problems; have observed that business calls the shots in Washington; and have concluded that major social changes are needed. According to the survey, millions of Americans have lost confidence in capitalism (33 percent), believe both major parties represent big business (57 percent), blame big business for the country's problems (49 percent), and favor public ownership of natural resources (44 percent). Very few saw the capitalist system or business itself as responsive to local community interests and needs.

A TAXONOMY OF GRASSROOTS GROUPS

Given the widespread disillusionment with existing institutions and the lack of government or corporate responsiveness at the local level, a tremendous surge of neighborhood vitality in the United States has expressed itself through grassroots associations. One of the striking things in looking at the array of groups across the country is their diversity—in type, scope, and choice of issue—as well as in their basic approach. Some feeling for this is conveyed by the examples given earlier, but in order to analyze the organizations, a typology is useful. The groups, then, may be classified according to approach: there are groups which use direct action to pressure existing institutions and elites to be more accountable; those which seek power electorally in order to replace the existing elites and institutions; and those which bypass existing centers of power by forming alternative institutions. These categories are by no means mutually exclusive; the most interesting, innovative, and successful groups often combine two or even all three approaches.

Within the *direct-action/pressure group approach* there are groups focused on a single issue (such as ... the women workers organizations or the Brown Lung Association in the Carolinas) and those which deal with multiple issues (such as ACORN in Arkansas, CAP in Chicago, and MACE in Mississippi). The groups also range in scope from the neighborhood level to citywide, to statewide, and even multistate. At present there are three multistate multi-issue organizations in the country, about a dozen statewide multi-issue groups, two dozen or more citywide groups, and hundreds of thousands of neighborhood associations and coalitions. In New York City alone there are some 10,000 block associations. Single-issue organizations number even more. In addition, a support network exists around direct-action organizations including organizer-training schools, research-action projects linked directly to the organizing efforts, and a national network of communications. A major part of this network is provided by a monthly called *Just Economics* (circulation 3,000) reporting the issues, struggles, and victories of mass-based, multi-issue, direct-action citizens' organizations throughout the country and carrying advertisements for organizers.

In the *electoral arena* a national network for coordinating progressive efforts exists as well—the Conference on Alternative State and Local Public Policies. Its goals are to "strengthen the programmatic work of the left ... end the isolation felt by elected and appointed officials, organizers, and planners who share a populist or radical outlook ... [and] enlarge the base committed to policies for a restructured American society from below."[1] Its first national conference was held in Madison, Wisconsin, in July 1975, with some 150 to 200 officials from 12 states around the nation. A series of six regional meetings were [held during the following year].... Among the participants [were] Jose Angel Gutierrez, the judge in Zavala County and major figure in the La Raza Unida victory in "Cristal"; early SDS founders Lee Webb (now on the Governor's Energy Committee for the state of Vermont) and Tom Hayden; explicit Marxists such as Judge Justin Ravitz in Detroit; and progressive young mayors such as Paul Soglin of Madison, Wisconsin, and Jeff Friedman of Austin, Texas. As Loni Hancock, a radical Berkeley city councilwoman, put it,

---

[1] From letter of invitation to conference.

their goal is to "turn the unthinkable into the inevitable."

Among *alternative institutions* there is also a wide variety. They range from large-scale, mostly urban community development corporations to rural agricultural cooperatives, to self-help housing projects (like U-Hab in New York City), to women's centers and self-help clinics, to the numerous food co-ops, credit unions, and consumers' cooperatives throughout the country.

Since a good number of community development corporations (CDC) were included in the study, it will be useful to look at this type of group in more detail. Community development corporations are community-based groups involved in service delivery and economic development. They came into being during the 1960s and early 1970s "typically in poor minority neighborhoods, with a central goal of developing new sources of strength and confidence in those neighborhoods ... [and] alleviating the economic and social distress caused by the malfunctioning of the private sector and the shortcomings of the public sector."[2] The more than 100 CDCs in the country are supported largely by federal programs and private foundations (especially Ford Foundation), although the ultimate goal is to be self-supporting through profits. They are located mainly in urban areas, although some of the most successful have been in rural counties where their impact is greater, and they are mostly Black or Hispanic, although the most recent ones have been white ethnic. Many of them grew out of the civil rights movement (such as Mississippi Action for Community Education and Southeast Alabama Self-Help Association in the South, and Mexican American Unity Council and Chicanos Por La Causa in the

Southwest). Others originated through the labor movement—specifically the United Auto Workers who tried to set up community unions with collective bargaining powers in their neighborhoods (for example, The East Los Angeles Community Union and Watts Labor-Community Action Council). Still others came about through coalitions of pre-existing local groups (such as the Southeast Community Organization, a white ethnic group in Baltimore, and the Hispanic Office of Planning and Evaluation, and the Spanish-Speaking Unity Council in Boston and Oakland, respectively). The two largest and most well-known are Black urban groups whose origins are unique: the Woodlawn Organization in Chicago which was originally organized by Alinsky in 1960 and the Bedford-Stuyvesant Restoration Corporation in Brooklyn, New York, which was launched in 1967 through the efforts of Senators Robert Kennedy and Jacob Javits.

Like the direct-action and electoral groups, the CDCs have a national network. In Washington, D.C., there is a national association of CDCs and in Cambridge, Massachusetts, a Center for Community Economic Development, which is a research and evaluation component.

Each of the approaches described above has its own particular problems. Direct-action groups often begin when people at the neighborhood level become aroused over some local grievance. But once the stop signs have been installed, the potholes in the street fixed, the abandoned building demolished, the massage parlor closed, or the highway rerouted, it is difficult to maintain their interest. People burn out and either victory or defeat can diffuse their energy. After a victory is won the tendency is to think that it's all over and everyone returns to "life as usual." On the other hand, failure reinforces pessimism, cynicism, and individualism and reconvinces

---

[2] *Search, A Report from the Urban Institute,* vol. 5, no. 5–6 (Winter 1975).

people that they "can't fight city hall." Either way people soon tire of marching, picketing, and coming out to meetings and hearings. Therefore, once the small-scale neighborhood issues have begun to wear thin, the group has to develop new directions to survive. The options are to take on broader citywide or statewide issues (through rapid growth of the original organization or through coalitions with other groups), to move into electoral politics, or to go into some form of direct service delivery or economic development for its constituency.

Likewise, each of these alternatives has its own problems. First, those groups that move on to large-scale issues generally use their best local leadership and staff energies to build the higher-level organization and fight the larger battles. If they are not particularly sensitive to the problems, they often withdraw so much of their resources and energy from the local-level activities that they may end up isolated with only paper organizations at their base. Second, electoral-type groups often spend enormous energies in getting their candidates elected only to discover that they can do very little once in office. Not only may they encounter strong opposition or be outvoted on a city council or board, but they also confront the built-in limitations of all local politics— namely, that many of people's most pressing demands, such as more jobs, or a better tax base (for improved services) are not controlled at the neighborhood or even city or state level. Disillusionment and accusations of "selling out" often follow the election of minority and/or progressive officials. The final option—the programmatic or alternative institution strategy—is an attempt to overcome that limitation in a small way: to create jobs, train workers and administrators, attract funds to the area, and provide direct services within the community. There is no doubt that any pressure group or electoral insurgency would benefit

immensely from the autonomy of having its own economic base. The problem is that this move from protest to program often leads to new forms of dependency and to the demise of the original participatory structure and mass base of the organization. As the energies, resources, and leadership skills of the organization are focused on "hard" programs, the role of the "soft" community side tends to diminish and may eventually wither away altogether. Furthermore, from the start there are built-in contradictions in trying to form a capitalist enterprise that will serve community welfare, that will be efficient in profit making and yet equitable in the distribution of those profits, and that will serve a community's needs rather than dictating them. Private profit and public welfare make strange bedfellows. And the ventures themselves are high-risk since they are generally in the most marginal sector of competitive capitalism, are located in communities with few resources and low purchasing power, and are often both undercapitalized and underexperienced from the start. Thus the odds of breaking even are low, and of generating profits for community use even lower. In fact, given that mere survival is a striking accomplishment, self-sufficiency would be a near miracle. It is no surprise then that CDCs and cooperatives might be dependent on the government and/or foundations. This may not be so bad given the multiple and possibly unique benefits they confer on the community; yet their very presence, like that of much self-help activity, takes regular institutions off the hook as far as providing equal services for their communities, and relieves a certain amount of pressure on them for what should be their responsibility.

AN OVERVIEW OF 60 GROUPS

The study of grassroots associations reported on here encompassed 32 direct-action groups (21 multi-issue and 11 single-issue), 5 research-action support groups, 3 electoral groups, and 20 alternative institutions (of which 11 were CDCs and 6 were agricultural co-ops). Groups were questioned on the following main points: how long they had been functioning, their origins, the constituency represented, leadership, number of members and staff, sources of funding, issues, and ideology. A summary of findings is reported below. More detailed information on individual groups is given in Table 26.1.

Length of Time in Operation

The first striking observation was that the grassroots groups studied were very young. The direct-action groups are no more than a few years old; most of the grassroots electoral victories have occurred over the past five years, and even the CDCs and co-ops are products of the late sixties. This raises the question, discussed in greater detail later, of whether the grassroots groups observed in 1976 will still be around in 1980 or 1986. Some believe that the life span of any community group is five years, after which time the "iron law of oligarchy" sets in and the group succumbs to the establishment. It will be interesting to observe over time not only whether these groups survive but whether they become rigid or go through "cultural revolutions" with new people charting new directions.

Origins

As suggested earlier, almost all of the direct-action and electoral groups and about half of the CDCs and co-ops had their origins in social movements. The welfare rights and antiwar movements (in addition to the "organizing movement" deriving from Alinsky's Industrial Areas Foundation Training Center) spawned

most of the direct-action multi-issue groups; the women's movement and labor movement generated a great many of the single-issue groups; and the civil rights and labor movements were the inspiration for those of the CDCs that started as authentic bottom-up groups rather than top-down welfare agencies.

Constituencies

The constituencies of the groups reveal some interesting differences. The direct-action groups have been focusing on developing a mass base which draws in moderate- as well as low-income people and which attracts working-class whites as well as racial minorities to the same side of the issues. The electoral groups—with the exception of Crystal City which was 83 percent Chicano before the La Raza takeover and now is 95 percent—try to put together liberal coalitions of professional people, students, minorities, and workers, and have had much better success in college towns (such as Berkeley, Austin, and Madison) than anywhere else. The CDCs are primarily Black and Hispanic with a very low income base and bourgeois leadership, although recently a few white ethnic ones have been established by groups pressuring the foundations and government about pluralism and reverse racial discrimination.

Leadership

The directors of CDCs and co-ops, the candidates in the electoral insurgencies, and the organizers and staff of direct-action groups tend to be better educated, younger, more often male, and from a higher class background than the base, although they are generally from the same racial or ethnic group. It is definitely out of fashion in the 1970s to have all-white leadership in an all-Black community, as was the case in many

TABLE 26.1
Typology of Grassroots Groups

TYPE OF GROUP	LOCATION	AGE	ORIGIN	CONSTITUENCY		
I. Direct-action groups A. Multi-issue	Headquarters	Date of Origin	Historic Antecedents	Rural or Urban	Class*	Race
MULTISTATE						
NPA (National People's Action)	Chicago, IL	1973	Organizer training	Urban	Low & moderate income	Mostly white
ACORN (Assoc. of Community Organizations for Reform Now)	Little Rock, AR	1970	NWRO**	Urban & rural	Low & moderate	70% white
NASP (National Assoc. of the Southern Poor)	Petersburg, VA	1968	Civil Rights, British parliamentary democracy; Jeffersonian democracy	Mostly rural	Poor	Black
STATEWIDE						
Massachusetts Fair Share	Boston, MA	1973	NWRO SDS	Urban & suburban	Low & moderate	Mostly white
CAL (Citizen Action League)	San Francisco, CA	1974	SNCC SDS NWRO Alinsky tradition	Urban	Low & middle income	Mostly white
Carolina Action	Durham, NC	1973	NWRO ACORN Organizer training	Urban & rural	Low & moderate income	Black & white
MAC (Maryland Action Coalition)	Baltimore, MD	1975	Organizer training	Urban	Working class	White
GROWTH (Grassroots Organizations with/without Tom Hayden)	Los Angeles, CA	1975	Antiwar movement	Urban & suburban	Working & middle class	Mostly white
IPAC (Illinois Public Interest Council)	Chicago, IL	1975	AFL-CIO & new left	Rural & urban	Working class	Mixed
PACC (People's Alliance for a Cooperative Commonwealth)	Chapel Hill, NC	1975	NAM (New American Movement)	Urban	Low & moderate income	Mixed

*The class base and issues are noted in the vocabulary of the groups themselves.

**Abbreviations: NWRO—National Welfare Rights Organization; SDS—Students for a Democratic Society; SNCC—Student Nonviolent Coordinating Committee.

TABLE 26.1
(Continued)

SIZE		FUNDING	ISSUES*	MEDIA PROFILE
Staff	Membership			
20–30	39 states, 104 urban areas, 11,000+ members	Churches, foundations, business, direct mail	Housing and neighborhood revitalization, redlining, S & L disclosures, variable-rate mortgages	High profile; uses the media
30–40	6,000 member families, 5 states (AR, SD, TX, MS, LA), 14 offices	Dues, foundations	Lifeline utility rates, generic drugs, Quorum Court, Wilbur Mills Exp., White Bluff Power Plant, tax assessments	Medium profile; work with local media
47	45,000, 900 active "conferences," 18 counties & 3 cities in VA, 9 counties in NC	Churches, foundations, direct mail	Racial discrimination, welfare and food stamps, municipal services, schools (curriculum, expulsions, suspensions), Black land loss, agricultural co-ops, tobacco allotment	Low profile; avoids media
35	600–1000, 8 affiliate groups around Boston	Canvassing, churches, foundations, fundraising	Utility rates, tax reform telephone rates, homeowner insurance, housing abandonment	High profile; good media relations
47 10 organizers	620–1000, 3 chapters (S.F., San Mateo, L.A.)	Foundations, membership dues, churches, canvassing, fund-raising	Utility rates, tax assessments, tenant organizing, child care, crime, nursing homes	High profile; works with media
12	700–1000, Durham, Raleigh, Greensboro	Dues, canvassing, churches	Lifeline fair share utility rates, property taxes, telephone rates, senior citizen bus service, city council, neighborhood revitalization	Low profile; wants more coverage
3	Just beginning	Canvassing	Utilities, taxes	Low profile
2	35 chapters, 15 new ones planned	Hayden campaign, direct contributions	Local neighborhood issues	Low profile
4	New group, 100 groups expected at founding convention	Canvassing, ad book	Housing, taxes, utilities, crime, economic justice	Medium profile; growing coverage
3	New group	Contributions	Neighborhood preservation, consumer protection, taxes, senior citizens, environmental issues	Low profile; very little media

413

TABLE 26.1
(Continued)

TYPE OF GROUP	LOCATION	AGE	ORIGIN	CONSTITUENCY		
I. Direct-action groups A. Multi-issue	Headquarters	Date of Origin	Historic Antecedents	Rural or Urban	Class*	Race
CITYWIDE CAP (Citizen Action Project)	Chicago, IL	1969–1970	Organizer training (Alinsky School) & ecology movement	Urban	Low & middle income	60% white, 30% Black, 10% Hispanic
COPS (Community Organizations for Public Service)	Phoenix, AZ	1974	Organizer training (Alinsky School-IAF)	Urban	Working & lower middle class	Chicano
Metropolitan Phoenix Indian Coalition	Phoenix, AZ	1975	Civil rights	Urban	Low	American Indian
NEIGHBORHOOD AMO (Adams Morgan Organization)	Washington, D.C.	1972	Civil and social action groups	Urban	Low & moderate income	Black, white, Hispanic
COPO (Coalition of Peninsula Organizations)	Baltimore, MD	1976	Organizer training, federated community, direct action	Urban	Working class	Mostly white
GO (Guadelupe Organization)	Guadelupe, AZ	1964	Catholic church, social work	Rural style in city	Low	Yaqui Indian & Chicano
I. Direct-action groups B. Single-issue	Headquarters	Date of Origin	Historic Antecedents	Rural or Urban	Class*	Race
MULTISTATE Carolina Brown Lung	Greenville, SC	1974	Black lung, United Mine Workers, Welfare rights	Rural & Urban	Lower working class	White
Minority Peoples' Coalition on the Tennessee-Tombigbee Waterway	Epes, AL	1975	Civil rights, Federation of Southern Co-ops	Rural	Low	Black
CITYWIDE WE (Women Employed)	Chicago, IL	1973	Union & women's movements	Urban	Working class	Mostly white
CAUSE (Campaign Against Utility Service Exploitation)	Los Angeles, CA	1975	Energy crisis, anti-war movement	Urban	Middle & working class	Mostly white
Nine-to-Five	Boston, MA	1973	Women's & labor movements	Urban	Middle & working class	Mostly white

TABLE 26.1
(Continued)

	SIZE	FUNDING	ISSUES*	MEDIA PROFILE
Staff	Membership			
4–6	8,000 members at peak, 35 neighborhood groups, 50 senior groups	Canvassing, dues, foundations	Pollution, tax reform, municipal services, redlining/greenlining, Crosstown Corridor Highway	High profile; good media relations
4	40,000, 300 groups	Churches, dues	Zoning, water rates, voter registration, neighborhood improvement	Medium profile; fair media
3–4	19 groups, 400 people at Spring Convention	Foundations, contributions	Intertribal cooperation, links between on- and off-reservation Indians, Indians empowerment, immediate needs	Low profile; very little media
2	4,000, 200 active	Fundraising	Housing & neighborhood revitalization, antispeculation, recreation, environment	Low profile; high locally
4	36 member organizations	Dues, fund-raising, contributions United Fund	Neighborhood issues with particular emphasis on housing, taxes, transportation	Low profile
14	425 now, 550 at peak	Foundations, churches	Incorporation referendum, neighborhood improvement (street lights, drainage ditches, roads, etc), land use	Low profile
Staff	Membership			
3	280 just starting 2 states: NC & SC	Dues	Occupational health & safety, compensation, factory condition improvement	High profile; good coverage
4–5	400 active members, thousands involved	Foundations	Jobs for local Black residents on the construction, land & water rights compensation	Low profile
6	300 dues paying, 1000 participants	Dues	Wage discrimination, working conditions, unionization, affirmative action in hiring & promotion	Medium profile
5	23 member organizations	Fundraising	Lifeline rates for water, gas & electricity, fight against Alaska Pipeline costs passed on to consumers	High profile; use TV especially
5 groups; 3 unions	450 dues paying, 800 on mailing list	Dues	Wage discrimination, working conditions, unionization, affirmative action in hiring & promotion, maternity benefits, job training	Medium profile

TABLE 26.1
(Continued)

	TYPE OF GROUP	LOCATION	AGE	ORIGIN	CONSTITUENCY		
NEIGHBORHOOD	I. Direct-action groups B. Single-issue	Headquarters	Date of Origin	Historic Antecedents	Rural or Urban	Class*	Race
	ROAR (Restore our Alienated Rights)	Boston, MA	1974	Neighborhood protection	Urban	Working class	White
	Co-op City	Bronx, NY	1974	Tenants movement	Urban	Working class	¾ White, ¼ Black
	II. Electoral efforts						
	Crystal City ("Cristal")	Zavala County, TX	1970	MAYO (Mexican American Youth Organization), La Raza Unida Party	Rural	Low	Chicano
	III. Alternative institutions A. CDCs	Headquarters	Date of Origin	Historic Antecedents	Rural or Urban	Class*	Race
MULTICOUNTY	MACE (Mississippi Action for Community Education)	Greenville, MS	1967	Civil rights voter registration, SNCC MS Freedom Democratic Party	Rural	Low	Black
	SEASHA (Southeast Alabama Self-Help)	Tuskegee, AL	1967	Civil Rights, OEO educational program	Rural	Low	Black
CITYWIDE	SSUS (Spanish-speaking Unity Council)	Oakland, CA	1963	Social work & services	Urban	Low	Hispanic
	Chicanos Por La Causa, Inc.	Phoenix, AZ	1968	Civil rights, Martin Luther King/JFK inspiration	Urban	Low & moderate	Chicano
	HOPE (Hispanic Office of Planning & Evaluation)	Boston, MA	1970	Civil rights, Social service	Urban	Low & moderate	Hispanic
	MAUC (Mexican American Unity Council)	San Antonio, TX	1968	Civil rights	Urban	Low	Chicano

TABLE 26.1
(Continued)

SIZE		FUNDING	ISSUES*	MEDIA PROFILE
Staff	Membership			
150 volunteers	1,000, 400 active, 200 "marshals"	Contributions	Fight against forced busing, neighborhood preservation, electoral politics, ABC's (anti-abortion, busing, communism)	Very high profile; national
5 full-time	55,000 people, 15,372 units	Withheld rents	Rent strike	Very high; Nat/local
Most all elected & appointed officials	10,000 500 active "Ciudanos Unidos"	Taxes, federal funds foundations	Housing, schools, health care, economic development (CDC), unionization of Delmonte	High profile
Staff	Membership			
10 offices 30 organizers	12,000, 14 counties	Ford Foundation	Equalization suit (Hawkins v. Shaw), electoral politics (former MS Freedom Democratic party), economic development, water and utilities	Very low profile; avoid media
20–25	8,000, 2 counties	Ford Foundation, federal programs, OEO	Feeder-pig co-op, credit union, housing, voter registration, Black land retention	Low profile; little media
13	13 organizations 47 at peak	Ford Foundation, federal programs	Information & job referral, business consulting, human-power training, housing & building management	Very low profile; almost no media
14	366 (just began)	Ford Foundation, federal programs, OEO/CSA	Zoning, housing, education, airport location, services, community economic development	Low; prefer more/better coverage
20	300, plan membership drive	Ford Foundation, federal programs, revenue sharing	Education (College-Bound program), anti-Southwest Corridor, prison, project	Low profile; little media
100+	None	Ford Foundation, federal programs, revenue sharing	Housing, hospital care, mental health, police brutality, alcoholism	Medium profile; runs own radio & TV spots

TABLE 26.1
(Continued)

	TYPE OF GROUP	LOCATION	AGE	ORIGIN	CONSTITUENCY		
	III. Alternative Institutions A. CDCs	Headquarters	Date of Origin	Historic Antecedents	Rural or Urban	Class*	Race
NEIGHBORHOOD	Bedford-Stuyvesant Restoration & Development	Brooklyn, NY	1967	OEO, Senators Kennedy & Javits	Urban	Low	Black & some Puerto Rican
NEIGHBORHOOD	TWO (The Woodlawn Organization)	Chicago, IL	1959	Alinsky school	Urban	Low	Black
NEIGHBORHOOD	SECO (Southeast Community Organization)	Baltimore, MD	1970	Organizer training civil rights "New Pluralism"	Urban	Low & moderate	white ethnic
NEIGHBORHOOD	WLCAC (Watts Labor Community Action Council)	Los Angeles, CA	1965	United Auto Workers	Urban	Low	Black
	TELACU (The East Los Angeles Community Union)	Los Angeles, CA	1965	United Auto Workers	Urban	Low	Chicano
	III. Alternative Institutions B. Cooperatives						
	SCDF (Southern Cooperation Development Fund)	Lafayette, LA	1969	Civil rights; rural co-op movement	Rural	Low	Black
	FSC (Federation of Southern Cooperatives)	Epes, AL	1967	Civil rights; rural co-ops	Rural	Low	Black

of the SDS (ERAP) organizing projects of 10 years ago. There are some white staff people in predominantly Black groups (like the staff director and organizers of NASP or the housing manager of SEASHA) but this is the exception, not the rule.

In all cases—from direct-action organizing groups to electoral campaigns to CDCs and co-ops—leadership is one of the most critical factors accounting for the success or failure of the group. Certain dilemmas arise with predictable consistency: (1) the different qualities of leadership associated with the founding of an organization as opposed to its institutionalization; (2) the question of accountability and the roles of organizer

TABLE 26.1
(Continued)

SIZE		FUNDING	ISSUES*	MEDIA PROFILE
Staff	Membership			
240 now, 300 peak	None, 26 "member" directors	Ford Foundation, federal programs, revenue sharing	Neighborhood physical & economic development, job creation, housing rehabilitation, tax issue, social programs	High profile; lots of media
288 staff (TWO & WCDC), 65 staff in organizing & services	115 groups, now beginning individual membership	Ford Foundation, federal programs, revenue sharing, social services money	Real estate/land use, economic development, housing, job training, employment, crime, shopping center employment	High profile; uses the media
35	70 groups	Ford Foundation, federal programs, revenue sharing	Expressway fight, neighborhood housing services, economic development	Increasing; cultivate media
150 staff, 350 employees	25 clubs	Ford Foundation, federal programs	Small business development, housing, Martin Luther King Hospital, humanpower training, seniors program	High profile; uses media
35 staff	15 clubs	Former Ford funding, federal programs	Economic development, research & planning, loan package, voter registration, incorporation	Low profile; little media coverage
8	35–50 co-ops	Ford Foundation, federal programs	Preventing Black land loss, creating humanitarian Moshav-style alternative, helping member co-ops with credit union, getting Blacks elected	Low profile; favorable coverage
50	30,000 families, 120 co-ops, 14 states	Rockefeller foundation, federal progams	Preventing Black land loss, providing "populist/socialist" technical assistance to co-ops, comprehensive rural economic development strategy, training center, demonstration farm (1,300 acres)	Low profile

or staff as opposed to local leaders and board members; (3) the issues of concentration or dispersion of decision-making power in an organization, and the importance of a strong single leader versus the development of good secondary leadership; and (4) the pros and cons of indigenous versus outside organizers and staff. Ulti-

mately, to understand all of these problematic aspects for leaders, one must raise the question of what's in it for them. Let us look at each of these points.

It has often been difficult for the same individual(s) who founded an organization to be effective in administering its everyday functioning. As Max Weber pointed out, the qualities of charismatic authority may be diametrically opposed to those of institutional/administrative authority. History has shown that those who make revolutions are often incapable of "keeping house" once the new order has been established. As many of the groups have moved from protest to program this has become an increasing problem. It has led to internal tensions and to major splits in some cases as new managerial personnel have been hired to positions of responsibility—and pay—over the heads of the initial vanguard group of activists, or as the organization has wrestled with the tension between focusing its principal energies on community organizing and/or activism, program development and negotiation. In two cases such conflicts led to severe organizational rifts in which the head organizers ended up setting up countervailing organizations on their own. In both cases the original organization has survived, but was much weakened by the internal and external consequences of the split.

The question of accountability and the need for role clarification between leaders and organizers in direct-action groups or between boards and staff in CDCs is not unrelated. Organizers and staffs are paid while local leaders and board members are expected to donate their time. However, the organizers and staff are theoretically working for and accountable to their membership as represented by the leaders and/or board members. This distinction is fraught with contradictions. In both direct-action organizations and CDCs the organizers, directors, and staff generally have greater expertise than the rank and file and thus tend to dominate when important decisions are made. This may result in increasing the feelings of inadequacy and powerlessness that the organizations are supposedly set up to combat. There is a wide range of behaviors of organizers and staff, from a case where the organizer, who clearly calls the

shots, puts the community leader into painful and humiliating situations, to a group run much like any large efficient corporation which does not waste time manipulating local people into its decision structure, to a case where the organizers' role is to facilitate the solving of local problems and implement group decisions rather than to suggest either issues or strategies of their own. Many groups have researchers developing issues and staff members deciding on strategies and tactics, but try (with varying degrees of success) to work closely with their boards and local leaders as they do this.

Clearly there is no perfect answer. But the problem is closely tied in with the next one—the parallel issue of concentration of authority within the organization itself and the development of secondary leadership. The problem is classic: a strong leader is often one of the key ingredients for a successful organization; yet often the individuals with sufficient drive and ego to play that role well are incapable of sharing power or delegating responsibility to others. A personal fiefdom has severe limitations in terms of the transfer of skills and a positive self-image to others, and as an alternative socialization model toward self-help and empowerment. Groups that have a dispersed internal power structure are assured continuity even if the original founder moves on to something else and are able to grow more and be more flexible because they are not limited by one person's strengths and weaknesses.

Concerning the pros and cons of indigenous leaders versus leaders recruited from the outside, the often successful outside organizer according to the Alinsky model has no vested interest in the community, no family or friends to protect, and no permanent ties. When local leadership is sufficiently trained and strong, such organizers move on and begin elsewhere. On the other hand, there are clear advantages of credibility, responsibility, and sensitivity which can accrue only to those from the community and planning to stay there and live with the effects of their actions. In this case, accountability stops being an abstraction and becomes much more concrete. The organizers and staffs of most direct-action organizations tend to come from outside, whereas over half the executive directors and staffs of the CDCs and agricultural co-ops come from the local community.

What benefits are derived by the leaders of these various types of groups? For the organizers of direct-action groups the very process of organizing is almost a form of addiction. They work incredibly long hours, get very little pay, and love it! The ego gratification, the feeling of power, and the sense of "moving the masses" and of accomplishment are their own reward. For the candidates of electoral efforts, power and prestige are the traditional inducements and the extra challenge of trying to provoke progressive changes makes it even more enticing. In the CDCs money is a factor as well as power, prestige, and the desire for change. The executive directors and top staff of CDCs are quite well paid, and like the antipoverty programs, there is often a degree [of] competition for the available jobs, which are viewed as channels for upward mobility. The danger here is that the inner circle will be enriched amidst a continuing base of community poverty. Yet one cannot ask well-trained minority professionals to work for low salaries, nor expect young minority college graduates to do the type of quasi-volunteer work that is the basis of most direct-action organization staffs.

Size

It takes a great stretch of the imagination to conceive of a range of grassroots activity encompassing a 45,000-person rural Black organization, a 10,000-person La Raza Unida city in Texas, a 1,000-person direct-action membership in Massachusetts, a 425-person neighborhood organization of Yaqui Indians and Chicanos near Phoenix, a 280-person Brown Lung group and a 25- or 50-person block club. There is tremendous variation in the size of these groups and the size of their staffs. It is also true that there are different organizing strategies within the multi-issue groups which affect their size: the Alinsky-type groups form their membership through coalition building among already existing groups, while others start out to recruit members on the strength of the issues alone. Among the CDCs membership ranges from zero (in Bedford-Stuyvesant and MAUC) to 115 affiliate organizations (in TWO), to 12,000 individual members (in MACE). Bedford-Stuyvesant, for example, does have a few storefront offices scattered around the neighborhood that do counseling and referral on a drop-in basis and transmit complaints, but that hardly qualifies as a mass-base or participatory organization. Furthermore, some of the CDCs which do claim to have a membership structure have it only on paper. In some cases, what their function seems to be is to hire and pay big staffs ranging from 12 to 500. Organizing staffs in direct-action groups get paid much less, and range from about 3 to 50.

Funding

To maintain staffs, to pay rent on offices, to print pamphlets and newsletters, to mount campaigns to promote candidates— in short to run an organization—all takes a substantial amount of money. In direct-action organizing the labor union has been an implicit model, and yet, unfortunately for community-based groups, there is no neighborhood equivalent of the dues checkoff on a paycheck, and it is very difficult to get members to pay dues at all. What community groups have traditionally done is cover their minimum expenses through local fund-raising events such as bake sales, picnics, dances, and the like. But that isn't sufficient to pay organizers' salaries. The Alinsky-style groups raised money mostly through the local churches or required each member organization to pay a yearly fee to be raised on its own. Other groups, like CDCs and co-ops, relied heavily on government and foundation financing.

One of the biggest breakthroughs in the new organizing of the seventies is the use of door-to-door canvassing. Using this method, groups have been generating not hundreds, but hundreds of thousands of dollars—money with no strings attached to churches, foundations, or government programs. In brief, the technique is that of the encyclopedia salesperson: it uses the slickest of modern entrepreneurial means for collective organizational goals. It began a few years ago when an encyclopedia salesman from Chicago named Mark Anderson grew increasingly concerned about pollution, started an organization called Citizens for a Better Environment, and realized he could apply the same techniques he had used in selling encyclopedias to selling his cause. Canvassers are well-trained and monitored. They go door-to-door telling briefly what their group has accomplished so far, explaining that it is supported entirely by contributions, and asking for about one to three dollars in low-income neighborhoods, three to five dollars in moderate-level communities, and five to ten dollars in middle-class areas. If there is a community meeting, they canvass earlier in the day so they can attend, and they keep closely abreast of events in the organization through weekly meetings with the entire staff. If they cannot collect a minimum of about $65 per night, or if they fail a weekly informational quiz on the issues and activities of the group, they are fired or asked to work in some other capacity. This method works very well. Not only do canvassers

raise up to a quarter of a million dollars per campaign, but also they come in contact with many people who are interested enough in the work of the group to want to be on the mailing list or to become local leaders themselves, which means getting 10 friends to join the organization and start a chapter. . . .

Issues

Housing, redlining, tenant organizing, neighborhood preservation, utility rates, telephone rates, generic drugs, tax assessments, public transportation, budget monitoring, zoning and land use, crime and safety, pollution, senior citizens issues, and health facilities are some of the most common items being addressed by direct-action groups all over the country. Let us look at some examples of grassroots activity in these areas.

Redlining has been a particularly newsworthy issue . . . and major national victories have been won on it. *Redlining* refers to the common practice by banks and savings and loan institutions of taking a city map and literally drawing a red line around those neighborhoods which they consider to be high risks. Consequently, no loans are made for home improvements and no mortgage money is available for home purchase within that area. . . .

One tactic that a community group in Chicago devised to combat redlining is cleverly called *greenlining*. It involves getting pledges from all of the neighborhood residents specifying how much money they have in specific local savings and loan institutions and pledging to withdraw and/or redeposit it in another savings and loan that will reinvest it in the area from which it came. The idea is that if a given percent of the assets of a local savings and loan comes from a given neighborhood, then it should invest that same percent back into that neighborhood and not in some wealthy suburb or downtown commercial plaza. The groups involved were able to get pledges that would mean the withdrawal of literally hundreds of thousands—in some cases millions—of dollars from specific savings and loan associations—which changed their tune rather quickly.

At the national level an organization called National People's Action, spanning 39 states and 104 urban areas, pressured for federal legislation forcing banks and savings and loans to disclose where their loans are made so as to expose redlining practices officially and publicly. After much pressure and negotiation they got the bill passed for savings and loan associations only (not banks) and for metropolitan areas only (not unincorporated or rural areas). By these compromises they sufficiently divided the opposition on the bill to drive it through, but they are still at work pushing for stronger measures in the future.

The issue of utility rates has also taken on importance nationwide. Almost every direct-action multi-issue group has waged some campaign on utilities toward the goal of restructuring rate structures. The present rate structure sets lower prices per unit for large industries and commercial users than for individual consumers. Groups have been demanding a reversal of this, either through a *lifeline rate* which establishes the basic minimum monthly gas and electric needs for an average family and provides that amount or under at a flat low rate, or a *fair share rate* which simply makes the structure progressive across the board. A statewide group called Citizen's Action League in California mustered enough pressure to get a state bill passed on lifeline utility rates; ACORN in Arkansas has launched a powerful campaign pressuring city councils in nine cities for lifeline electric rates; and Massachusetts Fair Share has gotten enough signatures to put the is-

sue on the ballot in the upcoming elections. Since the use and regulation of utilities is decentralized, the groups face different obstacles and opponents in each local setting, but they do have a common thrust.

Among single-issue direct-action groups many of the same issues arise. There are a number of groups fighting on utilities (such as Campaign Against Utility Service Exploitation in Los Angeles and the Georgia Power Project in Atlanta), many groups dealing with housing, . . . and a wide variety of environmental and consumer groups. Some other issues, however, are only taken up by single-issue groups, especially the occupational health, job discrimination, and women worker organizations.

In Boston and the Carolinas some very encouraging alliances and mergers have taken place between single-issue groups, multi-issue groups, and more politically oriented efforts in the community. Massachusetts Fair Share represents the merger of three potentially competing interests—a single-issue utility group called CAP-Energy, a neighborhood branch of it called Chelsea Fair Share, and a radical-oriented community school and community center. The new group also holds weekly meetings with the women worker organization, Nine to Five, so that they can coordinate efforts and support each other where possible. The same sort of complementary alliance exists among Carolina Action, a multi-issue group, the Brown Lung Organization, the Occupation Safety and Health Association, the union organizing attempts in the textile factories, and a newly forming radical statewide coalition called People's Alliance for a Cooperative Commonwealth.

Ideology

Most of the grassroots groups active around the country today share a loosely defined common ideological outlook. They are progressive pluralist and left-wing populist. They are reformist rather than revolutionary. The direct-action groups and electoral efforts tend to be more openly anticorporate and antiestablishment, but even the CDCs and the co-ops feel strongly that neither the public nor the private institutions of this society are concerned with meeting the needs of "the little guy." It is between the organizers of direct-action groups and the directors of CDCs that perhaps the greatest ideological difference exists. The direct-action groups generally have more radical leadership than the CDCs which, though sometimes started by charismatic minority movement types, now largely attract entrepreneurs, or are led by the original leaders whose energies have since turned in that direction with similar results. In both cases, however, the membership base tends to be more conservative than the leadership.

One striking exception to the ideological picture just sketched is a mass-based, single-issue direct-action membership group in South Boston called ROAR (Restore Our Alienated Rights). It is among the best known, largest, and most tightly organized neighborhood groups in the country. According to its age (1974), grassroots origin, working-class base, and neighborhood preservation stance, it fits well within the mainstream of the other groups in the study. Its ideology, by contrast, is explicitly and militantly anticommunist. It is the antibusing group fighting to keep white children out of Black schools and vice versa. It is backed by a paramilitary outfit called the Marshals. The group runs an open information center six days a week from 9:00 A.M. to 9:00 P.M. with at least six volunteers per shift, never has less than a few hundred people at its weekly meetings, and it is growing rapidly. Claiming to receive support mail from all over the United States, the group held a nationwide miniconvention earlier this year which was attended by thousands of people.

Most members are ardent Wallace supporters. In this regard it is important to remember that economic hardship and alienation have historically bred not only progressive radicalism but conservatism and even fascism.

THE FUTURE OF GRASSROOTS ACTIVITY

. . . The question has been raised time and again as to whether the members of such groups are involved only to satisfy their immediate self-interest and will drop back into passivity with the first major group victory or defeat, or whether their interest and participation will persist. Evidence thus far shows that not only have the groups been growing rapidly but also that participant turnover in the groups has been relatively low. This may be attributed to the fact that good organizers usually have a mixture of short- and long-range issues going simultaneously, so at no moment is there a sense of definitive defeat or permanent victory. Indeed, in grassroots activity there seems to be an emphasis on process—and the process offers unique rewards. A high degree of solidarity is created through group struggles; for many people this fills a void and creates satisfaction in and of itself. And in each struggle a few individuals cross the threshold between making life and making history; these few become leaders, making the struggle their lives.

Furthermore, the groups' individual accomplishments are adding up; each victory on each issue may not be earth-shattering, but the cumulative picture is one of ongoing progress toward more equity in the distribution of goods and services and more accountability to the consumers. Even in such cases where the achievement may only be temporary, such as the restructuring of utility rates or the curtailment of redlining, the experience of involvement remains an invaluable one. People are beginning to understand the issues, to see how power and politics operate, to grasp both the potentials and limitations in collective action and to feel a new sense of self-esteem.

Given this direction, one wonders whether grassroots leaders and groups will be able to develop more political content and ideological coherence without alienating portions of their membership. In part, the answer to this question is gradually evolving out of the struggles themselves, and local work-study-action councils called FDRs (Federations for Democratic Reconstruction) are being formed to deal explicitly with the theoretical and political lessons emerging from the practice of local groups. Through the Institute of Policy Studies, dozens of groups, each with 8 to 12 members, are beginning to work throughout the country on an experimental basis with the idea that each person in each group will mobilize more people and start a new group by the end of the year, thus multiplying the original groups' effect.

A third question concerns the limits of localism. It may be argued that even if people stay involved, there are just so many stop signs a neighborhood needs installed or potholes filled, and there are limitations to the effect they can have on the larger issues of housing, utilities, and job-creation built into the nature of the system. But what is significant here is that participation in even small issues gives people experience in dealing with and understanding the power structure of that system. It shows them who are their friends and who are their enemies. Taking on the larger issues then evolves from stage to stage, as understanding grows. It is essential to be involved in small local issues to raise consciousness for involvement in the larger ones.

This leads to a fourth question—that of the inevitable attempts at repression or co-optation once the issues are broad enough to pose a serious threat to entrenched interests. While these methods surely have the potential to render powerless certain grassroots groups, others may grow stronger and stronger as the opposition expresses itself. Ultimately, a national federation of community groups, which would be able to bargain from a position of strength, will be necessary to insure the continued integrity of grassroots associations. . . .

Even with a national grassroots alliance and an emerging political consciousness, certain questions remain. While alliances with organized labor would strengthen the power of a grassroots movement, thus far such alliances have been limited by the conservative character of labor union leadership. At the same time, one can foresee a linkup between the grassroots network and the more progressive elements of the labor movement which have shown themselves to be forces for social and economic change— namely, parts of the United Steelworkers Union, Chavez and the Farmworkers Union, certain elements of the American Federation of State, County and Municipal Employees (AFSCME), of the Oil, Chemical and Atomic Workers, United Auto Workers, and the Mine Workers.

Finally, it is possible to speculate that with a nationwide federation and the right alliances with other progressive groups, the local grassroots associations in all their manifestations—direct action, electoral, and institutional alternatives—may contain the seeds for a new radical party or a movement to transform the Democratic party. The Conference on Alternative State and Local Public Policies, mentioned earlier, is one step in that direction, and, no doubt, there will have to be a great many more. But in the interim it can be said that given current apathy to national politics, local grassroots associations have become a locus for putting the issues of redistribution, economic control, and political decentralization on the national agenda.

27.

Saul D. Alinsky

OF MEANS AND ENDS

That perennial question, "Does the end justify the means?" is meaningless as it stands; the real and only question regarding the ethics of means and ends is, and always has been, "Does this *particular* end justify this *particular* means?"

Life and how you live it is the story of means and ends. The *end* is what you want, and the *means* is how you get it. Whenever we think about social change, the question of means and ends arises. The man of action views the issue of means and ends in pragmatic and strategic terms. He has no other problem; he thinks only of his actual resources and the possibilities of various choices of action. He asks of ends only whether they are achievable and worth the cost; of means, only whether they will work. To say that corrupt means corrupt the ends is to believe in the immaculate conception of ends and principles. The real arena is corrupt and bloody. Life is a corrupting process from the time a child learns to play his mother off against his father in the politics of when to go to bed; he who fears corruption fears life.

The practical revolutionary will understand Goethe's "conscience is the virtue of observers and not of agents of action"; in action, one does not always enjoy the luxury of a decision that is consistent both with one's individual conscience and the good of mankind. The choice must always be for the latter. Action is for mass salvation and not for the individual's personal salvation. He who sacrifices the mass good for his personal conscience has a peculiar conception of "personal salvation"; he doesn't care enough for people to be "corrupted" for them.

The men who pile up the heaps of discussion and literature on the ethics of means and ends—which with rare exception is conspicuous for its sterility—rarely write about their own experiences in the perpetual struggle of life and change. They are strangers, moreover, to the burdens and problems of operational responsibility and the unceasing pressure for immediate decisions. They are passionately committed to a mystical objectivity where passions are suspect. They assume a nonexistent situation where men dispassionately and with reason draw and devise means and ends as if studying a navigational chart on land. They can be recognized by one of two verbal brands: "We agree with the ends but not the means," or "This is not the time." *The means-and-end moralists or non-doers always wind up on their ends without any means.*

The means-and-ends moralists, constantly obsessed with the ethics of the means used by the Have-Nots against the Haves, should search themselves as to their real political position. In fact, they are passive—but real—allies of the Haves. They are the ones Jacques Maritain referred to in his statement, "The fear of soiling ourselves by entering the context of history is not virtue, but a way of escaping virtue." These non-doers were the ones who chose not to fight the Nazis in the only way they could have been fought; they were the ones who drew their window blinds to shut out the shameful spectacle of Jews and political prisoners being dragged through the streets; they were the ones who privately deplored the horror of it all—and did nothing. This is the nadir of immorality. The most unethical of all means is the non-use of any means. It is this species of man who so vehemently and militantly participated in that classically idealistic debate at the old League of Nations on the ethical differences between defensive and offensive weapons. Their fears of action drive them to refuge in an ethics so divorced from the politics of life that it can apply only to angels, not to men. The standards of judgment must be rooted in the whys and wherefores of life as it is lived, the world as it is, not our wished-for fantasy of the world as it should be.

I present here a series of rules pertaining to the ethics of means and ends: first, that *one's concern with the ethics of means and ends varies inversely with one's personal interest in the issue.* When we are not directly concerned our morality overflows; as La Rochefoucauld put it, "We all have strength enough to endure the misfortunes of others." Accompanying this rule is the parallel one that *one's concern with the ethics of means and ends varies inversely with one's distance from the scene of conflict.*

The second rule of the ethics of means and ends is that the judgment of the ethics of means is dependent upon the political position of those sitting in judgment. If you actively opposed the Nazi occupation and joined the underground Resistance, then you adopted the means of assassination, terror, property destruction, the bombing of tunnels and trains, kidnapping, and the willingness to sacrifice innocent hostages to the end of defeating the Nazis. Those who opposed the Nazi conquerors regarded the Resistance as a secret army of selfless, patriotic idealists, courageous beyond expectation and willing to sacrifice their lives to their moral convictions. To the occupation authorities, however, these people were lawless terrorists, murderers, saboteurs, assassins, who believed that the end justified the means, and were utterly unethical according to the mystical rules of war. Any foreign occupation would so ethically judge its opposition. However, in such conflict, neither protagonist is concerned with any value except victory. It is life or death.

To us the Declaration of Independence is a glorious document and an affirmation of human rights. To the British, on the other hand, it was a statement notorious for its deceit by omission. In the Declaration of Independence, the Bill of Particulars attesting to the reasons for the Revolution cited all of the injustices which the colonists felt that England had been guilty of, but listed none of the benefits. There was no mention of the food the colonies had received from the British Empire during times of famine, medicine during times of disease, soldiers during times of war with the Indians and other foes, or the many other direct and indirect aids to the survival of the colonies. Neither was there notice of the growing number of allies and friends of the colonists in the British House of Commons, and the hope for imminent remedial legislation to correct the inequities under which the colonies suffered.

Jefferson, Franklin, and others were honorable men, but they knew that the Declaration of Independence was a call to war. They also knew that a list of many of the constructive benefits of the British Empire to the colonists would have so diluted the urgency of the call to arms for the Revolution as to have been self-defeating. The result might well have been a document attesting to the fact that justice weighted down the scale at least 60 per cent on our side, and only 40 per cent on their side; and that because of that 20 per cent difference we were going to have a Revolution. To expect a man to leave his wife, his children, and his home, to leave his crops standing in the field and pick up a gun and join the Revolutionary Army for a 20 per cent difference in the balance of human justice was to defy common sense.

The Declaration of Independence, as a declaration of war, had to be what it was, a 100 per cent statement of the justice of the cause of the colonists and a 100 per cent denunciation of the role of the British government as evil and unjust. Our cause had to be all shining justice, allied with the angels; theirs had to be all evil, tied to the Devil; in no war has the enemy or the cause ever been gray. Therefore, from one point of view the omission was justified; from the other, it was deliberate deceit.

History is made up of "moral" judgments based on politics. We condemned Lenin's acceptance of money from the Germans in 1917 but were discreetly silent while our Colonel William B. Thompson in the same year contributed a million dollars to the anti-Bolsheviks in Russia. As allies of the Soviets in World War II we praised and cheered communist guerrilla tactics when the Russians used them against the Nazis during the Nazi invasion of the Soviet Union; we denounce the same tactics when they are used by communist forces in different parts of the world against us. The opposition's means, used against us, are always immoral and our means are always ethical and rooted in the highest of human values. George Bernard Shaw, in *Man and Superman,* pointed out the variations in ethical definitions by virtue of where you stand. Mendoza said to Tanner, "I am a brigand; I live by robbing the rich." Tanner replied, "I am a gentleman; I live by robbing the poor. Shake hands."

The third rule of the ethics of means and ends is that in war the end justifies almost any means. Agreements on the Geneva rules on treatment of prisoners or use of nuclear weapons are observed only because the enemy or his potential allies may retaliate.

Winston Churchill's remarks to his private secretary a few hours before the Nazis invaded the Soviet Union graphically pointed out the politics of means and ends in war. Informed of the imminent turn of events, the secretary inquired how Churchill, the leading British anticommunist, could reconcile himself to being on the same side as the Soviets. Would not Churchill find it embarrassing and difficult to ask his government to support the communists? Churchill's reply was clear and unequivocal: "Not at all. I have only one purpose, the destruction of Hitler, and my life is much simplified thereby. If Hitler invaded Hell I would make at least a favorable reference to the Devil in the House of Commons."

In the Civil War President Lincoln did not hesitate to suspend the right of habeas corpus and to ignore the directive of the Chief Justice of the United States. Again, when Lincoln was convinced that the use of military commissions to try civilians was necessary, he brushed aside the illegality of this action with the statement that it was "indispensable to the public safety." He believed that the civil courts were powerless to cope with the insurrectionist activities of civilians. "Must I shoot a simple-minded soldier boy who deserts, while I must not touch a hair of a wily agitator who induces him to desert . . .? "

The fourth rule of the ethics of means and ends is that judgment must be made in the context of the times in which the action occurred and not from any other chronological vantage point. The Boston Massacre is a case in point. "British atrocities alone, however, were not sufficient to convince the people that murder had been done on the night of March 5: There was a deathbed confession of Patrick Carr, that the townspeople had been the aggressors and that the soldiers had fired in self defense. This unlooked-for recantation from one of the martyrs who was dying in the odor of sanctity with which Sam Adams had vested them sent a wave of alarm through the patriot ranks. But Adams blasted Carr's testimony in the eyes of all pious New Englanders by pointing out that he was an Irish 'papist' who had probably died in the confession of the Roman Catholic Church. After Sam Adams had finished with Patrick Carr even Tories did not dare to quote him to prove Bostonians were responsible for the Massacre."[1] To the British this was a false, rotten use of bigotry and an immoral means characteristic of the Revolutionaries, or the Sons of Liberty. To the Sons of Liberty and to the patriots, Sam Adams' action was brilliant strategy and a Godsent lifesaver. Today we may look back and regard Adams' action in the same light as the British did, but remember that we are not today involved in a revolution against the British Empire.

Ethical standards must be elastic to stretch with the times. In politics, the ethics of means and ends can be understood by the rules suggested here. History is made up of little else but examples such as our position on freedom of the high seas in 1812 and 1917 contrasted with our 1962 blockade of Cuba, or our alliance in 1942 with the Soviet Union against Germany, Japan and Italy, and the reversal in alignments in less than a decade.

Lincoln's suspension of habeas corpus, his defiance of a directive of the Chief Justice of the United States, and the illegal use of military commissions to try civilians, were by the same man who had said in

---

[1] *Sam Adams, Pioneer in Propaganda,* by John C. Miller.

Springfield, fifteen years earlier: "Let me not be understood as saying that there are no bad laws, or that grievances may not arise for the redress of which no legal provisions have been made. I mean to say no such thing. But I do mean to say that although bad laws, if they exist, should be repealed, still while they continue in force, for the sake of example, they should be religiously observed."

This was also the same Lincoln who, a few years prior to his signing the Emancipation Proclamation, stated in his First Inaugural Address: "I do but quote from one of those speeches when I declared that 'I have no purpose, directly or indirectly, to interfere with the institution of slavery in the States where it exists. I believe I have no lawful right to do so, and I have no inclination to do so.' Those who nominated and elected me did so with full knowledge that I made this and many similar declarations and have never recanted them."

Those who would be critical of the ethics of Lincoln's reversal of positions have a strangely unreal picture of a static unchanging world, where one remains firm and committed to certain so-called principles or positions. In the politics of human life, consistency is not a virtue. To be consistent means, according to the Oxford Universal Dictionary, "standing still or not moving." Men must change with the times or die.

The change in Jefferson's orientation when he became President is pertinent to this point. Jefferson had incessantly attacked President Washington for using national self-interest as the point of departure for all decisions. He castigated the President as narrow and selfish and argued that decisions should be made on a world-interest basis to encourage the spread of the ideas of the American Revolution; that Washington's adherence to the criteria of national self-interest was a betrayal of the

American Revolution. However, from the first moment when Jefferson assumed the presidency of the United States his every decision was dictated by national self-interest. This story from another century has parallels in our century and every other.

The fifth rule of the ethics of means and ends is that concern with ethics increases with the number of means available and vice versa. To the man of action the first criterion in determining which means to employ is to assess what means are available. Reviewing and selecting available means is done on a straight utilitarian basis—will it work? Moral questions may enter when one chooses among equally effective alternate means. But if one lacks the luxury of a choice and is possessed of only one means, then the ethical question will never arise; automatically the lone means becomes endowed with a moral spirit. Its defense lies in the cry, "What else could I do?" Inversely, the secure position in which one possesses the choice of a number of effective and powerful means is always accompanied by that ethical concern and serenity of conscience so admirably described by Mark Twain as "The calm confidence of a Christian holding four aces."

To me ethics is doing what is best for the most. During a conflict with a major corporation I was confronted with a threat of public exposure of a photograph of a motel "Mr. & Mrs." registration and photographs of my girl and myself. I said, "Go ahead and give it to the press. I think she's beautiful and I have never claimed to be celibate. Go ahead!" That ended the threat.

Almost on the heels of this encounter one of the corporation's minor executives came to see me. It turned out that he was a secret sympathizer with our side. Pointing to his briefcase, he said: "In there is plenty of proof that so and so [a leader of the opposition] prefers boys to girls." I said, "Thanks, but forget it. I don't fight that way. I don't want to see it. Goodbye." He protested, "But they just tried to hang you on that girl." I replied, "The fact that they fight that way doesn't mean I have to do it. To me, dragging a person's private life into this muck is loathsome and nauseous." He left.

So far, so noble; *but,* if I had been convinced that the only way we could win was to use it, then without any reservations I would have used it. What was my alternative? To draw myself up into righteous "moral" indignation saying, "I would rather lose than corrupt my principles," and then go home with my ethical hymen intact? The fact that 40,000 poor would lose their war against hopelessness and despair was just too tragic. That their condition would even be worsened by the vindictiveness of the corporation was also terrible and unfortunate, but that's life. After all, one has to remember means and ends. It's true that I might have trouble getting to sleep because it takes time to tuck those big, angelic, moral wings under the covers. To me that would be utter immorality.

The sixth rule of the ethics of means and ends is that the less important the end to be desired, the more one can afford to engage in ethical evaluations of means.

The seventh rule of the ethics of means and ends is that generally success or failure is a mighty determinant of ethics. The judgment of history leans heavily on the outcome of success or failure; it spells the difference between the traitor and the patriotic hero. *There can be no such thing as a successful traitor, for if one succeeds he becomes a founding father.*

The eighth rule of the ethics of means and ends is that the morality of a means depends upon whether the means is being employed at a time of imminent defeat or imminent victory. The same means employed with victory seemingly assured may be defined as immoral, whereas if it had been used in desperate circumstances to avert defeat, the question of morality would never arise. In short, ethics are determined by whether one is losing or winning. From the beginning of time killing has always been regarded as justifiable if committed in self-defense.

Let us confront this principle with the most awful ethical question of modern times: did the United States have the right to use the atomic bomb at Hiroshima?

When we dropped the atomic bomb the United States was assured of victory. In the Pacific, Japan had suffered an unbroken succession of defeats. Now we were in Okinawa with an air base from which we could bomb the enemy around the clock. The Japanese air force was decimated, as was their navy. Victory had come in Europe, and the entire European air force, navy, and army were released for use in the Pacific. Russia was moving in for a cut of the spoils. Defeat for Japan was an absolute certainty and the only question was how and when the coup de grâce would be administered. For familiar reasons we dropped the bomb and triggered off as well a universal debate on the morality of the use of this means for the end of finishing the war.

I submit that if the atomic bomb had been developed shortly after Pearl Harbor when we stood defenseless; when most of our Pacific fleet was at the bottom of the sea; when the nation was fearful of invasion on the Pacific coast; when we were committed as well to the war in Europe, that then the use of the bomb at that time on Japan would have been universally heralded as a just retribution of hail, fire, and brimstone. Then the use of the bomb would have been hailed as proof that good inevitably triumphs over evil. The question of the ethics of the use of the bomb would never have arisen at that time and the character of the present debate would have been very different. Those who would disagree with this assertion have no memory of the state of the world at that time. They are either fools or liars or both.

The ninth rule of the ethics of means and ends is that any effective means is automatically judged by the opposition as being unethical. One of our greatest revolutionary heroes was Francis Marion of South Carolina, who became immortalized in American history as "the Swamp Fox." Marion was an outright revolutionary guerrilla. He and his men operated according to the traditions and with all of the tactics commonly associated with the present-day guerrillas. Cornwallis and the regular British Army found their plans and operations harried and disorganized by Marion's guerrilla tactics. Infuriated by the effectiveness of his operations, and incapable of coping with them, the British denounced him as a criminal and charged that he did not engage in warfare "like a gentleman" or "a Christian." He was subjected to an unremitting denunciation about his lack of ethics and morality for his use of guerrilla means to the end of winning the Revolution.

The tenth rule of the ethics of means and ends is that you do what you can with what you have and clothe it with moral garments. In the field of action, the first question that arises in the determination of means to be employed for particular ends is what means are available. This requires an assessment of whatever strengths or resources are present and can be used. It involves sifting the multiple factors which combine in creating the circumstances at any given time, and an adjustment to the popular views and the popular climate. Questions such as how much time is necessary or available must be considered. Who, and how many, will support the action? Does the opposition possess the power to the degree that it can suspend or change the laws? Does its control of police power extend to the point where legal and orderly change is impossible? If weapons are needed, then are appropriate weapons available? Availability of means determines whether you will be underground or above ground; whether you will move quickly or slowly; whether you will move for extensive changes or limited adjustments; whether you will move by passive resistance or active resistance; or whether you will move at all. The absence of any means might drive one to martyrdom in the hope that this would be a catalyst, starting a chain reaction that would culminate in a mass movement. Here a simple ethical statement is used as a means to power.

A naked illustration of this point is to be found in Trotsky's summary of Lenin's famous April Theses, issued shortly after Lenin's return from exile. Lenin pointed out: "The task of the Bolsheviks is to overthrow the Imperialist Government. But this government rests upon the support of the Social Revolutionaries and Mensheviks, who in turn are supported by the trustfulness of the masses of people. We are in the minority. In these circumstances there can be no talk of violence on our side." The essence of Lenin's speeches during this period was "They have the guns and therefore we are for peace and for reformation through the ballot. When we have the guns then it will be through the bullet." And it was.

Mahatma Gandhi and his use of passive resistance in India presents a striking example of the selection of means. Here, too, we see the inevitable alchemy of time working upon moral equivalents as a consequence of the changing circumstances and positions of the Have-Nots to the Haves, with the natural shift of goals from getting to keeping.

Gandhi is viewed by the world as the epitome of the highest moral behavior with respect to means and ends. We can assume that there are those who would believe that if Gandhi had lived, there would never have been an invasion of Goa or any other armed invasion. Similarly, the politically naive would have regarded it as unbelievable that that great apostle of nonviolence, Nehru, would ever have countenanced the invasion of Goa, for it was Nehru who stated in 1955: "What are the basic elements of our policy in regard to Goa? First, there must be peaceful methods. This is essential unless we give up the roots of all our policies and all our behavior . . . We rule out nonpeaceful methods entirely." He was a man committed to nonviolence and ostensibly to the love of mankind, including his enemies. His end was the independence of India from foreign domination, and his means was that of passive resistance. History, and religious and moral opinion, have so enshrined Gandhi in this sacred matrix that in many quarters it is blasphemous to question whether this entire procedure of passive resistance was not simply the only intelligent, realistic, expedient program which Gandhi had at his disposal; and that the "morality" which surrounded this policy of passive resistance was to a large degree a rationale to cloak a pragmatic program with a desired and essential moral cover.

Let us examine this case. First, Gandhi, like any other leader in the field of social action, was compelled to examine the means at hand. If he had had guns he might well have used them in an armed revolution against the British which would have been in keeping with the traditions of revolutions for freedom through force. Gandhi did not have the guns, and if he had had the guns he would not have had the people to use the guns. Gandhi records in his *Autobiography* his astonishment at the passivity and submissiveness of his people in not retaliating or even wanting revenge against the British: "As I proceeded further and further with my inquiry into the atrocities that had been committed on the people, I came across tales of Government's tyranny and the arbitrary despotism of its officers such as I was hardly prepared for, and they filled me with deep pain. What surprised me then, and what still continues to fill me with surprise, was the fact that a province that had furnished the largest number of soldiers to the British Government during the war, should have taken all these brutal excesses lying down."

Gandhi and his associates repeatedly deplored the inability of their people to give organized, effective, violent resistance against injustice and tyranny. His own experience was corroborated by an unbroken series of reiterations from all the leaders of India—that India could not practice physical warfare against her enemies. Many reasons were given, including weakness, lack of arms, having been beaten into submission, and other arguments of a similar nature. Interviewed by Norman Cousins in 1961, Pandit Jawaharlal Nehru described the Hindus of those days as "A demoralized, timid, and hopeless mass bullied and crushed by every dominant interest and incapable of resistance."

Faced with this situation we revert for the moment to Gandhi's assessment and review of the means available to him. It has been stated that if he had had the guns he might have used them; this statement is based on the Declaration of Independence of Mahatma Gandhi issued on January 26, 1930, where he discussed "the fourfold disaster to our country." His fourth indictment against the British reads: "Spiritually, compulsory disarmament has made us unmanly, and the presence of an alien army of occupation, employed with deadly effect to crush in us the spirit of resistance, has made us think we cannot look after ourselves or put up a defense against foreign aggression, or even defend our homes and families . . ."

These words more than suggest that if Gandhi had had the weapons for violent resistance and the people to use them this means would not have been so unreservedly rejected as the world would like to think.

On the same point, we might note that once India had secured independence, when Nehru was faced with a dispute with Pakistan over Kashmir, he did not hesitate to use armed force. Now the power arrangements had changed. India had the guns and the trained army to use these weapons.[2] Any suggestion that Gandhi would not have approved the use of violence is negated by Nehru's own statement in that 1961 interview: "It was a terrible time. When the news reached me about Kashmir I knew I would have to act at once

---

[2]Reinhold Niebuhr, "British Experience and American Power," *Christianity and Crisis,* Vol. 16, May 14, 1956, page 57:

"The defiance of the United Nations by India on the Kashmir issue has gone comparatively unobserved. It will be remembered that Kashmir, a disputed territory, claimed by both Muslim Pakistan and Hindu India, has a predominantly Muslim population but a Hindu ruler. To determine the future political orientation of the area, the United Nations ordered a plebiscite. Meanwhile, both India and Pakistan refused to move their troops from the zones which each had previously occupied. Finally, Nehru took the law into his own hands and annexed the larger part of Kashmir, which he had shrewdly integrated into the Indian economy. The Security Council, with only Russia abstaining, unanimously called upon him to obey the United Nations directive, but the Indian government refused. Clearly, Nehru does not want a plebiscite now for it would surely go against India, though he vaguely promises a plebiscite for the future.

"Morally, the incident puts Nehru in a rather bad light. . . . When India's vital interests were at stake, Nehru forgot lofty sentiments, sacrificed admirers in the *New Statesman and Nation,* and subjected himself to the charge of inconsistency.

"This policy is either Machiavellian or statesmanlike, according to your point of view. Our consciences may gag at it, but on the other hand those eminently moral men, Prime Minister Gladstone of another day and Secretary Dulles of our day could offer many parallels of policy for Mr. Nehru, though one may doubt whether either statesman could offer a coherent analysis of the mixture of modes which entered into the policy. That *is* an achievement beyond the competence of very moral men."

—with force. Yet I was greatly troubled in mind and spirit because I knew we might have to face a war—so soon after having achieved our independence through a philosophy of nonviolence. It was horrible to think of. Yet I acted. Gandhi said nothing to indicate his disapproval. It was a great relief, I must say. If Gandhi, the vigorous nonviolent, didn't demur, it made my job a lot easier. This strengthened my view that Gandhi could be adaptable."

Confronted with the issue of what means he could employ against the British, we come to the other criteria previously mentioned; that the kind of means selected and how they can be used is significantly dependent upon the face of the enemy, or the character of his opposition. Gandhi's opposition not only made the effective use of passive resistance possible but practically invited it. His enemy was a British administration characterized by an old, aristocratic, liberal tradition, one which granted a good deal of freedom to its colonials and which always had operated on a pattern of using, absorbing, seducing, or destroying, through flattery or corruption, the revolutionary leaders who arose from the colonial ranks. This was the kind of opposition that would have tolerated and ultimately capitulated before the tactic of passive resistance.

Gandhi's passive resistance would never have had a chance against a totalitarian state such as that of the Nazis. It is dubious whether under those circumstances the idea of passive resistance would ever have occurred to Gandhi. It has been pointed out that Gandhi, who was born in 1869, never saw or understood totalitarianism and defined his opposition completely in terms of the character of the British government and what it represented. George Orwell, in his essay *Reflection on Gandhi,* made some pertinent observations on this point: ". . . He believed in 'arousing the world,' which is only possible if the world gets a chance to hear what you are doing. It is difficult to see how Gandhi's methods could be applied in a country where opponents of the regime disappear in the middle of the night and are never heard of again. Without a free press and the right of assembly it is impossible, not merely to appeal to outside opinion, but to bring a mass movement into being, or even to make your intentions known to your adversary."

From a pragmatic point of view, passive resistance was not only possible, but was the most effective means that could have been selected for the end of ridding India of British control. In organizing, the major negative in the situation has to be converted into the leading positive. In short, knowing that one could not expect violent action from this large and torpid mass, Gandhi organized the inertia: he gave it a goal so that it became purposeful. Their wide familiarity with Dharma made passive resistance no stranger to the Hindustani. To oversimplify, what Gandhi did was to say, "Look, you are all sitting there anyway—so instead of sitting there, why don't you sit over here and while you're sitting, say 'Independence Now!' "

This raises another question about the morality of means and ends. We have already noted that, in essence, mankind divides itself into three groups; the Have-Nots, the Have-a-Little, Want-Mores, and the Haves. The purpose of the Haves is to keep what they have. Therefore, the Haves want to maintain the status quo and the Have-Nots to change it. The Haves develop their own morality to justify their means of repression and all other means employed to maintain the status quo. The Haves usually establish laws and judges devoted to maintaining the status quo; since any effective means of changing the status quo are usually illegal and/or unethical in the eyes of the establishment, Have-Nots, from the beginning of time, have been compelled to appeal to "a law higher than man-made law." Then when the Have-Nots achieve success and become the Haves, they are in the position of trying to keep what they have and their morality shifts with their change of location in the power pattern.

Eight months after securing independence, the Indian National Congress outlawed passive resistance and made it a crime. It was one thing for them to use the means of passive resistance against the previous Haves, but now in power they were going to ensure that this means would not be used against them! No longer as Have-Nots were they appealing to laws higher than man-made law. Now that they were making the laws, they were on the side of man-made laws! Hunger strikes—used so effectively in the revolution—were viewed differently now too. Nehru, in the interview mentioned above, said: "The government will not be influenced by hunger strikes. . . . To tell the truth I didn't approve of fasting as a political weapon even when Gandhi practiced it."

Again Sam Adams, the firebrand radical of the American Revolution, provides a clear example. Adams was foremost in proclaiming the right of revolution. However, following the success of the American Revolution it was the same Sam Adams who was foremost in demanding the execution of those Americans who participated in Shays' Rebellion, charging that no one had a right to engage in revolution against us!

Moral rationalization is indispensable at all times of action whether to justify the selection or the use of ends or means. Machiavelli's blindness to the necessity for moral clothing to all acts and motives—he said "politics has no relation to morals"—was his major weakness.

All great leaders, including Churchill, Gandhi, Lincoln, and Jefferson, always invoked "moral principles" to cover naked self-interest in the clothing of "freedom," "equality of mankind," "a law higher than man-made law," and so on. This even held under circumstances of national crises when it was universally assumed that the end justified any means. *All effective actions require the passport of morality.*

The examples are everywhere. In the United States the rise of the civil rights movement in the late 1950s was marked by the use of passive resistance in the South against segregation. Violence in the South would have been suicidal; political pressure was then impossible; the only recourse was economic pressure with a few fringe activities. Legally blocked by state laws, hostile police and courts, they were compelled like all Have-Nots from time immemorial to appeal to "a law higher than man-made law." In his *Social Contract,* Rousseau noted the obvious, that "Law is a very good thing for men with property and a very bad thing for men without property." Passive resistance remained one of the few means available to anti-segregationist forces until they had secured the voting franchise in fact. Furthermore, passive resistance was also a good defensive tactic since it curtailed the opportunities for use of the power resources of the status quo for forcible repression. Passive resistance was chosen for the same pragmatic reason that all tactics are selected. But it assumes the necessary moral and religious adornments.

However, when passive resistance becomes massive and threatening it gives birth to violence. Southern Negroes have no tradition of Dharma, and are close enough to their Northern compatriots so that contrasting conditions between the North and the South are a visible as well as a constant spur. Add to this the fact that the Southern poor whites do not operate by British tradition but reflect generations of violence; the future does not argue for making a special religion of nonviolence. It will be remembered for what it was, the best tactic for its time and place.

As more effective means become available, the Negro civil rights movement will divest itself of these decorations and substitute a new moral philosophy in keeping with its new means and opportunities. The explanation will be, as it always has been, "Times have changed." This is happening today.

The eleventh rule of the ethics of means and ends is that goals must be phrased in general terms like "Liberty, Equality, Fraternity," "Of the Common Welfare," "Pursuit of Happiness," or "Bread and Peace." Whitman put it: "The goal once named cannot be countermanded." It has been previously noted that the wise man of action knows that frequently in the stream of action of means towards ends, whole new and unexpected ends are among the major results of the action. From a Civil War fought as a means to preserve the Union came the end of slavery.

In this connection, it must be remembered that history is made up of actions in which one end results in other ends. Repeatedly, scientific discoveries have resulted from experimental research committed to ends or objectives that have little relationship with the discoveries. Work on a seemingly minor practical program has resulted in feedbacks of major creative basic ideas. J. C. Flugel notes, in *Man, Morals and Society,* that ". . . In psychology, too, we have no right to be astonished if, while dealing with a means (e.g., the cure of a neurotic symptom, the discovery of more efficient ways of learning, or the relief of industrial fatigue) we find that we have modified our attitude toward the end (acquired some new insight into the nature of mental health, the role of education, or the place of work in human life)."

The mental shadow boxing on the subject of means and ends is typical of those who are the observers and not the actors in the battlefields of life. In *The Yogi and the Commissar,* Koestler begins with the basic fallacy of an arbitrary demarcation between *expediency* and *morality;* between the Yogi for whom the end never justifies the means and the Commissar for whom the end always justifies the means. Koestler attempts to extricate himself from this self-constructed strait jacket by proposing that the end justifies the means only within narrow limits. Here Koestler, even in an academic confrontation with action, was compelled to take the first step in the course of compromise on the road to action and power. How "narrow" the limits and who defines the "narrow" limits opens the door to the premises discussed here. The kind of personal safety and security sought by the advocates of the sanctity of means and ends lies only in the womb of Yogism or the monastery, and even there it is darkened by the repudiation of that moral principle that they are their brothers' keepers.

Bertrand Russell, in his *Human Society in Ethics and Politics,* observed that "Morality is so much concerned with means that it seems almost immoral to consider anything solely in relation to its intrinsic worth. But obviously nothing has any value as a means unless that to which it is a means has value on its own account. It follows that intrinsic value is logically prior to value as means."

The organizer, the revolutionist, the activist or call him what you will, who is committed to a free and open society is in that commitment anchored to a complex of high values. These values include the basic morals of all organized religions; their base is the preciousness of human life. These values include freedom, equality, justice, peace, the right to dissent; the values that were the banners of hope and yearning of all revolutions of men, whether the French Revolution's "Liberty, Fraternity, Equality," the Russians' "Bread and Peace," the brave Spanish people's "Better to die on your feet than to live on your knees," or our Revolution's "No Taxation Without Representation." They include the values in our own Bill of Rights. If a state voted for school segregation or a community organization voted to keep blacks out, and claimed justification by virtue of the "democratic process," then this violation of the value of equality would have converted

democracy into a prostitute. Democracy is not an end; it is the best political means available toward the achievement of these values.

Means and ends are so qualitatively interrelated that the true question has never been the proverbial one, "Does the End justify the Means?" but always has been "Does this *particular* end justify this *particular* means?"

28.

Bois d'Arc Patriots

ORGANIZING IN DALLAS

The Bois d'Arc Patriots were founded in late 1972 in deep East Dallas, as a response to rapidly deteriorating living conditions. The neighborhood is primarily a low-income inner-city community, and most of the residents are white and Chicano. The majority of people, approximately 80 percent, are tenants, and the majority of owners are absentee slumlords. As the neighborhood is located close to downtown, Dallas City Hall has begun making plans to replace its residents, via various redevelopment schemes, with upper-income residents, who would provide a stronger tax and political base for the downtown establishment.

Though City Hall, like local governments in most large U.S. cities, has had "revitalization" plans for all inner-city communities, East Dallas is first up, for several reasons. Much of the tenement housing had once been single family mansions, oc-

cupied by the elite and near elite of Dallas. As these people moved away, the area was zoned multi-family in hopes wholesale redevelopment would occur spontaneously. This did not occur. What happened instead was that the old mansions were chopped up into sometimes as many as twenty apartments, and low income residents, most of whom were recent migrants from the surrounding rural areas, moved in.

Some homes continued to be maintained, and in one small area, young professionals bought in, repaired the homes and got a historical designation for sections of two streets. This qualified the previous label given to East Dallas by City Hall, and cultivated a certain interest for the area by non-poor people.

Also, because of its location, because of its residential character, and because of its large white population (compared to other ghetto areas), East Dallas captured the imagination of city planners who felt that it would be more attractive to wealthy whites.

The largest majority of East Dallas citizens are low-income whites from whom,

Source: From Bois d'Arc Patriots "Organizing in Dallas" from the *Green Mountain Quarterly,* February 1977, pp. 9–24. Reprinted by permission of Green Mountain Editions.

because of a historical lack of organization, City Hall expected little resistance to territorial encroachment. In addition, a very large percentage of the Spanish-speaking population are Mexican aliens and are not in a position to resist.

In late 1972 plans for redevelopment had not yet been implemented. However, the writing was on the wall and on the rent receipts. Slum landlords, with the sanction of City Hall, were systematically milking buildings dry, steering neighborhood housing economics toward the point of no return: a point at which housing could no longer be repaired, but would have to be cleared. Here land values would reach their lowest ebb and developers would ride in on their gravy trains. Slumlords who had blocked up enough land would make additional profits.

The people who founded the Bois d'Arc Patriots were primarily residents of East Dallas. They understood essentially from the beginning what City Hall's plans held in stock for East Dallas, and why. They were aware of the fact that their neighborhood had been singled out for the first assault on the Dallas inner city, and why. They felt that it was necessary to organize themselves progressively and understood the value of developing alliances along class lines. They also knew that the Dallas city fathers,[1] in the wake of the civil rights-Vietnam antiwar movements, would be generally smug in their belief that the low-income white community would not be receptive to progressive organizing. The Patriot founders calculated strongly on this smugness, feeling that if organizing started from the ground up (rather than being initially "issue oriented"), it would already have a

[1]Dallas has been controlled politically by a tight-knit group of the city's wealthiest businessmen. Their organization, the Citizens' Council, has a secret membership. The Council's political wing is the Citizens' Charter Association.

strong base before City Hall realized its own error.

The name "Patriots" was chosen by the organization's founders because besides being a term people in the neighborhood related to, it provided the means of differentiating between allegiance to the people and allegiance to a government which is not representative of the people. "Bois d'Arc" was chosen to describe the quality of organizational commitment. The Bois d'arc tree, native to the North Central and East Texas regions, has one of the hardest and most durable woods of North American trees. It is of historical significance in that it was used by early white settlers to make plows, and by Native Americans to make long bows. The first streets of Dallas were paved with Bois d'arc wood and most of the houses in East Dallas still sit on Bois d'arc foundation blocks.

ORGANIZING

The Patriots began organizing upon an understanding of two basic principles: (1) the [trait] of "political backwardness" ascribed to low-income whites by everyone from political hacks to movement leaders had been incorrectly analyzed, generally. No ingrained reactionary philosophy dominated the political or social views of low income whites. Poor people who live in a system where property worth defines human worth tend to see themselves as worthless. Then, when they are ignored and even blamed for various social ills, the doors that get slammed in their faces make a very provocative noise. As a result, people tend to lack confidence in themselves and, in addition, tend to lack hope that they can do anything themselves to bring their circumstances under control. One of the results is cynical, reactionary political and social views. One of the best cures is meaningful involvement in political self-determination on a neighborhood basis. Politics, as defined by the Patriots, is "the process of people organizing on the basis of common needs." (2) The great majority of needs of the people in East Dallas were then, and are still, in immediate proportions. It is impossible to gear people up for tomorrow when they are unsure of whether they will get through today. The Patriots knew that in order to provide a foundation for ongoing organizing, they would have to get a handle on meeting immediate needs of people in the community. Then, once this had been accomplished, people would have the slack to dig into root problems. Politically speaking, organizing around immediate needs (which in many instances were extreme and involved confrontation and violence) would be a way of demonstrating to people in a concrete way that people are the priority. The process itself was inevitably a people-first exercise. Low-income people could establish the people priority only by pulling together, only by collectively struggling to project themselves and the needs shared by others of their class.

This dovetailed with traditional American pragmatism. It was not a talk oriented, but an action oriented approach. Then, once it developed a measure of success, people could begin to speculate: "What can we expect to gain by this in the long run?" Both the methods and the goals, no matter how short term, were geared at placing people of the lower classes in a position of greater "value" than the system of property—monopoly capitalism—which daily exploited them. It would not be hard to explain this as part of a revolutionary process.

ON THE STREETS

In early 1973 the Patriots implemented their first program: Free Pest Extermination. The neighborhood was infested with roaches and rats due to the degree of absentee ownership.

The program was designed not only to help meet an immediate need, but to demonstrate the Patriots' practical problem-solving commitment and to do so right in people's homes. Once the doors opened, contact was instantly established and communication and participation could and did follow. Residents were asked, (1) "What is the biggest problem in the community?" and (2) "Would you join in to help solve it?" The answer to the first question was: "Something has got to be done about these slum landlords—they're killing us." The answer to the second question was an overwhelming yes.

The Patriots had a core of four people then, and all worked, full or part time, at workaday jobs, ranging from construction and warehouse work to temporary labor. Core Patriots pooled resources to offset living expenses, cost of pest control chemicals, etc.

By the time a hundred or more units had been exterminated, the Patriots had enough support to start their next program: the East Dallas Tenants' Alliance.

Slumlords, historically, have never been receptive to the concept of tenants' (or homeowners') rights in the community where they have investments. Texas statutes and case law provide so few rights for residential tenants that slumlords did not even bother to familiarize themselves with the law. Basically, they did not have to: it was whatever they wanted it to be, if not in the way it was written, then in the way it was enforced.

Evictions were the critical problem. State law requires that no one can be evicted without the landlord's filing an eviction suit. However, on the landlord's signature an "immediate possession bond" went into effect, and this bond could legally remove a tenant from the premises before a court date. Appeals were prohibitive, averaging around $1,000 cash to file. (Eventually two lawsuits filed by the Alliance have succeeded in changing these laws to a more suitable form.)

More often than not, however, the law, such as it was, never entered into the eviction process. Landlords regularly intimidated tenants into moving immediately. Many times they used goons and simply threw the tenants' belongings into the street, stole the tenants' possessions, removed the doors, cut the utilities, or physically intimidated the tenants.

Causes of eviction usually fell into two categories: (1) the tenant had no money; or (2) the tenant refused to pay until the landlord made good on a promise to repair. In the first type of case, the landlord was often lenient for a while, figuring to get the money (or other compensation) at a later time. In the second category, landlords showed no leniency. (Texas has no "warranty of habitability" law as do over 30 states.)

The Patriots understood that the first priority was to stop slumlords from abusing tenants' legal rights. Once landlords began, in practice, to acknowledge legal rights of tenants, the issues of tenant organizing could be directed to expanding those rights. Until that time, day-to-day survival was the priority. Intimidation would have to be met with intimidation. Once landlords saw that the use of muscle could be effectively countered in such a way as to cause chaos for them, they would begin to withdraw to the plane where the law offered better protection.

Although this stage took over a year and a half, the incident that marked the turning point occurred in late spring of 1973. Two tenants had called Patriot co-ordinator Charlie Young at work (in a warehouse) and asked him to come by after hours to explain to their landlord that he would not be allowed to evict them by removing the door of their apartment. When Charlie arrived, the landlord grabbed a 12-gauge shotgun and declared "I'll show you what the law is." He fired, winging Charlie in the left arm. (Later, he would maintain that Charlie had not been shot, because "he didn't run." In fact, after promising the tenants he would be back, before going to the hospital, Charlie got a pistol himself and came back, but the landlord had run.) Tenants who witnessed the scene called the police who, after hearing the story, threatened to give the landlord a ticket for discharging a weapon in the city limits—but did not.

Subsequently, the landlord agreed to give the tenants proper notice, find them a new place, pay the first week's rent, plus move them himself. The Patriots knew it would be futile to take such a case to the D.A., as he would probably welcome the opportunity to turn the tables on these uppity tenants. So a suit for damages was filed in small claims court, which had an informal format. The Patriots decided to make the suit into a political case.

The suit was important not only because it was a Patriot who had gotten shot while doing his job, but for another reason. The landlord in question was the worst kind of slumlord. He rented to "down-and-outers" and figured he could get by with anything. He had a reputation for forcing winos who rented from him to work for him, and if they did not perform satisfactorily he would beat them with a billy club. In at least one instance after throwing a tenant's belongings into the street, he dragged the tenant down a flight of stairs and threw him into the street as well. If the Patriots could stop abuse of people who basically could not protect themselves, then the sun would surely break through the clouds on the tenant struggle in East Dallas. The landlord used every delay possible, figuring his former tenants were transients and would eventually leave town. He even bribed one witness, a retired prostitute who had moved out after the incident, by letting her move back in gratis.

Nevertheless, the trial date finally came up in March, 1974. All the witnesses came; most were nervous but visibly determined, and most had a taste or two stashed away.

The Patriots' strategy was (1) to have a jury trial (in Texas j.p. courts the jury is empowered to interpret the law *without* the judge's instruction); (2) to get all the witnesses on and get the story told in context; and (3) to anger the landlord so the jury could get a good look at a slumlord in form. Charlie was to be his own counsel.

The trial lasted five and a half hours. By the time it was over the judge had virtually thrown up his hands and the jury had been politicized. The landlord stated that the Patriots, in the eyes of East Dallas landlords, were "troublemakers," "rabblerousers," and "subversives." Charlie told the jury that if it ruled in the landlord's favor, then the tenant community would take the landlord's statement ("I'll show you what the law is") as a mandate. Charlie informed the jury that if this was the case, he would not spend any money on further legal action, but would buy a shotgun, as this would be the proper avenue of appeal. The jury, in less than fifteen minutes, returned a unanimous verdict against the landlord, and the word spread rapidly among slumlords.

Groups of tenants regularly began to band together to repel slumlord goon tactics, and tenant consciousness began to develop spontaneously. Before it was over, however, one East Dallas landlord had been killed and several others had gone to the hospital. In the case where the landlord was killed (stabbed through the heart with a butcher knife), the tenant, on the basis of testimony by neighboring tenants and homeowners, was no-billed (not indicted): "self-defense." . . .

Other regular occurrences of intimidation involved utility cut-offs. When a land-

lord who didn't want to file an eviction on a tenant took direct action and shut off one or more utilities, the Patriots in many cases would simply gather a group of people, enter the premises, and turn the utilities back on. Usually, this show of strength was enough to keep the utilities from being cut again.

It was during the "fight fire with fire" stage of the tenant struggle in East Dallas that the news media began to get interested. Newspapers, TV news and special programming, radio news and talk shows—all jumped onto the bandwagon. (The fact that 52 percent of the residents of Dallas are tenants guaranteed tenants' rights as a popular cause.) It seemed that after the ice was broken, there was something in the media daily concerning the East Dallas Tenants' Alliance. This lasted for about six months.

The Patriots utilized this new avenue of awareness to focus public attention on several critical aspects of the growing tenants' struggle: (1) tenants were now the majority in Dallas, and as such constituted a force to be reckoned with; (2) concepts of neighborhood stability now had to take tenants into account; (3) absentee and slum landlords were the enemy of every decent citizen; and (4) Warranty of Habitability with rent withholding provisions was needed, now.

The media were very responsive. Landlords (even those who projected themselves as being responsible) and government officials were not. This only heightened tenant consciousness. With Patriots focusing now on substantive issues of law, middle-income tenants began to join the struggle. (Though Dallas has many millionaires, it remains, per capita, a working class city, and thus its citizens have an ingrained hatred of the kind of overt, top-down political control that has been exerted by the Dallas Citizens' Council for the last forty years. In addition, Dallas has nearly completed the transition from town to city mentality, and the media, despite national stereotypes to the contrary, have been the first local institution to embrace the new maturity.)

Once the issues of tenants' rights became focused on reform rather than survival in the face of intimidation, the Patriots calculated that the middle-income community would begin to dominate the struggle. This had to be dealt with carefully, because of the middle-income community's tendency to transform such issues into an anti–poor people brand of consumerism.

The Patriots knew that they needed middle-class support, as this is where the biggest reservoir of political and economic power is located, at least as it concerns those who dominate the rental housing industry. And East Dallas, as well as other inner-city communities, desperately needs a warranty of habitability law for purposes of organizing a meaningful, ongoing offensive against slumlords and those who follow, viz., developers.

Tenants from all over Dallas, of all classes, were calling the Patriot office in search of assistance. An average day brought over eighty calls or walk-ins.

And now landlords and judges were beginning to use legal tools to forestall the tenant struggle. One Patriot was thrown in jail for contempt of court because he showed a j.p. a receipt for a jury trial and proceeded to inform several tenants of their constitutional right to trial by jury. (Judges and landlords dreaded jury trials in j.p. courts because of the statutory freedom given jurors in interpreting law. As the public developed more consciousness, many cases were won by tenants because the jury felt the existing law was simply unfair to tenants.)

After the Patriots had forced the warranty of habitability issue on the City Council in mid-1975, and after the council had made sympathetic noises, held hearings, and then dropped the matter in the face of

opposition by the housing industry, the media coverage peaked and began to decline.

At this point the struggle was so time consuming, in terms of both organizing and litigation (mainly through the Dallas Legal Services Foundation), it was clear that a new strategy was needed. Many middle-income tenants were willing to get involved, but had hesitations and fears about doing so from the East Dallas vantage point. They needed a structure of their own. Here, Patriot administrative coordinator, Lisbeth Stewart, conceived a new, city-wide organization, the Dallas Tenants' Union. The DTU was to address itself to substantive housing issues, be separate from the Patriots and East Dallas Tenants' Alliance, and develop the tenant struggle, citywide, from a case-by-case consciousness-raising effort into a movement.

The DTU was founded in January, 1976. Since that time, it has become self-supporting, through donations, and has proceeded to organize tenants in mass. Though it is still illegal, formally, to withhold rent in Texas, the DTU experience has shown that if enough people get together, they can do anything they want. The landlord is not so concerned about the law as he is about his pocketbook. This struggle reached fruition in the summer of 1976, when DTU organized thirty-one groups of tenants, negotiated out twenty-five cases of organized tenant groups, and led six rent strikes, all of which were won. The tenants' movement in Dallas is rapidly growing to steamroller proportions, and by the end of the summer, members of the housing industry, who largely determine the industry's statewide directions, asked to set up peace talks with DTU. They understood now, they said, the need for warranty of habitability. Dallas Tenants' Union organizers feel assured that there will be such a law in Texas in the near future.

OTHER PROGRAMS

Over the course of 1973–76 numerous programs were developed by and/or through the Patriots in response to community needs. Some programs, such as Emergency Clothing, a Food Buying Co-op, a Christmas program, a Free Health Fair, a monthly newspaper, "Four Walls," and an Emergency Food Pantry are largely self-explanatory. These programs are supplied with goods and services via pooling resources and hustling. The Emergency Clothing Program receives almost all material from community residents who have at one time or another benefited from this or other programs.

There are four more Patriot programs, however, which need additional explanation. These include the Free Legal Clinic, Free Medical Clinic, the Provisional Neighborhood Stabilization Program and related organizing activities, and the Labor Pool (to be discussed in a later section).

The Free Legal Clinic began in October, 1973, and since has been in continuous operation. It utilizes, primarily, volunteer Legal Services attorneys who come to East Dallas one evening per week. The clinic was originally open two evenings per week, but the Patriots felt that too much emphasis was being placed on attorneys and, as a number of Patriots became qualified as "paralegals"—particularly in regard to housing matters—the role of lawyers was relegated to litigation. It was obvious that poverty lawyers' greatest value to the East Dallas community was in the realm of major litigation (class action suits, etc.). And, as the low-income community has a basically defensive relationship with the legal system, the Patriots did not want to dilute this fact by bringing lawyers in on a day-to-day, person-by-person basis, when Patriot organizers (sometimes with benefit of counsel) could help residents just as well. The legal results were the same, the political results were much better.

The origins of the Legal Clinic are educational. When the Patriots realized that ultimately they would need legal support in the tenant struggle, they looked toward the Dallas Legal Services Foundation. DLSF (which is part of the National Legal Services Corporation) is critically underfunded, as are most poverty programs in the South. The gravy has for the most part ended up on the coasts. The DLSF program was (and is) understaffed, and some parts of town were excluded from representation on the DLSF Board. East Dallas, though statistically the second-poorest area in Dallas, was such an area, and no low-income whites had ever been on the board.

The Patriots, realizing that federal poverty programs were designed to appease rather than help, understood that the low-income white community, which had not been previously organized, had been excluded because it was not a threat to the status quo. However, the Patriots knew that in order to start a Free Legal Clinic, and to guarantee its continuation, they would have to have board representation. After talking to community representatives on the board, the Patriots persuaded the board to include the East Dallas area in a district. However, true to form, the board pitted East Dallas against an all-black area. The Patriots, from their beginning, had good relations with the liberation movement in the black community. Charlie Young, the Patriot coordinator and Fred Bell, Black Panther coordinator, had known each other before the Patriots or Panthers existed in Dallas. However, the two people who had represented the district into which the Patriots were placed were involved in some very questionable, non-movement-related activities. Consequently, the Panthers endorsed the Patriots in leaflets passed out in the black community. The Patriots, meanwhile, ran an issue-oriented campaign, stressing the need for a community Legal Clinic, de-emphasizing personalities, and explaining the whites needed representation, in the context of a broader explanation of how the government tries to set different races against each other and how no poor people of whatever race should begrudge other poor people fair representation. It has been the Patriots' belief, borne out time after time, that poor whites in this region, most of whom have had the experience of living close to blacks and browns, are more than willing to put aside racism if presented with a positive alternative. The Patriot definition of politics (organizing on the basis of common need) meets this criterion. Sipping tea at sensitivity sessions in the suburbs does not.

More people turned out to vote in East Dallas for representation than had ever turned out in the history of Legal Services and, shortly, the Legal Clinic was a reality.

A free medical clinic . . . is desperately needed. East Dallas leads the entire city in health problems in almost every major category: cancer, pneumonia, emphysema, tuberculosis, liver disease, and infant mortality. The reason is simple: it is the only inner-city community with no affordable, accessible medical facilities. A number of high-quality medical personnel have volunteered time, and some equipment has been obtained. A location has been secured, but some financing has yet to be raised.

The Provisional Neighborhood Stabilization Program was designed to integrate the struggle of tenants and homeowners who, because of specific circumstances, have common needs. These needs vary from the redevelopment threats via the city's Community Development programs, to the need of improved park facilities and a community center. (East Dallas is the only inner-city neighborhood with no community center).

In areas threatened by redevelopment, homeowners have provided the main leadership, as could be expected. This has been welcomed by the Patriots, as the struggle in East Dallas had, up until the inception of the P.N.S.P., been dominated almost completely by the tenant struggle and had tended at times to alienate homeowners. The P.N.S.P. has provided the necessary link (by establishing several neighborhood associations) between tenants, homeowners, and resident landlords.

Though the wealthier homeowners of East Dallas moved out, the working-class homeowners, who live primarily in small frame houses in the Santa Fe and Mt. Auburn areas, remain. Over 70 percent of these homeowners are now retired, and many are clinging to their homes for dear life. They represent a threat to City Hall's redevelopment strategy in that they are stable and don't want to move. When it was revealed in the spring of 1976 that the Santa Fe area had been designated, in a proposed Land Use Plan, for 70–100 percent redevelopment, the Patriots called a meeting, and the residents of this neighborhood turned out in mass.

Mass meetings have continued, and the people formed a committee to devise strategy. So far the committee has initiated a block-by-block petition drive for zoning change. This effort has spread into the adjacent Mt. Auburn area, making it possible for organizing efforts to begin there. The Santa Fe Committee has also been working on the Patriot Labor Pool program to devise means of assisting in minor home repair.

The Labor Pool, as it is presently beginning to operate, gets together those who need work done with those who need work. It is coordinated, in the form of a pilot project, by neighborhood contractors, through the Patriots. As the program is just getting under way, it is impossible to go into specifics. Theoretically, it will improve housing somewhat in the neighborhood, and by so doing, bring more income to those in the neighborhood who need it the most. The program will be more or less effective, depending on whether low-interest loans and grants are made available, in the future, through C.D.A., H.U.D., or other programs.

During the summer of 1976, the city hired forty temporary code inspectors. Their first target: the Santa Fe area of East Dallas. A bulletin was issued by the Patriots, informing people of their rights, viz., that they did not have to allow inspectors on their premises. The resulting confrontations generated news media sympathy for the senior citizens' plight in this neighborhood, and the city's code enforcement project put its tail between its legs. As a result, the city was forced to announce that it would not cite hardship cases to court, and that it would be willing to work with the Patriots in East Dallas to reverse some of its discriminatory practices in code enforcement.

In several other areas in or near East Dallas, the Patriots have also implemented the P.N.S.P. In one peripheral area, which is almost entirely black, a number of organizing successes have been achieved and

a committee has also been formed which works closely with the Patriots and the Santa Fe Committee. . . .

In related organizing activities, the Patriots were asked to come to the Southside of Fort Worth in November, 1975, and help the residents set up a community organization. This area is similar to East Dallas. Before the end of the year a Southside Neighborhood Alliance was founded, addressing itself generally to housing issues. The SNA is growing rapidly, has developed solid, principled leadership and is beginning to develop programs similar to the Patriots' (Tenants' and Homeowners' Alliance and Labor Pool).

Another related program focuses on the needs of the Chicano community in East Dallas. The Patriots have made it possible for a Chicano organizer from the Brown Berets to work, full time, using the Patriot office as a base, to organize an independent Chicano organization in East Dallas. This organization, Refugio, by the end of 1976 had begun to establish itself. On many issues and in many programs Refugio works in tandem with the Patriots, with the two organizations sharing resources. In many cases Refugio has begun to address itself to issues more specifically related to the needs of the Chicano community.

As Refugio matures, the two organizations will build a working coalition which will have the effect of bringing closer the white and Chicano communities for purposes of common struggle. . . .

29.

Warren C. Haggstrom

THE TACTICS OF ORGANIZATION BUILDING*

The organizer lives in a world in which everything is called into question, subject to change, where half-perceived and complex structures constantly dissolve and reform before him, a world of possibility in which he takes a hand to reshape the future. . . .

The organizer cannot afford to believe that he knows his world well because he is engaged in a course of action under barely tractable, constantly changing, and mostly invisible circumstances which contrast sharply with the neat flatland of the sociological theorist.

To build organization in low-income areas is something like playing a long game of blindfold chess in which no player is sure of the rules. The chess pieces move by themselves; skillful players help get this movement channeled into planned patterns, strategies, and tactics. There are standard beginning lines (e.g., house meetings vs. dramatic large public meetings) and some established principles of play ("rub raw the sores of discontent," "the social situation sets the limits for moves"), but much depends on attention to detail, immense energy, and individual brilliance in capitalizing on whatever happens. Finally, these chess pieces can throw an ineffective player right out of the game.

It follows that the question "How does one build an organization of the poor?" cannot be answered in the same way as the question, "How does one build a house?" or "How does one build a great football team?" One can only relate a history of past organizations of the poor, a description of those currently functioning, and principles to which some able organizers more or less adhere. The following remarks are directed to the [last-named] task.

THE STARTING POINT

The physical structure and location of a low-income area carry collectively held meanings to the people of the area, meanings which affect the relevance of the physical context to their lives. For example, a hospital may carry the meaning of being a slaughter house or of a place in which patients are "treated like dirt." A row of slum houses may mean at once inferiority and deprivation and reassuring familiarity to slum dwellers. Of seven unmarried mothers living in public housing, six may be respectable women and the seventh a scandal—all in accordance with criteria which are not known outside the neighborhood in question. . . .

The social situation in low-income areas, consisting of such collectively held sets of meanings, can vary tremendously around any physical situation. It is a key responsibility of the organizer to come to know the

*The following paper is a revised version of one read at the Annual Conference of the Greater Washington Chapter of Americans for Democratic Action on September 18, 1965. The content of the paper stems primarily from my own organizational experience. I am also particularly indebted to Fred Ross for helpful reactions to many of these ideas, and have benefitted from conversations with Saul Alinsky and Tom Gaudette.

Source: Warren Haggstrom "The Organizer." Previously unpublished. Reprinted by permission of the author.

social situation and, further, he must consider as well his own meaning as a stranger in the neighborhood. He starts work where he and the people of the neighborhood are in a social situation which slowly becomes intelligible to him. If people want their windows fixed and the welfare check increased, the organizer helps them to begin to act on these problems even though he may privately believe they would be better off working to open up additional jobs. He is limited by the fact that people consciously and unconsciously misrepresent where they are, and, sometimes, they do not understand how to be relevant to the organizer since he has not clearly defined himself and his purpose in the neighborhood. One can come closest to starting where the people are when one begins in an atmosphere of mutual trust which develops when the organizer places himself clearly on the side of the people with whom he is working and states as plainly as possible his purpose in the neighborhood, but does not presume to define for them their problems or the solutions to their problems.

The people, with the help of the organizer, start to work on problems. Very shortly, their action is contested and the problems are transformed into issues with established institutions opposing the action of people in low-income areas. For example, when a number of people in one city began to seek additional money for school supplies for their children, the Commissioner of Welfare at first acceded to the request. When the number of people making such a request becomes large enough, the commissioner began to deny many of the new requests. At that point, the requests became demands and the resulting struggle drew an increasing number of people into sustained activity of value in building organization. Through a process of struggle around issues perceived in the neighborhood as central the organization develops power which can be used to resolve problems of many varieties.

When an organizer helps people to begin to act on central problems, that is, to make their own decisions about resolving their own problems and to begin to implement those decisions, by that very fact the organizer deliberately creates conflict since the problems of low-income areas cannot be resolved without negative consequences for the self-perceived self-interest and traditional ways of thinking and acting of various advantaged minorities. Until the problems are resolved, so long as the organizer maintains neighborhood action he will by that fact maintain conflict, and requires no artificial strategies leading to artificial confrontations.

THE WAY TO BEGIN

People are usually immersed in private lives centered about work and home. The organizer pulls and jolts them into the public arena.

In the beginning, the organizer is simply another stranger trying to convince people to do something. He is like a salesman— and is met by the evasive tactics which people use to ward off salesmen. A salesman has only to persuade people to one act, to make one purchase. An organizer has the more complicated job of pulling people into new lives, into long-extended alternative lines of action. . . .

Because people do not yet know him, the organizer has to be credible, creating a convincing picture of what might be, relying on the emotional contagion produced by fire and enthusiasm as well as on the factual account that he gives. Since all this should be appropriate to the people with whom he is talking, he modifies his presentation at first as he talks with different persons and groups until working out an approach which is most effective for him (although not necessarily for other organizers) in the neighborhood in which he is working (although not necessarily in the other neighborhoods).

The organizer starts by persuading people to come to a meeting or begin action. He listens, describing the meeting or action as it is relevant to the situation of those with whom he is talking. He appeals to self-interest, builds anger, works along friendship and relationship networks and other formal and informal social structures. He recruits members without appearing too eager to recruit members; they must see themselves as acting on their own initiative. When people have decided to attend a meeting, join a delegation, etc., then an organizer does his best to make certain that their intention is carried out. People may be reminded again and again of the event, some are provided with transportation, etc.

Once at a meeting an organizer concentrates on moving those attending into decision and action through whatever formal structure may exist. He may make certain that decisions are made to do something concrete about sore points of acute concern: the speeding car that killed Bobby Smith, the lack of a policeman to protect Mrs. Jackson, the slum landlord who runs down the neighborhood, etc. He may ask action-oriented questions, or he may suggest alternatives by describing what other organizations have done in similar situations or on similar problems.

From the point of view of the organizer, the sole point of meetings is to prepare for action just as the sole point of organization is to provide a structure through which action takes place. Thus, he helps to clarify alternatives around concrete and immediate courses of action, makes certain that whatever process results in decisions is both legitimate (in accordance with the rules) and efficient (a course of action is undertaken which is likely to attain the objective

intended or otherwise to build the effectiveness of the organization).

At first, people defend themselves against accurately seeing their position in the community and against admitting their discontent to themselves and others. An early objective of action is to provide people with experiences which destroy these defenses. A second early objective is to provide people with experience in responsible planning in defining social paths along which they can make actual gains. . . .

The legitimation for action is provided in meetings, but specific action events may develop from the general responsibility of a committee or other group of work in some area, and not directly from meetings. . . .

For example, in one city, people representing a small neighborhood, with the help of the organizers of a large organization, went to a district sanitation inspector to appeal for better street cleaning. During the course of the discussion the supervisor mentioned that there was no point in putting additional equipment into such neighborhoods since the residents didn't care whether their streets were clean or dirty. When the story of this insult was widely reported (the organizer helping the report along), a large number of people wanted to do something to change street-cleaning practices which they had never before clearly understood to be deliberately discriminatory. They planned a series of actions, including sweeping their own streets while newspaper reporters recorded the event, had the implied backing of the large organization, and several times carried the debris to the homes or businesses of politicians who were responsible. They picketed the district sanitation office and protested at the central sanitation office of the city. Since the city had received national beautification awards and the mayor wanted to maintain its reputation and since the various politicians involved feared that their re-election would eventually be jeopardized, the embarrassment was enough to end the discrimination. . . .

During the course of the several actions, people for the first time saw their relationship to one city service with stark clarity; this alone drove them to action. The insights provided through the experience of people in action are the fuel for a dramatic and broadening rhythm of action. The landlord who denies that blacks are good tenants; the school principal who "confesses" that neighborhood parents do not want their children to get an education—both can become focal points around which a good organizer builds action. As groups of people become drawn into a series of actions, each group working on its own problems but in relation to a common organization, there develops a body of accurate knowledge, enhanced levels of skill, and a larger number of active persons. Together, these enhance to the greatest extent possible the opportunity for each member to resolve his problems through the organizational structure.

ORGANIZER RESPONSIBILITY

An enabler is relatively passive, accepting the prevailing views, and helping people with their problems as defined by current neighborhood perspectives. An organizer is sensitive to current neighborhood perspectives, but may disagree aggressively with people while he remains clearly on their side.

For example, it is common in low-income areas for people to scapegoat their neighbors: "they don't care," "they run down the neighborhood," "people around here will only complain, they never do anything," etc. In this fashion, people repeat the outside stereotypes of low-income areas and develop a rationale for not themselves venturing into organizational efforts. An organizer who agrees with the condemnation not only undercuts neighborhood confidence in the possibility of organizing, but also finds himself rejected as possibly concealing a negative opinion of *everyone* in the neighborhood. Or, the members of an organization may decide on an action that is certain to fail, or which is clearly in violation of the constitution of the organization, or clearly leads to violence, to a collapse of democratic process, etc.

In all these cases, an organizer may find it necessary to disagree aggressively with the members, not to convince people of his own point of view on issues, but rather to make it possible to organize, to build effective organization. The people provide the content of action. The organizer has the responsibility to create and maintain the effective democratic structure of action, that is, a structure through which each neighborhood person has as nearly as possible an equal opportunity effectively to secure self-realization. The organizer, thus, must sometimes assert vigorous, aggressive leadership, even though he is not a member of the organization, and although such leadership should never include projecting his own substantive orientations upon the neighborhood.

On the other hand, the organizer should always refrain from leadership or participation when his intervention is not clearly necessary. For example, when a delegation visits a city official, the preparation ahead of time may not have been enough and the meeting may threaten to dissolve into confusion. An organizer has the responsibility to intervene forcefully to ensure that an effective case is presented. Such intervention should occur rarely, and the organizer should refuse to participate above that minimal level even when urged to do so. To the extent that an organizer has to intervene, to that extent the members will not see the victories as *their* victories, will not maximally acquire knowledge and skills themselves, and will not develop effective organization.

Thus, the role of the organizer is extremely complex. He must stand by the side of the people and see the world from their perspective. But he must also be able to go outside that perspective to analyze and decide accurately what he should do in order to build organization. He should never be a member of the organization and should place the organization in the hands of the membership, but he also should know when and how to intervene to protect the essential characteristics which he is responsible for ensuring in the organization. He must be a passive enabler and an aggressive leader at the time when each is required of him, must use his own judgment to determine when he should do either, and therefore must not *need* to play either role.

In his role of energetic intervenor, an organizer does not actually place himself in opposition to the neighborhoods. Instead, he allies himself with the long-term objective self-interest of the people in building organization through which they can act effectively, and he seeks to break up collective distortions and orientations which make impossible the creation of such an organizational structure. With this one exception the organizer stays as close as possible to present neighborhood points of view. By this strategy he makes certain that it will be very difficult for enemies of the organization to isolate him from the neighborhood by attacking him as an outsider, as being on someone else's side, etc. Further, the gradual identification of neighborhood persons with their organization makes it increasingly likely that through, rather than outside of the organization, they will seek solutions to problems which for the first time become perceived as problems rather than as conditions of existence.

For example, where there is no organization, children playing on busy streets may be injured or killed without any response in the neighborhood. People assume that nothing can be done except, maybe, to watch the children more closely. "Life is like that." The presence of an organization provides a new remedy: "We can get a traffic light." Thus, getting a traffic light becomes a problem which, in the resulting struggle with the relevant city department, is itself transformed into an issue.

The organizer, therefore, not only creates issues and conflict; prior to that he creates problems where none were perceived before by creating opportunities where none had been before.

Inexperienced organizers typically fail to understand the necessary self-discipline, the requirement to act (or not) always to build organization and never through needs of the organizer which are irrelevant to or destructive of the building of organization. An organizer who is committed to racial integration cannot organize for racial integration in a community in which people oppose or are indifferent to this stance. . . . An organizer who admires a certain neighborhood leader cannot remain passive while that leader transforms the organization into his own political organization or social club. . . .

The people in a low-income neighborhood may decide not to adopt the kind of organizational structure recommended by an organizer. What then? Should the organizer try to manipulate or coerce the people into accepting what he recommends?

An organizer does not seek to impose himself on a neighborhood; instead he offers his services on the clearly stated basis that he will help build organization with certain characteristics, with the clear understanding that the organizer has responsibility to ensure that the organization meets certain criteria and that the organization is and will belong to the members. At first, the members do not yet understand the requirements of organization very clearly; they must be helped to clarity as rapidly as possible and should be made aware that at any time they can discharge the organizer. In short, the organizer must have a legitimated and mutually agreed upon relationship with the organization, a relationship which the organization can cancel whenever it may wish. When the organization achieves permanent status, it may be wise to outline in a written agreement the rights and responsibilities of the organizer and of the organization with respect to each other. . . .

THE STRUCTURE OF SOCIAL ACTION

Any structure through which the poor act on the sources of their problems will be under attack from local governmental and other established institutions. The attack may not be direct; it may consist of subtle attempts to talk organization members out of their concerns, to divert attention to other questions, to ridicule the organization in informal discussions, etc. Attacks by established institutions on an organization of the poor tend to be indirect as much as possible, while it is to the advantage of an organization of the poor to bring these subtle, half-concealed attacks into the arena of open confrontation.

An open attack on the organizational effort in low-income areas usually sharpens the issues and can be used to quicken the pace of organization. Established institutions, realizing this, may choose to attack the sponsors of organization (whoever pays the salary of and supervises organizers) rather than the organizational effort itself. . . .

The sponsor of organization may have any of a wide variety of structures providing only that it is able to refrain from emasculating the work. However, there are fewer alternatives for the structure of the

organization being built. It may be a direct membership neighborhood council or an organization of previously existing organizations. In any case, the point is to build a clearly defined structure through which people in low-income areas can act. Thus, although the organization of the poor may carry on social activities, provide services to members, and constitute a forum for militant rhetoric, the basic orientation has always to be the expression of power through the greatest possible number of members acting together to resolve the central problems of their lives.

For people to be able to act through a structure, it must be democratic. Any large number of people can act together democratically in complex activities only when the rules for their participation are clearly stated and equally applied to all members. Complex activities also require specialization of roles (e.g., the spokesman, the chairman, the secretary, the committee member, etc.) and a clear definition of the relationships among the roles. Thus, rules must be explicit and generally accepted in accordance with which members of the organization have a formally equal opportunity to participate in decisions and occupy various positions. The organizer is responsible to ensure that such a structure is developed and that formal equality is reflected as far as possible in actual practice. Since many low-income people are learning for the first time to maintain organizational roles, these structural requirements must be communicated and legitimated more vividly than would be necessary with memberships with more organizational experience.

It is common for an inexperienced organizer to attempt to develop movement through the natural relationships among people rather than to create an explicit structured set of interpersonal relationships and decision processes. The movement which results from the former course either is temporary and effective only in carrying out simple activities, or it becomes complex but the instrument of one person rather than of the widest possible portion of the general membership. In either case, the resulting organization is a relatively ineffective structure, relatively unavailable for collective action by the poor. . . .

One way to create [an effective] structure is to hold a series of preliminary unstructured small or large meetings with people in the neighborhoods in which organization is being developed (after organizers have been invited in by neighborhood persons and institutions). In those preliminary meetings issues can be clarified, leadership can become visible in the neighborhood, and a general interpretation can be made by the organizer of the nature of such a proposed organization. Then, an initial general meeting can decide whether to organize, can elect temporary officers, and provide preliminary committees (to develop a constitution, begin action, etc.). A permanent structure (officers, committees, constitution, by-laws, etc.) can be adopted at a later meeting. After such a beginning, there is a legitimated democratic process for replacing persons in various positions, a process which makes it less easy for the organization to become the captive of a single leader, and less likely that the organization will dissolve, turn into a social club, or meet others of the usual disastrous fates of democratic organizations.

THE SOCIAL SITUATIONAL CONTOURS OF CONFLICT

. . . The meaning of a move in a conflict depends on the nature of the move, its context, and may also vary to different audiences. For example, depending upon the context, when a Commissioner of Public Welfare increases clothing allotments this may be understood by everyone as an act of generosity or, alternatively, of weakness.

Or, it may be perceived as an act of generosity to members of the welfare establishment *and* as an act of weakness to members of the organization demanding the increase. Further, the divergence of interpretations of the same public act in a conflict situation tends to make the reactions of each side incomprehensible to the other. When the organization renews its pressure, persons in the welfare establishment may believe that the organized welfare clients are simple-minded puppets of organizer manipulation and agitation, and also amoral and naturally parasitic. The organized welfare clients, on the other hand, may believe that the commissioner is trying to deprive them of their rightful allotments, that this is why he is not giving straight answers to their questions.

In a conflict situation the objective consequences of an act by one side or by another, or the intentions behind the act, may be almost irrelevant. The act is one point around which conflict swirls, and a common interpretation may eventually be made as both sides, usually first really brought together by the conflict, begin to know one another better. . . .

SOCIAL ACTION AS MORALITY DRAMA

The organizer conducts the conflict which draws to itself the fascinated attention of a large portion of the entire community. The public conflict creates an audience and actors who play to the audience. The actors invent their own lives in a performance not to be repeated. The organizer ensures that the play is seen as a struggle between the forces of good and the forces of evil (although there will be no consensus concerning which side is which). Through helping keep the initiative with the organization of the poor, through breaking up existing perspectives by unforeseeable improvisations, through drawing the powerful into a conflict in the spotlight of public attention, the organizer enables that organization to begin to control the opponents, thus creating the first interdependency for previously dependent people. From that point, the organizer works with a process which includes the opponents; no longer does he work *only* with the organization of the poor. He conducts the play in which one group of actors (the organization of the poor) creates and controls the conflict, and in which the other mainly responds and attempts to avoid the conflict. The actors write their own lines, but the organizer helps them to improve the performance. There is rehearsal prior to a public event (role-playing) and an analysis afterward. As the play continues, the skills of the poor begin clearly to rival, and then to outstrip, those of the opposition. The public conflict then communicates the ability of the poor to the community which had previously depreciated that ability. . . .

Besides achieving a diminution in dependency and a lesson in equality, the organizer has the task of institutionalizing the new relationships so that, as the audience departs, the poor find themselves with a stable level of power, greater than before, and incorporated into the new community status quo.

The institutionalization of a new social position for the poor is possible because, although the conflict may subside, and the audience may leave, the ability of the organization to create the conflict and draw the audience has been established. Thus, the actions of the poor now acquire a new meaning. . . .

SYMBOLIC CONCESSIONS

When the organization becomes powerful enough, it will force concessions from opponents. The mayor will appoint a Human Rights Commission, the urban renewal agency will agree to more citizen involvement in relocation of people from the demolition area, the state legislature will pass a resolution setting forth state policy on housing code enforcement, the public education system will announce classes for adult poor, trade unions will state that they no longer exclude anyone from apprenticeship programs on racial grounds, public welfare publicly decides no longer to support slum landlords by paying rent for welfare recipients in slum housing, the police chief assures the organization that there is now a new complaint process to which he pays personal attention, etc.

All these are promissory notes, issued under pressure. It is a responsibility of the organizer to make certain that they are converted into the legal tender of actual changes in practice which benefit the people in low-income areas, that they are not merely used as symbolic substitutes for the actual resolution of problems. When the leaders of an organization of the poor are appointed to this committee and that board, the result is usually that they become part of the opponent apparatus by which the lives of the poor are controlled. Until enough experience develops in the organization it is often possible for opponents to take the edge off campaigns against them by making agreements which they intend never to keep. Especially in the early stages of organization, the organizer helps keep attention focused, not on promises and agreements announced with however much fanfare, but on whatever actually occurs in the lives of people in the low-income areas as a consequence of such announcements. When an opponent has agreed to a concession, a new line of action must usually soon be directed to force the opponent to carry out his agreement. Only after a period of time does it become clear to everyone concerned that agreements must be kept or painful sanctions will be imposed by the organization. The organizer repeatedly calls the attention of members, often by Socratic questioning, to what is actually happening within the low-income area, and brings out discrepancies between opponent promises and performances. The organizer agitates; the organization acts; a reluctant opposition is coerced into honesty.

KNOWING OPPOSITION TACTICS

Persons in positions of power have long experience in frustrating opposition to them. An organization of the poor gradually develops equivalent or even superior expertise through its own experience. The organizer helps members, and especially leaders, to think through the strategies and tactics of opponents.

He must, for example, understand the usual initial "cooling out" approach in which someone with a friendly and disarming manner attempts to persuade the neighborhood to accept something other than what is being demanded. He must know that opponents may replace an old and hated injustice with a new injustice about which anger has not yet been developed, as happened, for example, when alienation in public housing was substituted for exploitation by private slum landlords. He must be alert to the use of rules and regulations to confuse critics. For example, when a delegation went to talk with a welfare commissioner, the members were told that their demands could not be met because everything in welfare is done according to the rules—federal rules, state rules, county rules—and pointed to a huge manual to support his statement. If they had not been prepared the members would not have been able to describe numerous instances in which public welfare workers used wide discretion in interpreting and applying the rules.

The organizer must know the divide-and-conquer techniques, as, for example, when concessions are offered to leaders or to some portion of an organization in order to create illegitimate advantages and unfair disadvantages within the organization.

Opponents typically portray the organization to the rest of the affluent community as threatening some revered symbol: the nation, the American way of life, law and order, and the appeal for unity against subversion, for harmony rather than disruption, etc. They taunt the people for needing organizers, offer concessions provided the organizers are discarded, praise the people while attacking the organizers as outsiders trying to tell the people what to do. The organizer helps the people to understand the nature of the attack and to turn it back on the attackers in various ways. For example, the organization may publicize the extent to which the opponents violate other symbols: the right to equal opportunity, the value of self-help, the defense of mother and children. . . .

The current action requires development of moves against the vulnerable points of opponents. The organizer jogs members into thinking through what the opponent needs that the organization can provide, interrupt, or otherwise affect. Does a public agency fear public scrutiny? An organization of the poor can draw public attention to it. Does a city councilman need a thousand additional votes? An organization of the poor can affect many more than that number. Does a department store need a positive image? A margin of profit? A mass organization may be able to affect the one by bringing employment discrimination into the open; the other by a combination of picket lines and boycotts. Does a social agency need to pretend that it is meeting needs? A people's organization can demonstrate unmet needs by helping ten times as many people with legitimate need to apply for help as the agency has openings. Does a school claim that the parents of the neighborhood are not interested in education? The parents can seek public funds to sponsor their own school, picket and boycott the existing school, make it clear that their interest in education is as intense as their opposition to the existing school. Do a variety of people and organizations want to avoid the fray, to stay neutral? The organization can focus public attention on their neutrality, force them to examine the issues, force them to take sides. Since most people with detailed understanding of the issues will agree with the orientation of a mass organization of low-income people, or at least do not want the opposition of such an organization, forcing neutrals to take sides will result in increasing support for it in the affluent community.

Since low-income people lack resources, it is useful to get opponents to work for the organization. If persons in authority are drawn into attack on the low-income people or on the symbols dear to them, the attack itself will build organization more quickly than any number of organizers could do by themselves.

An organization has often to map possible lines of action by opponents in order to make it easiest for them to meet organizational demands. It is not enough only to attack the destruction by urban renewal of low-income neighborhoods; the organization may have to secure competent technical counsel to prepare alternative feasible plans for neighborhood rebuilding, plans which will not violate the professional standards of city planners while having the advantage of support by the people of the neighborhood. . . .

All the moves mentioned above have been tried and found useful in one or another context. No one can say whether they

would be useful again in other contexts. One could also consider modifications. Could clients or tenants engage in collective bargaining in order to work out new contractual agreements with a public welfare agency or a public housing authority? Could a low-income area organize to spend the bulk of its entire income in accordance with organizational decisions? What would happen if the poor used cameras and tape recorders to create a record of their treatment compared with that given affluent persons in shops, public offices, banks? Can low-income areas organize a "hiring hall" for jobs of all kinds, the analogue of industrial unionism on a community basis? . . .

THE KNOWLEDGE BASE OF ACTION

In a conflict situation, the organization does what is unexpected, dividing and confusing opponents, keeping them off balance. It seeks out and tackles points of weakness: the fact that bureaucratic organizations depend on clients or customers or constituents, provisions and communication, all of which may be affected at unpredictable times in unpredictable ways; the fact that powerful persons usually need to be jolted before they even begin to take seriously the lives of low-income people; the fact that people and organizations operating on routines cannot tolerate disruption. . . .

The knowledge base of social action must constantly be reformed; the organizer senses changes needed, inspires daily examinations and theoretical reanalyses of the event process. A series of demonstrations which had been projected for weeks may be abandoned without notice; an enemy of years' standing may become a friend; the major issue of one day may have been entirely replaced by another the next day; a drive to force landlords to repair housing may be replaced by a plan for public housing operated by the tenants. Academic observers may be surprised at the apparent lack of a predictable, consistent set of alliances, tactics, orientations, by the organization. However, the organization learns to follow the single principle of building power in the low-income area; it would be disastrous to that ambition if the organization were to become predictable to academic observers. . . .

CAMPAIGNS

The organization grows through actions and activities. Either is carried on by a series of campaigns of strictly limited duration. The actions may include a month of daily picket lines around city hall to protest police brutality, or a two-month period of voter registration and voter education ending in a massive directed vote, or a six-hour sit-in at a public official's office, or a two-hour play-in by children at city hall. The activities may consist of a two-day fund-raising barbecue, a week-long fund-raising carnival, a two-week chest X-ray campaign, a monthly tour of scenic places for elderly persons in the neighborhood, an annual one-day fashion show. Actions are directed toward securing change in the relationship of the low-income area to the affluent community; activities contribute only indirectly to this outcome: directly they occur within established inside-outside relationships. However, in either case, a large number of people will only become involved for what is known in advance to be a limited period of time after which there will be a time of relative quiescence. It is a responsibility of the organizer to make certain that a series of campaigns is developed, involving the problems and issues and interests and skills of the widest possible number of persons in the area being organized. And, since the organization exists primarily for action, the organizer should ensure that campaign *activities* do not come to occupy the major attention of the membership.

Through such a series of campaigns, the number of persons identified with the organization continues to increase. Provided there is maintained an action emphasis, the pressure on the opponents of the organization will continue to mount. . . .

SERVICES

To some extent, outposts of the affluent community in areas of poverty (welfare, medical care, public housing, private business) are not likely to be responsive enough to organizational demands to supply adequate services sensitively tailored to the self-perceived needs of low-income people. To that extent, the organization can itself sponsor temporary services which will eventually disappear when the area being helped is no longer one of poverty. From the point of view of the affluent community it is prudent to spend a given sum of money (a) more efficiently than it is now spent, and (b) without being open to blame for the inadequacies and inequities involved in the extension of services to a dependent and hostile population. It will therefore become attractive for the affluent community to finance services which will be operated under the direction of organizations of the poor. The organizer will need to acquire some understanding of the pitfalls and advantages of this eventual outcome, and help the organization to secure needed services in such a way that the organization is strengthened and retains its action orientation and in a way that avoids the stigma which attaches to many service programs operated by low-income people. . . .

The organizer should not get so involved in the tough daily struggle of creating organization that he loses sight of the minimum long-range outcomes which will validate the amount of effort by the organization.

WHAT WILL NOT WORK

... First, there is no easy or quick way to build powerful organizations in low-income areas. Power only comes to an organization after a large number of people have acquired the skill to work efficiently through the organizational structure. It takes several years to meet these conditions. Building mass demonstrations in a short-lived movement or campaign may leave a residue of change, but they do not provide a structure through which power is exercised. Or, one can pull together existing organizations and groups into an organization of organizations in a convention with mass attendance, but the people who attend such a convention are not yet organized. All that has happened is that groups which previously met separately now meet once together and maintain some subsequent communication. The long, hard work of building a single powerful organization will require additional years. It is important in organizational work that some power be exercised very nearly at the beginning, but the early exercise of power does not mean that a structure has yet been created through which the exercise of power is effective and routine.

Second, an organizer can "look good quick" by organizing at once a mass action effort. However, if he does not also concentrate on creation of a structure and decision process through which people themselves can act effectively, his flash flood of action will soon disappear or leave behind an organization run by one person or a clique, not a structure through which the neighborhood can act.

Third, an organizer may have made a brilliant analysis of the need for a revolutionary social transformation, or he may

have a beautiful vision of participatory democracy. But, if he projects these perspectives of his upon a low-income population with immediate and concrete problems, even if he also pays attention to these latter problems, he will find that his organization will be small, weak, sectarian, and easily isolated. An organizer must always be directly relevant to present neighborhood perspectives.

Fourth, it is sometimes argued that the appropriate structure for organizational work is that of the storefront church or some other type of organization [of] which low-income people are already members. This argument takes the culture of the poor into account, but not the fact that store front churches and other organizations in low-income areas do not *do* much, do not perform complex tasks. In addition to the requirement of conforming to neighborhood traditions there is the other requirement of creating a structure adequate to carry on action and activities and operate services simultaneously and efficiently on a wide variety of problems and issues. Over any length of time this requires a division of labor, specialization, differentiated explicit role structures. Primitive structures do primitive tasks.

Fifth, existing social welfare institutions usually cannot sponsor organizational work in low-income areas because they cannot tolerate the conflict, because they define the problems of low-income people from outside rather than working with the definitions of low-income people, because they start from a position above the poor and reach down rather than starting with a working respect for low-income people.

Sixth, an organizer cannot follow a political organizational model since such models are developed solely to deliver votes and since they deliver votes by the politician doing things for people rather than by people doing things for themselves. A neighborhood acts through a political organization only in a very limited way. . . .

AWARENESS OF CHANGE

. . . In social action, the power of the poor shifts imperceptibly through their efforts. The public welfare worker is a little more alert to guard their rights, the politician a little more concerned about their opinion, the police officer less inclined to acts of brutality or corruption in the low-income neighborhood and a little more inclined to protect the rights of the people. The neighborhood continues to see the public welfare worker, the politician, the police officer, on the basis of years of experience. It is one task of the organizer to arouse the people from their bad dream which includes an underlying fear of their own weakness and inferiority, to point out and describe the changes which are taking place even outside the areas of concrete actions by the neighborhood organization. It is a task of the organizer to go beyond the creation of an account of neighborhood action to helping the people in the organization create an alternative and more accurate view of their world and of their position in it. The assumption that blacks and women are excluded from an apprenticeship training program may be generally believed, no longer true, and an important belief for the behavior of young blacks and women. The assumption that the barriers to professional education are fixed and unchangeable may be important and no longer accurate. The organizer points out changes [and] possibilities and helps an appreciation of them to become incorporated in the everyday thinking of most people in the areas of poverty in which he is working.

THE NEW TRADITION

An organizer helps an alternative account of the world to develop in the orga-

nization. He may relate the story in detail again and again of how this leader stood right up to the commissioner and told him the truth, or how that demonstration led to an increase in police protection or how the voting power of the organization has the council passing ordinances which they never considered before. The action of neighborhood people becomes fixed in a positive account which creates a clear context whereby people can gain self-esteem through action, whether or not individual employment or other opportunities are open to them. . . . A positive collective identity becomes rooted in the past, and no longer subject to the vicissitudes of an uncertain world. This identity is publicly known throughout the neighborhood; it can be revived at any time as it bolsters self-esteem in contemporary actors.

An organizer who recounted traditions would normally be merely a neighborhood bore. But when the account is credible and about what neighborhood people have accomplished in combat on crucial issues against great odds, the account is often quickly grasped and long relished.

Thus, an organizer not only learns to listen carefully when he talks with people, but also learns to provide through his words a concrete, vivid, compelling, and credible picture of the situation, a picture that is intended to upset the existing definition, force people to take sides about a proposed course of action, and outline such a course with clarity. This concrete, vivid, compelling and credible picture is often essential for getting movement under way, even though it stereotypes a wide variety of people and events under single labels and thus distorts reality through oversimplification and selection. People learn first to think about action while making only the major distinctions. Later, and through their own experience, people make the exceptions and fill in the details. . . .

The fact that an organizer creates an oversimplified sketch of action space should not be taken to mean that the people of low-income areas think in simple terms. Rather, just as the first knowledge of university students about a new area is stereotypic, for the same reason people who begin collective action must begin on the basis of the major relevant ideas and would be immobilized by a complete and detailed account which would not be easily incorporated in action.

THE LOCUS OF RESPONSIBILITY

The success of action can be undermined in two major ways: (1) it does not attain its objectives, and (2) it attains its objectives, but someone other than members of the organization is seen as responsible for the result. If the enemy is perceived in the neighborhood as having simply decided to give the people what they want, the action may be seen as ending well, but it is a failure as social action. It only becomes a social action success when the outcome is understood in the low-income area to be a direct consequence of organizational activity. Similarly, if the intended outcome is perceived in the low-income area as directly due to the intervention of the organizer, it is a social action failure. The organizer must ensure that the responsibility for securing an intended outcome is always placed squarely on the organization membership. Thus, the organizer typically ensures that meetings are well attended, that the necessary work gets done, that the organization holds such an initiative that an action favorable to the organization by an opponent is perceived as stemming from this initiative. But, the organizer accomplishes these ends as unobtrusively as possible in view of the fact that he may sometimes need conspicuously to intervene and that he must maintain a relationship of candor and responsibility with the people

he helps. He interprets his role: "It is your organization, you will call the shots, do the work (and it's hard work)!" . . . Constant attention to placing responsibility with the people of low-income areas not only ensures that action has the most positive outcome for the skills and self-concept of the people involved, but also more people are more likely to become and remain active in an organization structured to increase their self-responsibility.

DEVELOPING THE PERSPECTIVES OF THE PEOPLE

People begin to act for themselves rather than have someone act for them. This requires that people also learn to think for themselves and not merely rely on the organizer's thinking. As much as possible, the organizer helps develop from the action itself a tradition of success; he does not only create the tradition and tell it to the people. . . .

Instead of outlining action possibilities for organization members, the organizer will often ask questions which help people to think through action alternatives for themselves and strategies of action by their opponents. Insofar as efficiency is not too greatly reduced, responsibility for thought as well as for action is placed in the neighborhood, not merely with leaders or with organizers.

For example, suppose that an organization is trying to stop the illegal distribution of narcotics by licensed pharmacists in its neighborhood. After learning that state officials will do nothing, the members begin to think of securing legislative remedy. The organizer could simply explain the difficulty of getting legislation, especially in the face of well-financed opposition. But this approach would leave him more vulnerable to the constant attack by opponents: "The idea behind your organization is a fine thing. But aren't you people grown up yet? Do you need an organizer to do your thinking for you?" It would also mean that members may agree, but would not act with much conviction on the basis of ideas that were not their own. An alternative is preferable. The organizer may ask a series of questions about exactly how the organization can use its energy most effectively. Can you put much pressure on the legislature at this stage? Are there any other ways to act? What about direct pressure on druggists in the neighborhood? What has the best chance to succeed? The organization may in any case seek legislation, but the decision will be made after a realistic examination of alternatives and will clearly be that of the organization itself.

A more complex problem arises when the organizer must respond to attempts (very common in organizational work) to isolate him from the members. For example, suppose that opponents of the organization spread the word that, although the organization itself is basically a good idea, it is hurt by the presence of an organizer who is a "communist." The line of questioning by the organizer must help the members to an accurate appraisal of the attack: that the allegation is false and that it is an attempt to weaken the organization. . . .

It is not easy to help people to think for themselves in areas outside their usual experience. The organizer can only do it well through self-discipline and great respect for the people (to prevent manipulation in . . . the direction of organizer biases) and through having become perceived in the neighborhood as responsible and trustworthy. People are often afraid to act, uncertain about whom they can depend on, ignorant of the extent to which they are vulnerable to one or another disastrous outcome. The organizer must be the kind of person who can be counted on. He helps them undertake actions on the basis of assumptions which, through their own experience, people discover to have been valid. Even when it would be easier to agitate people by building up unfounded fears, the organizer maintains a relationship of honesty with neighborhood people, helping them to see accurately the possible disasters as well as limitations in the successes before them. Any other approach would lead to initially dazzling demonstrations or other actions followed by a decline in the organization as its members lost confidence in the organizer. For example, suppose people in one area are considering a rent strike to force landlords to fix up slum dwellings. The rent strike would get started very quickly if the organizer stressed only the facts that attorneys will represent the tenants, that money is available for legal expenses, that rent strikes do not appear to be illegal, etc., but did not mention the fact that tenants could probably be evicted after thirty days for nonpayment of rent. After the first few evictions, the reputation of the organizer and of the organization would have been destroyed beyond recovery. Over time, a self-confident critical elaboration of an adequate neighborhood perspective stems from the experience of having acted on a reasonable appraisal of alternatives and possibilities with the help of an organizer who is responsible and honest.

TRANSFORMATION OF RELATIONSHIPS

The relationships in a low-income area are primarily: (a) friendship, familial, or neighbor relationships, all object relationships with persons within the area, and (b) ecological dependency relationships with persons and institutions outside. In the beginning, to some extent people simply shift their dependency from other persons and institutions to organizers. When an organizer first appears he is interpreted within the context of usual ways of relating. He is an outsider on whom people depend for the provision of skills and resources. He is also like a friend. Therefore, at first, he is likely to be loved at the same time hated, deferred to, and depended on. One task of the organizer is to transform this personal relationship (in which people find it difficult to accept a substitute for him) into a role relationship in a structure with which people identify. He is successful (a) to the extent that members value him as a resource, but in relationships of interdependence in which members make the important decisions and do much of the work; and (b) to the extent to which members want an organizer without needing a specific organizer, and (c) value him for his contribution to the organization rather than for the broad range of his unique personality characteristics. In other words, the relationship of an organizer to the organization becomes gradually depersonalized and egalitarian from a beginning point of personalization and dependency. . . .

SUCCESS

Success occurs when the people in low-income areas can, through organization, solve a wide variety of central problems which they could not solve before, when through organization they can become effective acting persons rather than passive objects of action. Many people are swept into action, not by direct active membership in the organization, but through identification with an acting neighborhood-based mass organization. The organizer has succeeded when he has ensured the creation of such a structure which expands the area of freedom for persons in the action area. . . .

As an organization accomplishes a number of things over a period of time, an organizer has to work actively against its decline into a bureaucratic skeleton going through routine motions while major collective problems remain unresolved. Because of the tendency of organizations to fossilize, organizers will very likely be needed to maintain an action emphasis for as long as one can plan ahead. . . .

30.

Studs Terkel

ORGANIZER: BILL TALCOTT

My work is trying to change this country. This is the job I've chosen. When people ask me, "Why are you doing this?" it's like ask-

Source: From WORKING: PEOPLE TALK ABOUT WHAT THEY DO ALL DAY AND HOW THEY FEEL ABOUT WHAT THEY DO, by Studs Terkel. Copyright © 1972, 1974, by Studs Terkel. Reprinted by permission of Pantheon Books, a Division of Random House, Inc.

ing what kind of sickness you got. I don't feel sick. I think this country is sick. The daily injustices just gnaw on me a little harder than they do on other people.

I try to bring people together who are being put down by the system, left out. You try to build an organization that will give them power to make the changes. Everybody's at the bottom of the barrel at this point.

Ten years ago one could say the poor people suffered and the middle class got by. That's not true any more.

My father was a truckdriver with a sixth-grade education. My uncle was an Annapolis graduate. My father was inarticulate and worked all his life with his hands. My uncle worked all his life with his mouth and used his hands only to cut coupons. My father's problem was that he was powerless. My uncle's problem was that he was powerless, although he thought he was strong. Clipping coupons, he was always on the fringe of power, but never really had it. If he tried to take part in the management of the companies whose coupons he was clipping, he got clipped. Both these guys died very unhappy, dissatisfied with their lives.

Power has been captured by a few people. A very small top and a very big bottom. You don't see much in-between. Who do people on the bottom think are the powerful people? College professors and management types, the local managers of big corporations like General Motors. What kind of power do these guys really have? They have the kind of power Eichmann claimed for himself. They have the power to do bad and not question what they're told to do.

I am more bothered by the ghetto child who is bitten by rats than I am by a middle-class kid who can't find anything to do but put down women and take dope and play his life away. But each one is wasted.

"I came into consciousness during the fifties, when Joe McCarthy was running around. Like many people my age—I'm now thirty-seven—I was aware something was terribly wrong. I floundered around for two years in college, was disappointed, and enlisted in the army. I was NCO for my company. During a discussion, I said if I was a black guy, I would refuse to serve. I ended up being sent to division headquarters and locked up in a room *for two years, so I wouldn't be able to talk to anybody.*

"At San Francisco State, I got involved with the farm workers movement. I would give speeches on a box in front of the Commons. Then I'd go out and fight jocks behind the gym for an hour and a half. (Laughs.) In '64, I resigned as student body president and went to Mississippi to work for SNCC. I spent three years working in the black community in San Francisco.

"At that point, I figured it was time for me to work with whites. My father was from South Carolina. We had a terrible time when I visited—violent arguments. But I was family. I learned from that experience you had to build a base with white people on the fringe of the South. Hopefully you'd build an alliance between blacks and whites . . ."

I came to East Kentucky with OEO. I got canned in a year. Their idea was the same as Daley's. You use the OEO to build an organization to support the right candidates. I didn't see that as my work. My job was to build an organization of put-down people, who can *control* the candidates once they're elected.

I put together a fairly solid organization of Appalachian people in Pike County. It's a single industry area, coal. You either work for the coal company or you don't work. Sixty percent of its people live on incomes lower than the government's guidelines for rural areas.

I was brought in to teach other organizers how to do it. I spent my first three months at it. I decided these middle-class kids from Harvard and Columbia were too busy telling everybody else what they should be doing. The only thing to do was to organize the local people.

When I got fired, there were enough people to support me on one hundred dollars a month and room and board. They dug down in their pockets and they'd bring food and they'd take care of me like I was a cousin. They felt responsible for me, but they didn't see me as one of them. I'm not an Appalachian, I'm a San Franciscan. I'm not a coal miner, I'm an organizer. If they're gonna save themselves, they're gonna have to do it themselves. I have some skills that can help them. I did this work for three years.

The word organizer has been romanticized. You get the vision of a mystical being doing magical things. An organizer is a guy who brings in new members. I don't feel I've had a good day unless I've talked with at least one new person. We have a meeting, make space for new people to come in. The organizer sits next to the new guy, so everybody has to take the new guy as an equal. You do that a couple of times and the guy's got strength enough to become part of the group.

You must listen to them and tell them again and again they are important, that they have the stuff to do the job. They don't have to shuck themselves about not being good enough, not worthy. Most people were raised to think they are not worthy. School is a process of taking beautiful kids who are filled with life and beating them into happy slavery. That's as true of a twenty-five-thousand-dollar-a-year executive as it is for the poorest.

You don't find allies on the basis of the brotherhood of man. People are tied into their immediate problems. They have a difficult time worrying about other people's. Our society is so structured that everybody is supposed to be selfish as hell and screw the other guy. Christian brotherhood is enlightened self-interest. Most sins committed on poor people are by people who've come to help them.

I came as a stranger but I came with credentials. There are people who know and trust me, who say so to the others. So what I'm saying is verifiable. It's possible to win, to take an outfit like Bethlehem Steel and lick 'em. Most people in their guts don't really believe it. Gee, it's great when all of a sudden they realize it's possible. They become alive.

Nobody believed PCCA[1] could stop Bethlehem from strip mining. Ten miles away was a hillside being stripped. Ten miles away is like ten million light years away. What they wanted was a park, a place for their kids. Bethlehem said, "Go to hell. You're just a bunch of crummy Appalachians. We're not gonna give you a damn thing." If I could get that park for them, they would believe it's possible to do other things.

They really needed a victory. They had lost over and over again, day after day. So I got together twenty, thirty people I saw as leaders. I said, "Let's get that park." They said, "We can't." I said, "We can. If we let all the big wheels around the country know —the National Council of Churches and everybody start calling up, writing, and hounding Bethlehem, they'll have to give us the park." That's exactly what happened. Bethlehem thought: This is getting to be a pain in the ass. We'll give 'em the park and they'll shut up about strip mining. We haven't shut up on strip mining, but we got the park. Four thousand people from Pike County drove up and watched those bulldozers grading down that park. It was an incredible victory.

Twenty or thirty people realized we could win. Four thousand people understood there was a victory. They didn't know how it happened, but a few of 'em got curious. The twenty or thirty are now in their own communities trying to turn people on.

We're trying to link up people in other parts of the state—Lexington, Louisville,

[1]Pike County Citizens' Association.

Covington, Bowling Green—and their local issues and, hopefully, binding them together in some kind of larger thing.

When you start talking to middle-class people in Lexington, the words are different, but it's the same script. It's like talking to a poor person in Pike County or Mississippi. The schools are bad. Okay, they're bad for different reasons—but the schools are bad.

The middle class is fighting powerlessness too. Middle-class women, who are in the Lexington fight, are more alienated than lower-class women. The poor woman knows she's essential for the family. The middle-class woman thinks, If I die tomorrow, the old man can hire himself a maid to do everything I do. The white-collar guy is scared he may be replaced by the computer. The schoolteacher is asked not to teach but to baby-sit. God help you if you teach. The minister is trapped by the congregation that's out of touch with him. He spends his life violating the credo that led him into the ministry. The policeman has no relationship to the people he's supposed to protect. So he oppresses. The fireman who wants to fight fires ends up fighting a war.

People become afraid of each other. They're convinced there's not a damn thing they can do. I think we have it inside us to change things. We need the courage. It's a scary thing. Because we've been told from the time we were born that what we have inside us is bad and useless. What's true is what we have inside us is good and useful.

"In Mississippi, our group got the first black guy elected in a hundred years. In San Francisco, our organization licked the development agency there. We tied up two hundred million dollars of its money for two years, until the bastards finally came to an agreement with the community people. The guy I started with was an alcoholic pimp in the black ghetto. He is now a Presbyterian minister and very highly respected."

I work all the way from two in the morning until two the next morning seven days a week. (Laughs.) I'm not a martyr. I'm one of the few people I know who was lucky in life to find out what he really wanted to do. I'm just havin' a ball, the time of my life. I feel sorry for all these people I run across all the time who aren't doing what they want to do. Their lives are hell. I think everybody ought to quit their job and do what they want to do. You've got one life. You've got, say, sixty-five years. How on earth can you blow forty-five years of that doing something you hate?

I have a wife and three children. I've managed to support them for six years doing this kind of work. We don't live fat. I have enough money to buy books and records. The kids have as good an education as anybody in this country. Their range of friends runs from millionaires in San Francisco to black prostitutes in Lexington. They're comfortable with all these people. My kids know the name of the game: living your life up to the end.

All human recorded history is about five thousand years old. How many people in all that time have made an overwhelming difference? Twenty? Thirty? Most of us spend our lives trying to achieve some things. But we're not going to make an overwhelming difference. We do the best we can. That's enough.

The problem with history is that it's written by college professors about great men. That's not what history is. History's a hell of a lot of little people getting together and deciding they want a better life for themselves and their kids.

I have a goal. I want to end my life in a home for the aged that's run by the state—organizing people to fight 'em because they're not running it right. (Laughs.)

CHAPTER VIII

Mixing and Phasing Strategies

Over the last three chapters we have explored three distinct strategies of community organization practice in some detail. In each case we treated a fairly unitary and internally consistent strategic mode. One might have assumed that these strategies were incompatible. While such "pure" forms of practice do exist, in the real world strategies tend to become intertwined. They alternate, disintegrate under external pressures, and are reconstructed in new forms. In this chapter we will consider how the practitioner may mix and phase strategies—how he may use them in combination or in sequence as stages in community change processes necessitate shifts in tactics.

Richard E. Walton discusses two strategies that he terms "power" and "attitude change." At first glance, severe contradictions appear to exist in using both simultaneously. Employing a power strategy may be detrimental to reducing perceived differences between groups and building trust, so necessary for attitude change and vice versa. Walton indicates that the dilemmas of utilizing both strategies may be resolved through such devices as arranging for different persons or subgroups to use each strategy, managing one strategy in such a way as to minimize the negative impact on the other, and using one strategy as an initial developmental stage leading to the successful use of the other. An outline, "Paradigm on Consensus and Conflict Strategies," prepared by Tex Sample, summarizes many of the points made by Walton.

The second selection, prepared by the Ann Arbor Women's Crisis Center, concerns the nuts and bolts of building a women's center from scratch. The coming together of women in the locality development mode gives way to rather careful and precise planning. Special attention is devoted to the articulation of short-, middle-, and long-range program goals at an early stage of organizational development. A variety of task functions is also explored.

A radical perspective is offered by Jeffry Galper in the final article. Despite the use of words that seem antithetical to planning and locality development strategies, all three models are explicitly used in the achievement of "nonreformist reforms." The creation of "collective, communal, democratic organizations that function to meet the needs of people in the community," for example, requires the building of trust through cooperation that is especially characteristic of locality development. The People's Fund, a social action alternative to Philadelphia's United Way, must engage in careful planning to get its message across to potential sources of support.

While these examples are relatively brief, the point should be clear. Most practitioners in most practice situations will need to use a blend of different strategic approaches. If one mode predominates, care should be taken not to neglect the potentials inherent in the others. If your own group or organization cannot use the interventive approach that seems most likely to get the job done, then a more appropriate body or association can be sought to take over the effort. Perhaps above all, the practitioner should not be bound by ideological commitment to a particular practice model, but consider which methods might best serve those people in whose name community work is being undertaken.

31a.

Richard E. Walton

TWO STRATEGIES OF SOCIAL CHANGE AND THEIR DILEMMAS

CHANGE SETTING

The type of intergroup setting which is of primary concern here is described by the following assumptions. First, assume a desire on the part of one group to change the allocation of scarce resources between two groups—these could be status, political power, economic advantage or opportunity, geographic occupancy, and so on. Alter-

nately, assume incompatible preferences regarding social institutions—such as the Berlin Wall, racial segregation, union shop. Second, assume that although the leaders of the groups recognize these areas of conflict they also want to establish a more cooperative set of attitudes between the groups. Third, assume further that there is neither law nor a compulsory arbitration mechanism which can accomplish the desired change or settle the conflict of interest.

Some of our most pressing problems of social change fit these assumptions almost completely and others meet them to a lesser degree. In international relations, for in-

Source: Reproduced by special permission from THE JOURNAL OF APPLIED BEHAVIORAL SCIENCE "Two Strategies of Social Change and Their Dilemmas," pp. 167–79. Copyright by NTL Institute, 1965. Reprinted by permission of the publisher and the author.

stance, the important substantive conflicts between the United States and the Soviet Union are accompanied by a general desire for more favorable internation attitudes. Moreover, in the present polarized world where the stakes of change can be enormously high, no international legal machinery is available to settle the important issues.

In race relations, the civil rights movement of the last decade has sought social change at times and in places where legal machinery could not be brought to bear to establish and enforce humane treatment for Blacks, to say nothing about equalizing their right to vote, to use public accommodations, to find housing, to apply for jobs, and so forth. At the same time, the majority of Blacks and white leaders have commented upon the necessity for improved intergroup attitudes.

In labor-management relations, also, there are important substantive issues, such as hours, wages, and working conditions, which are neither specified by law nor amenable to resolution by appeal to a higher order of common values. Often these differences are accompanied by a genuine and mutual desire for harmonious intergroup relations.

How does the leadership of a group behave in these situations when [it seeks] a change in the status quo? What actions are instrumental to the change effort?

Two groups of social scientists—viewing the same general situation—offer quite different explanations and advice. One change strategy is advanced by game theorists, diplomatic strategists, and students of revolutions. Their focus is on the building of a power base and the strategic manipulation of power. Another strategy is urged by many social psychologists and by many persons involved in human relations laboratory training. This approach involves overtures of love and trust and gestures of good

will, all intended to result in attitude change and concomitant behavior change.

TACTICS OF THE POWER STRATEGY

In recent years there has been an attempt to explicate the rational tactics of power and strategic choice (Schelling, 1969; Rapoport, 1960; Boulding, 1962; Walton & McKersie, 1965). The work in this area suggests that the fixed sum games—those situations in which what one person gains the other loses—require the following tactical operations.

First, in order to establish a basis for negotiation with the other and improve the probable outcome for itself, a group must build its power vis-à-vis the other. Group A can increase its relative power by making Group B more dependent upon it and by decreasing its own (A's) dependence upon B. Often the change is sought by groups with a relative power disadvantage. To command attention and establish a basis for a *quid pro quo,* they must threaten the other with harm, loss, inconvenience, or embarrassment. These threats in international relations range from nuclear war to unilateral cancellation of an official state visit. In civil rights they involve notoriety, demonstrations, consumer boycotts, and sit-ins, lie-ins, and the like. In labor relations they include wildcat strikes, authorized stoppages, unfavorable publicity campaigns. These tactics create a basis for negotiation only if the threats are credible. One important technique for increasing their credibility is to fulfill a given threat once or repeatedly, as required.

A second set of tactical operations is required in order for a group to make maximum use of its potential power. These include biasing the rival group's perceptions of the strength of the underlying preference functions. A leader of group A attempts to overstate his group's needs or preferences for various degrees of achievement of its stated objective. Also, leader A depreciates the importance to B of B's objectives. These operations require the skillful management of ambiguity and uncertainty. They involve manipulating communication opportunities such that B perceives A as being maximally (even if irrationally) committed to a course of action and that the leader of group B does not have a comparable opportunity to commit himself to a different set of actions.

An abundance of illustrative material from international relations is available for each of these tactical operations—for example, the Cuban missile episode, Berlin crises, and the crises over Suez, the Congo, and Viet Nam. Leaders of various civil rights groups have behaved in similar ways. Illustrative encounters are those in Montgomery (school-bus boycotts over public accommodations); Pittsburgh (consumer boycotts over employment); Chicago (lie-ins and demonstrations over de facto segregation in schools); Birmingham (demonstrations over public accommodations); Mississippi ("invading" the state in the interest of voter registration and freedom schools). Analyses of the negotiations in any of the major trade union strikes—such as those in steel in 1959, in rails in 1963, and in autos in 1964—would reveal labor-management behavior which conformed to the tactical operations of the power strategy.

TACTICS OF THE ATTITUDE CHANGE STRATEGY

Theoretical and empirical work in recent years has identified the conditions and actions which result in change in intergroup relationships (Naess, 1957; Janis & Katz, 1959; Osgood, 1959; Kelman, 1962; Berkowitz, 1962; Sherif, 1962; Deutsch, 1962;

Gibb, 1964; Walton & McKersie, 1965). The areas of agreement in these writings may be summarized in terms of the tactics of attitude change.

Increasing the level of attraction and trust between persons or groups involves the following types of operations, considering the leader of group A as the acting party: minimizing the perceived differences between the groups' goals and between characteristics of members of the two groups; communications to B advocating peace; refraining from any actions which might harm members of the rival group (inconvenience, harass, embarrass, or violate them in any way); minimizing or eliminating B's perception of potential threats from A; emphasizing the degree of mutual dependence between the groups; accepting or enhancing the status of the representative of the rival group; ensuring that contacts between groups are on the basis of equal status; attempting to involve many members in intergroup contact; attempting to achieve a high degree of empathy with respect to the motives, expectations, and attitudes of members of group B; adopting a consistent posture of trust toward the other group; being open about A's own plans and intentions; creating a network of social relations involving many mutual associations with third parties.

There is tension between the ideas which underlie the two change strategies outlined above. However, the two groups of social scientists who are associated with these respective change strategies tend to handle this tension either by ignoring it or by depreciating the assumptions, ideas, and tactics of the other. It is true that both systems of ideas treat certain realities of the total social field; and, admittedly, it is possible for one to center one's attention on those particular situations where his ideas by themselves are appropriate and upon those particular aspects of a more complex situation where his ideas apply. The practitioner himself cannot do this. He must deal with the total reality. The leader of a group who is advocating and seeking change directly experiences the tension between these two persuasive systems of ideas.

Social scientists can become more relevant and therefore more helpful to the practitioner if they, too, confront these tensions between ideas, these dilemmas in action programs.

It is important to identify still a third distinct process of change, namely, problem solving. This process can be used whenever the basic nature of the issue is one where there is the potential that arrangements can be invented or created allowing both parties to gain or where one party can gain without the other's sacrificing anything of value to himself. In other words, integrative solutions are logically possible (Blake, 1959). However, this alternative of problem solving is not applicable in the specific intergroup situations assumed here: The substantive conflicts are ones which by the nature of the issues and the parties' basic preferences can be resolved only by dominance-submission or some compromise outcome.

LEADERSHIP DILEMMAS IN PURSUING BOTH POWER AND ATTITUDE CHANGE STRATEGIES

If—as we have assumed here—a leader of group A has the objective both of obtaining important concessions from B and of reducing intergroup hostility, he would prefer to pursue simultaneously both change strategies discussed above. But in many respects the strategies place contradictory tactical demands on a leader, forcing him to choose between these strategies or to find some basis on which to integrate the two in some broader strategy of change. Several of the contradictions, dilemmas, and choice

points in the tactics of social change are discussed below.

Overstatement of Objectives versus Deemphasizing Differences

On the one hand, it is often tactical to the power strategy to overstate one's ultimate goals or immediate objectives—in effect, exaggerating the differences between the two groups. The strategy of attitude change, on the other hand, would deemphasize differences. Thus, the U.S. references to the status of Berlin which overstate our pertinent preferences, needs, and requirements may improve our position in bargaining for new terms there; but these statements run the risk of convincing the Soviet Union that our differences run even deeper than they do and that there is less basis for conciliation and trust than they had believed.

Stereotyping: Internal Cohesion versus Accurate Differentiation

Stereotyping members of the rival group, focusing on their faults, impugning their motives, questioning their rationality, challenging their competence—these are often employed by leaders and members of the first group to build internal cohesion and willingness to make necessary sacrifices. For example, these tendencies occurred in a moderate form as the Mississippi Summer Project prepared field staff and student volunteers for their work in "hostile" Mississippi.[1] The tendency to attribute negative attributes to members of the rival group may have aided in the implementation of the almost pure power strategy which characterized this particular project, but this tendency would have been a clear liability in another civil rights project where the objectives included achieving attitude change.

---

[1] Personal observation.

Emphasis on Power to Coerce versus Trust

If group A increases B's dependence upon A, this may enhance A's power to obtain substantive concessions, but it will not elicit more positive feelings. In fact, it can be argued that the trust-building process requires that A would communicate about A's dependence upon B. A labor union may enhance its power position by making management more aware of the company's vulnerability to a strike. But the same union might elicit more trust if it were to indicate instead how much the union must count upon management.

Information: Ambiguity versus Predictability

Whereas ambiguity and uncertainty are often tactical to the power strategy, openness and predictability are essential to the attitude change strategy. Similarly, the first strategy is facilitated when there is limited and disciplined interaction; the second, when there is a more extensive and more open contact pattern. Thus, the power strategy dictates that we restrict the flow of information and people between the Soviet Union and the United States and that the limited contacts be formal and structured and that the agenda of these contacts be quite guarded. Attitude change strategy, on the other hand, calls for freedom of travel, a variety of settings for international contact, and spontaneity and openness in these interchanges.

Threat versus Conciliation

Review of the tactical operations of the two strategies reveals another important choice point in dual or mixed strategies, namely, What should be the role of threat or harm? When A is primarily pursuing an attitude change strategy, he communicates peaceful plans, he reduces perceived threat to B, and he refrains from actions that harm B. However, to pursue a power strategy in the interest of obtaining substantive gains, A engages in quite different tactics.

Even instances of uncontrolled aggression out of frustration can build bargaining power for the frustrated group and serve as an implicit threat of more aggression if substantive gains are not forthcoming. The Harlem riots in the summer of 1964 illustrate this point. Although it was generally said at the time that these outbursts hurt the civil rights movement (i.e., "had set the movement back several years"), many changes which accommodated the Blacks' demands and needs were soon made in the budgets, plans, and organization of several commissions and departments of New York City. One column headline in the *New York Times*, July 1964, the week following the riots, read "City Accelerates Fight on Poverty: $223,225 Grant Made Amid Reference to Racial Riots." A casual content analysis of items in the news after the riots in Harlem, Rochester, Philadelphia, and elsewhere suggest that there were both substantive gains and attitudinal losses. Notwithstanding the fact that all responsible civil rights leaders deplored the wanton destruction of property and the indiscriminate defiance of legal authorities, their bargaining power was nevertheless strengthened in certain respects.

Hostility Management: Impact versus Catharsis

This dilemma is related to the preceding one but can present a somewhat more subtle problem for group leadership. Both change strategies involve the purposeful management of hostile feelings. In the power strategy the expression of hostile feelings is managed in a way which creates optimal impact on the other group, communicating strength of interest in the issue or making a threat credible.

The attitude change strategy also involves the expression of hostile feelings, but in a way which creates an optimal impact on the expressing group. Hostility expression is managed in a way which allows catharsis and the reevaluation of one's own group's feelings, but with minimum impact on the other group. Otherwise the hostility level will tend to be maintained or increased.

Coalition versus Inclusion

One final dilemma relates to the question of whether A tries to involve third parties or publics in a coalition *against* B or in a social group *with* B. Building bargaining power in the interest of substantive change may require A to isolate B and attempt to generate disapproval of B. This has been an important aspect of the strategy of the civil rights movement in the last decade. The movement has tried to identify and isolate those officials and power groups in the South who oppose integration and those national officials in the Republican Party who are unsympathetic with certain legislative and enforcement objectives. This has created a forced choice situation for the moderates and for the uncertain.

However, a strategy of attitude change involves creating a network of social relations among A, B, and others. Applied to the civil rights movement, an emphasis on attitude change would actively encourage dialogue, understanding, and mutual influence among (a) groups in the movement, (b) the middle-of-the-roaders, and (c) the segregationists and other right-wing groups.

Coping with the Dilemmas

How do those who seek both substantive changes opposed by another group and improvements in intergroup attitudes cope with these dilemmas?

If the group's leader sequences the emphasis placed upon these two objectives and their accompanying strategies, this does somewhat ameliorate the tension between the two sets of activities. In international negotiations between the East and the West, both sides have used a freeze-thaw approach. One may first engage in new initiatives intended to make substantive gains or to create a power base for the future, and then make peace overtures. As long as the cycle is not too short in duration and the initiatives and overtures are seen as genuine, a leader can engage in both sets of behaviors and still have them be credible. In race relations, a particular campaign may involve a street demonstration phase (power building) and a negotiation phase (a mixture of power bargaining and relationship building).

Another technique is to have the contradictory strategies implemented by different persons or subgroups. In international relations, power tactics occur in the confrontations between the United States and the Soviet Union in the United Nations General Assembly and Security Council, but their attitude change efforts are implemented by different groups involved in such activities as cultural exchange programs. In race relations, a similar distinction can be made between the programs of CORE and SNCC on the one hand and NAACP and the Urban League on the other. This technique makes it apparent that mixed or dual strategies can be pursued more readily by an organization than by a person, and more readily by a movement than by an organization.

Whether or not the activities are sequenced or assigned to different persons within a group, an important way of coping with these dilemmas is to choose actions which minimize them. Recognition of the tactical requirements of both strategies results in eliminating provocative acts which elicit negative attitudes and add nothing to the power strategy—for example, impeccable dress and demeanor in many civil rights demonstrations or the self-imposed norm of volunteers of the Mississippi Summer Project to avoid mixed racial couples' appearing in public even though eventual acceptance of such a pattern was one of the goals of the movement.

When the relationship between strategies is fully understood by the leader, he can select power tactics which have least negative impact on attitudes and choose attitudinal structuring activities which detract least from the power strategy.

Nonviolence is an attempt to meet the requirements of both strategies, but as a tactic it falls short of achieving an optimal integration. This is true in part because the distinction made between violence and non-violence is more meaningful to the acting group than to the target group. The distinction usually refers to whether or not there is a physical violation of members of the rival group. In fact, other violations may be experienced by them as equally devastating —such as violation of their traditions and other social norms (integrating schools), assaults on their power base (voting drives). In short, in some situations the only maneuvers which effectively increase bargaining power really do hurt.

OVERALL STRATEGY CONSIDERATIONS

Although in many situations one must engage in the tactics of power only at some disadvantage in terms of achieving attitude change and vice versa, this is not always the case. Especially when one takes a longer-range viewpoint, one may discover that the substantive objectives of the power strategy are more likely to be realized at a later date if an improvement in intergroup attitudes is sought initially. The point is that attitude change may result in some lessening of the substantive conflict. If Southern whites as a group were more accepting of Blacks (i.e., developed more favorable attitudes toward them for some independent reason), they would be less adamant on certain substantive issues—for example, segregated schools—and would, as a result, reduce the need for civil rights groups to utilize a power strategy. Moreover, in the case of many of the substantive gains which one may reach through the power strategy—an arms control agreement, a treaty on Berlin, an understanding reached regarding future employment practices affecting Blacks— the fulfillment of these arrangements is dependent upon the level of trust and confidence which exists in the relationship.

Similarly, a longer-range view point may show that the objective of attitude change is more likely to be achieved at a later date if one engages in the power tactics initially. The substantive gains obtained by the power strategy almost always result in temporary setbacks in terms of the level of friendliness and trust between the groups; but in the somewhat longer run, the result may be better affective relations. Consider race relations. One reason why more positive attitudes may develop via the initial power strategy is that the commitment and self-respect which the Blacks usually demonstrate in pursuing the power strategy may engender respect on the part of the larger white community—after the initial heat of conflict has subsided.

Another indirect and eventual way that the power strategy can lead to more favorable attitudinal bonds is through the mechanism of dissonance reduction. If as a result of substantive gains a group must be treated differently (more equal), there is a tendency to regard them differently (more equal) in order to make one's beliefs and attitudes congruent with one's behavior.

There is a third reason why a power strategy designed to obtain substantive concessions may achieve attitude change as well, particularly for a group which is currently less privileged and exercises less power. This refers to an important precondition for achieving a stable and healthy intergroup relationship—equal status and power between groups. This suggests that as long as group A remains at a power disadvantage and there is a potential for achieving power parity, A's mix of power and attitude change tactics will include relatively more power tactics. Thus, the power strategy for the civil rights groups during the last decade has dominated the attitude change strategy. This principle is also illustrated by the warlike actions of the Soviet Union during the period after World War II, when the United States alone possessed the atom bomb.

Whatever the existing balance of power, whenever B makes a move which would build his relative power, A will tend to act primarily in terms of the power strategy. This is illustrated by the United States's bargaining commitment moves when it discovered Soviet missiles in Cuba and when the Soviets attempted to make inroads in the Middle East and the Congo during the Suez and Congo crises respectively.

Implications

Recognition of these dilemmas is the first step toward developing a theory of social action which specifies the conditions under which one should conform to the tactical requirements of one strategy versus the other. But better theory is not enough. The agent of social change needs the behavioral skills required by simultaneously or sequentially mixed strategies. For example, international officials and civil rights leaders should be flexible enough to employ strategies of attitude change when a particular campaign reaches the negotiation phase.

What are the implications for training of leaders of groups advocating major social change? Human relations training generally and laboratory learning in particular are geared to developing insights and skills central to the strategy of attitude change and are less relevant to the power strategy. I suggest that the conception of the problem of change should be broadened to incorporate—as necessary and legitimate—the power strategy.[2] We must understand what demands on leadership behavior are

[2]In the interest of sharpening the issues about our conception of the problem, I offer the following assertions regarding the role of bargaining, power, and violence in social change:

First, bargaining and bargaining tactics (including tactical deception, bluff, commitment, promises, threats, and threat fulfillment) are often necessary in social change situations where there are basic conflicts of interest. Moreover, many of these tactical operations are amoral in such situations.

Second, attempts to create cooperative relations between parties are more effective if there is some parity in their power. Power of a party derives from its capacity to influence some aspect of the fate of the other—either rewards or punishments. Often the only avenue open to a party with less relative power is to increase its capacity to harm (embarrass or inconvenience) the other. Moreover, it may be necessary for the party to engage in a series of maneuvers which are increasingly persuasive in communicating to the other party both a capacity and a willingness to use the power.

Third, where they are used, tactics of nonviolence are effective at least in part because the other group perceives this method as an alternative to violence. The option of violence is indirectly suggested *by advocating nonviolence.*

Fourth, there is experimental evidence that a cooperative bid by A is more effective in eliciting a cooperative response from B when it occurs against a series of noncooperative moves by A. Maybe this paradox also operates in some social situations creating an incentive for initial noncooperation.

imposed by the power strategy of change both during the phase when power thinking necessarily dominates group leadership and the phase when preserving a power base is merely a consideration in designing an attitude change strategy. If these specialists deplore these power tactics simply because they violate their personal model of preferred social behavior, their advice which *is* appropriate and badly needed by the practitioner will be taken less seriously by him.

REFERENCES

Berkowitz, L. *Aggression: A Social Psychological Analysis.* New York: McGraw-Hill, 1962.

Blake, R. R. Psychology and the crisis of statesmanship. *Amer. Psychologist,* 1959, 14, 87–94.

Boulding, K. *Conflict and Defense: A General Theory.* New York: Harper, 1962.

City accelerates fight on poverty. *New York Times,* July 28, 1964, p. 15.

Deutsch, M. A psychological basis for peace. In Q. Wright, W. M. Evan, & M. Deutsch (Eds.), *Preventing World War III: Some Proposals.* New York: Simon & Schuster, 1962.

Gibb, J. R. Climate for trust formation. In L. P. Bradford, J. R. Gibb, & K. D. Benne (Eds.), *T-Group Theory and Laboratory Method: Innovation in Re-education.* New York: Wiley, 1964.

Janis, I. L., & Katz, D. The reduction of intergroup hostility: Research problems and hypotheses. *J. Conflict Resolution,* 1959, 3, 85–100.

Kelman, H. C. Changing attitudes through international activities. *J. Soc. Issues,* 1962, 13, 68–87.

Naess, A. A systematization of Gandhian ethics of conflict resolution. *J. Conflict Resolution,* 1957, 1, 140–155.

Osgood, C. E. Suggestions for winning the real war with Communism. *J. Conflict Resolution,* 1959, 3, 295–325.

Rapoport, A. *Fights, Games and Debates.* Ann Arbor: Univer. of Michigan Press, 1960.

Schelling, T. *The Strategy of Conflict.* Cambridge: Harvard Univer. Press, 1960.

Sherif, M. (Ed.). *Intergroup Relations and Leadership.* New York: Wiley, 1962.

Walton, R. E., & McKersie, R. B. *A Behavioral Theory of Labor Negotiations.* New York: McGraw-Hill, 1965.

31b.

Tex S. Sample

PARADIGM ON CONSENSUS AND CONFLICT STRATEGIES

CONSENSUS STRATEGY

1. *General Orientation*

a. *Search for things which unite* men by focusing on the commonalities all men experience and know.

b. *Faith* in the power and reality of ideas and values which men can discover if they will allow truth to emerge in a free and open encounter.

c. *Truth* is the correspondence of a statement with a state of affairs.

2. *Organization*

a. Collaborate.
b. Organize across interests.
c. Bring together various assortments of people to work on "real" problems which transcend divisions.
d. "Anti-ideological." Should be concerned with truth, not with ideological distortions. Organize people by helping them come to a common definition of a problem and a common solution through a collaborative process.

CONFLICT STRATEGY

a. *Search for things which divide.* Find structural cleavages which divide men and help them see their real interests. Develop strategies to divide men along those lines.

b. *Faith* in the power and reality of interests which can motivate men to organization and action.

c. *Truth* is loyalty to the interests of your group.

a. Fight.
b. Organize around structural interests.
c. Bring together people in same structural position. Make the interests manifest. *(Rub raw the sores of resentment.)*
d. Develop an ideology which supports your interests in conflict with other groups.

From "Consensus and Conflict Strategies: Their Implications for the League of Women Voters in Working with Powerless Groups in American Society," by Tex S. Sample. The complete paper was presented in March 1969 at the Conference for Joint Action on Urban Problems.

3. Communication[1]

a. A means of sharing. Use to clarify need, problems, and goals of all parties concerned.

a. A weapon. Use communication for strategic advantage to describe your interests in best light and to place enemy at a disadvantage.

b. Stress openness and honesty. Attempt to achieve clarity about oneself and others, to check perceptions by keeping communications open and free. Share real needs and problems and collaborate to achieve mutual goals.

b. Make strategic use of information. Understand what your own needs and interests are, but disguise them. Do not reveal them to the enemy. Do not reveal how much you are willing to give up to achieve a goal. Make the enemy think you are stronger than you are: overstate your objectives; bluff.

c. Use communication to develop trust and attraction between persons and groups.

c. Establish a strong negotiating base. Keep the situation ambiguous and uncertain for the opposition.

d. Be flexible and responsive. Keep all parties informed about what is going on.

d. Catch the opposition off guard. Surprise them. Create anxiety and confusion for them. But keep your own group well informed and on top of the situation.

4. Approach to Opponents

a. The opponent is one to be brought into dialogue so that a wider circle of relationship can be fashioned.

a. The opponent is the enemy. Polarize the relationship with him to your advantage.

b. Try to get as much clarity about the opponent as possible and to help him understand your group as well.

b. Attack the enemy.
—Question his competence.
—Impugn his motives.
—Stereotype and exaggerate his position.

5. Dealing with Conflict

a. Attempt to distinguish real from unreal conflict. Get at the real source of the problem.

a. The real source is in interest cleavages. Use real and unreal conflict to improve advantage.

b. Ventilate hostility. Humanize opponent.

b. Direct hostility toward the enemy.

c. Seek to resolve ill feelings.

c. Seek to achieve a better platform for negotiation.

---

[1]*In this section, I am indebted to a mimeographed paper entitled: "Some Alternating Modes of Behavior: Collaborate—Fight." Source unknown.)*

d. Keep conflict within some order. Attempt to institutionalize it into existing arrangements or differentiate those arrangements so as to be able to deal with it.

d. Use conflict but do not allow it to be institutionalized or channeled by established procedures, when those procedures are stylized by the privilege structure being opposed.

e. Keep distortion in the conflict to a minimum and prevent polarization.

e. Use distortion and polarization. Disrupt established procedures for handling conflict.

6. *Alliances*

a. Work with all those who are involved in a situation. Build alliances with those who *think* as you do or who will enter a process of working with you.

a. Build alliances with those who have same interests.

b. Build alliances across interest cleavages.

b. Build alliances across interest cleavages only on a temporary basis and only on specific issues where there is a convergence of interest.

7. *Attitude toward the System and Vehicles of Social Change*

a. Keep the system open.

a. Change the system.

b. The institutions of the system are the vehicles of social change. They are capable of responding to or setting up additional arrangements to deal with problems and needs.

b. The dominated groups of society are the vehicles of social change: the proletariat, blacks, students, etc.

8. *Criteria for Use of the Strategy*
Use consensus model when:

Use conflict model when:

a. Power is shared so that equals are dealing with equals.

a. Power disparities exist, one group dominated by another.

b. Goals are distributable, i.e., both sides can get what they need and want.

b. Goals are not distributable, i.e., the situation is win-lose.

c. People share values, interests, and goals, or it is at least possible to do so.

c. Sharp cleavages of interests exist.

32.

Women's Crisis Center, Ann Arbor

ORGANIZING A WOMEN'S CRISIS-SERVICE CENTER

SISTERHOOD VS. DOGOODY TWOSHOES

You've gotten together with several women friends and have all discovered that you share the same awful experiences in trying to solve personal and practical problems. Or you're upset and angry about what is being done to women in your community and the lack of resources available to them. As you share your feelings with more and more women, you become convinced that the suffering, the degradation, the deprivation, the isolation, and the powerlessness amount to a widespread crisis for women in your area. And you want to do something with the consciousness which you have so painfully raised in yourselves. The key to the process of translating awareness into feminist action is sisterhood: the perspective that self-interest and the interest of helping other women can be integrated.

As women we have always been taught to value the needs of others above our own. Our own needs, even when desperate, are labeled selfish, wrong, or sick. Most of the skills and competencies we have developed are aimed at improving the health, comfort, and happiness of our children, our men, our parents, the "disadvantaged"—always *other* people. At the same time we are told that we women are basically narcissistic, unreliable, and devious. So we work all the

Source: From "Developing the Need, Some Goals, and a Focus" in *How to Organize a Women's Crisis-Service Center,* pp. 1–8, 1974. Reprinted by permission of the Women's Crisis Center of Ann Arbor.

harder to show we care nothing for our own safety, comfort, knowledge, power, and even nothing for our own inner peace and joy. By this meatgrinding process we actually lose our capacity to be constructively and honestly subjective.

If there is any need for action by your group, it must first respect the need of women to recover the subjective parts of themselves. If you accomplish nothing else, you will in this have achieved a very important victory for yourselves. Whatever your eventual goals, you can start with the immediate need of your group for some kind of *mutual help organization* that maximizes your collective resources to fulfill shared wants. What is it that you all have to give one another? It could be the guarantee of help in an emergency, emotional support after a family blowup, an exchange of child care, help on academic work, help in dealing with difficult job situations, night escort —the possibilities are unlimited. Almost immediately you will have opened up options for yourselves. It is only a short step to opening up options for other women as well; this in turn will again increase your own resources and opportunities.

RESEARCHING THE NEED

In each community the crisis for women takes on different forms and dimensions. You may wish to rely solely on subjective sources of information about the community such as discussion meetings with groups of women, individual interviews, public hearings or "tribunals" (such as those held on abortion by women in New York), and telephone surveys, in which you advertise for women to call in anonymously and talk about their experiences with a problem (such as rape).

Obtaining objective, quantified information on these problems is not necessary but it can be extremely useful at some point in your development of action. Particularly when you are in the position of persuader, attempting to get money or free rent from a church or foundation, or trying to get an article published in the local newspaper, you will need some "objective" data to bolster your case. Be warned that even with watertight statistics many male listeners may laugh at you when you try to assert the facts of women's current crises. As a defense against their oppression of women, many men have convinced themselves—and many women too—that women "enjoy" a "privileged" status and like things just fine the way they are.

You may, if you have already gathered plenty of good subjective feminist support and/or money, ignore such male opinion. But if you do need funds and broader community support, you must convince some men and some skeptical, insulated women, as well, of the true depth of the problem. With these people you can try to discuss those problems having more "universal" sympathy, such as lack of health care, rape, unemployment, and loneliness of old age. Avoid fruitless efforts to enlighten people about the urgent need for preabortion and unwanted pregnancy counseling (unless yours is a very liberal community), for sexuality counseling, for mutual support groups for women (consciousness-raising groups), for child care, or for welfare rights. However, do find out about these problems in your own way. Following are some suggestions for objective information gathering. The data can expose issues you weren't aware of, reveal the extent of a problem, or

tell you more specifically who is and who is not likely to experience it.

1. Some public and social service agencies try to evaluate their own work. They should be able to tell you what services they provide and for how many people, per month and per year. Through this process you will also learn of community resources for future referral. Ask who is excluded from the service, and what proportion they constitute of the total group in need of the service. More rarely, a social agency or government bureau will try to assess the wider incidence of "emotional breakdowns," "social" diseases, child abuse, school leaving, and so forth. Ask for reprints of any studies done. Remember that even the best research usually yields a very low estimate of social problems, particularly those with stigma attached.

2. See if there is a government department that deals with the problem you are concerned about. There's a chance that it will have some relevant figures. The police department should have crime and rape statistics; the Friend-of-the-Court some records on divorces and child-support pay guidelines (and, perhaps, on delinquency in child-support payments); and the county clerk census data and records of births and marriages. Warning: Many of these agencies see no reason to break down their statistics by sex, even for salary records of their own employees. However, you might ask if you can obtain access to their files, and so compile your own statistics for women.

3. Check out back issues of newspapers and reports in the public library. (Newspapers may have better information on the courts than the courts themselves!) Look especially for feature articles or exposés.

4. Call or visit the local hospital(s) or clinics and find out the proportion of women to men patients and how many babies are born there. (Compare births to the

county clerk's figures—the discrepancy may reflect unrecorded "illegitimate" births.)

5. Call the school system and other adult education facilities, such as a university extension service. Find out how many women are dropping out of school because of pregnancy, how many are returning to adult education courses, and how many couples participate in childbirth education. Compare the latter to the total number of women having babies. ‘

6. If there is a mental hospital in your area, find out what proportion of its patients are women and what their diagnoses are in comparison to men. If women stay longer, ask why. Also, are there any resources for the women just released?

These are just some of the many ways you can retrieve data on below-the-surface trends in your community.

LONG-, MIDDLE-, AND SHORT-RANGE GOALS

By now, you are all well convinced that something must be done to improve things. You've extended your power by joining forces, but you are aware that, as a relatively small group with limited time and energy, you simply haven't got the clout to achieve vast and immediate changes—particularly in the powerful community agencies that are part of the problem. It will take time before we can eliminate all sexist doctors, lawyers, schools, and employers from our communities. And in the meantime, women are daily undergoing genuine agonies. What, then, can you do?

First of all, with what you know of some major problems, try to establish some goals. Goals are "what" you want to do as opposed to "how" you will go about doing it. Too often groups become bogged down arguing methods and means before a shared goal has really been established. Goals are

often easier to think about if stated as functions, such as:

1. To increase access to information
2. To provide a missing service
3. To decrease anxiety of women seeking to use existing services
4. To facilitate exchange of resources between private individuals in need

You can also state goals as roles you want to play in the community. For example:

1. Advocate for women
2. Broker of resources and information
3. Companion for individual women
4. Counselor in emotional problems
5. Consultant in problem solving
6. New image or model of personal change and competence for women
7. Skills trainer in organizational participation or political action

By expressing goals as functions or roles, you are on more solid ground in terms of agreement as a group. And the "goals language" does not of course dictate the means toward the goal. You will have the opportunity to brainstorm over how to get there.

Being able to distinguish your short-range goals from your long-range goals is also very important if your group is to take on realistic projects. The idea is to define the immediate projects so that they will clearly lead to your ideals—without their being so complicated and difficult that everybody gets discouraged and drifts away. Many of your initial goals will really be long-range, requiring over two years to accomplish. So after you have together set them forth, begin to think about the "how" of getting them done. Choose one of the "hows," and make that into a middle-range goal by wording it in the "goal language" shown above. A middle-range goal usually takes a period of one to two years.

After setting the middle-range goal, repeat the same kind of process in order to agree upon a short-range goal to be finished in several months. You may, perhaps, have several short-range goals on which to work in a series. And now that you've accomplished this most difficult planning phase, it should be easy for your group of sisters to work out the subsequent necessary details.

Bringing this all down to earth, Table 32.1 has some examples of such backwards goal setting from our own experience at the Women's Crisis Center in Ann Arbor.

When setting middle- and short-range goals, be careful not to duplicate what someone else is already doing in the community. If you don't like the *way* they are doing it, then go ahead yourselves, but be sure to clearly specify how your goal differs from theirs. If another group of women is tackling your goal in part, try to coordinate

TABLE 32.1

Long-Range (more than two years)	Middle-Range (one to two years)	Short-Range (several months)
A. To provide 24-hour total crisis counseling that is compassionate, nonsexist, free of charge, and controlled by women.	A. To provide telephone crisis counseling eleven hours a day, seven days a week by peer counselors giving short-term help on specific problems in an organization that is women-controlled.	A. To organize community women who are concerned and committed to women's rights and well-being, and who are willing to learn new skills in order to help each other.
B. To completely eliminate sexist or dangerous treatment of women by medical services.	B. To develop consumer control over local medical services. To set up a referral system so that women can be referred only to nonsexist doctors. To set up procedures for inspecting and evaluating local medical services.	B. To create a complete list of private and clinic doctors and medical services to accompany each entry by direct feedback from women consumers of that service. To give information and recommendations to other women using this list.
C. To create a large supportive community for women so that any woman in need can find resources close to where she lives.	C. To form an organization which is a supportive community for its members and in which callers needing help are then free to become members sharing in the work.	C. To list all resources and services of women in the group or known to the group. To share this information with each other.
D. To make sure that no woman is ever stranded without funds for essential food, child care, transportation, shelter, or medical care.	D. To have $200 in a fund for small emergency loans to women seeking an abortion, or postrape medical treatment.	D. To locate individuals or organization who might be willing to donate to the emergency fund. To speak to these people and/or submit proposals requesting donations or grants.
E. To make access to information regarding community resources and services easy and fast.	E. To create a computer-assisted information list which is updated weekly and can store a broad range of information indexed by name and subject.	E. To compile a notebook listing of all community resources and services relevant to women's needs. To accompany each listing by feedback and comments from consumers of the service. To share this information with other women.

with their efforts. And very importantly, check to make sure that the short-range goal *will* meet the long-range problem.

The importance of clear short-range goals—and good consensus among participants—cannot be overemphasized. It is much easier for group members to assert shared leadership when everyone knows what concrete steps must be taken and when. In contrast, if only one member or only an "in group" knows how the group gets from A to Z, others become dependent, confused, and tend to drift away. Furthermore, the existence of concrete goals—preferably in writing—tends to eliminate useless, vague philosophical arguments that consume so much time that nothing at all happens and the group disintegrates. You do not, of course, need to agree on all values in order to collaborate on a limited goal. And while you work together on a specific aim, what often develops is more shared values and a better understanding of differences that do remain.

FOCUS

So far you have struggled together—to define specific short-range strategy. Typically it takes several months to be able to spell out what you want to do and how to do it creatively. As women we have often had little experience in cooperating with each other—we've been taught to compete with each other and to avoid each other in preference to male company. Moreover, many of us have grown up with insecurities about our own competence and ability. Therefore, to work together we must unlearn a great deal as well as develop new sensitivities and assuredness. Furthermore, in working together we inevitably must influence each other. And each of us must assert personal leadership in various ways if guidance of the group is to be really shared. None of us is totally equal to any others—

thus at the same time we must help each other to develop in different ways.

No group, no matter how competent, can afford to ignore for long its members' own continuing personal development. This, along with your short-range goals, must be made a conscious focus from time to time. And focusing upon personal development can take many forms: you may decide to hold a specific meeting where you break down into small consciousness-raising groups, or you may plan special training sessions in order to practice shared leadership techniques and other skills in group process. During the planning stages this kind of attention to group processes will release far more energy, creativity, and commitment than would be released if everyone were simply working all the time.

Once your interests and realism have defined a short-range goal, you'll quickly find that supporting functions are needed. Some of these are:

1. Publicity (speaking at other groups and clubs, and writing announcements to release to the press)
2. Fund raising (benefits, sales, or writing funding proposals)
3. Internal communications (telephone chain, newsletter, or scheduling meetings)
4. Planning (coordinating task forces, scheduling meetings, making agendas, arranging for training, structuring budgets)

To get down to the nitty-gritty work of organizing it's best to break into task force groups of five to eight women. Over-large or overloaded groups fizzle out fast. You may have disagreements over how much can be accomplished in the time period for which you have planned—but it's better to take the most and least ambitious members' estimates and then aim somewhere in between. Overambition winds up discouraging everyone; remember that you can always take on new goals as you go.

Since many of these organizational "housekeeping" tasks are difficult, unrewarding, and time consuming, it is usually unwise to create long-term committees to tackle them. Particularly when no one is being paid for these essential tasks, it is better to simply rotate them. Accumulated experience can be passed on through the use of a job notebook, containing records kept from the very beginning. Usually, the more one woman learns about a job, the harder it will be for her to get rid of it. Instead, from the beginning, each task should be done by a pair at minimum, rather than by one woman alone. (Otherwise the job will be entirely avoided as others see the one job holder overwhelmed by the work. Such a precedent, in fact, makes job rotation difficult.)

As your organization attracts more women, you may want to change the division of labor for such "housekeeping tasks." Instead of pairs or committees specially designated for a function such as fund raising, you can divide the entire group into subunits or teams, each of which agrees as a team to raise a certain proportion of money for the overall center. In this way there is group responsibility for the maintenance jobs, and "many hands make light work."

Now that you have a clear idea of what to do, and have formed small groups ready to tackle it, you can begin the actual organization of your center.

33.

Jeffry H. Galper

ORGANIZING AND PLANNING

Few social workers are being hired specifically to do organizing work in the context of welfare state programs. The philosophical and financial support for such work conducted within the auspices of the welfare state reached its height in the mid-1960s, through the Office of Economic Opportunity's Community Action Programs. It tapered off in the late 1960s and early 1970s through the vehicle of the Model Cities Program (defined as a mayor's program, in contrast to the Community Action Programs which stressed grass-roots

Source: Jeffry H. Galper, THE POLITICS OF SOCIAL SERVICES, © 1974, pp. 217–24. Reprinted by permission of Prentice-Hall, Inc., Englewood Cliffs, New Jersey and the author.

activity and control) and is now virtually absent from official policy and programming. As a consequence, it is necessary to discuss organizing, and its radical potential, less as a formal assignment which some workers will be hired to fulfill than as a stance toward any social service activity. In one sense, the virtual death of a formal welfare state organizing role is a benefit because it forces us to develop the organizing role for persons in all service-delivery positions.

Social planners and social administrators have, to some extent, taken the positions once filled by organizers in the welfare state bureaucracies. They tend to be concerned with creating, maintaining, and further rationalizing some part of the superstructure within which social services operate from their positions in social agencies, planning councils, or departments of government. There is nothing inherently progressive about the social planning or administration role, though the radicals of the 1930s saw in their demand for government planning a critical handle on destructive private activity. However, it has become clear that private interests have made good use of the rationality and predictability that increased social planning has accomplished. The planner or administrator may be in a position to facilitate radical activity, though his or her possibilities are limited by higher general visibility and remoteness from grass-roots forces. Hopefully, this discussion will be of some use to persons in those positions who are developing a radical commitment.

. . . The notion of nonreformist or structural reforms . . . can be useful to radical workers in developing an orientation to organizing work. The criteria for nonreformist reforms . . . suggest ways to analyze and develop change strategies so as to circumvent the dilemmas of practice from within the liberal reformist position. They keep us alert to the dual concerns of practicing to further immediate well-being and to build toward the realization of a fundamentally transformed society.

DECENTRALIZING POWER AND CONTROL

The first characteristic of a structural reform . . . is that it encourages the decentralization of power and control and the simultaneous restriction of centralized power and control. That is, it tends to disperse power to local groups, collectives, and communities at the same time it weakens centralized power. The administrative decentralization of functions, as represented by some school decentralization plans and, in some measure, by revenue sharing, does not really meet this criterion since the final say about the overall shape of policy remains fairly centralized, though implementation of policy may be somewhat dispersed.

This criterion creates some dilemma for the planner-administrator in his or her traditional role. The assumptions of the planning-administration task tend to encourage faith in and pursuit of increased centralization of power and control. These assumptions may be based, in part, on decent motives, for example, on the notion that centralized rationality can produce more humane outcomes than can decentralized, disjointed, and perhaps somewhat less efficient efforts. Within the framework of liberal assumptions, this may be true. For example, in the public assistance program as it now exists, centralized control assures some uniformity and in the past has prevented local governments from instituting more repressive rules and regulations concerning client eligibility, standards of behavior, and so on.

However, our analysis has suggested that central control, while possibly more progressive in the short run, reinforces the welfare state superstructure within which it functions and, therefore, strengthens an inadequate and undesirable social mechanism. Central control may produce short-run gains within the boundaries of what is and simultaneously help ensure that those boundaries will be less easily transcended. The principle, therefore, is to struggle for the empowerment of local units. If we believe that we will achieve a decent arrangement for social services only in a transformed society and that the society should and can only be transformed from the bottom up, then all our actions must be directed to facilitating struggle at the local level. This guideline suggests a reasoning process for the social service worker, if not a specific set of tactics. It helps to identify the nature of most of the change or reform activity that organizers and planners are often called on to implement, namely, changes that call for some improved benefit schemes within the framework of centralized power and control.

Problems of developing a political strategy around the federal government's periodic retrenchment in levels of spending for social programs may be clarified by applying this criterion. In the effort to counter reductions in social spending that occurred in the early 1970s, coalitions of liberal and progressive forces struggled for a return to what would be, in effect, the Great Society days. They argued the "more is better" position. The lack of radical analysis and radical organization prior to those cuts left little alternative but for the liberal political forces to respond from the conservative position of calling for a return to the good old days. In so doing, their major allies were service providers. In building their case this way, they let the terms of political debate be set in a way that aided conservative forces. After all, the good old days were not so good; and Nixon, then President, was correct in suggesting that welfare state programming in the 1960s did not much help those for whom it was created (though his analysis of the reasons for this failure was faulty). He was also correct in identifying the self-serving nature of the objections raised by social service workers and organizations.

The struggle to enlarge social spending may be more or less successful in any period. To the extent to which it is more successful, more social service jobs will be saved. However, no more stable or meaningful organization to prevent the next round of reductions will have been created, nor will the reinstated programs, whatever their extent, be able to go beyond the earlier

generation of programs in their impact on social problems.

This suggests a dual focus for activity around social service budget cuts. On the one hand, it is important to struggle for increased government spending for people in need. It is also important, however, to raise questions about the locus of control of these programs and the underlying purposes they serve. Admittedly, social service cuts tend to occur in periods that are generally repressive, yet it is precisely at such times that a more aggressive stance is called for. A liberal stance plays into the criticism of self-interest on the part of service providers which politicians can level so successfully at the social service professions. That debate will be partially transcended and important political, educational, and organizing work will be done when the issue expands beyond more or less money to control at the grass-roots level. The social service professions have not stood for this, by and large. Their failure to do so has led to their vulnerability to political attack, and their effort to do so now could lead to a meaningful basis for long-term struggle in the future.

BUILDING ALTERNATIVE INSTITUTIONS

A second characteristic of nonreformist reforms is that they model and help build, in the present, the social units and values that would characterize the kind of society in which we would ultimately hope to live. This means that we must struggle to create, here and now, some examples, however modest, of a better way. This can help to show larger numbers of people what is possible, can renew our own faith in our ability to make a difference in the world, and can begin to build some units to serve as a nucleus for much-expanded activity in a more propitious period. As part of our work, we must attempt to create collective, communal, democratic organizations that function to meet the needs of people in the community and that are joyous and growth-producing for those who live and work in them. While we must struggle with the institutions that exist and attempt to move them forward, we must also try to create alternatives here and now. Increasing numbers of social service workers are discovering these possibilities.

One set of examples, from the health field, is the variety of people's health clinics that have sprung up in the United States in the last five years or so. One such effort, focusing on health care for women, is in Seattle, Washington. It is distinguished from traditional services in its provision of service free of charge to poor and working women; in its control by the women of the local community; in its antiprofessional stance (in the sense of being concerned with demystifying gynecology and making self-knowledge and self-help a reality); by putting a major emphasis on teaching-learning relationships among patients, staff, and doctors; and by a major emphasis on preventive medicine. While separate from major existing institutions, the free clinic relates to such institutions in several ways and thereby avoids isolation and containment that could unwittingly place the clinic in the role of alleviating pressures for change on conventional institutions. For example, it is active in seeking allies within existing institutions, both for help with the clinic and to encourage workers to raise challenges in their institutions along the lines suggested by the free clinic's operation. Also, it uses the clinic as a locus for organizing in the community among patient groups and with health-care workers to raise challenges to existing institutions about the cost, quality and control of traditional services.[1] This activity is being duplicated in many settings across the United States.

Counterinstitutions are also being developed in other areas of service. For example, a wide variety of services have sprung up for youth and counterculture people, generally organized and operated from the bottom. These centers not only provide service, but, again, serve as a locus for other organizing work. In one case of a free clinic in Long Beach, California, a group of workers organized a service for street people on the basis of a democratic communal form of organization. This clinic provided medical treatment, drug counseling, informal therapy, and a chance to pull together groups of people to think about and work on a variety of political issues, for example, draft counseling.[2]

Another exciting model of alternative services is the Women-in-Transition project, located in Philadelphia. This project was a response to the enormous number of requests for help the Philadelphia Women's Liberation Center was receiving from separated and divorced women. The project provides a variety of services to women. One of these is to engage women in small-group, support, and consciousness-raising sessions which are run by women trained by the project. Other services are legal assistance, referral to needed psychological-legal services, and outreach to already separated women, especially low-income women, about their legal rights. Several of the project's staff have social work training but find they have been

---

[1] See "An Approach to Women's Health Care," *The People's Health* (Voice of the Seattle, Washington, Health Movement), 9 (April–May 1972), pp. 2 ff.

[2] See Gerald R. Wheeler, "America's New Street People: Implications for Human Services," *Social Work,* 16 (July 1971), pp. 19–21.

best able to integrate their social work skills and their feminist orientation outside of a traditional agency structure. The staff functions as a collective and works in consultation with a project-planning group. The Women-in-Transition project not only provides a much-needed service, but does so in a way that orients and involves many "clients" to the women's movement. In addition, by teaching women to conduct their own divorce proceedings, the project is challenging both the Pennsylvania Bar Association and the laws of the State of Pennsylvania, which have attempted to impose legal hegemony on divorce proceedings to the enrichment of lawyers and at the expense of women.[3]

In a number of cities, alternatives to the local United Ways and United Funds have been created by radicals to serve as funding sources to movement groups. In Philadelphia, the People's Fund is such an organization. Organized in 1970 by radical social welfare professionals, the People's Fund raises money through a broad-based community fund-raising drive and distributes this money to grass-roots community groups working for radical social change. The People's Fund helps support over thirty groups, including the Welfare Rights Organization, the Addicts' Rights Organization, the Barbwire Society, the Black Panther Party, the Puerto Rican Revolutionary Workers' Party, the Philadelphia Resistance, the Women's Liberation Center, the United Farm Workers' Organizing Committee, the Black United Liberation Front, the Lawyer's Guild, and the Pennsylvania Abortion Rights Association. While the amount of money raised has not been large in comparison with the United Fund's efforts, even the smaller amounts of money have made a difference to a number of the recipient groups which operate on small, hard-to-come-by budgets. The People's Fund has been important in other ways as well. It has served as an information clearinghouse for some parts of the movement in Philadelphia and has been useful in educating people about the movement and about the shortcomings of the traditional fund-raising mechanisms. By its nature, it also lends support to the notion that radical forces must engage in a kind of internal community development process. This means getting to know one another, pooling information and resources, and learning to work cooperatively.[4] Alternative institutions like the People's Fund mobilize the energies and commitments of radicals who may also continue to work in "straight" agencies.

Many radicals with a social service background prefer to develop possibilities for full-time movement commitment. While not all their members are social service workers, the Movement for a New Society offers one model for full-time engagement in political work. The Movement for a New Society is a development of the Quaker Action Group and is now located in centers throughout the United States and in other countries.[5] By living collectively (in over a

---

[3]The project developed an important resource for divorced and separated women (which has proven useful to other women as well) entitled *Women in Transition: A Feminist Handbook on Separation and Divorce* (New York: Charles Scribner's Sons, 1975). A useful analysis of the relationship of *Women in Transition* to the effort to change established agencies is Miriam Galper and Carolyn Kott Washburne, "Maximizing the Impact of an Alternative Agency," *Journal of Sociology and Social Welfare*, 4 (November 1976), pp. 248–57.

[4]Information and analysis about the People's Fund is contained in Jeffry Galper and Barbara Hemmindinger, "The People's Fund: A Political Evaluation," c/o *The Journal of Alternative Community Services*, 3 (Summer 1977), pp. 7–15.

[5]Contact can be made with Movement for a New Society at 4722 Baltimore Avenue, Philadelphia, Pennsylvania 19143.

dozen homes in the Philadelphia area, for example); by conscious attention to reducing the cost of living (though by no means the quality); and by collective approaches to buying consumer goods, purchasing services, and so on, members of MNS are able to live quite inexpensively. For many, this means that a few days of straight work each month frees the rest of their time for direct political work.

Members of the MNS may engage in radical political activities as a collectivity or as individuals in other groups, as each person sees fit. There is no strict party line, although there is a point of view, of course. Part of what the MNS is able to do is to provide internal and external educational seminars on radical analysis and nonviolent radical change strategies. Members of this group have also been active in antiwar and antiimperialist work, ecology, education, Indian rights, and other issues. For those involved, affiliation with MNS provides emotional support, intellectual stimulation, and the opportunity to work directly on the issues they have come to see as critical to both personal and social survival. They suggest, by their nature, how far radicals can go in developing alternative institutions as they struggle within and against existing institutions.

Each of the examples in this section illustrates some of the possibilities for building new institutions within the old society.[6] Radicals in the social services have been attracted to these possibilities in the past. Hopefully, more will become involved in the future, as the awareness of the personal rewards and the political potency of this approach becomes more widely shared.

---

[6]A useful journal on such alternatives is *c/o The Journal of Alternative Human Services* (621 Fourth Avenue, San Diego, California 92101).

WORKING WITH MOBILIZED POPULATIONS

A further characteristic of nonreformist reforms is that they recognize that basic change occurs only when people are mobilized. This characteristic suggests, therefore, that radical organizers look for ways to provide resources to people who are already mobilized or have the potential to be mobilized. These resources may be money, personnel, or organizing skill and other expertise.

This does not imply that we should abandon the concept of providing resources where there is human need. It does mean that we take seriously the fact that our society will never truly meet people's needs unless it is basically changed. Therefore, orienting resources only on the basis of need may be humane in the short run, but self-defeating in the long run. . . . If resources can be used not only to meet need, but to facilitate political organization, a larger purpose is met.

If it became a choice, for example, of allocating resources for a deprived but unmobilized population (for example, alcoholics) or to a perhaps less deprived but mobilized group (the forces active around day care), the choice would have to be made on the basis of the long-range concerns for facilitating political activity. While the radical organizer may help to start activity in various settings, it is well to remember that, contrary to the liberal image of organizing, the radical worker does not see himself or herself primarily as a person with a bag of skills, capable of application through a problem-solving model. Given the sorts of problems that concern the radical, political mobilization or readiness for mobilization is critical, and no single or simple or traditional professional expertise or intervention technology can produce that readiness. The radical operates, therefore, where the action is.

POLITICAL EDUCATION

An ongoing part of all practice must be political education. The opportunity to do education and propaganda work further transforms what might be self-contained liberal efforts into an effort with larger potential. The radical practitioner must try to help more people understand the immediate situation in its larger light. This can involve discussion of all sorts and, at present, is leading to growing amounts of collective, organized, and self-conscious study. In practice situations, without manipulating situations for such purposes, it may well happen that efforts to create changes reveal underlying repressive dynamics, and these should be fully explored and interpreted by all participants.

These, then, are some of the ways in which the notion of nonreformist reforms can serve as guides to radical organizing practice. As a final note on such practice, we stress that the radical organizer, like the radical caseworker, needs to strive for mutuality in relations with those we have been accustomed to calling clients. This means that the worker is as ready to be influenced as to influence and to see himself or herself as an agent to be used in a common struggle rather than as a central figure in a larger plan of his or her own making. When the agenda is radical change, the worker is primarily an ally and a colleague, not a professional technician of the welfare state solving other people's problems within the framework of welfare state rationality.

The Challenges of Minorities and Students

John L. Erlich and *Felix G. Rivera*

The *Epilogue* to the Second Edition attempted a preview of what the near future might hold for community organization practice. Two areas were emphasized: bringing theory and research to practice; and some of the major tensions, strains and opportunities confronting practitioners in the 1970s. Many of the issues and questions addressed are now an integral part of this Third Edition. Since the late 1960s, the whole social welfare field has been in a period of retrenchment and close scrutiny in the political marketplace. The struggle for funding dollars has reduced the impetus for politically relevant innovations. We see no reason to alter the general statement of conditions as they were viewed in 1974:

> The range, depth and complexity of issues and problems facing the community organization practitioner in the coming decade constitute profound challenges, perhaps unequalled in the history of social work. At the same time, the varied social crises which embody these challenges also present a unique set of opportunities to create new programs and institutions, to rebuild and revamp those that are outmoded or in serious disrepair. However, there is no simple strategy, theory, or ideology that can set these challenges and opportunities in order so that the practitioner can easily address them. The debate among social scientists as to which way is forward (let alone how to get there) continues not only in the universities but at the highest levels of government.[1]

However, it seems to us that two arenas of community organization practice (and, in many ways, of the human services generally), often given lip service in the recent past, are in urgent need of thoughtful, serious consideration. The first concerns the role of community practice in serving oppressed minorities of color. The second deals with the destructive manner in which most students are trained for careers in social work.

---

[1]Cox et al. (eds.), *Strategies of Community Organization* Second Edition, Itasca, Illinois: F. E. Peacock Publishers, 1974, p. 411.

OPPRESSED MINORITIES

The 1970s have introduced a painful paradox for community organization practice: (a) the acceptance by most practitioners of a problem-solving technocratic perspective and (b) an increase in problems faced by minorities, coupled with the failure of community organization to deal successfully with those problems.

This decade has seen a zealot's use of general systems theory and methods of policy analysis and policy modeling consisting of such arcane approaches as input-output, linear programming, system dynamics and algebraic methods of operations research, to name but a few. Social planning and program development and evaluation, in attempting to gain more accountability, have embraced such methodologies as time-and-motion studies, cost effectiveness and cost-benefit analysis, social accounting, goal free evaluations, multiple dimensions of program effectiveness, etc. The loftier the methods—and the more reductionistic in their assessment of social problems—the more irrelevant have they become when contrasted with the realities of the *barrios* and ghettos of this country.

Attempts to understand minorities by putting them into smaller target population categories have created such a myopic view that social agencies have not been able to intervene successfully on their behalf.* For example, the unemployment rate for black youth continues to hover between 35 and 40 percent nationwide.[2] An alarming 33 percent of *all* Puerto Ricans between the ages of 16 and 64 are unemployed, and this does not take into account the underemployed.[3] Hispanic people, as shown in the 1975 Current Population Reports, number 11.2 million with 80 percent of them claiming Spanish as their mother tongue—and these are conservative estimates. Blacks are 11.4 percent of the total population, with 24 million being counted in 1974. The Asian American/Pacific Americans are another group that has yet to be totally recognized within the arena of disenfranchised people. The 1970 Census counted only 1.5 million Asians in the United States, but this count did not include Samoans or Chamorros (Guamanians).[4] Some eight hundred thousand native American Indians remain among the least served. The mass exodus from Viet Nam has placed these refugees' numbers at around one hundred fifty thousand in addition to the steady influx of Cambodians, Tongans and Filipinos into this country. The lieutenant governor of the state of California has estimated that, based on population predictions, California will have over 60 percent minorities by 1990.[5] What are social scientists and community organizers going to do about the continuing disenfranchisement of these groups?

---

*Rather than dealing with fundamental inequalities, the focus has been on problem sub-parts like pre-school education, job interview training, work-release programs and the like.

[2]Task Force Report. President's Commission on Mental Health, 1978, Vol. III, p. 825.

[3]"Puerto Ricans in the Continental United States: An Uncertain Future," Report of the US Commission on Civil Rights, October 1976, p. 53.

[4]President's Commission on Mental Health, op. cit., pp. 731–861.

[5]President's Commission on Mental Health, op. cit., p. 781.

The problems faced by minorities present an extraordinary challenge for community organization practitioners. If new census data begin to verify what is already known by minorities about the underestimation of their problems and numbers, it will be necessary to rethink the role community organization *should* have in beginning to impact this myriad of critical issues.

Part of this reassessment requires a redefinition of minority communities. Many ethnic minority communities maintain cultural practices based on inputs from home countries with their unique structural linkages as measured by kinship, political and economic organization. These communities develop a psychological identity that is quite different from neighboring ghettos or *barrios* whose inhabitants have been in this country for two or three generations. These communities are *neo-gemeinschaft* in their composition.[6] Such communities, with their informal rules and roles of members set by tradition, are increasing because of the heavy immigration into the United States and migration into these isolated pockets in cities throughout the country. Such cultural homogeneity may be observed in the Cuban section of Miami, the heavily Puerto Rican sections of New York and Chicago, the Chicano community of East Los Angeles, San Francisco's Chinatown, some of the towns bordering Mexico and the many Little Tokyos and Manilas. The inhabitants of these communities avoid contact with the dominant culture, relying on each other for economic and psychosocial support. The steady flow back and forth to the mother country (or other equally secluded areas in the United States) makes these isolated pockets as culturally homogeneous as is possible within the dominant society, given the pressures of cultural chauvinism. It is no accident that such communities are the poorest and most isolated in the cities, and are like colonies within the nation. Repressive approaches to locality development are an obvious outcome.

The recognition and acceptance of these realities by community organizers, social planners and policy analysts has profound implications for practice. No longer may a practitioner enter a *barrio* or ghetto with fixed ideas about the type of community in which he or she will be working. Cultural awareness is not enough; bicultural (and often bilingual) background are a must if community work is to be effective in these areas. Practitioners have to put the technological armamentaria aside in an attempt to relate to the unique cultural and psychological experiences of these communities.

In addition to understanding the psychosocial and cultural processes, community organization practitioners should involve themselves in the following: (1) an evaluation of the political economy of the *barrios* and ghettos, (2) an assessment of power relationships within cities and their impact on minority communities, and (3) an analysis of the community-elite and its patterns of communication in directing community affairs and information exchanges which systematically eliminate minorities.

---

[6]Anthony Panzetta, *Community Mental Health: Myth and Reality,* Philadelphia: Lea and Febiger, 1972; see especially Chapter 1.

EDUCATION FOR SOCIAL WORK

Despite ringing phrases of commitment to fight oppression and injustice, the overwhelming majority of social workers and social agencies still devote themselves to casework. Recent surveys suggest that over 85% of the social workers with master's degrees are employed by agencies that primarily provide services to individuals and families.[7] During the 1950's, Mary Antoinette Cannon offered a different perspective on an aspect of the same issue.

> As we look at our own scene and the small part played by social work in national social action, as we note its tenuous or slack ties to labor, to education, and to other movements, we must ask ourselves whether in our absorption process, we American social workers have not allowed ourselves to become the most backward of all national groups in action for the welfare of society.[8]

After having been a growth industry until the early 1970's social work has tightened up as a source of employment. During the 1960's, it was argued that students with radical orientations were systematically screened out of schools of social work. Now there seems to be little evidence that such an ideological means test is operative. To a large degree, the composition of student bodies at most graduate schools of social work seems to reflect the self-selective screening of people choosing to go into the profession. For most students, the appeal that social work had as a relevant profession for those interested in fundamental and substantial social change has dissipated. The constricted job market with its great emphasis on interpersonal helping and the resulting student preferences for marketable skills have strongly influenced the preponderance of clinically oriented people in graduate student populations. The weeding out of more radical instructors committed to change, and the disinterest of most faculty screening committees in recruiting such instructors, have also contributed to this trend.

The schools of social work, as has so often been the case in the past, are moving slowly and cautiously in the community change area. More often than not, leadership for change is provided by people beyond the campuses. Usually suspect in academia—too activist for conservatives and not militant enough for radicals—social work education seems often to be seeking a middle road that refuses to stay put.

Many graduate students say that they have been profoundly disappointed by their schools and their professors. A letter which one author recently received from a graduate student at one well-known institution of higher education sums up this feeling:

> . . . As you might have gathered, the school shattered my illusions that social work is a medium for aiding the organization and assertiveness of oppressed groups. This is not to say that our school is an exception. From my readings and contacts with other students, social work and social work education (as a professional socializing

---

[7]"Profile of Social Work Graduates," Report of the University of Michigan School of Social Work, 1975, p. 16.

[8]As cited in Marion Sanders, "Social Work: A Profession Chasing Its Tail," *Harper's Magazine,* March 1957, p. 57.

agent) appear to be woefully inattentive to social action and social change. The foundations of professionalism, objective mentality and monopolization of resources point away from political relevance ... (the limited) instruction and placements in planning, organizing and administration are taught solely within a bureaucratic and professional framework ...

Perhaps in the simplest terms it is the gap between what we say and what we do that students find so objectionable, especially because what we do so often violates the values which we claim to hold so dear.

Watching us closely, students have learned far more from what we do than what we say. Despite our vigorous posturing toward openness, honesty, sharing, caring and the like, students get contradictory messages quickly and clearly. We paraphrase the messages we get from our students as follows: Don't challenge your instructors. Just tell them what they want to hear. Your grade may depend on it. Don't confide in your field agency (or classroom) supervisors. Your words may come back to haunt you in an evaluation. If the pressures and strain of graduate school are getting to you, don't let it show. This may be evidence of your immaturity, instability or a sign of other incapacities to perform effectively as a social worker.

The general guidelines are widely understood—submit (intelligently, not obsequiously) and you'll be okay; question and confront classroom and field agency instructors and you may be in for a very rough program. These lessons are easily transferred by practitioners to authority figures—supervisors, administrators, etc. —in most social agencies. As Cloward and Piven point out:

> The infantilization of students is a fundamental mechanism by which the agents of oppression in the welfare state are created. Graduates of schools of social work, having been deprived by their training of much dignity or self-worth, often come to cope with this gnawing self-doubt by according the same treatment to others as was accorded to them. Infantilization serves another purpose as well. Students educated to mistrust their own judgment, life experience, and feelings are then ready to be trained to acquiesce to the authority of others.[9]

Faculty and administrative interrelationships is another area in which observant students note the chasm between verbiage and action. The much vaunted collegial sharing and cooperation is found largely absent as students watch their instructors deal with each other. Often, immediately below a thin veneer of congeniality, they detect deep hostility and antagonism. These feelings are not, most students will assure you, merely a function of scholarly and professional differences. Competitive and individualistic norms dominate. Models of true collegiality are few and far between.

These are difficult times for all—students, teachers, and administrators alike. There are no easy answers to making training more relevant, not only for students but also for the recipients of educational and social welfare services. Perhaps above all, we must be honest with ourselves and our students as to what we can

[9]Richard Cloward and Frances Piven, "Notes Toward a Radical Social Work" in Roy Bailey and Mike Brake (eds.), *Radical Social Work,* New York: Pantheon, 1975, p. xvi.

and cannot, will and will not, do. Strategies developed to confront the issues described earlier must be consistent with local conditions and the needs and interests of particular groups of students.

Like practitioners who advocate for minority clients' rights and teachers who advocate for their students, students who advocate for themselves and fellow students may be regarded as trouble-makers or even a serious threat to a school or social agency. Under these conditions, the need for structures of mutual support and aid cannot be underestimated. For the student, as for the agency practitioner or teacher, struggles for social justice and change are often lonely, debilitating and risky. Misunderstanding of one's motivation is much more likely than appreciation, chastisement and veiled threats more likely than reward and public approval.

Perhaps one of the major challenges of the 1980's will be for community organization practitioners and teachers to deliver on the social work rhetoric of self-determination, particularly in our efforts with minority communities and social work students. To try to do any less will be to back away from the cities, the poor, the handicapped and ethnic, racial and sexual minorities in their struggle for social justice. If we continue to follow the fast money, the faddish service populations and delivery systems, we will do so at the risk of abandonment by the very populations whose existence gives our community organization practice and teaching meaning.

Selected Readings

CHAPTER I. VARIATIONS, CONCEPTUAL AND HISTORICAL

CONCEPTIONS

1. Gilbert, Neil, and Harry Specht. "Social Planning and Community Organization: Approaches." In John B. Turner (ed.), *Encyclopedia of Social Work.* Washington, D.C.: National Association of Social Workers, 1977, pp. 1412–1424.
2. Harper, Ernest B., and Arthur Dunham. "What Is Community Organization? Selected Definitions." In Ernest B. Harper and Arthur Dunham (eds.), *Community Organization in Action.* New York: Association Press, 1959, pp. 54–59.
3. Heath, Monna, and Arthur Dunham. *Trends in Community Organization: A Study of the Papers on Community Organization Published by the National Conference on Social Welfare, 1874–1960.* Social Service Monographs, Second Series. Chicago: The School of Social Service Administration, 1963.
4. Kramer, Ralph M., and Harry Specht. "Introduction." In Ralph M. Kramer and Harry Specht (eds.), *Readings in Community Organization Practice.* 2nd ed. Englewood Cliffs, N.J.: Prentice-Hall, 1975, pp. 1–16.
5. National Association of Social Workers. *Defining Community Organization Practice.* New York: N.A.S.W., 1962.
6. Perlman, Robert. "Social Planning and Community Organization." In John B. Turner (ed.), *Encyclopedia of Social Work.* Washington, D.C.: National Association of Social Workers, 1977, pp. 1404–1412.

7. Ross, Murray G., with B. W. Lappin. *Community Organization: Theory, Principles and Practice.* 2nd ed. New York: Harper, 1967, pp. 3–99.

HISTORY

8. Addams, Jane. *Forty Years at Hull House.* New York: Macmillan, 1935.
9. Austin, Michael J., and Neil Betten. "Intellectual Origins of Community Organizing, 1920–1939." *Social Service Review,* 51:1:155–170 (March 1977).
10. Axinn, June, and Herman Levin. *Social Welfare: A History of the American Response to Need.* New York: Dodd, Mead, 1975.
11. Bremner, Robert H. *From the Depths: The Discovery of Poverty in the United States.* New York: New York University Press, 1956.
12. Chambers, Clarke A. *Seedtime of Reform, American Social Service and Social Action, 1918–1933.* Minneapolis: University of Minnesota Press, 1963.
13. Davis, Allen F. "Settlements: History." In John B. Turner (ed.), *Encyclopedia of Social Work.* Washington, D.C.: National Association of Social Workers, 1977, pp. 1266–1271.
14. Davis, Allen F. *Spearheads for Reform: The Social Settlements and the Progressive Movement, 1890–1914.* New York: Oxford University Press, 1967.
15. Dunham, Arthur. "Historical Perspectives." In Arthur Dunham, *The New Community Organization.* New York: Crowell, 1970, pp. 35–55.
16. Gilbert, Neil, and Harry Specht (eds.). *The Emergence of Social Welfare and Social Work.* Itasca, Ill.: F. E. Peacock Publishers, 1976.
17. Goldmark, Josephine. *Impatient Crusader: Florence Kelly's Life Story.* Urbana: University of Illinois Press, 1953.
18. Komisar, Lucy. *Down and Out in the USA: A History of Public Welfare.* Rev. ed. New York: Franklin Watts, 1977.
19. Leiby, James. *A History of Social Welfare and Social Work in the United States: 1815–1972.* New York: Columbia University Press, 1978.
20. Lewis, Verl S. "Charity Organization Society." In John B. Turner (ed.), *Encyclopedia of Social Work.* Washington, D.C.: National Association of Social Workers, 1977, pp. 96–100.
21. Lubove, Roy. *The Professional Altruists: The Emergence of Social Work as a Cause, 1880–1930.* Cambridge, Mass.: Harvard University Press, 1965.
22. Lubove, Roy. *The Progressives and the Slums.* Pittsburgh: University of Pittsburgh Press, 1963.
23. Pumphrey, Ralph E., and Muriel W. Pumphrey (eds.). *The Heritage of American Social Work.* New York: Columbia University Press, 1961.
24. Trattner, Walter I. *From Poor Law to Welfare State.* New York: Free Press, 1974.

CHAPTER II. COMMON ELEMENTS OF PRACTICE

KNOWLEDGE BASE

25. Bennis, Warren G., Kenneth D. Benne, and Robert Chin (eds.). *The Planning of Change: Readings in the Applied Behavioral Sciences.* New York: Holt, Rinehart & Winston, 1961.
26. Etzioni, Amitai. *The Active Society: A Theory of Societal and Political Processes.* New York: Free Press, 1968.
27. Kahn, Alfred J. "Social Science and the Conceptual Framework for Community Organization Research." In Leonard S. Kogan (ed.), *Social Science Theory and Social Work Research.* New York: National Association of Social Workers, 1960, pp. 64–79.
28. Lippitt, Ronald, Jeanne Watson, and Bruce Westley. *The Dynamics of Planned Change.* New York: Harcourt, Brace & World, 1958.
29. Maas, Henry S. *Five Fields of Social Service: Reviews of Research.* New York: National Association of Social Workers, 1966.
30. Maas, Henry S. *Research in the Social Services: A Five Year Review.* Washington, D.C.: National Association of Social Workers, 1971.
31. Rothman, Jack. *Planning and Organizing for Social Change: Action Principles from Social Science Research.* New York: Columbia University Press, 1974.
32. Rothman, Jack, and Irwin Epstein. "Social Planning and Community Organization: Social Science Foundations." In John B. Turner (ed.), *Encyclopedia of Social Work.* Washington, D.C.: National Association of Social Workers, 1977, pp. 1433–1443.
33. Schwartz, Edward E. "Macro Social Work: A Practice in Search of Some Theory." *Social Service Review,* 51:2:207–227 (June 1977).

VALUES AND ETHICS

34. Addams, Jane. *Democracy and Social Ethics.* Edited by A. F. Scott. Cambridge, Mass.: Harvard University Press, 1964.
35. Carr-Saunders, Alexander M., and P. A. Wilson. *The Professions.* London: Frank Cass, 1964.
36. Durkheim, Emil. *Professional Ethics and Civic Morals.* Glencoe, Ill.: Free Press, 1958.
37. Gaylin, Willard, Ira Glasser, Steven Marcus, and David J. Rothman. *Doing Good: The Limits of Benevolence in America.* New York: Pantheon, 1978.
38. Levy, Charles S. *Social Work Ethics.* New York: Human Sciences Press, 1976.
39. Pilsecker, Carleton. "Values: A Problem for Everyone." *Social Work,* 23:1:54–57 (January 1978).

PRACTITIONER ROLES AND SELF DISCIPLINE

40. Cheek, Donald. *Assertive Black . . . Puzzled White.* San Luis Obispo, Calif.: Impact Publications, 1976.
41. Epstein, Irwin. "Professional Role Orientation and Conflict Strategies." *Social Work,* 15:4:87–92 (October 1970).
42. Gilbert, Neil. "Neighborhood Coordinator: Advocate or Middleman." *Social Service Review,* 43:2:136–144 (June 1969).
43. Grosser, Charles. "Community Development Programs Serving the Urban Poor." *Social Work,* 10:3:15–21 (July 1965).
44. Grosser, Charles F. "Roles and Spheres of Activity." In Charles F. Grosser, *New Directions in Community Organization: From Enabling to Advocacy.* New York: Praeger, 1973.
45. Rothman, Jack. "An Analysis of Goals and Roles in Community Organization Practice." *Social Work,* 9:2:24–31 (April 1964).
46. Rothman, Jack. "Practitioner Roles: Variables Affecting Role Performance." And "Some Dynamics of Role Performance." In Jack Rothman, *Planning and Organizing for Social Change: Action Principles from Social Science Research.* New York: Columbia University Press, 1974, pp. 35–112.
47. Sanders, Irwin T. "Professional Roles in Planned Change." In Robert Morris (ed.), *Centrally Planned Change: Prospects and Concepts.* New York: National Association of Social Workers, 1964, pp. 102–116.
48. Schur, Edwin M. *The Awareness Trap: Self-Absorption Instead of Social Change.* New York: Quadrangle Books, 1976.

USE OF SMALL GROUPS

49. Cathcart, Robert S., and Larry Samovar (eds.). *Small Group Communication.* 2nd ed. Dubuque, Iowa: William C. Brown, 1974.
50. Corey, Gerald, and Marianne Corey. *Groups: Process and Practice.* Monterey, Calif.: Brooks, Cole, 1977.
51. Dean, John P., and Alex Rosen with Robert B. Johnson. *A Manual of Intergroup Relations.* Chicago: University of Chicago Press, 1955.
52. Hill, William. *Learning Through Discussion.* Beverly Hills, Calif.: Sage Publications, 1977.
53. Thelen, Herbert A. *Dynamics of Groups at Work.* Chicago: University of Chicago Press, 1954.

USE OF ORGANIZATIONS

54. Argyris, Chris. *Integrating the Individual and the Organization.* New York: John Wiley, 1964.
55. Caplow, Theodore. *How to Run Any Organization.* New York: Holt, Rinehart, 1976.

56. Ehlers, Walter H., *et al. Administration for the Human Services.* New York: Harper and Row, 1976.
57. Slavin, Simon (ed.). *Social Administration: The Management of the Social Services.* New York: Haworth Press and Council on Social Work Education, 1978.

PROGRAM DEVELOPMENT

58. Epstein, Irwin, and Tony Tripodi. *Research Techniques for Program Planning, Monitoring and Evaluation.* New York: Columbia University Press, 1977.
59. League of California Cities. *Handbook: Assessing Human Need.* Sacramento: League of California Cities, 1975.
60. Mager, Robert F. *Goal Analysis.* Belmont, Calif.: Fearon, 1972.
61. Masterman, Louis E. *The Applicant's Guide to Successful Grantsmanship.* Cape Girardeau, Mo.: Keene Publications, 1978.
62. *Where It's At: A Research Guide for Community Organizing.* San Francisco: Movement Press, 1967.

PROGRAM EVALUATION

63. Anderson, Scarvia, and Samuel Ball. *The Profession and Practice of Program Evaluation.* San Francisco: Jossey-Bass, 1978.
64. Patton, Michael. *Utilization-Focused Evaluation.* Beverly Hills, Calif.: Sage Publications, 1978.
65. Rutman, Leonard. *Evaluation Research Methods: A Basic Guide.* Beverly Hills, Calif.: Sage Publications, 1977.
66. Sze, William C., and June G. Hopps. *Evaluation and Accountability in Human Service Programs.* Rev. ed. Cambridge, Mass.: Schenkman, 1978.
67. Weisner, Stan. "The Impact of Community Intervention," *Social Service Review,* 51:4:659–673 (December 1977).
68. Weiss, Carol (ed.). *Evaluating Action Programs.* Boston: Allyn and Bacon, 1972.
69. Weiss, Carol. *Evaluation Research.* Englewood Cliffs, N.J.: Prentice-Hall, 1972.

CHAPTER III. COMMUNITIES

70. Banfield, Edward C., and James Q. Wilson. *City Politics.* New York: Vintage Books, 1963.
71. Beck, Bertram M. "Settlements and Community Centers." In John B. Turner (ed.), *Encyclopedia of Social Work.* Washington, D.C.: National Association of Social Workers, 1977, pp. 1262–1266.

72. Bourne, Larry S., and J. W. Simmons (eds.). *Systems of Cities.* New York: Oxford University Press, 1978.

73. Caputo, David A. *Urban America: The Policy Alternatives.* San Francisco: W. H. Freeman, 1976.

74. Coleman, James S. *Community Conflict.* Glencoe, Ill.: Free Press, 1957.

75. Dahl, Robert A. *Who Governs? Democracy and Power in an American City.* New Haven: Yale University Press, 1961.

76. Gans, Herbert J. *The Urban Villagers.* New York: The Free Press of Glencoe, 1962.

77. Gitlin, Todd, and Nanci Hollander. *Uptown: Poor Whites in Chicago.* New York: Harper and Row, 1970.

78. Goodman, Paul, and Percival Goodman. *Communitas.* 2nd ed. New York: Vintage, 1960.

79. Gottschalk, Simon. *Communities and Alternatives.* Cambridge, Mass.: Schenkman, 1975.

80. Greeley, Andrew. *Neighborhood.* New York: Seabury, 1977.

81. Hunter, Floyd G. *Community Power Structure.* Chapel Hill: University of North Carolina Press, 1953.

82. Jones, W. Ron. *Finding Community.* Palo Alto, Calif.: James E. Freel, 1971.

83. Kanter, Rosabeth Moss. *Community and Commitment.* Cambridge, Mass.: Harvard University Press, 1972.

84. Levin, Herman. "Voluntary Organizations in Social Welfare." In John B. Turner (ed.), *Encyclopedia of Social Work.* Washington, D.C.: National Association of Social Workers, 1977, pp. 1573–1582.

85. Poplin, Dennis E. *Communities.* New York: Macmillan, 1972.

86. Presthus, Robert. *Men at the Top: A Study in Community Power.* New York: Oxford University Press, 1964.

87. Stein, Maurice R. *The Eclipse of Community: An Interpretation of American Studies.* Princeton, N.J.: Princeton University Press, 1960.

88. Swanson, Bert, and Edith Swanson. *Discovering the Community.* New York: Irvington Publishers, 1977.

89. Tropman, John E., and Elmer J. Tropman. "Community Welfare Councils." In John B. Turner (ed.), *Encyclopedia of Social Work.* Washington, D.C.: National Association of Social Workers, 1977, pp. 187–193.

90. Vidich, Arthur J., and Joseph Bensman. *Small Town in Mass Society.* Princeton, N.J.: Princeton University Press, 1958.

91. Warren, Donald I. "Neighborhoods in Urban Areas." In John B. Turner (ed.), *Encyclopedia of Social Work.* Washington, D.C.: National Association of Social Workers, 1977, pp. 993–1005.

92. Warren, Roland L. *The Community in America.* 3rd ed. Chicago: Rand McNally, 1978.

93. Warren, Roland L. (ed.). *New Perspectives on the American Community.* 3rd ed. Chicago: Rand McNally, 1977.

CHAPTER IV. ORGANIZATIONS AND THEIR LINKAGES

ORGANIZATIONS

94. Blau, Peter M., and W. Richard Scott. *Formal Organizations.* San Francisco: Chandler Publishing, 1962.
95. Etzioni, Amitai. *A Comparative Analysis of Complex Organizations.* New York: Free Press, 1975.
96. Hall, Richard. *Organizations: Structure and Process.* Englewood Cliffs, N.J.: Prentice-Hall, 1972.
97. Hass, J. Eugene, and Thomas Drabek. *Complex Organizations.* New York: Macmillan, 1973.
98. Katz, Daniel, and Robert L. Kahn. *The Social Psychology of Organizations.* New York: John Wiley, 1966.
99. Litwak, Eugene. "Models of Bureaucracy Which Permit Conflict." *American Journal of Sociology,* 62:2:177–184 (September 1961).
100. Maccoby, Michael. *The Gamesman: The New Corporate Leaders.* New York: Simon and Schuster, 1976.
101. Maniha, John, and Charles Perrow. "The Reluctant Organization and the Aggressive Environment." *Administrative Science Quarterly,* 10:2:238–257 (September 1965).
102. March, James G., and Herbert Simon. *Organizations.* New York: John Wiley, 1959.
103. Messinger, Sheldon. "Organizational Transformation: A Case Study of a Declining Social Movement." *American Sociological Review,* 20:3–10 (February 1955).
104. Pfeffer, Jeffrey. *Organizational Design.* Arlington Heights, Ill.: AHM Publishing, 1978.
105. Pinner, Frank, Philip Selznick, and Paul Jacobs. *Old Age and Political Behavior.* Berkeley: University of California Press, 1959.
106. Rein, Martin, and Robert Morris. "Goals, Structures and Strategies for Community Changes." *Social Work Practice 1962.* New York: Columbia University Press, 1962, pp. 127–145.
107. Seeley, John R., et al. *Community Chest: A Case Study in Philanthropy.* Toronto, Ontario: University of Toronto Press, 1957.
108. Selznick, Philip. *TVA and the Grass Roots.* Berkeley and Los Angeles: University of California Press, 1949.
109. Sills, David L. *The Volunteers: Means and Ends in a National Organization.* Glencoe, Ill.: Free Press, 1957.
110. Thompson, James D. *Organizations in Action.* New York: McGraw-Hill, 1967.
111. Thompson, James D., and Arthur Tuden. "Strategies, Structures and Processes of Organizational Decision." In James D. Thompson et al. (eds.), *Comparative Studies in Administration.* Pittsburgh: University of Pittsburgh Press, 1959.

112. Turk, Herman. *Organizations in Modern Life.* San Francisco: Jossey-Bass, 1977.
113. Zald, Mayer N., and Roberta Ash. "Social Movement Organizations: Growth, Decay and Change." *Social Forces,* 44:327–341 (1966).

LINKAGES

114. Evan, William E. "The Organization Set: Toward a Theory of Interorganizational Relations." In James D. Thompson (ed.), *Approaches of Organizational Design.* Pittsburgh: University of Pittsburgh Press, 1966.
115. Fellin, Phillip, and Eugene Litwak. "The Neighborhood in Urban American Society." *Social Work,* 13:4:72–80 (July 1968).
116. Levine, Sol, Paul E. White, and Benjamin D. Paul. "Community Interorganizational Problems in Providing Medical Care and Social Services." *American Journal of Public Health,* 53:8:1183–1195 (August 1963).
117. Litwak, Eugene, and Lydia F. Hylton. "Interorganizational Analysis." *Administrative Science Quarterly,* 6:4:395–420 (March 1962).
118. Litwak, Eugene, and Henry J. Meyer. "The School and the Family: Linking Organizations and External Primary Groups." In Paul F. Lazarsfeld, William H. Sewell, and Harold L. Wilensky (eds.), *The Uses of Sociology.* New York: Basic Books, 1967, pp. 522–543.
119. Litwak, Eugene, and Jack Rothman. "Toward the Theory and Practice of Coordination between Formal Organizations." In William R. Rosengren and Mark Lefton (eds.), *Organizations and Clients.* Columbus, Ohio: Merrill Publishing, 1970.
120. Miller, Walter B. "Inter-Institutional Conflict as a Major Impediment to Delinquency Prevention." *Human Organization,* 17:3:20–23 (Fall 1968).
121. Morris, Robert, and Ollie A. Randall. "Planning and Organization of Community Services for the Elderly." *Social Work,* 10:1:96–102 (January 1965).
122. Reid, William J. "Interagency Coordination in Delinquency Prevention and Control." *Social Service Review,* 38:4:418–423 (December 1964).
123. Simpson, Richard L., and William H. Gulley. "Environmental Pressures and Organizational Characteristics." *American Sociological Review,* 27:3:344–351 (June 1962).

CHAPTER V. SOCIAL PLANNING

124. Banfield, Edward C. *Political Influence.* New York: Free Press, 1961.
125. Dudley, James R. "Is Social Planning Social Work?" *Social Work,* 23:1:37–41 (January 1978).
126. Fisher, Jack C., and Henry P. Henderson. "Regional Planning and Development." In John B. Turner (ed.), *Encyclopedia of Social Work.* Washington, D.C.: National Association of Social Workers, 1977, pp. 1175–1183.
127. Frieden, Bernard J., and Robert Morris (eds.). *Urban Planning and Social Policy.* New York: Basic Books, 1968.

128. Gans, Herbert J. *People and Plans: Essays on Urban Problems and Solutions.* New York: Basic Books, 1968.

129. Gibbons, Don, *et al. Criminal Justice Planning: An Introduction.* Englewood Cliffs, N.J.: Prentice-Hall, 1977.

130. Gil, David G. *The Challenge of Social Equality.* Cambridge, Mass.: Schenkman, 1976.

131. Gil, David G. *Unraveling Social Policy.* 2nd ed. Cambridge, Mass.: Schenkman, 1976.

132. Gilbert, Neil, and Harry Specht. *Dimensions of Social Welfare Policy.* Englewood Cliffs, N.J.: Prentice-Hall, 1974.

133. Gilbert, Neil, and Harry Specht. "Process Versus Task in Social Planning." *Social Work,* 22:3:178–183 (May 1977).

134. Golany, Gideon. *New Town Planning.* New York: John Wiley, 1976.

135. Green, Robert. *The Urban Challenge: Poverty and Race.* Chicago: Follett, 1977.

136. Greenbie, Barrie. *Design for Diversity.* New York: Elsevier, 1978.

137. Hansan, John E. "Social Planning, Governmental: Federal and State." In John B. Turner (ed.), *Encyclopedia of Social Work.* Washington, D.C.: National Association of Social Workers, 1977, pp. 1443–1448.

138. Hunter, Floyd, Ruth C. Schafer, and Cecil G. Sheps. *Community Organization: Action and Inaction.* Chapel Hill: University of North Carolina Press, 1956.

139. Kahn, Alfred J. *Planning Community Services for Children in Trouble.* New York: Columbia University Press, 1965.

140. Kahn, Alfred J. *Studies in Policy and Planning.* New York: Russell Sage Foundation, 1969.

141. Kahn, Alfred J. *Theory and Practice of Social Planning.* New York: Russell Sage Foundation, 1969.

142. Marris, Peter, and Martin Rein. *Dilemmas of Social Reform.* New York: Atherton Press, 1967.

143. Mayer, Robert R., *et al. Centrally Planned Change.* Urbana: University of Illinois Press, 1974.

144. Mayer, Robert R. "Environment and Social Planning." In John B. Turner (ed.), *Encyclopedia of Social Work.* Washington, D.C.: National Association of Social Workers, 1977, pp. 335–341.

145. Mayer, Robert R. *Social Planning and Social Change.* Englewood Cliffs, N.J.: Prentice-Hall, 1972.

146. Meltzer, Jack. "Environment: Urban Planning and Development." In John B. Turner (ed.), *Encyclopedia of Social Work.* Washington, D.C.: National Association of Social Workers, 1977, pp. 341–349.

147. Meyerson, Martin, and Edward C. Banfield. *Politics, Planning and the Public Interest.* Glencoe, Ill.: Free Press, 1955.

148. Moroney, Robert M. "Social Planning: Tools for Planning." In John B. Turner (ed.), *Encyclopedia of Social Work.* Washington, D.C.: National Association of Social Workers, 1977, pp. 1448–1452.

149. Morris, Robert (ed.). *Centrally Planned Change: Prospects and Concepts.* New York: National Association of Social Workers, 1964.

150. Morris, Robert, and Robert H. Binstock with Martin Rein. *Feasible Planning for Social Change.* New York: Columbia University Press, 1966.

151. Palmiere, Darwin. "Health Services: Health and Hospital Planning." In John B. Turner (ed.), *Encyclopedia of Social Work.* Washington, D.C.: National Association of Social Workers, 1977, pp. 595–602.

152. Rein, Martin. "Equality and Social Policy." *Social Service Review,* 51:4:565–587 (December 1977).

153. Rein, Martin. "Social Planning: Welfare Planning." In *International Encyclopedia of the Social Sciences.* New York: Macmillan, 1968, pp. 142–154.

154. Rein, Martin. *Social Policy: Issues of Choice and Change.* New York: Random House, 1970.

155. Tropman, John E., *et al. Strategic Perspectives on Social Policy.* New York: Pergamon, 1976.

156. Wenocur, Stanley. "A Pluralistic Planning Model for United Way Organization." *Social Service Review,* 50:4:586–600 (December 1976).

157. Zaltman, Gerald, and Robert Duncan. *Strategies for Planned Change.* New York: John Wiley, 1977.

CHAPTER VI. LOCALITY DEVELOPMENT

158. Arensberg, Conrad M., and Arthur H. Niehoff. *Introducing Social Change: A Manual for Americans Overseas.* Chicago: Aldine, 1964.

159. Batten, Thomas R. *The Non-Directive Approach in Group and Community Work.* London: Oxford University Press, 1967.

160. Biddle, William W., with Loureide J. Biddle. *The Community Development Process: The Rediscovery of Local Initiative.* New York: Holt, Rinehart & Winston, 1965.

161. Brager, George. "Organizing the Unaffiliated in a Low-Income Area." *Social Work,* 8:2:34–40 (April 1963).

162. Clinard, Marshall B. *Slums and Community Development: Experiments in Self-Help.* New York: Free Press, 1966.

163. Goodenough, Ward H. *Cooperation in Change: An Anthropological Approach to Community Development.* New York: Russell Sage Foundation, 1963.

164. Hester, Randolph. *Neighborhood Space.* Stroudsburg, Pa.: Dowden, Hutchinson, 1975.

165. Johnson, Harold R. "Neighborhood Services." In John B. Turner (ed.), *Encyclopedia of Social Work.* Washington, D.C.: National Association of Social Workers, 1977, pp. 986–993.

166. Lamb, Curt. *Political Power in Poor Neighborhoods.* Cambridge, Mass.: Schenkman, 1975.

167. Mead, Margaret, and Muriel Brown. *The Wagon and the Star: A Study of American Community Initiative.* Chicago: Rand McNally, 1966.

168. Mogulof, Melvin B. "Involving Low-Income Neighborhoods in Anti-Delinquency Programs." *Social Work,* 10:4:51–59 (October 1965).

169. Moynihan, Daniel P. *Maximum Feasible Misunderstanding: Community Action and the War on Poverty.* New York: Free Press, 1969.

170. Niehoff, Arthur H. (ed.). *A Casebook of Social Change.* Chicago: Aldine, 1966.

171. O'Brien, David J. *Neighborhood Organization and Interest-Group Process.* Princeton, N.J.: Princeton University Press, 1975.

172. Shostak, Arthur B. "Promoting Participation of the Poor: Philadelphia's Antipoverty Program." *Social Work,* 11:1:64–72 (January 1966).

173. Sorrentino, Anthony. *Organizing Against Crime: Redeveloping the Neighborhood.* New York: Human Sciences Press, 1977.

174. Sower, Christopher, *et al. Community Involvement.* Glencoe, Ill.: Free Press, 1957.

175. Spicer, Edward H. *Human Problems in Technological Change: A Casebook.* New York: Russell Sage Foundation, 1952.

176. Spiegel, Hans B. C. (ed.). *Citizen Participation in Urban Development.* Vol. 1, *Concepts and Issues.* Washington, D.C.: NTL Institute for Applied Behavioral Science, 1968.

177. Spiegel, Hans B. C. (ed.). *Citizen Participation in Urban Development.* Vol. 2, *Cases and Programs.* Washington, D.C.: NTL Institute for Applied Behavioral Science, 1969.

178. Spergel, Irving A. "Social Planning and Community Organization: Community Development." In John B. Turner (ed.), *Encyclopedia of Social Work.* Washington, D.C.: National Association of Social Workers, 1977, pp. 1425–1433.

179. Stern, Gloria. *How to Start Your Own Food Co-op.* New York: Walker, 1974.

180. Taber, Merlin A., *et al. Handbook for Community Professionals.* Springfield, Ill.: Charles C Thomas, 1972.

181. United Nations, Bureau of Social Affairs. *Social Progress through Community Development.* New York, 1955.

182. Warren, Rachelle B., and Donald I. Warren. *The Neighborhood Organizer's Handbook.* Notre Dame, Ind.: University of Notre Dame Press, 1977.

183. Weissman, Harold H. *Community Councils and Community Control: The Workings of Democratic Mythology.* Pittsburgh: University of Pittsburgh Press, 1970.

184. Wireman, Peggy. "Citizen Participation." In John B. Turner (ed.), *Encyclopedia of Social Work.* Washington, D.C.: National Association of Social Workers, 1977, pp. 175–179.

185. Zurcher, Louis A., *et al. From Dependency to Dignity: Individual and Social Consequences of a Neighborhood House.* New York: Behavioral Publications, 1969.

CHAPTER VII. SOCIAL ACTION

186. Alinsky, Saul D. *Reveille for Radicals.* Chicago: University of Chicago Press, 1946.

187. Alinsky, Saul D. *Rules for Radicals.* New York: Random House, 1971.

188. Bailey, Robert, Jr. *Radicals in Urban Politics: The Alinsky Approach.* Chicago: University of Chicago Press, 1974.

189. Berry, Jeffrey. *Lobbying for the People.* Princeton, N.J.: Princeton University Press, 1977.

190. Brown, H. Rap. *Die Nigger Die.* New York: Dial Press, 1969.

191. Burghardt, Stephen (ed.). *Tenants and the Urban Housing Crisis.* Dexter, Mich.: The New Press, 1972.

192. Cameron, William Bruce. *Modern Social Movements.* New York: Random House, 1966.

193. Camus, Albert. *The Rebel.* New York: Random House, 1951.

194. Carmichael, Stokely, and Charles V. Hamilton. *Black Power.* New York; Vintage Books, 1967.

195. Ellis, William W. *White Ethics and Black Power: The Emergence of the West Side Organization.* Chicago: Aldine, 1969.

196. Erlich, John. L. "Bibliography: Organizing the Poor." *Poverty and Human Resources Abstracts,* 1:6:167–172 (1966).

197. Galper, Jeffry. *The Politics of Social Services.* Englewood Cliffs, N.J.: Prentice-Hall, 1975.

198. Gamson, William. *The Strategy of Social Protest.* Homewood, Ill.: Dorsey, 1975.

199. Georgakas, Dan, and Marvin Surkin. *Detroit: I Do Mind Dying.* New York: St. Martin's Press, 1975.

200. Haggstrom, Warren. "Can the Poor Transform the World?" In Irwin Deutscher and Elizabeth Thompson (eds.), *Among the People: Encounters with the Poor.* New York: Basic Books, 1968.

201. Haggstrom, Warren. "On Eliminating Poverty: What We Have Learned." In Warner Bloomberg, Jr., and Henry Schmandt (eds.), *Power, Poverty and Urban Policy.* Beverly Hills, Calif.: Sage Publications, 1968.

202. Hartmann, Chester. *Yerba Buena: Land Grab and Community Resistance in San Francisco.* San Francisco: Glide, 1974.

203. Jackson, Larry, and William Johnson. *Protest by the Poor.* Lexington, Mass.: D.C. Heath, 1974.

204. Kleyman, Paul. *Senior Power.* San Francisco: Glide, 1974.

205. Kramer, Ralph. *Participation of the Poor.* Englewood Cliffs, N.J.: Prentice-Hall, 1969.

206. Kurzman, Paul (ed.). *The Mississippi Experience: Strategies for Welfare Rights Action.* New York: Association Press, 1971.

207. Levine, Naomi, with Richard Cohen. *Oceanhill-Brownsville: A Case History of Schools in Crisis.* New York: Popular Library, 1969.

208. Mandell, Betty R. (ed.). *Welfare in America: Controlling the "Dangerous Classes."* Englewood Cliffs, N.J.: Prentice-Hall, 1975.

209. Newton, Huey. *To Die for the People.* New York: Random House, 1972.
210. O. M. Collective. *The Organizer's Manual.* New York: Bantam Books, 1971.
211. Oppenheimer, Martin. *The Urban Guerilla.* Chicago: Quadrangle Books, 1969.
212. Oppenheimer, Martin, and George Lakey. *A Manual for Direct Action.* Chicago: Quadrangle Books, 1965.
213. Piven, Frances F., and Richard Cloward. *Poor People's Movements.* New York: Pantheon, 1977.
214. Quirion, Hughes. "Community Organization and Political Action in Montreal." *Social Work,* 17:5:85–90 (September 1972).
215. *Rights in Conflict: The Violent Confrontation of Demonstrators and Police in the Parks and Streets of Chicago during the Week of the Democratic National Convention of 1968.* New York: Bantam Books, 1968.
216. Schaller, Lyle E. *Community Organization: Conflict and Reconciliation.* Nashville, Tenn.: Abingdon Press, 1966.
217. Seale, Bobby. *Seize the Time.* New York: Random House, 1970.
218. Shockley, John S. *Chicano Revolt in a Texas Town.* Notre Dame, Ind.: University of Notre Dame Press, 1974.
219. Skolnick, Jerome A. (ed.). *The Politics of Protest.* New York: Ballantine Books, 1969.
220. Source Collective. *Organizing for Health Care.* Boston: Beacon Press, 1974.
221. Thursz, Daniel. "Social Action." In John B. Turner (ed.), *Encyclopedia of Social Work.* Washington, D.C.: National Association of Social Workers, 1977, pp. 1274–1280.
222. Trapp, Shel. *Dynamics of Organizing.* Chicago: National Training and Information Center, 1976.
223. Useem, Michael. *Protest Movements in America.* Indianapolis: Bobbs-Merrill, 1975.
224. Young, Alfred E. (ed.). *Dissent: Explorations in the History of American Radicalism.* DeKalb, Ill.: Northern Illinois University Press, 1968.

CHAPTER VIII. MIXING AND PHASING STRATEGIES

225. Braybrook, David, and Charles E. Lindblom. *A Strategy of Decision.* New York: Free Press, 1963.
226. Grosser, Charles. *New Directions in Community Organization: From Enabling to Advocacy.* 2nd ed. New York: Praeger, 1976.
227. Hunter, David R. *The Slums: Challenge and Response.* New York: Free Press, 1964.
228. Kaplan, Morton A. "The Strategy of Limited Retaliation." Policy Memorandum No. 19, Princeton University Center of International Studies. Princeton, N.J., April 9, 1959.
229. Kaufman, Arnold S. *The Radical Liberal: New Man in American Politics.* New York: Atherton Press, 1968.

230. Luce, Robert Duncan, and Howard Raiffa. *Games and Decisions.* New York: John Wiley, 1957.

231. Miller, S. M. "Criteria for Antipoverty Policies: A Paradigm for Choice." *Poverty and Human Resources Abstracts,* 3:5:3–11 (September–October 1968).

232. Peck, Harris B., Seymour R. Kaplan, and Melvin Roman. "Prevention, Treatment and Social Action: A Strategy of Intervention in a Disadvantaged Urban Area." *American Journal of Orthopsychiatry,* 36:1:57–69 (1966).

233. Riessman, Frank. *Strategies Against Poverty.* New York: Random House, 1969.

234. Rothman, Jack (ed.). *Promoting Social Justice in the Multi-group Society: A Casebook for Group Relations Practitioners.* New York: Association Press, 1971.

235. Schelling, Thomas C. *The Strategy of Conflict.* New York: Oxford University Press, 1963.

236. Snyder, Glenn H. "Deterrence by Denial and Punishment." Research Monograph No. 1, Princeton University Center of International Studies. Princeton, N.J., January 2, 1959.

237. Spergel, Irving A. *Community Problem Solving: The Delinquency Example.* Chicago: The University of Chicago Press, 1969.

238. Weissman, Harold H. (ed.). *Community Development in the Mobilization for Youth Experience.* New York: Association Press, 1969.

GENERAL TREATMENTS

239. American Association of University Women. *Tool Catalog: Techniques and Strategies for Successful Action Programs.* Washington, D.C.: American Association of University Women, 1976.

240. Brager, George A., and Francis P. Purcell (eds.). *Community Action against Poverty: Readings from the Mobilization Experience.* New Haven, Conn.: College and University Press, 1967.

241. Cox, Fred M., John L. Erlich, Jack Rothman, and John E. Tropman (eds.). *Tactics and Techniques of Community Practice.* Itasca, Ill.: F. E. Peacock Publishers, 1977.

242. Dunham, Arthur. *Community Welfare Organization.* New York: Crowell, 1958.

243. Dunham, Arthur. *The New Community Organization.* New York: Crowell, 1970.

244. Ecklein, Joan L., and Armand Lauffer. *Community Organizers and Social Planners: A Volume of Case and Illustrative Materials.* New York: John Wiley, 1972.

245. Green, Helen D. *Social Work Practice in Community Organization.* New York: Whiteside and Morrow, 1954.

246. Gurin, Arnold. *Community Organization Curriculum in Graduate Social Work Education: Report and Recommendations.* New York: Council on Social Work Education, 1970.

247. Harper, Ernest B., and Arthur Dunham (eds.). *Community Organization in Action: Basic Literature and Critical Comments.* New York: Association Press, 1959.

248. Hillman, Arthur. *Community Organization and Planning.* New York: Macmillan, 1950.

249. Kahn, Alfred J. "Trends and Problems in Community Organization." In *Social Work Practice, 1964.* New York: Columbia University Press, 1964.

250. King, Clarence. *Organizing for Community Action.* New York: Harper 1948.

251. Kotler, Milton. *Neighborhood Government: The Local Foundations of Political Life.* Indianapolis: Bobbs-Merrill, 1969.

252. Kramer, Ralph, and Harry Specht. *Readings in Community Organization Practice.* 2nd ed. Englewood Cliffs, N.J.: Prentice-Hall, 1975.

253. Lindeman, Eduard C. *The Community: An Introduction to the Study of Community Leadership and Organization.* New York: Association Press, 1921.

254. McMillen, Wayne. *Community Organization for Social Welfare.* Chicago: University of Chicago Press, 1945.

255. Murphy, Campbell G. *Community Organization Practice.* Boston: Houghton-Mifflin, 1954.

256. *One Year Later: An Assessment of the National Response to the Crisis Described by the National Advisory Commission on Civil Disorders.* New York: Urban American, Inc., and the Urban Coalition, 1969.

257. Perlman, Robert, and Arnold Gurin. *Community Organization and Social Planning.* New York: John Wiley, 1972.

258. *Report of the National Advisory Commission on Civil Disorders.* New York: Bantam Books, 1968.

259. Ross, Murray G. *Case Histories in Community Organization.* New York: Harper, 1958.

260. Ross, Murray G., with B. W. Lappin. *Community Organization: Theory, Principles and Practice.* 2nd ed. New York: Harper & Row, 1967.

261. Rothman, Jack, John L. Erlich, and Joseph G. Teresa. *Promoting Innovation and Change in Organizations and Communities.* New York: John Wiley, 1976.

262. Rothman, Jack, and Wyatt C. Jones. *A New Look at Field Instruction: Education for Application of Practice Skills in Community Organization and Social Planning.* New York: Association Press, 1971.

263. Schaller, Lyle E. *The Decision-Makers.* Nashville: Abingdon, 1974.

264. Spergel, Irving (ed.). *Community Organization: Studies in Constraint.* Beverly Hills, Calif.: Sage Publications, 1972.

265. Steiner, Jesse F. *Community Organization: A Study of Its Theory and Current Practice.* Rev. ed. New York: Century Co., 1930.

266. Stroup, Herbert H. *Community Welfare Organization.* New York: Harper, 1952.
267. Turner, John B. (ed.). *Neighborhood Organization for Community Action.* New York: National Association of Social Workers, 1968.
268. Warren, Roland L. *Truth, Love, and Social Change, and Other Essays on Community Change.* Chicago: Rand McNally, 1971.
269. Zald, Mayer N. (ed.). *Organizing for Community Welfare.* Chicago: Quadrangle Books, 1967.

NAME INDEX

SUBJECT INDEX